LIEBLING AT HOME

LIEBLING AT HOME

A. J. LIEBLING

INTRODUCTION BY HERBERT MITGANG

Most of the material in this book originally appeared in *The New Yorker*.

Manufactured in the United States of America
Wideview Books/A division of PEI Books, Inc.

Library of Congress Cataloging in Publication Data

Liebling, A. J. (Abbott Joseph), 1904–1963.
Liebling at home.

"Most of the material . . . originally appeared in the New Yorker"—copyright page, CIP galley.
Contents: The telephone booth Indian—Chicago—The honest rainmaker—[etc.]
1. United States—Miscellanea. I. Title.
E156.L532 1982b 973 81–70047
ISBN 0–87223–787–7 AACR2

Designed by Tere LoPrete

Contents

INTRODUCTION

Herbert Mitgang

The first glimpse I got of A. J. Liebling was in Algiers, right after the end of the Tunisian campaign, during the "good war" (good by comparison to such later dumb wars as Vietnam), and it took a little time to realize why something about him impressed me. Certainly, it was not because of his appearance; even in his war correspondent's khaki that spring, he did not cut a dashing figure. He had a slightly Falstaffian girth, and his uniform looked as if it had been slept in, which would have been a mark of honor instead of a sign of sloppiness at that particular place and time in history. As a correspondent for *The New Yorker*, Liebling had just returned from "the front," where he had covered the infantry in the djebels and wadis, being where the action was, under the strafing of the Luftwaffe and within range of the unpleasant German 88s. Dust and victory were in the air. He probably hadn't yet had an opportunity to visit the laundresses at Madam Fox's establishment off the Boulevard Baudin, but that might not have changed his appearance too much since laundry was not the specialty of the house.

No, what later struck me as being different about Joe Liebling's manner was that he was reading the local French newspaper, *L'Echo d'Alger*. Many of the other correspondents, who had recently graduated from the sports pages and reported the war as simply another noisy athletic contest, relied for their news solely on the Army's English-language paper, *Stars and Stripes*. We stood next to each other on an autobus of the *lignes urbaines* that circled the whitewashed city on the hill, talking about the prevalence of "pup-tent poets" in uniform who contributed to *Stars and Stripes*. It seemed that every corporal didn't carry a marshal's baton (as Napoleon said about his boys) in his knapsack; he carried an iambic pentameter. The autobus passed the Rue d'Isly, reminding him of a poem written by a sergeant that was titled "Ode to an MP, Chasing Me on the Rue d'Isly." Using the local transportation also enabled Liebling to listen to the *colons* and Arabs directly; others wearing war correspondent tabs too often obtained their views of the turbulent political situation through the censored filters of French and Anglo-American military communiqués.

After the war, I would sometimes run into Liebling at one of the wateringholes he frequented in midtown Manhattan, such as Gough's, the Blue Ribbon and the Pantheon. If he was dining alone, he'd still be doing the same thing that he did in North Africa or in Europe: reading the French newspapers and magazines. In Algiers, Paris, or New York (though not in Chicago, as he points out in this book), he was a cosmopolitan who responded to the tempo and panache of city life.

Writing about people and events at home or abroad, Abbott Joseph Liebling differed from the ordinary run of journalists for more reasons than one. Certainly, the freedom, independence, and astute editing offered to writers at *The New Yorker* helped to hone his instincts and talents. Most of the words in this collection of five books about the American scene first appeared in that magazine. Liebling had put in time—served time, as he talked about it, amusedly—on *The New York Times, The Providence* [R.I.] *Journal and Evening Bulletin,* and *The New York World-Telegram,* but they were places for him to get away from. On the *World-Telegram,* his feature stories sometimes ran unmolested, but newspaper rigidity blocked his skills more often than not; fine writing was suspect and neutralized by scared and tired editors sitting under green celluloid eyeshades. At *The New Yorker,* Liebling was allowed to break out of the ranks of the narrow-column paragraph troopers.

He was a scholar who could be spotted in newspaper morgues and libraries; he was a reporter who was unafraid to write elegantly if the subject required elegance; he could empathize with so-called unimportant men and women on the fringes of society and he could be acerbic about hypocrites and temporizers—especially in the American press. Whether on the fields of war or on the attack against pompous asses in the suites of the high and high-handed, he was courageous.

One of the main reasons why Liebling is so admired by younger journalists today is precisely because he practiced in print that old-fashioned virtue, courage. Few major newspapers or newsmagazines, and none of the television networks, allow their reporters the freedom to expose the venality of powerful corporations and conglomerates and commanding individuals, in and out of government, who direct or fail to regulate their fortunes and our lives. The watchword among modern news executives is "objectivity," which in their cowardly signal language means "cool it." Thank God Liebling was not "objective."

By the time Liebling came to write about the characters the reader meets in this collection, he had been through the mill of learning and experience. For those who came in late, he was born in New York in 1904 and lived into his sixtieth year. Liebling spent three years at Dartmouth, where the only course he flunked was one in English composition, and went on to the Columbia journalism school. "It had all the intellectual status," he later observed, "of a training school for future employees of the A. & P." At the same time, he studied French literature at Columbia, familiarizing himself with the classics. Reading Stendhal's *Le Rouge et le Noir* turned out to be better preparation for covering the Second World War than the apprenticeship served by some of his fellow war correspondents in the press boxes of professional football games. He spent a year studying "lightly" at the Sorbonne and at the Ecole des Chartes. The fluency he achieved in Paris stocked his mind with the riches of French culture, preparing him for the strange tongues and raffish personalities he encountered from New York to Chicago to New Orleans, the principal locales in this collection of Lieblingiana.

Turning to the books in this volume, the reader finds a Runyonesque world that is not fictional yet has all the virtues of lively storytelling. In "The Jollity Building" we meet a cast of characters who live by their wits on the west side of midtown Manhattan—hatcheck girls and hustlers, agents and talent scouts whose offices are holes-in-the-wall and sublets of sublets, Hymie Katz the Tummler who runs a horserace tipping service, orchestra leaders without orchestras, theatrical bookers without theaters, and miscellaneous promoters: "the petty nomads of Broadway." Here, too, is Paddy the Booster, who sells neckties he steals from haberdashers, and Mac the Phony Booster, who sells neckties that he pretends to have stolen but are really shoddy ties he has bought wholesale. A Mrs. Maida Van Schuyler comes under Liebling's scrutiny since she occupies an office near Hockticket Charlie, who pays off his acts in pawn tickets. Mrs. Van Schuyler provides novitiates in satin for pinching conventioneers. "Our girls must have poise, discretion and *savoy faire*," says their den mother-agent. Where Liebling differs from Damon Runyon is that, while explaining the exquisite manners of Hymie Katz of Brooklyn, he will throw in references to François Villon and Alexander the Great.

While some of these personalities have disappeared into the high rises or the next world, it is still possible to observe or at least imagine what Liebling calls the "Telephone Booth Indians." These are the mysterious whisperers who run their businesses out of the corner phone booth. "The glass side of the booth which forms the Indian's habitat affords a chance to observe all his significant activities," Liebling notes. "These in turn illustrate the Economic Structure, for the Indian is a capitalist in what my Marxian friends would call a state of pre-primary acquisition. He has as yet acquired not even the nickel with which to make a telephone call, and so must wait in the booth until another fellow calls him." The same volume includes Liebling at his most brilliant, writing about his old *World-Telegram* boss, press lord Roy W. Howard, "The Boy in the Pistachio Shirt." In it, he cuts up Westbrook Pegler, Howard's favorite reactionary (today, he'd be called a neo-conservative) columnist. "In addition to sensing the ideological kinship between himself and Pegler,"

Liebling says, "Howard found in Pegler one who sympathized with his belief that ignorance is an endearing quality."

Rough on big shots; generous to small-timers: Who else but Liebling?

One of the author's favorite characters appears in "The Honest Rainmaker": James A. Macdonald, whose pseudonym was Colonel John R. Stingo. The Colonel ran a thoroughbred-racing-tip service, wrote wisely about fast horses and loose women, promoted harmless games of chance, and could quote from La Fontaine. Where Liebling begins and Colonel Stingo ends is sometimes hard to tell; but they were obviously kinsmen in their admiration for the outer limits of language. The Colonel is quoted as proposing the notion of what to do with the then-existing Third Avenue Elevated: It should be converted into "a straightaway under glass, about five miles long . . . You could have mutuel-ticket sellers in the booths on all the stations and sell club-house badges to get into them." Unfortunately, the advice was not followed; instead they replaced Third Avenue with singles bars and gourmet food shops selling dollar croissants, and no chance of winning the daily double. Liebling generously says of Stingo, "I was to find that where he diverges from recorded history he improves on it."

In "The Earl of Louisiana," Liebling writes about Governor Huey Long's wayward brother with candor, offering the reader a lesson in Southern politics and personalities. Only a reporter with the ability to convey the trustworthiness of his own person and pen could obtain quotes such as these: "You know, the Bible says that before the end of time billy goats, tigers, rabbits, and house cats are all going to sleep together. My gang looks like the Biblical proposition is here." The conviction grew upon Liebling that the wily Long was the only effective civil rights man in the South, in or out of the governor's mansion. Another reason why Liebling came to admire Governor Earl Long was that both appreciated the better things in life, such as hearty dinners. He quotes Long on diet-faddists: "If there is to be a world cataclysm, it will probably be set off by skim milk, Melba toast, and mineral oil in salad."

Liebling showed himself to be less generous writing about "Chicago: The Second City." He was an outsider looking in, comparing it unfavorably to his own First City. "It's like a curdled New York," he told an interviewer, infuriating the natives. Still, the Liebling metaphors impress: "The railroad tracks are the cords that hold the Chicago Gulliver supine. They crisscross the town in a kind of ticktacktoe game in which the apparent object of each line is to stop its competitors from getting out of town." As for the University of Chicago: "[Its] undergraduate college acts as the greatest magnet for neurotic juveniles since the Children's Crusade." His loyalty to New York comes out a bit excessive, but then he did not appreciate the slogan that daily proclaimed the *Chicago Tribune* as "The Greatest Newspaper in the World."

Much has happened in the country since Liebling foresaw that there would eventually be monopolistic "one newspaper towns." He told his friends in the Newspaper Guild (echoing Heywood Broun) that "freedom of the press is guaranteed only to those who own one." He spotted slanted and ordered puff pieces when it was necessary to do so—and it still is—pointing out, for example, that the terminology used to describe collective bargaining in the newspapers and newsmagazines tilted toward the management side: Labor makes "demands" while management makes "offers." No one could detect a phony euphemism faster than Liebling.

One wonders what Liebling would be saying today about the modern Peglers in White House favor writing for *The National Review, Commentary*, and other neo-conservative spear carriers; about the half-million dollars a year paid to sportscasters and weathermen for reading on television—and about the effects of television itself on the country; about the gossip columns in gussied-up disguises that have gained respectability in the new editorial-merchandising sections of newspapers; about the editorials delivered on the usurped Op-Ed pages by Mobil and other pitchmen selling anti-environmental snake and banana oil. . . .

Liebling! thou shouldst be living at this hour.

THE TELEPHONE BOOTH INDIAN

Contents

Preface

THERE was once a French-Canadian whose name I cannot at present recall but who had a window in his stomach. It was due to this fortunate circumstance, however unlikely, that a prying fellow of a doctor was able to study the man's inner workings, and that is how we came to know all about the gastric juices, as I suppose we do. The details are not too clear in my mind, as I read the story in a hygiene reader which formed part of the curriculum of my fourth year in elementary school, but I have no doubt that it is essentially correct. I believed everything I read in that book, including the story of the three regiments of Swiss infantry who started to climb a mountain on a very cold day: the first regiment had been stimulated with a liberal ration of schnapps; the second had been dosed with about half an ounce of alcohol per man; the third had had only milk. The soldiers of the first regiment froze to death unanimously after marching only 223 yards; half the members of the second arrived at their destination, after losing their fingers, toes, and ears; the fellows in the third regiment not only raced to the top of the mountain feeling warm as toast, but took the mountain down boulder by boulder and threw it at a shepherd who was yodeling flat. This is a digression. What I meant to say is that the Telephone Booth Indians, a tribe first described by me in a monograph called "The Jollity Building," offer to the student of sociology the same opportunity that the fenestrated Canadian gave the inquiring physiologist. The glass side of the telephone booth which forms the Indian's habitat affords a chance to observe all his significant activities. These in turn illustrate the Economic Structure, for the Indian is a capitalist in what my Marxian friends would call a state of pre-primary acquisition. He has as yet acquired not even the nickel with which to make a telephone call, and so must wait in the booth until another fellow calls him.

The Telephone Booth Indians range over a territory approximately half a mile square, bounded longitudinally by Sixth and Eighth avenues in New York City, and in latitude by the south side of Forty-second and the north side of Fifty-second streets. This in part coincides with what is called humorously Broadway, the Heart of the World, and is in fact a sort of famine area, within which the Indians seek their scanty livelihood. Scattered about the district are a few large structures like the Jollity Building, but less imaginary, which are favorite camping grounds of the Indians because they contain large numbers of the telephone booths necessary to the tribe's survival. The Telephone Booth Indians are nomads who have not attained the stage of pastoral culture in which they carry their own shelter.* Like the hermit crab, the Telephone Booth Indian, before beginning operations, must find a habitation abandoned by some other creature, and in his case this is always a telephone booth. The numerical strength of the tribe is therefore roughly limited by the number of telephone booths in the district, as a sow's litter is by the number of her teats. Yet between the Telephone Booth Indian and the great man of the Indian's special world there is only the unessential difference between grub and worm. Instead of spending his working day looking at a coin box, the great man has from three to six telephones on his desk. In the land of the Telephone Booth Indians, according to the definition of my profound friend Izzy Yereshevsky, a successful man is one who knows how to get a dollar and the rest haven't got what to eat. All of the subjects of the sketches in this book come under one or the other heading. That is about all they have in common, but there is good deal that some of them have in common with some of the others. Mr. Yereshevsky thinks that the Telephone Booth Indian is a key figure in our city and age. He has always refused to allow the installation of a telephone booth in the I. and Y. Cigar Store which he owns at Forty-ninth Street and Seventh Avenue. "The store is open twenty-four hours a day," he says, "so if I had a booth how would I get the guy out of it?"

The only subject of a piece in this book who does not at least make his business headquarters in the territory of the Telephone Booth Indians is Mr. Roy Howard, the publisher. He dresses like a Telephone Booth Indian's idea of a fellow who knows how to get a dollar, and he likes to use the telephone. However, the main reason that he is in this book is that we needed the 15,000 words.

THE AUTHOR

* Example: Cheyenne, Sea Lapps, Bedawi, owners of trailers.

Masters of the Midway

ONE of the most distinctive periodicals published in the land of the Telephone Booth Indians is called the *Greater Show World*, a trade paper for outdoor showmen. It is edited in one room in the Gaiety Building, which is *not* a fictional edifice, by a man named Johnny J. Kline who has five typewriters in his office and usually has a sheet of copy paper in each of them. When he sits at one typewriter he is editor-in-chief, at another he is business manager and at a third a gossip columnist. He writes under different by-lines as two other reporters at the remaining typewriters. The magazine which he gets out all by himself every month is just as big as the *New Yorker*, he reminds me whenever I see him, and he says he wonders what the hell the *New Yorker* staff does for a living. Since the advertising and editorial departments of the *Greater Show World* are lodged in adjacent wrinkles of the same brain lobe, they sometimes get telescoped, and the result is a spontaneous eulogy for an advertiser. Through the years a pair of showmen named Lew Dufour and Joe Rogers have drawn more eulogies and paid for more ads than almost anybody else. The pair never got a chance to work near Telephone Booth Indian territory until Grover Whalen opened his World of Tomorrow over in Flushing Meadows in 1939. When that happened they showed they knew how to get a dollar.

Among the shows on the World's Fair midway presented by the firm of Dufour & Rogers, one, "We Humans," illustrated the grand strategy of evolution in a somewhat macabre fashion. A reverent, three-dimensional presentation of Da Vinci's "Last Supper," with life-sized models of the apostles, trick lighting effects, and a musical background of Gregorian chants supplied by a phonograph with an electrical record-changing device, was to have been another Dufour & Rogers offering. They could not find a suitable Catholic organization to sponsor the "Last Supper," so they dropped it. Rogers says, without any intended disrespect, "The nuns would not play ball with us." Dufour, the senior partner, saw no conflict in the subject matter of the "Last Supper" and "We Humans." He is a man of a speculative and scientific temperament. "We tell the customers about evolution," he says, "but we don't advocate it." Jang, a Malay boy with a tail six inches long, was a principal in "Strange as It Seems," another Dufour & Rogers attraction. Dufour wanted to invite all the inhabitants of Dayton, Tennessee, to come to see Jang and draw their own conclusions. Rogers, however, was against the necessary outlay for postage stamps.

As the partners had already rented a midway site for the abandoned religious spectacle, they substituted a hastily erected saloon and restaurant called the Rondevoo. The Rondevoo made its chief appeal to other concessionaires and their employees—an example of Dufour & Rogers resourcefulness, because, as Rogers said, "The attendance is off, but the boys have got to be here anyhow." The Rondevoo turned out to be their most profitable stab.

In deference to Dufour's scholastic leanings, Rogers, an earthy type, sometimes calls his partner "Dr. Itch." The firm believes in diversification of investments, as Dufour puts it, or, as Rogers says, spreading its bets. When the Fair opened, the partners had five shows and one ride, the Silver Streak, ready in the amusement area. They also had one of their evolution shows in operation at the San Francisco Fair. The New York shows were "We Humans"; "Strange as It Seems," which they described as a "de luxe Congress of Strange People, Presented in an Air-Cooled Odditorium"; the Seminole Village, the title of which is self-explanatory; "Nature's Mistakes," an exhibit featuring Adonis, the Bull with the Human Skin, and "Gang Busters," an epic depiction of the dangers and fascination of crime, with reformed gangsters reenacting the St. Valentine's Day Massacre and Juanita Hansen, a reformed movie actress, lecturing on the evils of narcotics, to which she said she was once addicted. They also added "Olga, the Headless Girl, Alive," and the restaurant. This list includes about every kind of proved midway attraction except a girl show, and that omission is due not to prudery but commercial principles. A girl show for a world's fair must have a rather elaborate installation, usually a name star, and always a considerable salary list. Moreover, one nude non-freak woman is much like another, and while it is certain that one or two of the dozen girl shows at a world's fair will make money, nobody can tell in advance which ones they will be. Freaks, crime, five-legged cows, and aborigines are staple midway commodities. At Flushing the five-legged cows came through for the firm, but the human freaks lost money.

Dufour and Rogers began their joint career at the Century of Progress Exposition in Chicago in 1933 and have figured conspicuously on the midways at San Diego, Dallas, Fort Worth, Cleveland, Brussels, and San Francisco since then. Long before 1933 they had worked separately in that curious world of sixty thousand outdoor show people, the "carnies," who travel from town to town with carnivals. A stranger once asked Joe Rogers whether he had started as a barker with a carnival. "Hell, no," Rogers replied. "I worked my way up to that." And anyway, he might have explained, no carnie says "barker." The man who holds forth outside the show to bring the people in is the "outside talker"; his oration is known as "the opening." The fellow who guides them about inside the exhibit is an "inside talker."

Banks, as might be expected, are reluctant to lend money to carnival people, so Dufour & Rogers finance their ventures largely by selling "pieces" of them to other men in the amusement business—owners of touring carnivals, manufacturers of slot machines, and retired circus proprietors. The ease with which they promote money from this skeptical investing public is evidence of their prestige in the profession. Outdoor showmen always refer to important sums as "paper money." When concessionaires with less of it ran through their bank rolls at past fairs, Dufour & Rogers bought them out. That way the firm wound up the second summer of the Greater Texas Exposition at Dallas with thirty-eight attractions on the midway, including the "Streets of Paris." The "Streets of Paris" was a girl show, but even a girl show may prove a good investment after the original proprietor's investment has been written off the books. The competition of pale-faced indoor showmen, like some of the concessionaires at the Fair who had a Broadway background, always makes Lew and Joe feel good. "Give me the sky for a canopy," Rogers once said, "and I will take Flo Ziegfeld and make a sucker out of him. How do you like that?" The difference between what will draw in Beloit, Wisconsin, and what will draw in New York, they think, is not basic, but is chiefly a matter of flash—the old vaudeville word for "class" or "style"—in presentation. "You can buy a ham sandwich at the Automat," Dufour says, "or you can buy it at the Waldorf. What's the difference? The Waldorf has more flash."

The partners have little of that pure enthusiasm for a freak as a freak that distinguishes some of their friends. A man named Slim Kelly, for example, who managed "Nature's Mistakes" for Dufour & Rogers, once spent three months and all his capital in the lumber country around Bogalusa, Louisiana, where he had heard there was a Negro with only one eye, and that in the center of his forehead. Kelly still believes the cyclops is somewhere near Bogalusa but that he may be self-conscious. Lew and Joe feel that the chance of finding a really new kind of freak is a tenuous thing on which to maintain a business.

Joe Rogers is a hyperactive man in his early forties, with contrapuntal eyes set in a round, sleek head. He has a boundless capacity for indignation, which he can turn on like a tap. Rogers' complexion, when he is in low gear, indicates rosy health. When he is angry, it carries a horrid hint of apoplexy. During the last few weeks before a fair opens, he carries on a war of alarums and sorties with contractors, delegates of labor unions, and officials of the concession department. His theory is sustained attack.

Once, on being approached by a stranger at the Fair grounds, Joe asked the man his business. "I'm a landscape architect," the stranger said. "Oh," Rogers yelled before beginning to bargain, "so you're the muzzler who's going to rob me!" He had a particularly bitter time with the contractor on one of his buildings in Flushing, a tall, solemn, chamber-of-commerce sort of fellow whose work Rogers regarded as slow and expensive. "He is a legit guy, a businessman," Rogers moaned one day, "and he tries to sell me a soft con!" "Con," of course, is a contraction of "confidence game." A soft con is one that begins with a plaint, as, "When I made this contract I didn't know the site was so marshy." A short con and a quick con are less humiliating variants because they are aimed at catching a victim off guard rather than insulting his intelligence. "Me, a showman, a snake guy!" Rogers continued. A snake guy is one who has exhibited snakes in a pit at a fair. The incongruity of the contractor's attempt to invert the natural order appeared to affect Rogers deeply. "Trying to cheat the cheaters!" he screamed. "I'll wrap a cane around his neck!" And he went out looking for the contractor.

Before he had gone three steps from his office in the "Strange as It Seems" building, however, he had become involved in a quarrel with two gypsies who sought employment in the Seminole Village. "Me Indian," said the first gypsy, who was swarthy enough to qualify. "You *gypsy!*" Rogers yelled. "You want to open a mitt joint in my concession! Get outa here!" A mitt joint is a booth for palm reading. Its bad feature, from the point of view of a respectable concessionaire, is the frequent disappearance of patrons' pocketbooks. This provokes beefs, which are bad for business. Rogers' life as opening day approaches is an assault in constantly accelerating tempo. Once a fair has opened, he goes to bed for twenty-four hours and wakes up thinking about the next fair on the international schedule.

Rogers was born in the Brownsville region of Brooklyn, but for the last fifteen years he has made his headquarters in the Hotel Sherman, a business and theatrical hotel in the Chicago Loop. He finds people out there more compatible. Dufour, however, lives in an apartment in Forest Hills. Between fairs the partners keep in touch by air line and long-distance telephone.

Lew Dufour is tall, sallow, and bland, and wears his dark clothes with a sort of mortuary elegance. Superficially, he does not resemble Rogers. "Mr. Dufour," a subordinate once said, "is a mental genius. Mr. Rogers is an executive genius." When Rogers fails to overwhelm an opponent in a business argument, Dufour takes up the task and wheedles him. It is a procedure used by teams of detectives to make criminals confess. As a unit, Lew and Joe are nearly irresistible. On propositions requiring dignity and aplomb, Dufour makes the first approach. At Chicago in 1934, however, Lew failed to impress General Charles G. Dawes, who was chairman of the finance committee for the Century of Progress. The partners had had a successful first season at the Fair, but the management wished to shift their "Life" show—an earlier edition of "We Humans"—to a less favorable site for the reprise of the Fair. When Dufour failed to move Dawes, Rogers leaned forward, pincered the general with his intercepting eyes, and shouted, "You can't do this to us, General! We are good concessionaires. We made a lot of money for the Fair." The general said, "How much did you make for yourselves?" "Oh," said Rogers, suddenly vague, "we made lots and lots." Rogers says he could hear the famous pipe rattling against the general's teeth from the force of the general's curiosity. "And what do you call lots of money, Mr. Rogers?" Joe's voice became a happy croon. "What I call lots of money, General, is lots and lots and *lots*." General Dawes permitted them to keep their old site. Presumably he hoped Rogers might relent someday and tell him. "I just worked on his curiosity," Joe says, "like I wanted him to come in and see a two-headed baby." The partners had made $111,000 on the "Life" show.

A favored type of investment among world's-fair concessionaires is an aboriginal village. Eskimos, Filipinos, or Ashantis usually can be hired at extremely moderate rates to sit around in an appropriate setting and act as if they were at home. The city dweller's curiosity about exotic peoples, built up by a childhood of reading adventure books, is apparently insatiable. Providing suitable food is not such a problem as it might seem once the concessionaire has learned the fact, unreported by anthropologists, that all primitive peoples exist by preference on a diet of hamburger steak. Dufour derives from this pervading passion a theory that all races of man once inhabited a common Atlantis, but Rogers does not go so far. He just says he is glad they do not crave porterhouse. Once engaged, the aborigine must be encouraged and, if necessary, taught to perform some harmless maneuver which may be ballyhooed as a sacred tribal rite, just about to begin, folks. This is ordinarily not difficult, as the average savage seems to be a good deal of a ham at heart.

Dufour & Rogers' debut as practical ethnologists was really caused by a large captive balloon that blew away from its moorings at the Century of Progress. The balloon had been one of the sights of the midway, and its taking off left a large site vacant. So Lew and Joe, who already had a couple of other shows, leased the space for a tropical village, which they called Darkest Africa. Some of the partners' acquaintances say they opened with a cast of tribesmen from South State Street, which is in the Chicago Black Belt, but Lew insists that he came to New York to engage them all. "Naturally, there was no time to go to Africa for performers on such short notice," he says, "but you would be surprised the number of real Africans there are in Harlem. They come there on ships."

By the time Dufour got back to Chicago with his company of hamburger-eating cannibals, Rogers had built the village, a kind of stockade containing thatched huts and a bar. "We had a lot of genuine junk, spears and things like that, that an explorer had brought from the bacteria of Africa," Joe Rogers says, "but this chump had gone back to Africa, so we did not know exactly which things belonged to which tribes—Dahomeys and Ashantis and Zulus and things like that. Somehow our natives didn't seem to know, either." This failed to stump the partners.

They divided the stuff among the representatives of the various tribal groups they had assembled and invited the anthropology departments of the Universities of Chicago and Illinois to see their show. Every time an anthropologist dropped in, the firm would get a beef. The scientist would complain that a Senegalese was carrying a Zulu shield, and Lew or Joe would thank him and pretend to be abashed. Then they would change the shield. "By August," Joe says with simple pride, "everything in the joint was in perfect order."

The partners bought some monkeys for their village from an importer named Warren Buck and added an outside sign which said, "Warren Buck's Animals." By the merest chance, the branches and leaves of a large palm tree, part of the decorative scheme, blotted out the "Warren," so the sign appeared to read "Buck's Animals." Since Frank Buck was at the height of his popularity, the inadvertence did not cut into the gate receipts of Darkest Africa.

The concession proved so profitable that Lew and Joe decided to open a more ambitious kraal for the 1934 edition of the Fair. They chose a Hawaiian village this time. Customers expect things of a Hawaiian village which they would not demand in Darkest Africa. They expect an elaborate tropical *décor*, languorous dance music, and a type of entertainment that invites trouble with the police. The few Hawaiian entertainers on this continent will not even eat hamburger, a sure indication that theirs is a vitiated type of savagery. All such refinements increase the "nut," or overhead. There was also a rather expensive restaurant. All told, Dufour and Rogers and their friends invested a hundred thousand dollars in the venture before it opened. The central feature of the Village was a volcano seventy feet high, built of painted concrete, near the restaurant. Joe Rogers in his youth had been much impressed by a play called *The Bird of Paradise*. In the big scene of the play the heroine jumped into the smoking crater of Mount Kilauea to appease the island gods. The Dufour & Rogers Chicago volcano was "gaffed" with steampipes. "Gaff," a synonym for "gimmick," means a concealed device. The verb "to gaff" means to equip with gaffs. Lew and Joe hired a Hawaiian dancer named Princess Ahi as the star of their Village. Twice nightly the Princess ascended the volcano, during the dinner and supper shows. As the Princess climbed along a winding path in the concrete, a spotlight followed her. The steampipes emitted convincing clouds; electrical gimmicks set around the crater gleamed menacingly, and the Princess, warming with her exertions, dropped portions of her tribal raiment as she gained altitude. The volcano was visible from all parts of the midway, a great ballyhoo for the Village and, incidentally, a free show for the small-money trade. When the Princess Ahi reached the top of the mountain, she whipped off the last concession to Island modesty and dived into the crater, which was only about four feet deep and was lined with mattresses to break her fall. "She would land right on her kisser on a mattress," Joe

Rogers says. The lights were dimmed; the steam subsided, and the Princess climbed out of Kilauea and came down again unobserved. Joe had to show the Princess how to dive into the crater, kisser first, instead of stepping gingerly into it. This astonished him. "She must have seen plenty other broads jump into them volcanoes at home," he says.

When interest in the Princess began to flag, the partners added Faith Bacon to their show. Miss Bacon did a dance in the N. T. G. show out at Flushing earlier that summer. "She was not a Hawaiian," Joe explains, "but she had once eaten some Hawaiian pineapple." At the Hawaiian Village, Miss Bacon did a gardenia dance, wearing only a girdle of the blooms and discarding them as she went along. This disappointed the customers, who expected her to start with one gardenia and discard petals. The partners also engaged a girl named Fifi D'Arline, who did a muff dance, using a small muff in place of an ostrich fan. She did not draw the crowds consistently, either. It was midsummer before the partners acknowledged to each other that the attendance at the 1934 renewal of the Fair consisted mainly of Chicagoans who came out to kill a day without spending any considerable sum. Lew and Joe ripped out the luxurious modernistic bar in the Village and installed a cafeteria that sold a cup of coffee for a nickel and a ham sandwich for ten cents. The cafeteria pulled the concession through. Lew and Joe made no money on the Hawaiian Village but at least were able to break even.

The Seminole Indians, Dufour & Rogers' contribution to the urban understanding of the savage, subsisted on buckets of hamburger exactly as the Kroomen and Dahomans did in Chicago. The Seminoles were not very cheerful, for long acquaintance with winter visitors to Florida had given them a peculiarly bilious view of the white man. The adult males wrestled with torpid alligators in the brackish water of a small swimming pool, and the women sold beads if visitors to the Seminole Village insisted upon it. When the Seminoles arrived at the Fair grounds, on a cold, rainy April day, they walked into a culinary crisis. The gas for their cookhouse range had not been turned on. The nonplussed Indians tried, rather ineptly, to build a campfire over which to fry their only known form of sustenance, but the World's Fair fire department raced to the midway and put out the fire. When the firemen went away the Seminoles built another fire. After several repetitions of the episode the firemen got tired and let them alone. By that time, Rogers had had the gas connected.

Another emergency arose when the World's Fair health officer insisted that the Seminole cookhouse be equipped with an electric dishwashing machine, required by Fair regulations wherever food was prepared and served. It was impossible to change regulations at the Fair, because they had all been printed in a booklet. The partners won an indefinite delay, however, by arguing that the Seminoles might accidentally mangle one of their papooses in a dishwashing machine, and so feel impelled to scalp Grover Whalen.

Joe Rogers liked the Seminoles. He understood them as intuitively as he understood General Dawes. Labor-union regulations prevented the Indians from doing any serious construction work on their village, but they did cover the tar-paper roofs of their lean-tos with palm leaves brought from Florida. They tacked overlapping layers of palm leaves to the tar paper, and in their lavish aboriginal manner used an inordinate number of tacks, which cost Dufour & Rogers money. Three or four days after the Seminoles got there, Will Yolen, the publicity man, arranged for them to make a tour of a New York department store. Yolen and the publicity department of the store hoped that some photographs of the Indians in the white man's trading post might get into the newspapers. Before the Indians went into town, Rogers, who had studied the Seminoles' mores, told his press agent to be sure that the party visited the hardware department. When the Seminoles returned, they brought plenty of tacks and even a few hammers which they had snitched en route, fulfilling their boss's expectations.

"You should have sent them to a jewelry store," said the admiring Mr. Dufour. "We could have cleared the nut before we opened."

Long before Lew Dufour and Joe Rogers became partners in the firm that once ran a half-dozen shows on the World's Fair midway, they had pursued separate careers with traveling shows. The men have been aware of each other's existence for at least twenty-five years, but until they started working together, during the Century of Progress in Chicago, their paths crossed so casually and so often that they can't remember where they first met or the occasion of the meeting.

Twenty years ago, Dufour was head of a carnival known as Lew Dufour's Exposition. The Exposition traveled in twenty-five railroad cars, and Lew's name was bravely emblazoned on each, although his equity was sometimes thinner than the paint. The carnival included a small menagerie, snakes, freaks, a girl show, several riding devices, and a goodly number of wheels on which the peasantry was privileged to play for canes or baby dolls. At the beginning of every season, the Exposition would leave winter quarters in debt to the butchers who had provided meat for the lions in the menagerie. If the weather was fair the first week out, the Exposition would make enough to go on to the second date on its always tentative route. On one occasion the organization was bogged down in mud and debt at a town in eastern Tennessee after two weeks of steady rain. The tents were pitched in a gully which had become flooded, but as in most outdoor shows, the personnel lived on the train. The sheriff came down to Dufour's gaudy private car to attach the Exposition's tangible assets. With the aid of a quart of corn liquor, Dufour talked the sheriff into lending him the money to pay off the local creditors. Then he got him to ask the creditors down to the car and talked them into lending him $1800 to haul the show as far as Lynchburg, Virginia. At Lynchburg he talked the agent of the Southern Railroad into sending the train through to Washington without advance payment. It was a mass migration of four hundred persons and six wild Nubian lions in twenty-five railroad cars, without other motive machinery than Dufour's tongue.

Shortly after that hegira, Dufour decided that while the show owners got the glory, it was the concessionaires traveling with the shows who got the money. So he became the proprietor of a "jam joint." A jam joint is a traveling auction store in which, as the climax of the "regularly scheduled sale," the auctioneer says, "Now, my friends, who will bid one dollar for this empty, worthless box?" A man in the audience says, "I will," and passes up a dollar. The auctioneer is touched. He says, "This gentleman has sufficient confidence in me that he offers one dollar for an empty box. I will not abuse his confidence. Here, mister, is the box. Open it in front of everybody." The box, it turns out, contains "a seventeen-jewel Elgin watch." "I don't want your dollar, mister," the auctioneer says. "Take this beautiful forty-five-dollar watch as a present." Then he asks how many people will give him five dollars for an empty box. A few five-dollar bills are passed up hopefully. He asks the people if they are perfectly satisfied to give him five dollars for an empty box. Sensing that it is a game, they shout "Yes!" He hands back their money and presents each of them with a "handsome and valuable gift," usually a wallet or vanity case worth about a dime, as a reward for their confidence in him. Next he calls for ten-dollar bids on an empty box. By this time the contagion of something for nothing has spread, and the countrymen eagerly pass up their bills. He asks them if they would have any kick if he kept their money and gave them nothing but an empty box. Remembering the previous routine, they shout "No!" "Nobody will have any complaint if I keep the money?" the jam guy asks. Nobody. The auditors expect him to return the money, with a present as a reward for their faith. The auctioneer assures them that he will *not* give them an empty box for their money. He will give to each and every one of them a special platinum-rolled alarm clock "worth ten dollars in itself." He makes a speech about the alarm clock. That is not all. He will give to each a beautiful Persian rug, worth twenty-five dollars, specially imported from Egypt. He makes a speech about the rug. That is not all. He adds a couple of patent picture frames "worth six dollars apiece." In short, he loads each of his confiding acquaintances with an assortment of bulky junk and then declares the sale at an end, retaining all the ten-dollar bills.

Jamming paid well and yielded a certain artistic satisfaction, but it did not content Dufour. He felt that it was not creative and that it had only an oblique educational value. It was at the Louisiana State Fair at Shreveport, in 1927, that Lew found his real vocation. He recognized it instantly; Keats felt the same way when he opened Chapman's Homer. There was a medicine pitchman at the Fair who carried with him a few bottles of formaldehyde containing human embryos. The pitchman used the embryos only as a decoy to collect a "tip," which is what a pitchman calls an audience, but Dufour, who was at the Fair with his auction store, dropped in on the medicine show one evening and at once sensed there was money in the facts of life. He must have had an intimation of that vast, latent public interest in medicine which has since been capitalized upon by Dr. Heiser, Dr. Cronin, Dr. Hertzler, Dr. Menninger, and all the other authors of medical best sellers. "A scientist may know a lot about embryology and biology," Lew has since said, "but it don't mean anything at the ticket window because it's not presented right. I felt the strength of the thing right away." From the day when he decided to present biology effectively, Lew began to collect suitable exhibits.

The important thing in assembling a cast for a biology show is to get a graduated set of human embryos which may be used to illustrate the development of an unborn baby from the first month to the eighth. The series parallels, as the lecturers point out, the evolution of man through the fish, animal, and primate stages. As an extra bit of flash, a good show includes some life groups of prehistoric men and women huddled around a campfire. Sometimes it takes months to put together a complete set of specimens. While it is true, as Lew sometimes roguishly observes, that you cannot buy unborn babies in Macy's or Gimbel's, there are *sub-rosa* clearing houses for them in most large cities. It is now a small industry, though seldom mentioned by chambers of commerce. The embryo business even has its tycoon, to borrow a word from graver publications, a man in Chicago who used to be chief laboratory technician at a medical school. The specimens are smuggled out of hospitals by technicians or impecunious internes. Hospitals have a rule that such specimens should be destroyed, but it is seldom rigidly enforced; no crime is involved in selling one. Dufour can afford to keep companies standing by. The actors need no rehearsal and draw no salary. Early in his biological career, Lew thought of a terrific title for his show—"Life." He did not pay fifty thousand dollars for this title, as Henry R. Luce did when he had the same inspiration. He did pretty well with his "Life" exhibits, playing state and county fairs and amusement parks, but he didn't get to the big time until he teamed up with Joe Rogers.

During Dufour's years of orientation, Rogers had been acquiring a comfortable bank roll by merchandising unbreakable dolls and cotton blankets in western Canada. His merchandising apparatus consisted of a wheel with fifty numbers on it. The customers paid ten cents a chance, and after every whirl one customer or another collected a doll or a blanket. In order to keep their midways free of swindlers, the Canadian fairs make contracts awarding all the concessions at each fair to one firm of concessionaires. Rogers' wheels were honest but allowed a nice margin of profit, and he usually got the concessions. Joe had established his headquarters in Chicago, and he used to travel through Canada west of Toronto in the winter, signing contracts with fairs. He was always a heavy bettor on sporting events, and on his journeys acquired an expert knowledge of professional hockey, which, in those days, existed only in Canada. When big-league hockey was introduced to the United States, Rogers was the only betting man in Chicago who really knew what the odds on the teams should be. He won consistently for several seasons before his friends began to catch on. In addition to all this, he ran the Link cigar store and restaurant on Michigan Boulevard, a rendezvous for sporting men and politicians.

Lew and Joe joined forces for the first time before the Century of Progress in Chicago opened. Lew had his "Life" show, and Joe was able to finance a flashy building for it at the Fair. Showmen are incessantly forming one- or two-season partnerships for a particular promotion, and neither Lew nor Joe realized at once the significance of their merger. The firm began its history just with "Life," but within a week it opened a second exhibit—the two-headed baby. The baby, one of those medical anomalies that never live for more than a few gasps, was in a large bottle of formaldehyde. For years it had been the chief ornament of a country doctor's study, and the partners had picked it up for a couple of hundred dollars from a Chicago dealer in medical curiosa. They built a fine front for this exhibit, with a wooden stork carrying a two-headed baby prominently displayed over the entrance. They got a female talker for the show, a motherly woman who wore a trained-nurse's uniform and made her ballyhoo through a microphone.

"Wouldn't you like to see a *real* two-headed baby?" the nurse would ask sweetly. "He was *born* alive."

"Get that," Joe says. "We didn't say it was alive. We just said it was born alive." The partners had arranged the entrance so that people on the midway could see past the door to a woman in nurse's uniform who bent over some object they could not discern. If the people inferred that the object was a baby and the nurse was trying to keep it alive, that was their own business. No deception could be imputed to Dufour & Rogers. And anyway, a look at a two-headed baby, even in a bottle, is well worth fifteen cents.

"Did you ever see a *real* two-headed baby?" Rogers sometimes murmurs euphorically, apropos of nothing except a cheerful mood. "It was *born* alive." The partners grossed fifty thousand dollars with their pickled star. Thirty-five thousand was clear profit.

"It wasn't a fake," Dufour argues earnestly. "It was an illusion, like when Barnum advertised the 'cow with its head where its tail ought to be,' and when the people paid their money he just showed them a cow turned around in her stall. Just a new angle of presentation, you might say."

The new angle of presentation is the essential element of success on a midway. There are virtually no novel or unique attractions. Even the most extraordinary freaks seldom remain long without rivals. Thus, shortly after the appearance of Jo-Jo, the Dog-Faced Boy, the show world witnessed the debut of Lionel, the Lion-Faced Boy. The appearance of Frank Lentini, the Three-Legged Man, was closely followed by that of Myrtle Corbin, the Four-Legged Girl. Lalou, the Double-Bodied Man from Mexico, soon had a rival in Libera, the Double-Bodied Spaniard. This is because when one victim of a particular deformity begins to get publicity, other similar freaks see profit in making themselves known.

Dufour and Rogers have deep admiration for a young man named Jack Tavlin, who managed three midgets at the San Diego Fair and made money with them by calling them "leprahons." "A midget is not worth feeding," Mr. Tavlin, who was also working at the Flushing Fair, wisely observed. "Everybody knows what is a midget—a little man. But when I said, 'Come and see the leprahons,' the customers came. Afterward some of them would ask me, 'What is the difference between a leprahon and a midget?' I would say, 'Madam, it is a different species. A leprahon cannot reproduce theirself.' " Mr. Tavlin's midgets were very small, because they were only six or seven years old, and a child midget is naturally rather smaller than an adult one. He dressed the midget boy in a high hat and a dress suit and the two girls in evening gowns. He didn't say they were full-grown. The customers assumed they were. In time the juvenile midgets got into the hands of a less conscientious impresario, and the picture of the boy appeared in the magazine *Life* as a "life-size portrait of the world's smallest man—age 18 years, height 19 inches, weight 12 pounds." The boy was only nine years old then, but, as Mr. Tavlin says, "There is always some unscrupulous person that will take advantage of a reporter."

For the two summers of the Century of Progress, Lew and Joe prospered. "Life," the Two-Headed Baby, and Darkest Africa, the Ethiop village that they opened the first season, all made plenty of "paper money." The Hawaiian Village, their most ambitious promotion, earned no profit, but the partners broke even on it. A vista of paper money and excitement opened before Dufour & Rogers in the fall of 1934. The only requisite to continued success was a steady supply of world's fairs. Brussels and San Diego had announced expositions for 1935. The firm divided its forces. Rogers went to Brussels with "La Vie," a variation of "Life"; "Les Monstres Géants," a snake show featuring rattlesnakes, or *serpents à sonnettes*, a novelty in Belgium; and, as a feature attraction, a show like "Gang Busters," called for the Belgian trade "Le Crime Ne Paie Pas." Dufour took the same line of shows to San Diego, and in addition had the firm's mascot, the two-headed baby. "Le Crime Ne Paie Pas" had a collection of tommy guns and sawed-off shotguns reputedly taken from *les gangsters américains*, a rogues' gallery of photographs featuring postmortem views of Dillinger and an old Pierce-Arrow sedan billed as "*L'Auto Blindé des Bandits.*" The old Pierce has especially thick plate-glass windows, and the doors and tonneau are indubitably lined with sheet metal. Its history is uncertain, but it must have belonged to somebody who was at least apprehensive of accidents. The car was like a box at the opera. In Brussels it passed on alternate Wednesdays as Dillinger's, on odd Fridays as Al Capone's, and at other times as Jack "Legs" Diamond's. Jack "Legs" Diamond was the most popular gangster in Belgium, Rogers says, because once he had tried to land at Antwerp from a freighter and had been turned back by the Belgian police. The Belgians felt they had had a personal contact with him. During the weeks before the Flushing Fair opened, Joe drove the armored car around the streets of New York, usually between the Fair grounds and the West Side Ruby Foo's, where he likes to eat.

The star of "Le Crime Ne Paie Pas" was a man named Floyd Woolsey, who sat in an electric chair and impersonated a murderer being executed. He had to give special performances for delegations of curious European police chiefs. Belgian journalists reported that "Le Crime Ne Paie Pas" gave them a fresh insight into American life. Dave Hennen Morris, at the time United States Ambassador to Belgium, found the show a fine antidote to nostalgia, but a few stodgy American residents of Brussels protested against giving Continentals such strange ideas of our culture. Therefore, acting on the Ambassador's suggestion, Rogers rechristened the show "Les Gangsters Internationaux." The inclusion of a few German gangsters in the rogues' gallery made everybody happy, and, as Joe says, "the heat was off." He thinks well of Europe except for the climate. "It is the wrong setup for snakes," he says. "Cold and rainy all the time." But the weather had no deterrent effect upon the crowds. The Belgians, Joe concluded, had given up hoping for fair weather.

During 1936 and 1937, Dufour & Rogers operated clusters of shows in the expositions at Dallas, Fort Worth, and Cleveland, but these were mere workouts: they had already begun to plan their layout for the World of Tomorrow. Throughout the Texas and Cleveland fairs, none of which was an unqualified success, Lew and Joe maintained a record of profit-making most unusual among concessionaires. Each time they emerged unscathed from another fair their prestige in the trade and the amount of paper money which they apparently had at their disposition increased.

The two men have divergent notions of pleasure. Rogers, noisy, pugnacious, and juvenile, likes to travel with sporting men. He will fly from a midway to an important prize fight a couple of thousand miles away and fly right back again when the fight is over. Dufour, despite his gauntness, is an epicure famous among carnival men. He has even invented two dishes—soft scrambled eggs with anchovies, and loose hamburger steak. He insists that his hamburger be made of a Delmonico steak cut into small pieces with a knife and that it be sautéed in a covered pan over a slow fire. Dufour's preoccupation with the finer things of life sometimes enrages Rogers. "I knew him when he had doughnut tumors," he says bitterly, "and now he has to have scrambled eggs with anchovies." Doughnut tumors are abdominal lumps which, carnies say, appear upon the bodies of show people who have subsisted for months at a time on nothing but coffee and doughnuts. "That Dr. Itch," Joe sputters at other times —it is his familiar name for his partner—"when trouble comes he lams and leaves me with the grief." But he values Dufour for his intellect. Both partners have been married for many years, and Mrs. Dufour and Mrs. Rogers hit it off well together.

The Dufour & Rogers reputation of always paying off stood them in particularly good stead when they bid for concessions at the New York Fair. Even an apparently flimsy building in the amusement area represented a big investment for the average outdoor showman. The buildings here had to be set on piles because of the low marshland; building specifications were strict; labor costs in New York were high. Would-be concessionaires had to furnish stiff guarantees of solvency. The "Nature's Mistakes" building, the least expensive of the Dufour & Rogers string, cost about $20,000. "Strange as It Seems," their most elaborate offering, cost nearly $100,000. Altogether, Lew Dufour says, their attractions at the Fair grounds represented an investment of $600,000. The partners usually incorporate each attraction separately and finance it by selling bonds. The corporation also issues common stock, of which around forty-nine per cent goes to the bondholders as a bonus, while the impresarios retain the rest. At the end of a fair, the corporation pays off the bondholders and the profits, if any, are divided among the holders of common stock. It is not a conservative form of investment, but the bank-roll men get action for their money.

Concessionaires paid a percentage of the gross receipts to the Fair, making a separate deal for each show. For "Strange as It Seems," for example, Dufour & Rogers agreed to pay around fifteen per cent on the first $500,000 of receipts. The show never reached that figure. The Fair administration provided either the ticket-taker or the cashier for each show—the option rested with the concessionaire. If the cashier was a Fair employee, the Fair collected the gate receipts at the end of the day and banked them, paying the concessionaires their share by check. Dufour & Rogers, with their usual acumen, prefer to have a Fair cashier and a Dufour & Rogers ticket-taker. "Then, if she takes any bad money, it is the Fair's hard luck and not ours," Mr. Rogers says.

"Strange as It Seems" is an example of an ancient American form of folk art, the freak show. Phineas T. Barnum was primarily an exploiter of freaks. He became a circus man late in life, and never got to be a good one. But after Barnum the freak show became a stale and devitalized art form. Syndicated cartoonists like Bob Ripley, who draws "Believe It or Not," and John Hix, Ripley's bustling young rival, who is author of the syndicated newspaper strip "Strange as It Seems," were instrumental in the revival, but the genius of the *risorgimento* was the late C. C. Pyle, a showman who realized that the American public loves to suffer. Pyle put on a large-scale freak show at the Century of Progress, calling it "Believe It or Not" and paying Ripley a royalty for the title. The selling point was that the highly peculiar principals in the show had been immortalized in the Ripley cartoons. The title had drawing power, but the unabashed appeal to the crowds' cruelty really put the show over. Women emerging from the exhibit advised friends not to go in. "You'll faint," they said. No stronger inducement to attendance could be offered—the friends went right in. Sally Rand topped the midway at Chicago during both summers of the Century of Progress, but the freak show finished a good second.

When Ripley's backers failed to come to terms with the World of Tomorrow, Lew and Joe moved in, using John Hix as a front man. Hix got five per cent of the gross for the use of his name and dutifully drew pictures of the freaks for his daily newspaper strip. Ripley, apparently peeved by the affront to his prestige, opened his own museum of curiosities on Broadway. Dufour & Rogers had exclusive freak-show rights at the World of Tomorrow, besides an excellent grasp of the neo-Frankenstein technique of breaking the audience down with horror. They had a man named Ellis Phillips in their show who drove a long nail into his nose, held up his socks with thumbtacks, sewed buttons onto his chest, and stuck hatpins through his cheeks. "It's a hell of an act," Joe Rogers said admiringly, "and we also have a very nice fellow who eats razor blades." The art of drawing up a bill for a modern freak show lies in alternating "strong" or "torture" acts in the layout, such as the tattooed girl, Betty Broadbent; the contortionist, Flexible Freddie, or the man who puts four golf balls in his mouth simultaneously. The customers move counterclockwise around three sides of the auditorium, and the strong acts are graduated in intensity, so that after passing the strongest of them the pleased patron will be within one bound of fresh air.

An ingenious gentleman named Nathan T. Eagle acted as manager. "The best ad for our show," Mr. Eagle said engagingly, "is the number of people who collapse or imagine they have delirium tremens after seeing it." The more important performers realize this and keep a painstaking record of how many people they cause to lose consciousness. Mr. Eagle's favorite performer was a Cuban Negro named Avelino Perez, who is always billed as the Cuban Pop-Eye because he can make his eyeballs pop far out of his head, either singly or in unison. Perez was a keen runner-up to the hatpin man in provoking comas. A gentleman who pulls weights on hooks passed through his eyelids was another close competitor

Perez was in especially good form one evening, and on performing his first, or left-eye, pop, caused a patron who had just dined at a midway restaurant to turn green. Perez popped his right eye, and the man went down cold. "A couple of our boys got hold of this fellow and started rubbing his wrists and pushing smelling salts under his nose," Mr. Eagle says. "Just as he started to regain consciousness—he was lying there on the floor in front of the Cubano, you know—Perez looked down at him and popped both eyeballs. The fellow passed right out again. Great sense of humor, that Cubano."

Sparring Partner

JOE LOUIS' knockout of Max Schmeling in their second match was a triumph for the theory that fighters should have tough sparring partners. Each of his bouts since has been a triumph for the same theory. Louis trained for Schmeling with the best colored heavyweights his handlers could hire. They included a man named George Nicholson, who is considered the best sparring partner in the business. Writers covering Louis' camp frequently reported that the partners were outboxing the champion. Schmeling's camp was run on quite a different basis. His sparring partners were four virtually anonymous human punching bags, on whom he practiced his blows with impunity. They seldom hit back except by mistake, and when they did the German punished them. Louis paid twenty-five dollars a day apiece for his sparring partners; Schmeling paid ten. A Schmeling victory, therefore, would have meant economic catastrophe for the sparring-partner industry.

"It goes to show that you got to be in the best of condition no matter who you fighting," George Nicholson says of the German's defeat. And getting in the "best of condition" implies to Nicholson sparring partners at twenty-five dollars a day. "You can hire any kind of cheap help to get theirself hit," says Nicholson. "What you got to pay good money for is somebody that is not going to get hisself hit. By not getting hisself hit, a sparring partner does more good to a fighter, because it sets the fighter to studying why he ain't hitting him." Nicholson's heartfelt interest in the defensive aspect of boxing, critics think, makes him an ideal sparring partner. It is this same interest which prevents him from being a great fighter. He is one of the kindest and least aggressive men who ever pulled on a boxing glove. "My one ambition," George sometimes says, "is to make my parents happy."

One reason he prefers sparring to fighting is that it keeps him out in the country for weeks at a time. George loves nature, usually soaking up its beauties through the pores of his skin, with his eyes closed. He is never more content than when he can sprawl his five-foot-eleven-and-three-quarter-inch body in one of the deep lawn chairs at Dr. Joseph Bier's training camp at Pompton Lakes, New Jersey, where Louis has trained for eleven Eastern fights and prepared for his match with Tony Galento at the Yankee Stadium. It is pleasant to watch Nicholson in his chair, a straw sombrero cocked over his eyes, which are further protected by smoked glasses with octagonal lenses. His torso slopes backward at an extremely obtuse angle to his thighs. One leg, with a size-thirteen shoe at the end of it, is negligently crossed over the other knee. Sometimes he drops off to sleep.

At two o'clock in the afternoon a brisk, pink-cheeked Jewish trainer named Mannie Seamon appears on the lawn and says, "C'mon, George, time to get going." The big man arises and starts for the gymnasium at the back of the house to prepare for the few minutes of acute discomfort whereby he pays for his leisure. Louis in training usually boxes against three sparring partners in an afternoon, two three-minute rounds with each man.

Nicholson is at home at Pompton Lakes. He has been there to help Louis prepare for four fights. In 1936 he spent three weeks in the same camp with Jim Braddock, when Braddock was getting ready to fight Tommy Farr. Now and then, Nicholson gets a fight on his own account, but he doesn't earn much that way. A sparring partner must be a pretty good fighter to give a star a workout, but if he is a financially successful fighter he will not work for training-camp wages. Since there are not many bouts available for a run-of-the-mill Negro heavyweight unless he has a powerful white promoter building him up, the best sparring partners are apt to be Negroes. White boys of commensurate ability are usually in training for their own fights.

A partner's life is not arduous when he has a camp job. He may take some hard punches in a workout with a hitter like Louis, but boxers in training wear headguards and sixteen-ounce gloves, and Nicholson has seldom received a cut. Nor has he ever been knocked down in a sparring match. The trouble with the calling is that stars usually train only four weeks for a bout and fight at most two or three times each year. Sometimes a heavyweight champion skips a year without fighting at all. In the intervals a sparring partner has slim pickings. This sometimes discourages Nicholson, but not for long. His is a sanguine nature.

"When it's no business in the fall," he says, "I go home to my parents' place in Mantua, New Jersey, and hunts rabbits and squirrels with a gun. And when it's no work in the spring I go there and work in the garden. And then, also, I might get a fight in-between-times." He does not say this last with any conviction. He had just fourteen fights in his first four years as a professional, and his net income from them was less than fifteen hundred dollars. George won nine bouts and thinks he got bad decisions in a couple he lost. He was twenty-eight—a ripe middle age for a fighter.

Boxers never start out to be sparring partners, any more than actors start out to be understudies. Fighters take sparring jobs to bridge over gaps between engagements, and even after a boxer has earned his living for years by sparring, he is apt to think of it as a temporary expedient. When Nicholson began boxing he thought he might be a champion.

George was born in Mantua, where his father was a teamster. Later his family moved to Yonkers, and there he played tackle on the high-school football team. His parents have moved back to Mantua since George left school, but he has a brother who still lives in Yonkers, "a govament man," he says, "WPA." One of George's earliest ambitions was to be a prize fighter, because he was always reading about boxing in the newspapers. The beginning of his true career was delayed, though. At Yonkers High he got to thinking he might be a lawyer. He abandoned this project for a peculiar reason. "I got out of the habit of trying to study law," he says, "on account of I saw I couldn't talk fast enough." For a few years he was bemused. He had got to thinking of himself as a professional man and he couldn't seem to readjust. Even today most of his associates believe he is a college graduate. The misconception, based upon his polished manner, is strengthened by the fact that he played for three seasons on a colored professional football team called the All-Southern Collegians. The Collegians accepted him without a diploma, George explains now. He quit his books after the third year of high school and took a job as porter in a hospital, playing professional football on autumn Sundays. He got the boxing fever again when he was twenty-three, an unusually advanced age for a debut.

George then weighed 243 pounds, which was far too much for his height. "I was so fat that one time I missed and fell right down," he says. "But I always throwed a good right hand anyway." He won two amateur bouts at smokers, both on knockouts, and then lost a decision to a fellow named Moe Levine in a big amateur show in Madison Square Garden. "I bounced him around, but I didn't know enough to finish him," George says now with a hint of cultured regret. A strange accident removed him from the ranks of the amateurs. He entered the 1934 *Daily News* Golden Gloves Tournament and was rejected because of a heart murmur. Soon after, he went up to Stillman's Gymnasium, where he met a matchmaker and got himself a preliminary bout on a card at a small professional club. The State Athletic Commission doctor found his heart action normal. Once he had fought this professional bout, he was no longer an amateur and after the fight, for which he got twenty-five dollars, he hit a long spell of unemployment. "I was so broke I didn't have *no* money," he says.

It is much easier for an amateur boxer to make a living than it is for a professional. Almost every night of the week several amateur shows are held in the city. Like bingo games and raffles, they are a recognized means of raising money for fraternal organizations. In most shows there are four competitors in each class. They meet in three-round bouts, with the winners competing in a final match later in the evening. There is a standard scale of remuneration. The winner of the final receives a seventeen-jewel watch, which may be sold in the open market for fifteen dollars. The runner-up gets a seven-jewel model, for which he can obtain five or six dollars. The two losers in the first bouts receive cheap timepieces known in amateur-boxing circles as "consolations." They have a sale value of two dollars. A preliminary boy "in the professionals" gets forty dollars for a bout, but opportunities for employment are much more limited.

Moreover, a State Athletic Commission rule restricts a professional to one bout every five days, whereas an amateur is free to compete every night.

Jim Howell, a Negro who is a frequent colleague of Nicholson as a sparring mate in the Louis camp, had a long career as an amateur. He remembers one week when he won four seventeen-jewel watches. "And it's funny," Howell says, "there's very few even the best amateurs that you can ask him the time and he got a watch. Or if it is, it's just a consolation." Now Howell is a professional and he hasn't had ten fights in the past year. But he still thinks he can break through into the big time.

Unemployment among professional boxers antedates the Hoover depression. There are about a thousand active prize fighters in Greater New York. At the height of the winter season seven boxing clubs operate, with from six to eight bouts on the average weekly card. Only about a hundred fighters out of the available thousand can possibly hope for weekly employment. When they do work most of them get from forty to seventy-five dollars, minus one third for their managers. The average boxer lives from one fight to the next on small loans. When he gets a match, he often owes his entire purse before he enters the ring. Colored boys have even bleaker prospects than their white competitors, but there is a high percentage of Negroes in any training gym. This is because their disadvantage, staggering as it is in the boxing world, is less than in ordinary industry. Even when they cannot get a match, they sometimes have a chance to spar with a white boy in the gymnasium, being paid from three to ten dollars for their trouble.

The plight of a starving boxer is particularly cruel because by his daily exertions he increases his appetite beyond ordinary human bounds. Worse than hunger is the fear of not being able to get up his dues, the dollar a week he must pay for the privilege of using the gymnasium and showers. There are other minuscular expenses which seem huge in the eyes of a boy with no match in sight: he uses ninety cents' worth of gauze and twenty-five cents' worth of tape a week to wrap his fists for sparring matches; he buys rubbing alcohol and Omega Oil, which he applies himself if he cannot afford a dollar for a professional rubdown. In order to avoid cuts he must buy a leather headguard.

Plunged into this athletic slum, Nicholson felt sad and lonely. He was about to go back to his job at the hospital when, in the fall of 1934, his solid frame and large white smile attracted the attention of Jim Braddock, at that time making his comeback, who also trained at Stillman's. Braddock had not yet got back to the point where he could pay experienced sparring partners. He noticed that the big colored boy "took a very good punch," a quality which Jim admired, and he offered to teach George some of the inner mysteries of the craft. Braddock got free workouts and Nicholson got free boxing lessons. Within six months Braddock was again in the big money, training for the fight in which he was to win the championship from Max Baer, and Nicholson had learned so fast that he qualified as one of Jim's paid sparring partners. Surprisingly enough, the heavy-set, oldish novice had innate style. He was a natural boxer with a willingness to take punishment when it was necessary. This is not the same as being a natural fighter, which calls for a certain streak of cruelty.

Nicholson still uses Stillman's as a business headquarters when he has no camp job and is running short of money. He loafs for three or four weeks after a training camp breaks up, then makes his appearance at the gymnasium, which is on Eighth Avenue between Fifty-fourth and Fifty-fifth. "More business is transacts there than anyplace in the world," he explains. Trainers and managers are always glad to see him.

"George is a good boy," says Mannie Seamon, who is a sort of personnel director for training camps. "Some sparring partners will throw a head [butt] or throw an elbow and maybe give a man a cut so the fight will have to be postponed, but George don't cross nobody up. He boxes quick so the fighter can't stay lazy, and he keeps throwing punches so the fighter can't make lax. A good boy."

When there is no camp job in sight George will sometimes box with a heavyweight training for a minor bout, receiving five or ten dollars for his afternoon's work, according to the fighter's prosperity. He can usually pick up fifteen or twenty dollars a week, which covers living expenses, until he gets more regular employment. George is a bachelor. "I can't see my ways through to getting married the way things are," he says. When he is in the metropolitan region, he stays with the WPA brother and his family in Yonkers. He doesn't go to Harlem much, because, he says, he doesn't want to change his ways and run wild. George doesn't smoke or drink. At Stillman's he observes the other heavyweights in the training ring. He makes mental note of their styles so that he will be able to imitate them on request. A sparring partner must be versatile. For example, when Louis was training for Nathan Mann his sparring partners were urged to throw left hooks like Mann. But when he was training for Schmeling the script called for George to throw right hands to Louis' jaw. Louis never did learn to block them, but his trainers felt that he would develop a certain immunity through inoculation. In 1939 Nicholson was emphasizing left hooks again, like Tony Galento.

His greatest benefactor, George thinks, was Jim Braddock. "There is no discrimination with Jim," Nicholson says. "When I was training with him in 1936 for that Schmeling fight that never come off he put rocks in my bed just like anybody else." This is a reminiscence of the refined horseplay that always distinguishes Braddock's camps from those of less whimsical prize fighters. A Louis camp is more restful. "All we does is play catch with a baseball and sometimes talk jokes," Nicholson says. He first trained with Louis when the present champion was preparing for his fight with Braddock in Chicago. Having boxed so often with Braddock, Nicholson could illustrate all his moves beautifully. Boxers do not consider such a transfer of allegiance unethical. You hire a sparring partner, and he does his best for you while you pay him. He may be in the enemy's camp for your next fight. Braddock hired Nicholson again before the Tommy Farr fight.

The worst sparring partner in all history was a young giant named James J. Jeffries, who joined Jim Corbett's camp when Corbett was training for his bout with Bob Fitzsimmons in Carson City, Nevada, forty-one years ago. Jeffries knocked Corbett out the first time they put on the gloves, which had an evil effect on Corbett's morale. He lost to Fitzsimmons. Later the ex-sparring partner knocked Fitzsimmons out and became champion of the world. Nicholson has never come near knocking out Braddock or Louis or even Primo Carnera, whom he trained for one of his last fights, but sometimes he is engaged to box with young heavyweights whom he must treat tenderly. A beginner can learn much from a good sparring partner, but if the partner knocks his brains out, as the boys say, the novice loses his nerve. George's most delicate client was a former college football player with the face of a Hollywood star and the shoulders of a Hercules, who was being merchandised by a smart manager. The manager had interested three Wall Street men in his dazzling heavyweight "prospect," assuring them that he was potentially the greatest fighter since Dempsey. The Wall Streeters actually put the boxer and the manager on salary and bought the youngster an automobile. This was before the boy had had even one fight. The manager, in order to prevent his backers from hearing any skeptical reports, arranged to have the football player train in a private gymnasium frequented only by fat businessmen. He then hired Nicholson to spar with him, and each afternoon the Wall Streeters and their friends visited the gymnasium and watched their hopeful knock George about. George got five dollars a workout. They were much astonished subsequently when, after supporting their coming champion for a year and a half, he was knocked out in a four-round bout they got him with another novice.

George says there was nothing wrong about his conduct. "That manager hired me to box with that boy," he says. "He didn't hire me to hurt him."

There isn't much money in the sparring business, George concedes, but there doesn't seem to be much in anything else, either. The prospect of injury doesn't bother him, because he seldom takes a punch solidly. He "gets on it" before it develops power, or else he takes it on his forearms or shoulders, or at worst "rolls away" from it as it lands. "I like the old word for boxing," he once said. "The manly art of *de*fense. And I don't fear no man. Now, that Joe, he really can punch. He can really punch. What I mean, he can punch, really. Yet he ain't never no more'n shook me. And when I feel myself getting punch-drunk I'm going to quit. I'm going to look me up a profitable business somewhere that's a profit in it."

Nicholson was in his chair at Pompton Lakes when he made this declaration. The chairs at his left and right were occupied by Jim Howell and another large colored man named Elza Thompson. Each of the three had his left leg crossed over his right knee. After a long interval they recrossed their legs in unison, this time with the right on top. There was no spoken word to suggest the shift, just telepathy. Undisturbed by the musical sigh of Nicholson's voice, Howell and Thompson were apparently asleep. Yet the triple movement was perfectly synchronized, like something the Rockettes might do, but in slow time.

At the phrase "punch-drunk" Howell had opened one eye.

"How you going to know you punch-drunk, George?" he inquired. "A man punch-drunk, he don't know he punch-drunk. That the sign he punch-drunk."

Nicholson thought this over in deep gloom for a while.

Then he said, "Sometime when I boxing with a fellow that hit me right on the button, and I know he ain't got no right to hit me on the button, and I boxing with him again and he hit me on the button again, then I going to quit."

After this the three sparring partners all fell asleep.

The Jollity Building

I—INDIANS, HEELS, AND TENANTS

IN THE JOLLITY BUILDING, which stands six stories high and covers half of a Broadway block in the high Forties, the term "promoter" means a man who mulcts another man of a dollar, or any fraction or multiple thereof. The verb "to promote" always takes a personal object, and the highest praise you can accord someone in the Jollity Building is to say, "He has promoted some very smart people." The Jollity Building—it actually has a somewhat different name, and the names of its inhabitants are not the ones which will appear below—is representative of perhaps a dozen or so buildings in the upper stories of which the small-scale amusement industry nests like a tramp pigeon. All of them draw a major part of their income from the rental of their stores at street level, and most of them contain on their lower floors a dance hall or a billiard parlor, or both. The Jollity Building has both. The dance hall, known as Jollity Danceland, occupies the second floor. The poolroom is in the basement. It is difficult in such a building to rent office space to any business house that wants to be taken very seriously, so the upper floors fill up with the petty nomads of Broadway—chiefly orchestra leaders, theatrical agents, bookmakers, and miscellaneous promoters.

Eight coin-box telephone booths in the lobby of the Jollity Building serve as offices for promoters and others who cannot raise the price of desk space on an upper floor. The phones are used mostly for incoming calls. It is a matter of perpetual regret to Morty, the renting agent of the building, that he cannot collect rent from the occupants of the booths. He always refers to them as the Telephone Booth Indians, because in their lives the telephone booth furnishes sustenance as well as shelter, as the buffalo did for the Arapahoe and Sioux. A Telephone Booth Indian on the hunt often tells a prospective investor to call him at a certain hour in the afternoon, giving the victim the number of the phone in one of the booths. The Indian implies, of course, that it is a private line. Then the Indian has to hang in the booth until the fellow calls. To hang, in Indian language, means to loiter. "I used to hang in Forty-sixth Street, front of *Variety*," a small bookmaker may say, referring to a previous business location. Seeing the Indians hanging in the telephone booths is painful to Morty, but there is nothing he can do about it. The regular occupants of the booths recognize one another's rights. It may be understood among them, for instance, that a certain orchestra leader receives calls in a particular booth between three and four in the afternoon and that a competitor has the same booth from four to five. In these circumstances, ethical Indians take telephone messages for each other. There are always fewer vacancies in the telephone booths than in any other part of the Jollity Building.

While awaiting a call, an Indian may occasionally emerge for air, unless the lobby is so crowded that there is a chance he might lose his place to a transient who does not understand the house rules. Usually, however, the Indian hangs in the booth with the door open, leaning against the wall and reading a scratch sheet in order to conserve time. Then, if somebody rings up and agrees to lend him two dollars, he will already have picked a horse on which to lose that amount. When an impatient stranger shows signs of wanting to use a telephone, the man in the booth closes the door, takes the receiver off the hook, and makes motions with his lips, as if talking. To add verisimilitude to a long performance, he occasionally hangs up, takes the receiver down again, drops a nickel in the slot, whirls the dial three or four times, and hangs up again, after which the nickel comes back. Eventually the stranger goes away, and the man in the booth returns to the study of his scratch sheet. At mealtimes, the Telephone Booth Indians sometimes descend singly to the Jollity Building's lunch counter, which is at one end of the poolroom in the basement. The busiest lunch periods are the most favorable for a stunt the boys have worked out to get free nourishment. An Indian seats himself at the counter and eats two or three *pastrami* sandwiches. As he is finishing his lunch, one of his comrades appears at the head of the stairs and shouts that he is wanted on the telephone. The Indian rushes upstairs, absent-mindedly omitting to pay for his meal. Barney, the lunch-counter proprietor, is too busy to go after him when he fails to return after a reasonable time. An Indian can rarely fool Barney more than once or twice. The maneuver requires nice timing and unlimited faith in one's accomplice. Should the accomplice fail to make his entrance, the Indian at the counter might be compelled to eat *pastrami* sandwiches indefinitely, acquiring frightful indigestion and piling up an appalling debt.

Morty, the renting agent, is a thin, sallow man of forty whose expression has been compared, a little unfairly, to that of a dead robin. He is not, however, a man without feeling; he takes a personal interest in the people who spend much of their lives in the Jollity Building. It is about the same sort of interest that Curator Raymond Ditmars takes in the Bronx Zoo's vampire bats. "I know more heels than any other man in the world," Morty sometimes says, not without pride. "Everywhere I go around Broadway, I get 'Hello, how are you?' Heels that haven't been with me for years, some of them." Morty usually reserves the appellation "heel" for the people who rent the forty-eight cubicles, each furnished with a desk and two chairs, on the third floor of the Jollity Building. These cubicles are formed by partitions of wood and frosted glass which do not quite reach the ceiling. Sufficient air to maintain human life is supposed to circulate over the partitions. The offices rent for $10 and $12.50 a month, payable in advance. "Twelve and a half dollars with air, ten dollars without air," Morty says facetiously. "Very often the heels who rent them take the air without telling me." Sometimes a Telephone Booth Indian acquires enough capital to rent a cubicle. He thus rises in the social scale and becomes a heel. A cubicle has three advantages over a telephone booth. One is that you cannot get a desk into a telephone booth. Another is that you can play pinochle in a cubicle. Another is that a heel gets his name on the directory in the lobby, and the white letters have a bold, legitimate look.

The vertical social structure of the Jollity Building is subject to continual shifts. Not only do Indians become heels, but a heel occasionally accumulates $40 or $50 with which to pay a month's rent on one of the larger offices, all of them unfurnished, on the fourth, fifth, or sixth floor. He then becomes a tenant. Morty always views such progress with suspicion, because it involves signing a lease, and once a heel has signed a lease, you cannot put him out without serving a dispossess notice and waiting ten days. A tenant, in Morty's opinion, is just a heel who is planning to get ten days' free rent. "Any time a heel acts prosperous enough to rent an office," Morty says, "you know he's getting ready to take you." A dispossessed tenant often reappears in the Jollity Building as an Indian. It is a life cycle. Morty has people in the building who have been Telephone Booth Indians, heels, and tenants several times each. He likes them best when they are in the heel stage. "You can't collect rent from a guy who hangs in the lobby," he says in explanation, "and with a regular tenant of an unfurnished office, you got too many headaches." He sometimes breaks off a conversation with a friendly heel by saying, "Excuse me, I got to go upstairs and insult a tenant."

As if to show his predilection for the heels, Morty has his own office on the third floor. It is a large corner room with windows on two sides. There is a flattering picture of the Jollity Building on one of the walls, and six framed plans, one of each floor, on another wall. Also in the office are an unattractive, respectable-looking secretary and, on Morty's desk, a rather depressing photograph of his wife. The conventionality of this *décor* makes Morty unhappy, and he spends as little time as possible in his office. Between nine o'clock in the morning, when he arrives and dejectedly looks through his mail for rent checks he does not expect to find, and six-thirty in the evening, when he goes home to Rockaway, he lives mostly amid the pulsating activity outside his office door.

The furnished cubicles on the third floor yield an income of about $500 a month, which, as Morty says, is not hay. Until a few years ago, the Jollity Building used to feel it should provide switchboard service for these offices. The outgoing telephone calls of the heels were supposed to be paid for at the end of every business day. This system necessitated the use of a cordon of elevator boys to prevent tenants from escaping. "Any heel who made several telephone calls toward the end of the month, you could kiss him good-by," Morty says. "As soon as he made up his mind to go out of business he started thinking of people to telephone. It was cheaper for him to go out of business than settle for the calls, anyhow. The only way you can tell if a heel is still in business, most of the time, anyway, is to look in his office for his hat. If his hat is gone, he is out of business." A minor annoyance of the switchboard system was the tendency of heels to call the operator and ask for the time. "None of them were going anywhere, but they all wanted to know the time," Morty says resentfully. "None of them had watches. Nobody would be in this building unless he had already hocked his watch." There are lady heels, too, but if they are young Morty calls them "heads." (Morty meticulously refers to all youngish women as "heads," which has the same meaning as "broads" or "dolls" but is newer; he does not want his conversation to sound archaic.) Heads also abused the switchboard system. "One head that used to claim to sell stockings," says Morty, "called the board one day, and when the operator said, 'Five o'clock,' this head said, 'My God, I didn't eat yet!' If there had been no switchboard, she would never have known she was hungry. She would have saved a lot of money."

As a consequence of these abuses, the switchboard was abolished, and practically all the heels now make their telephone calls from three open coin-box telephones against the wall in a corridor that bisects the third floor. The wall for several feet on each side of the telephones is covered with numbers the heels have jotted down. The Jollity Building pays a young man named Angelo to sit at a table in a small niche near the telephones and answer incoming calls. He screams "Who?" into the mouthpiece and then shuffles off to find whatever heel is wanted. On days when Angelo is particularly weary, he just says, "He ain't in," and hangs up. He also receives and distributes the mail for the heels. Angelo is a pallid chap who has been at various periods a chorus boy, a taxi driver, and a drummer in one of the bands which maintain headquarters in the Jollity Building. "Every time a heel comes in," Angelo says, "he wants to know 'Are you sure there isn't a letter for me that feels like it had a check in it? . . . That's funny, the fellow swore he mailed it last night.' Then he tries to borrow a nickel from me so he can telephone."

Not having a nickel is a universal trait of people who rent the cubicles, and they spend a considerable portion of the business day hanging by the third-floor telephones, waiting for the arrival of somebody to borrow a nickel from. While waiting, they talk to Angelo, who makes it a rule not to believe anything they say. There are no booths in the corridor because Morty does not want any Telephone Booth Indians to develop on the third floor.

Morty himself often goes to visit with Angelo and terrifies the heels with his bilious stare. "They all say they got something big for next week," he tells Angelo in a loud, carrying voice, "but the rent is 'I'll see you tomorrow.' " Morty's friends sometimes drop in there to visit him. He likes to sit on Angelo's table with them and tell about the current collection of furnished-office inhabitants. "Who is that phony-looking heel who just passed, you want to know?" he may say during such a recapitulation. "Hey, this is funny. He happens to be legitimate—autos to hire. The heel in the next office publishes a horse magazine. If he gets a winner, he eats. Then there's one of them heels that hires girls to sell permanent waves for fifty cents down, door to door. The girl takes the fifty cents and gives the dame a ticket, but when the dame goes to look for the beauty parlor it says on the ticket, there is no such beauty parlor at that address.

"We got two heels writing plays. They figure they got nothing to do, so they might as well write a play, and if it clicks, they might also eat. Then we got a lady heel who represents Brazilian music publishers and also does a bit of booking; also a head who is running a school for hat-check girls, as it seems the hat-check profession is very complicated for some of the type of minds they got in it. Those heads who walk through the hall are going no place. They just stick their potato in every office and say, 'Anything for me today?' They do not even look to see if it is a theatrical office. If they expected to find anything, they would not be over here. What would anybody here have to offer? Once in a while a sap from the suburbs walks into one of the offices on this floor thinking he can get some talent cheap. 'Sure,' some heel says, 'I got just the thing you want.' They run down in the lobby looking for somebody. They ask some head they meet in the lobby, 'Are you a performer?' They try the other little agents that they know. The whole date is worth probably four dollars, and the forty cents' commission they split sometimes four ways."

Morty's favorite heel of the current lot is a tall Chesterfieldian old man named Dr. Titus Heatherington, who is the president of the Anti-Hitlerian League of the Western Hemisphere. Dr. Heatherington for many years lectured in vacant stores on sex topics and sold a manual of facts every young man should know. "The line became, in a manner of speaking, exhausted," Dr. Heatherington says, "because of the increasing sophistication of the contemporary adolescent, so I interested myself in this great crusade, in which I distribute at a nominal price a very fascinating book by Cornelius Vanderbilt, Jr., and everything in it must be exactly as stated, because otherwise Hitler could have sued Mr. Vanderbilt for libel. Incidentally, I sell a lot more books than I have for years. I do particularly well at Coney Island."

Heels are often, paradoxically, more affluent than the official lessees of larger offices. Many fellows who rent the big units take in subtenants, and if there are enough of them, each man's share of the rent may be less than the $10 a month minimum rent a heel has to pay. One two-desk office on the fourth, fifth, or sixth floor may serve as headquarters for four theatrical agents, a band leader, a music arranger, a manager of prize fighters, and a dealer in pawn tickets. They agree on a schedule by which each man has the exclusive use of a desk for a few hours every day, to impress people who call by appointment, and the office is used collectively, when no outsiders are present, for games of rummy. All the fellows in the office receive their telephone calls on a single coin-box machine affixed to the wall. Subtenants often make bets among themselves, the amount of the wager corresponding to each bettor's share of the rent. The loser is supposed to pay double rent, the winner nothing. This causes difficulties for Morty when he comes to collect the rent. The official lessee always protests that he would like to pay on the dot but the other boys haven't paid him. Subtenants who have won bets consider themselves absolved of any responsibility, and the fellows who are supposed to pay double are invariably broke. Morty makes an average of fifteen calls to collect a month's rent on an office, and thus acquires a much greater intimacy with the tenants than the agents of a place like Rockefeller Center or River House.

Desk room in a large office has the advantage of being much more dignified than a cubicle on the third floor, but there is one drawback: Morty's rule that not more than two firm names may be listed on the directory in the lobby for any one office. Callers therefore have to ask the elevator boys where to find some of the subtenants. If the elevator boys do not like the subtenant in question, they say they never heard of him. Nor will the implacable Morty permit more than two names to be painted on any office door. Junior subtenants get around the rule by having a sign painter put their names on strips of cardboard which they insert between the glass and the wooden frame of the door or affix to the glass by strips of tape. "You cannot let a tenant creep on you," Morty says in justification of his severity. "You let them get away with eight names on the door, and the next thing they will be asking you for eight keys to the men's room."

Morty's parents were named Goldberg, and he was born in the Bensonhurst region of Brooklyn. He almost finished a commercial course in high school before he got his first job, being an order clerk for a chain of dairy-and-herring stores. In the morning he would drive to each of these stores and find out from the store managers what supplies they needed from the company's warehouse. Since he had little to do in the afternoons, he began after a while to deliver packages for a bootlegger who had been a high-school classmate and by chance had an office in the Jollity Building. The name on the door of the office was the Music Writers Mutual Publishing Company. About a quarter of the firms in the building at that time were fronts for bootleggers, Morty recalls. "Repeal was a terrible blow to property values in this district," he says. "Bootleggers were always the best pay." Seeing a greater future in bootlegging than in dairy goods and herring, Morty soon went to work for his old classmate on a full-time basis. The moment Morty decided that his future lay on Broadway, he translated his name from Goldberg into Ormont. " '*Or*' is French for gold," he sometimes explains, "and '*mont*' is the same as 'berg.' But the point is it's got more class than Goldberg."

By diligent application, Morty worked his way up to a partnership in the Music Writers Mutual Publishing Company. The partners made good use of their company's name. They advertised in pulp magazines, offering to write music for lyrics or lyrics for music, to guarantee publication, and to send back to the aspiring song writer a hundred free copies of his work, all for one hundred dollars. The Music Writers Mutual agreed to pay him the customary royalties on all copies sold. There never were any royalties, because Morty and his partner had only the author's hundred copies printed. They kept a piano in their office and hired a professional musician for thirty-five dollars a week to set music to lyrics. Morty himself occasionally wrote lyrics to the tunes clients sent in, and had a lot of fun doing it. At times the music business went so well that the partners were tempted to give up bootlegging. There were so many similar publishing firms, however, that there was not a steady living in it. "But you would be surprised," Morty says now, "how near it came to paying our overhead." The volume of mail made it look bona fide. They built up a prosperous semi-wholesale liquor business, specializing in furnishing whisky to firms in the Garment Center, which used it for presents to out-of-town buyers. "The idea on that stuff was that it should be as reasonable as possible without killing anybody," Morty says. "It was a good, legitimate dollar." The depression in the garment industry ruined the Music Writers Mutual Publishing Company's business even before repeal and left Morty broke.

The Jollity Building belongs to the estate of an old New York family, and in the twenties the trustees had installed as manager one of the least promising members of the family, a middle-aged, alcoholic Harvard man whom they wanted to keep out of harm's way. Morty had been such a good tenant and seemed so knowing a fellow that the Harvard man offered him a job at twenty-five dollars a week as his assistant. When the manager ran off with eleven thousand dollars in rents and a head he had met in the lobby, Morty took over his job. He has held it ever since. The trustees feel, as one of them has expressed it, that "Mr. Ormont understands the milieu." He now gets fifty dollars a week and two per cent of the total rents, which adds about two thousand a year to his income.

The nostalgia Morty often feels for the opportunities of prohibition days is shared by the senior tenant in the building, the proprietor of the Quick Art Theatrical Sign Painting Company, on the sixth floor. The sign painter, a Mr. Hy Sky—a name made up of the first syllable of his first name, Hyman, and the last syllable of a surname which no one can remember—is a bulky, red-faced man who has rented space in the Jollity Building for twenty-five years. With his brother, a lean, sardonic man known as Si Sky, he paints signs and lobby displays for burlesque and movie houses and does odd jobs of lettering for people in all sorts of trades. He is an extremely fast letterer and he handles a large volume of steady business, but it lacks the exhilaration of prohibition years. Then he was sometimes put to work at two o'clock in the morning redecorating a clip joint, so that it could not be identified by a man who had just been robbed of a bank roll and might return with cops the next day. "Was that fun!" Hy howls reminiscently. "And always cash in advance! If the joint had green walls, we would make them pink. We would move the bar opposite to where it was, and if there was booths in the place, we would paint them a different color and change them around. Then the next day, when the cops came in with the sap, they would say, 'Is this the place? Try to remember the side of the door the bar was on as you come in.' The sap would hesitate, and the cops would say, 'I guess he can't identify the premises,' and they would shove him along. It was a nice, comfortable dollar for me."

Hy has a clinical appreciation of meretricious types which he tries unsuccessfully to arouse in Morty. Sometimes, when Hy has a particularly preposterous liar in his place, he will telephone the renting agent's office and shout, "Morty, pop up and see the character I got here! He is the most phoniest character I seen in several years." The person referred to seldom resents such a description. People in the Jollity Building neighborhood like to be thought of as characters. "He is a real character," they say, with respect, of any fascinatingly repulsive acquaintance. Most promoters are characters. Hy Sky attributes the stability of his own business to the fact that he is willing to "earn a hard dollar." "The trouble with the characters," he says, "is they are always looking for a soft dollar. The result is they knock theirselves out trying too hard to have it easy. So what do they get after all? Only the miss-meal cramps." Nevertheless, it always gives Hy a genteel pleasure to collaborate, in a strictly legitimate way, with any of the promoters he knows. The promoter may engage him to paint a sign saying, "A new night club will open soon on these premises. Concessionaires interested telephone So-and-So at such-and-such a number." The name is the promoter's own, and the telephone given is, as Hy knows, in a booth in the Jollity lobby. The promoter, Hy also knows, will place this sign in front of a vacant night club with which he has absolutely no connection, in the hope that some small hat-check concessionaire with money to invest in a new club will read the sign before someone gets around to removing it and take it seriously. If the concessionaire telephones, the promoter will make an appointment to receive him in a Jollity cubicle borrowed from some other promoter for the occasion and will try to get a couple of hundred dollars as a deposit on the concession. If successful, he will lose the money on a horse in the sixth race at an obscure track in California. The chances of getting any money out of this promotional scheme are exceedingly slight, but the pleasure of the promoter when the device succeeds is comparable to that of a sportsman who catches a big fish on a light line. Contemplation of the ineffectual larceny in the promoter's heart causes Hy to laugh constantly while lettering such a sign. A contributory cause of his laughter is the knowledge that he will receive the only dollar that is likely to change hands in the transaction—the dollar he gets for painting the sign.

Musicians are not characters, in Hy's estimation, but merely a mild variety of phony. As such, they afford him a tempered amusement. When two impressive band leaders in large, fluffy overcoats call upon him for a communal cardboard door sign, toward the cost of which each contributes twenty-five cents, he innocently inquires, "How many of you are there in that office?" One of the band leaders will reply grandiosely, "Oh, we all have separate offices; the sign is for the door to quite a huge suite." Hy laughs so hard he bends double to relieve the strain on his diaphragm. His brother, Si, who lives in continual fear that Hy will die of apoplexy, abandons his work and slaps Hy's back until the crowing abates. "A suite," Hy repeats weakly at intervals for a half-hour afterward, "a huge suite they got, like on the subway at six o'clock you could get." Hy also paints, at an average price of twenty-five cents, cardboard backs for music racks. These pieces of cardboard, whose only function is to identify the band, bear in bright letters its name, which is usually something like Everett Winterbottom's Rhumba Raiders. When a Jollity Building band leader has acquired a sign for his door and a set of these lettered cardboards, he is equipped for business. If, by some unlikely chance, he gets an engagement, usually to play a week end in a cabaret in Queens or the Bronx, he hurries out to the curb on Seventh Avenue in front of Charlie's Bar & Grill, where there are always plenty of musicians, and picks up the number of fellows he requires, generally four. The men tapped go over to Eighth Avenue and get their instruments out of pawn. A musician who owns several instruments usually leaves them all in a pawnshop, ransoming one when he needs it to play a date and putting it back the next day. If, when he has a chance to work, he lacks the money to redeem an instrument, he borrows the money from a Jollity Building six-for-fiver, a fellow who will lend you five dollars if you promise to pay him six dollars within twenty-four hours. Meanwhile, the band leader looks up a fellow who rents out orchestra arrangements guaranteed to be exact, illegal copies of those one or another of the big bandsmen has exclusive use of. The band leader puts the arrangements and his cardboards under his arm and goes down to Charlie's to wait for the other musicians to come back from the hock shop. That night Everett Winterbottom's Rhumba Raiders ride again. The only worry in the world the Raiders have, at least for the moment, is that they will have to finish their engagement before a union delegate discovers them and takes away their cards. Each man is going to receive three dollars a night, which is seven dollars below union scale.

II—FROM HUNGER

IT IS LIKELY that when the six-story Jollity Building, so called, is pulled down, it will be replaced by a one- or two-story taxpayer, because buildings along Broadway now derive their chief incomes from the stores at street level, and taxpayers, which earn just as much from their stores, are cheaper to operate. When the Jollity Building comes down, the small theatrical agents, the sleazy costumers, the band leaders in worn camel's-hair overcoats, the aged professors of acrobatic dancing, and all the petty promoters who hang, as the phrase goes, in the Jollity Building's upper floors will spill out into the street and join the musicians who are waiting for jobs and the pitchmen who sell self-threading needles along the curb.

Meanwhile, day after day, small-time performers ride the elevators and wander through the grimy halls of the Jollity Building looking for work. Jack McGuire, who in the evening is a bouncer in Jollity Danceland, on the second floor, thoroughly understands the discouraged performers. "They're just like mice," he says, "they been pushed around so much." Jack is a heavyweight prize fighter who recently retired for the forty-eighth time in the last five years. He still looks impressively healthy, since few of his fights have lasted more than one round. "It was the greatest two-minute battle you ever seen," he said a while ago, describing his latest comeback, against a local boy in Plainfield, New Jersey. "For the first thirty seconds I was ahead on points." Jack's face is of a warm, soft pink induced by the prolonged application of hot towels in the Jollity Building barbership, which is just off the lobby. Sprawled in the sixth barber chair from the door, he sleeps off hang-overs. His shoulders, naturally wide, are accentuated by the padding Broadway clothiers lavish on their customers. Among the putty-colored, sharp-nosed little men and the thin-legged women in the elevators, he looks like an animal of a different breed. His small eyes follow the performers constantly. During the day, Jack is a runner for a great number of agents. He learns from them where there are openings for various types of talent—ballroom-dancing teams, Irish tenors, singing hostesses, and so on—and then steers performers to the agents handling the jobs. He has strolled about the Jollity Building so long that he knows hundreds of them by sight. "Such-and-such an agent is looking for a ballroom team," he will tell a husband-and-wife pair he knows. "A week in a Chink joint in Yonkers." He gives them one of the agent's cards, on which he writes "Jack." If the team gets the week, at forty dollars, it must pay a commission of four dollars to the agent, and another of two dollars to Jack. The second commission is entirely extralegal, since Jack is not a licensed agent, but Jack often steers performers to a job they wouldn't have had otherwise, so they don't kick. Agents are glad to have Jack work with them, because buyers of talent want instantaneous service and few acts can be reached by telephone during the day. Sometimes, when an act is held over for a second week and fails to pay the agent his additional commission, Jack is engaged to put the muscle on the unethical performer. When Jack encounters him, usually in Charlie's Bar & Grill or at the I. & Y. cigar store, which are both near the Jollity Building, he says, "Say, I hear your agent is looking for you." The hint is enough ordinarily. When it is not, Jack uses the muscle.

The proprietor of Jollity Danceland is the most solvent tenant in the building and he pays by far the largest rent. The dance hall has an entrance of its own on the street and is reached by stairway and elevators reserved for customers. Jack receives five dollars a night for bouncing there. At one time the proprietor planned to put the bouncers on a piecework basis, but he changed his mind, to Jack's lasting regret. "I would of bounced all the customers," he says. "I would of made my fortune sure." Between the hours of six and eight every evening, at a small gymnasium west of Tenth Avenue, Jack trains a few amateur boxers he manages. There is not much money in managing amateurs, who never earn more than sixteen dollars in a night, but Jack thinks that someday one of his protégés might show promise, and then he could sell the boy's contract to an established manager. With all these sources of income, McGuire would live in affluence, by Jollity Building standards, if it were not for his thirst, which is perpetual. When he drinks, he sometimes threatens to put the muscle on strangers who refuse to pay for his liquor. This detracts from his popularity at the neighborhood bars, and the bartenders resort to chemical expedients to get rid of him. Jack is proud of the immunity he has developed. "I got so I like those Mickey Finns as good as beer," he often tells acquaintances.

Although Jack has never paid any office rent, he is on familiar terms with Morty Ormont, the lugubrious renting agent of the Jollity Building, whom he encounters in the barbershop and at the lunch counter in the basement. He sometimes borrows a dollar from Morty, always giving him a hundred-dollar check on a bank in Lynchburg, Virginia, as security. Morty, of course, knows that Jack has no account in the bank. In the Jollity Building, checks are considered not as literal drafts on existent funds but as a particularly solemn form of promise to repay a loan, since it is believed that the holder of a bad check has it in his power to throw the check writer into jail for twenty-five years. When Jack repays the dollar, usually in four installments, Morty gives the check back to him. Practically everybody in the Jollity Building carries a checkbook. Fellows who cannot borrow from Morty even by giving him checks sometimes ask him to vouch for them so they can borrow from six-for-fivers, the chaps who lend five dollars one day and collect six dollars the next. "Will you O.K. me with a Shylock, Morty?" one of these suppliants will ask. "You know I'm an honest man." "In what way?" Morty demands cynically if he does not know the man well. If the fellow says, "In every way," Morty refuses to O.K. him, because he is obviously a crook.

The prize-fight managers who hang in the Jollity Building are, as one might expect, of an inferior order. The boys they handle provide what sports writers like to call the "stiff opposition" against which incubating stars compile "sterling records." "When the Garden brings in some fellow that you never heard of from Cleveland or Baltimore or one of them other Western states, and it says in the paper he has had stiff opposition," says a Jollity Building manager known as Acid Test Ike, "that means the opposition has been stiffs. In other words, the class of boys I got." It is Acid Test who manages Jack in all of his comebacks. For each comeback, Ike and Jack go to some place like Lancaster, Pennsylvania, or Wheeling, West Virginia, where there happens to be a novice heavyweight, and Ike tells the sports editor of the local newspaper, "My man will give this kid the acid test." Then Jack gets knocked out. Naturally, Ike also has to manage smaller fighters who will get knocked out by middleweights and lightweights. "A fellow could make a pleasant dollar with a stable of bums," he sometimes says, "only the competition is so terrific. There is an element getting into the game that is willing to be knocked out very cheap." Acid Test Ike always wears a bottle-green suit, a brick-red topcoat, and an oyster-white hat. "It don't take brains to make money with a good fighter," he says rather bitterly when he feels an attack of the miss-meal cramps coming on. "Running into a thing like that is just luck."

Performers, when they arrive at the Jollity Building looking for work, usually take an elevator straight to the floor on which the agent who most often books them is located. After leaving this agent, they make a tour of the other agents' offices to see if anyone else has a job for them. Only when rendered desperate by hunger do they stray down to the third floor, where the people Morty calls the heels hold forth in furnished offices each about the size of a bathroom. Since the heels constitute the lowest category of tenant in the building, no proprietor of a first-class chop-suey joint or roadhouse would call on them for talent. "The best you can get there," performers say, "is a chance to work Saturday night at a ruptured saloon for *bubkis*." "*Bubkis*" is a Yiddish word which means "large beans."

One of the most substantial agents in the building is Jerry Rex, a swarthy, discouraged man who used to be a ventriloquist. He has an unusually large one-room office, which was once the studio of a teacher of Cuban dancing. The walls are painted in orange-and-black stripes, and there are several full-length wall mirrors, in which the pupils used to watch themselves dance. Mr. Rex sits at a desk at the end of the office opposite the door, and performers waiting to speak to him sit on narrow benches along the walls. Rex has an assistant named Dave, who sits on a couch in one corner of the room. Rex always professes to be waiting for a call from a theater owner in, for example, Worcester, Massachusetts, who will want four or five acts and a line of eight girls. He urges all the entertainers who drop in at his place to sit down and wait with him. "Also, a fellow who owns the biggest night club in Scranton is going to pop up here any minute," he tells the performers confidentially. "You better wait around." The man from Worcester never calls up, but the performers don't mind killing a half-hour with Jerry. "It rests your feet," one woman singer has said, "and also you meet a lot of people you know." Jerry leaves Dave in charge of the office when he goes out. "If Georgie Hale pops up here looking for me," Jerry always says in a loud voice as he is leaving, "tell him that Billy Rose pulled me over to Lindy's for a bite." Then he goes downstairs to the lunch counter, where he may try to talk Barney, the proprietor, into letting him charge a cup of coffee. Rex, when he is not attempting to impress performers or rival agents, is a profoundly gloomy man. "You got only three classes of performers today," he sometimes says. "Class A, which means, for example, like Al Jolson and Eddie Cantor; Class B, like the Hartmans, for instance, or Henny Youngman, that can yet get a very nice dollar, and Class Z, which is all the little people. Small-time vaudeville is definitely out. All you got is floor shows, fraternal entertainments, and in the summer the borsch circuit. An entertainer who can average thirty dollars a week all year is Class Z tops. There ain't no such entertainer. A husband-and-wife team *might* make it."

Jerry does not consider his large office an extravagance, because he lives in it twenty-four hours a day, which is a violation of the building laws, and saves the price of a hotel room. He sleeps on the couch, while Dave, a blue-chinned young man with the mores of a tomcat, sleeps on one of the wall benches. Jerry occasionally buys a bottle of beer for the porter who cleans the offices. The grateful porter always does Jerry's first, so the agent can get a good night's rest. Every morning, Jerry washes and shaves in the men's room on his floor. Dave often contents himself with smearing face powder over his beard. Dave is of a happier temperament than his employer. He likes to think of himself as a heartbreaker and is full of stories about the girls who wander through the Jollity Building halls. He calls them heads and boskos. "Bosko" has a definitely roguish connotation. One may safely say to a friend, "That was a beautiful head I seen you with," even if one does not know who the head was. But if one says "bosko," and the woman turns out to be the friend's wife, one has committed a social error. Dave has a tried technique for forming acquaintanceships in the Jollity Building. "I know this head is a performer, or she would not be in the building," he says. "So I go up to her and say, 'What do you do?' If she says, 'I dance,' I say, 'Too bad, I was looking for a singer.' If she says 'sing,' I say, 'Too bad, I was looking for a dancer.' In that way we get acquainted, and if she looks promising, I pull her down to Barney's for a celery tonic."

Women performers have a better chance of getting cabaret jobs than men, because they mix with the customers. Jerry, who grew up in the sheltered respectability of vaudeville, resents this. "I booked a man with a trained dog into one trap in Astoria," he recently said, "and after one night they canceled him out because the dog couldn't mix. There never was such a tough market for talent. I book an acrobatic act in which, as a finish, one guy walks offstage playing a mandolin and balancing the other guy upside down on his head. The understander only plays a couple of bars, you see, for the effect. I booked them for an Elks' smoker in Jersey, and the chairman of the entertainment committee didn't want to pay me because he said the members don't like musical acts. To stand this business, you got to have a heart of steel." Most agents in the Jollity Building, when they supply talent for a whole show, book themselves as masters of ceremonies and collect an extra ten dollars for announcing the acts. Jerry has given up this practice.

"When I get out on the stage and think of what a small buck the performers are going to get, I feel like crying," he says, "so I send Dave instead."

A fair number of the performers who look for jobs in the Jollity Building have other occupations as well. Many of the women work as receptionists or stenographers in the daytime and make their rounds of agents' offices after five o'clock. Hockticket Charlie, an agent who is one of Jerry Rex's neighbors on the fourth floor, has a side line of his own. Hockticket Charlie is a tall, cross-eyed man with a clarion voice and a solemn manner. By arrangement with a number of pawnbrokers of his acquaintance, he sells pawn tickets. The chief reason anyone purchases a pawn ticket is that he holds the common belief that a watch accepted in pawn for ten dollars, for example, must in reality be worth around forty dollars. The fellow who buys a ticket for five dollars is therefore theoretically able to obtain a forty-dollar watch for a total outlay of fifteen dollars. Hockticket Charlie's pawnbroker friends, aware of this popular superstition, make out a lot of tickets to fictitious persons. Charlie sells the tickets for a few dollars each to performers in the Jollity Building. Each ticket entitles the purchaser to redeem a piece of secondhand jewelry—for not more than three times its value—which the broker has bought at an auction sale. Hockticket nearly always pays off colored performers with pawn tickets which will theoretically permit them to purchase diamonds at a large reduction. By paying ten dollars to a broker, the holder of one of these tickets can often acquire a ring easily worth three dollars. Sometimes Hockticket engages a number of performers to play a date in what he calls "a town near here," and tells them to meet him at the Jollity Building, so that they can all ride out to the date together. He loads them into a rickety bus which he has chartered for ten dollars, and the "town near here" turns out to be Philadelphia. If the acts traveled there singly, they would collect railroad fares for the round trip. Instead, Charlie collects all the railroad fares from the Philadelphia house manager who has booked the show. He often succeeds in paying the bus owner with hock tickets. Morty Ormont has a sincere admiration for Hockticket Charlie.

Another agent on the fourth floor, and the most sedate one in the building, is a woman named Maida Van Schuyler, who books stag shows for conventions and for the banquets large corporations give in honor of newly elected vice-presidents or retiring department heads. Mrs. Van Schuyler, a tall, flat-chested woman with fluffy white hair, was at one time a singer of arch numbers like "I Just Can't Make My Eyes Behave" and "Two Little Love Bees Buzzing in a Bower." As such, she recalls, she lent a touch of class to New England and Ohio vaudeville around 1912. The walls in an anteroom of her office are hung with numerous framed mottoes, such as "What Is More Precious Than a Friend?" and "Seek for Truth and Love Will Seek for You." A plain young woman sits in the anteroom and takes the names of visitors in to Mrs. Van Schuyler. When Mrs. Van Schuyler does not wish to see them, she sends out word that she is terribly sorry but one of her best-beloved friends has just passed away and she is too broken up about it to talk. If the visitor waits around a minute, he may hear a loud, strangling sob. Mrs. Van Schuyler, who is very much interested in spiritualism, often says that she would like to retire from the stag-show business and become a medium. "There isn't a dime left in this lousy business," she remarks. "The moving pictures have spoiled it, just like they did with vaudeville."

Every now and then, one of Mrs. Van Schuyler's shows is raided but the detectives give her advance notice because she provides the entertainments for a number of police banquets. "We have to make a pinch, Mrs. Van Schuyler," they say apologetically, "because the shooflies are working in our territory and we can't let a big brawl like this run without getting turned in." Shooflies, as all the world knows, are policemen in mufti assigned to make a secret check on the activities of other policemen. Within a week or two after the raid, which never results in a conviction, the friendly detectives return and say, "It's all right, Mrs. Van Schuyler, we got the shooflies taking now." With this assurance, Mrs. Van Schuyler can go ahead with her business. She seldom employs the ordinary entertainers who wander around the Jollity Building, but relies on specialists whom she lists in a large card file. "It is a highly specialized field of entertainment, darling," she tells gentlemen who are negotiating with her for their organizations. "Our girls must have poise, discretion, and *savoy faire*." To old friends like Morty Ormont, she sometimes says less elegantly, after an all-night party with a convention of textbook publishers or refrigerator salesmen, "You ought to seen those apes try to paw the girls."

Performers on their way to see one of the agents on the fourth floor are sometimes frightened by wild fanfares from an office occupied by an Italian who repairs trumpets. A musician who brings a trumpet to the Italian always blows a few hot licks to demonstrate that the instrument is out of true. When he calls for the trumpet, he blows a few more to see whether it is all right again. Once a swing dilettante stood in the hall for half an hour listening to the noises and then walked in and said that it was the best band he had ever heard and he wanted it to play at a rent party he was giving for some other *cognoscenti*.

Not all the transients in the Jollity Building halls are entertainers making the rounds of the agents. There is a fellow known as Paddy the Booster, who sells neckties he steals from haberdashers, and another known as Mac the Phony Booster, who sells neckties which he pretends to have stolen but are really shoddy ties he has bought very cheaply. Naturally, Paddy looks down on Mac, whom he considers a racketeer. "It takes all kinds of people to make up a great city," Jack McGuire sometimes tells Paddy, trying to soothe him. Also, every floor of the building has at least one bookmaker, who hangs in the hall. "In winter, the bookmakers complain because we don't heat the halls better," the beleaguered Morty Ormont says. A dollar is the standard Jollity Building wager. The accepted method of assembling it is to drop in on an acquaintance and say, "I got a tip on a horse, but I'm short a quarter." One repeats this operation until one has accumulated four quarters. It sometimes takes a long time, but there is always an oversupply of that. This system reduces the risk of betting to a minimum. On the infrequent occasions when some momentarily prosperous tenant bets important money on a race—say, five dollars—two or three of the hall bookmakers get together and divide up the hazard.

A stranger would be puzzled by some of the greetings exchanged by performers wandering between agents' offices. "Why, Zasu Pitts!" a gaunt young man wearing suède shoes and an overcoat of mattress filling will shout at a girl younger, twenty pounds heavier, and obviously poorer than Miss Pitts, whom she doesn't even faintly resemble. "Clark Gable!" the girl will shout, throwing her arms around him. "I haven't seen you since I thumbed a ride from that crumb in Anniston, Alabama!" The man and woman are not talking this way for a gag; they are survivors of a Hollywood-double troupe, a form of theatrical enterprise that has replaced the *Uncle Tom* show in out-of-the-way areas of the United States. In a double troupe, which usually travels in a large, overcrowded old automobile, all the members are supposed to be able to imitate Hollywood stars. They play in moving-picture theaters or grange halls, usually for a percentage of the receipts. Members of these companies seldom know each other's real names, even when they have heard them. In recounting their wanderings, they are likely to say, "Mae West was driving, see, and she goes to sleep. And only Ray Bolger seen the truck coming and grabbed the wheel, we would of all landed in some broken-down hospital in Henderson, North Carolina." The Hollywood doubles earn less and eat worse than the barnstormers of fifty years ago, but they have the pleasure of identifying themselves with the extremely wealthy. Some players are able to impersonate two or even three Hollywood stars to the complete satisfaction of an audience in Carbondale, Illinois. Sleeping on dressing tables, the doubles dream that they are lolling at Palm Springs, like in the *Daily Mirror*. A boy who impersonates Ned Sparks and Jimmy Durante once told Jerry Rex that he was downhearted only once in his mimetic career. That was at a county fair in Pennsylvania where some doubles were performing on an open-air stage under a hot sun. "I give them everything I had," the boy said, "and them apple-knockers just sat there from sorrow. They never even heard of Jimmy Durante or Ned Sparks. They broke my heart."

Summer, which used to be the dead season for entertainers, is now the period during which they eat most frequently. There are several rehearsal rooms in the Jollity Building, and throughout June they are full of uproar as the performers prepare for their migration to the Catskill Mountains resorts. "Up there the kids work for pot cheese," Jerry Rex says. "Here they don't even make themselves a chive." In the Catskills, a personable young man who can act as master of ceremonies, tell funny stories, give lessons in the conga, perform card tricks, direct amateur theatricals, do a screamingly funny eccentric dance, and impersonate stars of screen and radio can earn twenty-five dollars a week and room and board for ten consecutive weeks, provided he has a sensational singing voice. Performers at various hotels add to their incomes by uniting for occasional benefit shows, the beneficiary always being the entertainer at the hotel where the show is staged. "If a guy does not shoot crap with the guests," Jerry Rex says, "he has a chance to save himself a buck." Returning from the mountains after Labor Day, bloated with pot cheese, the actor sometimes survives until October, Jerry says, before developing doughnut tumors, a gastric condition attributed by him to living on crullers and coffee and which is usually a forerunner of the miss-meal cramps. By November, the performer no longer feels the cramps, because he is accustomed to being from hunger and not having what to eat. Then he starts talking about a job that has been promised to him in Miami if he can get there, and he tries, unsuccessfully, to promote somebody for railroad fare. Meanwhile, he plays any date he can get. Sometimes he doesn't work for a week and then has a chance to play a couple of dates in a night, perhaps a smoker in the west Bronx and a church party in Brooklyn, the first of which will net him $4.50 and the second $2.70, after the deduction of Jerry Rex's commissions.

The Jollity Building has at least a dozen tenants who teach voice, dancing, and dramatic art, and a few who specialize in Latin-American dance routines and acrobatics. The financial condition of the professors, which is solvent in comparison to that of the performers, musicians, and theatrical agents in the building, is a perpetual source of amusement to Morty Ormont. "The singers are from hunger," he says; "the performers are from hunger, and every day we get saps in the building who pay for lessons so they can be from hunger, too." Parents who believe their children are talented are the staple prey of the professional teachers. Seldom does a Jollity Building elevator make a trip without at least one bosomy and belligerent suburban woman, holding fast to the hand of a little girl whose hair is frizzled into a semblance of Shirley Temple's. Often several of the Shirleys and their mothers find themselves in a car together. The mothers' upper lips curl as they survey the other mothers' patently moronic young. The Shirleys gaze at each other with vacuous hostility and wonder whether their mothers will slap them if they ask to go to the bathroom again. All the Shirleys have bony little knees and bitter mouths and, in Morty's opinion, will undoubtedly grow up to be ax murderesses.

III—A SOFT DOLLAR

BARNEY, who owns the lunch counter in the basement of the so-called Jollity Building, never turns his head away from his customers for a second while working. Even when he is drawing coffee from the urn, he keeps looking over his shoulder, and this, in the course of his eighteen years in business, has given him a nervous neck twitch. "I know their nature," Barney says in explanation of this mannerism. "If I'll turn my head, they'll run away without paying." With all his vigilance, Barney cannot foresee when a client will eat two *pastrami* sandwiches and then say, after fumbling in a vest pocket, "Gee, Barney, I thought I had a quarter in my pocket, but it turned out to be an old Willkie button." Barney is a short, gray-faced man in his fifties who looks at his customers through thick, shell-rimmed spectacles that are usually clouded with steam from the coffee urn or with dabs of corned-beef grease. The customers see Barney against a background of cans of beans, arranged in pyramids. The cans, stacked on a shelf behind his counter, constitute a decorative scheme he never changes, except when he lays a fat, shiny stick of bologna across the can forming the apex of one of the pyramids.

Once, recently, Barney startled Hy Sky, the Jollity Building sign painter, and Morty Ormont, the renting agent, by announcing the return of prosperity. This was an event that neither of his listeners, confined for the most part in their associations to theatrical people, had suspected. "The taxi drivers who come in here are asking for sandwiches on thin bread, so they can taste the meat, and they are eating two sandwiches for lunch, usually," Barney said. "From 1929 until very lately, everybody was asking for sandwiches on thick bread, one sandwich should fill them up."

The lunch counter is at one end of the Jollity Building's poolroom, and most of Barney's customers are either people who work in the building or pool players. The taximen are his only customers from the daylight world.

"The bookmakers in the building are also eating regular," Barney said, continuing his survey of business conditions, "and even a couple of prize-fight managers recently came in and paid cash. With musicians, of course, is still the depression. Also with performers." Barney takes it for granted that anyone connected with the stage is broke, and if he can detect a speck of theatrical make-up under a woman's chin or behind an ear, he will refuse to give her credit. He even declines to believe that any performers receive regular remuneration in Hollywood. "It is all publicity," he says. "George Raft still owes me thirty-five cents from when he used to hang here." Musicians, although imperceptibly less broke, on the average, than actors or dancers, are almost as irritating to Barney. They sit at his counter for hours, each with one cup of coffee, and discuss large sums of money. Since most of the year musicians wear big, shaggy coats made of a material resembling the mats under rugs, they fill twice as much space as bookmakers or taxi drivers. Their coats overflow onto adjoining stools. "Three hours is average for a musician to drink a cup of coffee," Barney says, "and then sometimes he says he hasn't got the nickel, he'll see me tomorrow. Tomorrow is never."

Regulars who hang at Barney's counter may be identified by the manner in which, before sitting down, they run their hands under the counter. The are reaching for a communal dope sheet, a ten-cent racing paper giving the entries at all tracks. The regulars at Barney's chip in and buy one copy every day. This economy permits each of them to lose to bookmakers every week several dimes that would otherwise have been spent at newsstands. Barney has little contact with the pool players, although he does a good deal of business with them. A number of mulatto girls who rack up the balls on the pool tables also act as waitresses for the players. The girls pay Barney cash for all the cups of coffee they carry away. Presumably they collect from the players. "It is a pleasure they can have," says Barney.

One of the more conspicuous fellows who eat at the lunch counter and spend a good deal of time there between meals drinking coffee is called Marty the Clutch. Marty gets his name from his humorous custom of mangling people's fingers when he shakes hands with them. Strangers to whom he is introduced usually sink to their knees screaming before he releases their right hand. Casual acquaintances consider Marty a big, overgrown boy brimming with animal spirits. Only old friends really appreciate him. They know that when Marty has numbed a stranger's hand, he can often get a ring off the fellow's finger unnoticed. "It is very cute when you think of it," says Acid Test Ike, who is a manager of punch-drunk prize fighters. "I once seen the Clutch get a rock off a ticket broker big enough to use for a doorstop. By the time the scalper noticed the ring was gone, he thought a bosko he knew had clipped him for it, so he busted her nose." The Clutch is a big, square-shouldered man with a forehead barely sufficient to keep his hair from meeting his eyebrows. He used to be a prize fighter, but, he says, he worked with a gang of hijackers several nights a week and this interfered with his training, because he was always getting shot. Acid Test Ike considers this an amiable prevarication. "The Clutch never was a hijacker," he says. "He just gives that as a social reference. Really, the Clutch is a gozzler." This term means a fellow who gozzles people—chokes them in order to rob them. The gozzling business cannot be very good, because Marty is customarily as broke as most other patrons of the lunch counter. Every time Barney looks at Marty the Clutch, he rubs his throat nervously.

To Barney, the most interesting people in the Jollity Building are the promoters, the fellows who are always trying to earn, in the local idiom, a soft dollar. This is a curiosity he shares with Hy Sky and Morty Ormont, and sometimes the three of them get together at the lunch counter and discuss, with happy chuckles, the outrageous swindles perpetrated by fellows they know. One mental giant of whom all three speak with awe is a chap known as Lotsandlots, or Lots for short, who is in the land-development business. Lots's stock in trade is a tract of real estate in the Jersey marshes and a large supply of stationery bearing the letterheads of non-existent land companies and the Jollity Building's address. Prospects are carefully selected; generally they are close-fisted men with a few thousand dollars saved up. Each receives a letter informing him that he has won a lot in a raffle conducted by one of the land companies to publicize a new development. The winner, according to the letter, is now the owner, free and clear, of one building lot in some out-of-the-way district. With the lot goes an option to buy the lots on either side of it for a couple of hundred dollars apiece. The man receiving such a letter is distrustful. He knows that one house lot is not much use, and he suspects that the whole thing is just a dodge to sell him more land, so he doesn't even go out to look at his prize. In a week or so, Lotsandlots calls on the skeptic and says he hears that the man is the lucky owner of three lots in a certain undeveloped neighborhood. Lotsandlots says he represents a company that is assembling a site for a large industrial plant. He offers to buy the man's three lots for a good price, but begs him to keep the offer confidential, as publicity would interfere with his firm's efforts to pick up land. The lucky man of property always lets Lotsandlots think that he owns all three plots outright. He says that Lotsandlots should give him time to think the matter over and come back in a couple of days. Then, as soon as Lotsandlots leaves, the fellow hurries down to the land company's office in the Jollity Building to exercise his option on the two adjoining lots, which he expects to sell at a whacking profit. He pays four hundred dollars or five hundred dollars to the "office manager," an assistant promoter in Lotsandlots' employ. The manager gives him clear deed and title to two lots in a salt marsh. The man goes away happily, and then waits the rest of his life for Lotsandlots to reappear and conclude the deal.

"The art in it," Hy Sky says admiringly, "is the sap never knows Lots is running the land company. A good boy, Lots." Lots is a humorist, too. When anyone asks him if he does much business, he says, "Lots and lots," which is how he got his name. When he says it, he rolls his eyes so knowingly that Hy Sky, if he is around, suffers an attack of laughter resembling whooping cough.

Another respected promoter is Judge Horumph, a bucolic figure of a man who wears a stand-up collar, a heavy gilt-iron watch chain with a seal ring on it, and high, laceless shoes with elastic sides. The Judge's face is tomato red marked by fine streaks of eggplant purple. Barney and his customers are disposed to believe Judge Horumph's story that he was once a justice of the peace in a Republican village upstate, a region in which about one man in every three enjoys that distinction. The Judge, when he is working, sits at a telephone all day, calling various business houses that like to keep on the good side of the law—particularly firms with large fleets of trucks, because such firms are constantly dealing with traffic and parking summonses, and they don't want to offend anybody. He says, "This is Judge H-r-r-umph." The name is indistinguishable, but no layman knows the names of a tenth of the judges in New York, and it would be impolite to ask a judge to repeat. "I am giving some of my time to a little charitable organization called Free Malted Milk for Unmarried Mothers," the Judge says. "I know that ordinarily it would be an imposition to bother you people, but the cause is so worthy . . ." Rather often, the owner or manager of the firm tells the Judge he will send five or ten dollars. "Oh, don't say 'send,' " Judge Horumph booms jovially. "I know how prone we all are to forget these little things. I'll send a telegraph boy right over to get your contribution." The Judge is a man of real culture, Morty Ormont says, but he has one failing, and that is strong drink. Judge Horumph's one serious run-in with the law resulted from his throwing a whisky bottle at a Jollity Building wag who offered to buy him a malted milk.

The hero of the best stories that Barney and Hy Sky and Morty Ormont sit around telling one another is a promoter named Maxwell C. Bimberg, who used to be known in the Jollity Building as the Count de Pennies because he wore a pointed, waxed, blond mustache just like a count and because he was rather stingy except about gambling and women. The Count was a tiny, fragile man with large, melting eyes and a retreating chin. "He was a little wizened man that didn't look like nothing at all," Hy says, "but Maxwell C. Bimberg had a brilliant mind."

Hy recalls how he helped the Count de Pennies conduct a crusade against pari-mutuel betting in New York State in which the Count fleeced a prominent bookmaker who felt that his business was menaced by the movement to legalize the betting machines. The Count induced the bookie to finance a campaign of street advertising against the proposition, which was to be voted on at the polls. The Count was to have twenty signs painted, large enough to cover the side of a wagon. The signs were to say, "Mayor LaGuardia says vote 'No'!" Then the Count was to hire ten wagons, put the signs on them, and have them driven around the center of town the day before the referendum. The bookie peeled several hundred-dollar bills off his bank roll to pay for the operation. The promoter went to Hy Sky and ordered just two signs, allowing the painter a generous profit on them. He had the signs placed on a wagon that he hired for one hour. The wagon then drove a couple of times through the Duffy Square region, where the bookmaker hung, and returned to the stable. There the signs were shifted to another wagon, which made the same circuit, and so on. The bookie saw several wagons during the day and was happy. Count de Pennies saved the price of eighteen signs and reduced wagon hire by ninety per cent. "Maxwell C. Bimberg had a brilliant mind!" Hy Sky repeats when he tells of this successful promotion.

Morty Ormont's reminiscences about the Count are not all tender. "He was always borrowing a nickel for a telephone call, but one day he asked me for a loan of three dollars so he could get his teeth out of hock to con a sucker," Morty says. "I loaned it to him, and the next day I saw him looking very happy, with his teeth in. As soon as he spotted me he started with a small mouth. 'I am sorry, Morty,' he says, 'but the sucker didn't show, so I haven't got the three bucks.' So I turned him upside down—you know how little he was—and six hundred dollars fell out of his left breech."

The Count's admirers in the Jollity Building generally speak of him in the past tense, although it is improbable that he is dead. Some detectives employed by a railroad are looking for the wizened man as a result of one of his promotions, and consequently he has not been seen for some time around the Jollity Building. The project which irritated the railroad was known as the Dixie Melody Tours. The Count sold bargain-rate tour tickets to Florida which included train fare, hotel rooms, and meals. At the end of every month, the Count settled with the railroad and the hotels for the accommodations the tourists had bought through him. The tours were actually bringing the Count a fair income when, at the end of the third or fourth month, he decided to pay the railroad with a bad check. "It must have been a terrible temptation to him to stay honest," Morty says, "but he resisted it." "He always thought very big," Barney recalls affectionately. "I said to him lots of times, 'Be careful, Count. Nobody can promote a railroad.' He would say, 'What do you mean? This is strictly legitimate.' But I could see in his eyes he was thinking of larceny. 'Already I promoted some of the smartest people on Broadway,' he was thinking. 'Why not a railroad?' He always thought too big."

The Count made his first appearance in the Jollity Building a dozen years ago, when he was the manager of the widow of a famous gunman. He rented a furnished office, about six feet square, on the third floor and pasted on the outer side of the door a card saying, "Maxwell C. Bimberg, Presentation of Publicized Personalities." He booked the gunman's widow as an added attraction in burlesque theaters, and since that seemed to work out pretty well, he tried to sign up several acquitted female defendants in recent and prominent murder cases. The women were eager to sign contracts, but the Count found it difficult to make money with them. One reason, he said, was that "It is hard to write a routine for an acquitted murderess. If she reenacts the crime, then the public gets the impression that she should not have been acquitted."

One Wisconsin woman who had been acquitted of killing her husband with ground glass came to New York and rented an apartment to live in during her stage career under his management. She used to invite the Count to dinner every evening, and he had a hard time thinking of excuses which would not offend her. "Every time she says 'Home cooking,' " the Count would tell Barney, "I feel like I bit into a broken bottle." At last the life of the gunman's widow was violently terminated by one of her husband's business associates. An astute detective sat down next to the telephone in the murdered woman's flat and waited for the murderer to call up, which to a layman would have seemed an unlikely eventuality. The first person to call was the Count. He was phoning to inform his star that he had booked her for a week's engagement at a theater in Union City, New Jersey. The detective had the call traced. A couple of other detectives arrested the Count in the Jollity Building and pulled out his mustache one hair at a time to make him tell why he had killed his meal ticket. This experience cured the Count of his desire to make other people's crimes pay. After his mustache grew again, he decided to marry an elderly Brooklyn woman whom he had met through an advertisement in a matrimonial journal. The bride was to settle three thousand dollars on him, but the match fell through when she declined to give the Count the money in advance. "If you have so little confidence in me, darling," he said, "we would never be happy," "And also," he told Morty Ormont subsequently, "I didn't want to lay myself open for a bigamy rap."

The Count next organized a troupe of girl boxers, whom he proposed to offer as an added attraction to the dance marathons then popular. "It was not that the idea was any good," Morty Ormont says when he tells about the Count, "but it was the way he milked it. After all, what is there smart about selling a guy a piece of something that might make money? Smart is to sell a guy for a good price a piece of a sure loser. The Count went out and promoted Johnny Attorney, one of the toughest guys on Broadway, for a grand to pay the girls' training expenses and buy them boxing trunks and bathrobes. The Count trembled every time Johnny looked at him, but with him, larceny was stronger than fear. So he gives all the girls bus fare to Spring Valley, New York, and tells them he will meet them there and show them the training camp he has engaged. Then he takes the rest of the grand and goes to Florida." When Morty reaches this point in the story, Hy Sky can seldom restrain himself from saying, reverentially, "Maxwell C. Bimberg had a brilliant mind!"

"By the time the Count came back from Florida," Morty says, "Johnny Attorney was running a night club on Fifty-second Street. The Count walks into Johnny's joint as if nothing had happened, and in fifteen minutes he cons Johnny into making him a banquet manager. He booked a couple of nice banquets into there, but when Johnny would send the bill to the chairman of whatever club it was that held the banquet, the chairman would write back and say, 'I see no mention on your bill of the deposit I paid your Mr. Bimberg.' The Count had glommed the deposits. So after that he had to play the duck for Johnny for a couple of years. Whenever Johnny would get shoved in the can for assault or manslaughter, the Count would come back to town. That gave him quite a lot of time in town, at that."

Morty and Hy agree that the Count had a rare gift of making women feel sorry for him because he looked so small and fragile. "He made many a beautiful head," Morty concedes with envy. "If I had met a refined, educated girl like you when I was still young, my whole life would have been different," the Count would tell a head who might be a minor burlesque stripper. He would invite her to his tiny office in the Jollity Building to plan her Hollywood career. This office, he would assure her, was just a hide-out where he could get away from the crowds of people who besieged him for bookings at his regular place of business. The Count always made a point of stopping at the switchboard which then served the furnished-office tenants, collectively known to Morty Ormont as the heels. "Did that girl from the Paradise Restaurant call me this afternoon?" he would ask the operator. "You know, the one I got a job for last week? And by the way, if Monte Proser calls up in the next half-hour, tell him I'm out. I'm going to be busy." The mainsprings of feminine character, the Count used to tell his friends, were avarice and mother love. He would make extravagant promises of contracts in shows or moving pictures which he would tell every girl he was on the point of closing for her. Then he would say sadly, "Your success is assured, but I will never be happy. I am a Broadway roué, and no decent girl would look at me." "Oh, don't say that, Mr. Bimberg," a girl might beg, remembering she had not yet signed the contract. (The Count used to say, "You would be surprised how sorry a girl can feel for a man that is going to make a lot of money for her.") "Oh yes, I cannot fool myself," the Count would sob to the girl, and tears would flow from his large, protruding eyes as he grabbed for his protégé's hand. If the girl put an arm around his narrow shoulders to steady him, he would work into a clinch. If she pulled away from the lead, the Count would sometimes fall to his knees and sniffle. "Why should I live another day?" he would wail. "Tomorrow your contract is coming through. If I lived through tonight, I could collect my ten-per-cent commission, which would amount to perhaps a couple of thousand bucks. Is that a reason to live?" Usually the girl would think it was a pretty good reason. The Count did not always succeed. "When a bosko wouldn't have nothing to do with him," Hy Sky says, "Maxwell C. Bimberg became very emotional." He once offered a female boxer forty dollars to let him hold her hand. The boxer declined, saying, "I would rather wake up in a hole with a snake than in a room with Count de Pennies." The Count was very discouraged by her remark and hated to hear it quoted.

An enterprise which the Count's admirers remember with considerable pleasure was the Public Ballyhoo Corporation, Ltd. To launch this concern, the Count spent a couple of weeks promoting a bookmaker known as Boatrace Harry. The Count kept on telling Boatrace Harry about the great incomes that he said were earned by publicity men like Steve Hannagan, Benjamin Sonnenberg, and Richard Maney. Then he allowed Harry to invest a couple of thousand dollars in Public Ballyhoo, Ltd. He had letterheads printed saying that Public Ballyhoo, Ltd., would supply "anything from an actress to an alligator" for publicity stunts. The Count became so interested in his idea that he forgot to duck with Boatrace Harry's money. The manager of a theater showing the first run of a picture called *Eskimo* asked the Count to secure a genuine Eskimo to pose on top of the marquee with a team of huskies. The Count made a good try. He found in the telephone directory some kind of society for the preservation of the American Indian and obtained from it the addresses of two alleged Eskimos. One turned out to be a Jewish tailor in Greenpoint; this was obviously a wrong listing. The other, who lived in Bay Ridge, was a real Eskimo who had a job in a foundry. He turned down the job, however, and begged the Count not to give his secret away, because his girl would make fun of him.

The Count had a number of other disappointments. He saw a classified advertisement inserted in a newspaper by a man who said he wanted to buy cockroaches in quantity. The Count knew where he could buy some large tropical roaches which had been a feature of a recently raided speakeasy called La Cucaracha, where the customers could race roaches along the bar, instead of rolling dice, to see who would pay for their drinks. In his enthusiasm, the Count bought five hundred *cucarachas*, at a nickel apiece, from the prohibition agents who had raided the place. The Count knew some newspaper reporters from the days when he had exploited murderesses and boxing girls, so he called several of them up and told them of the big deal he had on the fire. They thought it was funny, and the story was published in the early editions of a couple of afternoon papers. The advertiser, however, did not want racing cockroaches. He wanted to feed the roaches to tropical birds, and the Count's acquisitions could have eaten the birds. Ordinary household roaches, obtainable from small boys in tenement neighborhoods at low cost, were better for the aviarist's purpose. The Count was stuck with five hundred hungry bugs. He turned them loose on the third floor of the Jollity Building and left for

Florida with what remained of Boatrace Harry's money. Barney attributes the unusual size of the bugs in the Jollity Building today to the thoroughbred outcross.

Morty was naturally quite angry with the Count at first, but after a few weeks began to miss him. "You have to hand it to him. He had a good idea all the same," Morty says now. "The story about the roaches was in all the papers, and with that kind of publicity he could have gone far. A week after he left, a guy called up and asked for Mr. Bimberg. I asked him what did he want, and he said he had read about Public Ballyhoo, Ltd., and he was in the market for some moths. So I told him, 'I haven't any moths, but if you'll come up here, I'll cut holes in your pants for nothing.' "

The Count de Pennies must have convinced himself that he was a publicity man. When he reappeared in the Jollity Building after he had lost Boatracc Harry's money at Tropical Park, he got a job with a new night club as press agent. The place had one of those stages which roll out from under the bandstand before the floor show starts. The Count decided he could get a story in the newspapers by sending for the police emergency squad on the pretext that one of the show girls had been caught under the sliding stage. The policemen arrived, axes in hand, and refused to be deterred by the Count's statement that there was no longer any need of them because he had personally rescued the girl. "You know very well that poor little girl is still under there!" the sergeant in charge roared reproachfully, and the coppers hilariously chopped the stage to bits. The Count lost his job.

What was perhaps the zenith of the Count's prosperity was reached during the brief life of the Lithaqua Mineral Water Company. Lithaqua was formed to exploit a spring on the land of a Lithuanian tobacco farmer in Connecticut. The water of the spring had a ghastly taste, and this induced the farmer to think it had therapeutic qualities. A druggist who was related to a murderess the Count had formerly managed organized a company to market the water. He gave the Count ten per cent of the common stock to act as director of publicity. The Count "sent out the wire," as fellows in the Jollity Building sometimes say when they mean that a promoter has had a third party act as go-between, to Johnny Attorney and Boatrace Harry. "Why be thick all your life?" he had his intermediary ask Johnny. "The Count has something big this time. If you will call it square for the few hundred he owes you, he will sell you ten per cent of the mineral-water company for exactly one grand." The Count had the same offer made to Boatrace Harry, and he sold his ten per cent of the stock to each of them for one thousand dollars. He sold his share in the enterprise to five other men, too, and was just beginning to think he had better go to Florida again when a chemist for a consumers' research group discovered that seepage from the vats of a near-by dye works accounted for the bilious flavor of the tobacco farmer's water. This got the Count out of a difficult situation. Even Johnny and Boatrace could understand that ten per cent of a worthless business was not worth quarreling about.

During this period of affluence, the Count lived in a hotel on West Forty-eighth Street. "There was even a private shower," intimates recall solemnly when they evoke the glories of that era. The Count took to wearing cinnamon-colored suits with pointed lapels that flared from his waistline to an inch above his shoulders and trousers that began just below his breastbone. Every day he bet on every race at every track in the United States and Canada, and he invariably lost. Almost four weeks elapsed, Morty Ormont recalls with astonishment now, before the Count again had to borrow nickels to make telephone calls.

The Dixie Melody Tours followed several promotions of an increasingly prosaic nature. "The tours was too legitimate for his character," Hy Sky says sadly. "There was nobody left for him to promote, only the railroad. So he went ahead and promoted it. Maxwell C. Bimberg was too brilliant!" Morty Ormont is more realistic. "In every class of business there has got to be a champion," he says. "The Count de Pennies was never no good to nobody, but he was the champion heel of the Jollity Building."

Mrs. Braune's Prize Fighters

IN TIMES like these, the lodginghouse conducted by Mrs. Rosa Braune on West Ninety-second Street, near Central Park, is a peaceful and comfortable place. It is almost entirely inhabited by prize fighters, who are the most tranquil of athletes. Unlike baseball players and jockeys, fighters seldom have noisy arguments. Not fighting is their avocation. Mrs. Braune's house gives a city dweller the same soothing sense of continuity that the round of seasons is said to impart to peasants. There are always new fighters coming up, old ones going down, and recurrent technical problems to discuss. I hadn't been to see Mrs. Braune and her lodgers since midsummer of 1939, and, as the world had gone through a lot in the interim, I visited the house a few days ago with certain misgivings. Happily, I found everything serenely unchanged.

Most of Mrs. Braune's lodgers are under the direction of Al Weill, a bulbous man who is the thriftiest and most industrious fight manager of the day. The two windows of his office—an indication that he is at least twice as opulent as any competitor—overlook the land of the Telephone Booth Indians, but he is too wise to stable his prize fighters in the vicinity. Fighters not in his charge occasionally stop at Mrs. Braune's house, but Mrs. Braune doesn't encourage them. Prize fighters are drawn inevitably to parks, and the Central Park reservoir, around which they can take their morning runs, makes the neighborhood especially popular with them. Weill has a family and a home of his own on the upper West Side; his viceroy at Mrs. Braune's is Charles Goldman, a trainer and an old friend of mine. Goldman is a brisk little man with a flattened nose and a thickened right ear. These add authority to his comments on professional subjects. He used to be a smart bantamweight and never lets any of his pupils forget it. Charlie opened the door and greeted me as soon as I had rung Mrs. Braune's bell. This was not strange, because he lives in the front parlor of the old-fashioned brownstone house. His wide windows are a strategic point from which he can see any fighter who comes home late at night or tries to bring a girl in with him. From them he can also check on the boys as they leave for their morning runs in the park.

We shook hands, then Goldman yelled up the stairs for Mrs. Braune and took me into his room to wait for her. It is a big room, and there are three beds in it. A French-Canadian fighter named Dave, who is not under Weill's management but lives in the neighborhood, was sitting on one of them talking in French to a Weill featherweight named Spider. Goldman introduced me, and then Spider said, raptly, "Go on, Dave, talk more French." "Spider don't understand him," Goldman said seriously, "but he thinks it sounds pretty." When Mrs. Braune came in a couple of minutes later, Dave stopped talking, because Mrs. Braune, a German Swiss, understands French and would not have liked what he was calling Spider. "It's better than double talk," Dave said to me with a grin. The two boys went out, and as they were leaving, Goldman said, "Don't get into no crap games." The house stands in a tree-shaded block of almost identical brownstones, all with high stoops, and usually there is a crap game in progress on at least one of them. Goldman disapproves of crap games because they take a fighter's mind off business. Whenever one of the boys is arrested and fined two dollars for shooting crap, Goldman gloats over his misfortune.

Mrs. Braune is about sixty years old and built like a large, soft cylinder with a diameter not greatly inferior to its axis. She has a pink face, sparse gray hair parted in the middle, and calm blue eyes. She is so much like the conventional idea of American motherhood that no fighter in his right mind would think of talking back to her. Mrs. Braune once ran a rooming house at 19 West Fifty-second Street—an address which disappeared some years ago when the next-door neighbors, Jack and Charlie, bought the building and added it to their restaurant at No. 21. Her clients in that house included a Fifth Avenue jeweler who had a lot of girl friends and suffered from a complaint that Mrs. Braune calls "the gouch," theatrical people, who were noisy and kept late hours, and a number of White Russian countesses, whom she calls in retrospect "the Countesses of Having-Nothing." The countesses were much the worst pay. Mrs. Braune prefers her present lodgers, who are in bed by ten o'clock except when they are professionally engaged. She is sure of getting the room rent from

Weill's fighters, at least, because Al pays it and takes the money out of their earnings. He is always urging his boys to live frugally and put their money in the bank. They have a hard time obtaining a couple of dollars a week from him for spending money. He telephones at ten every evening to ask Mrs. Braune if the boys are all in their rooms. Sometimes she covers up for a fighter she thinks must be staying on at the movies for the end of a double feature, but she doesn't condone any really serious slip. Weill has five-year contracts with his boys, and if one of them won't behave, even for Mrs. Braune, Weill simply declines to make any matches for him. This means that the fighter must get some other kind of work, a prospect so displeasing that discipline at Mrs. Braune's is usually perfect.

The one detail of Mrs. Braune's appearance that sets her apart from other landladies is a pair of miniature leather boxing gloves pinned high on her vast bosom. She likes to show them to visitors, for they have been autographed by Lou Ambers, twice lightweight champion of the world. Ambers, she explains, was her star lodger for years and was responsible for her entrance into the prize-fight business. In 1935, before he became illustrious, Ambers asked her for a room. He was training for a fight and had no money in the meanwhile. Mrs. Braune let him run up a bill of seventy or eighty dollars, a proceeding so extraordinary that after the fight Ambers induced his manager, Weill, to put all his fighters in her house. Ambers knew it was a lucky house, because he had won the fight. The boys living at Mrs. Braune's won a long series of bouts, and Weill began to call it, grandiloquently, the House of Destiny. It is impossible to tell how much Mrs. Braune's motherly discipline contributed to the winning streak, but the manager was sure it had some effect. Besides, the house is clean, and Mrs. Braune's rentals have always been reasonable. Now, after six years of it, she says, she feels like an old-timer in the fight game, and Goldman reports that once he even heard her telling a tall heavyweight how to "scrunch himself over so he wouldn't get hurted."

Weill practices a kind of pugilistic crop rotation. He has under his management fighters who are valuable properties now and others he thinks will be profitable in from one to four years. Fight people speak of a boy as being one or two or three years "away." Weill even has one towering youngster who hasn't yet had a professional bout but is living at Mrs. Braune's while he learns his trade. A manager gets from thirty-three and a third to fifty per cent of a fighter's purses, which, in the case of Ambers or Arturo Godoy, another Weill property, runs into considerable money. Often, however, a fighter on the way up doesn't earn his keep, and then Weill has to carry him. Weill pays Mrs. Braune the fighter's room rent and gives him a weekly five-dollar meal ticket. The ticket is good for five dollars and fifty cents in trade at a Greek lunchroom on Columbus Avenue. This arrangement keeps the boy from overeating, Weill explains. He makes his bookings in an office in the Strand Building, on Duffy Square. Usually he keeps a fighter working in towns like New

Haven, Utica, and Bridgeport until he seems ripe for a metropolitan career. The boys come back to the house on Ninety-second Street after each bout.

"I prefer fighters than any other kind of lodgers," Mrs. Braune said to me. "They got such interesting careers, like opera singers, but they are not so mean."

"She is just like a mother to them boys," Goldman said admiringly. "She presses their trunks for them, so they will look nice going into the ring, and sometimes when I tell a boy he is getting too fine, she fixes him a chicken dinner. They don't board here regularly, but she likes to cook for them now and then. A fighter can't stay down to weight all the time or he will work himself into t.b. Now and then he has got to slop in. Mrs. Braune is a restraining influence on them kids. They got too much energy."

A boy walked down the hall past the open door, and Goldman called him in to show me a sample of the student body. "This is Carl Dell, a welterweight," Goldman said. "He spends all his time writing long letters to dolls." "Charlie is always worrying about maybe I would have a good time," Dell said before acknowledging the introduction. "He is always beefing." Dell has a strong, rectangular head with the small eyes and close-set ears of a faun. Goldman, perhaps affected by some remote sculptural association, said, "Look at him. He has a head like an old Roman." He said Dell had been a good amateur and had won thirty-seven straight fights after turning professional. He had lost a couple of decisions in recent months, but that was natural, as he had begun to meet good men. "It is a lot in how you match a fellow," Goldman said, "but anyway, he is a great prospect." "I beat a fellow out on the coast that they said was the champion of Mexico," Dell said, "and when I was down in Cuba, I beat the champion of Cuba. That is two countries I am champion of already." Dell is twenty-three years old and is at least a year "away." He told me he came from Oneonta, New York, and had spent three years in the CCC, a government enterprise which develops fine arms and shoulders. Then he had won a lot of prizes in amateur tournaments and finally turned professional. He said he had never had any kind of job except boxing.

Goldman began talking to me about the importance of concentration in shadowboxing. Dell looked embarrassed, seeming to know that the little trainer was talking at him. Mrs. Braune just sat quietly, as if used to such seminars.

"One of the most important things in training is shadowboxing," Goldman said, getting into the middle of the floor and assuming a guard. "Most boys, now, when they are shadowboxing they are just going through the motions and thinking of some broad, maybe. Shadowboxing is like when the teacher gives you a word to take home and write out ten times, so you will know it. In the examination you only get one chance to spell the word. The best two moves I ever had come to me when I was shadowboxing, but I was not just going through the motions with a swelled head, thinking of some broad. I always used to have a move where I feinted a jab and stepped to the left to get away, and one day it come to me, 'Why not really jab when I step that way? If I hit, I am in position to throw a right, and if I miss, I got my right hand up anyway.'" Goldman went to his left, jabbed, and threw a right. "Then the thought come to me," he said, "'Why not throw a left hook for the body instead, and that will bring me in position for a right uppercut?' Now, when I straighten up with that uppercut the guy is going to cross me with a right, ain't he? Sure! He can't stop himself. So then, as I throw the uppercut, I duck to the left in one motion, see?" The little man moved his feet and swayed to his left. "And I come up under his right!" he exclaimed.

Dell had been watching with the detached interest of a boy who has no talent for mathematics but must pass a required course in trigonometry. "Do you get it?" Goldman asked him, abandoning his pretense of talking to me. "Sure," Dell said without enthusiasm, "but I guess I would rather just wear the guys down." He went away, saying he had to write a letter to his girl.

In addition to listening to Goldman's expositions of theory, routine for the prize fighters at Mrs. Braune's includes a long run around the reservoir early every morning and laboratory exercises at Stillman's Gymnasium on Eighth Avenue from noon until about three o'clock. At Stillman's, the fighters box against boys from other managers' strings, to avert possible upheavals in the Braune home. A boy who has had a hard workout is content to do nothing for the rest of the day, which is exactly what a trainer wants him to do.

Mrs. Braune, who used to take a normal matronly pleasure in promoting marriages between young people, has come to feel differently about marriage now that she is interested in prize fighters. Most managers don't like fighters to get married. "One manager is enough," they often say. Mrs. Braune concurs in this prejudice, because when the boys get married they stop living in rooming houses. Also, she takes a proprietary attitude toward any fighter who has lived in her house and she thinks that no young woman can give a pugilist proper care. Lou Ambers got married last year. He had lived in the rear parlor of Mrs. Braune's house for four years, remaining there even after he had become lightweight champion of the world and a great drawing card. The rear parlor has cooking arrangements, and a fellow named Skids Enright, an old short-order cook from Herkimer, New York, Lou's home town, used to live with him and do the cooking. The fighter was never extravagant. After his marriage Ambers went to live in Herkimer. A few months later he was knocked out by a lightweight named Lew Jenkins, who was also married but had been in that condition long enough to develop a tolerance for it. Another Weill fighter, Joey Archibald, won the featherweight championship, got married, and then lost a decision to a bachelor from Baltimore. Archibald is not acutely missed at Mrs. Braune's, however. Because of his unbearable erudition, her other lodgers never felt close to him. "Do you know what Archibald said to me?" Ambers once asked Goldman. "He said 'equilibrium.'" Goldman and Whitey Bimstein, Ambers' trainer, had a hard time restoring friendly relations. Arturo Godoy is also married, but Mrs. Braune feels that, being a South American, he can stand it.

I gathered that because of all the marriages and the absence of a couple of fighters who were on expeditions to the provinces, there are not as many boys as usual stopping at Mrs. Braune's. Goldman mentioned, besides Spider and Dell, a clever welterweight named Al Nettlow, Marty Serve, a coming lightweight, and Tony, the twenty-year-old heavyweight who hasn't fought yet. Tony came in while we were talking, and, after Goldman had introduced him to me as "possibly a future heavyweight champion if he's got the stuff in him," just sat there listening to us. He was bashful, I guessed, because he had not had a fight and so had nothing to talk about. "He is pretty big for a baby, only six feet five inches," Mrs. Braune said, "but he don't make no trouble at all. I was going to get him a special long bed, but he says no, he would just as soon sleep slanting." Some fighters are difficult about beds, Mrs. Braune said, and keep asking for new ones until they have tried every bed in the house. They sleep reasonably well in any of them, apparently, but there seem to be gradations in the profundity of a fighter's unconsciousness, caused by differences in bed springs and not explainable to other persons. Mrs. Braune's hands, while she talked to Goldman and me, were busy with a darning egg and a pair of socks undoubtedly belonging to a prize fighter.

There is a Mr. Braune, but, like most rooming-house husbands, he stays in the background. Until about twenty years ago, he and Mrs. Braune ran a stationery store. Then, she told me, she leased the Fifty-second Street rooming house which disappeared into Jack and Charlie's. The new business was somewhat in the family tradition, she felt, because one of her maternal uncles in Switzerland had kept a big hotel near Lake Geneva. "I would like to see again the Genfersee," she said parenthetically. "The Lake of Geneva, you know. But conditions must be pretty hard over there now. I got confidential postcards from the old country that every mountain is full of cannons. Still, what can they do now they got Hitler all around them?" She went on to say that the fighters are always offering her tickets to bouts but she never goes. She's afraid she couldn't stand the sight of blood. She does listen to fights on the radio, though, whenever she has a chance. When Ambers was fighting Henry Armstrong, the great colored boxer, Mrs. Braune prayed between rounds that her lodger would grow stronger. "And he did get stronger in the last," she said. "He won."

"Why don't you go upstairs and see Marty?" Goldman suggested. "I got to make some phone calls, but just say who you are, and he will be glad to see you. Marty is the baby of the house. He's only nineteen. He went up to Van Cortlandt Park Sunday and wanted to show the other boys how good he could play football. So he is laid up with a skinned nose and a sprained ankle." I climbed to the third floor to see Marty. Over the bed in which the boy lay hung a picture of the late Pius XI and, under the picture, a crucifix. Marty wore a large silver religious medal around his neck. His small, impish face made him look younger than nineteen, but his biceps and forearms were big and brown. He was restless, lying in bed with nobody to talk to, and was glad to see me. He said he had just been looking through an old scrapbook of newspaper clippings about his amateur fights. "I had ninety-three of them," he said. "I only got three or four dollars a fight. I was the highest-paid amateur in the Hudson Valley." Marty said his real name was Mario Severino and that he came from Schenectady. (Weill, since he got Ambers, has picked up several fighters from upstate.) "I didn't know anything before I turned professional," the boy said. "I thought I did, but I didn't. Amateur fighters aren't smart like my roommate, Al Nettlow. Al is a real cutie." Nettlow, he explained, is seldom around the house until the weather gets very cold because he is a "fishing nut." He leaves before dawn every morning he can get off training and takes the long subway ride out to Sheepshead Bay, where he boards one of the deep-sea boats that take fishermen out all day for two dollars. When he gets back, he tries to make the other fighters eat the fish he has caught, but only Tony, the heavyweight, who almost always uses up his weekly meal ticket in five days, displays any enthusiasm. Nettlow is a very clever fighter and is now of near-championship class. I gathered from Goldman that if he wins a title, he will probably want to pose in his publicity pictures with a dead swordfish.

Marty said that he had had thirty-nine professional fights and had won them all. "Mr. Weill gets me guys that I figure to lick," he said modestly. "He is a great manager. But he gave me hell for playing football. I don't like a sprained ankle. I got to fight once a week or I don't feel good."

I went downstairs and said good-by to Mrs. Braune and to Charlie Goldman, who by that time was clipping a newspaper account of the death of a preliminary boy in a Brooklyn prize ring. The boy had died of heart failure. Goldman collects newspaper stories he thinks will be instructive to his wards. "He was a nice kid," Goldman said to me, "but he never trained right. He relied on his ticker to get him by. He had plenty of moxie, but it is just like I am always saying to my kids. If the flesh is weak, the spirit don't mean a thing."

Turf and Gridiron

ONE OF THE pleasantest clubs in town, prior to 1940, was the Turf and Gridiron, which occupied the third and fourth floors of a narrow building at 20 West Forty-sixth Street. It cost thirty-three dollars a year to belong to the Turf and Gridiron, and it was not to be confused with the Turf and

Field, which has headquarters at Belmont Park and annual dues of a hundred dollars. The Turf and Gridiron was the social club of the New York bookmakers. It was exclusive in only one sense. In the hall on the ground floor—the club being the only tenant of the upper floors—there was an iron gate, such as used to protect speak-easies in the twenties. A colored elevator boy looked at visitors through the bars before admitting them. This precaution was taken because certain persons believed that the clubmen carried large sums of money. Most of the members were held up once or twice, and some of them so often that they became connoisseurs of criminal technique. It was all the result of a misconception. The bookmakers sent their funds direct from the race track to a bank every night in an armored car, and drew their working cash from another car at the track the next day.

The club came into being in 1934, when the state legislature rescinded criminal penalties for accepting bets at race tracks. Like the repeal of prohibition, a few months earlier, this action of the legislature restored an older order of things. Prior to 1909, when, at the urging of Charles Evans Hughes, then governor, the legislators made the practice of the bookmaking trade a misdemeanor, the bookies of New York formed an honorable and highly respected guild. Moreover, between 1909 and 1934, most of the present Turf and Gridiron clubmen took bets anyway. Their position, like that of bootleggers during the last years of prohibition, was delicate, although not exactly dangerous. The Restoration period was brief, for in 1940 the legislature legalized pari-mutuel machines and by that act outlawed the bookmakers again.

Turf and Gridiron members were for the most part substantial, conservative-looking gentlemen of at least middle age. Younger men, it seems, lacked the equanimity the profession requires. The wallpaper in the club lounge on the third floor was a fawn-and-brown plaid, like an old-time bookmaker's vest. There was a big American flag by the fireplace, and over the entrance to the bar a framed picture of a celebrated horse named Master Charlie, which was owned a dozen years ago by Tom Shaw, a prominent member. On a first visit, a casual observer might have thought the Turf and Gridiron a reform organization, for the club bulletin board was perpetually covered with newspaper clippings denouncing race-track betting. It was always the pari-mutuel form of betting that was attacked in these clippings, however, under headlines like "MACHINES TAKE WPA WORKERS' PAY" or "MUTUELS GUTTING TEXAS, SAYS GOVERNOR."

The guiding spirit of the club was its founder, Timothy James Mara, a large man with baby-pink cheeks and a square, massive jaw. Mara is a half inch over six feet tall, weighs two hundred and five pounds, and was fifty-four years old last August at Saratoga, when he gave himself his usual gargantuan, impromptu birthday party by inviting everybody he met during the evening to join his table. One summer, at the Arrowhead Inn there, he started out with his wife and wound up with a hundred and fifty guests. Mara lives in an eight-room apartment at 975 Park Avenue during most of the year, and he and Mrs. Mara also have a summer home in Luzerne, New York. He is one of eight honorary life members of Lodge No. 1, Benevolent & Protective Order of Elks. (The other seven include Nicholas Murray Butler, Governor Lehman, and former governors Charles S. Whitman and Alfred E. Smith.) In 1925, Mara established the New York Football Giants, the professional eleven which plays at the Polo Grounds. Later he presented the franchise to his two sons, Jack and Wellington, both Fordham alumni. It was because of the Giants that the club on Forty-sixth Street was called the Turf and Gridiron, rather than something like the Turf Association or the Odds Club. At various times in the past he has taken flyers in the liquor-importing business, the promotion of prize fights, and stockbrokerage.

The first dollar Mara bet on a horse started him on his way to all these glories. He was a twelve-year-old newsboy on Union Square at the time, and he lost the dollar. He forgets the name of the horse involved, but he remembers that it was ridden by an ex-newsboy named Micky Clemens. The experience taught him the irrelevancy of sentiment in horse racing. It also taught him that the bookmakers usually win. From that day on, his ambition was formed. The bookmakers to whom he delivered papers on his news route seemed to him singularly blessed among the people of the East Side. They dressed the best and worked the least.

His newspaper route ran along Broadway from Wanamaker's store to Seventeenth Street, and included several popular hotels, like the St. Denis and the Union Square. Sometimes hotel guests would ask him where they could place a bet, and he would take their money to the bookmakers he knew. If the bettors lost, the bookies would pay Tim a five-per-cent commission. If the bettors won, Tim would deliver the winnings, and often receive a tip. During that period Tim was a pupil in Public School 14, on Twenty-seventh Street near Third Avenue. He sold newspapers in the late afternoon, and in the evenings worked as an usher at the Third Avenue Theatre, a temple of melodrama. Tim's father died before Tim was born. In his neighborhood, therefore, he enjoyed the good will that falls to a bright, cheerful Irish boy who is at the same time the son of a poor widow. Among the early friends he made was Mike Cruise, the leader of the Tammany Central Association on East Thirty-second Street. Tim has been a good Tammany man ever since, and is frequently credited with great political influence, an impression he does nothing to discourage.

When Tim left public school he was thirteen. His first real job was with a lawbook firm on Nassau Street, delivering rebound volumes to attorneys. This gave him an opportunity to extend his betting business, for some of the lawyers played the races, and on days when they were busy in court they left betting commissions for him to execute. After working for several years for the lawbook dealers, he opened a place of his own, the New York Law Bindery, at 99 Nassau Street. More bookmaking than bookbinding went on there. By then he had established a regular following among bettors, and they telephoned their wagers to him.

His greatest patron was Thomas W. O'Brien, immortal in reminiscence as one of the few bettors who beat the races. Chicago O'Brien was this phenomenon's nom de course, and he was a retired bricklayer. At the appearance of O'Brien money in the betting ring, odds dropped like a barometer before a typhoon. Chicago therefore bet through agents, who placed thousands of dollars by telephone with poolrooms out of town. The agents were men who had established their credit in the gambling world. Young Tim was already in this class. Sometimes he placed $50,000 on a single race for the O'Brien account. Knowing that O'Brien was generally right, he would put $1000 of his own money on the same horse. If the horse lost, he had a five-per-cent commission, $2500, coming to him from the books, so he was certain of a $1500 profit anyway.

As his clientele grew, Tim began to cover the smaller bets himself, instead of passing them on to the bookmakers. The mathematical background he had gained at P. S. 14, although simple, was adequate for his needs. Bookmaking is based on a kind of arithmetical shorthand called "percentage." An even-money horse is said to be 50 per cent; a 2-to-1 horse, 33 per cent; a 3-to-1 horse, 25, and a 4-to-1 horse, 20. If there should be two horses in a race, both at even money, the book would be 100 per cent: if the bookmaker bet $1000 against each, he would break exactly even. If there should be three horses, and he laid $1000 at even money against each, he would stand to win $1000 no matter what happened. This would be a 150-per-cent book. Generally, the makers of the books aim at an arrangement of odds that will work out to about 115 per cent. A typical book on an eight-horse race might be arranged in this manner, if the bookmaker planned to lay $1000 against each entry:

ENTRY	ODDS	PERCENTAGE	RISK
Favorite	2–1	33	$1000 to win $500
Second choice	5–2	28	" " " 400
Third choice	4–1	20	" " " 250
Fourth choice	6–1	14	" " " 167
Long shot A	10–1	9	" " " 100
Long shot B	10–1	9	" " " 100
Outsider A	30–1	3	" " " 33
Outsider B	50–1	2	" " " 20
		118	

If the favorite should win, the book would have to pay out $1000 of the $1070 it took in from the bettors on the other horses. If the second choice should win, the profit would be $100 greater. A victory for the extreme outsider would mean a profit of $550 for the book.

The bookmaker's troubles come in filling the book. His customers always insist on betting more than he wants to cover on certain horses and on ignoring others, so his system of checks and balances is shattered. The bookmaker lowers the odds against the horses most in demand, but often this expedient does not suffice. He cannot afford to turn away trade, so he tries to place some of the money with other bookmakers. This form of hedging, also prevalent among insurance underwriters, is called laying off. Concomitantly, other bookmakers lay off with him. Bookmakers bet against bookmakers, like the people of the Hebrides who lived by taking in one another's washing. Odds sometimes change so radically in response to the market that by post time the book's percentage has been erased, and the bookmaker has become a bettor on a rather large scale.

From the beginning, Mara displayed an exceptional flair for this form of mathematical catch-as-catch-can. In 1921, he made up his mind to abandon city betting and go out to the track. It was like the decision of a stock-company actor to invade the big time. Tim didn't begin at the bottom, by accepting the two- and five-dollar bets of the ordinary grandstand patrons. Optimistically, he set up business in the enclosure at Belmont, ground usually restricted to bookmakers of long experience. A ticket to the enclosure costs twice as much as one to the grandstand; it is assumed that enclosure patrons bet more heavily.

A bookmaker's success in the long run depends on the size of his clientele. If a man has a following, bookmakers believe he will eventually cash in on what is called the hidden percentage. Hidden percentage is a thing distinct from ordinary percentage. It is the tendency of bettors to be content with modest gains when they are winning but, when losing, to insist on betting more than they can afford in an effort to recoup. After a day of beaten favorites, Tim has great faith in this psychological ace in the hole.

A bookmaker on a New York track needed a considerable sum for overhead expenses, as well as his capital for betting. For the privilege of operating, he had to pay a daily fee averaging ninety dollars to the racing association that owns the track. He also paid a few dollars a day to John Cavanagh, a gentleman known as a "racing stationer," who provided him daily with a few pencils, blank sheets of paper, and cardboard slips bearing the names of all the entries, which were usually tacked up at one side of the bookmaker's slate. Besides selling cardboard, Cavanagh acted as arbiter of the betting ring. All sorts of disputes arise about bets. Cavanagh's decision was final. A bookmaker needed a crew of from five to eight assistants, each of whom drew from ten to twenty-five dollars a day. With him constantly were a sheet writer, who recorded all his bets; a cashier, to handle the money, and a ticket writer, who kept track of transactions with credit customers. Most bookmakers also employ a bet caller, who receives the money of cash bettors. The caller bawls out the bet and the badge number of the customer, such as "Aneroid, sixty to fifteen, badge 1347." Tim did not employ a caller, preferring to call the bets himself. He enjoyed the feel of the bills in his palm, and was not opposed to the sound of his own voice. In addition to these employees on fixed post, every bookmaker had two "outside men." One outside man scouted around the betting ring, noticing what odds other books were laying, and particularly whether the professional betting men were placing large amounts on any of the entries. He reported to his boss at brief intervals. The other outside man bet for the book; his job was laying off. On an average weekday, Mara handled bets amounting to between ten and fifteen thousand dollars; on a Saturday or holiday, as much as thirty thousand dollars.

In Mara's quality of surface good humor he excelled all his confreres. Unlike most of the Turf and Gridiron members, he managed to look like the popular conception of a sporting man, even without wearing a fancy vest. His big, pink, happy face, with its frame of wavy, ginger-colored hair, is that of a man who would give anyone a break. Perched on his high stool in the enclosure betting ring, he met all comers joyfully, with a robust voice and feeble jokes. "Where did you dig that one up?" he would ask a client who bet a long shot. "I'll give you my watch if it wins." If the bettor was a steady customer, he sometimes gave him an extra point. Ignoring the odds of 17 to 5 marked on his slate, he would magnanimously make it 18. This was usually a sign he was sure the horse would lose. Win or lose, however, Tim maintains his smile. It did not come off even after a filly called Sally's Alley won the Futurity Stakes in 1922. Tim, who had been contemptuous of the filly, dropped sixty thousand dollars on the race. "I been shot at by sharpshooters," he said afterward. Wise bettors have found him a more difficult target since.

Because of his apparently excellent connections, Tim in 1926 became a figure in national politics as manifested in the professional prize ring. James A. Farley was then Chairman of the New York State Athletic Commission. Farley, who had always dreamed of luring the colored voters away from the Republican party, had recognized Harry Wills as the leading contender for the world's heavyweight championship, then held by Jack Dempsey, who was in notoriously poor shape. Gene Tunney, an Irish-American heavyweight born in Greenwich Village, also was challenging Dempsey. Tex Rickard, the promoter, preferred this match. But since the New York Irish always voted Democratic anyway, there were no votes to gain by aiding Tunney. Tunney's manager, Billy Gibson, was a bookmaker of the common grandstand variety. Scrambling for political support, Gibson thought that Mara could induce Governor Smith to overrule the Athletic Commission. In return for Tim's influence, Gibson and Tunney promised him twenty-five per cent of the fighter's earnings as champion if Tunney beat Dempsey. The influence didn't work. Eventually, however, Rickard put the match on in Philadelphia, where it drew more than a million dollars, and Tunney won the title. When Mara asked for his share of the earnings, Tunney said that since Mara had not done anything for him, he owed nothing to Mara. After Tunney retired as champion, in 1928, the bookmaker brought action against him for $405,000. The Mara-Tunney suit came to trial in the New York Supreme Court in the fall of 1930. The jury found for Tunney. Mara's attorneys appealed for a new trial. Tunney in 1932 paid Mara $30,000 to settle the case, and since then both men have claimed a victory.

Before the autumn of 1925, Mara had never seen a football game. In that season he became the owner of New York's first big-league professional football team. Bookmakers, like clergymen and physicians, are famous for their susceptibility to new forms of investment. So when promoters of the National League of Professional Football Clubs, which had begun in the Middle West, decided to invade New York, they offered the franchise to Mara. He bought it because it cost only $2500. He hired Bob Folwell, former coach at the Naval Academy, to assemble a team.

The first edition of the Giants included a glittering set of names, but wasn't a particularly good team by professional standards. Mara's publicity man distributed vast numbers of complimentary tickets. He even supplied a band and a cheering section of small boys to simulate college atmosphere. But the Giants lost money until the postseason game against Red Grange and the Chicago Bears. In 1925, Grange was America's leading hero. When, at the end of the 1925 intercollegiate season, he turned professional and his New York debut was announced, the ticket line began to form at Mara's office in the Knickerbocker Building. Thousands of enthusiasts were turned away from the Polo Grounds on the Sunday of the game. The contest drew $56,000 and gave Tim such a millennial vision of what professional football might eventually be that he became an irrepressible football fan. On one occasion, when his Giants beat the Bears in Chicago, 3–0, he rushed out on the field like a freshman to grab the ball from the referee. "The winning team gets the ball!" he yelled, a stickler for campus tradition. The referee didn't know him and waved him away. Tim grappled with him; some Chicago players joined the scuffle, and when Tim broke away, there were cleat marks on his habitual spats. But he had the ball under his arm.

The president of Mara University, as those whimsical fellows, the sports writers, sometimes term the football Giants, usually watches the games from a window of the baseball Giants' clubhouse behind center field. He gets enough fresh air at the race track in summer, he says. Ever since Tim started the team, his immediate family has gone football-mad. Mrs. Mara, an attractive, young-looking woman whom Tim married in 1907, made an important suggestion at the first game she saw. She noticed that the Giants' bench was on the south side of the field, and as twilight came on was in shadow. She said the Giants ought to move to the warm side and let the visiting postgraduates suffer. Tim's sons, although neither played football at Fordham, have developed into subtle theorists from attending Giant practice.

Mara's most startling peculiarity does not at once meet the eye. It takes time to explain, and most people are incredulous even after he explains it. Mara is destitute. His only assets are about one hundred dollars in pocket cash and two watches. This poverty, in which he takes a good deal of honest, jovial pride, stems from another law suit, which closely followed his wrangle with Tunney. In 1928, after Al Smith had been nominated for President on the Democratic ticket, out-of-town Democrats showed a marked reluctance to contribute to the Smith campaign fund. John J. Raskob, National Chairman of the party, turned for aid to the County Trust Company of New York, a bank friendly to Tammany. A state law forbids banks to lend funds to political parties. The County Trust officers, however, said they saw no objection to lending money to responsible Democrats on their own notes, endorsed by Raskob. In spite of Smith's having disappointed him in the Tunney affair, Mara signed a note for $50,000, and the bank turned the cash over to the Democratic National Committee. Other Tammany men of substance signed similar notes. After the election, the bank moved to collect on the notes. Mara and several of the other signees were at first astonished, then indignant. They protested that the notes had been dummies, made so that the bank might have collateral to show for its loans to the party. They admitted an agreement that, if the National Committee failed to raise $4,000,000 for its campaign, it might use the notes. But, Mara said, the records of the committee showed it had raised $4,006,000 in cash. The bank sued Mara and Patrick Kenny, a Yonkers contractor, in a test case. Smith administered the *coup de grâce* to his beautiful friendship with Mara by appearing on the stand for the County Trust.

"The jury didn't believe him," Tim recalls with relish. "They believed me." But although the jury absolved Mara and Kenny, the bank wouldn't. For two years the case dragged through the higher courts, and the County Trust won its appeal. When it tried to collect, the bank found that Mara was legally destitute, although he appeared the picture of prosperity. He had founded a large and flourishing coal firm, the Mara Fuel Company; his wife and his brother owned all the stock in it. His sons owned the football team, now consistently profitable. As for the bookmaking business conducted under his name, Tim said he had no financial interest in it; he was just a manager. Tim's credit customers of the track received weekly statements and settled by check, but he had no bank account. When the customers won, they got checks signed by Walter Kenny, Tim's cashier, who is a son of his codefendant.

Tim's destitution does not interfere with his enjoyment of life. Daily he visits the various business enterprises in which he has no financial interest. During the racing season, he still spends all his afternoons at the track, nowadays in the character of a simple bettor. Periodically he makes trips to Washington, from which he returns with casual anecdotes of what he said to important politicians and what they said to him. Occasionally he plays golf. Last fall, shortly before the Elks made him an honorary life member, he presented them with an organ. Jimmy Walker accepted the gift in the name of the lodge.

Tim has his sentimental side. He enjoys singing ballads like "The Rose of Tralee." He even has his softer moments at the track. During one spring meeting at Jamaica, he was touched to the core by the fine spirit of a man who insisted on paying him fifty dollars which the man said he had borrowed from Tim fifteen years before. Tim accepted the money under protest. In the next race, the mysterious stranger bet him two hundred dollars on a horse named Galloping, 2 to 1 to show, and won four hundred dollars from him. "Maybe," Tim says, "it would have been better if I'd never seen the bum."

Your Hat, Sir?

IN THE YEAR 1904 a man named Harry Susskind, then in his early twenties, looked through a window of Captain Jim Churchill's crowded restaurant at Forty-sixth Street and Broadway. He noticed that the male patrons laid their overcoats and hats on chairs and balanced their walking sticks precariously against tables. This represented a loss of income to Captain Churchill, a retired police officer, since obviously if every third or fourth chair was occupied by an overcoat, the space available for customers was reduced by a third or a quarter. To Susskind, the overcoats represented a financial future. He went in and proposed that Captain Churchill set aside a corner of the vestibule for coat racks. He offered to provide a couple of girls to help customers off with their coats, to check them, and return them as the customers went out. This would, incidentally, relieve Captain Churchill of responsibility for hats that customers sometimes exchanged by mistake and for canes that bibulous owners insisted they had brought into Churchill's when as a matter of fact the sticks were safe in the umbrella stand at home. Susskind promised to wear a uniform and personally supervise the checking. Over and above all the services he proposed to render, he offered Captain Churchill three thousand dollars a year. Churchill had considered hiring a couple of wardrobe attendants himself, but had boggled at the extra expense. He accepted Susskind's offer on the spot, and the young man became the first lessee of a hat-check concession in New York. Susskind made a profit of about twenty-five thousand dollars in his first year at Churchill's.

Susskind had a good idea of the true value of such a concession because he had worked as a hat-check boy, in pea jacket and tight pants, at the Café Martin on Fifth Avenue, and later at the brand-new Astor. At these smart resorts and a few others, hat-checking had existed for a long time, but the managements had never thought of renting out the concession. In some places, attendants were allowed to retain their tips in lieu of salaries. In others, hat-check rights were granted to a headwaiter or doorman as a perquisite of office. The owners of these gratuitious concessions paid the salaries of the hat-check boys and received from them what proportion of their tips the boys thought it prudent to yield. Only an ex-hat-check boy could understand the vastness of the possibilities.

The titular *vestiaire* at Martin's was an old retainer named Louis, who paid nothing for the concession. Louis' boys used to palm alternate tips and drop the coins inside their uniforms. They wore long underdrawers in those days, and coins would remain safe between the legs of the drawers and the skin of the wearer. Despite the leakage of silver, the concessionaire grew wealthy. Susskind had had opportunity to study the Broadway mentality at the Astor and decided that pretty girls would draw heavier tips than boys. He had also learned that it was extremely flattering to regular patrons to memorize their faces and say, "No check," when they gave him their wraps. Recognition enhanced their self-esteem, and they tipped generously. He taught this mnemonic method of boosting tips to his employees at Churchill's, where he paid his girls twenty-five dollars a week.

When the concessionaire, wise to the ways of checkers, was in personal charge of his business, he could exercise a vigilance impossible to a hotel functionary with other duties. If he thought a girl was stealing an unreasonable amount, he could discharge her. By trial and error he could build up a fairly reliable personnel. Susskind bought more concessions with his profits from Churchill's. When George Rector seceded from his father's restaurant and opened his own place on Forty-eighth Street, Susskind paid him three thousand dollars for his coatroom concession before he opened. Shortly before the United States entered the World War, Susskind, in partnership with his brother Joe, ran the cloakrooms of sixty restaurants and employed six hundred men and women. Harry continued to wear his uniform at Churchill's, which had moved to larger quarters twice since he opened shop there. Joe wore the livery of the Hotel Knickerbocker, where the brothers had an extremely profitable concession. The Susskinds put managers in their concessions in other restaurants, paying them a small percentage of the profits. Complete honesty is not expected in the hat-check business, and most of the managers stayed within reason.

The public was more ingenuous then than now, and most restaurant patrons believed that the Susskinds' girls retained their tips. The girls wore a kind of musical-comedy French-maid costume and put their tips in their apron pockets as they received them. The Susskinds were wise enough not to install the locked boxes into which many present-day hat-check operatives drop their tips as soon as they get them. But the arrangement could not be kept a secret indefinitely. S. Jay Kaufman of the old *Globe* and Karl K. Kitchen of the *Evening World*, who were the Broadway columnists of circa 1917, gave the true state of affairs considerable publicity. Harry Susskind began to sense an undertone of antagonism. People kidded him about driving to work in a special-body Cadillac and then donning a hat-check attendant's uniform. Susskind lived in style in those days. He had an apartment on Riverside Drive, then fashionable, a house in Pelham, and a camp in the Adirondacks. His two children attended the Edgewood School in Greenwich, where, he likes to recall, they were classmates of a Rockefeller child.

Hat-checking was no longer a dignified business, the Susskind brothers decided when the criticism increased. Even worse than the effect of the publicity on tipping, which fell off sharply, was the invasion of the hat-check field by cloak-and-suiters with money to invest. Bids for concessions rose and the margin of potential profit decreased. By that time the brothers had accumulated about one million dollars and they retired. Joe Susskind died in 1930. Harry opened several large restaurants, invested in real estate, played the stock market heavily, and lost virtually everything he had. Then, a small, gnomish, gray-haired man, slightly cynical about everything, he was back in the hat-check business. He leased the concession at a minor night club on West Fifty-second Street, until it closed.

There is practically no illusion about the hat-check business now. A well-founded skepticism governs most patrons' reactions. Resentful customers often say to girls, "Here's ten cents for you and ten cents for the greaseball you work for"—a remark as unsound as it is wounding, for the girl has to surrender the twenty cents anyway. A few out-of-town visitors may retain their naïveté, but there is little consolation for the concessionaire in them. Some are so naïve that they do not tip at all. Hat-checking has evolved into a cold, calculating, highly competitive industry.

The girls have a union—Wardrobe and Checkroom Attendants' Union, Local No. 135—with a scale of minimum wages. Its office is at 1650 Broadway. If a member is caught by her employer "knocking down" a tip, her union card is suspended. Mr. Benny Jacobs, business secretary of the local, acts as a casting director for night-club proprietors. Some like blonde girls, some brunettes, to match the color schemes of their places. Jacobs gets requests for pert girls or cultured types to fit places with swing or class atmosphere. John Perona of El Morocco, for example, insists on tall, cultured brunettes, although the local argued him into taking a young woman with dark chestnut hair as an experiment. Concessionaires usually let proprietors specify the type of comeliness they require. The union has seven hundred members, and there are seldom more than four hundred employed simultaneously, so a considerable range of types is always available. Many of the girls are members of Chorus Equity too.

Girls earn twenty-five dollars a week in what Local No. 135 calls Class A clubs. In this group it includes El Morocco, the Stork Club, Fefe's Monte Carlo and like places. In the smaller Class B clubs, girls get twenty dollars. Not only cloakroom girls but cigarette and flower vendors and washroom matrons belong to the union, which is affiliated with the Building Service Employees' International of the American Federation of Labor. Checkroom workers in the hotels are not organized and earn less than the night-club girls, a condition for which various excuses are offered. Union girls in night clubs work approximately nine hours a night for six nights a week. They are entitled to one week's vacation with pay for every nine months they work, if the club lasts nine months.

All night-club concessions now include the doorman, the washroom attendants, the cigarette girls, the girls who sell stuffed dogs, limp dolls, and gardenias, programs in places vast enough to have them, and any other little item the concessionaire chooses to peddle.

"For every girl up front taking clothes from the customers and giving them back, you got to have two people behind the counter putting coats on racks and seeing they don't get mixed," one entrepreneur says. "If the front girl kept the tips, who would pay the hangers? And then how about the washroom attendants? In the average night club, they don't take in as much as you pay them." This is a routine defense among concessionaires.

Reputedly the most successful concessionaire is a vehement, youngish man named A. (for Abraham) Ellis, who does business under the name of Planetary Recreations, Inc., from an office on an upper floor of the Manhattan Opera House, which he now owns. He bought the old theater with profits from the hat-check business. He operates the ballrooms and banquet halls at the Opera House, and his customers check a lot of coats. Ellis leases the concessions at half a score of other restaurants. He became involved in theatricals in 1935 when he paid $15,000 for concessions at *The Eternal Road*, the big Reinhardt production that was delayed for a year by money troubles. Before the show could open, Ellis had to contribute $4000 toward the Equity bond to cover actors' salaries. He lost $10,000 on the deal. If the show had had a long run, he says, he would have made "a fortune of money." For the three years of the French Casino's success, Ellis had the concession there. He paid a flat sum of $31,000 a year, with a percentage arrangement that brought the total up to $50,000 annually. When Billy Rose took over the place during the winter he raised Ellis' rent to $40,000 in advance and a percentage. Ellis paid about $20,000 for the Cotton Club.

The Stork Club concession was rented for $15,000 to a syndicate of employees. The proprietors of "21" long ago presented their concession to Jimmy, a doorman who is said to have saved them from infinite grief during the prohibition period. Renée Carroll, the red-haired girl at Sardi's, pays nothing for her concession, because the management values her gift for remembering the names of moving-picture publicity men and making them feel like celebrities.

The most conservative concessionaires operate in hotels. A painfully sedate and now defunct graduate doorman named J. Bates Keating had the concessions at the Astor, the Pierre, and the Edison for many years. He liked to talk about the unobtrusiveness of his service—no vulgar, obstreperous flower or cigarette girls pushing sales. Cigarette girls in hotels work for the lessee of the stand in the lobby. The Waldorf retains its own checkrooms, but pays ten per cent of the gross receipts to the manager, an experienced concessionaire.

The strangest feature of the hat-checking business is the complete absence of tangible merchandise or a fixed charge. The stock in trade consists of cardboard checks, worth two dollars a thousand wholesale, and the customer is not allowed to retain even the check when he leaves. A patron who takes his hat and walks out, paying nothing to the check girl, is liable to no pursuit, physical or legal. In reputable resorts, the contract between concessionaire and proprietor specifies that no patron is to be caused embarrassment. Yet less than one per cent of the people who use checkrooms omit the tip.

Shortly before the war, there was a national crusade against tipping. The shocking discovery that many tippees turned over their take to a third party spurred the crusaders. Governor Charles S. Whitman of New York was a leading anti-tipper, and the city had a Society for the Prevention of Useless Giving. A man named William Rufus Scott, of Paducah, Kentucky, wrote a book called *The Itching Palm* which urged the human race to give up tipping. Scott said that the psychological basis of tipping was one part misguided generosity, two parts pride, and one part fear of being unfavorably noticed. The last motive is unquestionably important. During the hours when checking is desultory, the patron walking up to the counter feels that he has the undivided attention of the cloakroom staff. He probably tips a quarter. When patrons are leaving in a hurry at the close of a floor show, men sneak in dimes. The more efficient concessionaires keep hour-by-hour graphs that prove this.

"A tip is what one American is willing to pay to induce another American to acknowledge inferiority" was another of Scott's dicta. Largesse exalts the ego of the tipper in almost exact ratio to the inconsequence of the service. Heralds in the Middle Ages had a nice living in gratuities from feudal landlords who would hang a peasant for holding out a ducat of rent. The state of Washington once passed a law against tipping, but repealed it after a couple of years because people tipped anyway and juries wouldn't convict.

The most plausible hypothesis of modern tip motivation was promulgated by Louis Reverdy, a French lawyer, in his thesis, "Le Pourboire," for the Doctor of Laws degree of the Sorbonne in 1930. Reverdy says that men first tipped for display. Now, he thinks, they tip from a sense of duty, since they realize that the tips constitute the tippee's means of livelihood. This is true even when the customer knows that the cloakroom girl works for a concessionaire and when he feels that it is the duty of the restaurant to check his coat free. For he knows that the individual girl will lose her job if nobody tips her. By withholding his tip, he would sacrifice an amiable individual to a cold principle. The chances are that he is inspired to even greater sympathy if the girl happens to be comely. Concessionaires, of course, are aware of this and pick their girls accordingly, but they place no premium on actually beautiful girls. "A girl who's a real knockout gets herself a guy in a couple of weeks," Abe Ellis once explained, "and then you got to break in another girl."

The contemporary tipper gets little positive pleasure from tipping. Less than one per cent of the patrons at the French Casino tipped fifty cents, and there was no significant correlation between the amount patrons spent in the restaurant and the size of the tips they gave in the lobby. Most men oscillate between the dime and quarter levels, the average tip at a large Broadway place being sixteen cents. Girls report that at East Side clubs like El Morocco there may be a slightly higher ratio of quarter tippers to dime tippers. But fifty-cent-plus tippers are as rare on the East Side as on Broadway. Perhaps twice a week, in any club doing a large volume of business, eccentric patrons tip girls five dollars or more. The recipient is allowed to keep half of any tip in this class, turning the rest in to the concessionaire.

Men in the hat-check business admit that the customers don't enjoy tipping. But, they say, nobody ever went to an unpopular place merely because of free hat-checking. And conversely, when people want to attend a certain club, they don't stay home because of the cost of checking their hats. They are fond of telling how the Café Savarin on lower Broadway once abolished tipping, only to have the patrons force the money on the girls, and how the Hotel Algonquin had the same experience.

At private banquets in the Astor, hosts sometimes stipulate there shall be no tipping of cloakroom attendants. Keating, the concessionaire, used to cite one such affair attended by the late Nathan Straus, the free-milk man. Mr. Straus gave the girl a dollar. She handed it back to him. The thwarted philanthropist threw the dollar behind the counter and walked out. The experience of the Hotel Pennsylvania conflicts with these happy reminiscences of concessionaires. The Pennsylvania and all the other Statler hotels abolished hat-check concessions and hat-check tipping in 1933. Far from resenting this change, the Statler people say, patrons now check thirty-three and a third more articles per capita than they ever did before. At the restaurants Longchamps, where the hat-check tip is included in the ten-per-cent service charge, most patrons seem content to let it go at that.

The most skilled operatives of the concession business are not the young women of the cloakroom or the hangers who work behind the counter but the cigarette and novelty girls. They need salesmanship to maintain their level of sales and tips, and tact to avoid arguments with customers. If a girl is the subject of a complaint to the management, she generally loses her job. The worst sin a girl can commit is to recognize a man accompanied by a woman and remind him of a previous visit. The woman may be his wife and his previous companion may not have been.

Standard brands of cigarettes sell for twenty-five cents in night clubs, and a girl's tips are expected to equal her gross sales. In the large Broadway clubs, the girls are sometimes demure, but at East Side places, the girls say, "a girl has got to talk very direct." "If you want to sell cigarettes to those guys," one girl reported, "you got to say things that would shock a medium-class man." The business of being a cigarette girl is so complex and requires so much ingenuity that a star can sometimes command thirty dollars a week.

"A good cigarette girl," Abe Ellis has said, "is far and in between. She has got to know just when to lay off and when to knock the customer down. And selling stuffed dogs to grown-up women is an art in itself."

The chief technical problem of the hat-check industry since its inception has been the safe conveyance of the customer's quarter to the pocket of the concessionaire. The girl receiving a tip can seldom conquer the atavistic notion that it was meant for her personally. Even hiring a watcher for each girl would not preclude collusion. Since there are no fixed rates of tipping, it is impossible to tell from the receipts on any given evening whether the girls have held out anything.

When the Susskind brothers ran virtually all the concessions in town, they used a common-sense personal-confidence sort of system which kept their help from robbing them too flagrantly. But since they obtained their leases cheaply, they could afford a good deal of tip leakage. Competitors, bidding against the brothers, reduced the margin of profit. Consequently they worked harder to protect their receipts, putting the girls in tight, pocketless uniforms and making them drop their tips through a slot in the counter as soon as they got them. Under the counter was a locked box.

Modern concessionaires, more efficient, use a variation of the Bedaux System. They keep charts from which they establish a norm of production for each girl and location. The concessionaire knows, when he goes into a new restaurant, approximately what to expect. If there is a minimum charge of $1.50, for example, the tipping should compare with that at the old Paradise. He will then expect, from each hundred tippers, a return of about thirteen dollars. The first crew of girls he puts in his new concession are reasonably safe if they approach that standard. The girls do not know exactly what their boss expects, so the assumption is they will try hard to make a good showing. After a few weeks, the concessionaire switches the girls to another place and brings in a new set. If the receipts fall off noticeably, he suspects the replacements. If receipts rise, he suspects the first group. He shifts individual girls in the same way. If a hypothetical Billie, checking hats at a certain club for a month, turns in an average of eleven cents a customer, while an equally hypothetical Mamie over a similar period averages sixteen cents, he bounces Billie. By continued shifts, he establishes an average for the place. This may not turn out the same as the average at the Paradise, however. The new club may get a high ratio of Southern patronage, which brings the average tip down, or of "collegiates," notoriously poor tippers, or of race-track men, notoriously good ones.

After each tour of the house, a cigarette girl turns in all the cash she has received. In this way she has no chance to hoard her tips for the evening. She might decide, if they were unusually good, that she could safely knock down a dollar for herself. Even at that, most cigarette girls manage to keep some part of their tips. Concessionaires never know exactly how much, but if the girl is a "producer," they don't care.

"Better a kid who takes ten in tips and knocks a buck," a pillar of the industry once said, "than a dummy who gets half the tips and turns in all she gets. But please don't use my name, because on such a question I hate to quote myself."

The Boys from Syracuse

COMMONLY, when a family achieves such fame that it has a street named in its honor, it moves to a better part of town. There are no Roosevelts on Roosevelt Street, no Astors within blocks of Astor Place, and no Vanderbilts on Vanderbilt Avenue except when Brigadier General Cornelius Vanderbilt pays an occasional visit to the Yale Club. Lee and J. J. Shubert, however, live almost entirely in, above, and around Shubert Alley, which runs from Forty-fourth to Forty-fifth Streets between Broadway and Eighth Avenue. The Alley, although it has a sidewalk and a roadway for automobiles, is a private street, part of the property rented to the Shuberts by the Astor Estate in 1912 on a lease which still has sixty-nine years to run. The rest of the leased area is covered by the Shubert, Booth, Plymouth, and Broadhurst theaters. Lee Shubert's private office is in the turret at the southeast corner of the Shubert Theatre building. His desk is directly above the "u" in the theater's sign. J. J., who long ago conceived a seignoral disdain for his given name of Jacob, lives just across Forty-fourth Street, on the tenth floor of the Sardi Building, which the Shuberts own; the sixth floor is given over to his offices. J. J. often says that he likes to live upstairs from his business. Lee has an apartment adjoining his offices on the fifth floor of the Shubert, but he seldom uses this suite except for shaves and sun-ray treatments, both endured in a barber chair with he has had installed there. He prefers to sleep in the Century Apartments, on the site of the old Century Theatre on Central Park West. Even there he is not outside the Shubert sphere, for the brothers hold a second mortgage on the apartment building.

The Messrs. Shubert have been the largest operators in the New York theater for so long that only a few persons remember that they were once boy wonders in Syracuse, where both of them were running theaters before they had reached their twenties. City records in Syracuse show that Lee was born there sixty-six years ago and J. J. five years later, but the brothers still have the brisk and querulous quality of two combative small boys who feel the teacher is down on them. A few years ago they addressed a manifesto to New York dramatic editors, insisting that they be referred to by the collective designation of "the Messrs. Shubert." "Lee and Jake," they felt, sounded much too flippant. Lee takes a quiet pride in being known as the fastest walker on Broadway. He walks fast even when he doesn't know where he is going. J. J. is distinguished for his bitter vehemence at rehearsals. "There is only one captain on this ship," he once shouted while rehearsing a musical, "the director and me!"

When Lee, in his office in the Shubert Theatre, wishes to communicate with J. J., in the Sardi Building, he summons Jack Morris, his secretary, and says, "Take a letter to Mr. J. J." When J. J. wishes to communicate with Lee, he says to his secretary, "Take a letter to Mr. Lee." This custom has given rise to a theater-district legend that the brothers are mortal enemies and do not speak at all. The legend is not founded on fact. When either of the Shuberts is really in a hurry to discuss something with the other, he walks across the street to do so. An even more fanciful theory has it that the story of animosity between the two has been fostered for business reasons by the Shuberts themselves. The exponents of this theory contend that when Lee wants to get out of a deal, he says that J. J. will not allow him to go through with it, and that when J. J. wants to get out of a deal, he blames Lee. Actually there is no overt hostility between the brothers. Mr. J. J. says that it was the intention of the Messrs., when they collaborated in the construction of the Sardi Building in 1926, to move all their executive offices there from the somewhat constricted quarters on the upper floors of the Shubert Theatre. That summer, Mr. J. J., who sometimes explains a predilection for foreign musical shows by saying, "I am more dynamic and Continental than Mr. Lee," made his annual trip to Europe to inspect the new vintage of operettas. When he returned, he found that his office furniture had been moved into the new building, but that Mr. Lee had treacherously remained in the Shubert Theatre. The Shubert enterprises have been a two-headed organism ever since, with Mr. Lee's casting department and executive staff on the north side of Forty-fourth Street and Mr. J. J.'s on the south side. The publicity and auditing departments are on Mr. J. J.'s side of the street; the real-estate, theater-booking, and financial departments are on Mr. Lee's. The balance of power is worked out to the last milligram: Mrs. Lillian Duffy, the plump, white-haired receptionist in Mr. Lee's office, has the authority to hire all girl ushers for Shubert theaters; Mrs. Loretta Gorman, Mrs. Duffy's practically identical sister, is Mr. J. J.'s receptionist and hires all the theater charwomen. But the brothers, like most two-headed creatures, have a single life line. All their real estate is held in common, and they have a joint checking account. The separate-office arrangement resembles one of those dual households advocated by married female novelists. The Shuberts retain community of interests, but avoid friction; each produces shows without interference from the other. Failure of one of Mr. J. J.'s shows is made easier for Mr. Lee to bear by the knowledge that it was Mr. J. J.'s idea. Success is sweetened for Mr. Lee by the reflection that he will share in the profits. Things work out the same way on the other side of the street.

The brothers' chauffeurs amicably share the parking facilities of the Alley, which are also made available to producers and stars of companies playing the Shubert Theatre if the shows are hits. Katharine Hepburn, for instance, parked her car there regularly during the many months *The Philadelphia Story* filled the theater. Mr. Lee has three automobiles, all of them foreign—a Rolls-Royce, a Hispano-Suiza, and an Isotta-Fraschini. Mr. J. J. favors American cars. Mr. Lee explains that he has never owned any but European automobiles because when he is in this country he is too busy to go shopping. He finds his only moments of relaxation during cruises and trips abroad, when he sometimes has half an hour to spare. It was during one such trip that he signed up Carmen Miranda in Rio de Janeiro and brought her to New York to star in *The Streets of Paris.*

Mr. Lee comes to work every day shortly before noon. He leaves his desk to go home to the Century Apartments at three or four o'clock in the morning. When people ask him why he works such long hours, he says, "I am not a loafing kind of boy." The habit goes back to the days of the great commercial rivalry which existed for fifteen years between the Shuberts and the firm of Klaw & Erlanger. Abe Erlanger was an early riser. Once he told a friend, "I am up and at my desk while the Shuberts still are sleeping." Mr. Lee decided that the only way to beat Erlanger was to stay up all night. Erlanger and Marc Klaw, his partner, are now dead, but Mr. Lee still can't sleep nights. J. J. attributes his brother's outrageous workday to the fact that Lee has always been a bachelor. Although J. J. himself has not had a wife since he was divorced in 1918, he says that the experience of marriage, no matter how far in the past, so changes a man's metabolism that he never again wants to work more than twelve hours at a stretch. Shubert employees—house and company managers, play readers, and publicity men—have the sympathy of their professional colleagues, because they must remain virtually on call until Mr. Lee decides to go home. The Shubert play-reading department gets about fifty manuscripts a month throughout the year and filters the best ones through to Mr. Lee's office. Authors of these promising works are sometimes summoned at a grisly hour shortly before dawn to read their scripts aloud. Mr. Lee never reads a play himself; he merely looks at synopses drawn up by his readers. During an author's reading, Mr. Lee sometimes appears to fall asleep. This is a frightful experience for the playwright, who is afraid to offend the producer by awakening him and, in desperation, continues reading. Mr. Lee always maintains that he has heard every word. The concentration of the Shuberts on their business is looked upon by most theatrical people as unsporting. If the brothers were going to work so hard, these critics think, they should have taken up a trade instead of the theater. Mr. Lee's incessant activity, even though some of it is undoubtedly superfluous, has served him well during his forty-two years on Broadway. He has simply outworn most of his opponents.

Mr. Lee is a short man whose appearance is so ostentatiously youthful that he is usually suspected of being very old. His face is a deep copper red all year round, a result of the sun-ray treatments and sun baths which he takes whenever he gets a chance. A musical-comedy director, strolling near the Mazzini statue in Central Park one morning, saw Mr. Lee asleep in the open tonneau of one of his automobiles with his face turned toward the sun. Mr. Lee's chauffeur, also asleep, lolled in the front seat. Before the invention of the sun-ray lamp, it was customary for writers to mention Lee's "midnight pallor." Because of his high cheekbones, narrow eyes, and lank black hair, it was also customary to say that he looked Oriental. Now that he can take sun-ray treatments, his upturned eyebrows and the deep wrinkles at the corners of his eyes make him look something like a good-natured Indian—Willie Howard, perhaps, in war-chief make-up. Mr. Lee always wears conservative, well-fitted suits made for him by Gray & Lampel, on East Fifty-third Street, at $225 each, and he has a liking for thick-soled, handmade English shoes and pleated shirts, which he wears with stiff collars. He admires his extremely small feet. There is a sedulous avoidance of flashiness in his dressing, but nothing pleases him better than a compliment on his clothes. Joe Peters, Mr. Lee's valet, shaves him at eleven in the morning and at seven in the evening. When Mr. Lee needs a new valet, he goes to the Hotel Astor barbershop and hires a barber. It was there he got Peters and Peters' predecessor. He has had only three valets in thirty-two years. Mr. Lee takes good care of his figure. He often lunches on half a cantaloupe and an order of sliced tomatoes.

In contrast to his older brother, Mr. J. J. seems dumpy and rumpled. While Lee's hair is preternaturally black and lank, J. J.'s is gray and wavy. Although he is a small man, there is something taurine about the set of his neck and head, and there is a permanent suggestion of a pout on his lips. Mr. Lee's voice has an indefinable foreign intonation; he is always polite, tentatively friendly, and on guard. Mr. J. J., who has no trace of accent, can be an unabashed huckster, choleric and loud, but he can be warmer and more ingratiating than his brother when he wants to.

It is pretty nearly impossible to make a living in the American theater without encountering the Shuberts because they own, lease, or manage twenty of the forty-odd legitimate theaters in New York and control about fifteen theaters in other cities, a very high percentage of the total theaters, considering the low estate to which the road has declined. As theatrical landlords, the Shuberts have practically no real competitor in New York

City, although Sam Grisman occasionally gets his hands on two or three theaters at a time. Theaters not owned or controlled by the brothers are for the most part in the hands of independent producers. Since the producer of a play usually turns over at least thirty-five per cent of the gross receipts as theater rent, the Shuberts, even if at any given time they had no show of their own running, could still conceivably be sharing in the profits of twenty attractions. This would give them by far the largest single take in the success of any theatrical season. In point of fact, however, they do produce shows. Like the movie-makers, they have to schedule their product with an eye to the number of theaters they must keep busy. If they have six theaters empty and only one manuscript of promise, they must go ahead and produce six shows anyway.

To make tenants for Shubert theaters, Lee, who is more active in theater management and real estate than his brother, will often finance another producer by lending him Shubert money on condition he brings his show into a Shubert house. The Shuberts have backed such disparate enterprises as the Group Theatre production of *Success Story* and a *jai-alai* tournament at the late Hippodrome. They supplied most of the money for *The Children's Hour* and *Shadow and Substance*, both earnest plays that the public would consider out of the Shubert line. Several years ago Mr. Lee backed Olsen and Johnson, a pair of vaudeville comedians, in expanding their seventy-minute unit show into a knockabout entertainment called *Hellz a Poppin*, which is still keeping the Shuberts' Winter Garden comfortably filled. When the Messrs. were sounded out on the production of a musical comedy for the World's Fair, Mr. Lee's reply—"Why should I make competition for my own houses?"—was typical. His creative instincts are weighed down by several thousand tons of concrete and twenty long-term leases. Inevitably the Shuberts make more bad bets than good ones. This does not mean that they lose money. "If we could hit one out of three," Mr. J. J. says very reasonably, "we would be doing fine."

When the Shuberts produce shows on their own account, they are likely to fall back on formulas that have served them well in the past. *The Student Prince* is typical of the Shubert tradition—the darling of the firm in retrospect and its present ideal. It made more money than any other show the Shuberts ever produced. When, in the season of 1925–26, there were nearly a dozen road companies of *The Student Prince* out, covering North America and Australia, the production sometimes grossed as much as $250,000 a week. Yet *The Student Prince* was only a musical adaptation of a German play that had already served the Shuberts well. On the first occasion, in 1903, they produced the play done into English and called *Old Heidelberg*, at the Princess Theatre. It was not conspicuously successful. Then they changed the name of the show to *Prince Karl*, got Richard Mansfield to play the title role, and put it into the Lyric, where it became a very remunerative hit. After the war a musical version of the original play appeared in Germany. The Shuberts commissioned Sigmund Romberg to write another score for the American edition. The late Dorothy Donnelly did the American book. Even today *The Student Prince* is not dead; he merely slumbers. The costumes for ten complete *Prince* companies hang in the Shubert storerooms at 3 West Sixty-first Street. In the Shuberts' opinion, *The Student Prince* is still a great show. Lee thinks it is not yet quite the time for a revival. He says that the time has to be right for any kind of show and that if the time is right for it, any kind of show is likely to catch on. "The trouble with a lot of producers," he has been known to explain, "is they have a couple of hits because the time is ripe for that sort of a show, and then they think they are geniuses, so they do the same sort of a show right over again, and it flops." A piece like *Hellz a Poppin*, for example, is not so much an innovation as a type of fast, unsubtle comedy which had been absent from Broadway so long that by 1938 it was new to a whole generation of playgoers. The Shuberts, true to form, followed through by having Olsen and Johnson more or less repeat themselves by working out gags for *The Streets of Paris*. If the brothers accept Mr. Lee's own advice, however, they won't attempt the same thing again—at least not right away.

The Shubert clichés are like an assortment of dry flies on which they try the public periodically. They don't expect a strike every time. J. J. is strongly committed to operettas, even though, as a concession to modernity, he will accept Cole Porter lyrics and an interpolated dance by the Hartmans now and then. Lee is more susceptible than his brother to current influences, because he gets around more. He takes advice from Harry Kaufman, a blocky, Broadway sort of chap with a wide, shining face, who began in the cloak-and-suit business and progressed into ticket brokerage. Kaufman, now in his middle forties, is active in the Tyson and Sullivan theater-ticket agencies, but he has a desk conveniently across the hall from Mr. Lee's in the Shubert Theatre. He divides his time between the agencies and Mr. Lee. Kaufman, through his ticket-selling connections, keeps his patron informed of box-office trends. "Mr. Shubert is the greatest affection of my life," says Kaufman. "He built the entire midsection of town, which is a weighty accomplishment. There is a bond of affection between us, and we have certain mutual ideas which we believe to be mutually sound, and in the long run we hope it will win." Kaufman serves as a scout for new talent. He saw some young people giving an impromptu Sunday-night revue in a camp at Bushkill, Pennsylvania, one summer and suggested to the Shuberts that it would be an inexpensive way of filling one of their theaters. Mr. Lee agreed, brought the show to New York as *The Straw Hat Revue*, and made a reasonably successful production of it. Kaufman also acts as a buffer between the Shuberts and stars already under contract to them. Kaufman has been known to send flowers to a sulking comedienne at his own expense. He is always the first to suggest that the star or the director of a Shubert company accept a cut in pay because the business is falling off. In one busy evening, Kaufman will go to dinner at a Broadway night club, where he hears a singer do a single number; to a play, to catch the big scene, and to a prize fight, timing his arrival to coincide with the round that promises the most action. In the intervals between these high spots he will stop in backstage at a couple of Shubert shows to see how things are running.

After such an eclectic three hours, Kaufman will return to Mr. Lee's office to play pinochle with him. Toward midnight, Mr. Lee's conferences with press agents and company managers begin. He often sandwiches hands of pinochle between conferences. When he has seen the last of his visitors, he and Kaufman sometimes make excursions to new night clubs to watch performers. Mr. Lee drinks very little—perhaps one brandy in the course of an evening—but he gets a certain stimulation from seeing lots of people around him. He returns to his office at three, to look at telegrams giving the receipts at theaters on the Pacific coast, where the time is three hours behind ours. Mr. Lee and Kaufman sometimes wander about the streets even after that, with a Shubert limousine trailing a short distance behind them. They wind up at Reuben's, on Fifty-eighth Street, where Mr. Lee usually drinks three cups of black coffee before heading for bed. These nocturnal walks have long been a habit of Mr. Lee's, and Kaufman is not the first of his walking companions. In former years, it is said, Mr. Lee on these walks paced off the dimensions of sites he intended to assemble for theaters. Now, at any rate, he walks just for exercise.

It was Kaufman who introduced Vincente Minnelli, the young designer and director, to Mr. Lee. Some of Minnelli's revues at the Winter Garden, like *At Home Abroad*, in 1935, and *The Show Is On*, in 1936, called for an investment entirely alien to the conservative Shubert tradition and shocked Mr. J. J.'s sensibilities. Mr. J. J. persists in preserving costumes and props, as well as ideas, from old productions. He sometimes escorts parties of contemporary chorus girls to the Sixty-first Street storerooms to try on the high headdresses and sequined pseudo-Orientalia of the 1913 Winter Garden show.

The Messrs. have entirely different styles of behavior at rehearsals. Mr. Lee is undemonstrative but insistent. Upon seeing a rehearsal of a play, he often commands the author to make the second act the first, the first act the last, and put the third act in the middle. This sometimes improves a play immeasurably. In theatrical matters, Mr. Lee has a tender heart. The late Sam Shipman once wrote a play about a boy brought up by his mother, whom the boy supposed to be a widow. In reality the mother was a divorcée. The brutal father returned and won the boy's sympathy. The boy deserted the mother at the end of the second act, before discovering what sort of cad the father had been. In the third act, of course, son came back to mother. Mr. Lee wouldn't stand for the boy's being away from the mother during the intermission. He made Shipman arrange to have the reunion before the second act ended. "What will I do for a third act?" Shipman asked him. "That's your business," Mr. Lee said. "I have a lot of other things to think of."

Mr. Lee often acts out bits in backstage corners for the benefit of his directors. "Look," he once told one of them, "anybody can play Cyrano. See?" He turned a chair around and straddled it, arms folded on the back, legs thrust out stiffly, as if in jack boots. Then he leaped lightly to his feet, flung an imaginary cape over his left shoulder, took two or three long strides, and jumped to *en garde*, an imaginary rapier in his right hand. "Da dill de-da," he said, thrusting briskly at an imaginary opponent. "Deedle dee dum! That's the way Mansfield used to do it. An actor like Everett Marshall can't miss!" When Mr. Lee feels that something is lacking in a musical show, he often says, "What we need here is a song that goes like this: 'Da, dum, de-dum-dum—dada, dada, de-dum, de-dum-dum.' " The tune always turns out to be "Sing Something Simple," but he never says so. Mr. Lee admires good actors, although he has spent the better part of his life trying to conceal that fact, because he does not want to pay them more than is necessary. Once, discussing actors, he said, "They are not an everyday-going class of people. They are very conceited, but the intelligence is still above the conceit." His respect for actors is tied up with his inability to picture himself as one. "Myself," he says, "I can't make an after-dinner talk even to half a dozen people. I must have some kind of complex."

Mr. J. J. screams at the chorus people in the shows he produces; to principals he is often polite. He has always admired tall women, and his shows are the last stronghold of the statuesque type of showgirl. No matter how engrossed he may become in the difficulties of putting on a show, he never forgets that he is first of all the owner of the theater. At the dress rehearsal just before the opening of *You Never Know* at the Winter Garden a couple of seasons ago, he was violently excited over the jerkiness of the production. "Such a stupid people," he repeated mournfully as he wandered, an incongruous little figure, among the ranks of showgirls, most of them six feet tall in their high heels. The chorus people were in costume; Mr. J. J., in his wrinkled gray suit, looked like a comedian about to liven up the scene. "Walk around some more!" he shouted. "Don't I get any use out of these dresses?" All at once he stopped the rehearsal and pointed in horror to a seat in the third row on which a Shubert underling had left a wet overcoat. Then he scrambled down off the stage, grabbed the coat, and held it aloft for the assembled cast to see. "Ruining my beautiful theater!" he howled. Shows come and go, their fate a matter of almost pure chance, but theater seats are the foundation of the Shuberts' fortune.

II

BEFORE the Shuberts rose to eminence, the American theater was governed in totalitarian fashion by an organization known as the Syndicate, headed by Marc Klaw and Abe Erlanger. In 1905, when the Shubert brothers—Lee and J. J.—first defied the Syndicate, there were 5000 legitimate theaters in 3500 American cities. The Syndicate controlled the bookings of 1250 of these theaters; its list included almost every house that a first-class attraction could play with profit. The theaters were variously owned, but the Klaw & Erlanger booking office was the clearinghouse for shows, so Klaw & Erlanger could put any owner out of business by refusing to send him productions. They could put a producing manager out of business by denying him a route. The Shuberts fought this "malign octopus" (as the Shubert press agents usually referred to the Syndicate) until they had built up a benign octopus of their own, including nine hundred theaters that got shows through the Shubert office. Naturally, Mr. Lee and Mr. J. J. feel that the theater owes them a debt of gratitude for thus destroying a monopoly, but since few of the younger men in the trade remember the Syndicate, they are likely to consider the Shuberts themselves rather tentacular. This makes for what the Shuberts consider misunderstandings. During the jihad, or holy war, between the Shuberts and Klaw & Erlanger, the moving pictures gradually destroyed the legitimate theater in the provinces. Then the depression put a terrific crimp in it in New York. The theater in recent years has become a minor form of enterprise localized on Manhattan. But even though their army has shrunk to a squad, the Shuberts comport themselves like field marshals of industry. They have never taken to moving pictures. Mr. Lee says that the cinema is "a kind of make-believe."

The Shubert preoccupation with the theater dates back to 1885, when Sam, the eldest brother, now dead, made the only recorded appearances of a Shubert on the American stage. He was eleven years old, and his part was a walk-on in the first act of a Belasco production called *May Blossoms*, which at the time happened to be playing the Wieting Opera House at Syracuse. *May Blossoms*, a treacly thing, called for the engagement of four child actors in every town the company visited; this was much cheaper and less troublesome than taking children on the road. The company manager had picked Sam Shubert out of his classroom in the public school nearest the theater. The boy received a dollar a performance for a whole week, and the entire Shubert family, including ten-year-old Lee and five-year-old Jake, attended every night, on passes. The boys were entranced by this factitious world, so unlike the Seventh Ward, where the Shuberts and most other poor Jews in Syracuse lived. David Shubert, the boys' father, peddled notions, underwear, and sundries among upstate farmers, riding out to the country on a train from Syracuse and then trudging from door to door with his wares on his back. *May Blossoms* gave Sam, Lee, and Jake their first intimation that there might be a pleasanter way of making a living. It was such a milestone in the Shuberts' lives that they later devised two operetta titles from that of the Belasco show. The operettas were *Maytime* and *Blossom Time*, both illustrious money-makers.

Sam was a precocious, imaginative boy. Since his death in 1905, the surviving brothers have agreed to consider him the family genius, and a portrait of him hangs in the lobby or lounge of every theater they operate. Soon after his dramatic debut, Sam became program boy at the Grand Opera House, the second-best theater in Syracuse, at $1.50 a week. Immediately his younger brothers' ambitions switched from the artistic to the commercial side of the theater, where they have been ever since. Sam was still wearing short pants when the manager of the Grand promoted him to assistant treasurer, which meant relief ticket seller. He had to stand on a box to reach the ticket window. When Sam moved over to the more elegant Wieting Opera House, at a higher salary, Lee succeeded him at the Grand. Lee, in his early teens, already had been an apprentice cigar maker and shirt cutter, and a haberdasher's clerk. The haberdasher was named Jesse Oberdorfer, and he, too, had theatrical inclinations. He was destined to be the first in a line of Shubert bank-roll men which since then has included George B. Cox, a Cincinnati millionaire; Andrew Freedman, Samuel Untermyer, and Jefferson Seligman. Syracuse had four legitimate theaters in the nineties. A job in a good provincial theater was the best possible introduction to the profession, for stars spent most of their time and earned most of their money on the road. Sam and Lee Shubert met actors like Richard Mansfield, Nat Goodwin, and Joe Jefferson in Syracuse. Before Sam and Lee were twenty, they rented road companies of *A Texas Steer* and *A Black Sheep* from Charles H. Hoyt, the author-manager, guaranteeing him a fixed return for the use of the productions which he had assembled and trained. The boys managed the companies, sent them wherever they could get a profitable booking, paid the actors' salaries, and made money on the deal. The formative years of the Shuberts resembled a piece by Horatio Alger or the editors of *Fortune*. They ran a stock company in Syracuse, cornered all four theaters there, and added houses in near-by Buffalo, Rochester, Albany, Troy, and Utica, and in Portland, Maine. Of these cities, only Buffalo and Rochester have so much as one legitimate theater now.

Sam and Lee drafted Brother Jake into the business when he was fourteen. Sam was not content with prosperity upstate; he wanted to produce plays, and a producer had to have a theater in New York City as a show window. Then, as now, an attraction could obtain few bookings on the road unless it had had a New York run. So, in 1900, Sam Shubert went down to New York, accompanied by the faithful haberdasher Oberdorfer, who had a bank roll of some thirty thousand dollars. Sam leased the Herald Square Theatre, a small, unpretentious house just across

Thirty-fifth Street from the present site of Macy's. Lee followed Sam from Syracuse, leaving Jake in charge of the theaters upstate. Sam and Lee cajoled Mansfield into opening their theater for them with his production of *Julius Caesar*, an event which left little profit for the brothers because Mansfield took virtually all the receipts, but which immediately gave their theater prestige. The brothers followed up by leasing two more theaters and producing *Arizona, A Chinese Honeymoon*, and *Fantana,* all highly profitable shows. *Old Heidelberg*, a Shubert enterprise that looked like a failure at first, became a great success when, after the show had been renamed *Prince Karl,* Mansfield took over the leading role. The Shuberts, like everybody else in the industry, booked through Klaw & Erlanger.

All the Shubert hits up to this point, as Sam and Lee well understood, had been achieved by sufferance of the Syndicate. Klaw & Erlanger had established their dominion over the theater industry by performing a real service. Before their advent in the late eighties, the business had been in an impossibly confused state. It was then the custom of every house manager in America to come to New York and bargain for attractions with producers, usually in saloons around Union Square. Producers often booked their shows into two theaters for the same week, so that they would be sure to find one theater available when the playing date arrived. Managers just as often booked two shows for the same week, so that they would be sure of having some sort of production in their houses. If both attractions arrived on schedule, the manager would pick the better of the two. If a show had booked two towns for the same week and both theaters were available, the producer would pick the one promising the greater profit. It was practically impossible to enforce a contract. The owner of the Opera House in Red Wing, Minnesota, for example, could not very well abandon his theater and chase out to California to sue a defaulting road company even if the troupe had any assets worth attaching. Nor could the manager of a traveling company abandon his show while he waited upon the slow processes of the law in some Iowa town where the theater owner refused to honor a contract.

The Syndicate changed all this. It offered a steady supply of shows to member theaters and a full season's booking to producers in good standing, and it was in a position to enforce its rulings in case of dispute. By the time the Shuberts arrived upon the scene, however, Klaw & Erlanger had turned their control of the industry into a tyranny. Ordinarily, producers paid the Syndicate seven and a half per cent of their gross receipts in return for bookings, but when Erlanger "asked" the producer for a higher percentage, the producer had to comply or fold up. In the same way, a theater owner who wanted a particularly strong attraction had to pay a high premium to the Klaw & Erlanger office to get it.

The Syndicate, in order to protect its supremacy, had only to see to it that no one built up a chain of theaters powerful enough to support a rival booking office. When it began to look as if the Shuberts might do just that, Erlanger tried to curb them by refusing to route their musical comedy called *The Girl from Dixie* unless the brothers would agree to lease no more theaters.

The youthful Shuberts interpreted the refusal as a challenge. They announced the opening of an independent circuit of theaters that would play any man's show. The public had not yet forgotten the Boxer Campaign, and the Shubert press agent, J. Frank Wilstach, revived a slogan that John Hay had made popular in those days, "The Open Door." As a nucleus for their enterprise, the Shuberts had leases on three theaters in Manhattan and eight more upstate, and they had found a few other theater owners who were angry enough to pull out of the Syndicate with them. The brothers filled their circuit by renting vaudeville and burlesque houses in a number of towns and using them for legitimate shows. They had two principal allies among the producers in their campaign. One was Harrison Grey Fiske, the husband of Minnie Maddern Fiske. He had already offended the Syndicate, and for years his wife had been refused road bookings, although she was so great a star that she had been able to play steadily in New York. The other Shubert ally was David Belasco, who accused Abe Erlanger of muscling in for half the profits of his success *The Auctioneer*. The new combination wasn't much competition for the Syndicate at first, but after the Shuberts had confounded predictions by staggering through one season, they began to get more support. Any theater man could see the advantage of maintaining a competitive market.

At the beginning of each theatrical season during the great war for the theatrical Open Door, newspapers in every city in the land carried reports that the local playhouse was "going Shubert" or "staying Syndicate." It was a question of enormous import in one-theater towns. If the house went Shubert, the town might see David Warfield, Mrs. Leslie Carter, and Mrs. Fiske. If it stayed Syndicate, the matinee girls would be permitted to ogle William Faversham and the young men would have a chance to gape at Anna Held. Within a very brief time the boys from Syracuse became national figures. As underdogs, anti-monopolists, and employers of a succession of good publicity men, they had public sentiment with them. Editorial cartoonists usually drew them as three very small Semitic Davids (Jake, twenty-three, was by now almost an equal partner) squaring off to a corpulent Goliath labeled "Syndicate." To offset the Shubert good will, the Syndicate had most of the material advantages. Klaw & Erlanger had seldom built theaters, for they had been able to control enough of the houses already existing. The Shuberts had to build theaters in cities where they could not otherwise get a foothold, and they had to find financial backing for these theaters. Cox, the moneyed gentleman from Cincinnati, was one of their principal stand-bys in this phase of the fight. Lee Shubert has always had phenomenal success in raising money when he really needed it.

Sam Shubert was killed while trying to add a link to the chain of "open-door" theaters. The Shuberts wanted the Duquesne, in Pittsburgh, to break the jump between Philadelphia and Chicago, in which cities they already had good houses. Sam was on his way to Pittsburgh with William Klein, who is still the Shubert lawyer, when the train they were on collided with a car full of dynamite outside Harrisburg. It was one of the worst wrecks in railroad history. Sam Shubert was so badly burned that he died two days later. For a time after this, Mr. Lee and Mr. J. J. called every theater they built the Sam S. Shubert Memorial Theatre. That was the official title of the Shubert here, too, until the brothers found that the funereal connotation was bad for business. Mr. Lee and Mr. J. J. have never traveled together since Sam's death. They take no chances on the extinction of the firm. If they have to go up to Boston to watch a show break in, Mr. Lee leaves New York on one train and Mr. J. J. follows him on another. After the show they return by separate trains. Each has made one or two trips by plane, but the same rule applies to air travel. They have never flown together.

Sam Shubert left such an impress on Mr. Lee that the latter has even taken over some of his brother's idiosyncrasies. One of these is his fast walk, with head thrown forward. Another is a custom of giving alms to every panhandler who accosts him. It was more than a custom with Sam; it was a compulsion. If he had no change in his pocket when approached by a beggar, he would hurry into a store to break a bill and then return to look for the man. Lee feels this compulsion too. He was walking up Broadway with a subordinate one day a year or so ago when a down-and-outer asked the underling for the price of a cup of coffee. "You asked the wrong man!" Mr. Lee shouted indignantly, almost pushing his employee off the sidewalk in his eagerness to get to the tramp. The Shuberts are always being approached by theatrical veterans hoping to make a touch. They are the only managers still active on Broadway whom the troupers of the period from 1900 to 1910 know personally, and both brothers are rated as generous. Their loyalty to aging chorus girls, who appear in Shubert shows year after year, has occasionally furnished first-nighters with material for humorous comment, but it has been a lifesaver for the girls.

The biliousness with which Mr. Lee and Mr. J. J. regarded the world during their struggle with the Syndicate was not assuaged by the newspapers. True, the Shubert press department hornswoggled a great many favorable editorials out of provincial journalists, but it was harder going here. *The Morning Telegraph*, at that time the great theatrical trade paper in New York, once ran a headline asking, "WHY IS LEE SHUBERT AND WHEREFORE?" The Syndicate, in the beginning of the controversy, had a much larger volume of theatrical advertising to place than the Shuberts, and that, in those days, determined the *Telegraph*'s news policy. When Sam Shubert first came to town, he had hired one of the *Telegraph*'s critics as his *sub-rosa* publicity man. This unscrupulous fellow took Sam's money and puffed his shows. The *Telegraph*'s subsequent reversal of policy left the Shuberts with a Continental slant on newspaper ethics. Mr. Lee ordered all Shubert advertising out of the *Telegraph* and kept it out for almost thirty years, although the newspaper changed hands several times in the interim. The *Telegraph* of that era referred to A. Toxen Worm, who had succeeded Wilstach as the Shubert press agent, as "Lee Shubert's vermiform appendix." As a medium for rebuttal, the Shuberts founded their own weekly trade paper, the *New York Review*, in 1910 and kept it up until 1931. "That newspaper which is bounded on the north by a saloon, on the south by a saloon, and facing a carbarn" was one of the *Review*'s more flattering references to the *Telegraph*. "The Shuberts, who evidently are trying to pile up a world's record of theatrical disaster, have added one more attraction to the long list of companies which have brought their tour to an end for lack of patronage" was a *Telegraph* comment on the demise of a Shubert show, and again, "This paper will never libel the Shuberts. It would be as cruel as unnecessary."

The *Telegraph* took particular pleasure during the hostilities in calling Shubert shows salacious, and hinting that they should be raided. Mr. Lee was particularly sensitive on this point; he felt black despair one November night in 1911 when he heard that the patrol wagons were being backed up to the curb in front of the Maxine Elliott Theatre, a Shubert house that had been rented to George C. Tyler and the Abbey Players of Dublin. The American première of Synge's *Playboy of the Western World* was taking place there, and Mr. Lee must have suspected that the show included something like a Dance of the Seven Veils. What the trouble really was, as any historian of the theater knows, was an old-fashioned Irish riot. Irishmen here resented Synge's "slander" on an ancient race and had gone to the opening to egg the actors. Mr. Lee, who had been attending another opening, rushed down the street to the Maxine Elliott and arrived in a dead heat with a man whom he recognized as a reporter for the *Times*. "If I had known there was one thing off-color about this show," Mr. Lee shouted to the reporter, "I wouldn't have let Tyler have the house!"

Mr. Lee concedes grudgingly that newspapermen today are probably honest, but he cannot for the life of him see why a hundred-dollar-a-week employee of a publisher should be allowed to impair a Shubert investment of fifty thousand dollars in a show. This does not prevent him from exploiting to the full any favorable reviews that accrue in the course of a season. He feels newspaper reviewers are naturally perverse, and admiration is wrung from them only by the supreme artistry of a particularly great production.

The Shuberts' feeling against the critics came to a head in 1915, when the brothers ordered the doormen of their theaters to bar Alexander Woollcott, the reviewer for the *Times*. Woollcott, then twenty-eight, had said about a farce called *Taking Chances*, "It is not vastly amusing." To the Shuberts the remark was evidence of violent animosity. They ordered the *Times* to send another reviewer to their attractions. The *Times* replied by throwing out all Shubert ads and Woollcott, backed by his bosses, applied to the United States District Court for an injunction restraining the Shuberts. He said he was being prevented from earning his livelihood as a critic. It was a glorious day for William Klein, the Shubert lawyer, who filed a brief listing all Woollcott's unfavorable criticisms of Shubert shows, with dissenting reviews by Woollcott's colleagues. Woollcott filed an equally long brief with concurrent opinions by the colleagues. The court ruled, to the astonishment of everybody, that the critic's fairness had nothing to do with the case; if the Shuberts wished to bar a man from their property, they had a right to do so. Admission to a place of amusement, the court found, is not a civic right but a license granted by the owner and revocable upon refund of the admission price. On the basis of this decision, the one sort of critic a theater may not bar is a Negro, because when a Negro is refused admittance there is a presumption that he has been so treated on account of race or color and he can sue the management for damages. Woollcott was white. Always realistic, the Shuberts soon made friends with Woollcott and the *Times*, which they had found the best medium for theatrical advertising.

A dozen years later, the Messrs. Lee and J. J. barred Walter Winchell, then dramatic reviewer for the *Graphic*, for writing "flip reviews." Presently Winchell began to write a Broadway column. Mr. Lee feels that Winchell's promotion was the result of their row and often reminds him that he should feel grateful. Three years ago, Winchell, by his ecstatic plugging of *Hellz a Poppin*, a Shubert enterprise, counteracted the almost unanimous scolding which the other daily reviewers gave the show and had a good deal to do with turning it into the hit it is. Mr. Lee refused to be inordinately thankful. "Winchell has roasted some very good shows," he said.

The Shubert relations with actors, as with reporters, have been subject to frequent emotional disturbance. "The actor is a person so naturally conceited as to become unconsciously ungrateful," Lee once pronounced officially. "In most cases what passes for art is unmitigated self-assurance. It is a difficult thing to explain briefly how much the actor owes to the manager." It is hard to reconcile this low estimate of the actors' art with what the Shuberts said for the record about Joe Smith and Charles Dale of the Avon Comedy Four, who tried to break a contract with them. Attorney Klein's brief stated, "Defendants are novel, unique, and extraordinary. At every appearance they are received with long, loud, and practically continuous applause." The court ruled that Smith and Dale were irreplaceable. The Shuberts won a case on similar grounds against Gallagher and Shean. The comedians argued forlornly that they were terrible and that the Shuberts could hire any sort of turn to take their place. For a while after that, Shubert actors' contracts used to carry the clause, "I now admit I am unique and extraordinary." Mr. Klein says proudly that these cases, like the one against Woollcott, created legal precedent. He thinks that the Shuberts have had a considerable part in the development of American jurisprudence. Mr. Klein has been the Shubert lawyer for thirty-seven years and he says, in endorsement of his clients, "Nobody can show me a single case in which the Shuberts have failed to pay a judgment against them."

Consistency has never hampered the Shuberts. They have had many wrangles with actors, but they were among the first managers to sign a closed-shop agreement with Equity in 1924. Approximately four times a year, during the busiest period of his life, Mr. Lee used to issue a statement that the time was ripe for the emergence of American dramatists; four times a year, just as regularly, he would announce that the theater was doomed unless the playwrights agreed to reduce royalties. Whenever the owner of a string of one-night stands quit the Shuberts during the Syndicate war, either Mr. Lee or Mr. J. J. would declare that first-class attractions could not play one-night stands profitably. When the same man returned to the Shuberts, one of the brothers would tell the press that the one-night stands made all the difference between a profitable tour and an unprofitable one. Once, when Chicago newspapers complained about the quality of the shows sent there, the Shuberts' *Review* announced, "Chicago does not realize she is in the position of a beggar who ought to be happy for every penny dropped in her tin cup." A couple of years after that, Mr. J. J. said that Chicago was the best theater town in the country and that he was going to make it the dramatic center of America. Self-consciousness is not a Shubert trait either.

III

BY THE MID-TWENTIES, a quarter of a century after the first of the Shubert brothers came to New York from his home in Syracuse to do battle with the forces that were monopolizing the theater, the enemy, personified by the Klaw & Erlanger Syndicate, was groggy. The Shuberts owned or had long leases on about 150 theaters, and they controlled the booking of 750 more. They didn't have enough dramatic attractions to go around, even though two thirds of the important producing managers were now booking their shows into Shubert houses. A weakness of drama on the road is that provincial audiences demand the original Broadway casts. Operettas, on the other hand, are not so dependent on individual talent and get along all right on the road without first-string stars. The operetta, therefore, became the favored art form of the Shubert Theatre Corporation. Those were the days and nights when the Shuberts' publicity office never closed. Claude Greneker, their press agent, employed a lobster shift of assistants who went to work after midnight and pounded their typewriters until the day men began to come in. Time was beginning to help the Shuberts in their fight. Marc Klaw and Abe Erlanger, the Syndicate leaders, had been mature men in 1903, when the struggle started, while the Shuberts had been prodigies in their twenties. Now, as their rivals aged, the Shuberts were just hitting their stride. Klaw retired in 1926, and Erlanger died in 1930. Erlanger at his death was regarded as a wealthy man, but his estate, as it developed, consisted of two million dollars in assets and three million dollars in liabilities.

The operetta industry reached an all-time high in the winter of 1925–26. During that lush season, the Messrs. Shubert had ten companies of *The Student Prince* on tour in North America and one in Australia. The paths of the *Prince* companies often crossed those of five companies of *Blossom Time*, another Shubert operetta, which had been produced in 1921 and was hard to kill. By 1927 there weren't so many companies of *The Student Prince* and *Blossom Time* as there once had been, but five road companies of *My Maryland* had joined the survivors and the nation was still filled with song. The coffers of the Shubert Theatre Corporation were filled with cash, and in 1928 its stock, listed on the Exchange, reached a high of 85¼.

The manufacture of operetta companies for the road became a mechanical process with the Shuberts, like making new prints from the negative of a moving picture. Operettas had the advantage of sound effects, which the movies of 1925 hadn't. A man named Jack C. Huffman, who, before he retired in 1929, was the Shuberts' favorite director, staged the No. 1 productions. Two subordinate directors rehearsed the road companies, retaining all Huffman's stage business. The road units went out at intervals of about two weeks. It was customary to give each *Student Prince* cast a single break-in performance at the Jolson Theatre, where the No. 1 company played. No audience ever objected to the substitution, if any even noticed it. This gave the road companies self-assurance and permitted them to be billed as coming "direct from Broadway." Each *Student Prince* unit required forty male and twenty-four female choristers. *Blossom Time* and *My Maryland* called for less choral singing but increased the strain on the supply of prima donnas, ingénues, and presentable male singing leads. The Shuberts' musical-casting director, a motherly little man named Romayne Simmons, combed the chorus of the Metropolitan and the glee clubs of every police department in the land for recruits. Fortunately, Simmons says, the costumes worn by ladies in the early-nineteenth-century and Civil War eras, with which the operettas were respectively concerned, covered the figure from neck to ankle, so that the Shuberts did not have to worry much about the figures of the singing women they drafted. Friends at the Met sent Simmons young people who had tried out there but whose voices were not quite good enough for grand opera. There were even sinister rumors of singers waking up on the train to Toronto with a No. 5 company when the last thing they remembered was taking a drink with a Shubert representative at Hughie McLaughlin's bar on Forty-fifth Street.

It was during the time when Lee and his brother Jake, who now prefers to be known as J. J., were the most important men in the American theater that a type of humor classified as the "Shubert story" attained its vogue in the way that similar anecdotes have since automatically become part of the life and works of Samuel Goldwyn. There are three possibilities about the origin of any Shubert story. The incident may have involved a Shubert; it may have involved a less widely known producer and been credited to the Shuberts to make it sound funnier; and it may have been invented out of whole cloth at the bar of the Players Club or some less exclusive loitering place of actors.

One of the favorites is the story of the actor walking up Broadway, shaking his head and repeating aloud, "The rat!" Another actor stopped him and said, "So is his brother Jake!" A subtler variant concerns the actor at the Players who was hanging over the bar and ranting about the Shuberts when a confrere interrupted him. "They're not so bad," the second actor said. "No?" said the first actor. "Then why do they call them Shuberts?" A bit of counterpoint to this is the true anecdote about the Shubert press agent who warned Mr. Lee that a certain interviewer was inclined to be tart. "What can he possibly think of bad to say about me?" Mr. Lee asked earnestly.

Concerning the Shubert appreciation of the arts, there is the story of how Mr. J. J. attended a rehearsal of a musical show and thought the orchestra played too loudly. "Very softly!" he told the violins. "Play only on one string!" The quotation is accurate, but the attribution is wrong. It was Erlanger who said it at one of his rehearsals. On the same pattern is the tale of an actor in a Shubert drama who read a line beginning, "I am Omar Khayyam." "You don't know anything," Mr. Lee is supposed to have told him. "You should say, 'I am Omar *of* Khayyam.'" "'I am Omar *of* Khayyam,'" the submissive actor intoned. Later one of the more literate Shubert subordinates apprised Mr. Lee of his error. Next time the actor said, "'I am Omar *of* Khayyam,'" Mr. Lee stopped him. "Let's cut out the 'of,'" he said. "The act's a little too long already." This story might have been told of any producer at any period in history and in a related form was probably familiar to the boys who hung out with Menander in the Athenian equivalent of Lindy's.

Such stories have never bothered the Shuberts. They have never pretended to any rich cultural background and they know that their shrewdness in affairs of the theater is often underestimated because of their lack of polish. They see business as a form of combat. Mr. Lee recently said, "I like to take a play and bet my money *against* it." Money, Mr. Lee thinks, is the best measure of success in the theater. There is no doubt that the brothers, beginning at the bottom, have made more money out of the legitimate stage than any other two men who ever lived. Mr. Lee acknowledges, however, that they have lost a great deal of it in bad real-estate investments and in the stock market.

When there was a European theater of consequence, the Shuberts liked to buy shows that had already succeeded abroad. They would sometimes buy by cable without having seen the script. Afterward they would Americanize their purchases by introducing James Barton into the second scene as an American sailor who had lost his way in the grand duke's palace. "The advantage of a play that you bought in Paris," Mr. Lee says now, "was that it was usually a German play that had been translated into French, so that by the time you had it translated into English, you got the services of three great authors on one script." He is sorry that because of the collapse of the Central European theater it is now usually necessary to start from scratch. Even Czecho-Slovakia, he reminds friends, was occasionally the source of a play. "Bill Brady got one there," he recalls, "the bug play." By this Mr. Lee means *The Insect Play*, which was produced here as *The World We Live In*.

The Shuberts, to quote Mr. Lee again, have never been loafing boys. The brothers, as nearly as he can remember, built the Forty-fourth Street, the Lyric, the Shubert, the Booth, the Broadhurst, the Plymouth, the Morosco, the Bijou, the Ritz, the Forty-ninth Street, the Nora Bayes, the Ambassador, the Forrest, the Jolson, and the Maxine Elliott theaters. They converted a horse exchange, where New Yorkers used to buy carriage horses, into the Winter Garden. The Empire is the only theater now showing legitimate plays in New York which was in business before the first Shubert came here. Shubert competitors built the rest of the local theaters, so Mr. Lee in a way feels responsible for them too. Once, riding on Forty-sixth Street in his Isotta-Fraschini, he said, "If I hadn't built all these theaters, they would be dark today."

The brothers made two invasions of England—the first in 1904, when they built the Waldorf Theatre in London, which they had to abandon two years later, and the second in the early twenties. They acquired six London houses on their second try, but again they lost out. London was the only city in the world that rejected *The Student Prince*. British critics said it was pro-German. The Messrs. Shubert also made two attempts to break into vaudeville, in 1906 and in 1921, and both were expensive failures. A kind of recurrent stubbornness is a Shubert trait. They retreat, but they come back for more. In the early thirties they tried a show called *A Trip to Pressburg* three times with different stars. It never got further than Pittsburgh, but the Shuberts still own it, and someday it will reappear.

The resilience of Mr. Lee and Mr. J. J. is magnificently illustrated by the tangled affairs of the old Shubert Theatre Corporation, which vanished as a result of receivership proceedings in 1931. The Shuberts might have been spared this financial embarrassment if a prediction made by Mr. Lee in 1910 had come true. In that year he said he did not believe the shares of any theater corporation would ever be listed on the Stock Exchange. Times and the Shuberts' minds changed, and in 1924 the brothers organized the Shubert Theatre Corporation, with 210,000 shares of common stock. This was duly listed on the Exchange, and during the first five years the corporation consistently reported earnings of over one million dollars. In organizing this enterprise, the Shuberts turned over to it many of their theaters but withheld certain valuable properties, which included the Winter Garden, Shubert, Broadhurst, Booth, Plymouth, Cort, and Daly theaters as well as the Sardi Building and considerable other non-theatrical real estate. They explained that they had partners in these holdings who were opposed to entering the corporation. The brothers still own or have long leases on these personally held properties, which never became involved in the ups and downs of the corporation.

In 1933, two years after the receivership, Mr. Lee, with his brother as partner, bought in all the assets of the defunct corporation for four hundred thousand dollars, a price which barely covered the costs of the receivership. The creditors were glad to receive even that small amount, however. They had discovered that the leasehold on a theater is practically worthless in the eyes of bankers, who know neither how to produce a play nor how to put such a property to any other profitable use. The Shuberts lumped together all that could be salvaged from the Shubert Theatre Corporation in a new company called the Select Theatres Corporation. They kept fifty per cent of the stock of the new organization for themselves and distributed the rest among those who had held stock in the old corporation. The Select stock never has paid dividends, either to the Shuberts or to anybody else. Through Select, the brothers maintain their control over a large number of theaters, and this protects their strategic position in the industry. Among the theaters now owned by Select are the Barrymore, Ambassador, Hudson, Maxine Elliott, Forty-sixth Street, Golden, Longacre, Imperial, Morosco, and Majestic. Lee is president of Select, and J. J. is general manager. The overhead costs of all Shubert enterprises, including the salaries of Lee and J. J., are charged to Select and the Shubert personal holdings; each Shubert production is a new corporation in which Mr. Lee and Mr. J. J. usually own all the stock. The precise financial status of the Messrs. is one of the thousand and one topics of idle speculation in Broadway taverns. Recently, from Mr. William Klein, who has been their attorney for thirty-seven years, came the nearest thing to an official statement yet heard on the subject. "Neither of the Messrs. Shubert," he said, rubbing his hands together vigorously, "will ever be buried in potter's field."

The brothers have great confidence in each other's integrity; one never questions the other's drafts on the joint Shubert cash account. On the other hand, they are seldom in agreement about business policies and twice a year they meet in Mr. J. J.'s apartment atop the Sardi Building for a formal dinner and argument. They are attended by attorneys on these occasions. During the rest of the year they lead separate social existences. Mr. J. J. lives in his apartment alone except for a cook and maid, and he seldom goes out at night. The living room, which runs the whole width of the building, is adorned with lighting fixtures from the old Hotel Knickerbocker and with a great deal of Louis XIV furniture. All of the furniture, he likes to assure visitors, was bought especially for the apartment—none of the pieces are leftovers from shows. At the west end of the room there is a wrought-iron door from a Venetian palace, on which the most noticeable adornment is a female figure with six breasts. The door weighs three and a half tons. The space behind one of the dining-room walls is hollow and filled with a large supply of liquor which Mr. J. J. acquired at reduced prices during prohibition and which he has as yet barely sampled. He isn't much of a drinker, but he never could resist a bargain. The dining room has Syrian furniture inlaid with mother-of-pearl and ivory, and on a terrace in front of the living room there is a fountain from the Knickerbocker lobby. Despite these and other attractions of his apartment, Mr. J. J., when he's at home in the winter, spends most of his time in the bathroom, reading in an armchair which he has installed there. This is because the bathroom is the only comfortably warm room in the place. The heat in the Sardi Building, above the first floor, is turned off at seven o'clock in the evening and all day on Sunday. Since it is impossible to warm the apartment on the top floor without heating the whole building, Mr. J. J. retires to the bathroom, which he has fitted up with an elaborate battery of electric heaters. He does all his play-reading there. When he occasionally goes out, it is usually to Lindy's for a cup of coffee at about midnight. He also likes to sit through double features at fourth-run movie houses. Mr. J. J. prefers to lunch in his apartment, but when he has to talk business with someone at noon, he eats with the person at Sardi's, on the first floor of his residence. Vincent Sardi, the proprietor, used to be a captain of waiters at the Little Club, a night place that the Shuberts owned many years ago. He is a good tenant now, and the Shuberts always believe in patronizing people who do business with them.

Mr. Lee almost invariably lunches at Sardi's. Actors who want him to notice them eat there too. Lee often convinces people who work for him that they also should live in the Century Apartments, where he lives and in which the brothers have an interest. *Hellz a Poppin* had hardly become a hit when Mr. Lee induced Chic Johnson, one of its stars, to take an apartment in the Century. Both the Messrs. Shubert like to say that they "never learned to play—never had time," but Mr. Lee at least gets about a good deal. He says he does so to maintain contacts. "Maybe I would like to play," he says plaintively, "but there is no one around I care to play with."

Mr. Lee's office in the Shubert Theatre Building is in a turret and therefore circular—not more than twelve feet in diameter. Into it is squeezed the desk he has used ever since he came to New York, a chair, a sofa, a gilt statue of a nymph and faun, and an autographed photograph of Colonel Lindbergh. A short passageway leads from Mr. Lee's office to that of his secretary, Jack Morris, which in turn opens into the waiting room, a bleak place with French-gray furniture grouped around a snake plant, and two unchanging, disregarded signs—"No Smoking" and "No Casting until August." The gray chairs usually are occupied by a queue of petitioners waiting to see Mr. Lee. It is a point of pride with him that he never refuses to see anybody who is willing to wait a few hours. The passageway between Mr. Lee's office and his secretary's has an extra door leading directly into the waiting room, but only the experienced understand this door's significance. When Mr. Lee is ready to grant an audience, he pops out at the Morris end of the passageway and beckons to the man who has advanced to the head of the queue. This hopeful comes forward, thinking that Mr. Lee is going to conduct him into his private office. Mr. Lee takes him by the arm, leads him into the passageway, says, "I'm sorry, I can't do anything now," and steers him out through the extra door and into the waiting room again. This maneuver is known in the trade as the Shubert brush-off.

Nothing confuses Mr. Lee more than to be caught without anything to do. "It just happens you catch me at a time when everything is very quiet," he will apologize, scratching his head energetically with a paper cutter. When his embarrassment becomes extreme, he scratches himself under the armpits and behind the ears. "You should have seen it yesterday. I didn't have a minute to myself." On summer afternoons when there are only a few persons waiting to see him, he has been known to sneak out of his office, go downstairs to his limousine, and so off to the baseball game, returning when a queue of more flattering length has formed. "Business won't wait," he says when reproached for spending most of his time in the vicinity of Shubert Alley even during the dog days. During intervals of quiet, Mr. Lee often plays rummy with Peters, his valet. If Harry Kaufman, the ticket broker upon whom Mr. Lee relies for companionship as much as for advice, is available, they change the game to three-handed pinochle. Peters reads Mr. Lee's personal correspondence as a matter of duty and answers it. Mr. J. J. sometimes refers to Peters as "the Crown Prince."

Mr. Lee's insistence upon running all the Shubert theaters himself, even down to the smallest detail, is a carry-over from a period when theater treasurers and house managers consistently robbed their employers. Larceny was considered a perquisite of their jobs. The house manager would issue "complimentaries," and the treasurer would sell them. It was the Shuberts who devised the present method of accounting for tickets. Under this system, there are separate racks for unsold tickets, for the stubs of tickets that have been paid for—known in the trade as "the hardwood"—and for stubs of complimentaries, or "deadwood." Every seat in the house must be accounted for in one or another of the racks; by deducting unsold seats and deadwood from the house capacity, the theater owner knows exactly what should be in the cash drawer. The only subordinate who can issue complimentaries in the whole Shubert organization here is the publicity chief, Greneker, and he is exceedingly frugal with them. Most passes to Shubert shows are signed by Mr. Lee himself. Many Shubert employees have been with the elderly Syracuse boys for a long time. Mr. Lee has faith in them but can't get over his distrustful nature. Some years ago, he recalls, he was standing in Shubert Alley when a Negro walked up carrying a pair of shoes. The Negro asked him for a wardrobe woman who worked for the Shuberts. The Negro complained that the woman had sold him the shoes, which he was returning because they were misfits. They were Shubert shoes. The incident proved to Mr. Lee that a man of property must be on the alert all the time.

Just as the Shubert empire has two chiefs, so it has two heirs apparent. One is Mr. J. J.'s son, John, who, the father likes to remind Lee, is "the only direct-line Shubert of his generation." On Mr. Lee's side of the firm, the young hope is Milton Shubert. Milton, however, is not "direct line." He is a nephew who adopted the avuncular name for business reasons, and he is the only member of the family who has shown any interest in moving pictures. He used to be head of the Shubert dramatic department in New York, but now spends most of his time in Hollywood, where he is helpful in directing Shubert affairs on the West Coast. Milton's mother was a sister of Mr. Lee's and Mr. J. J.'s; his father was named Isaacs. John, who is very tall for a Shubert—five feet ten inches—is thirty-one and lives at the Hotel Astor in a suite overlooking Shubert Alley. Milton, short and small, is forty-two; he stays at hotels when he is in New York. John is supposed to take charge of Shubert interests in New York when both Mr. Lee and Mr. J. J. are out of town, but this has happened only once since John left the University of Pennsylvania twelve years ago. His regency lasted for two weeks. At least twenty other Shubert relatives, of various degrees of consanguinity, are employed in lesser jobs in the organization.

Because of their fear of assuming responsibility, Shubert employees in general are the most literal-minded attachés of the American theater. Their attitude has given rise to some famous yarns of niggardliness. When the cast of *You Can't Take It with You* was rehearsing in the Booth Theatre, the supply of drinking cups at the house's water cooler gave out, and Sam Harris, producer of the play, called for more. He got them, with a bill for $1.15. A representative of the Shubert auditing department pointed out that the contract of rental did not specifically obligate the Shuberts to provide drinking cups. Harris wrote an indignant letter to Lee Shubert, who had gone to considerable effort to get *You Can't Take It with You*, a prospective hit, into a Shubert house. He reprimanded his underling for sending the bill. "Before doing a thing like that," Mr. Lee said, "you should consult me!" Of a piece with this story is the one about Noel Coward. He was playing in *Point Valaine* at the Barrymore Theatre, and asked to have the paint in his dressing room freshened up. He got a bill for seven dollars for the painting job, again apparently from an auditor drunk with power. Coward vowed never to play another Shubert theater. Even among men who dislike Mr. Lee, few believe him guilty of these small, miserly touches. They are not in his style. "I paid Sarah

Bernhardt eighteen hundred dollars a night," Lee says. "Do you think I need a couple of dollars?" When he is particularly vexed, he sometimes bursts into tears. "How could you do this to me?" he will ask the person who has displeased him. "I would rather have given you fifty thousand dollars."

Despite such demonstrations, well-trained Shubert subordinates continue at every opportunity to save money for their bosses. There is an interlude in *Hellz a Poppin*, a show which will probably earn over a million dollars for the Shuberts, in which all the lights go out while members of the cast pepper the audience with dried beans. Olsen and Johnson, the stars of the show, introduced this subtle bit of business long ago, when they were managing their own company in vaudeville. From the beginning, Olsen and Johnson bean throwers had used large paper cups holding half a pint of beans. Shortly after the show opened in New York the comics were approached by the company manager. "If we used ordinary drinking cups to throw the beans out of," he said, "we would get the cups cheaper, because we buy them in such large quantities for the theaters. Also, with the smaller cups we would use less beans. Altogether, I figure, we would save at least a dollar a week."

No Suave Inflections

ON THE DAY that *Hellz a Poppin*, the refined revue which began its run at the Forty-sixth Street Theatre, was scheduled to move to the larger Winter Garden, Ole Olsen and his partner, Chic Johnson, loitered sadly in front of the Fulton Theatre. The Fulton is also on Forty-sixth Street, and *Oscar Wilde* was playing there that season. "It will be a terrible thing for that show when we move," Olsen said with a wave of his hand. "They been living on our overflow." Johnson nodded in agreement. Both men were quite serious. This overweening modesty has carried Ole and Chic through twenty-four seasons of show business—as entertainers in a Chicago rathskeller, as a two-act on the Pantages and Orpheum time in vaudeville, and latterly as the proprietors of a "unit show" which has toured the country every year as regularly as *Uncle Tom's Cabin* used to in the eighteen-eighties. Vaudeville has been dead for a decade, but Olsen, the thin partner, and Johnson, the fat one, have never known enough to lie down.

An Olsen and Johnson unit show used to carry about forty people, including musicians and a line of twelve girls. There was always a quartet, members of which doubled in bits of slapstick; there were always a couple of specialty acts, and there were always Olsen and Johnson themselves, working like mad through the duration of the piece, just as they do now in *Hellz a Poppin.* A unit ran seventy minutes, approximately half the length of a musical comedy, and there was no intermission. Olsen and Johnson and their assistants in the unit would play four or five shows a day, depending on business in the movie palaces where they were booked. When business was good, the house manager would ask the partners to speed up their show so that he could get more customers in and out of the seats. Olsen and Johnson would then rush the performance through in sixty minutes. When the unit was teamed with an unusually short feature picture, the partners would sometimes be asked to extend their running time to eighty minutes. Those actors in the present Winter Garden show who have worked with Olsen and Johnson on the road have found it difficult to overcome the habit of asking, "Long or short version tonight?" when they hear the opening chords of the overture. They are just beginning to realize that they are now working on a fairly static schedule. The first half of *Hellz a Poppin* is, with a few emendations, the unit show which Olsen and Johnson opened in Fort Wayne, Indiana, in July 1938. The second half is made up of material from the unit show with which they opened in Denver several years ago. Lee Shubert, their financial backer, saw the first half of *Hellz a Poppin* at a moving-picture theater in Philadelphia, but the partners had a hard time explaining the second half to him because they had no script. Olsen and Johnson carry on by ear, and it seems unnecessary to dwell upon their obvious relation to the *commedia dell' arte.* In order to copyright their present show after it became a hit, they had to have a stenographer sit in the wings and take down the dialogue in shorthand.

From the beginning of their career, Olsen and Johnson have been surefire between Cleveland and California. Intimate acquaintance with their art, which New York has tardily recognized, induces a patronizing bonhomie among the Western visitors who swarm backstage at every performance of *Hellz a Poppin.* These out-of-towners, frequently accompanied by their wives or nieces, casually invade the partners' dressing rooms in such numbers that the hospitable comics, crowded out by their visitors, have to change their trousers on stair landings. Olsen's room usually fills first because he has long been the front man and speechmaker for the team. His room presents the greatest cross section of inland America to be found anywhere on Manhattan outside the lobby of the Hotel Taft. "The boys have been big stars for the last twenty years out where I come from," said Stephen F. Chadwick, a National Commander of the American Legion, during one of his frequent visits to New York. The commander lives in Seattle. Olsen is constantly inviting callers from Spokane to shake hands with callers from Green Bay, Wisconsin, and prominent executives from Akron to shake hands with prominent executives from Columbia, Missouri. Most of his visitors, in fact, belong to that nebulous but exalted class, the American executive. Olsen and Johnson themselves are honorary members of the Executives' Club of Portland, Oregon, and Olsen is fond of executive turns of phrase. "My thought on this matter is . . ." he says frequently before advising Johnson to hit a stuffed skunk with a hammer instead of his hat or to use a dressed turkey instead of a dressed chicken for a hunting bit.

The partners are honorary members of the Gyro Club of St. Paul and Minneapolis, the Gray Gander Club of Seattle, the International Association of Police Chiefs, and the Chicago Police Lieutenants' Association. They belong to the Yellow Dogs Club and Ace of Clubs of Columbus, Ohio, organizations of downtown quarterbacks who live for the Ohio State football team. They also hold membership in the Couvert Club of Cincinnati, the Arnama (Army, Navy, and Marine) Club of Los Angeles, the Atey (80) Club of San Francisco, the Round Table of Spokane, and the Breakfast Clubs of Seattle, Portland, Los Angeles, and Denver. All of these are endemic variants of Rotary, Kiwanis, and the Lions. Olsen and Johnson are honorary Rotarians, Kiwanians, and Lions, too, and are aspirants to the Dutch Treat Club of New York City. They are Elks, and each has been made a Kentucky colonel twice, the second time by a governor who did not know that a predecessor had already commissioned them.

Through their perfect adaptation to the Midwestern terrain where they were born, Olsen and Johnson managed to survive and prosper there for years, preserving the art of hokum for its present brilliant revival. They prefer the word "gonk" to "hokum." "Gonk is hokum with raisins in it," they say. "Gonk is what we do." For a long while survival wasn't easy; Olsen and Johnson once rose at seven in the morning to ride sacred white Arabian stallions in a cattle roundup conducted by the Shriners of Sioux City, Iowa. They never missed an opportunity to play an Elks' smoker, even after having given their regular five shows that day. A glass eater who was with their act in 1929 complained that the benefit shows were ruining his digestion. Johnson convinced him that some chile con carne which he was in the habit of eating late at night was responsible. During one tour, Olsen sold 114 supercharged Auburn sport models for dealers along the route. Auburn salesmen in each town promised prospects a final demonstration by Ole Olsen, the matinee idol of the Northwest. In gratitude for Olsen's services, the Auburn dealers organized year-round Olsen-and-Johnson clubs. "It rendered the territory Olsen-and-Johnson-conscious," Olsen says.

Neither Ole nor Chic has the intrinsic comic quality of a Harpo Marx or a Frank Tinney. They were never as funny, individually, as Clark and McCullough, Duffy and Sweeney, or the members of half a dozen other gifted combinations, and Olsen and Johnson readily admit it. But they have worked for laughs with a grimmer determination than any of the others, and there is something in the forthright earnestness of their attack which is in itself pleasing. The chief comic asset of the team, considered merely as a team, is Johnson's face. It is a wide, lardy, fat-man's face with bulging eyes that resemble poached eggs with pale blue yolks. These curious, anxious eyes belie the jaunty tilt of the derby he wears onstage; they are the eyes of a restaurateur watching a customer eat a bad egg. When the egg goes down without complaint from the customer, the face registers a vast and ingenuous relief. Johnson's expression oscillates between terror and insecure joy. It is impossible not to think about eggs when you think about him—he has a Humpty-Dumptyish personality. Olsen holds himself stiffly and is rather thin; only the wide, mobile mouth marks him as a comic. He is the straight man—glib, arrogant in a loutish way, but intermittently softening his arrogance with an ear-joining grin, like a circus clown. Olsen prepares the way for the laughs his stooges get—he is as much a ringmaster as a principal comedian.

One advantage the team possesses over contemporary combinations is its timing. Comedians who work in the films or before the microphone lose the sense of tempo which makes a vaudeville act click on the stage. Since Olsen and Johnson now are almost the only vaudeville team that has been working right along *as* a vaudeville team, they are among the few to retain this knack. An even more important asset when they are central figures in a show is their flair for contriving bits of comic business in which they utilize props and other actors. An exemplary Olsen and Johnson bit is the man who tries vainly to free himself from a strait jacket for practically the whole of *Hellz a Poppin* and winds up in the outer lobby when the customers are leaving after the show. Olsen and Johnson began using that bit in 1926. The timing of the escapist's repeated appearances makes each seem more comical. "The gag builds," Johnson says. "You have to know how to humor a gag like that." When the partners have an audience in their grip, they can make it laugh even at this sort of dialogue:

Q—What part of Ireland do you come from?
A—Staten Ireland.
Q—How old are you?
A—Sixteen.
Q—What do you want to be?
A—Seventeen.
Q—How much would you charge to haunt a house?
A—How many rooms?

"After a few more years," Johnson says of the final sally, "I think we will change that gag. I will ask, 'How much would you charge to sour some milk?' and the stooge will say, 'How many quarts?' "

"We don't go for suave inflections," says Olsen, the intellectual of the team. "We go for the ocular stuff. Suave inflections are poison in Youngstown, Ohio." It is his theory that if you once get a man laughing hard, you can keep him laughing all evening by talking fast. Babe Ruth never had to bunt. "To hell with chuckles," Johnson says. "Only belly laughs count."

Until *Hellz a Poppin* became a hit, producers and managers had considered this type of comedy too corny for present-day New York. "Corny" is a cultural term meaning crude, obvious, and the antithesis of what Noel Coward would do in a given situation. The corn taboo had been so fixed in Broadway minds by a succession of smart musicals, all the way from *The Band Wagon* through *I Married an Angel,* that the man who books acts for Loew's State Theatre, where there is a seventy-five-cent top, scorned the Olsen and Johnson unit. The partners were playing four shows a day in Philadelphia when the Loew's booker turned thumbs down on them. They were paying all the salaries and other expenses of their unit and would have been willing to bring it into New York for a price of five thousand dollars a week, out of which they would have taken a profit of around twenty-five hundred dollars. During the Philadelphia run, Olsen went to a night club for a steak sandwich and encountered Nils T. Granlund, a New York night-club operator who is a tenant of the Shuberts. Granlund thought the unit might have possibilities as a longer revue. He got Lee Shubert to come down from New York and look at the strange provincial charivari, and Shubert, who had several empty theaters in New York, rather dubiously agreed to back Olsen and Johnson in a full-length piece. "If I hadn't gone out for a steak sandwich and run into Granlund, we wouldn't be in New York today," Olsen says. "Big things always happen to us like that. We are creatures of destiny." The Shuberts did not invest much money in the show—probably something like fifteen thousand dollars. They provided it with a collection of sets from defunct Shubert musicals such as *The Show Is On* and *Hooray for What*, a smattering of secondhand costumes from their warehouse, and exactly three new sets of dresses for the chorus girls. Olsen and Johnson could have easily financed the production themselves, but they have always been frugal. "If we had had to buy everything new, it might have cost us twenty-five thousand dollars," Olsen says, "and that's not hay. The way it was, we figured that if the show folded in New York, we could open the unit in Baltimore the next week anyway, without having lost anything except our time."

The curious trade prejudice against a hearty laugh almost spoiled the opening at the Forty-sixth Street Theatre. The partners took especial pains to insure the success of their Broadway debut as author-actors. They had even provided a string trio to play in the men's lounge. On the old Orpheum circuit Chic Sale had been their only rival for popularity, and, like him, Olsen and Johnson have always specialized in smoking-room humor. They installed an intricate system of rubber tubing whereby stagehands could blow air under the skirts of the women customers seated in the orchestra. No detail had been overlooked, and the audience laughed incessantly for three hours. This reassured Olsen and Johnson. As they waited up to read the record of their triumph in the morning papers, they kept telling each other that New York was just a department of the sticks. After all, they reasoned, Richard Watts, Jr., of the *Herald Tribune*, was a native of Parkersburg, West Virginia; John Mason Brown, of the *Post*, hailed from Olsen-and-Johnson-conscious Louisville; Brooks Atkinson, of the *Times*, from a small place in New England; Richard Lockridge, of the *Sun*, from Kansas City (a great Olsen-and-Johnson town), and John Anderson, of the *Journal & American*, from some place in Florida. The critics should have felt at home at *Hellz a Poppin*. It turned out that no one is so bashful in the presence of the corny as a fugitive from a cornfield.

Mr. Watts, of Parkersburg, wrote, "The greater part of it depended on the mere fact of its madness and didn't succeed in being funny." Mr. Brown, of Louisville, said, "Its lapses from taste are almost as frequent as its lapses from interest," and the Floridian Mr. Anderson called *Hellz a Poppin* "steadily vulgar and anesthetic." *Hellz a Poppin* seemed to embarrass the boys like a visit from a home-town cousin, and, among the Manhattan newspaper critics, only the native and uninhibited Walter Winchell dared to risk an outright plug for the show. Winchell plugged it so hard and so often that a rumor started that he owned the production. He didn't, of course, but when the show became a hit he began to think of himself as a major prophet. Olsen and Johnson are abjectly grateful, but it is probable that *Hellz a Poppin*'s success helped Winchell as much as Winchell helped *Hellz a Poppin*.

Life began for John Sigvard Olsen and for Harold Ogden Johnson when they met in the professional department of a music publisher's office in Chicago in 1914. They had existed, after a fashion, as individuals, but neither had as yet found his groove. Olsen and Johnson had come to the publisher's office in search of music for their respective acts. Olsen was with the College Four, a quartet of music-making comedians who played beer halls and rathskellers. He had been graduated from Northwestern, at Evanston, Illinois, in 1912 and was the only member of the College Four who had even been near a college. Ole played the violin, sang with illustrated slides, and did a bit of ventriloquism as his contribution to the act. Johnson was primarily a ragtime piano player, but he had a funny face. He was doing a two-act in small-time vaudeville with a girl named Ruby Wallace. Both the boys had had serious musical ambitions. Olsen's pattern, in his boyhood days in Peru (pronounced Pee-ru), Indiana, had been Jan Kubelik, the Czech violinist. Johnson had gone out into the world from Englewood, Illinois, to eclipse Paderewski. Olsen's parents were born in Norway, Johnson's in Sweden. Chic and Ole immediately saw each other as great men. "I knew as soon as I saw him that Ole was a genius," Johnson, the less articulate, says today. "He wore high yellow bulldog shoes that buttoned up the sides, and he was the first man I ever heard imitate a busy signal on the telephone. I knew I had to have him as a partner." Olsen experienced a similar recognition of destiny. "Chic had the most powerful right hand I ever heard on a piano," he says reverently. They could not sever their old associations right away, but they played a few dates together at the North American Café on State

Street—violin, piano, ventriloquism, and harmony. They played together the following season and got a booking on the Pantages time. History does not record what became of Ruby Wallace or of Ole's three associates of the College Four.

Pantages shows were booked intact, a combination of five acts traveling together all season. Two of the four acts that traveled with Olsen and Johnson in their first year together were Victor Moore and Emma Littlefield, and William Gaxton and Anna Laughlin. A vaudeville act in those days grew gradually, the way a folk play or a legend does; it was not a static thing, like a play that a man writes on a typewriter. After the manner of a human body, it discarded dead cells and built up new ones. The more it was apparently the same thing, the more it changed. An act started with half a dozen gags; at the end of the first season, a couple of them might be dropped in favor of some experimental material. Some acts, while retaining their basic characters, changed all their material in the course of a few years. In others, one particularly strong comic bit would stay in for twenty or thirty years and become a kind of trade-mark. Olsen and Johnson still do a ventriloquist bit that was in their first act in vaudeville—the interlude in which Johnson sits on Olsen's knee. They dropped it for about fifteen years, then picked it up when Charlie McCarthy brought ventriloquism back. In their first act on the Pantages time, the curtain rose with Johnson seated at the piano, on which there was a telephone. The telephone rang, and Johnson, answering it, said, "Mr. Olsen? Is there a Mr. Olsen in the house?" Olsen entered and picked up the telephone. When he picked it up, the cord dangled free, and the audience could see that it was not connected. That was a sure laugh. Olsen sang into the telephone, "Hello, Frisco, Hello," with Johnson pounding the piano. Then Ole pretended to talk to someone on the telephone, producing the replies by ventriloquism. The bit included his immortal imitation of a busy signal. Olsen and Johnson got two hundred fifty dollars a week during their first season and then were booked on the Orpheum time, a more important circuit. The Orpheum was the Western division of the Keith-Orpheum system, the Big League of vaudeville, and their joint salary rose until it hit twenty-five hundred dollars. Orpheum acts that wanted to come East for the first time had to accept a cut in salary until they made themselves drawing cards here. The same thing was true of Eastern acts wishing to establish themselves in the West. So Olsen and Johnson stayed west of Chicago most of the time. Occasionally they accepted temporary cuts just for the glory of playing the Palace, but they never felt sure of themselves in New York. On one of their last Palace engagements, they brought along a 1912 Hupmobile with a Negro chauffeur. They would drive from the Palace to the Hotel Astor to buy a couple of cigars, and every time they got out of the old car the chauffeur would run before them and lay a ragged red Turkey carpet across the pavement for them to walk on. The Palace *cognoscenti* remained unimpressed by these high jinks, preferring the subtler comic style of entertainers like Frank Fay and Bea Lillie. When the great circuits cracked up and Olsen and Johnson had to take to the road at the head of their own units, they were compelled to widen their territory. Movie houses that will gamble on a stage show nowadays are sometimes far apart. Running out of big towns to play, Olsen and Johnson once tackled the one-night stands of the South, playing sixty-five nights, as Olsen elegantly expresses it, "in cow barns and illuminated outhouses." They made money. On a similar divagation from the beaten track, they acquired the title for their present show. The beaten track, for Olsen and Johnson, includes Phoenix, Arizona, and while they were playing there in the fall of 1937, they were waited on by a delegation from Buckeye, Arizona, which is far afield, even for them. The delegation sought successfully to engage their unit as the chief feature of the annual Buckeye Cotton Carnival. This sagebrush Mardi Gras is always called "Helzapoppin," with one "l." The partners adopted the name of the Arizona festival for their 1938 unit, but they put a second "l" into it.

Offstage, Olsen and Johnson are serious types, resembling the European circus performers who reserve their eccentricities for the ring and remain solid *petits bourgeois* outside. The partners save their money; they rarely drink; they are good family men. They are in the European tradition, too, in that they make their enterprises a kind of family affair. Olsen has been married for many years and has a son, John Charles Olsen. He is a lank youth with cavernous cheeks and sad eyes, and he is quite the busiest stooge in the show. He acts as his father's dresser between his own cues. John Charles went to Ohio State and the University of Southern California, his father says, "in order to wind up as a shot offstage." He fires at least fifty rounds of pistol ammunition during the evening. Chic's wife, Mrs. Catherine Johnson, is the apparently suburban woman who wanders in the aisles of the Winter Garden during the show, yelling, "Oscar!" The Johnsons were married twenty-one years ago and have a daughter who is an ingénue in Hollywood. Mrs. Johnson used to play in stock in St. Louis, and her husband says she can yell "Oscar!" better than any woman they ever tried in the role. The inspiration for the Oscar gag was a woman Johnson saw five years ago wandering up and down the aisles at a boxing match in Hollywood looking for her husband and getting in the fans' line of vision. Olsen has a home at Brentwood, California, near Hollywood, and another at Malverne, Long Island. He bought the Malverne house sixteen years ago, and it comes in handy now that he is working in the East. He lives there and commutes to the Winter Garden. Johnson has a house at Santa Monica, California, and a farm at Libertyville, Illinois, which he uses mostly for shooting. He likes to hunt and fish; he also likes to talk about his health and is addicted to chiropractors. "My health comes first," he often says. He has never missed a show on account of illness. In town, the Johnsons live at 25 Central

Park West, an apartment house largely populated by successful actors.

Throughout the last ten or twelve years, Olsen and Johnson have managed to average forty weeks' work a year, earning about twenty-five hundred dollars a week between them. Since they have held on to a sizable share of this, both are well-to-do. The Shuberts now meet all the expenses of *Hellz a Poppin*, and Ole and Chic together collect eighteen per cent of the gross receipts. The show is drawing around thirty-four thousand dollars a week, so the partners split about six thousand dollars. Besides Olsen and Johnson's six thousand dollars, the show costs around ten thousand dollars a week to operate, stage hands' and electricians' salaries accounting for a good proportion of the total. This leaves a profit of almost eighteen thousand dollars a week for the producers. By risking a little of their own money, Olsen and Johnson might have kept the whole show in their hands, but Ole and Chic say they were never gamblers and profess to be well satisfied with the present arrangement.

In off hours the partners like to sit in Dinty Moore's restaurant at a table plainly visible from the street and there receive the adulation of the profession. If no actors are present, they gladly accept the adulation of the laity, for whom they write innumerable autographs. "It's the ham in us," Olsen cheerfully remarks. On days when there is no matinee, they sometimes spend all the afternoon in Moore's, drinking coffee and devising new bits of gonk. Or they may pass the time by speaking condescendingly of the hardhearted booker at Loew's State who refused to book *Hellz a Poppin*, or of Mr. Watts, the supercilious critic from Parkersburg, West Virginia, who is not yet Olsen-and-Johnson-conscious. Johnson looks in the full-length mirrors, picks his teeth, and spits on the floor. Olsen invariably wears a large sprig of artificial flowers as a boutonniere. One of their favorite subjects of reminiscence is the offstage practical joke, a specialty of the firm, which brightened their dark years in the Rotary belt. One Christmas they sent pregnant rabbits to all the critics in San Francisco.

"No suave inflections," Olsen says when he tells the story of the rabbits, which is usually interrupted by convulsions of laughter.

"Sure," says the moon-faced Johnson, picking his teeth. "With us it's a belly laugh or nothing."

The Boy in the Pistachio Shirt

BUSINESSMEN like Baron Axel Wenner-Gren, the Swedish manufacturer of iceboxes and anti-aircraft guns, and Bruce Barton, the advertising executive, who know Roy Wilson Howard, head man of the Scripps-Howard newspapers, think of him as primarily a Great Reporter. Howard frequently assures them that he would rather cover a good story than do anything else in the world. Most of the newspaper reporters who know Mr. Howard think of him as primarily a Great Businessman, and this misconception, as he terms it, pains him. "I'm still just a newspaper boy," Howard democratically informed a former employee he met at the Philadelphia convention of the Republican party. He was at the moment waiting for Wendell L. Willkie, who had just been nominated, to pack a spare shirt and join him aboard the Howard yacht, the *Jamaroy*, for a weekend voyage of relaxation. While waiting, Howard called the ex-employee's attention to his green hatband, made of the neck feathers of a rare Hawaiian bird. "You can only use six feathers from a bird, and it takes two hundred birds to make one of these bands," he said with modest satisfaction. Abercrombie & Fitch sold a total of two or three of these bands for one hundred fifty dollars apiece.

The *Jamaroy*'s fantail was draped in red, white, and blue for the Willkie cruise, and Mrs. Howard, a plump, pleasant woman, who looks a little like the first Mrs. Jimmy Walker, wore seagoing togs of the same colors. Howard stuck to an ensemble of bright green suit, shirt, tie, and hatband. He adopted loud clothes as a trade-mark when he first went to work nearly forty years ago, believing that they would prevent superiors from forgetting him. The clothes serve no practical purpose now, since he has no superiors, but they have become a habit. Barton, an old friend, explains them by saying, "When a product is going well, you don't change the package." Soon after Willkie arrived on the *Jamaroy*, newspapermen who came aboard with him to say good-by discovered that Helen Worden, a reporter on Howard's *World-Telegram*, was on the yacht as a guest. Fearing that Miss Worden might write a series of exclusive feature articles, possibly entitled "Wind, Waves, and Willkie," the other reporters kept complaining to the candidate until he gave in and ungallantly asked Howard to order her ashore, which the publisher did. Howard thought of this as one more instance of the unjust suspicion with which other journalists sometimes regard him. He is extremely sensitive.

One evening, during a particularly acrimonious phase of some negotiations with the American Newspaper Guild, the CIO union of editorial and business-office workers which now has contracts with fourteen of the nineteen Scripps-Howard newspapers, Howard learned that a Guild leader had spoken harshly of him at a meeting. Around midnight he called up a subeditor who lived in Yonkers and asked him to come to the Howard home in the East Sixties immediately. At about two o'clock the employee arrived. "Joe," the publisher shouted before the Howard butler had had time to take the man's hat, "tell me, am I a son of a bitch?" The man said no, and Howard seemed reassured. The same sensitiveness came to light after the passage of the lend-lease bill, which Howard and his editors had vigorously opposed. The Scripps-Howard chief telephoned to a number of acquaintances friendly to the administration and asked them if they thought he was an appeaser. "If you ever think I'm getting too far off base," he told one man, "I wish you'd call up and tell me."

Despite this concern over other people's opinions of him, the publisher frequently follows courses of action that strangers might consider dictated by self-interest. There was, for example, the time in 1937 when a Congressional committee was about to investigate loopholes in the income-tax law and, it turned out, to name Howard and several other Scripps-Howard officers, along with still other wealthy men, as having set up personal holding companies to cut down their taxes. Howard's particular device, entirely within the law, had saved him eighty thousand dollars in taxes on his taxable income of five hundred thousand dollars in 1936. For weeks before the committee met, Westbrook Pegler, Howard's favorite Scripps-Howard columnist, blasted away at the highhanded and inquisitorial methods of the government's income-tax men. Howard must have been tempted to ask Pegler, as a favor, to stop, on the ground that the world might think the excitement more than a coincidence, or to omit some of the Pegler columns from his newspapers. However, the publisher steeled himself against such tampering with the liberty of the press, and the columnist's opinions appeared.

Something in Howard's stature and carriage suggests a jockey, but he would be too big to ride in anything except a steeplechase. Howard blames the late Arthur Brisbane for spreading the impression that he is ridiculously short. "Brisbane once tried to get me into the Hearst organization," he says, "and he never forgave me for turning him down. After I got well known, he always referred to me in his column as 'little Roy Howard.' Arthur could never understand a man who wasn't interested in money." Sometimes, to prove that he is not really small, Howard invites new acquaintances to stand up beside him in front of an immense mirror in his office. The publisher stands straight, lifts his chin, and waits for the caller's cheering assurance that he isn't such a very little fellow after all. He looks a trifle shorter than he is because his head, covered with gray hair that he parts in the middle, is large in proportion to the rest of him. He is five feet six.

Howard has a wedge-shaped face, broad at the temples and tapering toward the chin, and has a short, close-cropped, graying mustache. His face is youthful in a curious way, reminding one of a prematurely old boy. He is actually fifty-eight. One of Howard's characteristics is a high, banjo-string voice that plucks at a hearer's attention, dominates it, and then lulls it until, like the buzz of a mosquito returning from a swing around a room, the sound increases in intensity and awakes the listener again. He is acutely conscious of prolixity in others. He once telephoned a Scripps-Howard editor in Washington from New York to tell him of a long-distance conversation he had just had with Joseph P. Kennedy, who was in Boston. "That Kennedy talks your ear off," Howard complained. "I was paying the charges, and he had me on the phone for forty-five minutes." When Howard hung up, the editor looked at his watch. The publisher had been talking to him for just about forty-five minutes. Howard occasionally times his telephone calls with a stop watch so that he can later check his bills. Even with the expensive minutes fleeting before his eyes, he has the same emotional difficulty in hanging up a receiver that a fat woman has in waving away a tray of chocolate éclairs.

When Howard is on a local wire his pleasure is uninhibited by economic considerations, and there are days when he practically edits the *World-Telegram*, which is at 125 Barclay Street, from his own office at Scripps-Howard headquarters, on the twenty-second floor of 230 Park Avenue. On these days, Lee B. Wood, the executive editor of the *World-Telegram*, squirms at his desk in a corner of the newspaper's vast city room, holding the receiver against his ear and repeating "Yes, Roy," at irregular intervals until his voice sounds as mechanical as the clack of the news tickers. Wood, an extremely tall man, slides forward and down in his seat as such a day progresses, until finally he appears to be resting on his shoulder blades. Howard's voice sometimes seems to have a narcotic effect on the cerebral processes of his subordinates. An irreverent *mot* of the *World-Telegram* city room defines a Scripps-Howard editor as "a man who walks briskly, smiles a lot, and rearranges furniture." Top editors have an additional function: keeping down expenses. A good Scripps-Howard editor is never too tired to walk around a newspaper plant at the end of the day and turn out unnecessary lights.

This frugality is a heritage from the reign of Edward Wyllis Scripps, the founder of the newspaper chain, who was accustomed to go into towns where there was an established conservative newspaper and start an opposition sheet on a minimum budget. The Scripps entry would plump for labor as a matter of business principle. Its chances of survival depended on keeping expenses low. The Scripps formula, as expressed by a cynical veteran, was to "hire a shed down by the railroad station, put in a press that Gutenberg had scrapped and some linotype machines held together with baling wire, then put in a kid for twelve dollars a week to be editor and promise him one per cent of the profits as soon as the circulation hit a million." Scripps's thesis, as he himself expounded it, was that a heavy outlay on a newspaper put a publisher at the mercy of bankers and advertisers. Only a shoestring newspaper could afford to be pro-labor, he used to say, but if a pro-labor paper could survive for a while, it was bound to catch on. He once said that ninety-five per cent of all newspaper readers were not rich and would read a daily published in the interest of the have-nots. A profitable amount of advertising would follow circulation. Scripps remarked late in life that he had founded about forty papers on this shoestring basis and that a third of them had been great financial successes. When he died, in 1926, his newspaper chain was estimated to be worth forty million dollars. Since his death, there have been changes in the business concepts as well as in the editorial doctrines of the firm, but a vestigial frugality remains.

None of this frugality is evident in Howard's private office, which is a loud version of an Oriental temple in red-and-black lacquer and gilt, with a chandelier in the form of a Chinese lamp trailing red tassels. The walls are decorated with scrolls addressed to the publisher by admiring Celestials. They are long, vertical strips of parchment covered with large calligraphy, and Howard, who reads no Chinese but knows an English version of each of the texts by rote, likes to translate them for visitors. "The Chinese send them instead of autographed photographs," he says. "That one there, for instance, is from my old friend Tong Sho-yi, who was slated to be President of China if Wu Pei-fu had beaten the Kuomintang, but the Kuomintang beat Wu Pei-fu, and Tong Sho-yi was killed by hatchet men in Shanghai. He was a great friend of Herbert Hoover's. The scroll says, 'To make love to a young woman is like feeding honey to a baby on the point of a knife.'" In his house in the East Sixties, which looks something like a branch public library, he also has a Chinese room, and Mrs. Howard has a three-hundred-year-old Ning-po lacquer bed that was imported in a hundred and twenty-three pieces, with directions in Chinese for putting it together. "The only Japanese stuff in my house," Howard says, "is a dressing-table set of pigeon's-blood cloisonné that Mrs. Matsuoka gave Mrs. Howard." Until recently, Mr. Matsuoka was the Japanese Foreign Minister.

The surface of the huge desk at which Howard works in his office, and which looks long enough for him to sleep on, is so brightly polished that it mirrors his face, and a caller sitting across from him may have the sensation of being talked at simultaneously by two identical faces, one perched on Howard's neck and the other spread out on the desk. There is always a small bowl of dark magenta carnations on the desk, and Howard usually has a carnation of the same shade in his lapel, day or night. When he dines out, he has been known to wear patent-leather Russian boots, an evening cape, a red tie, a checked waistcoat, and a dinner jacket. His business suits are short-waisted and double-breasted, and have long, pointed lapels like the ears of an alert donkey. Although the suits in themselves are notable, people usually remember them only as accessories to his haberdashery. Beholders recall chiefly the wine-red shirts with large plaids of shrill green; the shirts of turquoise-and-gold squares; the orange, mauve, and pistachio shirts; the shirts of jade, rust red, and tangerine, lovingly picked out with electric blue, and, invariably, the matching bow ties and pocket handkerchiefs cut from the shirting. A fascinated colored washroom attendant who once observed him in the clubhouse at Saratoga stared for a minute and then said with awe, "All that man need is a gold horseshoe front and back and he have the prettiest racing colors in America."

Whenever Howard gets an idea he considers good, he walks into an office adjoining his own and tries it out on William W. Hawkins, chairman of the board of the Scripps-Howard newspapers, who has been his closest ally inside the organization since both were youngsters working for the Scripps wire service, the United Press, thirty years ago. Hawkins is a broad-bodied, placid, red-faced man who gazes at you benignly through gold-rimmed spectacles. There is nothing exotic about his office. It is traditionally American-executive in motif, and is adorned with a large portrait of Will Rogers by Leon Gordon. Howard owns 13.2 per cent and Hawkins 6.6 per cent of the stock of the E. W. Scripps Company, which holds over fifty per cent of the voting stock of each of the more than fifty separately incorporated Scripps-Howard enterprises. According to its financial statement for 1939, the E. W. Scripps Company's net worth was $43,161,753, making Howard's and Hawkins' stakes in it roughly $5,611,027 and $2,805,513, respectively. Its net earnings in that year were $1,530,000. The other 80.2 per cent of the stock is owned by the Edward W. Scripps Trust, which was established by the Scripps will. Robert Paine Scripps, last surviving son of the founder of the company, was sole trustee during his lifetime. The stock now is held by the trust for his three sons. The present trustees are Howard, Hawkins, and George B. Parker, the editor-in-chief of all the newspapers. The three are to be relieved of their duties in turn as Robert Paine, Jr., Charles Edward, and Samuel H., the three sons of Robert Paine Scripps, reach the age of twenty-five. Hawkins will retire as trustee in 1943, when the eldest boy reaches that age. Parker will yield his place to the second son in 1945. Howard is slated to remain until 1952 before giving way to the youngest Scripps son. Since Howard and Hawkins always vote alike, the arrangement leaves the two partners, as complementary and alliterative as a gentile Potash and Perlmutter, effectively in control of a property which includes nineteen newspapers, several newspaper syndicates, and the great United Press. Parker is a stern-looking, white-haired man, conspicuously decorated with a Phi Beta Kappa key. He was graduated from the University of Oklahoma in 1908 and is the cultural force of the triumvirate.

Until shortly after Robert Paine Scripps' death, Howard and Hawkins had no share in the parent E. W. Scripps Company, but possessed large interests in several of the individual properties it controlled, particularly the *World-Telegram*. Since, as trustees of the Edward W. Scripps Trust, they might have been suspected of favoring certain subsidiaries at the expense of others, they exchanged their holdings for shares in the E. W. Scripps Company.

If Howard and Hawkins constituted a vaudeville team, Howard would be known as the star and Hawkins as the feeder. Flashy, mercurial, and enormously energetic, Howard, in conferences with Hawkins, characteristically walks around his seated partner like an ocean traveler circumambulating a deck. Hawkins intones only brief, bass responses to Howard's rapid tenor litany and speeds or slows Howard's gyrations by increasing or diminishing the degree of what seems to be apathy in his voice. Howard expresses great faith in his intuition, but he usually seeks reassurance from others before he acts on it. He doesn't expect to be contradicted, but he does gauge the intensity of an associate's approval. A couple of unadorned yeses from an editorial writer, for example, would indicate the man's deep conviction that Howard was wrong. Hawkins is actually four months younger than Howard, who was born on January 1, 1883, but he sometimes refers to his partner as "the boy." "We would have had the boy dressed up if we'd known you were coming," he once said to a visitor when Howard stepped into his office wearing a relatively subdued arrangement of suit, shirt, and tie all in a large black-and-white hound's-tooth pattern. Hawkins has an idea that Howard's yacht is bad publicity for the firm and does his best in conversation to make it sound like a dory. "It's really not much of a yacht," he says. "I don't know what the hell he wants it for." The *Jamaroy* is a 110-foot power vessel which once belonged to C. F. Kettering, a vice-president of General Motors.

Howard and Hawkins made their way up in the newspaper world with the United Press, which the elder Scripps established in 1907 after buying out a news service known as the Publishers' Press Association. They both went to work there that year. Howard's flashier qualities got him off to a faster start than Hawkins, and they assumed their present roles in the combination almost instinctively. When Howard became president and general manager of the United Press in 1912, Hawkins became second in command. When Howard resigned in 1920 to become chairman of the board of the Scripps newspapers, Hawkins succeeded him as president of the United Press. Hawkins followed Howard to the Scripps-Howard main office in 1923. The current *Directory of Directors* lists Hawkins as an officer or director of fifty separate organizations, all within the Scripps-Howard group. Howard, possibly because of diffidence, is listed only forty-seven times.

Among the eighteen Scripps-Howard newspapers, aside from the *World-Telegram*, are the Cleveland *Press*, Pittsburgh *Press*, Cincinnati *Post*, Memphis *Commercial Appeal*, San Francisco *News*, Washington *News*, and papers in Birmingham, Indianapolis, and Columbus. Of these, the Cleveland, Pittsburgh, and Memphis papers are believed in newspaper circles to be extremely profitable and the others less so. The combined circulation of the nineteen papers is about 1,500,000, which is around three quarters that of the New York *Daily News* and approximately three times that of the New York *Times*. Howard and Hawkins have said repeatedly that the profits of the *World-Telegram*, despite its 400,000 circulation, have been negligible. On one occasion in 1935, Howard, addressing a group of editorial employees, said that Heywood Broun's salary of approximately forty thousand dollars was larger than the profits of the newspaper in the previous year. The United Press, a news-gathering organization that sells its news to 1460 papers in the United

States, South America, and Japan, as well as to five hundred radio stations, has been said to earn a million dollars a year. There are also complementary organizations, like the Newspaper Enterprise Association, or N.E.A., a syndicate which sells newspaper features; the Acme picture service, which sells news pictures, and the United Feature Syndicate. Every Scripps-Howard paper pays a fee to the central office for "national management." Sometimes a paper which, considered as a single corporate enterprise, is just breaking even is actually a profitable Scripps-Howard property because of this fee and the fees it pays as a customer of the Scripps-Howard syndicates.

Howard says that he has not been in an office of the United Press for years and that its policy is controlled entirely by Hugh Baillie, its president, who has a much larger financial interest in that organization than either Howard or Hawkins. The E. W. Scripps Company, which Howard runs as an officer and trustee, although he owns only about thirteen per cent of its stock, holds over half of the stock in the United Press. Baillie has worked for the United Press for thirty years. It now has fifteen hundred full-time correspondents and fifty-five thousand contributing part-time correspondents. The subscribers include a hundred and fifty-one papers in twenty-one Latin-American countries, the Japanese-government news agency, the Osaka *Mainichi* and Tokio *Nichi-Nichi*, which are two of the most widely circulated newspapers in the world, and a cluster of customers in Europe, including thirty-three papers in Germany.

Howard and Hawkins are less inseparable in social life. This may be because Howard tries to regulate the big-bodied Hawkins' intake of food and drink for what he considers Hawkins' own good. He takes a maternal interest in the private life of everybody he knows. A United Press correspondent, explaining a fondness of his employer's for Orientals, once said, "Roy likes to teach them how to use chopsticks." Another time, when Howard was on a cruise ship, the vessel's social director fell ill, and the publisher spent a satisfying week introducing apathetic men to patently antagonistic women and making people play deck tennis when they didn't want to. Not long afterward he bought the *Jamaroy*, on which he could be social director officially. He is never happier than when he has guests on his yacht to organize. Merlin H. Aylesworth, former president of the National Broadcasting Company, who was an important Scripps-Howard official for about two years after he left the radio corporation, says he once saved a leading Howard columnist from being killed by the publisher's solicitude. "Roy wanted him to go on the wagon," Aylesworth says, "and I told him, 'Roy, if that fellow goes on the wagon, he'll die.'" The columnist is still in good health.

The publisher freely volunteers advice to political candidates, plans complete careers for young women he has known three minutes, and for a year tormented a Russian portrait painter he knew with instructions for the improvement of a left eye in one of the painter's works. The maddened painter finally turned on him and shouted, "Yah, and I know who designs your shirts! The Congoleum Corporation of America!" As a matter of fact, Howard has them made for him by Walter-McCrory, on West Forty-sixth Street. Howard's willingness to run things sometimes rises to the international plane. Matsuoka, whose wife sent Mrs. Howard the cloisonné, was chief of the Japanese delegation to Geneva at the time Japan withdrew from the League of Nations. Howard was also in Geneva then. "Matsuoka never could sell me on the idea of taking Japan out of the League of Nations," Howard says, "but he tried like hell." Another Japanese project of which Howard disapproves is the appointment of Wang Ching-wei as puppet President of China. "I am personally acquainted with Wang Ching-wei," he says, "but I do not think he would make a good president."

Howard prefers as friends men whom he considers leaders in their field. This includes not only businessmen like Barton, Bernard M. Baruch, and Bernard F. Gimbel but Howard Chandler Christy and Leon Gordon, the artists; Lowell Thomas, the broadcaster; Rex Beach, Rupert Hughes, John Erskine, and Hendrik Willem van Loon, the writers; and Kent Cooper, general manager of the Associated Press. Of the entire group, Baruch is the only one who might be called a representative of finance capital. Howard grew up in Indiana with a pious, Midwestern fear of Wall Street. In general he finds the Eastern or pseudo-English type of rich man a bit stiff and prefers the company of transplanted Midwesterners like himself. Many of his friends are members of the Dutch Treat Club, a sort of Kiwanis of the arts. Howard likes the Rotarian congeniality of the club and doubtless approves of the house rule that every man pays for his own lunch. He has a feminine reluctance to part with money for anything except clothes. Sometimes he tries to make this characteristic amusing, saying blithely, "I'm Scotch," as one of his employees pays the fare for the taxi in which they have been riding or picks up a check for drinks. On other occasions, in restaurants, he determines the tip by dividing the amount of the check by ten and leaves the exact tithe, down to the penny. "The so-and-so gave us the worst service I ever saw in my life," he is likely to say afterward.

The event in his life to which Howard most frequently refers in ordinary conversation is the time he had an audience, in 1933, with Hirohito, Emperor of Japan. This privilege, as the United Press was careful to explain in sending out Howard's account of the meeting, had never before been enjoyed by an American newspaperman. Howard was unfortunately unable to quote the Emperor in his newspapers, because court etiquette forbade it. However, his account of the colloquy, which ran on the front pages of all Scripps-Howard papers, left no doubt that the publisher had favorably impressed the Emperor. Howard often dates events by the momentous day. "That was two and a half years before my interview with the Emperor of Japan," he will say to a woman he meets at a dinner party, while discussing almost anything, and one associate unkindly says that Howard thinks of the Christian era as something that began 1933 years before the historic encounter.

According to Howard's own story of the interview, Matsuoka, who, after maneuvering the Japanese out of the League of Nations at Geneva, barnstormed the United States in a dignified fashion, explaining Japan's position, suggested that the publisher come to Tokio sometime and meet the Mikado. One gathers that, having business there a few months later, he dropped in on Matsuoka casually and the statesman practically dragged him through the palace gates, insisting that Hirohito would be offended if he didn't call. Newspapermen who were stationed in Tokio at the time are wont to state openly that however easy it had been for Howard, it hadn't been much of a cinch for Miles Vaughn, the United Press correspondent there, who had gone through months of diplomatic toil arranging the audience. Howard was not permitted to write much more than such general statements as "Japanese-American friendship, understanding, and cooperation are of the utmost importance to peace not only in the Far East but in the world, in the opinion of His Imperial Majesty Hirohito, Emperor of Japan." As one looks back, it is doubtful if the interview can be considered a milestone in the old endeavor of the Occident to understand the Orient.

Howard, in some moods, likes to deprecate the importance of his scoop as a journalistic accomplishment, although it is naturally impossible to deprecate anything without mentioning it. He does not wish it to obscure other achievements. "Nobody ever says anything about my knowing anything about Russia," he often complains. "I interviewed Stalin too." The Stalin interview was in March 1936. The publisher submitted a written list of questions before the interview, and the dictator was ready with prepared answers which were read off by an interpreter. Stalin spoke harshly of Hitler and the Japanese. "The interview was devoid of forensics and dramatics," Howard wrote. ". . . the informality and ready humor which characterized the conversation are silk gloves covering an often-demonstrated iron will." Although Stalin didn't divulge much information, Howard felt that his time had not been wasted. He believed that he had a clearer understanding of the Russian situation. On his return to New York he told ship-news reporters that Russia had the kind of government the people wanted and that any businessman could see that it was going to last, a statement he has since referred to as illustrating his open-mindedness. "Stalin is a little fellow," he told the ship-news men, "not as tall as I am."

Howard also had an interview with Hitler in 1936, but his impression of him was not so happy. "I only got a chance to say four or five words," he says. "Every time I said something to the interpreter Hitler let loose with an oration in German." It was one of the rare occasions in Howard's life on which he has been talked down.

II—THE PAX HOWARDIENSIS

EARLY the morning after last Election Day, a message went out on the wires of the United Press, the Scripps-Howard news service, to editors of the nineteen Scripps-Howard papers scattered over the United States, saying, "Kill Talburt Cartoon Out at Third—R. W. H." The cartoon, drawn by Harold Talburt, an artist employed by a Scripps-Howard feature syndicate, showed Franklin D. Roosevelt in baseball togs sliding for a base marked, with the usual Scripps-Howard subtlety, "Third Term." The third baseman, marked "American People," was, presumably upon Scripps-Howard advice, tagging him out. The precautionary message was a typical tribute from Roy Wilson Howard to the alertness and intelligence of his editors. He wasn't taking any chances. A few weeks after this, Howard paid a friendly call on Mr. Roosevelt at the White House. Ever since the first Wednesday of last November, a sign above the desk of the President's secretary, Stephen T. Early, has proclaimed, "We ain't mad with nobody." It is unlikely that any other critic of the President as acrid as Howard took the sign literally so soon.

As Howard left the President's office after the interview, reporters from the press room in the White House gathered around him on the chance of picking up a few quotations. The publisher waved the newsmen away with a twanging "Nothing to say, boys." As he headed for the door, somebody called out, "Mr. Howard, did you call to report another armistice?" "Who said that?" Howard asked. Nobody answered, and the publisher hurried on with his short, quick stride. The anonymous voice had recalled the most gigantic *gaffe* in newspaper history, the false armistice report Howard sent over from France on November 7, 1918. The fellow who had asked the question may have reflected on the possibility that the false-armistice episode was the clearest proof in Howard's career of his ability to survive experiences that would have proved mortally discouraging to other men.

The report that set the country to celebrating the end of the first World War on the afternoon of November 7 was received by the United Press in New York and said, in the customary newspaper cablese: "URGENT ARMISTICE ALLIES GERMANY SIGNED ELEVEN SMORNING HOSTILITIES CEASED TWO SAFTERNOON SEDAN TAKEN SMORNING BY AMERICANS." It was signed "HOWARD SIMMS." Howard, then president of the United Press, was supposed by his subordinates here to be in Paris. William Philip Simms, now foreign editor of the United Press, was then the organization's manager in Paris, and it was a rule that all United Press messages from France had to bear his signature. When Howard sent the cable, he was not in Paris but in Brest, where he had just finished having a chatty lunch with Vice-Admiral Henry B. Wilson, commander of the American naval forces in France. According to Howard's subsequent account of the affair, he had concluded that the World War was about washed up and had obtained permission to return to America on a transport scheduled to sail from Brest on November 8. Armistice was in the air. The German government had appointed a delegation to meet with representatives of the Allied powers and receive terms. The two delegations were due to come together sometime on November 7, but Howard did not know the exact hour. When he met Admiral Wilson, the naval officer told him that he had just had a telephone call from a friend in the United States Embassy in Paris. The friend had told Wilson that the armistice had been signed. Howard promptly wired this interesting item from Brest, which was the cablehead of the transatlantic cable. The Brest censors were in the streets celebrating the armistice rumor, which had spread rapidly from the officers of Admiral Wilson's staff to American sailors and from them to the inhabitants. The telegraph operator assumed the censors had passed Howard's dispatch and simply transmitted it. Howard had added Simms's signature *ultra vires* as Simms's boss, and because of Simms's name the United Press office in New York assumed that the message came from Paris via Brest, instead of directly from Brest. Simms, if consulted, might have advised his superior to double-check his information, a naïve procedure habitual among journalists of lower voltage.

Newspapers in the United States passed the news along to the public under headlines like the New York *Journal*'s "GERMANY GIVES UP, WAR ENDS AT TWO P.M." and the *Evening Post*'s "REPORT ARMISTICE SIGNED; CITY IN WILD DEMONSTRATION." Factory whistles blew; church bells rang, and office workers began throwing paper out of windows. It cost New York eighty thousand dollars to clear the debris of the celebration off the streets. The State Department issued a statement in the afternoon denying that the war was over, but the public refused to be balked. The Associated Press, older and more conservative rival of Howard's pushing organization, denied the report from the first, but newspaper editors suspected that it was covering up its own lack of enterprise. An angry crowd tried to wreck the office of the Associated Press at 51 Chambers Street, shouting that it was a nest of German spies. Outside the headquarters of the United Press in the Pulitzer Building, an air-raid siren, vintage of 1918, shrieked at one-minute intervals.

During the twenty-four hours that followed the publication of Howard's report, other, lesser American correspondents in France were desperately chivied by their editors, who plaintively cabled, "CAN YOU CONFIRM WAR END?" A *Times* man at the headquarters of the American Second Army received twenty-seven messages from Carr Van Anda, his managing editor. The correspondent kept asking Major General Robert L. Bullard, the army commander, if the war had ceased, and Bullard kept insisting it hadn't. Each denial, when cabled to America, apparently made Van Anda more suspicious. The *Times* headlines on November 8 furnish a concise chronicle of the previous day: "FALSE PEACE REPORT ROUSES ALL

AMERICA," "CITY GOES WILD WITH JOY," "SUPPOSED ARMISTICE DELIRIOUSLY CELEBRATED HERE AND IN OTHER CITIES," "CROWDS PARADE STREETS," "JUBILANT THRONGS REJECT ALL DENIALS AND TEAR UP NEWSPAPERS CONTAINING THEM," "JUDGES CLOSE THE COURTS," "MAYOR ADDRESSES CROWDS AT CITY HALL," "SALOONS CLOSED AT NIGHT TO CHECK DISORDER," and "UNITED PRESS MEN SENT FALSE CABLE."

The afternoon newspapers on November 8, particularly those that had been taken in the day before, attacked the United Press. A Brooklyn *Eagle* editorial, typical of the milder approaches to the subject, began, "The United Press, its news dupes, and the French censors must get out of this muddle as best they can." The *Post* deplored the heavy loss of working hours incurred when shipyard workers knocked off to celebrate. The *Sun* said, "The responsibility is serious in the extreme." The *Globe* wondered, "Will the public dare to rejoice over the real news when the armistice comes or will the celebrations be an anticlimax?" During the following week, United Press news disappeared almost completely from the pages of American papers.

All through the false-armistice excitement, William W. Hawkins, Howard's phlegmatic second-in-command, who was in charge at the New York United Press office, fought to defend the Howard message. Hawkins had collaborated with Howard from the first year of the United Press's existence and was two years later to succeed him as president of the organization. Five or six hours after the State Department's denial of the story, Hawkins, at his office in the Pulitzer Building, said that the United Press would stand by the report until it was disproved. The State Department said that German and Allied delegates to a conference on armistice terms had not even met at the time the report was released. Hawkins replied that it was lucky Howard had got his story past a momentarily relaxed censorship. Twenty-four hours after the false report, the United Press sent out another dispatch just received from its president, saying, "URGENT BREST ADMIRAL WILSON WHO ANNOUNCED BREST NEWSPAPER ARMISTICE BEEN SIGNED LATER NOTIFIED UNCOMFIRMABLE MEANWHILE BREST RIOTOUSLY CELEBRATING. HOWARD SIMMS." Subsequently it sent out a message from Admiral Wilson admitting that the report had originated in his office. Years afterward, when the *Tribune* had been taken in by a fake report of a fleet of gambling palaces off the Atlantic coast, Howard, playing golf on a Westchester course, shouted to a *Tribune* man named Montague, who was playing near by, "Where did you get that scoop?" "Admiral Wilson told us," Montague answered. Howard was struck dumb for five or six seconds.

The signing of the real armistice on November 11 saved Howard and the United Press from any prolonged humiliation. Americans were too pleased with the real thing to stay angry over the false. Howard ordinarily thinks of the incident lightheartedly. In 1928, on the first anniversary of his acquisition of the New York *Telegram*, a purchase which marked Scripps-Howard's entry into the New York newspaper field, the editorial staff held a beefsteak dinner at Cavanagh's Restaurant. The publisher acted as master of ceremonies. Francis Albertanti, a sports writer, heckled Howard freely. At last, Howard happily yelled, "Shut up! I once stopped a war and I can stop you!"

The false armistice and its aftermath did nothing to estrange Howard from Edward Wyllis Scripps, the odd old man who owned fifty-one per cent of the stock in the Scripps newspapers and the United Press and had been Howard's employer for thirteen years. The way Howard bounced back after the nightmare of November 7 increased Scripps's respect for him. Scripps, in his spare time, used to dictate for his own amusement notes he called "disquisitions" on anything that came into his mind. He had already dictated one on Howard in 1917. Howard, then thirty-four years old, had been president of the United Press for five years. "Right from the start, Howard's self-respect and self-confidence was so great as to make it impossible for it to increase," Scripps had said. "Doubtless to himself his present situation in life, his successes and his prosperity, all seem to be perfectly natural, and to be no more nor less than he expected." Describing the young man at the time of their first meeting, Scripps dictated, "His manner was forceful and the reverse of modest. Gall was written all over his face. It was in every tone and every word he voiced."

Scripps never tried to build a large metropolitan newspaper. He remained true all his life to a formula of establishing liberal, shoestring newspapers in towns so much alike in their outlook that the publications could have practically interchangeable parts. The national policies of the papers were determined at annual conventions of Scripps editors held at French Lick, Indiana, where Scripps would berate them all on general principles. The editors could determine their own local policies, provided they favored labor. In the eighties, Scripps, as a young man, had tried to run a newspaper in St. Louis and had found Joseph Pulitzer's *Post-Dispatch* too well intrenched in the liberal field in that city. He had thereupon decided that he was destined to be a newspaper Woolworth rather than a Tiffany. Except for St. Louis and Chicago, where he launched a small-scale experiment with an intentionally adless newspaper just before the World War, Scripps tried no city larger than Cleveland. There, in 1878, he founded the enormously profitable *Press* with an initial investment of $12,500. Howard, while he worked under Scripps, was a liberal too. He was frantically adaptable.

The town of Gano, in southwestern Ohio, where Howard was born in 1883, is so small that it does not appear in an ordinary library atlas. Howard usually refers to himself as a Hoosier because his family moved to Indianapolis seven years after he was born. William Howard, his father, was for several years a railroad brakeman and later became a conductor. Railroad pay was low in the last century, and the Howards had a harder time than most railroad families, even though Roy was an only child. William Howard was tubercular, and a good part of his income went for medical care. When a friend a few years ago made fun of Howard for tipping a Paris taxi driver only fifty centimes, the publisher declared solemnly, "If my father had had a thousand dollars saved up, he could have gone out to Colorado and been cured." Howard sometimes speaks appreciatively of the railroad labor brotherhoods, because, he says, his father's pay and working conditions were terrible in those old non-union days. Roy went to Manual Training High School in Indianapolis, and became the school correspondent for the Indianapolis *News.* William Howard died during his son's senior year, and after the boy graduated he went to work as a reporter on the city staff of the *News* at eight dollars a week. He soon transferred to the *Star*, the opposition paper, where he became sports editor at twenty a week. Supporting his widowed mother, the boy, small, tense, determined to get on, adopted his now well-known uniform of gaudy shirts and patent-leather shoes as an outward disclaimer of his inward forebodings.

On the Indianapolis *News*, Howard met several men who became more or less fixtures in his life. Among them was the late Ray Long, a slightly older Hoosier, who was already city editor of that paper. Long, about Howard's size, was shallow, quick, energetic, and hedonistic. Howard always admired him as a pattern of worldliness and *savoir-vivre.* For twenty-five years, from 1910, when Long left Indianapolis to be a magazine editor, until 1935, when he committed suicide, he and Howard were inseparable companions after working hours. During that period Long edited *Red Book, Cosmopolitan,* and other magazines. Another friend Howard made in Indianapolis was a reporter named Lowell Mellett, a Hoosier born in the Elwood that Wendell L. Willkie subsequently made famous. Mellett, present director of the Office of Government Reports in Washington, is one of Franklin D. Roosevelt's principal advisers on public relations. Men who worked with Howard in Indianapolis remember most his eagerness and the neat manner in which he always draped his jacket on a hanger before sitting down at his typewriter. An older man on the *News* named Charles Stewart, who liked Howard, presently got a job as telegraph editor of the St. Louis *Post-Dispatch* and took the cub with him as assistant. Howard's mother rented a house in St. Louis, and Stewart boarded with the Howards. When Ray Long became managing editor of Scripps's Cincinnati *Post* a couple of years later, he sent for Howard to be news editor, and mother and son moved to Cincinnati. Mellett also joined the *Post* staff. Scripps's Midwestern papers were then known as the Scripps-McRae League; the McRae was Milton McRae, a junior partner who owned a relatively trifling amount of stock. Howard, who had been reading O. Henry, was eager to move on to New York and become a New Yorker. Long managed to have him appointed New York correspondent for the Scripps-McRae League, and Howard took the train for the big city. When he became proprietor of the New York *Telegram* twenty-one years later, he put notices on the bulletin board in the city room that said, "Remember! New York is Bagdad on the subway." O. O. McIntyre, when he eventually began writing his column, seemed to Howard the only authentic interpreter of the New York scene.

The twenty-three-year-old Howard who came to New York with an assured thirty-eight-dollar-a-week job, a beginning most of his colleagues would have envied, had already acquired a species of bantamweight dignity. "When you're my size," he sometimes says, "you can't afford to be a comedian." Newspapering, despite urgent prodding from schools of journalism, has always lagged behind the learned professions on the march to seemliness. Lawyers wrestled and played practical jokes on each other in Lincoln's time, but newspapermen continued to rough each other up for many decades thereafter. Howard, small, obstreperous, and glossy, had had to put up with an unusual amount of mauling during his Indianapolis and St. Louis days. One contemporary remembers seeing him tossed across the city room of the *Star* by a fat-headed giant giving a demonstration of jujitsu. Another time a colleague on the *Post-Dispatch* playfully touched a lighted match to the nape of the cub's neck. Howard, unfortunately, had that morning drenched his hair with a tonic that contained alcohol. A blue flame flickered over him, and for a moment he resembled a crêpe Suzette *flambée*. He never entered into the spirit of these high jinks, and finally his special brand of dignity came to be respected.

The Hoosier *boulevardier* was just beginning to settle into his role as the Babylonian correspondent of the Scripps-McRae League when Scripps, in 1907, acquired the Publishers' Press Association, a decrepit news-gathering service which he made the nucleus of a new agency he called the United Press. The Publishers' Press, which had its headquarters in New York, cost Scripps about $180,000. The Associated Press has always been a cooperative enterprise which will issue no new franchise on its telegraphic news service in a city where there are member papers unless the members consent. Since at that time there was no other large-scale telegraphic agency in the country, a non-member paper was at a tremendous disadvantage. Scripps said that the U.P. would buck the A.P. and sell news to anybody who would pay for it. He considered it his greatest contribution to a free journalism, and it proved to be one of his most profitable accomplishments. Shortly before his death he wrote, "Perhaps the greatest reason, however, for my objecting to becoming an integral part of the Press Association [the A.P.] in the crisis was that I knew at least ninety per cent of my fellows in American journalism were capitalists and conservatives. In those, my youthful days of pride, I swelled up with vanity at the thought that I was to be the savior of the free press in America. Of course, I have learned since that it requires more than one man to guarantee such freedom." Howard decided, soundly enough, that he would have more future as an executive with the new organization than as the solitary correspondent in Gomorrah of a group of Ohio newspapers.

The first president of the United Press was John Vandercook, a former Cincinnati *Post* official who knew Howard. Howard made his interest in the U.P. known, and Vandercook hired him as New York district manager. Mellett soon came on from Cincinnati, too, and for a while the two Indianapolis boys, both thin, shared a single bed in the apartment he and his mother rented. Hawkins came on from Louisville, where he was working on the *Courier-Journal.* The United Press was guaranteed against loss in the first few years by dues Scripps levied on the score of papers he controlled to cover the news agency's operating costs. Scripps, following his custom, reserved fifty-one per cent of the stock for himself, giving an option on twenty per cent to Vandercook and an option on another twenty per cent to Hamilton B. Clark, the business manager. Minor executives had chances to acquire smaller blocks of stock. The executives were to pay for their stock out of the profits of the new venture, if profits developed. This was a system Scripps had developed for giving executives of his newspapers an extra incentive. Even today Scripps-Howard executives of importance usually have an agreement with the management that they call "a deal," which means that they are rewarded with stock in the corporation employing them, if the corporation shows a profit. When an executive leaves one Scripps-Howard corporation for another, or for the outside world, he is compelled to surrender his stock at a price fixed by an "appraisal board" of other Scripps-Howard brass hats. His successor then has a chance to acquire the same stock. Vandercook, a newspaperman of great ability, died suddenly just as the United Press profits began to come in. Howard, already conspicuous for his push, begged for a chance at Vandercook's job. Gilson Gardner, Scripps's secretary, has described Howard as "busy as a wasp trying to get through a windowpane." Clark backed the youngster. Scripps was at Miramar, his California ranch. He spent most of his time there because he didn't like other rich men and couldn't abide poor people, he once told one of his associates. The old man had never seen Howard, but Scripps's wife and Howard's mother had been chums as girls, and Scripps had heard a good deal about him. "I was surprised at being urged to let Howard be tried out," Scripps later wrote. But he gave him the job. "My fancy was tickled with the idea," the old man continued; "my propensity to try experiments demonstrated itself again. However, Howard made good. Howard continued to make good. The United Press . . . began to grow into a property that had an actual value." Soon Howard got a chance to buy Vandercook's twenty-per-cent share of the company's stock, and did so. Clark resigned to found a Philadelphia paper, and Howard also picked up his twenty per cent. In 1909, Howard made a trip abroad to report to Scripps on the foreign-news-gathering arrangements. Some time before, he had met a young freelance newspaperwoman named Margaret Rohe in New York. Miss Rohe, tiring of letters, had gone to London in the cast of an American show called *The Chorus Lady*, in which she had a small speaking part. Howard met her again in London and married her. Howard's mother took a second husband a few years after her son's marriage and moved to the Pacific coast, where she died in 1931.

The United Press started off with the same independent Left Wing slant for which the Scripps-McRae newspapers were known. That was because, in the beginning, most of its clients were members of the chain. In its handling of the strikes of the Danbury hatters in 1912 and the Paterson silk workers in 1912 and 1913, the U.P. was noticeably more pro-labor than the Associated Press. The contrast gradually disappeared. Howard was not slow to recognize that a news service has a market unlike that of a newspaper. Scripps had once remarked that ninety-five per cent of all newspaper readers are not rich even though ninety per cent of the publishers are "capitalists and conservatives." When, in 1912, Howard was made president of the United Press and was in a way to become a rich man, old friends in Indianapolis considered him a great success in the East. In New York, unfortunately, there was no Scripps paper and nobody seemed to know him. As an ambitious young man of twenty-nine aspiring to take his place as a prominent metropolitan figure, he was pained scarcely less that few New Yorkers had ever heard of E. W. Scripps, either. He indicated a feeling that Scripps's indifference to Broadway showed a blind spot.

The first World War brought the United Press the big newspapers of South America as customers. Before the war they had been clients of Havas, the agency subsidized by the French government. Also, during the war, newspapers all over the United States felt the need of more wire service, and the United Press, which was selling its service to five hundred clients in 1914, had seven hundred newspapers on its list in 1918. Howard's false armistice had no effect on his fortunes, which unexpectedly improved further when Scripps quarreled with his eldest son, James, publisher of the Seattle *Star* and several other Western papers. James gained control of the stock of these papers and broke with his father. James's death in 1921 came before a reconciliation was possible. A second son, John, died in 1914. James's defection in 1920 left only Robert Scripps, twenty-five years old and profoundly uninterested in the newspaper business, as an heir. The elder Scripps had to pick a practical newspaperman as a running mate for his son, and since most of the editors who had helped him build his newspapers had short life expectancies, Howard was the logical choice. Old Scripps made him chairman of the board of the Scripps-McRae newspapers in 1920. Howard resigned as president of the United Press in order to accept the new job. McRae, the second barrel of the Scripps-McRae name, was already out of the firm. The following year Howard's name replaced McRae's on the mastheads of all the papers in the chain, which added to Howard's prestige. The resplendent young news-service man was nevertheless looked upon with some suspicion by the older set of Scripps's followers among newspaper publishers, Midwestern liberals who thought Howard had been corrupted by his residence in the East. Scripps gave up active direction of the Scripps enterprises in 1924, but retained a controlling financial interest.

The combination of Howard and Robert Paine Scripps, who together took over the direction of the news empire when the elder Scripps retired, was once compared by a company eulogist to "the two blades of a pair of shears." It was an accurate metaphor only if the writer was thinking of a tailor's shears, which has one flat and one cutting blade. Robert Scripps was the flat blade. Originally planning to be a nature poet, he had been drafted into the newspaper business because his father believed in keeping his properties in the family. Robert Scripps used to say, "I hate to make decisions. Roy loves to make them. So I let him." E. W. Scripps died aboard his yacht, *Ohio*, off the coast of Liberia on March 12, 1926, at the age of seventy-two. He left his newspapers, valued at a total of forty million dollars, to his son and three grandsons in a trust which would be dissolved upon the death of the last surviving grandson. Eleven months later, Howard acquired the New York *Telegram* for the Scripps-Howard chain. At last, by stretching a point, he could call himself a New York publisher. It was a little like the gesture of a turf-struck movie actor who buys a lame old horse for the sake of wearing an owner's badge. Ever since he had come to this city, Howard had wanted a New York paper, but E. W. Scripps had forbidden him to buy one. The *Telegram* was literally a museum piece. Frank Munsey had willed it along with the *Sun* to the Metropolitan Museum of Art, which had sold both to William T. Dewart. Dewart kept the *Sun*, which he still owns, and sold the *Telegram* to Howard for $1,800,000. The *Telegram* was housed in a rat-infested old barracks at Washington and Dey streets, where its personnel was strictly forbidden to smoke lest the Fire Department condemn the building. The paper, founded in 1876 by James Gordon Bennett as a raffish afternoon running mate to his morning *Herald*, had a circulation of 195,000, which depended chiefly on the racing news and Tammany political gossip that it published. It had been adopted by Tammany as a kind of house organ and got considerable political advertising. Howard was so impatient to own a New York newspaper that he closed the deal before he persuaded Robert Paine Scripps to string along with him. Young Scripps acceded to the *fait accompli*.

Howard, having restlessly kibitzed the New York newspaper business for twenty-one years while working for the United Press and Scripps-Howard, had a number of ideas about what a metropolitan newspaper should be. He completely revamped the character of the *Telegram*, although he retained several members of the staff, and started out to show New York a supercharged version of, say, the Evansville *Press*, with trimmings from *Smart Set.* The publisher believed that news stories in New York papers were too long. Shorter, crisper stories would be more widely read, he told his editors. The space saved on news stories could be devoted to feature articles with the accent on fine writing. The first effect of Howard's doctrine was a reduction almost to the vanishing point of news matter in the paper. The second was a mass invasion of New York by fine writers, recommended by Scripps-Howard editors in twenty-five cities, including Albuquerque, New Mexico; Youngstown, Ohio, and Covington, Kentucky. They wrote in a style which has been classified by historians of English literature as Oklahoma Byzantine. Since they were unacquainted with the gags that press agents had sold to previous generations of feature writers, the *Telegram's* pages began to look like a retrospective show of publicity wheezes. Some of the young men were encouraged to shine in the high aesthetic line, while others wrote, for the first page of the second section, in-the-know biographies of sterling Wall Street characters, most of whom subsequently jumped bail. Howard's first managing editor was a man named Sturdevant, who once had been happy as the editor of the Youngstown *Telegram.* Sturdevant was followed in office by Ted Thackrey, present executive editor of the *Post,* who was then fresh from Cleveland. Lee B. Wood, who had made a name in Oklahoma City, eventually displaced Thackrey. None of them could do anything to make Howard's venture profitable, and the *Telegram* finally declined to the point of losing a million dollars a year. It was steadily losing readers, too, many of them people who had developed hallucinations from reading its prose and were dragged from subway trains slapping at adjectives they said they saw crawling over them. This did not shake Howard's confidence in himself. He can take a beating and come back with the undiminished aplomb of an actress blaming her last flop on an unsuitable vehicle.

He made his first spectacular move toward establishing the new *Telegram* by hiring Heywood Broun in the spring of 1928. Broun was at liberty because, after a long wrangle with the late Ralph Pulitzer, publisher of the *World,* over his columns on the Sacco-Vanzetti case, he had written an article for the *Nation* which Pulitzer considered "disloyal." The first sentence of that article was "There ought to be a place in New York City for a liberal newspaper." Howard gave Broun a two-year contract at twenty-five thousand dollars a year. By hiring him, Howard got a name for broad-mindedness and at the same time gave a large number of people one reason for reading the *Telegram.* Broun was the best-known columnist in the country, with the exceptions of O. O. McIntyre and Arthur Brisbane. The glory reflected on the employer of a public figure pleased Howard, and he began to be seen in speak-easies with Broun, wearing a grin, like the minstrel men who used to sing, "I've Got a White Man Working for Me Now."

III—AN IMPROMPTU PULITZER

EDWARD WYLLIS SCRIPPS, founder of the Scripps newspaper empire, was content to create the second- or third-best newspaper in each of a couple of dozen cities. When Roy Wilson Howard, chairman of the board of the Scripps-Howard newspapers, bought the Pittsburgh *Press* in 1923 for $6,200,000, *Editor and Publisher*, the trade magazine of the newspaper industry, observed that this purchase of a ready-made daily marked a change in a Scripps policy almost fifty years old. Howard bought the paper and announced its acquisition while old E. W. Scripps, who had retired from active supervision of the chain, was on his yacht *Ohio* somewhere in the South Seas. Robert Paine Scripps, his son, was with him. The younger Scripps had succeeded his father as titular head of the Scripps-Howard newspapers, but Howard was generally permitted to do about as he pleased. Colonel Oliver S. Hershman, who had published the *Press* for twenty-three years, wanted to retire but drove a hard bargain for his paper. Howard and a retinue of other Scripps-Howard executives, including William W. Hawkins, his administrative alter ego, checked into a Pittsburgh hotel, secretly, in order to mask their movements from possible competitive bidders, about a week before the deal was closed, all the executives registering under the names of their secretaries. They bargained with Colonel Hershman and his lawyers almost continuously for a week, and finally reached a point where Howard's offer was within twenty-five thousand dollars of Hershman's asking price. Hershman flipped a coin to decide who would pay the difference, borrowing a quarter from Howard for this ceremony. Howard called and lost.

As Howard's control of the Scripps-Howard interests became more nearly complete, he continued this policy of buying going papers. In making an acquisition of this sort, he sometimes had to go to a bank for money. Old Scripps had a horror of borrowing from a bank, a practice which he feared might affect a paper's editorial independence. Howard feels that his own integrity is superior to such considerations. The *Press* has paid heavy dividends on the Scripps-Howard investment. A couple of other Howard purchases, like the Denver *Rocky Mountain News* and the Denver *Times*, which he bought and merged in 1926, and the Buffalo *Times*, which he got in 1929 and discontinued in 1939, turned out to be heavy losers. There were twenty-five Scripps-Howard newspapers when E. W. Scripps died in March 1926. Howard added four to the chain within the next year. Since then the number has declined to the present nineteen. In the same period the total number of dailies in the United States has dropped from 2333 to 1998. Howard's fourth addition to the chain after E. W. Scripps's death was its first New York newspaper, the *Telegram*, acquired in 1927. He paid something less than two million dollars for this property. When, in 1931, he made a bid for the New York

World with a view to merging it with the *Telegram*, the gesture seemed slightly presumptuous. It was as if the Knott hotel chain had offered to take over the Waldorf-Astoria.

The *World, Evening World*, and *Sunday World* were properties of the Press Publishing Company, of which almost all the stock was held by the estate of Joseph Pulitzer. Pulitzer's will forbade the sale of the Press Publishing Company stock "under any circumstances whatever." He had written, "I particularly enjoin upon my sons and my descendants the duty of preserving, perfecting, and perpetuating the *World* newspaper (to the maintenance and upbuilding of which I have sacrificed my health and strength)." Ralph, Joseph, Jr., and Herbert Pulitzer were directors of the Press Publishing Company, as well as trustees of their father's estate, but the will had assigned a six-tenths interest in the newspapers to Herbert, the youngest son, so in a pinch he could outvote his brothers. The papers earned a handsome income for sixteen years after the senior Pulitzer's death in 1911, and the profits were distributed among his sons and the other beneficiaries of the estate. By 1931, these included fifteen Pulitzer grandchildren. Pulitzer, perhaps in the belief that the papers would make money *every* year, had neglected to provide for a reserve fund. Money flowed from the newspapers into the estate, but there was no way of getting it back from the estate again. When, after a succession of business mistakes, the Press Publishing Company lost the relatively small sum of $474,000 in 1928, Herbert Pulitzer and his brother Ralph, who was editor of the *World*, became alarmed. Joseph Pulitzer, Jr., was giving all his energy to another Pulitzer paper, the St. Louis *Post-Dispatch*. Ralph retired as editor of the *World* in 1930, and Herbert took charge. When the company's balance sheet for 1929 showed a somewhat larger deficit, Herbert began looking for exits. At the *World* papers' lowest ebb, the *World* had a circulation of 320,000, the *Evening World* had 285,000, the *Sunday World* had 500,000, and their joint annual revenues were in excess of twelve million dollars. However, Herbert Pulitzer was neither a gambler nor a newspaper enthusiast. Howard was behind seven million dollars in his operation of the *Telegram* and in the position of a poker player so far in the hole that his best chance of pulling out was to double the stakes. He had a dream of acquiring the competing *Evening World*, the *Sunday World*, and the *World*, and of then scrapping the last two and absorbing the first into the *Telegram*.

Howard had met Ralph Pulitzer aboard the *Paris* on a transatlantic crossing in the summer of 1928. The publishers had talked half jokingly of swapping the *World* for the *Telegram* and then merging the *Telegram* and *Evening World*. A year later, in New York, Herbert Pulitzer had promised Howard not so jokingly that if the brothers ever wanted to sell out they would tell him before anybody else. Pulitzer kept his word in January 1931, and on January 31 a contract of sale with Howard was signed. Howard promised nothing more definite than that he would continue the *World* papers "in spirit." It is not certain that Herbert Pulitzer gave a hoot. The deal became public only on February 24, when, as trustees of the Pulitzer estate, the brothers asked permission of the Surrogate's Court to go through with the sale. On such short notice it was almost impossible for other potential buyers to prepare competitive offers for the property, but the 2867 employees of the *World* papers, their jobs threatened, banded together to make a cooperative offer for it. They held a mass meeting at the Astor, a few pledging their savings and all promising to turn back a portion of each week's salary to the paper if the cooperative plan went through. At a hearing before Surrogate Foley, Howard argued that any delay would have a bad effect on the *World* staff's morale and that the paper's good-will asset would depreciate. Wearing a wasp-waisted, double-breasted brown suit, the publisher appeared at his most incisive. Upholding the Pulitzers' right to sell, the surrogate blandly ruled that, notwithstanding Joseph Pulitzer's own lucid words, "the dominant purpose of Mr. Pulitzer must have been the maintenance of a fair income for his children and the ultimate reception of the unimpaired corpus by the remaindermen, permanence of the trust and ultimate enjoyment by his grandchildren, as intended." This, naturally, would have been obvious to any surrogate. Foley added that he had no right to instruct the Pulitzers whether or not to accept the Howard offer, because in selling the Press Publishing Company they were acting not as trustees but as directors of the Press Publishing Company selling its assets. This would have been equally obvious to any good legal mind. Howard's offer was a definite three million dollars and the possibility of an additional two million. The money was to be paid a half million down, a half million in ninety days, and two million in eight payments of two hundred and fifty thousand dollars, to begin in 1934. The final two millions were to be paid out of the profits of the new paper, the *World-Telegram*, if and when it earned any profits.

"No one possessed of a drop of the milk of human kindness could view with disinterest the situation of the many employees of the *World* who face at least temporary unemployment," Howard said in a prepared statement after the transaction was closed. He had Lee Wood, managing editor of the *Telegram*, set up a registration office in the ramshackle Telegram Building on Dey Street for survivors of the *World* publications.

In the first issue of the new *World-Telegram*, Heywood Broun, the *Telegram*'s columnist graduate of the *World*, wrote, "It is my sincere belief that the Scripps-Howard chain is qualified by its record and its potentialities to carry on the Pulitzer tradition of liberal journalism." His optimism was based on his own relations with the *Telegram* before the merger. For several years, Broun, like a star pitcher with a last-place baseball club, had been allowed a flattering latitude of opinion in his column. The *Telegram* circulation had risen only infinitesimally in four years of hard pulling with Howard as coxswain, but it was probably true, as the publisher said, that a new set of readers had replaced the old ones who had bought the *Telegram* for the racing news and Tammany items. The new *Telegram* readers were people willing to pay three cents to see what Broun had to say.

The *World-Telegram*, which made its first appearance on the day after the merger, resembled a colored houseman wearing some of his dead massa's old clothes. Rollin Kirby, Denys Wortman, and Will B. Johnstone, the cartoonists, were retained from the *World*, along with Harry Hansen's book column and J. Otis Swift's nature notes. On the whole, it was an amorphous publication that looked like the result of physically telescoping two totally different newspapers. It bulked large because Howard had taken over the *Evening World* advertising contracts. Since the advertising rates had been based on a circulation of less than three hundred thousand and that of the merged paper hovered for a while around a half million, the *World-Telegram* lost money on every advertisement printed. When Howard later raised the rates in proportion to the new circulation, many advertisers quit. They have had to be wooed back over a stretch of years, a factor which some critics contend has had a perceptible influence on the newspaper's policy. Within a few months after the merger, the *World-Telegram* had returned to the appearance and editorial formula of the Scripps-Howard *Telegram*, except for the three new cartoonists, and Swift, and Hansen. A number of *World* reporters and sports writers hired at the time of the merger were not with the new paper long. That summer, the *World-Telegram* moved into a new building at 125 Barclay Street. At about the same time, Howard, finally the important and full-fledged New Yorker he had long looked forward to becoming, with a major local paper of his own, gave up his suburban home, which was on Pelhamdale Avenue in Pelham, and moved into the heart of town. The Pelham house had seventeen rooms and five baths; the one he took on the East Side, near Central Park, has sixteen rooms, six baths, and an elevator. The elevator is not quite high enough for a tall man to stand upright in. The diminutive publisher enjoys seeing his tall executives, such as Lee Wood, stoop when they ride in it.

When Howard had bought the *World*, he had told the press that the transaction meant not "the death of the *World* but its rebirth." However, the *World-Telegram* made no serious effort to carry on the *World* tradition. The foreign staff of the *World*, which even in the paper's last years included such correspondents as John Balderston and William Bolitho, went out of existence. The *World-Telegram* rarely sent members of its own staff farther out of New York than, say, Hopewell, New Jersey, mostly relying on the Scripps-Howard United Press and out-of-town Scripps-Howard newspapers to cover it on more distant assignments. The Scottsboro, Alabama, trials, for example, were described for the *World-Telegram* by a reporter on the chain's Birmingham *Post*. The great droughts, the West Coast shipping strike, and the trial of Al Capone got the same modest attention. The feature writers gave the paper a façade of knowingness. The feature men's most important work appeared on the first page of the second section, known in shoptalk as the "split page." Every week one of them wrote a series of articles on such topics as Powers models, soldiers of fortune, voodoo rites, and prison reform. Howard decreed that there should also be a feature story about a woman, with accompanying photographs, on the third page of the first section every day. He said that people were interested in women. The *World-Telegram* consequently published daily a story about a woman who made powder compacts out of flattened tomato cans or was making good in some Broadway show, which usually closed by the end of the same week. The only requirement was that the subject should be as good-looking as a muskrat, and this was frequently waived. Appearing on the split page along with the polychromatic prose of the feature men were Broun's column and Alice Hughes's shopping notes. It was on the split page that Howard eventually developed one of his major contributions to newspaper strategy, the practice of letting columnists more or less express a paper's editorial policy while the editorial writer *en titre*, whom comparatively few people read anyway, remains free to hedge at the publisher's discretion. In the beginning, however, the page resembled the continuous entertainment at a pretentious Coney Island restaurant.

There had been slight rifts at the *Telegram* between Howard and Broun in the first years of the depression. The publisher, for example, had asked Broun not to devote so many of his daily columns to *Shoot the Works*, a cooperative musical revue the writer had put on with unemployed actors. Commercial producers, who paid for their advertising, were complaining. In the summer of 1930, Howard, in a *Telegram* editorial, had chided Broun for running for Congress on the Socialist ticket. The *Telegram* had backed Norman Thomas for mayor in 1929, but in 1930 Howard seemed to imply in his reproof to Broun that a few decent people were beginning to read his paper. Neither of these quarrels lasted long, since *Shoot the Works* soon ran out of audiences and Broun failed by a wide margin to get elected. The strain between the two men increased after Howard merged the *World* with the *Telegram*. Howard's paper was no longer an outsider trying to attract attention but an insider trying to hold on to everything it had suddenly fallen heir to. Broun, instead of being a magnet to draw readers from the competing *Evening World*, was now merely an employee who might say something to offend the advertisers. He could not possibly draw readers from the conservative *Sun*, and the *Evening Post*, as run by the Curtis-Martin Newspapers, was crumbling to powder without outside assistance. Liberal readers in New York had to take the *World-Telegram* because they had no alternative.

Most successful New York newspapers began their runs from the liberal position that the *World-Telegram* now held almost by default. James Gordon Bennett, when he founded the *Herald* in 1835, was labeled a scurrilous radical. Joseph Pultizer cast himself in the same role in 1883, when he began to edit the *World*. Hearst made his first impression here as an imitation radical. The *Daily News*, the most profitable newspaper of our period, has from the first been on the whole the city's most forthright champion of social legislation. Howard abandoned his strategic ground as casually as he had attained it. The *World-Telegram* differed from the *Herald*, the *World*, and the *Journal* in one important historical respect. It turned conservative *without* making big money.

The sole form of liberalism that Howard thought it safe to emphasize in New York was something called Fusion, which is somehow usually popular with large taxpayers. Fusion furnished Howard with his one opportunity to feel like a kingmaker. The king he indisputably helped make was Fiorello H. LaGuardia, who was elected Mayor in 1933, the *World-Telegram* furnishing his only outspoken newspaper support. The tone of numerous Howard-inspired editorials in the same paper has since suggested that the Mayor is not sufficiently grateful. Likewise, Howard has given LaGuardia numerous pointers, which are generally conveyed to him through the *World-Telegram*'s City Hall reporter. To these LaGuardia has paid little attention. Whenever the publisher sends an emissary to tell him how to run the city, the Mayor lectures the City Hall man on editorial policy. LaGuardia asks for the heads of reporters with the same assurance that Howard asks for those of city commissioners. The two little men obtain equally negative results and are in a fairly constant state of reciprocal exasperation.

The *World-Telegram* split page rose to journalistic eminence side by side with the United Feature Syndicate, a Scripps-Howard subsidiary organized in 1921 principally for the purpose of marketing weekly articles by David Lloyd George. As the first World War receded in public memory and Lloyd George in prominence, the articles became more difficult to place. A United Press man named Monte Bourjaily was delegated to take charge of the syndicate. He hired Benito Mussolini, Camille Chautemps, and a now nearly forgotten German statesman named Wilhelm Marx to write monthly letters about European politics and offered the fourfold service to non-Scripps Sunday newspapers. The syndicate feature sold moderately well. Upon the accession of Pius XI, Bourjaily obtained the American newspaper rights to an authorized biography of the new Pope by an Italian cardinal. This feature sold extremely well, and the cardinal used his share of the payments to rebuild a church. United Feature later bought the American newspaper rights to Charles Dickens' *The Life of Our Lord*, an unpublished manuscript that his heirs made available for publication in 1931. *The Life of Our Lord* earned a quarter million dollars for the Scripps-Howard syndicate. Bourjaily next bought the rights to Napoleon's letters to Marie-Louise, until then never published. This feature did not go well, apparently because few newspaper readers knew who Marie-Louise was. A competing syndicate scored handsomely by dressing up Napoleon's letters to Josephine with illustrations and selling them to more newspapers than bought the letters to Marie-Louise, although the letters to Josephine had been in the public domain for a century.

Bourjaily also tried to sell Broun's column to newspapers outside the Scripps-Howard chain, but never with great success, because, from fifty miles outside the city limits, Broun in those days assumed the aspect of a gin-drinking Communist with loose morals. United Feature entered the syndicated columnist field in a serious way in December 1933, with the launching of Westbrook Pegler. This writer had some years earlier worked for Howard, almost totally unremarked, as a reporter, a war correspondent, and finally as a sports editor of the United Press. He had then switched to the Chicago *Tribune* syndicate as a sports columnist, and his work had been sold to a number of other papers, including the *Post* in New York. In 1933, Colonel Frank Knox, publisher of the Chicago *Daily News*, who wanted Pegler's stuff for his own paper, suggested to Howard that the *News* and the *World-Telegram* combine to engage Pegler as an essayist on general subjects. Howard agreed, and Pegler was signed up at a salary of thirty thousand dollars a year and half of all syndicate sales in excess of sixty thousand dollars. Pegler, as a sports writer, had been philosophical rather than technical, presenting the wrestling and boxing businesses as a sort of parable of *Realpolitik*, which had only a slight literal relation to anything that would interest a sports fan. As an essayist, Pegler was assigned a spot on the split page with Broun.

Pegler wrote several practice columns to prime himself for his new job, and showed them to Howard. They included one approving the lynching by a mob in San Jose, California, of two men charged with kidnaping. The publisher thought that this was about right for a new columnist who wanted to attract attention. The lynching column was the third to appear under Pegler's by-line in his new column. It drew a great deal of indignant notice, which was just what Howard had wanted. One of the hottest reactions was Broun's. He asked, in his neighboring column, "Is this to be the measure of justice in California? Men with blood and burnt flesh on their hands are to be set free. Mooney must remain in jail. Freedom for the guilty. Punishment for the innocent." It was generally conceded that a rave review of a lynching represented a fresh point of view.

Howard's own writing is undistinguished. In Pegler, he evidently grew to feel, he had found his voice. Pegler was to Howard what Jenny Lind had been to Barnum. Some years ago a volume of Pegler's columns was published under the title of *The Dissenting Opinions of Mister Westbrook Pegler*. By a rare phenomenon, he almost always dissents from the side where the money isn't. In the last presidential campaign, for example, Pegler fearlessly dissented from the majority of his fellow citizens by plumping for Wendell Willkie. It was a happy coincidence that eighty-one per cent of the newspaper publishers who buy columns were on the same side. Dorothy Thompson, whose candidate won, lost about fifty per cent of her syndication during the campaign. Pegler is a courageous defender of minorities—for example, the people who pay large income taxes. Just the same, he has devoted around twenty columns to attacking the American Newspaper Guild, which Howard loathes. Pegler's idea of a demagogue, to judge by his columns on Senator Wagner, is a senator who favors labor laws. One of the columnist's favorite irritants is a character known as "the boss-hater." On the other hand, Pegler may dislike sycophants but he never writes any columns against them. He has written thousands of words about labor-union officials who employ violence or have criminal records, but he has never touched on the incidence of criminality among company guards or strikebreakers. During the last campaign he wrote several columns about the godlike virtues of Hoosiers, without mentioning specifically either the Republican candidate or Howard. In January, shortly after Willkie split with Howard over the question of giving aid to England, Pegler wrote a column denouncing Willkie as a fake Hoosier. This was the case of dissent from himself.

Howard, in addition to sensing the ideological kinship between himself and Pegler, found in Pegler one who sympathized with his belief that ignorance is an endearing quality. This is the basis of the Artemus Ward school of humor. There is nothing, except perhaps Mrs. Roosevelt, on which the columnist can grow more bitterly satirical than the subject of college professors, who, he implies, are parasites on society and had better keep their noses out of public business. He calls psychoanalysts "Viennese head feelers," and once wrote a column voicing his suspicion that Einstein was a fraud since he, Pegler, couldn't follow Einstein's reasoning. His top effort in this line was a column last summer fearlessly deploring false sympathy for Paris. Paris, Pegler wrote, was a city famous only for naked women.

Howard's second important addition to the split-page menagerie was another United Feature discovery, Brigadier General Hugh S. Johnson, a Reserve officer who had been administrator of NRA for the first sixteen months of its existence. General Johnson, who had finally broken with the President, brought away from Washington a conviction that Mr. Roosevelt had fallen among evil advisers, along with a vocabulary culled from among the ruins of the *Decline and Fall of the Roman Empire*. The enterprising Bourjaily read a speech that General Johnson had made before a group of businessmen and went to see him at the Hotel St. Regis, where he was then living. Bourjaily told Johnson that the speech, properly cut up and pasted together again, would have made five syndicate columns and that it was uneconomical to give the stuff away. The General was pleased to learn he could sell what he had to say. He signed a contract with United Feature which gave him an advance and fifty per cent of the money received from the syndication of his articles. As a columnist, the General warmed up slowly, with the thesis that the President was a possibly honest fellow who had been kidnaped by Stalinist janissaries. This was too mild to appeal to most publishers, and it was not until the General got down to painting Mr. Roosevelt as a he-witch hurrying the nation to a massacre that the column became a really popular number in the syndicate salesmen's line. By the time the Supreme Court fight was at its hottest, Johnson's share of the syndicate sales had risen to forty thousand dollars a year. The King Features Syndicate hired Johnson away from United Feature early this spring for a flat guarantee of fifty thousand dollars a year, but the column is still appearing in the *World-Telegram* and in Howard's Washington *News*, without, however, any mention of the fact that the General is now working for Hearst.

The most incongruous member of the split-page collection is Mrs. Roosevelt, still another Bourjaily literary find. Mrs. Roosevelt had, when her husband became President, accepted the editorship of a new Bernarr MacFadden magazine called *Babies, Just Babies*. The proceeds from her contract had gone to a couple of her favorite charities, but, all in all, the venture had not been happy. Bourjaily suggested that she write a column in the form of a daily letter to a woman friend relating the events of her day. He then signed her to a ten-year contract. The feature, at the last report, was grossing about eighty thousand dollars a year, of which forty thousand dollars is retained by United Feature and forty thousand dollars goes to Mrs. Roosevelt, who turns it over to a number of charities. Mrs. Roosevelt is not only a business asset for Howard but also, in his frequently expressed opinion, a proof of the *World-Telegram*'s impartiality. "If I were such a hell of a Tory as people say," he protests, "I wouldn't have Eleanor there, would I? But I don't think she ought to write about politics."

When the split page began to attract notice, Broun's column, "It Seems to Me," appeared in the upper right-hand corner of the page, that position being considered the most prominent. Later, Broun was shifted to the left side of the page, and Pegler, the new arrival, received the place of honor at the right. As Howard accumulated columnists, he began to pack them into layers, like Chinese in an opium den. They were all stacked together in a tier on the left side of the page, and their relative levels indicated the importance the management attached to their output. Pegler, for economic and symbolic reasons, has been from the beginning of this arrangement what racing men would call the top horse. He brings in the most money, about one hundred and fifty thousand dollars yearly. Broun, who once wrote, "The underdogs of the world will someday whip their weight in wildcats," at first ran directly under Pegler. Broun complained that his pieces were often shortened, sometimes by the excision of sentences or clauses that he considered vital to continuity, and was told that this was done not from malice but because it was necessary to make the tier of columns come out even at the foot of the page. Johnson had the third position from the top, and Mrs. Roosevelt, possibly because she was an avowed Democrat or because Howard felt a lady should have a lower berth, occupied the nethermost position. As differences between Broun and the publisher developed, the heavyweight columnist's specific gravity appeared to pull him toward the bottom. When the day came that Howard moved Johnson above Broun, a memorandum informed all Scripps-Howard editors, "General Johnson is a columnist of increasing importance, as indicated by the change in his relative position on the page."

IV—ONCE AGAIN SHE LORST 'ER NIME

A SERIES of articles which appeared in the Philadelphia *Record* and the New York *Post* last winter referred to Roy Wilson Howard, head man of the Scripps-Howard newspapers, as "the mastermind of appeasement." This irritated Howard but scarcely astonished him. He ascribed it to the *Post*'s desire to take away the *World-Telegram*'s department-store advertising. Howard also said that Robert S. Allen, the author of the articles, was angry at him because he had never run Allen's daily column, "Washington Merry-Go-Round," in the *World-Telegram.*

William R. Castle, Under-Secretary of State during the Hoover administration, and General Robert E. Wood, chairman of the board of Sears, Roebuck and national chairman of the America First Committee, two of the country's outstanding and least apologetic appeasers, are among the few prominent citizens with whom the publisher does not admit close acquaintance. "Why, I only met Castle once in my life, and that was about eight years ago on a beach in Hawaii," Howard recently said. As the Senate debate on the lend-lease bill was nearing its close in March, he said, "I wouldn't know General Wood if I saw him." Nevertheless, Howard wrote a first-page editorial on the lend-lease bill in which he made verbatim use of one of the mail-order General's most narcotic arguments: "If six million men, well trained and well equipped, cannot cross twenty miles of water and conquer 1,500,000, how could they possibly cross three thousand miles and successfully invade the United States?" The first part of this proposition implied that Great Britain was safe from invasion, the second that the larger the expanse of water to be defended by a given force was, the easier the defender's task would be. Howard introduced Wood's double-barreled paralogism with the casualness of a teacher making an allusion to accepted truth. The editorial was a retreat from Howard's all-out opposition to the bill; its thesis was that since the measure was bound to pass anyway, the country should support the President. The *World-Telegram* then eased into a campaign of opposition to convoys and reproof to detractors of Charles A. Lindbergh. While Howard has made no frontal attack on aid to Britain in principle, he has fought a continuous delaying action against every concrete proposal of aid. Of the thirty-one members of the America First national committee who first appeared on its letterheads last winter, three—General Hugh S. Johnson, John T. Flynn, and Major Al Williams—were Scripps-Howard columnists. Howard said at the time that it was a coincidence. Feverishly isolationist senators like Burton K. Wheeler of Montana, Gerald P. Nye of North Dakota, and Robert R. Reynolds of North Carolina are treated with conspicuous respect in the Scripps-Howard press. The collective efforts of this group of senators, so faithfully cheered on by Howard, delayed the passage of the cash-and-carry bill of 1939 for two months. They held up the Selective Service Training Act until the end of last summer, which caused a still longer delay in the expansion of the army, since men could not be sent to training camps in fall weather until barracks had been built for them. Howard, however, has never joined forces with the isolationists. He calls his procedure "maintaining detachment." In a parallel manner, from 1935 through 1937, he called himself a supporter of the President but opposed many of his specific projects and said he hoped Roosevelt wouldn't get a large majority of the electoral vote in 1936 because too much power is bad for anyone. Similarly, last fall, while Howard was in agreement with Wendell L. Willkie in principle, Westbrook Pegler and General Johnson, in their Scripps-Howard columns, seemed to develop a temporary attack of non-partisanship every time Willkie refused a Howard suggestion about campaign strategy. Whenever Willkie complained, Howard explained that the most effective support was the least obvious.

Howard's position on the country's foreign policy has possibly been influenced by a feeling that the President has never taken him seriously enough. He once related with some indignation part of a conversation with the President at the White House. He had told Roosevelt that a certain stand he had taken was a serious mistake, and the President had replied, "Horsefeathers, Roy, horsefeathers!" The publisher's attitude toward the war, like that of some of the America First leaders, is possibly affected by the simple fact that he is a wealthy man who does not wish to be disturbed. In addition he regards himself as intuitive and a repository of confidential information. If he were a race-track plunger, he would never look at horses or form charts. He would put his faith in his hunches and conversations with dopesters. Some of the dopesters he has listened to, like Al Williams, have a high opinion of German prowess and may have influenced him to put a bet on isolationism. Munich, in Howard's estimation, was good business sense. He has said that Neville Chamberlain has not yet been fully appreciated. Howard visited Europe in the summer of 1939 and filed a series of dispatches to his papers belittling the danger of war. Some people accused him of acting, like Senator Borah, as if the world crisis were a political gimmick rigged by Roosevelt. It usually takes Howard, on a foreign reporting tour, around four days to learn the truth about a major power, but he can fathom a nation of less than twenty-five million inhabitants in one afternoon. Before going on such a trip, Howard, who tells new acquaintances that he is "primarily a reporter," bashfully asks his subordinates if they think it worth while for him to cable some stories. They invariably think so.

It is impossible to imagine Howard playing Harun-al-Rashid on the Bowery, as hulking Captain Joseph Medill Patterson, publisher of the *Daily News*, sometimes does. Howard's contacts with the people are generally those he makes on Pan American clippers, at de luxe hotels, and at dinner parties. One acquaintance who made a considerable impression on him in the thirties was Baron Axel Wenner-Gren, the Swedish industrialist, who is heavily interested in the Electrolux and Servel corporations and whose European holdings include timberlands, paper mills, and munitions factories. Wenner-Gren was at the time a friend of Edward VIII, Mrs. Simpson, and Von Ribbentrop, then German Ambassador to London. He had also known Hermann Göring during the German's sojourn in Sweden after the first World War. Wenner-Gren's viewpoint, as recorded in the *World-Telegram* and elsewhere, seemed to be that though there were labor unions in Sweden they knew their place, whereas in Germany and Italy the workers, by insisting on too much, had made necessary a totalitarian revolution, and that he feared the same thing might happen in the United States. Whenever Wenner-Gren was coming to New York, Howard was apt to have a reporter sent to meet his ship, with advice on what opinions to look for in the statement the Baron had not yet made. The Baron believed that Germany and the United States could get along beautifully with the right people running both countries. Senator Wheeler was another whose interviews were frequently "front-office" assignments. Not only such officially protected game as Wenner-Gren and Wheeler but almost all *World-Telegram* interviewees wearing suits that cost more than one hundred dollars would begin by asking the reporter, "How is Roy?"

In the years between his purchase of the *World* and the beginning of the second World War, Howard succeeded in becoming a fairly well-known New York figure, although he never got to be a celebrity *du premier plan*, like Jimmy Walker or Walter Winchell or Dutch Schultz. He is certainly the only publisher of a New York newspaper except William Randolph Hearst whose photograph would be recognized by the average newspaper reader. Captain Patterson, Ogden Reid, Arthur Hays Sulzberger, and William Dewart are men without faces as far as the public is concerned. Returning to his hotel from one of the sessions of the Democratic convention in Chicago last summer, Howard and a few of his employees, unable to get a taxi, climbed aboard a crowded streetcar. A large, sweaty fellow in work clothes looked down at the small, iridescent publisher and snarled, "Say, you look like that so-and-so Roy Howard." Howard seemed thoroughly pleased. In the early years of his career as a publisher, he often accepted appointments to public bodies; he was once, for instance, on the board of judges in a Camel-cigarette essay contest.

Now, while he is more conservative, he is still receptive to the right kind of appointment. It was the belief of several political writers during the last campaign that he would have liked to be Willkie's Secretary of State. He does not allow his name to appear in the society columns of his own papers, because, he says, "Shucks, I'm not society," but he is constantly interviewed by other papers climbing in and out of planes, and he used to be a minor staple for ship-news reporters. Mrs. Howard, a tranquil, friendly woman, does not appear at all the gatherings he attends. The schedule would be too rigorous for almost any woman. The Howards have two children, a son and daughter. The son, Jack, was graduated from Yale in 1932 and is now president of Scripps-Howard Radio, Incorporated, which operates two broadcasting stations in Memphis. Jane, the daughter, is married to Lieutenant Albert Perkins of the United States navy.

Howard has paid less and less attention to his out-of-town newspapers in recent years. The national headquarters of the chain are in New York, instead of in Cleveland, where they were in E. W. Scripps's day, and editorial conventions are now held in Washington more often than in French Lick, the traditional site. Old-timers say that the programs at these get-togethers are quite uniform. One of the officers makes a speech denouncing the Reds; another complains about taxes, and a third delivers a rousing plea for more concentrated, punchy writing. After that, everybody plays poker.

The chain's papers have become increasingly orthodox, and they no longer reveal any of the Scripps crotchets about the dangers of monopoly or the right of labor to organize. When Scripps-Howard bought and merged the Denver *Times* and the *Rocky Mountain News* in 1926, Howard announced that the chain had come to Denver "to correct a sinister journalistic situation" which was caused by the domination of the Tammen and Bonfils *Post*. Three years later he told the Denver Chamber of Commerce he was in town primarily to sell advertising. When the chain acquired the Memphis *Commercial Appeal*, a rich, conservative newspaper, a few years ago, it retained the *Appeal's* make-up, typography, and syndicate features, as well as its traditional editorial policy and, as a consequence, its advertisers. The Scripps-Howard San Francisco *News* has supported a referendum proposition to make the franchises of a traction company perpetual. So it goes, more or less, with other Scripps-Howard papers.

One of the publisher's amusements is hunting. "Roy loves to shoot a moose," William W. Hawkins, the second man in the Scripps-Howard organization, says. Howard democratically plucks the birds he shoots on Bernard M. Baruch's estate in South Carolina and takes pride in the way he dresses a rabbit. Even as a hunter, he is financially conservative. He went to New Brunswick with a group of his associates a couple of years ago, and their guide showed them fine sport. The other huntsmen gathered in the Scripps-Howard offices the day after their return to decide what to send the guide as a mark of appreciation. They had just about settled on a rifle when Howard entered the conclave. "Now, wait a minute, boys," he said. "Let's not be so splendiferous. Let's call in one of our artists from N.E.A. and have him draw a picture of a moose's head crying big tears. Then we'll all sign it and send it to Jean so he can hang it in his cabin." The guide got the picture.

Howard's present political course was determined in 1937, the year Franklin D. Roosevelt began his second term in the White House. That year the publisher broke with his old friend Lowell Mellett, the editor of the Scripps-Howard Washington *Daily News*, who had been something of a final link with the Scripps days. Mellett saw the New Deal as an expression of the old Scripps progressivism. In the early twenties he had written a series of articles denouncing what he called "government by the courts," and limitation of the power of the Supreme Court had become almost a Scripps copyright theme. When, in 1937, Howard wanted the *News*, like the other papers of the chain, to campaign against Roosevelt's scheme to reorganize the Court, Mellett resigned, giving up an income of twenty-five thousand dollars a year to take a government job at eight thousand dollars. That same year Howard broke irrevocably with Broun. The precipitating cause was a document in the form of a letter "to a famous newspaper publisher," which Broun contributed to the *New Republic*. Broun, addressing his purportedly fictitious publisher as Butch Dorrit, wrote:

> Do you honestly think that the great American public is all steamed up about your income tax? Take off the false whiskers. There's nothing immoral or unethical in your espousing the conservative side all along the line, but doesn't that pretense of progressivism sometimes cleave to your gullet? All your arguments are based upon the premise that you're a great success. You've scrapped some great papers and what have you got to show for them? What's left is an eight-column cut of the Quints asking permission to go to the bathroom.

This last sentence was a reference to the full-page layouts of pictures of the Dionne Quintuplets with which the *World-Telegram* had been embellishing itself about once a week. The Newspaper Enterprise Association, a Scripps-Howard feature syndicate known as the N.E.A., had triumphantly obtained exclusive American rights to newspaper photographs of the sisters. Perhaps more cutting was Broun's allusion to Howard's tax affairs. Broun's contract still had two years to run, but after this incident he and Howard did not make even a pretense of mutual tolerance. "I wouldn't pour water on Broun's leg if he was on fire," the publisher once said to some *World-Telegram* men. The Bureau of Internal Revenue, in an attempt to illustrate loopholes in the tax law, had named Howard and several of his associates, along with other wealthy men, at a hearing by the Congressional Joint Committee on Tax Evasion and Avoidance, as creators of personal holding companies. The Treasury subsequently maintained that the choice of names was accidental, but some observers thought the accident well planned. The testimony, they figured, was aimed to forestall a Scripps-Howard newspaper campaign for downward revision of the surplus-profits tax. A newspaper owner who was already taking full advantage of a wide gap in the law would make an awkward figure as crusader for further tax reductions.

Old Scripps had anticipated an economic revolution within a hundred years and had been accustomed to say that it was up to people of wealth to make the change painless. Howard once said, "I wonder if the old man would have been such a liberal if he had had a pistol up against his belly the way I have." Howard was referring to the American Newspaper Guild. Broun was one of the founders and the first national president of this union of newspaper editorial and business-office workers. The coming of the Guild to the Scripps-Howard papers brought a general rise in minimum wages and the establishment of severance pay in proportion to length of service. The Guild also protected the forty-hour week established by NRA. These changes cost the newspaper chain about a million dollars a year. Restrained editorial support, in the old days, of unions in other industries had cost precisely nothing, and Scripps himself might have balked at paying this much in cash for his franchise in the friend-of-labor business.

In 1934, when Broun's original contract with the *World-Telegram* expired, the Guild, which had not yet arrived at the *World-Telegram*, had still seemed innocuous. It had not yet joined even the American Federation of Labor, from which it later seceded to affiliate itself with the CIO. Westbrook Pegler, who had been placed on the famous "first-page second-section," or "split page," with Broun toward the end of 1933, had not yet established himself as more than a side dish, and the older columnist remained the *World-Telegram*'s chief claim to prestige. During the honeymoon months of the first Roosevelt administration, Broun even began to look a little like a prophet. There was a popular enthusiasm for the sort of governmental innovations that would have been called radical a couple of years earlier. Business in general showed signs of improvement, and William Randolph Hearst, foreseeing a period of commercial expansion, began a campaign to hire away his competitor's editorial assets. Broun was getting about five hundred dollars a week, but Hearst's King Features Syndicate offered him a contract at twelve hundred dollars and a cash bonus of twenty-five thousand dollars if he would sign it. Howard offered Broun a contract at seven hundred dollars a week, which, with the columnist's share of his rather modest syndicate sales, would bring his annual income to forty thousand dollars. The idea of working for Hearst was not pleasant to Broun, so he took the Howard offer even though it was lower.

When the Guild joined the American Federation of Labor in 1936 and started its campaign to get the *World-Telegram* to sign a contract with it, Howard told the Guildsmen that the public would have no confidence in reports of labor disputes by writers who belonged to unions. Broun argued that the public had no confidence in journalists who had to reflect the views of anti-labor publishers. Howard always treated as coincidental, extraneous, and without importance the fact that in general the level of salaries on the *World-Telegram* was far below that on the *Daily News*, whose management welcomed union organization. Around that time a favorite anecdote in the *World-Telegram* city room was about a depressed and impoverished reporter who in 1934 scooped the entire country by obtaining facsimiles of the signatures on the Lindbergh-kidnaping ransom notes. Lee B. Wood, the *World-Telegram*'s executive editor, told the reporter that in recognition of his coup the paper had decided to reward him with a due bill on a chain clothing store entitling him to a thirty-dollar suit of clothes. The reporter went to the store, got a suit, and, when he looked in the glass, acquired enough confidence to try to find another job. He landed one at two and a half times his *World-Telegram* salary.

Howard issued a long statement to the *World-Telegram* staff in 1936 saying that he would never negotiate with the Guild, although he would welcome a company union. The following year, however, he signed a contract with the Guild, which had become powerful enough to make him eat his words. Even without the Guild, Howard, at fifty-eight, might today be a well-established conservative, but the fight probably speeded up his natural metabolic changes.

In 1928, Howard, overruling the Scripps-trained editors like Mellett, had his papers back Hoover for the presidency when most liberals supported the Democratic ticket of Alfred E. Smith and Joseph T. Robinson. Howard argued that Hoover was a great progressive in disguise. The depression did not make Howard change his mind. Moreover, since it enabled him to absorb the competing *Evening World* and to pick up a few shreds of the morning *World*'s prestige at bargain rates, he had no cause to be heartbroken, and in his enthusiasm he was probably inclined to believe the bankers when they predicted that prosperity might return almost any week end. He said, however, he felt that the voters would demand a change of administration and that he wanted a safe one. He went to the Democratic national convention in Chicago in 1932 to collaborate with John F. Curry of Tammany and John McCooey, the Democratic leader of Brooklyn, in a stop-Roosevelt drive. Tammany was angry at Roosevelt because while he was Governor of New York State he had forced Mayor Jimmy Walker out of office. Howard, whose editorial writers had howled for Walker's removal, evidently now felt that he was nearer to Tammany than to Roosevelt. The *World-Telegram* announced that it favored the nomination of Al Smith. A widely accepted theory held that Howard figured Smith would block Roosevelt, after which, with the convention in a deadlock, the publisher could effect the nomination, as a compromise, of Newton D. Baker, Secretary of War under Woodrow Wilson and then, incidentally, general counsel for the Scripps-Howard newspapers. This apparently boyish attempt to name a President of the United States amused James A. Farley, who was managing Roosevelt's campaign. "Howard thought he could take off a few afternoons from his newspaper duties to nominate a presidential candidate," Farley wrote in his memoirs. "The game is somewhat more complicated."

After the Republicans had renominated Hoover, the Scripps-Howard editorial convention at French Lick endorsed him. The publisher showed no warmth for Roosevelt until the summer after the inauguration, when "New Deal" had become a password to popularity. He then threw himself on the President's neck with all the shyness of a hostess in a navy café. "Roy is a fellow who likes to climb aboard a band wagon," one politician said awhile ago, "and then gets mad if the fellows who were on first won't let him drive and play the bass drum at the same time."

Howard's infatuation with the President ended with the "breathing-spell" letters they exchanged in the summer of 1935. Alarmed by the administration's tax program and quietly relieved by the Supreme Court decision which terminated the NRA, Howard proposed to Stephen Early, the President's secretary, that Mr. Roosevelt grant him an exclusive interview. The President was to furnish prepared answers to a questionnaire previously submitted by Howard. The affair was to be on the grand scale. There would be photographers, newsreel cameramen, and probably a broadcast, and the purport of the President's answers would be that recovery had already been achieved and that reform was something business might thenceforth cease to worry about. The President demurred, but agreed to answer a letter from Howard and permit publication of the letter with his reply. The publisher wrote that large-scale industry, harassed by taxation which it considered "revengeful," felt there should be "a breathing spell and a recess from further experimentation until the country can recover its losses." The President answered, "The 'breathing spell' of which you speak is here—very decidedly so." He also said, "The tax program of which you speak is based upon a broad and just social and economic purpose—this law affects only people who have incomes over fifty thousand dollars a year." Howard published Roosevelt's reply, but his editorials soon indicated that he thought the President had trifled with his affections. "I was never so thick with the President as people said," he now remarks modestly, and adds, rather defiantly, "and I'm not so thin with him now as some people would like to have you think."

In the 1936 presidential campaign, Howard gave nominal support to the administration. George Morris, a shrewd old political writer whom he had inherited with the *Telegram* when it was a wardheelers' Bible, assured him from the start that Landon would carry only two states. The publisher nevertheless took occasion during the campaign to visit Landon on his special train in Buffalo to pay his respects. "Our bark is worse than our bite," he told the Republican candidate. The fight over the Supreme Court made the division between Howard and Roosevelt definite. In the course of this struggle, the *World-Telegram* expressed extravagant admiration for Governor Herbert H. Lehman of New York, who helped beat the President's proposals. The praise bounced back in Howard's face in 1938, when Lehman ran for reelection against Thomas E. Dewey, the publisher's favorite adolescent Republican. A typical *World-Telegram* editorial of those days might begin with some such statement as "The State is indeed fortunate to have a choice of two such equally remarkable candidates" and then go on to the end praising Dewey. After Lehman's reelection, Howard may have felt that both men owed him gratitude, but the Governor refused a request of his to remove the Brooklyn district attorney from office. This proved that Lehman was no more to be depended on than Roosevelt or that earlier ungrateful protégé, LaGuardia.

The great German offensive of 1940 may well have annoyed Howard, as it practically insured the President's nomination for a third term. The publisher, who had looked to 1940 to deliver him from the insubordinate Roosevelt, suddenly found himself in the dilemma of a racing trainer who has to beat something with nothing. Dewey, whose prestige had steadily declined since his defeat by Lehman in the gubernatorial campaign, was too callow for a crisis President. Senators Taft and Vandenberg had demonstrated a remarkable knack of inspiring apathy. The kingmaker was standing on a corner waiting for a hitch on a band wagon when Oren Root, Jr., and Russell W. Davenport, Henry R. Luce, and a group of other men on the staffs of *Time* and *Fortune* came along with Wendell L. Willkie. Howard's wooing of the large, talkative Indianan was tempestuous. He appeared so consistently at the same dinner parties Willkie attended that Willkie, trapped once into playing a free-association parlor game and suddenly presented with the word "Howard," answered, "Soup." "Howard wore those nineteen newspapers in his lapel with that red carnation," a member of the original Willkie group has said. "He talked about them as if he were going to give them to us." Howard now says that he is sorry the election provided no clear-cut test of public opinion on intervention in the war. When Howard went to the Republican convention in Philadelphia as one of Willkie's most vociferous rooters, Willkie had already declared himself for full aid to Great Britain, but Howard, like many other Willkie admirers, may well have believed that Willkie was not really in earnest. One close friend has said, "Roy doesn't believe anything that is not told to him confidentially." At any rate, Howard seemed to think of the candidate's later demonstration of consistency as one more betrayal. As in the case of Roosevelt, Howard saw the first sign of ingratitude when he moved to help take charge of his new protégé.

Davenport, Root, and Luce, discoverers of the new white hope, refused to cut Howard in for a big enough piece. Howard, the *Time-Fortune* people say, seemed to think that about ninety-eight per cent would be right. Howard encouraged General Johnson to make a trip to Colorado Springs, where the candidate was resting, to write Willkie's acceptance speech for him. This was a mistake, because if there is one thing Willkie is sure he can do, it is write. The clash of literary temperaments was intensified by Johnson's insistence that Willkie include a plan for farm relief the columnist had thought up and that he should mention the Virgin Mary someplace in his speech. The Elwood, Indiana, stylist felt hurt, and said so. Johnson returned to the East and wrote a couple of columns calling Willkie's advisers political amateurs. Howard, boarding the campaign train soon after Willkie's first tour had started, remained enough of a businessman to complain that the candidate was timing his speeches to break in morning papers (eighteen of the nineteen Scripps-Howard newspapers appear in the evening). As a political expert, he also gave some constructive criticism about the setup of the train and the itinerary.

Meanwhile, Pegler and Johnson, after the General had recovered from his irritation, wrote columns in boiling oil, invoking the wrath of a just deity who had destroyed Sodom and Gomorrah upon the subversive activities of Mrs. Roosevelt, who belongs to the American Newspaper Guild. They discussed the third term in a clinical style that reminded readers of the *Daily News* campaign against syphilis. The General fumed over the appointment of Elliot Roosevelt to a captaincy in the army. For comic relief, he went on the radio and told funny stories in Jewish dialect, a lapse which brought a disclaimer of responsibility in the *World-Telegram*. Howard, talking recently about the activities of his columnists during the election, said that they had run away with him. "You know, I would not interfere with any man's freedom of expression," he said solemnly, "but I thought they were very unfair to Franklin." Among the columnists, Raymond Clapper, the *World-Telegram*'s accredited liberal, in a relative sense, remained almost neutral until near the end of the campaign. Finally he came out for Willkie, too, like the white horse in the circus chariot race who loafs along behind the others until the last lap. "When I looked in the paper and saw that Clapper had come over too," Howard says, "I said, 'Oh, my God!' It made us look partisan."

In his experience with public men, Howard has been betrayed so many times that he sometimes must feel like the cockney girl in the song "Once Again She Lorst 'Er Nime." Last January, when the administration began to propose a lend-lease bill, Howard telephoned to Willkie at his home, asked him to prepare a statement attacking the bill, and indicated that this was a chance to make up for the mistakes he had made during the campaign. "All the other boys are going to jump all over this bill, Wendell," Howard said in effect, "and I don't want you to get left at the post. I have a reporter with Tom Dewey writing his statement for him now, and I'm having lunch with Hoover tomorrow." (Howard has always had a tender spot for Hoover. He has given unlimited publicity to all the Hoover projects for sending food through the British blockade, despite the possibility of embarrassing the administration, which has tried to coordinate its foreign policy with Great Britain's.) Willkie told Howard that he could not decide until he had read the bill. The next day, after he read it, he said he would be for it if minor changes were made in it. The publisher and the ungrateful candidate had a resounding argument later at a dinner party given by John Erskine. It wound up by Howard's telling a blackface story to Willkie. The punch line of the story was "Wait till I get my razor on you tomorrow!" Willkie, more ingenuous than a LaGuardia or a Roosevelt, was astonished at such disrespect. "A man like that is too flippant to have so much power," he told friends later. He has as large a capacity as Howard's for feeling that his affections have been trifled with. Immediately after Willkie's return from England, Howard sought a reconciliation. He succeeded in getting Willkie to come to dinner at his house, but their twanging wrangle continued all through the intended love feast. "To tell you the truth," Howard afterward remarked to a friend, "as long as one of them had to be elected, I'm glad it was Roosevelt. Willkie is a fellow you can't depend on."

"Pull His Whiskers!"

FEW AMERICAN INDUSTRIES have suffered so spectacular a decline as wrestling, which had its happiest days during the early years of the general depression. In the winter of 1931–32 ten wrestling shows were held at Madison Square Garden, and drew an average gate of twenty-four thousand dollars. These indoor shows merely served to prepare the wrestling public for outdoor bouts at the Yankee Stadium and the Garden Bowl, which occasionally drew sixty thousand dollars. The last match in the Garden was promoted on March 30, 1938, by an old acquaintance of mine named Jack Pfefer, and it attracted less than five thousand dollars' worth of patronage. If a promoter tried to rent the Yankee Stadium or even Ebbets Field for a wrestling show this summer, sporting people would think he had been overcome by the heat. Pfefer, however, is still conducting wrestling matches in a small way, and feels that from an artistic point of view they are superior to those of the great era. The trouble, according to him, is that the moneyed clientele has ceased to believe in wrestling as a sport and has not yet learned to appreciate it as a pure art form, like opera or classical dancing.

Pfefer holds shows in neighborhoods like Ridgewood, in Queens, and the region just south of the Bronx Zoo, and they draw fairly well at a general admission of a quarter or forty cents. Several nights a week he leads his wrestlers out of the state to places like Jersey City and Bridgeport. Pfefer's wrestlers do not make big money, but most of them work five times a week even in summer. The promoter has been celebrated for years as the most unrelenting foe of the English language in the sports business. "You never heard it of an unemployment wrestler, didn't?" he asked me when I visited him awhile ago in his office on the tenth floor of the Times Building. "For wrestlers is no WPA."

In the trade, Pfefer is believed to have retained money despite the debacle. He was one of the four partners who controlled the wrestling business in New York in the golden era, and when the money was rolling in he lived frugally. His present enterprises, although on a very small scale, are often mildly profitable. He is a tiny, slight man, weighing about a hundred and twenty pounds and possessing the profile of a South African vulture. His eyebrows rise in a V from his nose, and he wears his hair in a long, dusty mane—a tonsorial allusion to a liking he has for music. On the walls of his office, among pictures of wrestlers, he keeps a death mask of Beethoven and signed photographs of opera singers.

He never opens a window in this office and wears a vest even in summer. In the street he always carries an ivory-headed cane presented to him by an Indian wrestler named Gafoor Khan. Pfefer's entire office staff consists of a worried, middle-aged ex-newspaperman named Al Mayer, at one time a successful manager of prize fighters. When the wrestling business was in its majestic prime, the partners in the local syndicate, besides Pfefer, were the late Jack Curley, a promoter named Rudy Miller, and a former wrestler called Toots Mondt. Miller and Mondt are among the little man's competitors. In the good days, it was Pfefer who had charge of the department of exotica—he was responsible for such importations as Ferenc Holuban, the Man without a Neck, Sergei Kalmikoff, the Crashing Cossack, and Fritz Kley, the German Corkscrew. Most of the foreigners were built up into challengers of Jim Londos, the syndicate's perennial champion, who would throw them with his spectacular "airplane whirl."

Ffefer blames Londos' rapacity for the decline of the wrestling industry. After the syndicate had for several years informed the public that Londos was the greatest wrestler on earth, the Greek began demanding most of the gate receipts. The promoters had but two equally unpleasant alternatives. They could become virtual employees of Londos or destroy the edifice of legend they had built around him by declaring he was not much of a wrestler after all. They chose the second course. Within a year the country swarmed with champions, each group of wrestling promoters recognizing its own titleholder. At last reports, there were in different parts of the United States fifteen wrestling champions, including Londos, who has been performing for at least twenty-five years. The New York State Athletic Commission acknowledges no world's champion, and for that matter refuses to admit that wrestling is a competitive sport. The commission refers officially to all wrestling bouts as "exhibitions," and will not allow them to be advertised as contests. Pfefer says he is glad the commission doesn't permit a champion, because it saves hard feelings among his wrestlers. When they perform, they know it is just a night's work and they can concentrate on their histrionics.

I went up to Pfefer's office late one Wednesday afternoon a couple of summers ago, having made a date by telephone to go out to the Ridgewood Grove Arena with him and see his current band of wrestlers in action that evening. He was in a bad mood when I entered. A rival promoter had hired a wrestler to hit Pfefer in the jaw on the previous evening, as Jack sat in a restaurant on Forty-fourth Street. Evidently, to judge by the absence of facial wounds, Pfefer had been able to fall down before being seriously damaged, but it wasn't the blow that had hurt—it was the insubordination the blow had implied. "A wrestler should hit a promoter!" Jack wailed. "Because they don't like me, those loafers are breaking the wrestling business down to little pieces!" The chief reason for the bitterness between Pfefer and his rivals is his agreement with the Athletic Commission that wrestling is a form of show business. "A honest man can sell a fake diamond if he says it is a fake diamond, ain't it?" he yelled, appealing to me. "Only if he says it is a real diamond he ain't honest. These loafers don't like that I say wrestling is all chicancery—hookum, in other words."

There are three small rooms in Pfefer's suite of offices. While he was telephoning to a couple of city editors who, he felt, had underplayed the news of the assault upon him, I went into one of the outer rooms and talked to two wrestlers who were sitting there. They were looking at their own pictures in a copy of *Ring*. Both of them were in their middle twenties, a couple of solid young men wearing slacks and sports shirts. Both had the fantastically mangled ears which mark their trade. They were heavily tanned, because, one of them explained, they were living at Coney Island for the summer and exercised on the beach every morning. One introduced himself as the Italian Sensation. He came from up Boston way, he said, and had started wrestling ten years ago in the Cambridge Y.M.C.A. "The girls like these ears," he said self-consciously. The other wrestler, blond and jolly-looking, said he was the Mighty Magyar. He came from St. Louis and had begun wrestling in a boys' club there. "Both my parents were born in Hungary, though," he said.

People of foreign birth provided the chief support for wrestling during the pre-Londos era, before the general public became interested. It was a popular form of vicarious suffering in Europe before boxing was known there. Now that the public has abandoned the industry, it again depends largely on the foreign-born, and to excite the small clubs a performer must claim some European affinity. "You can't get rich wrestling nowadays," the Mighty Magyar said, "but you can afford to drive a car." After a while the boys went out to eat. I was to see both of them wrestle later in the evening.

Not long after the Italian Sensation and the Mighty Magyar left, Pfefer said it was time to start for Ridgewood. Al Mayer, Pfefer's factotum and publicity man, came with us. Mayer, a short, plump man with graying hair and mustache, carried a large framed picture of a wrestler named King Kong, the Abyssinian Gorilla Man, which was to be hung in the lobby in Ridgewood. The picture restored Pfefer's spirits. "Look at him," he said to me, pointing to King Kong with his cane, "a great funny maker!" King Kong wears a full black beard, and the picture showed him in a kind of regal robe, with a crown on his head, looking a little like Haile Selassie. "He's a Greek," Pfefer said, "but during the Fiopian war I made him for a Fiopian." We took the B.M.T. under the Times Building and rode down to Union Square. En route, I asked Jack how the wrestlers knew who was supposed to win each bout. Jack Curley used to evade this question with a grin. Mr. Pfefer, however, is forthright. "I tell them," he said. "I treat them like a father, like a mother beats up her baby. Why should I let some boys be pigs, they should want to win every night yet?"

Pfefer said that the Italian Sensation, whom I had met in the office, was to wrestle in the feature event of the evening against a fellow known as the German Superman. They would divide ten per cent of the house, which on a warm night like this would probably mean twenty-five or thirty dollars for each of them. In the next show, Jack said, they would both wrestle in preliminaries, while two other members of the troupe appearing in preliminaries tonight would meet in the feature attraction. Performers in supporting bouts receive ten dollars each, a minimum fixed by the Athletic Commission. A wrestler working five nights a week, including one feature exhibition, can count on about sixty-five dollars. Ridgewood is a neighborhood where a great many German-Americans live, so the card for the evening stressed the Axis powers. Besides the German Superman, the program listed a German Apollo and a German Blacksmith, and in addition to the Italian Sensation, it included a Hollywood Italian Moving-Picture Star and an Italian Idol. Pfefer, Mayer, and I changed to the Canarsie line of the B.M.T. at Union Square, and as we walked down the ramp connecting the two platforms a big shirt-sleeved fellow rushed up to Pfefer and squeezed his arm. "Hollo, Jack!" he shouted. "Got work for me soon?" Pfefer told him to drop around to the office. The promoter explained that the big fellow was the Siberian Wolf, who now had a job in a Brooklyn shipyard but liked to pick up extra money at his old trade. Pfefer and Mayer left me at the door of the Ridgewood Grove Arena, a low, widespread, wooden building, and I walked over to a German saloon on St. Nicholas Avenue and had my supper.

When I returned, the crowd was beginning to arrive at the Grove. Most of the men were in shirt sleeves, and about half of them wore stiff straw hats. They moved forward heavily, with the experienced air of men going to church on Sunday and prepared to criticize the sermon. There were a good many women with them, most of them shapeless and wearing house dresses.

Pfefer had given me a working-press ticket, which calls for a seat directly at the ringside. The ushers looked surprised when I sat down there. No newspaperman had covered a wrestling show at the Grove for years. The only other person in the first row at my side of the ring was one of the judges, an old boxing referee whose legs have gone bad. Although the Athletic Commission concedes that wrestling exhibitions are not contests, it insists on the presence of two licensed judges and an inspector, as well as a referee and a doctor. The referee gets fifteen dollars and the others ten dollars each.

The first exhibition brought together the Polish Goliath, a vast and bulbous youth who, according to the announcer, weighed 310 pounds, and the Italian Idol, a strongly built fellow weighing a mere 195. As soon as the Goliath appeared, wearing a dingy bathrobe with a Polish eagle sewn on the back, the crowd began to boo. This was partly because he had such an advantage in weight and partly because of Poland's anti-German foreign policy. When the bout began the Italian Idol clamped an arm lock on the Goliath's left arm and started to twist it. The Goliath contorted his face in a simulation of agony. A fellow in the crowd shouted to the Italian Idol, "Break it off!" Soon the rest of the audience took up the chant, "Break it off! Break it off!" The Italian Idol seemed to put a great deal of pressure on the arm, but when the Goliath merely waved his wrist the Idol not only lost the hold but fell flat on his back. From what I could recollect of a few painful experiments in college wrestling, this seemed a remarkably easy way to break a hold, but it convinced a man behind me. "Jeez, he's strong!" the man exclaimed in an awed tone. I could hear variations of the same comment all over the hall. But the Pole seemed as stupid as he was powerful. He just stood there glaring at the prostrate Idol instead of pouncing on him. Then he turned to the audience, raised one fat fist, and solemnly thumped it against his nearly hairless chest. The crowd exploded in fury, booing and whistling. The Goliath turned toward the Idol and waddled slowly forward. He put his feet together and made as if to jump on the Idol. The Italian wriggled out of the way and got to his feet, and the referee, a lively young man, shook a finger warningly at the Goliath. The putative Pole demanded loudly, "What's the matter with that?" He said it in good clear Brooklynese, for, as I later learned, he is a native of South Brooklyn. But the crowd, convinced in spite of their own ears that a Polish Goliath talks with an outlandish accent, shouted back mockingly, "Vot's der mottur vit dot?"

While the Goliath was talking to the referee, the Italian Idol, miraculously revitalized, rushed across the ring and butted his opponent in the rear. The Goliath fell partly through the ropes. When he disentangled himself, he turned to the referee. "Why don't you watch that, ref?" he bellowed. The fans shouted in unison, "Vy don't you votch dot, ref?" It was a kind of litany. The wrestlers repeated the arm-lock routine three times, and then the Goliath got both arms around the Idol's head, pulled him forward and pushed his head down. The Goliath's face reflected an ogreish pleasure. The Idol stamped as if in acute pain. I looked up under the ropes and saw the Idol's face, which was invisible to the crowd. He was laughing. The sympathetic fans shouted, "Referee! Referee! Strangle hold!" One fellow screamed, "We had a good referee here last week, you butcher!" Then the man behind me yelled, "Step on his feet!" The Italian Idol promptly stepped on the Pole's feet, and the Goliath let him go. One of the Goliath's most effective gestures for inciting boos was to stand back, place his hands on his large, womanish hips, and puff out his chest and stomach. Another was to put his left hand on the Italian's right ear and then, with his right hand, twist his own left thumb. This looked as if he were twisting the Idol's ear off. After about fifteen minutes of such charades, the Goliath grabbed the Idol by the hair on top of the head and threw him over his left shoulder. I thought the Idol must have cooperated in this maneuver, but the crowd took it literally. The Idol lay as if stunned, and the Goliath fell on him. The referee slapped the Goliath on the back to signify victory. The fans booed angrily, but there was a note of anticipation in their howls, as if they knew that sooner or later they would have the pleasure of seeing the Goliath ground in the dust. In the meantime they would continue to come to the shows whenever he was billed.

The principals in the second exhibition were the Irish Wild Man and the German Apollo. In some neighborhoods, Irish athletes are presented in an endearing light, but not in Ridgewood. This was immediately apparent when the Irish Wild Man refused to shake hands with the German Apollo before they came to grips. The man behind me yelled, "Make it short and snappy, Fritz! He wouldn't shake hands with you!" The Wild Man, a stocky fellow with a considerable paunch, evidently had been in the navy or a side show, for he was almost covered with tattooing. Soon after the bell rang he hit the Apollo on the jaw with his fist and knocked him down. From my seat, I could see that the blow had really landed on the Wild Man's own left hand, which he had carefully placed on the Apollo's neck before swinging his right. The crowd booed frantically, because hitting with the fist is a foul. The Apollo got up, staggering. The Wild Man knocked him down again, with a terrific blow that missed him. The referee intervened and held the raging Wild Man away while the Apollo got up and walked around the ring, apparently in quest of consciousness. Then, when the referee turned the Wild Man loose, the Apollo hit the villainous Irishman a ferocious punch on the breastbone. The Wild Man went down with a crash, which he produced by kicking the mat with his heels. The fans shouted triumphantly. "How do you like that, you mick?" the man behind me cried.

When the Wild Man got up he immediately started to run away from the Apollo, who followed him relentlessly. Every time the Wild Man got into a corner of the ring, he would turn and hold both arms wide, as if disclaiming evil intent. Occasionally he would hold out his hand to shake, but the Apollo, who played his role straight, would disdain the proffered clasp. Then the Wild Man would jump out of the ring and stay outside the ropes until the referee argued him into returning. The referee pleaded with the Apollo, who finally nodded a majestic forgiveness. The Wild Man held out his hand again in friendship, and the guileless German reached to grasp it. Instantly the Wild Man hit him on the jaw again. I saw his fist pass behind the Apollo's head, but anyway the German fell down. The Wild Man loosed a peal of depraved laughter and then started to kick the Apollo's prone form. The Apollo sat up moaning and rubbing his groin. A lynching seemed imminent. Suddenly the Apollo, galvanized by righteous anger, jumped up, seized the Wild Man by the head, and threw him down. Then he began to twist the Wild Man's left foot, to the accompaniment of a cadenced chant of "Break it off!" in which all the lady spectators joined with shrill fervor. The Irish Wild Man rolled his eyes and groaned, rather incongruously, "Ach! Ach!" He pounded the mat with his hands, but got no sympathy. Shortly afterward the Apollo pinned the Wild Man's shoulders to the mat, amid hosannas of Teutonic triumph. Mr. Pfefer had slid into a seat beside me and was observing the Wild Man's *moues* with the intent appreciation of a McClintic watching a Cornell.

"A nice boy, the Wild Man," the promoter said as the Irishman climbed down from the ring, shaking his fists at the crowd. "He got five children, and he's so good he couldn't hurt a fly on the wall. But in the ring he acts like a wildcap. He is a good villain, the dope. In every match must be a hero and a villain or else a funny maker. The villains and the funny makers are the hardest ones to develop."

Both of my acquaintances of the afternoon, the Italian Sensation and the Mighty Magyar, appeared to fall within the hero category. The Magyar threw the Hollywood Italian Moving-Picture Star, a large gentleman who seemed to me a poor reflection of the Polish Goliath, employing the same comedy technique but less effectively. The Italian Sensation lost to the German Superman. Of all the wrestlers on the card, the Superman, a recent *émigré*, seemed the one most puzzled by the proceedings. When he grabbed the Sensation and the latter came off the floor as lightly as the woman in an adagio team, the Superman was obviously astonished. But he did the only thing feasible—he let the Sensation fall with a crash. This produced an impression of boundless strength. "He'll learn," Pfefer said. "He'll be someday a wonderful funny maker."

Earlier in the evening, I had turned around to look at the vociferous man in the row behind me, and had been surprised to recognize in him an outwardly cynical waiter from the Gaiety Delicatessen near Longacre

Square, a place I go to occasionally. As the principals in the final exhibition climbed into the ring, I stole another glance at the waiter. He was white with emotion, and his tongue protruded between his lips. He stared at the Abyssinian Gorilla Man with the horror that suggestible visitors to the Bronx Zoo reptile house sometimes show before a python. As the exhibition was about to begin, the waiter plucked at the arm of the man next to him. "That man's a murderer," he said. "I seen him wrestle before. It shouldn't be allowed—not with a human being."

The Gorilla's opponent in the closing turn was the German Blacksmith, a creamy-skinned, blue-eyed, and golden-haired youth who could have posed for an illustration in a Hitler primer. The Gorilla Man dragged this Aryan god toward the ropes and pretended to rub the Blacksmith's eyes out against the top strand. The referee tore the Gorilla Man from his prey. The Gorilla Man made a motion to strike the referee. The Blacksmith held his arm over his eyes. The fans expected to see a couple of bloody sockets when the arm dropped. But his eyesight had been miraculously preserved. The Gorilla Man treacherously extended his hand. The fans shouted, "No, no! Don't shake!"

The Gorilla Man then sneakily got behind the Nordic and began to strangle him. The referee made him release his unfair hold. The Blacksmith coughed desperately to indicate the degree of strangulation. The Gorilla Man grabbed him from behind again. It seemed unlikely that he understood the referee's English. He was an untrammeled savage. "Stop it!" my friend the waiter shrieked. "For God's sake, stop it!" The German did not seem to know what to do. Suddenly my friend had an idea. "Pull his whiskers!" he shouted. The German Blacksmith appeared to hear. He reached behind him and pulled at the Gorilla Man's long black beard. The Gorilla Man let out a wild scream and released his hold. He jumped up and down in the center of the ring clutching his whiskers. Then, with another shout, he leaped at the Blacksmith again and got another strangle hold. But now the fans had the answer. "Pull his whiskers!" they shouted joyfully. The Blacksmith pulled; the Gorilla danced and then took another hold. "Pull his whiskers!" came the chorus. The sequence was repeated four more times. At length the Blacksmith butted the Gorilla Man in the stomach. The latter fell down, still holding his whiskers, and the Blacksmith pinned his Graeco-Abyssinian shoulders to the mat. On the way to the nearest exit I caught up to my friend the waiter and greeted him. He looked at me a trifle sheepishly and said, "How did you like the show? I never take it serious." Mr. Pfefer, at my other elbow, said, "We did only about six hundred dollars, the bums."

CHICAGO: THE SECOND CITY

To R. R. McC.

Contents

FOREWORD

THE DAY after the first of my series of three pieces on Chicago appeared in *The New Yorker* I began getting letters from Chicagoans and people who had merely been there. The letters from the visitors, and from expatriates, were almost all favorable—those from people who were still there weren't. The most catamountainous of all came from the suburbs; the people who wouldn't live in the city if you gave them the place rose to its defense like fighters off peripheral airfields in the Ruhr in 1944.

There was for example the woman from Oak Park, Illinois, who wrote:

> If my old sainted grandmother, in her eighties, who having borne eleven children, reared them successfully to maturity, now spends her life in prayer and uncomplaining illness, had been brought upon a dias [*sic*] and examined dispassionately by a jury of casting directors I could not have been more dismayed or indignant.

All the letter-writers together found just two, or perhaps three, small factual errors, which I have signalized in the present book by footnotes in the appropriate places. The most considerable was that I had placed the Bahai temple in Evanston, the suburb just north of Chicago, when it was really in Wilmette, a mile farther on. But most of the objections were directed against the spirit of the reporting, which the objectors found too objective: *De mortuis nihil nisi bonum*, and "Don't cheer, men, the poor devils are dying," were the two main lines of rebuke. Both are too pessimistic, for Chicago is neither dead nor dying; it is, as the sideshow men say, "Alive, Alive—did you ever see a two-headed baby?"

("The gaff in that line," a sideshow man once told me—he happened to be a Chicagoan—"is that you don't say you got a live two-headed baby. You just ask them have they seen one." But this is a digression.)

Another kind of unobserved fire, thrown in my general direction, was the charge that I was a flitting viewer, writing about the place after a visit of a few weeks, days, or hours (according to the degree of indignation of the writer). The extreme example of this form of criticism I have preserved in a postcard from a lady named Swift. It bears the simple legend: "You were never in Chicago."[1]

But the fact is that I lived in Chicago for nearly a year in 1949–50 and went back to check up in May, 1951. So this isn't a between-trains job. I gathered a lot of material which I discarded; the report is packed down rather than built up, and I think it is exact, in the same sense as El Greco's picture of Toledo, not the one in Ohio. The suppressed detail would, if retained, merely have messed things up. I don't say it is as good as the El Greco, but Saul Steinberg has tried to bridge the gap with his illustrations.

The least easily answerable comment came via postcard from a man in Bergenfield, New Jersey, who had read the first section to appear in *The New Yorker*.

"Re Chicago:" the message read, "Okay, we give up, . . . who asked you?"

To which I can but rejoin, "Who asked Lemuel Gulliver or Marco Polo or Tocqueville or Sir John Mandeville or Abyssinian Bruce? Who asked Dam Trollope or Son Trollope, Birkbeck (who got to Illinois in 1817) or Mungo Park or William Dampier? In fact, what travel writer ever waited to be asked?"

Lest these precedents be thought insufficient, I invoke that of Colonel Robert Rutherford McCormick. Annually, or almost, the Colonel quits his atomic-bombproof eyrie in his Symphony in Stone, the Tribune Tower, to soar off into the Wild Blue Yonder on a mission of aerial reportage. From the places where he alights, the Colonel tells *Tribune* readers what the world outside looks like to him, generally pretty awful. The average time it takes him to cover a country is twenty-four hours. And if the Colonel can tell Chicago about the outside world, why can't a fellow from the latter tell the outside world about Chicago? To borrow a line from Judy Holliday, it's a free country.

Some of the letters I got, even from Chicago, took a more sympathetic turn. As one of these put it:

> It is, and most apparently so, that Chicago is not what it should or could be. It is not, however, in need of more bitter criticizing, rather in need of intelligent and honest aid at the front.
>
> I should like to know Mr. Lieblings true humanitarian capacity—if any!! It is hardly likely that he throws automobile tires at his wife, beats same, plus children,—nor would he, upon encountering a person of lowest circumstances,—"a beggar on the street" (New York version)—"a bum" (Chicago version, and quite the more vivid and descriptive term)—probably be captured with the near obsesion of just how he could further lead this be-beggared one into still further depths of any worse condition which might be possible to

[1] I replied with a quotation from "Take Back Your Mink": "It all seems a HORRIBLE DREAM."

bring about.—It is entirely enough that there are now, so many others, world wide, who are only too willing to trample any of the falling, hesitant, or be-clouded—without dwelling so long, hard and sarcasticly upon such an accumulance of dowdy and brutal remarks, which in the end, are certainly not much of a shock to anyone,—

Is Mr. Liebling forming a "Be Nasty to Chicago Club"??? Is he perhaps trying to gain followers—those who are also inclined towards sarcasium, slicing throats,— Or is he by some maddening theme—perhaps without knowing, himself endeavoring to inspire helpful people to action at the Chicago front!! If this is so and I almost entirely doubt such a pleasant ulterior motive, then I should adore to board the next plane possible and be first in line to tenderly and encouragingly grasp the hand of Mr. Liebling as he staggers (I hope) backward from reading such reactionaries as this one of many of which he must be in recipience daily!

Leave us not without exception, stamp on the discarded cigarette—if it is out, it's quite ridiculous.—

Sincerely,

A first emotional letter to the editors writer.

First-Emotional-Letter-To-The-Editors-Writer has divined, although with pardonable incredulity, the true intent of this report, which is kind. I stagger forward (I hope) to tenderly and encouragingly grasp his or her hand. His or her reactionary is most perceptive.

Even kinder was a man who might have claimed a just grievance, since he had to carry pounds of my prose on his daily rounds, as well as pay for his own copy.

"Mr. Liebling," he wrote, from an address far out on the North Side:

By this time no doubt you'll have batches of mail excoriating you for your series on Chicago. Well, here's one reader (subscriber) who finds little sniffishness in your pieces. . . .

I'm not a literary person; I don't know any writers or hang around book stores. I'm a mailman (we dislike *postman*—for the same reason editors sneer at *journalist*). Born here in '96, a few blocks from where the Chicago fire started in '71, I have lived here practically all my life, with the exception of about five years in New York and the East. So I can honestly cast my vote for your excellent reporting as a native son.

I have embodied a considerable amount of the more pertinent correspondence in my footnotes to this present text, and added a few of my own reactionaries to those of which I have been in recipience.

A. J. LIEBLING

1 / So Proud to Be Jammy-jammy

In the summertime, the Gold Coast of Chicago, that strip of opulent apartment houses and mansions along Lake Shore Drive, takes on some of the aspects of the streets leading from the Brighton Beach station of the B.-M.T. line out in coastal Brooklyn. Large numbers of bathing-suited inhabitants of the steamy interior of the city arrive by trolley at a point a couple of blocks from Lake Shore Drive, bearing beach balls, babies, lunch hampers, and fudgicles. Making their way through fine streets served by private garbage collectors (public collection is worse than irregular), the beachers pass under the marquees of buildings whose tenants drink water from which the chlorine taste of ordinary Chicago tap water has been filtered. (This service costs two dollars a month per apartment and is a more satisfactory solution of the taste problem, from a Gold Coast point of view, than having the city bring palatable water from afar for everybody, which would mean higher taxes.) The beachers do not come in automobiles, although a substantial proportion undoubtedly possess them. ("No Money Down, No Credit Standing Necessary. Even If You Have Been Blacklisted, See Me," Chicago second-hand dealers advertise.) They would find no place near the Drive to park. The streets are bordered with "No Parking, By Order of the Police Department" signs, which are obtained from the office of a city alderman at the rate of eleven dollars a year and insure that any man who pays for one will always have a place to park his car. The beachers go through a tunnel under the Drive and emerge on a strip of concrete and sand. The sun is strong even in June, when the water is still paralyzingly cold. Lying on their backs, the beachers gaze out at the great empty surface of Lake Michigan, and the girls compare the discolorations of their legs. When they turn over on their bellies, they are able to look back at what skyline Chicago has to offer—a serrated wall of high buildings aligned along the lakeward side of the city. One among them is the Tribune Tower, a Gothic skyscraper equipped with a carillon of editorial tocsins.[1] So viewed, Chicago seems a big city instead of merely a large place.

[1] I am informed by two correspondents that the Tower, though one of the serrated wall of buildings, all right, is not visible from the Gold Coast Beach, being concealed by a curve in the shoreline. I have not been back to check.

But the beachers are not fooled. They know that what they see is like a theatre backdrop with a city painted on it. Immediately behind the precise middle of the palisade of tall buildings lies the Loop, a rectangle only seven blocks long and five wide, holding most of the major stores, theatres, and big hotels and office buildings, as well as the financial district, components of a city that in Manhattan are strung out from Central Park South to the Battery, a good five miles, and in London from Albert Hall to the Tower, about the same. The Loop, with its lakeside screen, forms a unit like the Kremlin as described by Richard Harding Davis when he attended the coronation of Nicholas II, in 1896—a small city surrounded by a boundless agglutination of streets, dramshops, and low buildings without urban character. The Loop is like Times Square and Radio City set down in the middle of a vast Canarsie. Moreover, the façade is no more functional than a billboard turned away from the road; it might impress travellers if they approached the city from the Lake, but nobody does. The stranger arrives by car from the airport, approaching the Loop across a tundra of industrial suburbs unchanged in character by the city line, or else comes in on one of the railroads that run through slums of their own making. The railroad tracks are the cords that hold the Chicago Gulliver supine. They crisscross the town in a kind of ticktacktoe game in which the apparent object of each line is to stop its competitors from getting out of town. Thus the Baltimore & Ohio, connecting the city with the East, has been obliged to head due west for five or six miles to find a chink to slip through.

This Chicago is not like the one I used to visualize in my provincial East Coast youth, but it is certainly less alarming. My first intimations of Chicago were missionary and literary, and made me feel I could do without it. When I was about eleven, a boy of around my age moved with his parents from Chicago to the town on the south shore of Long Island where I lived. He was an enthusiastic Boy Scout, and he used to tell me and other uninterested Long Island boys about the fine boulevards and parks they had in Chicago. He also said the aquarium was a lulu. The football pennants tacked to the walls of his room bore exotic names, such as Northwestern, Iowa, and Purdue, instead of names everybody knew, like Yale, Columbia, and Rutgers. That same year, my mother gave me a ten-volume set of Kipling for my birthday, and I read straight through it. The volume that contained "Wee Willie Winkie," "Baa Baa, Black Sheep," and "The Drums of the Fore and Aft" (which, I decided on reading them, were the three greatest short stories ever written) also contained "American Notes"—correspondence describing a voyage the author had made to the United States in 1889. Of Chicago, my new idol had written, "Having seen it, I urgently desire never to see it again. It is inhabited by savages. Its water is the water of the Hooghly, and its air is dirt. Also it says that it is the 'boss' town of America. I do not believe that it has anything to do with this country." Kipling caught Chicago at possibly its most terrifying moment. The census of 1890 showed that it had displaced Philadelphia as the second city of the United States, and it was preparing to go right through the roof.

It was considerably later, when I was a college senior, that I again thought of Chicago. There was some kind of literary revolution going on there. All the prose coming out of the place was highly carbonated. I read a book called "Midwest Portraits," by Harry Hansen, about this Chicago literary *Spritzer*, a book that Laurence Stallings had reviewed in the New York *World* under what I thought the side-splitting heading "Write 'Em, Cowboy." (Stallings, a native of Georgia, was evidently under the influence of the common illusion that it is in the Far West. In reality, it is in the easternmost third of the continent.) Among the chapter headings were "Carl Sandburg, Poet of the Streets and of the Prairie," "Sherwood Anderson, Corn-fed Mystic, Historian of the Middle Age of Man," "Robert Herrick and Edgar Lee Masters, Interpreters of Our Modern World," "Harriet Monroe, Priestess of Poetry," and "Ben Hecht, Pagliacci of the Fire Escape."

Until 1938, however, I never got to see Chicago, although I had by then met the Pagliacci of the Fire Escape, who had moved to Nyack, and Hansen himself, who was doing a book column for the New York *World-Telegram*. Among the places I had seen were Angers, Funchal, Cappoquin, Youghal, Spitzbergen, and Gevrey-Chambertin, but I hadn't been west of Buffalo. By 1938, the Chicago literary revolution had ceased, except for parting bursts from the tail guns of angry young novelists flying East. The writers left behind them the question of whether what had been written about the place had ever actually existed—for example, Sandburg's city "with lifted head singing so proud to be alive and coarse and strong and cunning." From all reports, the place was still reasonably coarse, but the pride and the singing had been muted. And instead of "laughing even as an ignorant fighter laughs who has never lost a battle," Chicago wore a grin that might have indicated punch-drunkenness.

There is an opinion, advanced by some men who worked in Chicago transiently during the twenties, as well as by many native Chicagoans, that the city did approximate the great, howling, hurrying, hog-butchering, hog-mannered challenger for the empire of the world specified in the legend, but that at some time around 1930 it stopped as suddenly as a front-running horse at the head of the stretch with a poor man's last two dollars on its nose. What stopped it is a mystery, like what happened to Angkor Vat. There are only theories, most of them too materialistic to satisfy me, such as "Sam Insull took this town for all it had" and "The depression hit this town a wallop it never shook off."[2] Some skeptics have

[2] A woman with a plaintive voice, calling me on the telephone after this appeared, dated Chicago's decline from the day Jane Addams boarded the Henry Ford peace ship in 1916. The intellectual life, as well as the social conscience, of Chicago, centered on Jane Addams and Hull House in the years before World War I, the woman said.

their own explanation of the disparity between the Chicago of the rhapsodists and the Chicago of today. It is that the rhapsodies were merely the result of mutual suggestion, like the St. Vitus's Dance epidemics of the Middle Ages. There may be some truth in that theory, too. "It was a wonderful place when I was a kid," a fellow who writes a column on foreign affairs for a Chicago paper once told me. "Guys would be shot down every day on the busiest street corners. It was romantic." He admitted, when I put the direct question that he personally had not seen anybody shot, but I sensed that he did not like to acknowledge this, even to himself. (I might as well have asked a Charleston lady how she knew that everybody in the South had been rich before 1860.) Mary Garden says that in 1910 she found in Chicago a great audience and almost unlimited backing for grand opera in French. There is some tangible support for these reminiscences of the Grande Epoque—in the files of the Chicago *Tribune*, for instance, and in the existence of the now silent Civic Opera House. The *Tribune* in the twenties used to print daily on its editorial page a "Program for Chicagoland," of which Article 1 was "Make Chicago the First City of the World." Now it doesn't bother.

When I first got to Chicago, in November, 1938, I didn't even know that anything had changed. I was simply relieved to find in the city neither the newness nor the briskness that I dislike and that I had been led to expect. The Midwestern friendliness that I had been warned I would have to put up with was well dissimulated by the airport personnel. Seen from the taxi, on the long ride in from the airport, the place looked slower, shabbier, and, in defiance of all chronology, older than New York. There was an outer-London dinginess to the streets; the low buildings, the industrial plants, and the railroad crossings at grade produced less the feeling of being in a great city than of riding through an endless succession of factory-town main streets. The transition to the Loop and its tall buildings was abrupt, like entering a walled city. I found it beguilingly medieval.

I first noticed something like what I had been warned to expect when I reached, on a thoroughfare called Ashland Avenue, a point near which the city begins to look like a city. The street there is lined with bizarre stone houses that were once family residences, but of what class I have

---

Miss Addams's pacifism destroyed her prestige, consequently that of her whole group. Momentum carried some of the writers through the early twenties, and then they dispersed, having nothing to hold them together.

A couple of weeks later I had a letter from a writing friend. "Many years ago I made Chicago my home for a little more than a year," he wrote, "having left college to do social work in what was then still Jane Addams's town. And during that period I saw Chicago through the eyes of the Dell-Anderson-Masters-Sandburg-Monroe coterie. They were at the white heat of their creation in a town that was momentarily blessed with greatness. As the years have passed by my Chicago Dream has faded slowly but steadily."

The stranger on the telephone may have had something.

never been able to decide. They aren't mansions, but they aren't smack up against each other, either, and most of them have little spires and turrets that make them look all the more desolate now, like a bedraggled old woman in the remains of a spirited hat. The first you strike as you come from the airport have Negro tenants, who bulge out of the windows and spill down the stoops. The last are given over to far shabbier whites. On a street corner along Ashland Avenue, I noticed a large sign proclaiming, "Chicago has the finest system of boulevards and parks in the world." That sounded to me like the Boy Scout with the Purdue pennant. This form of civic self-approbation is not extinct in Chicago. A huge sign on Michigan Boulevard reads, "This is the Magnificent Mile. It is lined with the most beautiful buildings and the finest and most luxurious shops in the World." Such vestiges of the old spirit, like the *Tribune*'s unchanging subtitle, "The World's Greatest Newspaper," are regarded by the inhabitants with the same kind of affection they bestow upon the old Water Tower, which survived the Fire of 1871. They are links with the plangent past. "Heiress of all the ages, she stands in the foremost files of time," the *Tribune* editorialized about Chicago in 1893.

A thing about Chicago that impressed me from the hour I got there was the saloons. New York bars operate on the principle that you want a drink or you wouldn't be there. If you're civil and don't mind waiting, they will sell you one when they get around to it. Chicago bars assume that nobody likes liquor, and that to induce the customers to purchase even a minute quantity, they have to provide a show. Restaurateurs, I was to learn, approach the selling of food from the same angle. The Porterhouse, a restaurant in the Hotel Sherman, when I last looked in on it, had six cowboy violinists in fringed pants to play "Tales from the Vienna Woods" at your table in order to sell you a hamburger, and the menu listed credits for costume and scenic design. The urge to embellishment found literary outlet in the listing of things to eat, such as:

> Ah, the PORTERHOUSE! Aristocrat of steaks . . . most delectable of steaks. Greatest of all the steaks, for within it are encompassed the Tenderloin, the Sirloin, the meaty bone of the full loin. Small wonder that in this fabulous steak, ERNEST BYFIELD found inspiration for the name of the last . . . and the finest room he was to conceive!
>
> Carved from vintaged corn-fed beef, your PORTERHOUSE is broiled under a high heat that seals in the flavor-giving juices . . . sears the rich fat to a crispy-edged succulence. Specify to your Captain the precise degree of "doneness" you require—and tell him, too, whether you wish it to be graced with garlic's subtle savor.

One of the more modest items on the menu was "Chuck Wagon Beef Stew, Sautéd Julienne of Beef Tenderloin in Hot Sour Cream Sauce with Rice." Walking through a cocktail lounge and into another dining room in the Sherman, known as the Well of the Sea, I was handed a bill of fare proposing "Bahama Conch Chowder with Barbados Rum, said to be a favorite soup of Ernest Hemingway, believed by the natives of the Bahama Islands to promote virility and longevity" and "Scallops in Season: Called St. James Shells in England. Says Elliot Paul, 'Cleverest and most tasty of Mollusks.'" The Sherman menu writer is in the great tradition of a Chicago restaurateur named Dario Toffenetti, who opened a New York *succursale*, where, in season, he sells "Autumnal Pumpkin Pie in an Avalanche of Whipped Cream."

The smallest bars provide an organist or a pianist or two organists or two pianists, or a pianist and an organist back to back, both backs, if female, bare to the coccyx. The musicians work on a small dais behind the bottles. Places slightly larger furnish a singer and a comedian, as well. Their art makes conversation impossible, but on my first visit to Chicago I had no one to talk to anyway, so I found it a pleasant custom. It wasn't until I went back later and made some friends in the city that I learned to long for the sociable quiet of a New York bar, in which you can snarl at your companions without having to use a microphone.[3]

The Chicago bars also employ blondes known as dice girls, who stand behind small green baize layouts and keep score on customers attempting a ten-dice game called Twenty-Six. In this game, you try to roll any number from one to six twenty-six times or better in thirteen tries, the odds against such an achievement, according to experts, being slightly less than five to one. The customary bet is a quarter, but you can play higher. If you win, the house pays four to one, which gives it a seventeen-percent edge. This is about the same as the take of the parimutuel machines in New York State. The bar, however, pays its four to one in trade, on which there is a profit of perhaps three hundred per cent. One of my most astute Chicago friends, a native, is sure the girls can control the dice with magnets. I do not believe this for a minute, but it illustrates the working of the Chicago mind. It is inconceivable to my friend that the house should be content with the monumental advantage it already has. Yet he plays the game steadily, mostly in bars around the Loop. He loves that grim rectangle, bound in its iron crown of elevated-railroad tracks, and says that during the war, when he was overseas and he thought of Chicago, it was always of the Loop in the rain, with the sound of the low-pitched, bisyllabic police whistles, like sea birds' cries.

I began my investigation of Chicago's saloons the first evening I spent in the city, and wound up by wandering out from the center of the Loop along a street called West Madison, which resembles a Bowery of a more raucous sort than the one we know. Toward the end of my run, I found myself in an area where whiskey was two shots for a quarter—and the entertainment was more copious than ever. I have never heard "Mexicali Rose" sung so well as that night on West Madison Street. I arrived back

[3] Of late, television has been cutting into the number of good snarling spots, even here.

in my hotel filled with that tranquil satisfaction that follows a revel in a strange town, in which nobody will turn up next day to remind you how dull you were.

The following afternoon, I went out to Sportsman's Park, which was—and is—a half-mile race track, such as one would expect to find at a county-fair meeting. Because hardly anybody will risk a good horse on such short turns, the long spring and fall meetings there attract a class of stables usually seen only in places like Puerto Rico (among the winners last year was a horse just off a successful campaign at Raton, New Mexico), and the size of the purses and the grade of the jockeys are scaled to the class of competition. Only the crowds and the betting pools are city-size; there is no other racing in Chicago while Sportsman's is in operation. A year or so ago, the track auditor, a man named Hugo Bennett, testified before the Kefauver Committee that he had lent eighty thousand dollars of the track's funds to Paul (The Waiter) Ricca, for no special reason. Ricca is reputedly a gangster with power to influence the awarding of racing dates. Edward J. O'Hare, the first president of Sportsman's, was shot and killed on the street in 1939. The track was built originally for greyhound racing and scaled to dogs rather than horses. The gyp (for gypsy) horsemen who race there now are small owners trying to win their living in purse money and from clients who will pay for a tip. Half the horses, in my time, apparently spent race mornings with all four feet in tubs of numbing ice. Few horses are worked under saddle at Sportsman's, for fear they will break down; they are "ponied," which means that a mounted man gets out in front of them and gallops them on a lead line. To bear up under a jockey's inconsiderable weight for the duration of a race once a week is about all the trainers expect of their steeds.

Sportsman's is beyond the city line, in Cicero, a town devoted to the cult of Al Capone, who did much to put it on the map. Cicero looks no more or less sinister than any other Passaic—tarpaper roofs, frame dwellings flaking paint, and beer signs. It was in a saloon there one evening that I met a wonderful woman with a gift for capsule autobiography. She was the daughter of a Lithuanian saloonkeeper, and was flanking her father behind the bar when I stopped in. The bar was on the ground floor of their house and had surely been a home-brew or needle-beer joint before repeal came and they opened the front door. "I was once married to a rich man who manufactured printing ink," this lady told me. "But he was always too potst. So I came home to Dad."

In the barbershop at Sportsman's one morning, I saw a colored man cornered by another, whom he had pretended skillfully but unsuccessfully not to see. "How come you haven't been around since you hit that daily double?" the interceptor said. "You used to be so jammy-jammy with me." I never say potst or jammy-jammy without thinking of a city with lifted head, singing.

* * *

The second time I visited Chicago was in the early spring of 1941. My purpose in going there then was to talk with General Robert E. Wood, chairman of the board of Sears, Roebuck, and with a young man named Robert Douglas Stuart, Jr., son of a vice-president of Quaker Oats. They were chairman and national director, respectively, of the America First Committee, an organization devoted to keeping the United States from aiding Great Britain in her war effort. This was also the official line of the Communist Party, for the Soviets and the Third Reich were still jammy-jammy, but there was no reason to suspect America First of Leninism. General Wood looked more like a general than most generals get to look, somewhat resembling Warren Gamaliel Harding. He was also even more positive than most generals get to be, and told me that a German victory could not possibly endanger the United States, then as naked of armament as a garden worm. The General had served in the Quartermaster Corps during the First World War and he knew. He expressed no concern over what a German victory would mean to Europe; he considered preoccupation with any country other than America treasonable. He said the Eastern seaboard didn't represent America, whose rich, red heart, he let me understand, beat within the walls of the Chicago Board of Trade Building, on the eighteenth floor of which we sat talking, in the America First offices.

General Wood was obviously a decent man, but he gave me a feeling of remoteness from the world I knew that was even stronger than the one I had had in Franco Spain the day I crossed the French frontier after Pétain asked for the armistice of 1940. The Spanish civilians at least could understand from their own experience the meaning of conquest. The national director, nearly forty years the General's junior, was even more disquieting, because, despite his youth, he was equally assured. All things, national and international, were manifest to the manufacturers of overalls and breakfast cereals, and the America First letterhead showed that the General and the oatlet had behind them the man who made Spam and a man who made steel and a man who had investments in salt, teletype machines, and wristwatches. As intellectual reference, they offered Robert Maynard Hutchins, the president of the University of Chicago.[4]

After we entered the war, I have been told, Chicago was gloriously

[4] General Wood has a Winnetka lady fan who wrote to me:

> Your affinity for truth reminds me of Mister Truman's affinity for integrity. Since you second-guess, with such moral righteousness, our General Wood [she must have been in the Quartermaster Corps] you evidently were and are convinced that other peoples' welfare is commensurate with our own. [Author's note—I had always thought that accepted Christian doctrine.] And that "America First" is either morally evil or politically impractical. An amazing conclusion from one who labels himself a "New York City first" advocate.— New York: Pinnacle of Culture . . . Phonies . . . and All The News That's Fit to Print. It never ceases to scratch your bloated pomposity, does it, that Chicago publishes the World's Greatest Newspaper? [The Chicago *Tribune.*]
>
> Besides evoking the above thoughts, your article inspired little regard for

hospitable to service men and at least as bellicose as any other city in the country where people were making money hand over fist. But I could not understand why what was so plain, in the spring of 1941, in New York and Washington and Lisbon and London should be so bitterly denied by so large a segment of the dominant group in this particular city and region. They appeared to live in a pressurized cabin, unaffected by the weight of the outside air. It was not until long afterward that I began to think I understood those men. As much as any unreconstructed Confederates, the mail-order giants and puffed-fluff kings have found themselves the leaders of a lost cause. Their personal fortunes may be great, but the world has not gone as they willed it. Chicago's bid for grandeur has failed, and they remain permanently dissident; whatever happens anywhere else is wrong. As a matter of fact, most of the men who think of themselves as leaders have, physically, abandoned the city out of office hours, and so have most of their assistants. The relatively small white-collar population converges daily on the Loop by rail and at night leaps over the surrounding sprawl of city wards—dreary clusters of frame houses and factories—to go home to suburbs like Oak Park, to the west, and Evanston, to the north. Upper- and lower-middle groups commute together, leaving behind them each night the exiguous skyscraper core and the vast, anonymous pulp of the city, plopped down by the lakeside like a piece of waterlogged fruit. Chicago after nightfall is a small city of the rich who have not yet migrated, visitors, and hoodlums, surrounded by a large expanse of juxtaposed dimnesses.[5]

---

your accuracy and perception. You grazed, sans insight, the periphery. [This, apparently, refers to Winnetka's geographical position re Chicago.]

A friend of Mr. Stuart's wrote: "I saw a great deal of Bob Stuart in Lake Forest throughout 1941. We argued America First by the hour. He was in my home for Sunday lunch when the news of Pearl Harbor came over the radio. He was in the army within forty-eight hours."

I hadn't thought of the young man since 1941, but it seems to me that his prompt enlistment only pointed up the contrast between reality and the world-picture that the America Firsters tried to impose—like a new breakfast food. And I wasn't second-guessing in 1951, or first-guessing in 1941. I didn't have to guess, because I had spent the first year of World War II in France and knew. Wood and Stuart were guessing. General Wood also assured me that for logistic reasons the United States Army could play no decisive role in a war on the continent of Europe, and I am to assume therefore, I suppose, that everything I saw happen there, beginning on the morning of June 6, 1944, never occurred at all because it was impossible.

[5] This is a sensitive point with the migrators. Dr. Hutchins, leaving the University of Chicago for a job with the Ford Foundation, recently emptied *his* tail guns in a series of articles in the Chicago *Daily News*, and he wrote, among other things: "The leaders of Chicago business and professional life have moved to the suburbs. Nobody cares about Chicago."

This aroused an accredited local grandee named Holman D. Pettibone (I invent nothing), president since 1931 of the Chicago Title & Trust Company, and a past president of the Chicago Association of Commerce and Industry, to reply, on the first page of that publication: "In making this statement Dr. Hutchins conveys the impression that when a citizen takes up his residence in a suburb he loses all interest

By the time of my second visit, I knew at least one Chicago couple. They were a New York woman I had worked with on the old *World* and her husband, a Chicago man, who was employed by a textbook publisher. The city was marvellously dilapidated, they reported when I went to call on them. New York, in retrospect, seemed to the wife a kind of Spotless Town. Chicago was amusing for one year, she said, but after the arrival of the baby she was expecting, they would move to Evanston, which has a Bahai temple, Northwestern University, and no saloons.[6]

When I returned again to Chicago, in 1949, it was with the soon regretted design of settling down there for some time. So did various of Hakluyt's venturers, on one voyage sighting a coast afar and on a second putting ashore a boat's crew who shot an Indian with a gold ring in his nose, return a third time for a full-scale settlement, with women, hens, and demiculverins, only to perish of shipwreck, arrows, or malaria. On this voyage, I took with me a wife and stepdaughter, and by then I had a considerable circle of Chicago acquaintances—a psychiatrist, whom I had come to know in North Africa during the war, and his wife; a war correspondent, retired, and *his* wife; the textbook people, who had moved to the aseptic suburb of Evanston; and an assortment of others, whom my wife and I had met at cocktail parties in New York. A friend's friend had found for us, after weeks of intelligence work, a furnished apartment. (Housing was tighter in Chicago than even in Washington, we were informed.) We had abandoned a New York apartment, and it struck us that the one the Chicagoan had turned up for us was incomparably more elegant, though far less comfortable than the one we had left. It was on the Gold Coast, two short blocks from the Lake, in a building of which the upper floors command a lacustrine vista that increases rentals. Unfortunately, we were on a lower floor. It was a sixteen-story coöperative building with two apartments on each floor, and the woman just above us, with whom our landlord had left the key, said it was as friendly as an old-time boarding house. "All the apartments are laid out just alike," she told us, "and that makes it homey, because no matter whose apartment you're in, you know where everything is. Last New Year's Eve, eleven of us got together and gave a party in all our eleven apartments one above the other. One apartment was South American, with a rumba band, and another was Wild West, with a square-dance caller, and another French, with an accordionist, and you just took the elevator from one to another, and lay where you fell."

---

in Chicago; he fails to carry his share of public responsibility; he is some sort of a disloyal renegade. As a suburban resident, I disagree."

The fiercest epistolary defenders of Chicago live in places like Winnetka and Lake Forest.

[6] My Winnetka admirer and another woman have both signalized my dislocation of the Bahai temple. Northwestern is in Evanston, all right, but the Bahai temple is in the next town, Wilmette. No saloons are in both of them. "It happens to be in Wilmette, not Evanston, for all your erudite eastern enlightenment!" It is humiliating.

The woman across the hall was even friendlier. On being introduced, she suggested to my wife that after we had moved in, we leave our door on the latch and she would leave hers, so we could wander in and out like one big family. We ducked that one, and laid ourselves open to an imputation of Eastern snobbishness. It is uncertain, however, whether the woman wanted us to act upon her proposal. A transplanted Philadelphian we met later said that at his first Chicago parties everybody he met insisted they must get together again within a week. None ever called. "It's just a way of talking they have," he said. "I don't think they're very warm. They mix less than they say they will, and perhaps less than they think they do. They're not given to meeting friends in restaurants, which means that their social repertory is fixed by their facilities for entertaining. A family able to manage two dinners for six guests each every month, for instance, will soon find itself limited to friendship with six couples, for each couple will invite it back every month, and the next month it starts all over again. This means a snug schedule, and the only way to break it without making two enemies is to leave town."[7]

2 / *At Her Feet the Slain Deer*

WHEN I was in Chicago a couple of months ago, a friend of mine who lives out there and manufactures roulette wheels, craps layouts, wheels of fortune for carnivals, shuffleboard games, and juke boxes—he looks like Samuel Seabury and is considered an elder statesman of the amusement-devices business—told me a story about a simple fellow called Porky, whom the boys at Clark and Madison enlisted to shove synthetic di-

[7] This statement apparently aroused passionate resentment. One of my wife's best women friends in Chicago, while challenging little in the piece, wrote: "You know that everybody knows more than six couples." The woman in question, however, has a big house, and so have most of her friends. It is therefore probable that she maintains relations with seven couples, or eight if one husband and one wife are midgets.

I checked on this social impression with a man I met in Chicago last May, an outlander like myself, but engaged in business there. He said he had temporarily reversed the usual outward drift by moving his family back from a suburb into Chicago. (It had been easy for him because he was a hotel man. He could therefore shunt them around among vacant suites.) "We had to move in to get away from the little circuit of people we knew there," he said. "After a while we can move out to some other suburb and meet some other people it will take us a couple of years to get sick of. I figure there are enough suburbs to last us until the youngest kid goes away to college, and then my wife and I can move into a double and bath and pretend we're transients."

Because of this roundrobinnical social life, a family can live in any suburb and have as many friends as in the city itself, or in the city and know as few people as if it inhabited the smallest suburb. It eliminates one of the great pleasures of urban living and spreads boredom as evenly as cream cheese on a drugstore sandwich.

amonds. My friend's father was a successful gambler of the nineties who invested his savings in real estate and got cleaned out. To recoup his fortunes, he began manufacturing gambling equipment. His son carries on with the roulette and craps lines because they are a family tradition; he continues to turn out a well-balanced roulette wheel as an exercise in filial piety, for the real money now is in coarser ware. Chicago is the center of coin-machine manufacture, including coin-operated gambling games; it accounts for twenty per cent of the nation's total volume. "Most of our stuff is sold to fraternal organizations and churches," my friend says. "I always advise them to stay away from roulette and craps. They're hard games for amateurs to run, and a gambler might take them. What they want is a nice wheel of fortune with plenty of flash."

"It was around 1905," my friend began when he told me the Porky story. "Some guy in Germany had invented these rocks that would meet about every test for a natural diamond, except there was just something about them that would give them away to an expert. When they were mounted in rings, they were even harder to tell from the real thing. So the boys were unloading them on pawnbrokers. A pawnbroker takes a quick look at a ring, guesses it's worth around two hundred dollars, and offers to lend maybe fifteen on it. If he was going to buy it, it would make a difference exactly what the stone was worth, so he would size it up more closely. But he didn't think he was going to buy it. So one of the boys would walk into a hock shop as if he needed a stake in a hurry, leave the ring, take the fifteen, and never go back. When it became the pawnbroker's property, he would find the stone was worth seventy-five cents. Porky had the kind of dumb face that wouldn't make a broker suspicious, and the boys were trying to give him courage to go into this dodge. 'You can't hardly tell them from the real thing,' they were telling him, and giving him reasons why. 'Stop, fellows!' Porky says. 'I don't want to hear anything more. When I go into that store, I want to believe they *are* real.' "

My friend also told me how a fair-sized industry, the manufacture of the fruit-symbol slot machines known as one-armed bandits, was captured for Chicago. The first slot machines, he said, were electrically operated, and were always getting out of order. Then a machinist named Charlie Fey, in San Francisco, hit upon the notion of a machine that operated by gravity, and, using that principle, built the first fruit-symbol machine. He sold it to a saloonkeeper, and it made such a hit that he received more orders than he could fill working by himself in his basement shop. Fey got in touch with a manufacturer in Chicago, who agreed to make the machines for him. You can't patent a gambling device, but before sending the plans for his machine to the Chicago man Fey exacted a promise from the fellow that the first five hundred machines he produced would be shipped to him, as the inventor, in San Francisco, where he had orders for most of them. The Chicago manufacturer put the machine in production, and shipped the first five hundred to Fey, all right, but routed them by ordinary freight via his agents in Halifax, Tampa, Banff, Chattanooga, and a few dozen other places, and while they were en route, he sold the second, third, and fourth five hundred, a lot of them in California. Chicago has been the center of the one-armed-bandit business ever since.

Faith like Porky's and imaginative enterprise like the slot-machine manufacturer's are ingredients lacking in contemporary Chicago. When, in 1857, a Chicago *Tribune* editorialist wrote of this city, "The sign is still onward until the last rival in the race for greatness is left behind," the chances are he meant it. So, probably, did another *Tribune* man, who wrote, thirty-six years later, during the Columbian Exposition, "In her white tent like Minnehaha, the arrow maker's daughter, stood Chicago yesterday morning and gazed out on a sapphire lake, under a blue and cloudless sky, and her Hiawatha, her World Lover, came to her, and laid at her feet the slain deer, the tribute of universal admiration and love." At the world's feet, Chicago, in return, laid a butchered hog. The city was certified the third biggest in the United States by the census of 1880, and the second biggest by that of 1890, having more than doubled its population in the intervening decade. The figures were 503,000 in 1880 and 1,100,000 ten years later. Chicago's relative position has remained the same ever since; Los Angeles is now a serious threat to its hold on even second place.[1] The hopes for all-round preëminence, to come as an automatic bonus for being biggest, have faded, too. Still, the habit of purely quantitative thinking persists. The city consequently has the personality of a man brought up in the expectation of a legacy who has learned in middle age that it will never be his.

The kind of buccaneering drive that won the slot-machine industry for the city has been lacking since a date that is hard to fix definitely but that preceded the rise of the automobile. "Chicago could have had the automobile industry if Chicago money had gone out after it," a Chicago stockbroker assured me. "We're nearer than Detroit to both iron ore and coal, and we had the greatest supply of skilled and unskilled labor in America when Detroit was still a small city. But the big boys let it go by default; they didn't want an industry in here that would dwarf them. The

[1] The population of Chicago in 1940 was 3,396,000; of Los Angeles, 1,504,000. The census of 1950 showed Chicago with 3,606,000, a gain of about 6 per cent; Los Angeles with 1,957,000, a gain of 30 per cent. If population growth continues at these rates the two cities will be neck-and-neck in about twenty-five years. It isn't certain that Los Angeles will continue to grow that fast, of course. It was upon precisely such a calculation that the Chicagoans of 1890 based their hopes of overtaking London and New York.

Philadelphia, by the way, still clung to third place in 1950, with 2,064,000, a gain of 133,000 over 1940.

Chicago, as of today, is the seventh biggest city in the world, outranked only by London, New York, Shanghai, Tokyo, Berlin, and Moscow. It has a big edge over Paris in population.

arteries had already hardened." The financial community has accepted its secondary position. All the Midwest Stock Exchange aspires to, its president, James E. Day, told me, is a top minor-league rating, specializing in Midwestern issues of not quite national magnitude. Many stocks listed on the big board in Wall Street are also bought and sold on the Chicago exchange, of course, but it is like play away from the race track. When a Chicago corporation—International Harvester, for example—is so big that it is listed on the New York Stock Exchange, the New York volume of transactions in its shares exceeds the Chicago volume by as much as twelve to one. According to some Chicago businessmen with whom I have talked, the city's two great banks—the First National and the Continental—which flex their two-and-a-half-billion-dollar muscles in trade publications, no longer undertake ventures on the grand scale without the assent of the still biggest banks in the East. The old nineteenth-century dream of making Chicago a great port, from which ships would carry grain and ore direct to Europe, has subsided to such an extent that the *Tribune* last year editorially opposed the St. Lawrence Seaway scheme because it might bring a lot of foreign shipping to the Great Lakes. Foreign ships, the *Tribune* feared, might drive American lake steamers from the Canadian trade. From "Let me at him!" the city's cry has changed to "Hold him offa me!"

The collective sense of disappointment is evident in the utterances of the town's tutelary deity, Colonel Robert R. McCormick, the *Tribune*'s publisher. The Colonel was a youth in the era of the city's greatest expectations (he was born in 1880), and the few scores of millions of dollars that he has been able to add to the family fortunes since have been unable to reconcile him to his position as first citizen of a not-quite metropolis. Even the circulation of the New York *Daily News*, more than twice that of the *Tribune*, must annoy him sometimes with its constant reminder of status, although he inherited control of the *News* after the death of Captain Joseph Medill Patterson, his first cousin. It is too late for the Colonel to leave Chicago now. The office of tutelary deity is not elective. The god just sets himself up, and then starts pitching thunderbolts at anybody who laughs. Colonel McCormick hurls a delightfully reverberant thunderbolt, flavored with sassafras. When, for instance, the Montreal *Star* recently took exception to one of his dicta, the *Tribune* countered with an editorial headed "The Kicked Dog Howls," which read, in part, "The Montreal *Star*, howling like a kicked dog, has endeavored to reply to a radio speech by the publisher of the *Tribune* on Canada and Canadian-American relations. Since the *Star* could not reply with candor to his remarks on the efforts of the Union Nowers and Rhodes scholars to destroy the sovereignty of Canada along with that of the United States—because the *Star* is deeply involved in that movement—it adopted more devious tactics." I do not know whether the *Star*, itself no maiden's sigh, responded with an editorial headed "The Stuck Pig Squeals." The Colonel would not have blenched, in any case. He is accustomed to think of himself as the man most feared by the British Empire, which for him begins at the Hudson River.

The opportunity to view a tutelary deity should never be passed up by an explorer, so during the winter of 1949–50, while my wife and I were living in Chicago, I arranged to attend one of the weekly ceremonies at which the Colonel manifests himself to his people. These are the broadcasts of what is known as "The Chicago Theatre of the Air," from nine to ten every Saturday evening over WGN (for World's Greatest Newspaper), the *Tribune*'s radio station. They are put on in a broadcasting hall, which is sometimes also called the Chicago Theatre of the Air and adjoins the Tribune Tower, an example of Wedding-Cake Gothic that the Colonel considers the equal of the Taj Mahal, although to me it has a look of incompleteness. The architect, I have always thought, should have finished it off with a gigantic double scoop of ice cream, topped by an illuminated cherry.

Among Chicagoans of more than grade-school education, there is a disposition to deprecate the Colonel, just as in Periclean Athens there doubtless was an intellectual clique that made discreet jokes about owls. Some of the scoffers among my acquaintances in Chicago greeted my project of attending one of his séances with exclamations of disbelief, like New Yorkers learning that an out-of-towner wants to visit the Statue of Liberty. "I never read the *Tribune*," "I never believe anything I read in the *Tribune*," "I read the *Tribune* just for laughs," and "Colonel McCormick never wins an election" are four passwords used by enlightened Chicagoans to establish their affranchisement. The Colonel, nonetheless, has been the chief molder of the city since the nearly simultaneous, though unrelated, withdrawals of Al Capone and Samuel Insull, twenty years ago.

I was not to be dissuaded. Tickets for the broadcast, I was informed when I telephoned the radio station, must be applied for by mail at least four weeks in advance. I overcame this difficulty, which I had scarcely anticipated, by appealing to the WGN press agent. My surprise at the demand for seats arose because I had been preparing for the occasion by reading the texts of some of the Colonel's previous broadcasts, transcripts of which are available, free, to anybody who drops in at the Tribune Tower and asks for them. Most of the broadcasts were on historical topics, like "Nathanael Greene, Strategist," "John Paul Jones (I and II)," and "The Boston Massacre," not to be confused with the 1929 Saint Valentine's Day Massacre in Chicago. Others were on international affairs, such as the importance of the Panama Canal, where, Colonel McCormick told his WGN audience in 1947, he had caught Trygve Lie "spying out the land." The Colonel commented at that time, "I am glad it is not Henry Luce, who could spy it out just as well and not be so obvious." Colonel McCormick is an authority on espionage; his best script purely from the point of view of entertainment, I thought, was one entitled "Mata Hari's Innocence." It began: "Mata Hari has so long been known as a spy that it is too late to change her undeserved reputation. This is the truth of the matter." The climax of the truth of the matter was:

> Mata Hari also was tried as a spy. Malvy, reputed to be her lover, persuaded her not to confess or testify, saying he would take care of her. When she was convicted and condemned to death he again persuaded her not to confess or testify, guaranteeing that the guns of the firing squad would not contain bullets. He told her that as an actress she could fall as if dead, that she would be picked up and put into a coffin, and at the cemetery she would be transferred into an automobile and driven to Spain. The simple woman believed him. She went before the firing squad at the fortress of Vincennes. All of the rifles were loaded with bullets. She fell dead, was taken to the cemetery and buried. Her secret was buried with her and she has borne to this day the false accusation of being a spy.

Another script, apparently the Colonel's favorite, since he repeats it on an average of once every three months (the *Tribune* prints it in full each time, as it does all his broadcasts), was about the 1st Division, in which, I knew, he had served briefly in the First World War. The peroration went: "March on, then, First Division! March over the sunny hills of France; march thru the flaming towns of Picardy, up the shell-swept slopes of Lorraine, thru the gas-filled forest of Argonne—on to everlasting glory." I liked it, but I didn't think that anybody who had been in some other division would care to hear it more than once a season.

I soon learned that in assuming there would not be a capacity turnout to listen to such oratory I had underestimated the Colonel, an error into which it is easy to fall. Among other things, "The Chicago Theatre of the Air" presents condensed versions of musical shows like "The Student Prince" and "No, No, Nanette," and the Colonel's speeches are usually sandwiched in between the well-buttered slices of divertissement, so that to hear the second half of the show the studio audience has to sit through the homily.[2] The attraction on the evening I was to attend was Rudolf Friml's "The Vagabond King," running fore and aft of a talk by the Colonel on "The American Navy." "The Vagabond King," as you probably remember, is the musical comedy containing the song about "And to hell with BurgunDEE!" It tells how François Villon is made ruler of France for a day, after which he is to be executed, and how he saves France and wins a fair lady's hand and escapes unscathed.

The Chicago Theatre of the Air looks very much like the usual broadcasting studio, with a stage but no scenery, and a couple of hundred

[2] An anonymous Chicagoan, thinking I missed the point, typed on a postcard: "People don't listen to hear McCormick's asinine speeches. They want to hear Nancy Carr's singing. You know: music!"

comfortable seats, and it was full when I arrived there, a good fifteen minutes before the performance. My fellow-spectators in the audience were well-dressed, suburban-looking people (the system of application by mail allows the studio officials to pick guests with nice addresses), quite evidently grateful for the opportunity to see something resembling theatre without paying for it. There is, by the way, little opportunity to see theatre in Chicago even if you do pay for it. As a theatrical center, it is outclassed by Oslo, which has a population of four hundred thousand.

The members of the cast, in evening clothes of various degrees of formality, were seated about the stage—rabble of Paris and nobles of Louis XI's court dressed out of the same department stores. There was a good-sized orchestra, as well as a female chorus in delft-blue dresses. At the beginning of the show, the master of ceremonies-*cum*-narrator introduced the performers, none of whose names I remember. There were two François Villons—one in tails, who sang, and a black-tie one, who spoke lines. The narrator had some very poetic things to say about eyes. "The lowering dusk with flaring eyes of impending war" was one I think I noted on my cuff, but, my shirt having been washed before I transcribed the notes, I can't be sure that it wasn't "glaring eyes." One I am sure of, though, is "The King's eyes betrayed his evil scheme."

"Fear not, milady," the black-tie Villon would say. "My men have taken over this balcony en masse." Then the white-tie Villon would step to the microphone and intone "Only a Rose." The girls in delft blue would back him up. I liked it fine.

Presently, however, my attention was diverted to a control booth at the left side of the stage. Through its glass window I could see the profile of a tall old man with a long gray face and puffy eyes. He wore an unpointed gray mustache designed to break the sweep of an overlong upper lip, and he looked rather as if he were about to cry. I attributed this to the effect of Rudolf Friml's music, but it was more probably, I ascertained a little later, the result of a cold in the head. The old man first looked at the audience, as if counting the all-paper house. Some chamberlain's head would have rolled, I suppose, if he had descried any empty seats, but probably a platoon of spares—wives and children of *Tribune* editors—is held in reserve for such emergencies. He then turned an appreciative grandfatherly eye on the young woman singing the part of Huguette, the girl of the people—she was wearing a strapless silver evening gown with an ermine thing around her neck—and at last concentrated on reading over a typed script he was holding in his hand. This, I heard afterward, is a precaution he has scrupulously observed ever since a time when, reading a script he had not previously seen, he was overcome by emotion and burst into sobs before his audience. The script that so moved him was about the scalping of a pioneer mother by an Indian who had got drunk on rum purveyed to him by an English nobleman.

Precisely as the studio clock showed twenty-five minutes past the hour, with the pack in full melodious cry ("Onwood! Onwood! On ta face tha ff—"), the narrator stepped to the mike, swallowing a fifteenth-century accent, and said, "We will now hear an address on 'The American Navy,' by Colonel Robert Rutherford McCormick, publisher of the Chicago *Tribune*." The old man walked out of the booth and onto the stage. I thought I could see on the faces around me a certain resentment at the interruption, but the faces' owners applauded politely. The singers closed their mouths as unobtrusively as possible. The speech was the kind of résumé that could have been culled from a couple of public-library books in an hour, embellished by a few digs at Great Britain. The Colonel read it completely without expression, pausing only to sniffle. In fifteen minutes, he got the American Navy out of the Bonhomme Richard era and into that of the internal-combustion engine, and finally "guid-id miss-siles." As he finished reading each sheet, he let it flutter to the floor, and as he dropped the last one, the conductor was already giving the orchestra the come-on. The Colonel had talked more slowly than usual, because of his cold, and the Duke of Burgundy waited impatiently at the gates of Paris. "Onwood! Onwood! On ta face tha foe!" shrieked the blue ladies as the lecturer moved toward the wings, and the members of the audience again looked happy.[3]

[3] Another, disaffected, Chicagoan who did sign, has written:

> I felt obligated to express my sympathy at the fact you were so unfortunate as to see just a second rate performance of Col. McCormick reading a speech.
>
> Somewhere in the years between 1943 and 1947 I was forced, or shall I say strongly encouraged, to attend a special performance of the Chicago Theatre of the Air presented at Medinah Temple in honor of the Reserve Officers' Training Corps (ROTC), a special love of the Colonel's.
>
> That evening, in uniform, we arrived at the Temple somewhat early, and were seated close to the large stage, whence I was able to see (and resist the temptation of throwing a spitball at) the Colonel.
>
> The Chicago High School ROTC is close to the heart of the Colonel, as he told us that evening, for he was, for all intents and purposes, its founder. It is to the credit of the Army that our instructors gave the Congress more credit than the Colonel, but perhaps they knew who paid their salaries. On the selfsame evening the Colonel also informed us (he was lecturing on things military) that he had saved the U.S. from Canadian invasion during World War I, and that he had invented the machine gun. As oldtime Chicagoans, we had heard all this before, but we listened respectfully.
>
> The really entertaining part of the show, however, was the manner in which the speech was delivered.
>
> In contrast to the way he was sandwiched in at your performance, in this instance he came on within the first fifteen minutes of the show. Wearing a dinner jacket, he was accompanied by a pleasant young man who carried his speech, a glass, and a pitcher of water. The Colonel apparently wasn't quite up to snuff, for he had a cane in each hand, though they appeared to be merely surplus, for he stood quite erect. As he would finish a page, the young man would turn the pages, and when he wanted a drink, the young man would pour the water, hold a cane, and the Colonel would drink. I would give a better report of what he said if I hadn't been so engrossed in these mechanics.

The Colonel's fortitude when duty's to be done is well illustrated in this reminiscence, as well as his knack of being prepared for all emergencies. Two canes are better than one, even when you don't lean on either, because if you did happen to lean on one it might break.

It was typical of the Colonel to appear and read his speech despite his cold. He would not let his people down. The cultural wool fat in which he has chosen to embed his talks characterizes his own taste. The *Tribune* recently ran a front-page cartoon, in color, labelled "The Three (Dis) Graces"—"Depraved Art" (an obvious foreigner, in a beret and smock, carrying a smeared canvas intended to represent an abstract painting), "Sedition" (an unattractive lady of Levantine features, wearing a red Liberty cap), and "Pornographic Literature" (another female, round-faced and bespectacled, hauling a manuscript from a garbage can). Art, according to the *Tribune*'s canon, has been depraved since Landseer, literature has been pornographic since James Whitcomb Riley, and sedition begins with a wish to redraft the Illinois Constitution of 1870, which, in effect, bars a state income tax. The Colonel's conviction that the world is going to the dogs antedates the New Deal; it was Herbert Hoover upon whom he made his famous pronouncement "The man won't do." His pessimism weighs heavily on his city.

It is a miasmic influence, discernible in the conviction of every Chicagoan that he is being done. Plays at Chicago theatres, for example, are always locally assumed to be inferior versions of the New York productions, or, if they *are* the New York productions, with original casts intact, the actors are presumed to be giving inferior performances. Taking an interest in the Chicago theatre, therefore, is regarded as naïve, as my wife and I discovered when, attending a party shortly after our arrival in the city, we innocently inquired what shows in town were worth seeing. Chicagoans with the price of airplane tickets do their theatregoing here in New York, where, along with people from Boise, Chillicothe, and Winnemucca, they pay such exorbitant premiums for tickets to hits that most of the natives never see them. It is not considered smart to admit having seen any play in Chicago, because this implies either (a) that you haven't seen the *real* play or (b) that you haven't the airplane fare or (c), and possibly worst of all, that you are indifferent to nuances and might, therefore, just as well go back to Fond du Lac, Wisconsin, where you went to high school. Whether this approach to the theatre originated with the *Tribune*, whose current critic, Claudia Cassidy, is its high priestess; with those producers who have in fact sent out bad shows; or with the airlines' sales-promotion departments, I do not know. But it interested me that the Chicagoans who do their playgoing in New York say they never take the *Tribune* seriously. What I suspect they mean is that they never take the *Tribune* seriously consciously. While my wife and I were in Chicago, a company of "Death of a Salesman" put in an appearance and proved to be, according to a reliable friend of mine who had seen the play in New York, better than the original company; the show lasted for only a hundred and seventy-five performances and closed in midseason. In this particular case, I believe, Miss Cassidy had praised, but the Chicago theatre has fallen below the point where an individual review can do much for a show.

With the best-heeled and most knowing slice of the potential Chicago audience thus eliminated, actors have become aware of a curious sensation when playing the place. An actress who appeared there in "The Madwoman of Chaillot" during my stay said that she had a feeling the audience meant to be kind, but that it always laughed in the wrong places. Another large portion of the potential audience is incommunicado overnight in the suburbs, to which train service after commuting hours is awful beyond a Long Island Railroad trustee's fondest vision of what it is feasible to get away with. (The suburbanites go in for amateur theatricals coached by professionals; a young man of my acquaintance became the central figure of a taut situation in Glenview by putting on "Springtime for Henry," the antiseptic 1931 chestnut. The local Catholic priest found it scandalous.) And those great, silent, though densely populated, spaces, the outlying city wards, are peopled by frequenters of neighborhood movies who are now turning to television.

Whoever started the ball rolling, it's under the truck now. A summary of the season of 1950–51 by Miss Cassidy herself lists twenty-three attractions, which played a total of a hundred and fifty-two weeks at seven theatres. The most successful was the national company of "South Pacific," and the three next were, in order, a revival of "Diamond Lil" and holdover-from-the-previous-season runs of "Lend an Ear" and "Two Blind Mice." Among the rest were "Ti-Coq," something called "Mike McCauley," which ran four performances, and "Borscht Capades." During the season, there were seldom more than four theatres open concurrently, and sometimes only three. "Look over your shoulder, if you can bear it, and contemplate what purported to be our season," Miss Cassidy wrote last June before taking off on a three-month tour of Europe to see some shows and hear some music. (She is the *Tribune*'s critic of music and the dance, as well.) The lot of drama critics in Chicago is an enviable one, for they are expected to visit New York to see the new shows; they see eight or ten a week, at a glob, just like out-of-town paying customers. Their advantage over their New York colleagues is that while working they live on an expense account. Looked at from this angle, nothing could be more disastrous for Chicago theatre critics than a revival of the Chicago theatre.

Chicago's wariness extends to women's clothes, I discovered through my wife. Women who wouldn't think of going to a show in Chicago told her they wouldn't think of buying a dress in a Chicago store, either. New York stores like Saks Fifth Avenue and Bonwit Teller have Chicago branches, but these women distrust them, too. They suspect that the clothes at the Chicago Saks and Bonwit differ from those at the New York Saks and Bonwit, having, presumably, been chosen in accordance with some patronizing New York notion of Chicago taste. They circumvent this presumed strategy by buying clothes during their New York trips, on afternoons when there are no matinées. My wife thought this remarkable, because she herself found a lot of dresses she wanted in Chicago. It's a field in which I have no competence. Only the repetition of the motif of distrust interested me.[4]

Opera has succumbed completely to the lack of faith. The gloriously sonorous old Auditorium, home of Chicago's own opera companies from 1910 until the late twenties, when the monster Civic Opera House, on Wacker Drive, was opened, stands disused and out of repair. The Civic Opera House itself is occupied only now and then, by such travelling attractions as "Peter Pan" and the Sadler's Wells Ballet; the Metropolitan gave four performances there last May after the close of its New York season. The Chicago Symphony bears up, or has borne up so far, under a constant fire of criticism based on its supposed inferiority to the Boston, the Philadelphia, and the Philharmonic. That it is a pleasant orchestra to listen to when it plays good music is seldom mentioned in print or over cocktails.

The drawbacks of the first-or-nothing psychology in a city that, it now seems certain, will never be first, impress a visitor to the dejected macrocosm gradually, one by one.

Chicago is the country's foremost printing town, but little publishing is done there. Giant printeries turn out billions of telephone directories,

[4] A correspondent suggests an interesting but discouraging theory about this shopping. "The Chicago taste for clothes is different from New York," he writes. "So actually it makes little difference where Chicago buys, for inevitably their taste will predominate. I suspect that every New York store has clothes for Chicagoans. But, except for the labels, the styles are the same as those on sale on the shores of Lake Michigan—flamboyant, scrumptious, frabjous. You can turn that picture around, too. New York women would be dressed as well no matter where they bought, even in Chicago."

This would explain how my wife found clothes she wanted in the Chicago stores, but the double treachery it ascribes to New York retailers—stocking Chicago-taste clothes for sale to Chicago women at both ends of the airline—is a little hard to swallow. It is a theory the passenger departments of the airlines must explode, for if it stands up, the intercity fares expended by shoppers are demonstrably a waste. And, after all, how is the New York vendeuse to know that the customer is from Chicago, so that she can bring out the frabjous little number or the scrumptious model? My correspondent has an answer for that, too, but I do not believe him.

"Chicago ladies apply makeup to their cheeks with equal abandon," he writes. "In New York the women gild the lily lightly."

I found Chicago women pretty and they looked well-dressed to me. It just interested me that so many didn't *think* they were well-dressed unless they had bought their clothes somewhere else.

A very smart (in both senses of the word) Chicago woman I know looked around her in a New York restaurant a few years ago and said, "There's something about New York women that simply makes me feel awkward." The restaurant, as it happens, is little more than a saloon, and the "New York women" were for the most part newspaper reporters not long out of smaller places than Chicago. They were wearing, I should think, ready-made clothes of brands the visitor wouldn't look at in Marshall Field's, since they would be in some kind of a popular-prices department. Her feeling about them had no objective basis.

Frenchwomen cast something of the same spell over female visitors from across the railroad timetables, and copies of *Time* and *Life*, but the most talked-about national magazine edited in Chicago is the spry Negro monthly *Ebony*, with its affiliates *Jet* (the size of *Quick*) and *Tan Confessions* (rather like *True Confessions*).[5] Even *Esquire* has moved its editorial offices to New York, where most of the writers are. Nor has the city one major publisher of general books. There is, though, Rand, McNally, which specializes in atlases and "Kon-Tiki," and a new firm, the Henry Regnery Company, which makes a specialty of anti-Roosevelt "revelations."

There are four newspapers of any consequence in Chicago, of which only the *Tribune* is, in its own peculiar way, exceptional. Its rival in the morning field, Marshall Field's *Sun-Times*, is a tabloid, ordinarily Democratic in national politics (though it has just endorsed General Eisenhower), cleanly edited, and not without enterprise, but, for mechanical reasons, cursed by limited space, so its out-of-town and foreign coverage is uncomfortably concise. It sometimes raises a great row with stories about local political graft, which have a circulation value, since the contemplation of municipal corruption is always gratifying to Chicagoans. They are helpless to do anything about it, but they like to know it is on a big scale. This is a point the *Tribune* seems to have forgotten in recent years. Although Chicago municipal graft is necessarily Democratic, since the city's government is Democratic, it is the *Sun-Times*, rather than the *Tribune*, that gets indignant. There is, indeed, a widespread belief that the *Tribune* is on good terms with the Democratic city machine; certainly it reserves its foam-flecked-lips editorials for Governor Adlai E. Stevenson, a liberal Democrat who was nominated, and won, in 1948, when the state leaders thought they could not stem "the Dewey tide" with a Party hack. Dewey, in the same fashion, is responsible for the liberal Democratic United States Senator Paul H. Douglas, who was nominated in the same campaign.

Channel. WAF officers who had felt themselves belles in London would walk into cafés in Paris after the Liberation and for the first time in their lives become conscious of their wrist joints. Yet the competition might not be much.

It's a hoodoo, which might be mathematically expressed: NYW: CW: FW: EW.

[5] Most staff members, however, feel ill at ease in Chicago, and there is hot competition for out-of-town assignments. A couple of them explained to me, awhile ago, that Negro Chicago is like its white counterpart, a bit heavy and materialistic. Writers don't rate as high as they do in Harlem, and all the Negro stars of the entertainment world make their headquarters in New York or Hollywood. Chicago's Negroes have a different recent geographical origin from New York's, they pointed out—most of them have come north along the line of the Mississippi River and the Illinois Central Railroad, from Alabama, Mississippi, Tennessee, and Arkansas, while New York's Negroes are mainly from the South Atlantic states, with a strong leavening of West Indians. The general level of Negro education is lowest in the lower Mississippi states, and the mass immigration into Chicago is on the whole newer than that into New York. "But Chicago's a better town for a Negro to make a living in, if he could find someplace to live," my *Ebony* men conceded. "There are more jobs in heavy industry than there are in New York."

The *Tribune*'s circulation, which stood at 1,076,000 in 1946, has dropped off to 925,000, while the *Sun-Times* has established a solid and apparently profitable circulation of almost 600,000 where no morning circulation except the *Tribune*'s existed in 1941, when Field started his paper, as the *Sun*. (He later acquired the Chicago *Times*, an afternoon paper, and made his present newspaper out of the pair.) In Chicago proper, the *Tribune* has only 60,000 more readers than the newcomer, the rest of its superiority lying in its suburban and out-of-town circulation. The *Sun-Times* buys the New York *Herald Tribune*'s foreign and Washington services (it has a Washington bureau of its own, too) but hasn't the space to print more than a small part of them. Its limit is ninety-six tabloid pages, and advertisements, features, photographs, and funnies reduce its news space below the intellectual subsistence level even when it prints the full ninety-six with a proud house ad announcing that *x* columns of paid advertising have had to be refused. In contrast, the unlimited bales of advertising the *Tribune* carries are its greatest circulation asset. As long as large masses of women pine to know what goes on in the department stores, Colonel McCormick's editorial policies won't hurt his paper much. The growth of the *Sun-Times*, however, is evidence of the resentment he has built up. The only alternative to the Colonel's dream world is the *Sun-Times*' world—neat, if limited.

In the afternoon field, there are the *Herald-American*, a Hearst paper that is like every other Hearst paper on earth, and the *Daily News*, a good-looking, fundamentally negative newspaper owned by John S. Knight, who also owns papers in Detroit, Miami, and his home town, Akron, Ohio. (As I write this, I learn that the *Sun-Times* has just expanded its operations and is now publishing on a round-the-clock basis, but it is too early to say how this policy will be received.) Literate Chicagoans speak wistfully of the time when the *News*, under the ownership before last, was a "great newspaper," by which they mean that it was Chicago's own and amusing to read. Right now, it is neither. Even so, it has been moving ahead in the vacuum left in the afternoon field by the *Herald-American*, which is aimed at the intellectual level of a slightly subnormal strip-tease girl.

The reader who stays on Chicago newspapers exclusively for a month (I made the experiment) feels, on seeing his first New York *Times* or *Herald Tribune* after the ordeal, like a diver returning to the light. A year of this underwater swimming and he must surely have forgotten what it was like on the surface. In this subaqueous atmosphere, at least two columnists move like relatively big fish. They are Irv Kupcinet, of the *Sun-Times*, and Sydney J. Harris, of the *News*.

Kupcinet, generally known as Kup, is a large, powerful man, a former professional football player, whose chief material is the interview with the Hollywood movie star on his or her way through Chicago to New York or the New York stage performer on his or her way through Chicago to Hollywood. The arrival of these celebrities by train is a sign that they desire to be interviewed, since otherwise they would simply fly over. On getting to town, they check in at one of the two Ambassador Hotels, which stand on opposite sides of North State Street and are connected by a passage under the pavement. They post themselves at tables in the Pump Room of the Ambassador East in order to be "run into" by Kupcinet and by his imitators on the other three papers. ("Ran into Charles Boyer last night in the Pump Room. . . .") The pretext for the actor's presence in Chicago is the layover between trains; the traveller arriving in Chicago must get out of his incoming train and station and travel across town to an outgoing train, in another station. (He sometimes has the privilege of staying in his car, if he wishes, but this involves several dull hours as the car is shunted from one railroad yard to another.) The late Ernest L. Byfield, a partner in several Chicago hotels, founded the Pump Room in the confident expectation that the railroads would never improve their service. When, shortly after the war, Robert R. Young, the chairman of the board of the Chesapeake & Ohio Railway, began a campaign of newspaper advertisements urging through passenger trains ("A hog can cross America without changing trains—but YOU can't"), Mr. Byfield, always a profoundly sad man, grew even sadder. "If they ever have through trains, *nobody* will stop here," he said. "How could a guy admit he was taking an extra day just so he could happen to be run into by columnists from four papers with a total circulation of a couple of million and nothing to write about?" The well and gratuitously advertised presence of the celebrities keeps the Pump Room crowded with less illustrious but more profitable guests, who come in the hope of recognizing the current attraction. Incidentally, the Pump Room serves as a center for the spread of sophistication. "It was here in this place I first ate snails," I heard a man say there.

I saw a more indigenous brand of knowingness displayed at the Sirloin Room of the Stockyards Inn during the run of the annual International Livestock Show and Chicago Horse Show, which flourish concurrently each November. The chairs in the Sirloin Room are covered with red-and-white cow fur, in the interior-decorator manner. A party of stockmen came in, high on a distillation of the stuff they feed their cows, and one of them wanted a *black* cow fur to sit on. "I want to sit on an Angus," he bawled. "I won't sit on a Hereford." He was loyal to the breed he made his money on.

The International, by the way, is a congenial affair, perhaps the pleasantest on the Chicago calendar. The New York Horse Show makes the mistake of treating the horse as a creature apart, instead of showing him in a setting of other domestic animals. The International has hogs, sheep, cattle, and, I think, rabbits for you to go next door and look at during the harness classes, and the Horse Show part of the enterprise gives working horses a turn in the ring—eighteen-hand Clydesdales, and range-cutting horses ridden by cowboys. It has more of a circus atmosphere than New York's, first because it smells stronger and second because it is jammed with 4-H-Club kids in from the real Middle West for corn- or calf-judging contests. The added spectacular attraction, when I was there, was also authentically circusy—maneuvers by a club of Midwestern Arabian horse fanciers, dressed like mounted nobles of the Mystic Shrine. The bifocals bounced on the noses of the Sheiks-for-a-night and their ladies as the pearls of the Iowa desert bore them swiftly past the hot-dog stand, and everybody seemed to be having a good time. This is not true of the solemn military equitation groups that perform here, every man wondering what the C.O. will say to him if his horse breaks wind.

But to get back to our newspapers—

Harris, the antithesis of Kupcinet, is an in-print introvert. His column, on the *News* editorial page, is titled "Strictly Personal," and he often fills it with lists of "Purely Personal Prejudices," in the manner of H. L. Mencken's "Prejudices" in his *Smart Set* days. "Why doesn't some bright manufacturer put on the market a spiked platter from which a roast or a ham can't slip while it is being carved?" he wrote in a typical column not long ago. "All the clumsy-fingered carvers like myself would give him eternal thanks." But he is no mere clown. In the same column, he showed himself to be profound ("The greatest enemy of progress is the fanatical reformer—because he makes the world believe that all reformers are fanatics"), instructive ("No commonly-used word is so frequently mispronounced as 'irreparable' which should be accented on the second syllable"), esoteric ("The new summer styles for women boldly illustrate the truth of Lin Yutang's remark that 'all women's dresses, in every age and country, are merely variations on the eternal struggle between the admitted desire to dress and the unadmitted desire to undress' "), aesthetic ("One of the most passionate and defiant pieces of chamber music is the Schubert string quartet No. 15, as played on the new LP recording by the Vienna Konzerthaus Quartet. It's more shaking than a symphony"), and iconoclastic (" 'Oklahoma!' is perhaps the most overrated of all American musical plays; 'Dark of the Moon,' while not one-hundredth so successful, was far superior in almost every way"). Harris gives you a lot to think about. In any gathering of bright young Chicagoans, you are likely to find yourself arguing with Sydney Harris all over the place, even though he isn't there in person. And at any cocktail party to which you, as an out-of-towner, are invited to meet writers, you are almost sure to find him in person.

These cocktail parties, after I had been to several, began to remind me of a time in the spring of 1944 when a whole swarm of American war correspondents, including me, were spirited out of London by the Army and dropped at a place called Fowey, in Cornwall, where we were left on the hands of the commanding officer of a base for naval landing craft. The purpose of this excursion was to deceive any German spies who might be watching the war correspondents. The spies, seeing us disappear, would theoretically notify their bosses that the invasion was on. When we came back from Fowey, they would feel silly. The plan, I suppose, was for us to wear them out by a succession of such false alarms, but the real invasion started before we could complete the project. The C.O. at Fowey, who liked parties, caused it to be represented to the county families of the region that we were influential journalists who, for the sake of promoting international amity, should be entertained in their baronial keeps. The families were decent about it, but caused it to be represented to him that they had neither whiskey nor rations for hospitality. Accordingly, one afternoon, at the first baronial keep we were suffered to enter, the chatelaine, a blonde, steered us to an ancestral board presided over by a colored Navy messman in a white jacket, impersonating a feudal retainer. The board was laid out with ham sandwiches and the least expensive grade of Schenley's whiskey. We were then led out to the moat to have our pictures taken by a Navy photographer, and by the time we had said goodbye to the chatelaine and got over to the next keep, the same messman was all set up with some more ham sandwiches and a fresh supply of Schenley's. He must have raced ahead of us in a jeep. After our fourth keep, a correspondent with a vast appetite for Schenley's asked me if I didn't think it was funny all these country families having colored butlers. "And be damned," he said, sitting down in a bed of ancestral nettles, "if I don't think they all look the same."

At every party my wife and I went to in Chicago, we met Nelson Algren, whose novel "The Man with the Golden Arm" had just been published and well reviewed. Algren, who had never before had a popular success, had stuck by his West Side Poles after all the rest of the stark Chicago realists had fled to Hollywood, and he was still wearing steel-rimmed spectacles and a turtle-neck sweater. He made no attempt to look grim, however, and a diet of turkey, Virginia ham, and cocktail shrimp apparently agreed with him; I don't believe that for months he had an opportunity to eat anything else. We were always glad to be introduced to each other, and even went out in private a couple of times between parties. A man named Milton Mayer, who writes articles for magazines, was another standard act. The rest of the party was usually made up of admiring patrons of the arts and members of the faculty of the University of Chicago. For a city where, I am credibly informed, you couldn't throw an egg in 1925 without braining a great poet, Chicago is hard up for writers.

The Chicago baseball teams of the National and American Leagues have long languished, ignored, in the second divisions of their organizations. Chicago sports pages and taxi-drivers alike denounce them, but without hope. Here is no spirit like Brooklyn's, perennially reviviscent through disastrous years and rising to ecstasy every time the Dodgers take both halves of a doubleheader. Even last spring, sports-writers tell me, when the White Sox had a long winning streak and took the American League lead, the suspicious crowds were slow to repair to the ball-park.[6] The fans don't want to believe in their teams. It's the same in boxing; no Chicago fighter has been a big Chicago drawing card since Tony Zale, who emerged in the middle thirties. (Zale was "out of" Gary, Indiana, but Gary is one of the series of industrial suburbs that blend imperceptibly into the larger city.) In much smaller cities, like Youngstown, Hartford, or Providence—or, for that matter, in New York—a fighter has only to win a few bouts to get a neighborhood following, and a few more to be a town hero. Chicago skepticism about home talent is, in my estimation, a sign not of maturity but of a premature old age.

It is true that the *Tribune*, by devoting a preponderance of sports-page space to the huge annual amateur-boxing tournament called the Golden Gloves, a newspaper-promotion device, has helped put the professional game in the shade. Yet amateur boxing itself arouses no enthusiasm in Chicago. The *Tribune* now has to import boxers from places as remote as Memphis and Los Angeles for its "regional" championships. In the last of these championships that I witnessed, only one Chicagoan reached even the semifinal round.

Chicago is not particularly blessed with good restaurants. Byfield, its most energetic restaurateur until his death in 1950, used to say with pride that he was an engineer by training and a showman by inclination. He would invent dishes primarily for their spectacular possibilities—crabmeat wrapped in bacon and served flaming on a skewer, for example, or a salad of hearts of palm, Chinese water chestnuts, capers, bananas, and a highly spiced sauce. The first four ingredients of the salad cancel one another out, and the sauce makes the whole thing taste like the barbecued sandwiches the customers really like. "They won't come out to eat," Byfield told me sadly, a fortnight before his death. "They can eat at home. To get them out, you have to give them a show." Curiously, however, his fellow-citizens would come out for a show only if it was billed as a dinner.

[6] This was the occasion of a rebuke from a friend:

> Where did you ever get the idea that this town was not excited about the White Sox? You must have talked to some particularly weary sports-reporter by the name of Legion. I have never seen the damned town so excited over anything. I was offered twenty-five dollars a pair during the early summer for upper-deck box seats. When the Sox were leading the League, crowds gathered early around LaSalle Street newsstands listening to the vendor's radio. The Sox became temporarily a symbol of revived faith.

I shall not reveal his name, because he added, "Your general thesis, however, is better than okay."

They would not patronize the shows he put on at his College Inn night club and billed as shows; a Chicagoan knows enough not to believe anything he sees in print. Byfield's restaurants became so theatrical they obliged him to abandon show business.

To compensate for the paucity of good restaurants, there are thousands of barbecues—usually spelled "Bar-B-cues"—that sell pig ribs roasted on a spit over a gas fire. These are appetizing, but always the same, and the natives eat them smothered with a hot sauce. To compensate for the lack of ordinary theatre, there are scores of strip-tease joints. The performances, like the pig ribs, are always the same, but they are invariably unpleasant. The most common form of strip joint is a long, narrow barroom with a rectangular or oval bar running up the middle; the girls work on a platform in the center, almost, but not quite, within the patrons' reach. The regular customers sit glumly on stools around the bar, trying to make a bottle of beer—priced at fifty cents—last all night. They must not concentrate too attentively on the girls, though, because the bartender sometimes tries to snatch the bottle while it is still a quarter full. The customer then has to buy another to retain his franchise. A master or a mistress of ceremonies introduces the girls and, in the course of his remarks, listlessly insults a stooge in the audience. ("Why don't you borrow two dollars and go out and get rid of them pimples?" the m.c. may ask a youthful gawk.) One of the girls, introduced as "Mlle. Yvonne Le Vonne, straight from Paris—and I mean Paris, Illinois, ha, ha," then goes through the familiar business of removing most of her specially constructed clothes, which have none of the sexual quality of other clothes. She does this with idiot gravity, and as a climax puts one foot on each side of the microphone shaft and does several kneebends. She then shakes herself as if she had just sat down on a spilled beer, and ends up by posing on one foot, with the other leg bent behind her. After that, she comes down into the crowd to cadge a drink, but she will settle for a cigarette if only the regular customers are present. Why they are present, night after night, is their own pathologically mysterious business. They are sad types, either adolescent or middle-aged, and though they are willing to pay a high price for the beer they drink, they are shabbier and of a more discouraged appearance than the clientele of other saloons.

The remunerative targets for the girls are the unknown drunks, wanderers from respectability, who come into the places in pairs or parties. Every joint has a permanent window sign reading, "Welcome, Conventioneers." No particular convention is specified; there are nearly a hundred of them a month in Chicago, and the joints are one of the principal, if usually unwritten, arguments in the selling of the city to convention secretaries. The girls attach themselves to the visiting drunks like tugboats to an incoming liner. They hustle them for drinks, and insult them if they're shunted off. But generally the drunks buy. After all, that's what they're there for. A girl granted the privilege of ordering a drink will have three in one—a shot glass of rye, a second of sweet vermouth, and a third of Coca-Cola. This retails for a dollar and thirty cents, or whatever multiple of it the bartender thinks fit to ask; he may set up a claim that the drunk has authorized drinks for two, three, or four girls besides the drink for the girl who has engaged him in conversation. The girls do not drink "downs"—soft drinks represented to the customers as whiskey. They apparently feel a need to stay as drunk as they can get without paying for it.

Two atypical conventioneers, one from North Hollywood, California, and the other from Old Greenwich, Connecticut, gave the newspapers ground for a good deal of fun a couple of years ago. It began on the night of April 19, 1950, when they declined to pay $28.35 for what they claimed were only eight drinks at a place called the French Casino, on North Clark Street. They finally paid, under what they interpreted as duress, but lest their indiscipline affect the behavior of future conventioneers, parties who eventually turned out to be unknown set upon them on the sidewalk outside and beat them senseless with small baseball bats. The conventioneers were under the impression these parties included the proprietor and his assistants. The use of small bats, in order not to kill the fellows, was an example of moderation, but they both proved unworthy of it. When they recovered consciousness, they crawled to a taxicab and asked to be taken to a police station. There was one practically right around the corner, on Chicago Avenue, but the driver, with fine presence of mind, drove them to a station a couple of miles away, where the lieutenant in command informed them he had no jurisdiction over North Clark Street. They had not specified *what* police station, the driver probably explained to them as he collected a fare of several dollars.

The unsporting pair persisted, and next morning they brought about the arrest of the proprietor of the Casino and the rest of the batting order as they remembered it. The police, perhaps stimulated by the Chicago Convention Bureau, which is opposed to local slaughter, at least before the guests have checked out, suspended the license of the establishment (its owner was reported in the newspapers to have an interest in three other places in the same police district, which were not affected), and the whole softball team, or at least the conventioneers' version of the lineup, was charged with felonious assault.

The case was set for hearing, and the battered guests stayed on to testify. But defense attorneys objected to the judge who was to preside at the trial and applied for a change of venue. A new judge was named, and on May 9th granted a continuance until May 22nd. The complainants thereupon went home, promising to return on the new date, which, undoubtedly to the defendants' astonishment, they did. The judge then granted another postponement, until June 27th, and the plaintiffs again went home, and again came back. It took three days to select a jury, and by that time the batting-practice targets, deciding it looked like all summer in Chicago for them if they stuck it out, had had enough. They went home for good. Municipal Judge Oscar S. Caplan, the presiding jurist, dismissed the jury, with sympathetic indignation. "It's a travesty on justice to waste your time and mine," he told the jurors, apparently not considering the time spent by the plaintiffs wasted, since travel is always instructive. The then Police Commissioner, John Prendergast, was more emphatic. "They are just out-of-towners who come in here and raise a lot of hell," he said to reporters. "They only raise hell to see what they can get out of it. We go ahead and do our part, and they fall flat on their faces." The captain of the Chicago Avenue police station had declared, upon first hearing of the case, that there were no clip joints in his satrapy, and that the battered men had probably been slugging each other. The effect of the affair upon the consuming public was excellent from the point of view of the North Clark Street strip-and-clip proprietors. Subsequent customers, knowing the penalty for adding up a check, have thought twice before being so vulgar.[7]

The Clark Street batting bee had an unfortunate social effect on my wife and me. A couple of days after it took place, a French friend, a member of the cultural service of the Embassy, visited Chicago to address a convention of language teachers, and came to our house to dinner. Later in the evening, desiring to show him native culture, we escorted him to a strip-tease joint. We selected for this purpose a place of a slightly friendlier, as well as more pretentious, cast than the Casino, called the 606 Club, at 606 South Wabash Avenue. The 606 has a bar, but it is in the rear of the place, and there are tables between it and the blanket-size stage on which the girls perform. As evidence of character, there is a card on every table, reading:

[7] Recalcitrance has reared its ugly head again, according to the following story from the *Sun-Times* of January 19, 1952.

Chicago Briefs
CONVENTIONER'S BUDDY SINGED,
TAVERN RAIDED

A conventioner from Fairfield, Conn., drew a map Friday to show police where his companion was singed in a brush against Chicago night life.

Gail C. Smith, 31, said he was struck by the "push button" entrance to the place when he visited it the other night with William H. Arnold, 31, of New York.

A press of a hidden button, he said, opened a steel door to a night club offering all the presumed conventioners' delights, including feminine companionship.

Smith said he left the place early and Arnold came back to their hotel later missing $125 in cash, a $100 check, a cigaret lighter and a wrist watch. Smith added that he diagnosed his companion's condition as a case of knockout drops.

With the aid of sketches Smith prepared of his taxi trip to the place, police found the button at the Coconut Isle Tavern, 3345 N. Western.

They pressed it and the door opened on a scene in which were six taxi drivers, five conventioners, five women and five employes of the place, including Lawrence Falco, 29, of 1025 Claremont, the manager.

All except the conventioners were arrested.

It just shows that you go easy with some jerks and they creep all over you. Internal medicine is no good with a conventioneer. (I reject the *Sun-Times'* shortened spelling.) What them apes need is surgery.

Table No. Waiter No.

$2.00 MINIMUM

PER PERSON

FOOD INCLUDED

Guest please check your table number with the waiter's check, any discrepancy please see Cashier or Floor Man.

The spaces after "Table No." and "Waiter No." on our card, however, were left blank.

The girls in the 606 appear a trifle better fed then those in the Clark Street places, and consequently exhibit a bit more spirit. On the evening we took our Frenchman, the first girl introduced walked onstage fully clothed. We smiled at our friend, and he smiled back with complicity; he had been told what was to come. He would be able to describe this strange rite to his friends in Paris when he next went home. The girl walked back across the stage, paused, and walked back without discarding so much as a glove. The conventioneers at the tables around us clapped to encourage her. She walked across again, still fully clothed, and for three minutes she just kept on walking. I have seldom seen a woman's face record such embarrassment. Remaining clothed was obviously as much of an ordeal for her as stripping in public would have been for a dowager. Our friend regarded us with an air *étonné*; the conventioneers looked gloomy. Six successive girls went through practically the same performance. One of them made a lamentable attempt at a tap dance; another, coaxed by the master of ceremonies, sang a couple of lines of a song and then broke into a nervous giggle.

"But it's very *moral*," our Frenchman said. "It is like the commencement exercise at a seminary for young ladies. I feel almost as if I were to present the prize for proficiency in Romance languages."

After finishing our two-dollar minimums, including no food (the only food that could possibly fit into the minimum, if you had one drink, would be a cherry, if the drink happened to be a Manhattan), we headed for the door. Remembering the boys' baseball bats, I hesitated to complain, but I timidly asked the man who guides you to your tables if the show wasn't somehow different from the way I remembered it.

"Sure," he said. "The lid's on."

A *Tribune* editorial cartoon, celebrating the award last May of the national Republican convention for 1952 to Chicago, showed "Chicago, the Convention Queen" as a female figure draped in long robes of virginal white. I hope it is not a forecast.

3/*The Massacree*

THE CITY of Chicago, on the west shore of Lake Michigan, is less one town than a loose confederacy of fifty wards. To bind them together, the wards have not even climate, since the waters of the Lake retain warmth on into the fall and intense cold through June, with the result that there is sometimes a difference of as much as twenty degrees in temperature between the Lake shore and the interior. The inhabitants of the city, therefore, cannot use the weather as a common topic of conversation. The heart of the city, as small in proportion to its gross body as a circus fat lady's, succeeds in pumping most Chicagoans through it barely more than once a year, and then just to view the Christmas decorations set out by the department-store owners on State Street. The people in the majority of the wards, remote from this heart, work in the wards they live in—those living near the Stockyards, for example, work in the Stockyards, and those near Inland Steel at Inland. If a man has a job outside the ward he sleeps in, it is likely to be in one just as far from the center of town. In this, Chicago is the antithesis of Washington and New York, where there is a universal movement of the working inhabitants—toward the center of the city in the morning, centrifugal in the evening.

Communication between the residents of the different wards is further limited by the pronounced tendency of immigrant groups in Chicago to coagulate geographically. In Chicago, a man known as a Pole or a Norwegian may not have been born in Poland or Norway, or of parents born there. If even only his grandparents were so born, he refers to himself as a Pole or a Norwegian if he wants to sell coffins or groceries or life insurance to others like himself. A national identification is absolutely essential if he wishes to enter politics. A Chicago party ticket is an international patchwork, like Europe after the Treaty of Versailles. Most of the members of the Chicago national blocs, however, think of Europe as it was cut up by the Congress of Vienna. The great waves of immigration that carried them or their forefathers to their jobs in this country ended with the beginning of the First World War, and they lack the sense of contact with Europe that is sustained by the coming and going of ships, as in New York. To Chicago Norwegians, Norway remains a backward peasant country—"with goats on the roof," as one social-service worker puts it. These Norwegians were isolationists during the war, while their Brooklyn compatriots, who were in a position to talk with Norwegian sailors, were interventionists. To Chicago Croats or Chicago Serbs, Yugoslavia is an unexperienced concept. Poland, to Chicago Poles, means Catholicism and street parades. Chicago has no liberal Italian-American political leaders, like LaGuardia, Poletti, or even Pecora; to be Italian in Chicago means to be loyal to the Italian political machine in the Italian wards. The Irish continue to boil over about the famine of 1846–47. The national blocs are as entirely cut off from Europe as they are from the rest of America—or from the next ward. And the division between the Negro wards and the white is even more drastic.

To make the wards breathe as one calls for an event like the Fire of 1871 or the Columbian Exposition of 1893. The Haymarket riot of 1886, when somebody or other threw a bomb that killed several policemen, and the Black Sox scandal of 1920, when the city learned that its American League team had sold the World Series of the previous year, were other happenings of the magnitude required. The wards are as jealous of their political sovereignty as Ulster or the Union of South Africa. The aldermen do not hesitate to snub the Mayor, a moving-and-storage man named Martin H. Kennelly, who looks like a bit player impersonating a benevolent banker. Kennelly, the aldermen are fond of saying (as if they had never head of Samuel Insull), "must be honest, because he doesn't need the money," but when he tries to assert himself, they react as if they had been kicked by a stained-glass window.

I have been a visitor to Chicago several times in the past few years, but it was only during the winter of 1949–50, when my wife, my stepdaughter, and I were residents, that I had a chance to get to know the aldermen well. At that time, they gave an entrancing display of their free spirit by blocking a plan to provide low-cost housing for twelve thousand families, out of the two hundred thousand who, according to one reliable estimate, are in need of it. The federal government had earmarked the necessary funds for this purpose, and the Mayor had appointed a Chicago Housing Authority, which, after study, had approved sites for the buildings. But every site lay within some alderman's ward—a difficulty impossible to avoid, since all Chicago is divided into wards. Few aldermen wanted new housing within their own wards; it might loosen the landlords' grip on their established constituents. Even worse, it might bring an influx of new voters to upset the ward's political balance and the alderman himself.

An idea of how serious the subject of housing is in Chicago may be gathered by this passage from a piece that Walter White, Executive Secretary of the National Association for the Advancement of Colored People, wrote for the New York *Herald Tribune* following the Cicero riots last summer:

> As part of the background, let's look at the plight of Harvey Clark and his wife Johnetta, also a college graduate, and their two children, aged eight and six. The Clarks moved to Chicago from Nashville, Tenn., in 1949. At first he worked as an insurance salesman and later as a bus driver for the Chicago Transit Authority.

> Because as a Negro he was restricted in finding a home, the best accommodation he could secure was one-half of a small two-room apartment on Chicago's South Side, for which he paid $12.50 a week, or approximately $56 a month. The Clarks occupied a tiny bedroom while another family of five occupied the equally small living room. The apartment was located in a vermin-infested building which can most charitably be described as a firetrap.

Many of the white wards are almost as congested, and the spillover of Negroes from their intolerably crowded neighborhoods into the scarcely less jammed wards around them sets the stage for the racial violence that is Chicago's greatest present danger. Racial feeling is harsh; it isn't just a matter of the riots that get into the newspapers, but a continual edginess.

For example, I have seen a white couple, laden down with bundles after an afternoon's Christmas shopping, pass up a colored taxi-driver on State Street, though cabs were scarce. They apparently preferred to stand and shiver until they could get a white man. I got into the cab after they, to my amazement, had waved it on, and on the way home I asked the driver if I had rightly understood the little scene. He said I had. "They passed me up because I was colored," he said. "A lot of them do."[1]

Chicago crowding is still a crowding into one- or two-story, one- or two-family dwellings, as it was in 1906, when Upton Sinclair brought out "The Jungle," describing the Lithuanian and Polish workers in the Stockyards. The slums look more like Hoovervilles than Harlems. In this horizontal crowding, the proprietors of all the tar-paper-and-matchwood buildings fear the economic threat of the multiple-family housing development.

One of the advantages of this type of housing, from a landlord's point of view, becomes evident in the following story from the Chicago *Daily News*, sometime last June:

> *Authorities Pass the Buck*
>
> QUERIES ON FIRETRAPS
>
> GET REPORTER NOWHERE
>
> BUILDING IN WHICH 3 DIED
>
> UNSAFE, CORONER'S JURY RULES
>
> Who is going to investigate the "unsafe and hazardous condition" of the 3-story building at 1736 N. Clark in which three elderly men lost their lives in a fire May 11?
>
> A Daily News Reporter set out to find the answer to that question. He got nowhere.
>
> A coroner's jury ruled Wednesday that the three men—Thomas

[1] I will concede the possibility that there are New Yorkers who will take a white driver in preference to a Negro when either is available; but I have never seen one who would freeze for his ill feelings.

McGeeghan, 80; John Nordlund, 80, and Carl Laubengaier, 68—died accidentally in the fire in the house owned by Mrs. Anna Anbach, 69, who lived in the building.

The jury found also that the building was kept in an "unsafe and hazardous condition" and recommended an investigation by "proper authorities."

But just who are the "proper authorities"?

The building had never been inspected by the city because buildings of that size are considered private residences if they have less than 10 tenants. This building had nine.[2]

The aldermen, who constitute the City Council, rejected the Housing Authority's sites and turned the quest for new ones into a form of slapstick. At one point, they proposed to place all twelve thousand family units in the vicinity of the University of Chicago, far from the worst overcrowding. This was a broadly comic dig at Bob Merriam, the young alderman from the Fifth Ward, which includes the University. Merriam had been one of the few members of the Council to support the Housing Authority's sites. It was all good, clean fun, and the housing never got built, although the Council has since approved some sites, on three or four of which work may commence this spring. Meanwhile, the two hundred thousand families continue to live in sub-standard homes.

Merriam is a town character—an honest alderman. In any of the better residential neighborhoods, one meets him at practically every party one attends; it is typical of well-off Chicagoans to be passionately interested in good government. Merriam is a lively man in his mid-thirties, who has inherited his taste for politics from his father. The elder Merriam, a professor emeritus of political science at the University, once ran for Mayor of Chicago on a reform ticket. In the son, the delighted observer frequently gets ahead of the idealist. "Chicago is unique," he said to me the first time I met him. "It is the only completely corrupt city in America." When I told him I had heard a couple of other places equally ill spoken of, he said defensively, "But they aren't nearly as big."

This ambivalence is a Chicago characteristic. People you meet at a party devote a great deal more time than people elsewhere to talking about good government, but they usually wind up the evening boasting

2 The story, as it chanced, ran on an inside page of the same issue of the *News* that contained Mr. Pettibone's paean, part of which I cited earlier. In another portion of his piece Mr. Pettibone listed some recent advances made in Chicago civic life.

Among them was: "Adoption of a modern building code and a start on enforcement of minimum housing standards through adequate inspection."

The 1700 block on North Clark, by the way, is not in some outer Bronx or Newlots of Chicago, but spang in the middle of the city, no farther from the Loop than 75th Street is from Times Square.

about the high quality of the crooks they have met. At every social gathering, abuse is heaped upon the head of every politician in public view, the standard complaint being that the fellow is not sufficiently idealistic. The male guests carry five-dollar bills folded in their drivers' licenses. Upon being stopped by a traffic policeman, they present the license, the cop takes the fin and returns the license, and the transaction is closed. "He had me, all right," is the customary explanation. "Why should I bother to go to court to pay a fine?"

These same people are constantly in quest of intellectual improvement. "We'd like to invite you over to dinner tonight," one of our best Chicago friends told us on the telephone the second day we were in town, "but we've turned over our house for the evening to our Group for an informal discussion of the devaluation of the pound." Everybody you meet belongs to a Great Books Discussion Group; the study of the Great Books can last a lifetime, even when the samplings taken of them are exceedingly small. (Two chapters of Gibbon, thoroughly digested in a discussion group led by one's chiropodist, are supposed to be the equivalent of the whole work merely read.) In Chicago intellectual circles, a man who can't do a psychoanalysis between two Martinis ranks with a fellow who can't change a tire. A man condemned to earn his living by writing, and therefore accustomed to talk about football or the proper temperature of beer, finds himself conversationally impaled by determined ladies who want to discuss Lionel Trilling. Intellectual Chicagoans are all desperately earnest and seem as wholly isolated as the second-generation Croats. The wards stretch out around the lakeside apartment houses, or Gold Coast, and around the University and the pleasant detached houses near it, where the serious thinkers live, and the wards are unaffected by anything the people in those houses think or say.

Because there is very little low-priced housing, Chicagoans have set up a Housing Council, and because there is much crime, they have set up a Crime Commission, and because relations between whites and blacks are bad, a Commission on Human Relations, but everything remains very much the same, for these organizations operate in a vacuum. The conviction that anything in the world can be ameliorated by setting up a council or forming a committee is as much an article of faith with Chicagoans of good will as the notion that there is a short cut to every intellectual objective (except business success, which, of course, demands full-time thought in all waking hours not set aside specifically for culture). The city is not only the home of the short analysis and of the theory that a liberal culture can be acquired by reading arbitrarily chosen slivers of a number of arbitrarily chosen books; it also has the only large university that awards a liberal-arts degree for an undergraduate course that starts after the second year of high school and ends after what would anywhere else be the second year of college. As a result of this generous stand, the University of Chicago's undergraduate college acts as the greatest magnet for neurotic juveniles since the Children's Crusade, with Robert Maynard Hutchins, the institution's renovator, until recently playing the role of Stephen the Shepherd Boy in the revival. Walking inadvertently (I can't imagine anyone's doing it on purpose) into any of the campus taverns along Fifty-fifth Street, the University's equivalent of the Boulevard St. Michel, the adult stranger finds himself in a kind of juvenile Alsatia, where the male voices haven't changed yet. By conversation with the inmates, he may learn, as I did from one lad, that "the strong point about Chicago is it's the only university where you can hold a full-time daytime job and still get your B.A. You don't have to go to class at all. Just read the Great Books and work up a line for the comprehensive examination at the end of the year." There is no general public institution of higher learning in Chicago, and the opportunity to work full time is often necessary to the earning of tuition fees. But a B.A. is a B.A., and if Dr. Lawrence A. Kimpton, who not long ago succeeded Hutchins as chancellor of the University, decides to accept candidates out of the third grade instead of the tenth, he will probably be hailed on the Midway as an even greater educational innovator.

ACADEMIC AMPLIFICATION

[A DOCTOR in Urbana, Ill., wrote to me that talking to the undergraduates about a college was as vain as trying to learn about an army from the enlisted men, or, as he put it, EMs. I am in favor of both procedures.

[A learned office boy at *The New Yorker* (B.A. University of Chicago, 1950) has contributed the following amplification:

> The real truth is that, in the College—and not the "Divisions" (junior year of regular college and up), *no* papers are required. The mark in the course is determined entirely by a six-hour objective exam, which is given at the end of the year. This is called a "Comprehensive" ("comp" for short) and consists of complete-the-statement-correctly questions, and sometimes there is a short essay question, the subject of which is never given out in advance. On the English composition exam, two essays are assigned—their subject is not known until the student is in the examination room. Sometimes, however, the Board of Examination cannot resist the scientific instinct and gives a short section of objective questions on English style. This section, like all objective sections—is marked by an IBM machine, which is apparently the newest thing in education since the Great Books. (Incidentally this gives rise to a strange academic occupation. During examination periods, the Board of Examinations finds it necessary to hire a girl for eight hours a day

for the sole purpose of sharpening the special pencils needed to make out the IBM answer sheets, which are graded electrically.) To get back to papers, none, even in English composition, are compulsory except those on the comps.

This system of comprehensive exams usually makes the student say—when describing the system to his friends and relatives back home—"All you gotta do is pay the fees and pass the comp." Reading books, writing papers, studying, are overshadowed by the comp.

[From a graduate student of Government now at an Eastern university, who spent last year in Chicago:

I went to the U. of C. with the suspicion that Laski had been harsh in his cracks about Hutchins and the neo-Thomists looking to the Middle Ages to forget the slums, stockyards and gangsters on the South Side. He wasn't.

[I had a reproving note from a Harvard faculty wife who, she said, was Chicago-born. It ended:

P.S. As I think back it is *how* you have said a lot of things—not always what you have said. I find myself a critic of Hutchins, and I thought the students I knew at the University of Chicago dull socially and Neurotic—and—and—and I was sick when I thought my husband might take a job there,—and I'd half to live around there. ["Half" for "have" from an educated woman is a revealing slip; she may have felt that she would be only half alive if compelled to inhabit her home town.] But the way you said it made me want to defend the whole kit and kaboodle of them. And I don't like them at all.

[The bearer of one of the premium names in the meat-packing industry, who describes himself in his letter as "a graduate of the University of Chicago, and expatriate who has no desire to go back," writes in part:

One of my pet theories is that the flatness of the region is largely responsible for the city as it is.—The spreading flatness made possible those wooden slums and the dreary houses and apartment buildings of the ordinary folks. Indeed the curiously futile darts of many Chicago people up towards culture may be partly due to their flat foundation.—Hutchins and the Hundred Books are like attempts at synthetic books and mountains.

[No portion of my *New Yorker* series provoked more hot written words than my brief allusion to this intellectual foundling asylum, the undergraduate college of the University, whose inmates I viewed with sympathy, like the Little Princes in the Tower, or Hänsel and Gretel in the cage.

[The graduate faculties, which resisted *Gleichschaltung* with open rebellion against the impresario some years ago, are still on a pinnacle of prestige, especially in the natural sciences, about which I am not qualified to have an opinion.

[This reminds me of a French restaurant-owner I knew in Paris during the static *drôle de guerre*. He took a dim view of the British, who as yet had sent no troops into the line. But even he approved of the headlines telling about the sinking of the *Graf von Spee*, the German pocket battleship, by two British cruisers. "It appears they are superb," he said, "but not where I can see them!"]

A superb specimen of a Chicago alderman is Paddy Bauler, who represents the Forty-third Ward. Bauler's De Luxe Gardens, at North Avenue and Sedgwick, is as sedate a groggery as you will come upon in the city of Chicago. It occupies the former premises of the Immigrant State Bank, which went under in the crash, and the original lavatory solemnity of the interior's marble décor has never been altered. The high ceilings, the grilles barring the way to the vaults, and all the other accessories designed to nurture unfounded confidence remain to warn of the uncertainty of appearances, and the patrons conduct themselves as discreetly as men about to solicit a loan. It is here that the Alderman, who is also a member of the Cook County Democratic Committee, holds court, like Saint Louis of France under his tree of judgment, from nine to eleven each evening, when he is not travelling in Europe. Paddy travels often, and always in style; he says that trips to places like Rome and Palestine help him to understand the different kinds of people in his ward. The saloon's license is in his brother's name. Paddy has apparently done well at making his aldermanic salary of five thousand dollars a year stretch.

The Alderman is a mountain—or, rather, since his contours are soft, a gravel dump—of a man, with a wide pink face wearing an expression of mock truculence. Twenty years ago, when he was courting the attention of Mayor Tony Cermak, he used to roll about the floor in wrestling matches with himself to make His Honor laugh; he weighed two hundred and seventy-five pounds then, and he has put on several ounces since. He is essentially decorous, however; a few nights before Christmas of 1933 he shot a policeman who wanted him to serve a drink after hours. Paddy had locked up and was depositing the receipts from a Forty-third Ward Democratic Christmas Fund benefit show in the bank vault when the policeman came to the door raucously demanding admittance. Paddy went out to quiet him. "Johnny, why have I got this coming to me for?" the Alderman roared plaintively. "I never done anything to you." Then he shot the policeman, and nobody has used bad language or tried to get a drink after hours in the De Luxe Gardens since. Only a few years ago, a man named Kane, who was opposing Paddy in the Democratic primary in the ward, complained because the store he was using for his headquarters was bombed one night. Kane claimed to be a close friend of Mayor Kennelly's. The Alderman said things were coming to a pretty pass when a fellow would bomb his own headquarters for publicity. "I wouldn't have minded it so much," he told reporters, "if the guy hadn't run up there and stuck Kennelly's picture in the broken window before the cops came." Paddy's posters in a recent election campaign said, with elegant restraint, "Elect Mathias J. Bauler. He will appreciate your vote." Paddy doesn't have to make himself known to the voters in the Forty-third. Once, he says, he told a campaign audience that he had been the first child ever christened in St. Teresa's Church, in his ward. The pastor looked up the baptismal record and, sure enough, Paddy had been.

Paddy's father was born in Germany, and his mother in Illinois, of German descent. Like many other men of non-Irish descent who spend their lives in politics, he has acquired a Celtic manner that sometimes imposes on him, just as some non-Frenchmen who work their way up in the restaurant business begin to think of themselves as French. Paddy's ward, it happens, is so ethnologically scrambled that there is no great political profit in being any particular kind of European, but among politicians the rule is: When in doubt, be Irish. "I've almost forgotten my name is Mathias," Paddy says.

There is no entertainment—not even a dice girl—in the De Luxe Gardens. North Avenue, which begins near Lake Michigan and runs straight west through the dimness until it hits the city line, lies only a little over a mile and a half north of the Loop, but it is the axis of an autonomous dreariness. The eastern end of the avenue, which is in Paddy's ward, has a small night life, with a German-language movie house, one or two German restaurants with zither players, and some Hungarian saloons, through which wander, in the course of the evening, a few fiddlers, who say that they are gypsies but that they have forgotten the Old Country music, because they are never asked for it. The favorite request numbers of Chicago Hungarians are "Tennessee Waltz" and "When Irish Eyes Are Smiling." Also, there are numerous bars that use low prices as their chief sales argument. These places seem purposely bare and flimsy, as if to assure the customers that nothing is being wasted on overhead. The liquor-license fee is low in Chicago, and the sheer number of saloons, even in backwash neighborhoods, is amazing. Curbstones are high, often consisting of two steps instead of one, and drunks sometimes take astonishing falls. These are seldom fatal. "You're like all us Polacks," I once heard a North Avenue bartender say to a patron who had had all he could drink. "One ain't enough and a thousand ain't enough." Then the patron went out and crashed on his head. "You can't kill a Polack," the bartender said.

The Forty-third Ward is one of the most diversified in the city, containing in its lakeward corner half of the Gold Coast, including the two Ambassador Hotels, the Cardinal's Residence, and Colonel Robert R. McCormick's town house. Toward the ward's southwest frontier there is a Negro slum (not the great one but an isolated growth), in its center is the residue of the original German colony, and within its boundaries are also blocs of Nisei, Finns, Hungarians, Italians, Irish, Syrians, Armenians, Swedes, and Poles, and a couple of neighborhoods of flats and one-family residences inhabited by solid settlers of the middle class from Iowa and Nebraska. Parts of the ward look like a city, parts like a pleasant suburb, and large tracts like the less favored sections of a blighted mill town. The principle of Paddy's rule is simple. "Everybody gets something," he says.

During one of my longer stays in Chicago I lived in the Forty-third, and I ran across a friend of mine—and a constituent of Paddy's—who volunteered to take me over to the De Luxe Gardens to meet the gentleman. The friend, a fellow named Martin, was brought up in the ward, where his father, a carpenter and novelist born in Finland, owned a house. Martin started out to be a novelist, too, but somehow landed in the advertising business, which keeps him prosperous and embarrassed. He is a victim of his present environment, in which literature no longer flourishes; if he had been born ten years earlier in Chicago, I am convinced, he would have been a novelist, proud and famishing. We found Paddy sitting at a table with one of his executive assistants, a younger man, who also owns a saloon and is training to be an officeholder. "I am always here at nine o'clock, in case anybody has a brother that has been arrested or a relative he wants to get into Cook County Hospital or anything like that," the Alderman said. "I am A-1 with the Hospital," he went on, and explained that without support, a candidate for admission has to wait his turn. "You got to keep in touch," he said. "Things like that the precinct captain should be on the lookout for, if they are in his precinct, but you can't always depend on them."

Paddy told me that there were forty thousand votes in his ward, and that in his capacity as Democratic Committeeman he had seventy-six precinct captains, each with a city, state, or county job. "We have some very nice jobs to give out, from two hundred and seventy up to three hundred and fifty dollars a month," he said. "And all the fellow has to do is keep track of the votes in his precinct and get out the Democratic voters when it counts. If he says there will be one hundred votes for us and eighty for the other fellow, I would rather have it come out that way than one hundred and fifty to twenty, because if it comes out the second way, it shows the precinct captain don't know his business, or he is faking. I got to know within one per cent. That's how I know if I got good precinct captains. Then I got to tell the county chairman how the vote will be in the ward. That's how he knows if he's got a good committeeman. Naturally, if I got a bum precinct captain, I got to get rid of him and give that city job to a hustler, because if I got enough bum captains, it will throw my figures out. Then I am a bum, too."

"And have you always been able to tell what the vote in the ward will be?" I asked.

"I never been off the public payroll in forty years," the Alderman replied, with modest indirection. "The second big thing a precinct captain has to do is get out the vote. The way he does that is by knowing everybody in his precinct and being nice to them. Everybody needs a favor sometimes, but some people are too dumb to ask for it. So I say to my captains, 'If you notice a hole in the sidewalk in front of a fellow's house, call on him a week before election and ask him if he would like it fixed. It could never do any harm to find out.' When you got a good precinct captain, you got a jewel. Like last year. It was an off year and hard to get people interested, but we needed some votes to elect local candidates. I asked a young fellow named Barney McGuirl how many votes he thought he'd get out in his precinct and he said about ninety-five. 'Well,' I said, 'Barney, I know you got five beautiful little children and a bailiff's salary does not go as far as it should,' I said, 'although I hope to get you something a little better soon. But if you get me a hundred and fifty votes just this time, I will present them angels with ten dollars apiece.' He got me a hundred and ninety-seven.

"We got nice people in this ward," Paddy went on. "Nice Germans, nice Poles, nice Irish, nice Jews, nice colored people, and so on, and recently we been getting a lot of Japanese, which are moving north across Division Street, and they are a very nice high-class class of Japanese. I try to see that nobody gets shut out on the jobs. The Forty-third Ward, I always say when I make a speech, is like the United Nations."

The Gold Coast, although it confers social éclat on the ward, is not Paddy's favorite corner. "The type people you got over there don't need a job as bailiff, so you got to rely on amateurs for your organization work," he said. Moreover, he holds that the inhabitants of the Gold Coast, many of whom are Republicans, expect more than their share of service. "They complain about dirty streets and bad lighting and fads like that, and about they never got enough cops, and when you come right down to it, they got only one vote apiece, like everybody else," he told me. "But it's a fine ward. We had the Massacree in this ward. Did you know that?"

"The what?" I asked.

The effect of my failure to comprehend was unfortunate. "*The St. Valentine's Massacree*, of course!" Paddy shouted. Then, regaining control of himself, he added, "Right over in a garage in the 2100 block on Clark. I knew some of the fellows." The Alderman's manner, if not his tone, was that of Dr. Douglas Southall Freeman saying, "There stood Pickett's men."

I was impressed. I had, naturally, heard about the St. Valentine's Day Massacre of 1929, in which some gangsters lined up seven competitors against a wall and slaughtered them, and I was familiar with the 2100 block on Clark, for it was just around the corner from the Francis W.

Parker School, which my stepdaughter was attending, but I had not been aware that there was any connection between the two or that I had frequently walked past a shrine.

"Were the fellows you knew shot?" I asked the Alderman. "Or did they do the shooting?"

"They were shot," he said, giving me my first intimation that the home team had lost.

"The Gusenbergs weren't bad kids," Paddy said. "Just wild. They were working for a bootlegger, that's all." Now he sounded like a man who had known General Custer. Frank Gusenberg, a boy from the ward, had been the hero of the Massacree, although I didn't know it then. I have since learned that Frank, left for dead among the corpses, was found still breathing and was transported to the Alexian Brothers' Hospital, where he survived for an hour, and then died "true to gangland's immemorial code," as one newspaper put it, refusing to say who had shot him. Local historians resolutely reject the hypothesis that he didn't know. Someday he undoubtedly will have his statue.

I tried my story of Paddy Bauler and the Massacree on a non-practicing lady novelist, sixtyish, of distinguished Chicago lineage and social position, who once won a Pulitzer Prize and is on most subjects a well-balanced woman. With gay excitement, she cried, "How I remember that afternoon! I went around to Francis Parker to call for my daughter. But all the children had cut classes and gone to view the scene! Those were wonderful times!" A matron who, as a young newspaperwoman, did a feature story on the bloodstained garage spoke of the day with the same nostalgia. I could well believe that since then life for her had been an anticlimax.

Feeling that I was for the first time on the verge of discovering something that would help me understand Chicago, I hurried to the morgue of the *Sun-Times* to enrich my recollection of the local epopee. The Massacree had occurred, I read, in a garage at 2122 North Clark Street. Seven men—six thugs and an optometrist who was, like many Chicagoans of his day, a crime buff with a penchant for impressing his friends by dropping names—had been lounging around some trucks in the garage on the morning of the 14th when, at about ten o'clock, an automobile drove up to the curb and four men got out. Two of the men from the automobile were wearing police uniforms and carrying submachine guns and the other two were in ordinary clothes and were armed with sawed-off shotguns. The four men entered the garage. After about half an hour, they came out, first the pair in ordinary clothes, who were now unarmed and walked with their hands over their heads, as if prisoners. The two in police uniforms were right behind them, and kept their guns pointed at their backs. A Mrs. Alphonsine Morin, street-watching from a window of

No. 2125, across the way, had seen it all. North Clark must have been an interesting street to live on at that time, for she didn't think the scene unusual enough to call to her neighbors' attention. Presently, somebody walked into the garage and found Frank Gusenberg wallowing in his blood, and the corpses of six men, including Dr. Reinhardt H. Schwimmer, the name-dropper.

The way the victims had fallen indicated that they had been lined up facing a wall, as if to submit to a search for arms. Noting this, and hearing about the men in police uniforms, the first reporters on the scene decided that the Forty-third Warders had been betrayed by their confidence in the Chicago police. The victims, so the reasoning went, had assumed they were going to be taken to a station house for a shakedown, which wasn't worth fighting over, and had therefore not resorted to their own weapons. The police, in denying this theory, were highly indignant about the executioners' ruse, evidently fearing no gangsters would ever trust them again. The next morning's papers reported all the town's speakeasies closed, "criminals missing from their usual haunts," and "a relentless investigation unclenched." (Who, I have often wondered, clenches an investigation?) Arthur Sears Henning, the Chicago *Tribune*'s chief Washington correspondent, viewing the event from the capital, blamed "alien gangs that have been terrorizing Chicago."

Crime reporters wrote like Lippmanns and Alsops in those days, and one of these seers of the bigger picture asserted that the North Side gang had been stricken by its "historic antagonist, as history goes in the swift careers of gangsters"—the South Side gang. It was, almost all the reporters agreed, a tragic chapter in the bloody story of the North Side Dynasty of Dion O'Banion, Hymie Weiss, Schemer Drucci, and Bugs Moran, who had already been done in or had disappeared and who, in long biographical résumés, were pictured as victims of their own chivalry. Their opponents, the Colosimo-Torrio-Capone Dynasty, were deprecated as consistently unethical. Their latest demonstration of this quality, the writers predicted, might well affect the balance of power in International Gangdom. Meanwhile, a lady reporter wrote that she had watched detectives strip large diamond rings from the stiffening fingers of the victims, proving that not robbery but revenge had been the motive. It also proved that the killers had not been bona-fide detectives, who would have got the rings in the first place for sure.

It was my impression that nobody had ever been punished for taking part in the Massacree. I found, consulting the *Sun-Times*' clippings, that this was correct. The police eventually decided they knew who the shooters were, but by the time they had made up their minds, all the putative marksmen had themselves been massacreed, except a man by the name of Burke, who was then at large and later wound up in prison for killing a police officer in St. Joseph, Michigan. Burke died in stir in 1940—true, the press noted, to gangland's immemorial code.

In the *Sun-Times'* morgue, I came across some very beautiful retrospective pieces about the Massacree, most of them written on anniversaries of the event. One, by a man named Larry Kelly, in the *Sun* of February 14, 1943, began, "St. Valentine's Day in Chicago doesn't always call up thoughts of heart-shaped boxes and pretty verses. Forever linked with that day is the memory of that morning of February 14, 14 years ago. . . ." The tenderest, I thought, was by a fellow named Clem Lane, of the Chicago *Daily News.* "There had been snow flurries that morning as the mailmen made their rounds, their loads made heavier by the lovers' missives," he wrote, also in 1943. Further on, his style hardened: "There was talk of a reward of $100,000 for the apprehension of the killers. The City Council voted $20,000 for such a reward, but spent it on something else when the heat died down." There was no lack of fresher shooting to write about in 1943, I reflected, and thousands of Chicagoans were abroad in the thick of it. But the spell of the Massacree persisted. It was Chicago's own.

When I felt myself sufficiently documented, I made a pilgrimage by taxi to 2122. There is not even a modest historical plaque on the exterior of the building, which has been converted into a warehouse. The driver, to whom I explained the purpose of my trip, was much impressed. "I've heard Al Capone was a good guy," he said. "He run soup kitchens during the depression."

There have been gang homicides in Chicago since the Massacree—at least a hundred and eighty-eight since 1932, according to an estimate published in 1950. Public interest, however, has flagged. On September 25, 1950, for example, a former Chicago police lieutenant, William J. Drury, who had been acting as a tipster for the Kefauver Committee in Chicago, was shot to death as he sat in his car in the garage behind his home. The story had attractive features: Drury was said to have owned "a little black notebook" with all the dope about Chicago crime in it, he had received threatening telephone calls, and he had got in touch with the Kefauver people a few hours before his death to say he needed protection. Chicago didn't rise to the bait. "The police investigation followed the routine pattern in gang killings," the *Tribune* reported, two days after the crime. "The inquest into Drury's death was continued after his widow testified she knew of no reason why anyone should want to kill her husband. All law enforcement authorities pledged co-operation in the man hunt. No one was arrested." In due course it was reported, "The investigation of the shotgun slaying of former police lieutenant William Drury [seems] to be fading out," and on November 28th the coroner declared the inquest formally closed. I missed the fine frenzy of the old Massacree stories, with their talk of dynasties and immemorial codes. Nowadays, nobody in Chicago even mentions the Drury murder.

The city's tendency to live in the past since the Massacree—as shown by its muted reaction to the Drury case, which in the twenties would have been considered a creditable murder—is a peculiar one. I have tried to account for it by the hypothesis that the Massacree, like the Dionne quintuplets, set too high a standard of performance for the maintenance of public interest in the future. Just as no multiple birth short of six will ever again seem newsworthy, so the Chicago gangster ambitious to make an impression is confronted with the task of killing at least *eight* people at a clip, preferably including a minimum of *two* professional men—perhaps a chiropractor and a podiatrist—and preferably on Mother's Day or Christmas Eve. (The Fourth of July, by the way, also offers tempting possibilities for a massacree. I know a man in Rhode Island whose father used to go out and shoot a deer every time the date came around, on the safe assumption that the game warden would think the shot part of the celebration.)

The hold the Massacree has on the civic memory is not entirely dependent on the number of casualties. A couple of years ago, a streetcar collided with a gasoline trailer tank truck and thirty-two passengers were burned to death, but the event shows no signs of entering into legend. Nor has it had any effect on the life of the community. The streetcars still run at the same insane speed and the trailers are of the same unwieldy length as before; Chicagoans view such hazards with equanimity, like the railroad crossings at grade that intersect their principal streets. The gasoline companies deserve the same consideration as the railroads, sensible Chicagoans say; after all, nobody contests the Stockyards' right to smell. The *Tribune* no longer bothers to print its editorial "Program for Chicagoland," which included, as Points 4 and 5, "Abolish the Smoke Pall" and "Grade Separation on Thru Streets and Boulevards." The smoke pall is the town's concession to the steel plants. As Paddy says, "Everybody gets something."

The Massacree has held Chicago's interest partly because the gangster years coincided with those of the Great Bubble. That was when Insull built his pyramids of holding companies, Cutten and other heroes slaughtered invaders in the grain market, and the world looked as promising as a pool table with a hanger on every pocket. All that ended soon after the Massacree. Primarily, the Massacree focussed attention on the town. I have known Chicagoans who claim that they are embarrassed, when they are travelling abroad, at being quizzed about *les gangsters*. I have never believed them, because they invariably tell it like a funny story. They remind me of a movie star telling what a bore it is to be recognized. As for the kids in the drearinesses of the wards, they have always loved Chicago's reputation. Citizens of a city celebrated in the movies, they are little Scarfaces as they sit with their molls in the darkened cinemas and identify themselves with the glorious past.

* * *

The great tradition has left its mark. Only the real gangsters and their molls no longer dress like gangsters and their molls, if the witnesses before the Kefauver Committee were samples. Thousands of Chicago girls still try to look like Jean Harlow, although they may never have heard of her. They style themselves on their older sisters, who picked up the idea from their youngish mothers. All the men you see in bars along streets like Rush and Division are in uniform as hoods. The hair shines, the hats are down over the eyes, the well-spaced-out orders for beer escape from the corners of the mouths, and with no need to punch the time clock in Goldblatt's department store until eight o'clock next morning, the boys are at liberty to listen to the two-piano team and look sinister. They also look terrified, because most of them believe that the other fellows in the bar, who probably work in Marshall Field's, may be what they are disguised as. The bar customers are loath to enter into conversation with strangers, lest they betray their own harmlessness and so become victims. Faith in the omnipresence of crime is like a belief in voodoo. It makes the believer cautious. I have witnessed a similar aloofness at gatherings of unacquainted Englishmen, each afraid to betray by his accent that he has gone to a less important school than the others. Britons so situated open their mouths as hesitantly as poker players turn up their hole cards. The pleased smile of the fellow who finally takes the pot—perhaps an old boy of a small public school—is a lovely thing to watch. Now all he has to think of is something to say.

Chicago's working gangsters have gone mysterious. They are referred to as the Syndicate, and it is accepted as gospel by congenial people that the Syndicate owns most of the good restaurants in the city, one or two of the race tracks, and the laundry, dry-cleaning, candy, soda-water, baby-linen, night-club, antique-glass, and beauty-parlor businesses, as well as the labor unions, the public utilities, and any hotel a visitor happens to be stopping at. "Did you know that was a Syndicate place?" is a staple of small talk. The answer is "Sure. Who doesn't know that?" The out-of-towner's accompanying mental reservation is "Who does?," but he should not voice it if he wishes to be popular.

A while ago the *Sun-Times*, in a series that purported to expose the Syndicate-operated call-girl system, yielded so unreservedly to Chicago's honest adulation of its gangsters that the installments could have been reprinted as a brochure for distribution by the Chicago Convention Bureau. The girls, the *Sun-Times* reported, were beautiful and well dressed, and, thanks to efficient Syndicate administration of the system, the out-of-town customer was reasonably free from worry about blackmail, larceny, or venereal disease. All of these were discouraged, the *Sun-Times* recorded, because of their effect on customer good will. To meet a girl, the reader was advised, the visitor applied to the bell captain in his hotel. The day after the first article appeared, Milburn P. Akers, who was then the *Sun-Times'* managing editor, got a letter from a girl who said she was a waitress and would like to know how to get a job as a call girl.

Syndicate administration of the saloon-with-entertainment business is equally smooth, a man on a theatrical publication told me. "In the twenties, two or three different outfits might try to muscle in on the same place," he said. "If the fellow didn't pay off, they went in for rough stuff, and even if he did, they might get rough with each other. Now just one man arrives and says he is from City Hall, and he is a partner, drawing down a hundred and a half a week, or two hundred—whatever the club looks good for. It's a part of the nut, like the rent. After all, if everybody has to pay, nobody has an unfair advantage."

"And if the place doesn't pay off?" I asked.

"The police send a delinquent female minor into the joint to buy a drink," my informant replied. "Some kid who looks over eighteen and will do anything they say because she's out on parole. The law is death on selling drinks to minors. Then they close the place."

"But is the fellow who declares himself in really from City Hall or from the Syndicate?" I asked.

"Well, he's known as a Syndicate fellow, but the police enforce what he says," the man said. "I don't know what the split is."

"Maybe the Syndicate is just a front for the city government," I suggested, "instead of its being the other way around."[3]

And maybe, I have thought since, the city government is just a front for Colonel McCormick and for the railroads that don't want to be moved off the streets and for the landlords who don't want to lose the swollen rents from their hovels and for all the nice, earnest people who constantly form committees but really don't want anything changed if it costs money. If no Syndicate existed, it would be necessary to invent one, to blame it for the way things are. The leaders of the Syndicate, whoever they may be, hardly ever shoot each other in public any more, even one at a time, and Chicagoans are left in the plight of the Greeks at the beginning of history, when the gods commenced ceasing to manifest themselves.

3 The story of Sammy Rinella, murdered last December, several months after the above was written, seems to lend some support to this hypothesis. Rinella, a night-club promoter, had not included in his 1945 income-tax return a bank deposit of $157,000. When the Internal Revenue people, reviewing his return, challenged this omission in 1951, Rinella said the money hadn't been his. He said it had been part of $205,000 he had borrowed from a police captain so he could open a new night club. Rinella was shot to death soon after he told his story. The police captain admitted having lent him some money—a mere $100,000. But he denied any connection with the shooting.

In the old days the boys staked the cops. Now, it appears, the cops stake the boys.

Newspapers made much of the fact the police captain, who is now retired, never made more than $5,200 a year. The implication was that he must have been a paragon of thrift. But suppose the $100,000 or $205,000 had been his only in part, or not at all. Might he not have been acting for a departmental investment fund, a kind of police-force Morris Plan?

THE HONEST RAINMAKER

The Life and Times of Colonel John R. Stingo

To the Châtelaine

Contents

THE LEGEND

There was once a sheik, the richest and most puissant in all Arabia, and he owned thousands of swift dromedaries, the best in all Arabia, and thousands of thoroughbred Arabian steeds, the fastest in all Arabia, and his years were four score and nineteen, and his sons long since had reconciled themselves to his demise. So when, one eve, as the sun sank sad on the west side of the Euphrates, the old sheik summoned his eldest son to the side of his couch, the son sensed that it was the finish, although the word "official" had not yet flashed on the odds board.

"Draw near, my son," the old man croaked, "for my voice is feeble with years, and I would have you hear me."

The son, who was himself a green three score and ten, inclined obediently above his sire, and placed his right ear near the old sheik's mouth.

"You know, my son, that I own thousands of swift dromedaries," the old man said, "the best in all Arabia."

"Yes, Father," the eldest son said, "I know."

"And you know I own thousands of fat-tailed sheep, the fattest in all Arabia."

"Yes, Father," the eldest son said, "I know."

"And you know I own thousands of thoroughbred Arabian horses, the fastest in all Arabia."

"Yes, Father," said the eldest son, "I know."

"Well, Son," the old sheik said, "I bet on those horses.

"And now the First National Bank of Mecca holds a mortgage on the thousands of swift dromedaries, the best in all Arabia.

"And the First National Bank of Medina holds a mortgage on the thousands of fat-tailed sheep, the fattest in all Arabia.

"And the First National Bank of Trans-Jordan has foreclosed on the horses, and they are to be sold at auction in the paddock at Babylon tomorrow.

"So I have no material goods to leave to you."

The eldest son's heart was heavy within his breast, but he was a dead-game sport.

"It is well, Father," he said.

Then the old man, with a last mighty effort, sat up straight on his couch of gazelle skins and said:

"But I have something more precious to bequeath to you, my counsel."

"Yes, Father," the eldest son said, "I hear."

"My son," the old man said. "Never work a day. And NEVER, NEVER, take an honest dollar."

—Favorite barroom recitation of
Colonel John R. Stingo

1 / The Plug in the Door

When the New York *Times* published the news a while back that 169 towns and individuals upstate had filed damage claims against New York City for $2,138,510 and no odd cents, Colonel John R. Stingo was politely amused. The claims rested upon the city's efforts to produce rain from clouds over its Catskill Mountain reservoirs during a water shortage in 1950. These involved seeding clouds with dry ice, and were carried out by a meteorologist named Dr. Wallace E. Howell, who had a contract from February, 1950, until February, 1951, to help it rain. The upstaters accused Dr. Howell of drowning them out, even charging him with the tornado which swept the whole Atlantic coast on November 25. It seemed to be up to the city to prove Dr. Howell's experiments hadn't worked, although at the time they were made it had intimated they were at least partially successful.

Colonel Stingo sometimes refers to himself as the Honest Rainmaker, as in the phrase, "the Honest Rainmaker, who is among those with the Prattle of a Babe and the soul of Jimmy Hope the Bank Robber." When he read the story in the *Times* he said, "I'm astonished that these modern professionals, men of authenticated science, wind up with damage suits and hard feelings. When my rain-inductive colleagues and I concluded a campaign, we were invariably the guests of the benefited community at a banquet where *sec* and *brut* flowed like the showers in the dressing room of the St. Louis Cardinals after a sixteen-inning game on a day of record heat. We would all get stiff as boards and they would invite us to come back next season."

Colonel Stingo is a nom de plume, but hardly anybody calls the Colonel anything else, and not many of his casual acquaintances know he has another name. He has been a newspaperman, off and on, for sixty-five years by his own count, and is now, for that matter, but he has never seen a future in it. The Colonel has always believed that fortune swims, not with the main stream of letters, but in the shallows where the suckers moon. In pursuance of this theory, he has acquired a varied experience, which he willingly shares with his friends.

Colonel Stingo's real name is James A. Macdonald, and half a century ago, when he was writing about horse races for the New York *Evening Journal*, he used to sign it J.S.A. Macdonald, which led critical colleagues to call him Alphabet. The S stood for Stuart, a name he has since discarded, because, he says, it made him seem a Young Pretender. In that dawn age of Hearst journalism in New York he was a favorite of Arthur Brisbane, who saw in his damascened style the making of a Hearst editorial writer. "But I stuck to the turf," Colonel Stingo says. "I knew the money was in the side lines." Reminded that Brisbane died with around twenty million dollars, the Colonel comes up with a correction. "Thirty-nine million," he says. "But it was a fluke." The Colonel himself lives in what he terms a "one-room suite" in a hotel built over a bus terminal.

During the Hearst days a competitor, outraged by the Colonel's exclusive report of a projected hundred-thousand-dollar match race between Irish Lad and a kangaroo backed by a millionaire Australian, wrote: "Alphabet Macdonald never permits facts to interfere with the exercise of his imagination." The Colonel rightly considered this a tribute to his mastery of his material.

"The sculptor," he says, "imposes his design on the Parian marble." But in most of his tales there is an element of truth which passes through the finest filter, so it is impossible to class them as fiction.

It is a matter of taxonomy, and immaterial.

The Colonel is a small, lively man with a back as straight as the wide part precisely in the middle of his hair, which becomes wider but no less precise with the passage of the years. His straightness, his neatness, and a certain old-fashioned formality of diction befit an old military man, and there are a good many impressionable bartenders on Broadway who believe he is. He wears bow ties, clothes that have an archaic dash, even when they are a trifle worn, and pointed shoes that show off his elegantly diminutive feet.

"When I was young," he sometimes says, harking back to what he calls "the days of halcyon, before Charles Evans Hughes leveled a deathblow at gracious living in America—I wore shiny patent-leather shoes with sharp points, and if I didn't like you I'd kick you and you'd bleed to death." This is by some of his acquaintance considered an allegorical allusion to the power of the press. But the Colonel has not elucidated it.

Hughes, while Governor of New York, signed a bill abolishing betting on race tracks here. A few years later the bookmakers found a way around it which tided them over until track bets were again legalized in 1934. But the Colonel still thinks of the late Chief Justice of the United States Supreme Court as the man who ushered in the Dark Ages of Hypocrisy. "Prohibition was an inevitable sequelae," he says, "and so was the sordid pari mutuel." Hughes was also indirectly responsible for the Colonel's withdrawal from the New York scene. When the unplucked statesman was elected Governor in 1906 he was already pledged to stop racing. There didn't seem to be any future for a racing writer in New York, and so the Colonel snapped at a chance to go out to Los Angeles as sporting editor of Hearst's *Examiner*, in that then distinctly minor-league city. He didn't get back for twenty-three years, and it is in this period of *wanderung* that he places many of his most picturesque and least checkable anecdotes.

There is usually a white carnation in the Colonel's buttonhole, and almost invariably, when he is seen in public, a beer glass in his right hand. For a period before lunch, which is customarily his first meal of the day, he devotes himself to gold gin fizzes, which are made with the yolk of the egg. During this process of remedial imbibition he is morose and does not appreciate company. "I met a villain last night," he will say in explanation of his mood, "and he led me down the path of dalliance Gambrinian." If the bartender in setting down the shaker bangs it against the wood, the jangled Colonel will say, "Doctor, don't cut too deep! I have been riding the magic carpet." But he eats his lunch with good appetite. He often says he is a "good doer." On surveying the menu he says, "The entry list seems to have filled well," and then he goes down the line with few scratches. After lunch he makes what he calls "the Great Transition," switching from hard liquor to beer, which he continues to drink from then until he goes to bed, unless he meets a villain who induces him to deviate.

In periods when Colonel Stingo is what he describes as "non-holding," or financially straitened, he spends a large part of his time in the reading room of the New York Public Library, seeding the clouds of printed erudition above his already overflowing reservoir of odd information. Such knowledge he refers to verbally as "esatoric," although he can spell the word all right. When he ceases to be non-holding, and has an adequate amount of what he refers to as "Tease," he makes his *rentrée*, usually telling his favorite bartenders in detail about conditions in some place he has been reading up on in the Public Library. "Glad to get back," he says. "There's no place like New York."

He doesn't like to be in bars when he can't buy his share of the drinks or undergo an occasional small bite. "I am a man of money," he likes to say when he has any at all. "The next round is on me."

Since the Kefauver committee began its revival of the Hughes Inquisition, the Colonel has had time to do a record amount of reading. His job, writing a column for a newspaper called the New York *Enquirer*, is irreproachably legitimate, but carries no salary. His income has been derived from its perquisites, which are commissions on the ads he attracts to the paper's sports pages. Nearly all of these are from turf analysts, which means tipsters. Their profession too is irreproachably legitimate, since freedom of opinion is guaranteed by the Bill of Rights. But nobody is going to pay for a tip when he can't find a bookmaker to play it with. The harder things get for the bookies, the more nearly impossible they become for the purveyors of purported information. As the latter drop their ads, the Colonel's absences from his Gambrinian haunts become longer and more frequent, until at one time they threatened to merge in one long continuous hiatus, like that induced by the Hughes Law. Some of his friends, making an erroneous inference from his age and the protraction of his nonappearance, began to refer to him in the past tense.

At the moment of his remark about the decline of good feeling in the rainmaking business, I knew by a sure sign he was non-holding: he asked me how he could earn some money. I have known Colonel Stingo for five years, during which I had occasionally heard him allude to his career as a rainmaker, but I had never heard him tell the full story. I therefore suggested that he set it forth.

"If you write it," I told him, "you might be able to sell it."

"It's a strange idea, Joe," he said, "but I'll try it."

Before he would begin, though, he insisted that I promise to stand by to help.

We took rendezvous for that day week at Gough's, a bar on West Forty-third Street where there is a life-size oil portrait of John L. Sullivan wearing a frock coat. The Colonel was to bring with him a rough draft of at least a substantial part of the story of the Honest Rainmaker.

"While I am about it," he said, "I might as well write my autobiography, of which this is only one of the episodia minora. I shall call it *The Plug in the Door.*"

"It is an ominous title, Colonel," I said.

"It is indeed," he said. "A phrase fraught with fear for hundreds of thousands of habitual hotel inhabiters. What mockery lies in the word 'guest' as employed by the average flinthearted hotelier! His so-called hospitality is limited by the visible extent of the inmate's liquid assets. He has a memory as short as a man who borrows five dollars; the months of faithful acquitment of obligations by the patron avail him nothing,—the hotel man's recollection extends back only as far as the last presentation of the bill. The sealed keyhole," he said, in his emotion mixing metaphors as smoothly as a bartender blends gin and vermouth, "is the sword of Damocles suspended by an economic hair over a large proportion of the American people.

"And yet," he added, a gentler light suffusing his rugged countenance, for the Colonel is a man of everchanging mood, "I have known the plug in the door once to save a friend of mine from trancelike despair. It was a snowy night in January, and he had just descended from an office where he had been trying for hours to write a story that seemed to him of less moment every time he looked at it. Ultimately he had thrown it into the wastebasket. He had bet on fourteen consecutive losers at Hialeah, his wife had left him to run off with an advertising man, and from a vertiginous pounding in his ears he felt himself due for a coronary occlusion. Proceeding but a few yards, he found himself at the corner of Forty-fourth Street and Times Square, the southeast one. He had had some idea of seeking out a place to eat, but he had no appetite and he could not decide where to go. Then it began to seem to him that it wasn't worth the trouble to go anywhere. The snow continued to fall, and he began to assume the aspect of a well-powdered Christmas tree.

"The discordant laughter of a party of revelers, outward bound from some dispensatorium of cheer, recalled him to a sense of his situation. He cringed at the thought of being accosted by a copper solicitous of his compos mentis, and the hilarity suggested to him a possible source of assuagement. So he entered the bar of the old Hotel Cadillac, which at that time still stood at Forty-third Street.

"The Cadillac was a hotel harboring a most Bohemian motley, particularly in the last phase of its existence; it was the last stand of many old show people fallen from high estate, and also of elements more riffraffian. My friend entered the bar. A mere partition set it off from the lobby. It was thronged with raucousness; the atmosphere was most convivial. He wedged his way between two blondes to attain contact with the mahogany; they evinced no indignation, although he ignored them. He drank one, two short scotches before he even began to look about him. By the seventh he was on terms of pleasant familiarity with his neighbors adjacent; he took them out to dinner and had a hell of an evening, winding up by inviting them to visit his apartment, solitary since his wife's defection. When he awoke next morning they were both still there. They had returned to their room at the Cadillac on the previous evening only to find their door plugged, they explained, and had adjourned to the bar, the habitat of wisdom and inspiration, to reflect upon their situation, when they made the happy encounter. Had the management not locked them out, my friend might have succumbed to despair and self-destruction, which would have been a pity because his wife left the advertising man and came back to him three days later. They lived happily ever after, until she ran away with the night manager of an automat."

We shook hands and parted.

2 / *The Pasha Strikes Out*

GOUGH'S IS a saloon which has been on Forty-third Street for only five or six years, but the portrait of Sullivan gives it an air of maturity. One item of *décor* like that can make a place. I remember when a man I know opened a speakeasy in 1925 and put a suit of armor in it. As soon as you saw the armor you knew the proprietor had confidence he would last, investing in such superfluous elegance. And it couldn't be a clip joint, or they would never have anything around that a drunk who got rolled could come back and identify. The armor established the place. A lot of saloons are open for years without getting established.

A life-size portrait of Sullivan is of necessity a big thing. He was six feet tall and the artist naturally had to leave something for him to stand on and something over the head so you can see he isn't wearing a hat. This is a very dark portrait, so it is hard to see in places whether the black is frock coat or background. The picture looks as if it had been painted in the nineties, after Sullivan had lost the title and gone on the wagon. His face is fat, he is wearing a fine moustache, and his right hand is on his belly, as if he is going to begin a temperance lecture. There is a light at the top of the frame and a little sign at the lower right-hand corner of the picture which says, "John Lawrence Sullivan, Heavyweight Champion of the United States, Born, Boston, Mass., 1858—Died, 1918."

The sign was put there a couple of months ago, after a stranger had come in and looked at the portrait for a while and then burst out laughing. The stranger had walked over to the bar and said to the bartender: "I know who that is, it's John L. Sullivan."

"Who else would it be?" the bartender had asked.

"Well, I'm from Naval Intelligence," the stranger had said, and he had a card to prove it, "and some fool reserve officer was in here and reported to us that there was a bar on Forty-third Street with a life-size portrait of Stalin and a votive light over it."

The sign went on next day.

The portrait is signed by somebody named Daunton, but the Colonel, who has a scheme to sell it to a millionaire Texan with an Irish name for a quarter of a million, believes that this is a case of wrong attribution.

"Daunton may have been some dauber engaged to clean the picture," he once told me. "I never heard of him. I believe the painter to be Copley. Much better price." When I reminded him that Copley had lived in the eighteenth century, he said, "I meant Copley the grandson." He has an answer for everything.

The Colonel, by his own account, was born in 1874 in New Orleans, and there is no reason to quibble over the date. He has no trace of southern accent, and this has led certain friends to the assertion that his true birthplace was considerably north of Louisiana, in Montreal or Brooklyn, and that his present version of his origin was suggested by the name of the hotel where he now lives, the Dixie. But if his cradle was not bowered by magnolias, it should have been. He is a true romantic.

Personally, I believe the New Orleans story, even though one of the Montreal-theory men who knew the Colonel fifty years ago insists that from the day of his arrival here the Colonel was a good ice skater. "There were no artificial rinks in the nineteenth century," he says. The way I figure it, what the man really remembers is that the Colonel *told* him he was a good ice skater, which is not the same thing.

The Colonel himself has spoken to me of his regret at losing his Louisianian accent, by a process he describes as slow attrition. "It got rubbed off, Joe, like pollen off the bee, by contact with a thousand charming flowers," he said. "In the speech of each I left some trace of my native music. From each I received in return some nasal diphthong or harsh consonant. It was a heavy price." In a more practical vein he added, "The accent would have been of great assistance if I had wished to set up on my own as a turf adviser. A southern accent is an invaluable asset to a tout.

"Also," he said, "it would have aided me in religious work. The great Dr. Orlando Edgar Miller, an evangelist who took in more money at Carnegie Hall than Paderewski, used to say to me, 'Jim, if you were a taller man and you hadn't lost your southern twang, you'd be a hell of a revivalist.'" Religion has played a large part in the Colonel's life. I once heard him say, "It's the strongest thing man ever invented, with the possible exception of the Standard Oil Company."

As in journalism, Colonel Stingo believes, the real money is in the side lines. "The immediate collection is of little import," he says. "The Rev. Dr. Hall, with whom I was once associated, had a self-exegetic Bible, which he sold for a hundred dollars a copy, but only on the written agreement of the subscriber that it would remain in his personal possession until transmitted to his heir. It was a masterwork superb. I wrote a chapter myself. To be eligible to buy a copy you had to be a graduate of the salon classes for ladies, six lessons for fifty dollars; or of the esatoric course for men, twelve sessions for two hundred and fifty. We sold 412 Bibles in the first month of one race meeting at Seattle. The bookmakers made us a proposition to leave town because we were getting all the Tease. That was before the Reverend Doctor began betting on the horses. After that they offered to pay the rent on a hall if we would stay."

The Colonel's habitual expression is that of a stud-poker player with one ace showing who wants to give the impression that he has another in the hole. He looks as if he knew something amusing that he didn't have the right to say. In poker this may be either a bluff or fake bluff, designed to induce other players to get into the two aces. In the Colonel's case, however, the expression means only that he finds the world a funny place.

When he showed at Gough's with the first section of his manuscript, he made me think he was a veritable Georges Simenon or Edgar Wallace, or that in the manner of the elder Dumas or Henry Luce he had placed himself at the head of a literary factory, for he produced from the diagonal slash pockets of his nubbly blue jacket two long manila envelopes bulging with manuscript.

"I suggest that you have a look at the autobiography first," he said, handing one of the envelopes across the table to me.

On the first sheet, under a neat row of asterisks, he had typed the title:

PLUG IN THE DOOR

and then, after four blank lines:

Projected Story in Book Form of Everyday People in Everyday Life.

On the next page it said:

Characters in the Story Play
The Duchess
The Millionaire Kid
Dynamite Jack Thornby
"Wild Bill" Lyons
Harry the Coupon King
Mike The Bite
Senator Casey
Mary The Martyr
The Singing Kid
Madame Alda
&
Colonel John Adams Howard,
Circle C Ranch
Cheyenne, Wyoming

On the third page, a memorandum on procedure, it said:

Establish Personal Basis.
Developing Story to Bring in Alluring Events Over the Chronological Sequence.

The fourth page said just:

Chapterial Outline

and led to twelve pages each headed by a chapter subject but otherwise bare. On the page following the Colonel had taken a fresh start.

Plug In The Door

This one said:

A Story of a Life Variegated

Finally, on about the twentieth page, the Colonel had apparently taken his spring.

The Stories and Rhymes heard at Mother's knee in the prattling days of childhood persist and live to the end of the recipient's tenure here below.

The inclining influence there exerted upon the delicate tendril of babydays shapes and directs the Fate and Destiny of all men, of all women, no matter who or what they may be; as illustrious as a Caesar, as squalid as the Thief of Bagdad.

But, strange as it may be, it is of my Grandmother and my Great Grandmother that, perforce, I must talk in getting along with the Story of A Life, my life, we've, you and I, thought up under the aforementioned titleage of Plug In The Door, a circumstance and a terror uncounted multitudes of ordinary mortals know so well.

All the remaining pages were blank.

"I couldn't go on after that," the Colonel said. "I was overcome by emotion. But the lead is the main thing, Joe. Everything will follow along nicely after I once barge into the episodia."

I was, quite truthfully, not much disappointed. What I had wanted him to write was a story about rainmaking. To set down his life from its beginning, I felt, might be a valuable spiritual exercise for my friend, but the years stretching from his great-grandmother's knee to early manhood could have only a limited popular appeal. They wouldn't help much to keep the plug out of his door at the Dixie.

"It reads very well, what there is of it, Colonel," I said. "But how about *The Honest Rainmaker?*"

The Colonel smiled and handed over the second well-stuffed envelope. The pages in this one were covered with typescript. The first began:

"Rain,—it's abundance, it's paucity,—meant Life and Death to the Ancients for from the lands and the flocks, herds, the fish of the sea, the birds of the air, the deer and mountain goat they found sustenance and energized being. All the elements depended upon the Fall of Rain, ample but not in ruinous overplus, for very existence.

"Through all human history the plenitude of Rain or its lack constituted the difference between Life and Death, the Joy of Rain or existence and misery."

"That's the first part of a speech I used to deliver to chapters of the Farmers' Guild in California when I was clinching deals for Professor Joseph Canfield Hatfield," the Colonel explained, gesturing to the waitress to bring him a second bottle of delight Gambrinian. "The next ten pages are on the same high level, but I would not suggest they are of the highest interest to our potential readers. Anyway, it will give you an idea of what I can do when the Ark of the Covenant falls upon me.

"Rain has always made the difference between plenty of Tease and non-holding for those farmers in the California valleys, a circumstance of which I was made much aware in July, 1908, when I was one of three hundred guests of a rich man named Captain James McKittrick on his stupendous estate, the Rancho del McKittrick, twenty miles from Bakersfield, at a party to celebrate the advent of Sudi Witte Pasha, a rainmaker the Captain had imported at vast expense from the Sudan. The episode begins on page ten."

I found the place and read:

"This enormous Rancho comprised 212,000 acres, an area so large that it required a Cowhand, with many pinto relays, two days and two nights to cross it, West to East or North to South.

"But the world's prime essential, golden Wheat, remained the prime crop. With rain precipitation at the very right moment the year for Rancho del McKittrick, with its 62,000 acres to Wheat, would be beneficently happy. Otherwise, no Rain no joy in Mudville, mighty Casey, he struck out. So the expansive Capt. McKittrick had brought on Sudi Witte Pasha, the World's Heavyweight Champion Rainmaker, to see what he could do about the anguishing situation in the Lower San Joaquin Valley,—no rain and ruin around the corner.

"The old Pasha had twenty-two Professors and Holy Men in his Mob and a whole mobile Library of Books with imploring Cantors, bewhiskered Priests, Bell Ringers, Soothsayers and Pricemakers,—all quartered in the lap of luxury in the Santa Clara Villa, an adjunct of the Manor House, with a retinue of Chefs, Servitors and Body Guardsmen at command. We all understood that the Captain agreed to pay Pasha and his lads the sum of $150,000 and all expenses, to and from Cairo, Egypt, for a three months' service and demonstration of his magic Bag O'Tricks.

"In the middle of July, 1908, with $2,000,000 worth of Wheat just beginning to ripen off in the field, the Egyptian Rainmaker went to work to bring on the aqueous dispensation. His chatty Camp Followers first greeted the Morning Sun and took a dip in the cold waters of Cherry Creek before going into the big Two-Day Fast, touched off by a little body lashing, and a sort of an ear piercing Indian War Dance, much like those you see done by the Indians in Arizona.

"The real Kick-Off came the third day with a series of Incantations and the throwing about of quite a deal of reddish colored powder and sweet smelling myrrh. The pretty Samia never swung such belly convulsions in her Royal Court Dance at Hotel Mecca, beneath the Pyramids, as did little Miss Matti, the Pasha's apple of eye, towards the end of the Exhortation to the Spirits of Rain. We were told by Interpreters what the dance meant.

"The fourth day was given over to the throwing upon the Runways, surrounding the miles of Wheat Fields a brownish sort of little nut, known as the Kofu Bean from the Eufrates Country in ancient Persia,—all ground up fine. It was done en masse, the Pasha in command, and with his impressed Rancho help of about 200 cowboys, cowgirls, and field workers going down the furrows ladling out the seeds, right and left, one might recall the ancients sowing their fields in biblical times out of shoulder bags with a blessing and hope of a fruitful harvest in the months to follow.

"That night in the Great Hall of the Manor House was staged a feast of Food, Fun and Frivol, the likes of which I had never seen before or since. It was for about 300 persons, and lasted until sundown the following day. Chefs down from San Francisco "curried" everything within sight,—even Sherry's ice cream, rushed through by special train from New York. Choice vintage of Paul Masson, one of California's choicest, flowed like water. The Feast of Belshazzar was pikish compared to this Orgy in Imploration for Rain; yet dire was the choleric ranchero's reaction when nothing happened.

"After 56 hours we were to see results, affirmed the Pasha; meantime, to engage in supplication and reverent prayer. Well, we waited and waited for exactly nine days but not a sign of rain; then came the Blow Off. The jolly Captain,—the Show had cost him an additional $40,000—came to a sudden and drastic decision; "Enough is enough," he said while forthwithedly ordering prepared at once his two special railroad cars, the 'Erma' and the 'Sally Jane,' lying in the Southern Pacific Railroad siding, a mile down Cherry Creek, for an immediate emergency itinerary,—to take the whole caboodle of Oriental scientists and rainmakers to the nearest station on the Sunset Route, the Old Santa Fe town of Barstow, where arrangements had been made to attach the cars to the outgrowing Pelican Express for Phoenix, Fort Worth and New Orleans; with a stop over for a resumpton of egress by Cromwell Line steamer from the Crescent City through the Straits of Gibraltar to the palm-waving beaches of dear old Cairo and the verandah at Shepherd's Hotel."

So it ended. I went back and reread that one tremendous climactic sentence, in which the irate millionaire sweeps the whole caboodle from the shores of the Pacific to the palm-waving beaches of old Cairo, with glimpses in transit of Barstow, Phoenix, Fort Worth, New Orleans, and the Straits of Gibraltar. Eight thousand miles or so in a few seconds. It made me visualize the soothsayers, price makers, and dancing girls picking themselves up off their rumps on the beaches and waving *their* palms in astonishment, as if they had been dropped by a Djinn, or Genius. The genius in this case is the Colonel's.

"It must have been quite a party," I said. Colonel Stingo gave the barmaid a sign of the hand to bring on another round for both of us, and when he had seen this signal honored, he acknowledged that I was right. "It was a stupendous quaffery," he said. "Of course, my interest in the proceedings was purely cultural and Belshazzarian. I was engaged in the promotion of race tracks, and our mutual interest in the turf, rather than agriculture, had brought me into contact with Captain McKittrick, a grand fellow. But I could see the strength of the Pasha's racket immediately. If the Fates had been kind enough to vouchsafe a normal rainfall, he could have parlayed it into an empire like Pizarro's. Where there is a need, someone will arise to fill it. I didn't think his presentation was particularly adapted to the American market, though. The exotic inspires distrust. A display of cold science, with impressive paraphernalia, is more effective, especially if combined with a spiritual note."

The Colonel had by now emptied a third bottle of the Gambrinian amber. "The subsidization of the Pasha was not the first attempt to influence the rain gods in California," he said. "For years wheat growers had been bringing in bands of Apaches from a reservation at Douglas, Arizona, to do rain dances. It didn't cost much and they figured it couldn't do any harm. That's why I was intrigued by this clipping,"—and he handed me a paragraph that looked as if it had been cut from a Sunday magazine section:

"OLD ORDER CHANGETH: Navajo Indians near Gallup, N.M., have become skeptical of—or just plain bored with—their ancient rain-making rites. During a recent drought, they hired professional rainmakers to seed the clouds over their reservation. Result: one-and-a-half inches of rain."

3/*Toad in Spring*

"MY OWN ENTRY into the rainmaking arena did not immediately follow my perception of its potentialities," the Colonel said. "I followed after false gods. I started a race track at Salt Lake City in 1909; had to do business with the elders of the Mormon Church to get the green light. Our track was out at a place called Lagoon. After we got our track going nicely an outraged husband, an old-time Mormon, shot our track manager for the usual reason. The Mormons, although sub roseately polygamous, were monopolistic in their conjugal views. This caused a scandal, and the elders shut down our track and opened one of their own. Afterward I got a heavyweight prize fighter named Tommy Burns, who is now a faith healer in Coalinga, California. We are still dear friends and correspond incessantly."

As if in evidence, the Colonel displayed a calling card which read:

Compliments of
TOMMY BURNS

FORMER WORLD'S HEAVYWEIGHT BOXING CHAMPION

A demonstrator of Universal Love

PHONE 442 BOX 566

Coalinga, California, U.S.A.

Scrawled over the print was a line in handwriting: *God is Life & God is Love & not a human being up in the sky.* On the back of the card was a printed message, headed: THINKING KINDLY MAKES PERFECTION.

"He's a dear old Tommy," the Colonel said. "We severed our professional connection in Reno, Nevada, the day after the fight between Jim Jeffries and Jack Johnson on July 4, 1910. Jeffries never hit Johnson a punch. Burns and I had previously agreed he should retire, but Tex Rickard, the promoter of the Jeffries–Johnson fight, offered us twenty-five thousand dollars to fight Stanley Ketchel, the Michigan Assassin. I put it up to Tommy. 'You fight him,' he said. 'I'm going fishing.' "

The Colonel sighed. "We could have beaten Ketchel, too," he said. "After that I engaged in a variety of promotional ventures too multifarious to recount now. I would see an enterprise that needed the services of a good public relations man, and I would talk myself in, always for a piece. It was in that manner I encountered Professor Joseph Canfield Hatfield, in about 1912. I was in a town called Modesto, California, where the chief attraction of the particular evening was a cocking main, to be held in the auditorium of the Salvation Army Temple following a meeting of the Modesto local of the Farmers' Guild.

"Cockfighting is not my idea of the sport supreme, but having nothing better to do I attended, and for the same reason I got there early. Here this tall angular individual, Professor Joseph Canfield Hatfield, a squinty-eyed old fellow around fifty or so—was up on the platform lecturing about 'the induction of rainfall by vibratory detonation.' He had already been around for perhaps fifteen years with his theory, but had never yet made a major score.

"The first wheat growers in California had been the owners of huge ranches, but after the introduction of Turkey Red wheat to California between 1875 and '90, a variety that could grow on poor and semi-arid lands, there got to be more and more 'small' wheat growers with ranches of about twenty-five hundred acres. These made up the membership of the Farmers' Guild."

This was a field on which the Colonel had me completely at his mercy, since it was impossible to check his statements by reference to the American Racing Manual or Nat Fleischer's Ring Record Book, my usual editorial resources.

I ordered up a replenishment of the Gambrinian, and Colonel Stingo continued.

"Always the dread of the wheat grower in California in the valleys of the San Joaquin and the Sacramento River and further north in the terrain of the Columbia River and the tortuous Fraser River is lack of rain precipitation. But the Professor didn't quite know how to transmute their apprehension into auriferous deposit."

I cite, from his manuscript:

"In all sincerity this old Prof. Hatfield believed that Cannon Detonation at certain times under certain conditions would induce Rainfall; he said he had been successful in South Africa, round about Pretoria and Ladysmith and along the Tugela River bottoms in creating Rain Precipitation at the very precise time when the downpour saved the Boers vast crops of grain and fodder. He claimed credit for prolonging the Boer War a whole year.

"This incongruous Hatfield, a highly religious man, continuously bespoke the Deities in his exhortations as though his Gatling Gun would more surely serve scientific expectations through the kindly office of the Occult. He availed fasting and a wing and buck salute to the Morning Sun as a means to further favorable propituary. At the same time, I would remark at this juncture, recollection suggests the Professor knew the practical difference between the Net and the Gross and the possibilities thereof.

"Marco Polo returned from Cathay with an explosive yellow powder to the Savants Salon in Venice with the story of the first known attempts at Rain Precipitation through chemical action or physical impact according to Prof. Hatfield.

"Before not fewer than 4,000 curious long-haired gentry in Angelus Temple, Los Angeles, Calif., in his first days in the Golden State the mystic Prof. Hatfield, put to it by a Platform Barnyard Committee on Science, stated that it was his understanding that the Ancients exploded the powder by centralizing the sun's actinic rays but that he, 'the master,' used a more effective modern device,—'the awful Gatling Gun with it's discharge of pure dynamite: the gun which had won the Battle of San Juan Hill in the Spanish-American War and elected a Rough Rider to the appalling office of President of the United States of America.'

"The yokelic audience evocated in unison 'Amen, crack again.'

"I did the spade work and brought the situation to a near climax by assembling two representatives from each of the 80 Locals of the Guild with power to sign up on the Professor's neatly contrived contract of service and payment. We signed the contract at Tulare.

"The proposition was for each Local to guarantee Prof. Hatfield just $1,000, to be deposited at the Title Guarantee Trust Company in Tulare in advance. On the part of the Hatfield Rain Precipitation Corporation, through device and services of our scientific Detonationary Method, we were to assume all expenses and full direction. The official Gauges, Containers and Measuring Paddles were approved and the centrifical point of test and calculation to be the Roof of the Court House at Visalia, Calif., in heart of the Drought Wheat Lands with crops, in case of Rain, worth at least $2,000,000 in jeopardy.

"We, the Rainmakers, the Party of the First Part, always Innocents Abroad and Unsuspecting, had 32 days and nights in which to deliver 4.10 (four decimal ten) inches' depth of rain water. Rainmakers were to receive $10,000 an inch for every inch from 3 inches and below, up to 4.10 inches. If 'the can' ever showed as much as 4 inches we, the Rainmakers, were to receive the sum of $20,000 an inch for the whole amount of precipitation. We could win $80,000 and the Professor's expenses for the 30 days' Preliminary Campaign had been just $6,120: we got $1,200 of this back from the Sunny Jim Breakfast Food Co.'s advertising campaign, —so that our Nut was about $5,000.

"There was not one of the Delegates, and not a Wheat Grower in the Valley but wished heartily for the Rainmakers' success; they did not begrudge the money and wished us well. The women prayed in the churches for our success and a score or more Barn Dances and Picnics were given in our behalf, for the Professor was a natural friend maker and great alround wonderful old thief and grand good fellow. I wore off the O'Sullivan rubber heels from French, Shriner & Urner twenty-dollar shoes that month of July dancing with the buxom farm girls. And what hoedowns they were,—from sunset to sunrise. Their homemade whiskey and kitchen beer would cure cancer first time at bat.

"They say all first-class Boob Traps must contain a real smart Ace-In-The-Hole. The Rainmakers on this occasion, as well as on all other similar occasions, possessed that desideratum to a high degree.

"It was just the Meteorological Tables and Rain Precipitations for Central California issued by the Weather Bureau of the United States and the Analytical Charts and Study Averages issued by the Department of Agriculture, Washington, D.C. Then there were the Tables on Rain Precipitation from Sacramento and the Merchants Exchange, San Francisco. Many the long-hour midnight vigil I spent over those masses of demonical figures and equations in collaboration with Mr. 'Kid' Bloggs, a mighty man with Horse Figures, who was, and is, a smart Handicapper of the Gees at home and abroad.

"Without going into a labyrinth of meaningless Figures to the layman it may suffice to state the Rundown showed that for the 32-Day Period it was 55 per cent in the Rainmakers favor, viz., that 4 inches of Rain would fall regardless of Prof. Hatfield and his Gatling Guns and stores of 'pure' dynamite.

"Before an immense gathering on the North Slope of Mount Meadows, a sort of junior mountain, foregathered State, Civic and Departmental officials and the Locals turned out to a man,—about 5,000 persons on a hot dry afternoon beneath a burning Mid-California 'desert' sun. After the speeches and the Band had droned its last brassy blare Prof. Hatfield announced his retirement with Staff and ascent, not to heaven, but to the mountain's apex and bade the crowds retire to safe distance on the lower slopes. The double Battery of Gatlings went off like the Clap of Doom with a repeat, every five hours under Director of Ordnance Dr. G.A.I.M. Sykes.

"Just about midnight a perfect deluge suddenly engulfed the countryside causing Prof. Hatfield to swell his chest and bleat his salutations like a toad in springtime. The old boy thought in his inner soul that he had something on the ball but was not thoroughly convinced the Occult Powers had not framed up on him by staging a Show for his benefit and especial delight; perhaps he deserved the indulgence of the Fates, he thought. The Precipitation was 1⅛ inches, which is a lot of rain in anybody's country. Next day all the newspapers were full of the story and the Professor became slightly deified; the whole Valley stood enraptured and the fields and the ripening grain bloomed forth in gentle freshness wonderful to behold. The farmers were so happy, and even the banks began to loan money.

"Three times more during the thirty-odd days and nights we had real heavy downpours. We made a Gross Total of 3⅝ inches;—just under the full 4 inches. The overjoyed Locals held a Special Meeting and voted us the full $80,000 and invited Prof. Hatfield to return next season. The crop came in most beautifully. It was a bumper. That winter many a California wheat grower spent Christmas at New York and the childhood home in New England.

"We were paid all O.K. My cut was about $22,000. On the strength of our success the Hatfield Outfit was invited by the Farmers of the Columbia River in Oregon to a conference the following year in Salem. Meanwhile the puffed up Prof. Hatfield had received overtures from interests in the Sudan in Egypt and accepted the offers but he left us all behind.

"It was a great opportunity for Dr. Sykes and myself to go ahead on our own hook. Overnight the Doctor became the Miracle Man and I the Chief Salesman. We kept on our Staff of nine people and a Battery of Cannon used in the Civil War. Same old deal and once again we are hoping for good luck with the lay of the cards all in our favor or comparatively so based on the Rain Precipitation Figures covering the Oregon Territory. To make a long long story short we win again and the world is ours. My take is $9,200. Paid off the Boys and Girls and disband for further orders.

"But we never did come together again for the reason that the Guildsmen found out they could do just as well themselves provided they had the right sort of Cannon.

"While shooting off their Cannon one Guildsman lost his leg and several Farmers were chewed up a bit. The rain fell just the same and the jig was up. The idea cooled off to a whisper and a story of the yesteryear."

The rain, the cold November rain, beat down on Forty-third Street as I finished reading the Colonel's story.

"In this climate," I said, forgetting 1950, "they ought to pay somebody to prevent rain."

"I was in that business too," Colonel Stingo said.

4 / *The Third Palace*

THE PALACE BAR and Grill, on Forty-fifth Street off Longacre Square, has not, like Gough's, the air of a shrine. It is a salon. Sophie Braun, who presides over it, suggests a collaboration between Vigée-Lebrun and Rubens, with soft white hair, pink skin, and substantial proportions. She is a woman whose quiet courtesy inspires courteous quiet in a potentially obstreperous clientele, and it was this power of Mrs. Braun's that first attracted Colonel Stingo to the place.

Joe Braun, her consort, has an equally restful personality. A sallow, stocky man of fixed habits, he goes to the races on each of the 198 afternoons of the New York season and bets five dollars on every horse Ted Atkinson rides. This is in addition to his otherwise-motivated betting, —a sort of left-hand bass to his play on the other side of the piano. He also places much faith in the advice of a friend who sells pari-mutuel tickets at a hundred-dollar window. It is impossible to tell from Joe's expression at the moment of encounter, however, whether Atkinson is on a winning or a losing streak, or whether the hundred-dollar bettors are doing any better than the herd. He smokes cigars and removes them from his mouth for only brief lapses into speech. Once an unfortunate fellow player, who had borrowed a considerable sum from Joe, paid him off with a number of plots in a Jewish cemetery. "I thought I might as well take them before he bet them on some pig," Joe said.

This left Mr. Braun with several surplus resting places, as he and Sophie had no children. So he presented one to Colonel Stingo, who accepted. "I couldn't be in better company," the Colonel declared, with feeling.

It was at the Palace that I awaited the arrival of the Colonel with the second installment of his story.

He arrived, smiling as he showed off an envelope as rounded on the sides as a rye loaf.

"Joe," he said, "if I say so myself this is a *pisseur*." The Colonel frequently lends elegance to an old-fashioned turn of speech by Frenchifying it. Thus he will sometimes refer to a figurator, or man who sells ratings on horses, as a *rateur*. "A touch of French here and there challenges the reader," he says. He often speaks of a rich man as a member of the *bourgeoisie*, pronouncing the *s* as a second *g*. "A rich man, a powerful man, plain as an old shoe, and as sweet a fellow as you would ever want to meet," he will say describing some prestigious figure of his youth. "A member of the *bourgeoigie*, and a great old thief." *Pisseur* is reserved for objects of his highest approval, like P. T. Barnum's Jumbo or the swindler George Graham Rice.

We took possession of one of the Palace booths, and the Colonel said, "I would suggest, if I might, a libation to the Goddess Pluviosa, synonymous, in the life of the Honest Rainmaker, with Fortune. In the summer of 1930, having transferred my pursuit of the Golden Fleece back to the eastern theatre of operations, I was decidedly non-holding. Old Dr. Orlando Edgar Miller, my principal in a campaign of religious education, had been laid by the heels in California. He was in durance vile, as a result of persecution by the American Medical Association, which contended he could not prolong people's lives by swinging them in a hammock, thus extending their vertebrae. An ice-skating rink which I promoted in San Francisco had been eclipsed by the subsequent erection of a larger rival, and it was too late to arrange a comeback for Tommy Burns, even had he been willing, because he was by now on the half-century mark. A storm cloud lowered over the American economy, and the moment seemed inauspicious for any kind of a score.

"Hearing of my lack of immediate projects, an old California friend of mine who had himself scored handily in New York had written to me, urging me to challenge the big city once again. I recalled a phrase I had once heard from the lips of Elbert Hubbard, also about New York. 'It's a hard place to live, Little Mac, but the money's there.' I had a house near Golden Gate Park, in San Francisco, staffed by a Chinese couple, man and wife, whose stipendia were somewhat in arrears. I presented them with the house and came on like the Argonauts, by a slow ship through the Panama Canal. But venture capital had apparently taken refuge. The depression of October, 1929 refused to rescind itself, and the old town had changed. I had a room at the old Hotel Imperial and office space in the Knickerbocker Building at Forty-second and Broadway, but I was beginning to worry about the plug in the door.

"When without specific objective, I have often found it rewarding to go to the race track. I have made it a lifelong rule, since the age of fifteen, never to bet on horses. Freed of this vulgar preoccupation, a man at the track can sometimes see opportunity beckon."

"Didn't you ever bet a horse?" I asked, incredulous.

"At an early age I learned the futility of the practice," the Colonel said, reminding me, as he spoke, of another friend, Izzy Yereshevsky, the proprietor of the I & Y Cigar Store, which remains open twenty-four hours a day except on Yom Kippur at Forty-ninth Street and Seventh Avenue. There is a cigar box on the counter which also remains open twenty-four hours a day, into which customers drop contributions toward the burial expenses of old horse players. "Don't any of the boys win?" I once asked Izzy, who is, like the Colonel, a non-player.

"How did you think them horses gets feeded?" Mr. Yereshevsky asked me.

"I have just finished a section of my autobiography," the Colonel said, "which will shed light on what you seem to regard as an eccentricity." Before I could steer him back onto the story of the Honest Rainmaker, he had planted in front of me a chapter of *The Plug in the Door*, and since he then turned all his attention to a *delice Gambrinienne*, I had nothing to do but read.

5/ *Baptism of Fire*

"IT WAS 1888. Back home in New Orleans my destiny became the live subject of commentation at all family gatherings. What to do with him? In those times Springfield Lodge, my ancestral home, filled me with delight always. It cost my Grand Father a great deal of money and was regarded as one of the most typical and palatial in the whole South.

"My dear Mother finally announced that she had achieved the brave heights by securing 'James Aloysius,'—that's me, a job with a weekly Irish Catholic newspaper. A fine kindly gentleman was Father John Quinn, the Editor of the New Orleans *Catholic Register*. I'm assigned the task of securing Data and writing pieces about the 'dear departed' of St. Jerome's Parish and collecting sales returns from the news stands based upon the prior week's sales. I would have been much more at home keeping score of the Southern League games at Heinneman Park for the Pelicans.

"After writing a few dandy pieces about prominent decedents of the Parish, and after aggrandizing $20 or so from the downtown news stands and top carriers, a comforting discovery came to me,—I learned, much to my surprise and delight, that a perfectly adorable spot to rest the body and cool the fetid brow from much deep-sea thinking and unremitting pave-pounding, was 'Sitting Bull' Bush's barnlike Poolroom, where business was done on five different Fields of Horses in five different cities. Also, the newly established Young Men's Gymnastic Club's tremendous Training Quarters for Pugilists, Wrestlers & Chicken Fighters provided elegant and restful surcease for a young and aspiring journalist who, after all, liked the finer and higher things of life.

"But one day Fate stepped in. On this occasion a prominent Parishioner had gone on to his paradisical reward. He was big, he was top news. To acquire the facts and picture necessitated a trudge away out Canal Street and here I was some $60 winner on the horses in Mr. Bush's cool-off Poolroom. All based on the 'monetary leverage' for I was utilizing the News Stand collections to sustain my speculative moves. To tear myself away from such idyllic environment and engaging occupation would be unthinkable to most mortals, and it certainly appealed to me in that direction. I figurated there was justifiable cause.

"So a way out popped from the box.[1] I consulted the Town Oracle who stood at my right side where he could get a clearer view of the chalked-up prices on the First Three of the last heat at Latonia. 'Why Mr. John Sidney White, the guy you say has kicked off, I knew him well. I can and will tell you all you wish to know about him.' This was comforting and everything I might hope for in realization. Said I, hastily getting Pad and Pencil together, 'That is fine. You have saved my neck. Please let me have it in gobs.' And the considerate Horse Player just did that little thing. 'The late Mr. White,' said he, 'was cut down in the very prime of life. He was one of the most athletic and herculean types of men our city had ever known. He could beat 10 flat in the hundred and put the 16-pound shot at Yale in his Sophomore Year no fewer than 59 feet. And how those women in the Rotunda of the French Opera went for White, a walking Adonis. And you say it was Heart Disease. Well, well I so regret to hear the sad intelligence.'

"After close of the Poolroom operations, and, bye the way, I may say my speculation turned out to be a stalemate,—quit even,—I repaired to McConkey's marble-tabled short-order Bazaar in Commercial Alley and transposed the above facts as related by the Town Oracle into a right nice piece for the *Catholic Register*, wherein it duly appeared the next Sunday. Recently, the dear Father had complimented me by suggesting I should take the Junior Class at Sunday School next week. Looked like I am standing high in his estimation.

"Rather early on the succeeding Monday the Reverend Father sends for me.

"So I look into the eye of Father Quinn wonderingly. What wrong had I done anyway? You could see he intended to be stern. So here goes. Here is what he said to me. 'Mr. Macdonald you have been doing very nicely on our *Register*' said the Editor, 'but in reference to that glowing symposium on the late Mr. White's physical perfection, I recall you said he was the modern Adonis, I must call to your attention that Mr. White had lost his left leg at the siege of Port Hudson and the absence of his

[1] The Colonel is fond of figures of speech taken from the game of faro (originally *pharaon*, another example of his Gallic predilection). He will bet this game or bank it whenever he gets a chance. "The percentage is almost nil," he says, "unlike the pari-mutuels with their fearful sixteen-per-cent bite. The complexity of the game and its equality, however, militate against its survival. Gambling houses, even in Nevada, are full of slot machines now. It is an age debased and mechanical."

nose was due to the ravage of malignant cancer. Now, Mr. Macdonald we who have the destiny of the *Register* in hand do not claim to rank in journalistic brilliance with "Marse" Henry Watterson, Horace Greeley, or Charles A. Dana, but we are sticklers for authenticity. We're very aggrieved Mr. Macdonald.'

"Some time went on and I'm a regular at Bush's Poolroom. Somehow I'm never much loser, never much winner. But one Saturday night when the Deadline for News Stands Collections is at hand I'm short $18, current exchange, and no fussing around. Like a brave bull in the afternoon, I walk into Father Quinn's study with the salutation: 'Father Quinn may I ask an indulgence please sir. I find myself incommoded in the sum of $20.00 which I extracted from Collections this very day. Shall come in with it next Monday noon. Is that all O.K., Father?' This kindly man and fine Editor looked at me with his two saucer-shaped blue eyes, rejoining: 'My boy, worry no further. Mr. Bush sent for it and I've paid him the $18.00. I'm busy, I'll be seeing you later.'

"But one day this very human and monumental spirit of goodness said, 'My boy don't you know this is no paper for you to be working on. I've gotten a new position for you this coming Monday on Mr. O'Malley's very sedate New Orleans daily *Item*. I'm sorry to see you go but destiny for you beckons to other and larger fields of newspaper endeavor.'

"And, so it was that I reported to the *Item* front boss and was assigned a desk and utensils. No sooner had I gotten well set in my work than two belligerent Editors began shooting at the visiting Chief of Police, the slugs skimming over my head but some of them bouncing merrily off'n a steel pictorial cut extended in front of me for final check up and O.K.

"And that was my beginning in a chosen field of Destiny, the newspaper business, a story of a Lifetime in the pursuit of the Fourth Estate."

6 / A Day with Dominick O'Malley

"YOU SEE what race-track betting brought me to," the Colonel said when he perceived I had finished. "Do you blame me for refraining in the intervening years?"

"On the contrary, I admire you," I said. "But what brought you into the line of fire?"

"Mr. O'Malley had abandoned his desk at the usual hour of twelve and betaken himself for prandial relaxation first to the bar of the St. Charles Hotel, where he had a three-bagger of Sazeracs, then to Hymen's bar on Common Street, where he increased his *apéritif* by four silver gin fizzes and after that over to Farbacher's saloon on Royal where he had a schooner or two of Boston Club punch. O'Malley was not of that *sang-pur* elegance which would have got him past the portal of the august Boston Club, the most revered in New Orleans, but he had bribed a fancy girl to wheedle the formula from the Boston Club bartender. It consisted of twelve bottles of champagne, eight bottles of white wine, one and one half bottles raspberry syrup, one half bottle brandy, one half bottle kirschwasser, one quarter bottle Jamaica rum, one quarter bottle Curacao, two pineapples, two dozen oranges, two and one half lbs. sugar, seltzer and ice. This was enough to serve several persons.

"When he had finished his preparations bacchanalic he strolled over to Antoine's, where he had four dozen freshly shucked oysters without any muck on them, a red snapper flambée in absinthe, a salmis of three woodcock and four snipe, a chateaubriand, *bleu*, six bottles of Bass's ale, and a magnum of La Mission Haut Brion of the comet year. After that he smoked a made-to-measure cigar, as long as his arm from the inside of the elbow to the tip of the middle finger, and drank a dipper of Calvados from a cask that had been brought to Louisiana from Normandy with the first cargo of sparkle-eyed Cyprians in 1721. Not more than one quart had been drawn from the cask in any one year since, and it had been carefully replenished each time. Having effectuated the *trou normand*, O'Malley consumed an *omelette au kirsch* and a small baked alaska, followed by a *caffè espresso* for which he sent the maître d'hôtel to a dive operated by the Maffia. 'The hardest thing to get in New Orleans,' he always said, 'is a decent cup of coffee.' He then started to walk back toward the office, which was on Camp Street, with some vague notion of pausing on the way to drape a beautiful octoroon's ivory throat with pearls, and would have arrived at his usual hour, after half-past four, had he not met with an unforeseen vicissitude."

The Colonel paused and looked about him with an expression that approximated distaste. When he is in such moods his current Gambrinian haunts seem to him to lack éclat.

"I'll settle for another beer," he said, and when it had been brought continued.

"I, a mere kid, had been entranced from the moment of Mr. O'Malley's exit by the notion of seating myself in his swivel chair and cocking my feet on his desk," he said. "Expecting momentarily his return, for I had heard that secular newspaper men ate, so to speak, *sur le pouce*, I refrained for the first four hours and fifteen minutes. Then, deciding that he might not be back at all, I yielded. I made my way furtively to his desk, sat down, swung my legs up, and encouraged by the smiles of the older men, even took the boss's green eyeshade off the blotter and placed it on my towish potato. I then raised a steel line cut from the desk and, pretending to inspect it, held it in front of my face, thus veiling my identity. I did not know it was the habit of Mr. David Hennessy, the Chief of Police of New Orleans, to arrive at the *Item* office each afternoon at four thirty-five to shoot at Mr. O'Malley. The fellows in the composing room set their watches by it and sent the second edition to press.

"It was a tryst. O'Malley would arrive at four-thirty, hang up his frock coat, lay out his revolvers on the desk in front of him, and start to write a leader taking the skin off Hennessy. He would indite daily a virulent editorial charging the Chief with official dereliction by permitting the poolrooms, policy bazars, brothels and bagnios, the stews and knocking shops, to run wide open every day including Sunday, a day of extreme reverence south of the Tennessee River. Mr. O'Malley was in political control of the city and figured that any madame who wanted a Sunday turn at bat should apply to him personally. At four thirty-five the Chief, who had been steaming up on Creole coffee laced with contraband Cuban rum at McConkey's in Commercial Alley, would proceed across Camp Street and ascend to the first landing in the *Item* building. He gave Mr. O'Malley five minutes to get set. With little knowledge of trigonometry, but with natural copperial intuition, Mr. Hennessy would select a likely angle of trajectory through the wooden partition screening the city room and the corner where Mr. O'Malley sat in pontifical augustity.

"These first shots were a long price to wing Mr. O'Malley but a good bet to drive him under his desk in search of cover, a position from which he could not efficiently retaliate. Advancing behind the barrage, Mr. Hennessy would reach a spot from which he could survey the city room. But there he would be caught in a cross fire between the sports editor and the editor of the religious page, and after emptying both revolvers would be impelled to retreat. It was a lesson in logistics which I have never forgotten.

"But do not think that Mr. O'Malley had not his troops in elegant *élan* and precise readiness for these manoeuvres. At the first muffled roar and crackling sound of timber rendered, all hands except the enfilading pair, from the city editor to the meekest copy boy,—would secure shotguns conveniently placed for the purpose and rush to the front windows looking out on the street below, knowing full well that the miscreant Hennessy must, perforce, make egress and present briefly a target. After I had survived my first payday I was initiated into the routine. But on this first day of employment I was completely unprepared when a bullet from a Smith and Wesson whammed into the steel plate I held in front of me, knocking it from my hands and me *derrière dessus* behind Mr. O'Malley's desk. I learned afterward that it was the most accurate opening shot Mr. Hennessy had ever fired. 'A perfect carom,' the religious editor said. 'He played it off that new machine, the typewriter. I always said they had no place in a newspaper office.'

"After Mr. Hennessy had retreated, shrinking up close to the front of the *Item* building so as not to give the boys with the fowling pieces a clean shot, all my seniors apologized profusely for not having tipped me off. They hadn't thought I was in any real danger, they explained, and had just wanted to see some of the cockiness taken out of me when the first missile whistled overhead. 'It is ceasing to be fun,' the sports editor said. 'Also, I suspect the Chief of wearing the cover of a wash boiler inside the seat of his pants. The man in the slot had what looked like a clean hit on him day before yesterday and the only result was a loud clang. What worries me, though, is what has happened to the boss? He is either in the clink or some panelworker has stolen his trousers again.' "

The Colonel's wide, generous nose is slightly retroussé, and when he looks up at me his nostrils form a deeply indented M. They have a look of unshakeable sincerity.

"The first surmise was correct," he said. "Mr. O'Malley, returning to the office from his last mysterious port of call, had been hurrying through Commercial Alley, a narrow lane between St. Charles and Camp Streets, in order to arrive at the rendezvous before Mr. Hennessy. Had Hennessy got there first, Mr. O'Malley would have found himself cut off from his base. But in making his way through the alley, the editor, a man of generous girth, came into abrupt collision, like a crack flyer of the Southern Railroad meeting a freight train of the Louisville & Nashville, with the editor of a rival newspaper, the New Orleans *States*, headed in the opposite direction. The two had exchanged acrimonious ink about a suggestion, publicized by Mr. O'Malley, that a bank of which his fellow editor was a director was on the point of failure. Mr. O'Malley had been refused a loan. The bank was the Hibernia National, known in New Orleans of the epoch as the Irish Rock.

"The editor of the *States*, whose name, as I recollect it, was Ewing, invariably carried an umbrella with a sharp ferrule, vouchsafing it served him as a sunshade in the summer. He thrust it immediately at Mr. O'Malley's left eye, being resigned to an exchange of shots and thinking that by this preliminary he might impair Mr. O'Malley's aim. He missed the eyeball, however, although he put a nice hole in Mr. O'Malley's brow, and forthwith the fusillade began. Of course down there in those days there was so much shooting the general public knew just what to do. The patrolmen on St. Charles and Camp detoured all traffic headed past the ends of the alley, and a number of shopkeepers on Commercial reached out from their doorways and grabbed the right hands of the contestants, an efficacious method of terminating hostilities. Sometimes they made a mistake; one of the duelists was left-handed. The effect of the error could prove lethal. Both Mr. O'Malley and Mr. Ewing, however, were conventionally orientated, and there were no casualties beyond the effusion of gore from Mr. O'Malley's punctured pumpkin.

"The police escorted both men before a magistrate, and from the clutches of these Dogberries O'Malley would soon have talked himself free, had not Ewing, himself a political power, sworn out a warrant against him for impairing the credit of the Hibernia National and causing a run on the Irish Rock. The judge happened to own stock in that institution. O'Malley was therefore immured, soon to be joined by a Mr. Kiernan who published the New Orleans *News*, and who had joined in his campaign of retribution against the Hibernia. A swift messenger informed us at the *Item* office of their predicament."

"What happened to Ewing?" I asked. "He started the fight, didn't he?"

"He was released," the Colonel said. "In those days a mere felonious assault was considered of no moment."

I found this easier to believe because of a conversation I once had with a leading member of the Bar in Nevada, where the law still has a decent respect for human combustibility. We were talking about a friend of ours in Reno who had got shot in an argument about something or other a couple of years previously. "Harry got it in the liver," the jurist said. "They were laying five to one against recovery in the morning line at the Nevada Turf Club. But there happened to be an ace surgeon in town who still had a couple of days to wait for his decree, and he got the slug out without hurting him."

"What happened to the other fellow?" I had asked then, and the legal light had answered:

"He's fine, just fine. Saw him down at the Golden Hotel bar last week."

"Did they arrest him?" I asked.

Eminent counsel looked at me with some astonishment. "Why, no," he said. "If Harry had *died* we would have arrested him, though."

"A high bail had been set," the Colonel said, unaware how far west my thoughts had strayed, "and while the senior members of the staff sought bond for the captives, I was despatched to the St. Charles Parish Prison, where they were incarcerated, in a hired hack with a case of vintage Irroy *brut*, and Mr. O'Malley's English bulldog, Mike, whom he had left tied to the umbrella stand when he went out to lunch. I found the prisoners in good spirits and left them in better after they had emptied the first three bottles, kindly inviting me and the turnkey to have a glass with them. I went out thinking I had landed in the pearl of professions. And so it was, in those days of halcyon, the very cap and zenith of American journalism."

The Colonel appeared to ruminate for a while, and I thought I could visualize the procession of eminent zenithians, like Marse Henry Watterson and the youthful William Randolph Hearst, that must be passing behind his eyelids. But he was thinking of something else.

"I have never ceased to regret, Joe," he said, "that on my first day at the *Item* I was the indirect though innocent cause of Chief Hennessy's death. The bullet that struck the plate in my hand ricocheted through the flimsy ceiling and hit an old-style southern gentleman in the business office in the calf of the leg. His name, as I remember it, was Mr. Troup Sessams, and he had withheld his fire previously because he considered the shooting downstairs a strictly editorial matter. When the bullet arrived, Mr. Sessams said, 'This is no damn joke.'

"He closed up his roll-top desk, hung his alpaca office coat on a hook, put on his long-tailed frock coat and a hat with a five-inch brim, and withdrew from the lower drawer of the desk a rosewood case containing two long-barreled dueling pistols with which he had eliminated all antebellum rivals for the hand of his wife, at that time heiress to a plantation Faulknerian, but since, like so many of us, non-holding. He loaded the pistols and placed one inside each breast of his frock coat, in the long pockets provided for that purpose by antebellum tailors. He then walked downstairs, limping a little,—the shot had only grazed him,—and followed Hennessy out into the night. It was the end of the Chief. His perforated body was discovered next morning. The year was 1889; the precise date eludes me."

"But wasn't Hennessy the New Orleans police chief who was killed by the Maffia?" I exclaimed, beginning to think I remembered something I had once read.

"That was the common theory, Joe," the Colonel said, "and the citizens of New Orleans acted upon it to the extent of shooting eleven Italians and then hanging them to trees. But those foreigners were desperate characters anyway, and doubtless deserved their fate."

In the course of a recent visit to New Orleans, I sought corroboration of Colonel Stingo's recollections. My research there seems to indicate that while the years may have blurred his memory in regard to some of the facts and caused it to embellish, if not invent, others, there is a certain hard core of veracity in what he remembers and no doubt at all that at least some of his cast of characters did exist in roles more or less akin to those he ascribes to them. There is the matter of Mr. O'Malley's *embonpoint*, for instance; I learned of one editorial fracas in which it served him ill and rather more gravely so than in the one recounted by Colonel Stingo. This was a duel between Mr. O'Malley and Colonel Harrison Parker, editor of the *Picayune*. Mr. O'Malley had published in the *Item* a cartoon representing Colonel Parker as a dog led on a string by the governor of Louisiana, whom Mr. O'Malley disliked. The newspaper offices were on opposite sides of Camp Street. One day, both editors emerged into the street at the same time, bound for lunch—apparently the lunch hour was reserved for shootings in that miraculous city. "O'Malley fired first and winged Colonel Parker, crippling his accustomed pistol arm," a local historian who described the incident to me said. "Colonel Parker took his pistol in his left hand, but knowing he could not shoot accurately with it, walked across the street to get close to O'Malley before pulling the trigger. Colonel Parker had commanded a regiment in the Confederate Army, and the pistol was a Tranter .52, a monstrous weapon throwing a slug as big as a heavy machine gun. Mr. O'Malley, not caring to confront his fire, tried to scrounge himself up behind a telegraph pole, of which we then had many in the downtown section. But he was so big and fat his belly protruded beyond the defilade furnished by that improvised position of defense, and Colonel Parker, advancing to the opposite side of the telephone pole, leaving a trail of sanguinary testimony to his courage as he walked, took careful aim and shot his man right through the protuberance, the bullet entering under one end of his watch chain and emerging from under the other. Both men were seriously discommoded."

As for Mr. O'Malley's connection with the *Item*, it appears that he did not become proprietor of that newspaper until 1894 or '95, half a dozen years after Chief Hennessy's death. A police reporter emeritus, almost as old as the Colonel, told me that there was a New Orleans Chief of Police who sometimes used to shoot O'Malley (although you couldn't set your watch by it), but his name was Ed Whitaker, and he didn't become chief until 1906, when Stingo was thirty-two years old. However, Whitaker was a recorder, or police magistrate, during the nineties, and he may have started shooting O'Malley then. Hennessy and O'Malley were deadly enemies during the Maffia days, but at that time O'Malley was a private detective, not yet an editor. It is suspected that O'Malley bribed a juror during a trial of the eleven Italians for Hennessy's murder, and so secured a hung jury and a mistrial. The lynching followed. O'Malley's fee is said to have provided the capital with which, when things had quieted down, he bought the *Item* and set up as a reforming editor. O'Malley lisped. He had an old iron safe in his editorial office which he used to say contained dossiers on every outwardly respectable citizen of New Orleans, accumulated during his days as a private detective. "You see that safe?" he used to say to callers when he was premeditating a front-page attack on some particularly saintly target. "It's full of that sonofabits."

It would seem that the Colonel has intertwined elements of the Hennessy-O'Malley cycle with others of the O'Malley-Whitaker cycle, to produce a result artistically superior to either. The Tristan legend underwent an analogous development. The roles, and even the identities, of the two Iseuts are inextricably confused, like those of Hennessy and Whitaker. Only the hero, O'Malley-Tristan, remains a constant.

7 / *Reunion at Belmont*

"THIS HAS BEEN a labyrinthian digression," Colonel Stingo said, with a handkerchief dabbing the Gambrinian foam from beneath his nostrils, and signaling his readiness for a refill. "But here I am, this fine though overcast early afternoon in September, 1930, if memory serves, the Wednesday following the opening on Monday, Labor Day, when the Fall Highweight Handicap had been won by that marvelous sprinter, Balko, under a hundred and thirty-six pounds. The second day's racing had been marred by a torrential downpour beginning after the second race, and the question of weather for the rest of the short meeting, only twelve more days, but including the Grande Semaine of American racing, was naturally a subject of managerial preoccupation. The Westchester Racing Association was offering a generous stake list,—the purses had been announced at a period when the country looked financially impregnable, —but for the first time since the end of the First World War attendances at all sporting events had fallen off, a circumstance imputable to the quasi-disappearance of Tease from public circulation. The pari-mutuels were not yet grinding out their vast gist of vulgar gelt for the New York tracks, though they were in operation in other regions, and not even bookmaking had been formally legalized, as it was in a few years to be. The hand of Charles Evans Hughes still lay heavy on the state that had gifted him with its highest office.

"The tolerated bookies, who discreetly received bets on the track, presumably only from members of their acquaintance, bought their operating franchises from the Association by paying a high rent, nominally for boxes in the grandstand. But the income from this source was limited. So the gate money was vital if Belmont was to meet the nut, and the directors of the Association, although all millionaires, had not got that way by losing money, an ordeal to which they were still painfully unaccustomed although in many cases recently initiated. The president, Mr. Joseph E. Widener of Philadelphia, was even less accustomed than the lesser millionaires who surrounded him. He was a Prince of Good Fellows, attired in atelier-like clothes, and possessed of the divine inflatus for money-getting. I knew him from the happy days preceding the advent of Charles Evans Hughes, when I had frequently chronicled the triumph of his racing colors, the red and white stripes.

"From here on, Joe, you may as well read my account of the sequelae." And the Colonel, leafing through his manuscript, found a jump-off spot for me, passed the bundle across the table, and signaled to Louie, the lunch-counter man who doubles as waiter, to bring him another Gambrinian libation.

"Upon arrival at the Park," I read, "I made my way to Mike the Bite's lucky Shoe Shine Stand just in off the Betting Ring, the scourge of the Pari-Mutuels not having descended upon the tranquil scene of the Oralist, as yet, in 1930, in fact, it was not to be for 10 years later. The proprietor, a slightly colored man, perhaps an octoroon, was of true name William Beeson, but styled Mike the Bite because he was such an easy fellow to promote for a loan. This was because of native generosity, not lack of business acumen, for Willie had built up for himself a considerable fortune by his occult activities. The stand provided but a small portion of his revenues. He paid $300 a month rental for the two-seated stand and charged 25 cents for a slap-dash polish with quick brush-off. But he also sold, to customers both male and female, a daily rabbit's foot for $2 and an agreement to bet $2 for him on his third-race selection. He must have been quite a figurator, or else quite a salesman, because he put out around 50 rabbits' feet per diem. Not all the rabbits' feet customers took shines.

"On two long hanger racks in the rear the Bite undertook to care safely your overcoat or umbrella; his way of assuring himself the customer's return and, above all, payoff. If the Bite's selection came down in front in the third, it requires no great computation to see he was a sure thing to become rich.

"The second dodge of the Bite was quite classic. Early in life his back was broken during a Tornado at his place of nativity down South, notoriously the home of high winds, viz., Gainesville, Georgia. Nobody ever had such a magnificently large Hunch as the Bite believe me.

"And be assured the Bite made the Hunchback Business pay him better than it had Lon Chaney, who played Quasimodo in the silent films. He made a play for the lady Horseplayers only. He bought two suits a year, one for the summer and one for the chilly days of autumn, generally at $35 each. But he paid $5.00 extra for a very special alteration. Where the coat rested plumb atop the Hunch this mastermind contrived a large Patch Pocket that opened and closed on a shiny zipper about six inches long.

"For years, the Bite held to the psychic fixation, in effect, experience had shown him, that only women could enjoy good luck in playing the horses by the laying on of the hands upon the prodigious Hump. He would say oftentimes that under no circumstance would he sell 'a tough,' as he termed the merchandise, to a man, only to a woman, and never less than $10.

"As the years went by the Bite built up a large and steady patronage among the women turf speculators. They would come sidling up quietly to the Shoe Shine Stand and back in the rear of the hanger racks. The Bite would follow, tip toeish like, and in a flash a tug on the zipper would bring exposure of the Hump. By a quick and dexterous move the lady Horseplayer reached down a 'pinky' and 'the touch' became achieved.

"I climbed up on Mike's stand not because I was a candidate for the eleemosynary department, still less to get a horse in the third, but because it provided a perch from which I might survey briefly the hurrying throng, all panting with greed, intent on the accumulation of unearned increment. Also I liked to exchange a greeting with the Bite, who had a particular esteem for me because I always addressed him as Willie, his real given name. And from my perch I perceived a friend of olden times, the tall, gaunt, Professor George Ambrosius Immanuel Morrison Sykes, D.D. (Zoroastrian), whom I had known first as assistant to Dr. Joseph Canfield Hatfield, the father of artificially induced precipitation, and later as my own partner in the Honest Rainmaking business.

"He was hurrying with long strides, but not in the direction of the betting ring, from which I judged he was on some tryst intent. Since he was not given to extra-conjugal romance I took it that his appointment was with a solvent boob. I followed with my eyes his progress across the clubhouse lawn, and to my astonishment recognized the resplendent form encountering his as that of Mr. Widener, who was accompanied by the Racing Secretary of the meeting, a Mr. Schaumberg, since, like his boss, gone under the wire.

"The incongruous three joined in colloquy and shortly moved away to a tree surrounded by benches, where they seated themselves. I, having by now felt the tug at my trouser-leg which was the Bite's signalization of the completion of his onceover, descended from the chair and followed them. It was a cinch, I had already estimated, that Mr. Widener would not wish Dr. Sykes to bring on *more* rain, so I wondered if the good Doctor had found a method of keeping it away.

"The gentlemen had selected for the talk the Joyner Oak, set within a richly verdured parkway enclosed by four brightly striped benches of heavy hickory wood and spiked in the supporting headpieces by wooden stanchions, instead of modern steel clavers.

"The benches had been presented to the Westchester club by the late Pierre Lorillard, the Master of Rancocas Farms, Jobstown, N.J., as an ornament to Belmont Park when it was first opened.[1]

"Across the Lawn stood the entrance to the private elevator which would take Mr. Widener to his offices in the upper reaches in the Club Preserves within the huge grand stand, and quite apart from the expensive Turf and Field Club in the ancient Manice Mansion further along and across the green swarded Paddock with it's celebrated group of Old English Trees and Rose Bushes in hedge formation. Suddenly, the knot of earnestly conferring men became restive, and Mr. Widener made his adieu with a gentle move towards the elevator entrance. Messers. Sykes and Schaumberg would be obliged to cross my path if they directed their way to the Racing Secretary's Office.

"Sure enough, that was the direction they took. Almost abreast of me, Dr. Sykes suddenly saw and recognized me. An effusive greeting followed.

"Suddenly, from here, there and everywhere, occurred a rush of persons from beneath the Paddock trees, from underneath the grandstand and out of the recesses of the Racing Administrative Building, all towards the trackside rail, all in answer to the thrilling alarum, 'They're off.' Like a red coon dog catching high scent, the Secretary broke into a run and was gone.

"That was the cue for me to isolate Dr. Sykes from the mass of possible interference round about; I edged him away to Mike the Bite's stand and manoeuvred him back behind the hanger racks, where we could talk

[1] This is the kind of thing on which I never know how far the Colonel is spoofing, if at all.

unobserved. He came quickly to the point; he had been doing business in late years as the Weather Control Bureau, of Burbank, Cal. Out there, he said, he had received a letter from a lady in New York with a name fragrant of millions, asking whether he could prevent as well as cause rainfall. If so, she said, she would be willing to defray the expense of a conference here in New York. On arrival here he was to report to the offices of the Westchester Racing Association, when a meeting would be arranged between him and Mr. Widener. The good Doctor had come on speedily.

" 'My latest apparatus has proved as efficacious in driving away rain as in inducing it,' he said with a perfectly straight face. 'But I would appreciate your assistance with the meteorological data. It's a good thing to know what you have to contend against.' He had reported on arrival, and Mr. Schaumberg had made the appointment for him with Mr. Widener.

" 'Funny thing about him, though,' the Doctor said, 'He said he couldn't make up his mind on the deal until we'd both talked it over with the lady. Said he had great confidence in her intuition. So we made another appointment for tomorrow, same time, but out at the Widener barn, where the lady's car will be parked. These rich Easterners are very suspicious. He seemed to doubt my good faith.'

" 'That's because he has never done business with an Honest Rainmaker,' I said, and we both laughed. 'I have known Mr. Widener for many years,' I added, 'and I am prepared to corroborate whatever assertions you may make, within reason, about your past accomplishments. Also, as you may recollect, I have an adroitness in handling the feminine component, a way with the ladies, and I suspect that Mrs. Harriman,'—that was the fair one's name,—'will have the determining voice.' So I was in like Flynn, for 45 percent of the whole deal, which like a promising but untried mining claim we did not yet know the full value of, yet it bore a Bonanza aspect. The old Doc stipulated 10 percent for Mrs. Sykes, who he said had accompanied him to New York, and 45 percent for himself. I contributed my office facilities, desk space and mail service at the Knickerbocker Building, so that the Weather Control Bureau could offer a New York address, always a denotation of substantiality. I was to be the outside man, or talker, and old Doc was to profess the zealot, unapproachable and hard to understand.

" 'Now,' I said, 'I would suggest that Mr. Widener, who has in his life drag-netted a vast accumulation of profits, is more attracted by the possibility of making money than of guaranteeing against loss. I would therefore suggest that we offer him a forfeit for non-fulfillment of our promise, —something like double his money back if it rains.' I had in the back of my mind that it rains less than once a week on the average in early September, a hot, sultry time in the vicinity of New York usually, but I was going to check it before I made the price.

"So the Good Doctor and myself left Mike the Bite with his Lares &

Snares; making headway to the Doctor's brand new Buick we soon found ourselves speeding along the Boulevard en route to New York; we felt no desire to see the rest of the races, having matters more emergent on our minds. I for one had to see what Weather reports for the Long Island district in past years were available at the New York Public Library, my source of avail in an endless variety of situations. The appearance of the Doctor's vehicle did not deceive me; I was acquainted with the liberal credit arrangements available in a time of increasing automotive merchandising difficulty.

"'Are you holding, Doctor?' I asked him. He shook his head. 'Just enough to live nice for a couple of weeks,' he said. My resources were similarly limited. I thought that some small capital might be necessary to launch the enterprise. But I had already fixed in my mind a potential source for such collateral. '*Semper Paratus*' is the motto of the Long Riders."

"The Long Riders" is a term the Colonel likes to apply to himself and all his associates, past and present, in allusion to the train robbers who used to ride out of the Indian Territory of Oklahoma with Al Jennings, a character Colonel Stingo claims as a boyhood friend. The analogy is purely poetic, however. The only gun point at which the Colonel has ever taken money is the muzzle of Professor Hatfield's cannon.

"Doctor and Mrs. Sykes had taken a month's lease on an old brownstone house in the West Eighties," the manuscript went on. "There I joined them in the late evening, after a long afternoon profitably spent in meteorological figuration. We could afford to lay Mr. Widener 2 to 1 and still have a percentage of .7499 in our favor, I had discovered, while the greediest bookmakers content themselves with .15 and .20, and the remorseless parimutuel as at present constituted but .16. But by a subtlety in the wording of our wager I could bring the real odds down still further for the Grande Semaine, beginning with Saturday, Sept. 6, the date of the Lawrence Realization and Champagne Stakes, and running through Saturday the 13, Futurity Day, on which the best two-year-olds in the country were to vie for the championship and a prize of more than $100,000. It turned out to be $121,670. We had an edge in our favor beyond the dreams of avarice.

"But this old joker Sykes maintained the pretext that his manipulations were in fact capable of affecting the result, and that my calculation of probabilities was only supplemental. 'A lot of things have developed in our profession since your time, Little Mac,' he told me, 'including radio.'

"That night we dined with fine gusto, and remained at table for hours at Café Conte on Astor Place recalling old times and old friends. Mrs. Sykes was a big woman with a blarney and a swagger that would have been useful in a sideshow of Adam Forepaugh's Three-Ring Circus of ancient time. In the Rainmakers' Campaigns in the Far West it had been her specialty to attend gatherings of the women of the Farmers in their churches and Meeting Houses where she would lead the exercises and the prayers. This time, she said, she would exercise another talent. She could mix drinks as expertly and diabolically as any leering Night Club Bartender I ever knew. 'It should help with public relations,' she said.

"With a freshening shower and spanking breakfast, I was in fine fettle as Dr. Sykes and myself stepped into his car for the long ride to Belmont Park next morning.

"And now the Bugle Call for the opening race of this drizzling murky day here at Belmont Park clarioned through the Paddock and across the vast stretches of the Queen of All Racing Courses in the New World.

"We knew that within ten minutes we would be at Mrs. Harriman's side, along with Messrs. Widener and Schaumberg."

8/"*Long, Lissome, Lucreferous*"

"PRECISELY on the dot, we kept our appointment with Mrs. Harriman at the Turf & Field Club. A very gracious lady and one of the real beautiful women of her day and time, she chose to receive us upon the Driveway leading up to the Clubhouse verandah while seated in a handsome custom built, 8-cylinder, imported Hispano-Suiza.

"I afterwards learned this motor car cost, laid down in New York from Toledo, Spain, the surprising sum of $22,000, one of the most luxurious and expensive jobs in the United States in 1930. On the direction of Madame, the tonneau's side door swung ajar, revealing a vista of rich and ravishing splendor;—upon her Golden Barge in the simmering moonlight of a sheening night on the Nile, I am sure Cleopatra never looked more completely devastating than does dear Mrs. Harriman as she reclines her elongated figure lissomely strewn, lengthwise upon the satin-cushioned coach seat while smoking a costly heaven-scented Carolina Perfecto, à la Panatela, with the poise of a Winston Churchill tweezing a Wheeling stogie.

"In quiet souciance, a quick glance measured Dr. Sykes and myself for her Ladyship, and we were evidently satisfactory for she said, 'Now boys what may be your first name,—yes you blue eyes—yours?' Timidly abashed, I squeaked up,—'Jim.' Dr. Sykes merely suggested, 'Just call me Doc.' Then came the first imperial command from the Royal Divan's purpled folds to a Club attendant,—'Please, immediately, chairs for the gentlemen from the Clubhouse.'

"Now, all of us are nicely grouped about Mrs. Harriman and her Throne Room in commodious club chairs awaiting the opening phases of the impending Grand Symposium.

"Tall, slim and elongated she was, and her wide wondering eyes were in shade the color of sea shells along the Caribbean beachway at sunrise; her honey-tone-colored hair, bunched in braids after the affectation of Elizabeth Barrett Browning, generally matched up with a single California pink rose in long tendril, while her every physical movement bespoke the Della Sarte motif in its fullest synchronization,—albeit she appeared languorously and coquettishly lazy."

I paused in my reading to congratulate the Colonel on his descriptive powers.

"It reads like Dr. Faustus casing Helen," I said. "Mrs. Harriman must have been a remarkable woman."

"She had a weakness, however, Joe," he answered,—"an inquiring mind. She was curious of the occult, and had landed on the mailing list of every peddler of the esatoric, from Father Divine to the Omnipotent Oom and the Rosicrucians. It was through one of her yogi cronies, no doubt, if not through a Bahai, that she had learned of Doctor Sykes's prowess, for the old boy ranked high in the mystic confraternity. She was therefore predisposed in our favor."

The Colonel is a strong rooter for the opposite sex, whom he considers it impossible to buck.

"Since you cannot defeat them," he sometimes says, "it is necessary to win them over to your side. There is not a man, however intelligent, who is one half as smart as any woman."

The Colonel's ideal of feminine beauty remains constant.

In this he resembles an old wartime friend of mine named Count Prziswieski, a minor figure in the exiled Polish government.

"All my life I have been faithful to one woman," the Count once said to me,—"a fragile blonde with a morbid expression."

He found this woman in every country, and she never aged, although the Count did. The fragile blonde with a morbid expression, wherever she turned up, was in her twenties.

My knowledge of the Count's predilection saved us both embarrassment one week end when I was away from my London hotel and returned to find he had been a guest there during my absence.

"Do you know the Count Ginwiski?" the night porter, an inquisitive sort, asked me. "Said 'e knew you. Rum cove."

"I certainly do know him," I said. "One of the county families of Poland."

"And do you know the Countess?" the porter asked artfully.

"Very well," I answered. "Thin blonde woman, much younger than he is, speaks English perfectly."

"Good night, sir," the porter said in a disappointed tone.

The Colonel's ideal is a dashing woman, tall, lissome, understanding, and, above all, loaded down with Tease. He represents her in a prototype called the Duchess, who appears throughout his writings columnistic and his reminiscences, but who is not permanently identified with any individual. Like the fragile blonde, she stays the same age, but the Colonel's ideal is thirty-five rather than twenty, for at thirty-five a woman has at once more dash and more understanding. The Colonel's affair with the Duchess began, he says, when he was getting out a weekly paper called the *Referee* in San Francisco, in the period following the retirement of his pugilistic meal ticket. The *Referee* dealt largely with night life,—"which was in those days variegated," the Colonel says. It was his sharp, shiny-shoe period. He wrote a column of night-spot notes under the signature of the Duchess, "a woman of the world, well heeled and a hell of a good fellow, who visited the resorts both advertising and non-advertising and commentated on the personalities she encountered there. There soon ceased almost totally to be non-advertisers." He has revived the Duchess many times,—she was the only woman present at the Gans-Nelson fight in 1906, according to one of his columns for example, and also the most beautiful spectator of the finish of Middleground's Kentucky Derby in 1950, not a grayed-eyelash older.

His description of Mrs. Harriman conforms to this type, and possibly Mrs. Harriman did. I have not looked her up in a picture morgue.

The *Referee*, with many enterprises of vaster commercial import, was submerged, the Colonel says, in a reform wave which swamped San Francisco just previous to the Panama-Pacific exposition. There was a conflict of maelstrom proportions before the reformers won out, he says, with a slight shudder at the recollection, but in the end they shut the town tighter'n a drum.

"And what was the editorial policy of the *Referee* during this struggle for righteousness?" I once asked him.

" 'Let Paris be gay!' " he answered.

But this is what the Colonel himself would call a labyrinthian digression.

9/ *"The Detonatory Compound"*

I RETURNED to the manuscript. Mrs. Harriman was speaking.

" 'Here at Belmont Park this season we're confronted by a severe Depression and a continued period of rain would ruin us,' explained Mrs. Harriman, 'and I thought you California experts might be able to prevent it. What may be your reaction?'

"The nudge that Dr. Sykes trained into my ribs was quite unnecessary for I realized my time at bat had come to hand. Slowly from my brief case emerged the Syllabus which I had prepared the night before on Rain

Prevention and what we could do for the panicky top people at Belmont Park.

"'The new and most modern method of meteorological control and precipitation engenderment will be utilized, the Silver Iodine Spray based on Canalized Wave Vibration,' I intoned. 'The cost of installation for the term of ten racing days or less will not exceed $5,000 and it is our firm belief, after many years in the ancient and honorable profession of the Rainmaker, you will not have more than two days with a perceptible rainfall.'

"Syllabus explained that our Proposition is based solely upon an ability to prevent rain. It is *not* a bet, like rain insurance as offered by Lloyds of London, but a measure designed to insure good racing conditions as well as protect the sportsmen backing the meet from loss. However, as a guarantee of our seriousness, we included an indemnity provision.

"Then came the all-important Denouement: 'the terms.' They embraced simply this: 'We, the U. S. Weather Control Bureau, hereinafter to be styled party of the first part, agree to induct, maintain and operate the Iodine Silvery-Spray and Gamma-Ray-Radio system, the cost to us not to exceed $5,000, cost of buildings and labor to be defrayed by the Westchester Racing Association. The party of the second part agrees to pay party of the first part $2,500 on Saturdays, Sept. 6 and Sept. 13, and $1,000 on each intervening weekday for its services in preventing rain. Party of the first part agrees to pay to party of the second part $2,000 on any day on which United States Weather Bureau reports rain, even a trace, within purlieus of Belmont Park between 11 A.M and 5:30 P.M. Payment to be made each day at 6 P.M. at the Office of the Westchester Racing Association, Belmont Park.'

"This looked like a two-to-one bet but it wasn't. It was even money on weekdays and we couldn't lose if we tried on Saturdays.

"When I read off, 'cost of buildings and labor to be defrayed by the party of the second part,' the Good Doctor Sykes shifted nervously while his face assumed the ghastly aspect of an Egyptian mummy. If we had had to get up that Tease we would have been in trouble. But Mr. Widener acceded. He said though that he thought we should get up a certified check for $2,000, the amount of our forfeit in case we failed on the first Saturday, as earnest of our corporate responsibility. It was up to me to find the two grand, as I was handling the business side of the enterprise.

"Mr. Widener still hesitated, as one who feared a trap. The sum involved could to him be of no consequence, a fleabite, but he fancied himself a sharp guy.

"Sharply sudden came a lull in the negotiative colloquy with all eyes and attention veered upon Mrs. Harriman; her brow bore a knitted texture just for a fleeting second or two, then came a faraway look evidently penetrating the distant realm of occult portent, for with beatific transition she suddenly exclaimed: 'Joe, my boy, it comes to me as clear as crystal, the augury is for you and fine success. Close the Deal with the gentlemen.'

"That was a lucky trance for us Rainmakers I may assure you. Without further ado, Mr. Widener accepted terms, extended a handshake to me along the diameter of the friendly little circle. The deal was a bet and was on as sure as you live. On Mrs. Harriman's suggestion we adjourned to the Turf & Field Club for a snack and a service of illicit but authentic Irroy *brut*.

"With laughter and banter the gathering broke up, Mrs. Harriman, womanlike, having the last word. She expressed the thought to Dr. Sykes; —said she, 'Well Doc, your partner, Jim, is quite a lawyer fellow, isn't he?' The Good Doctor said I was not a man of the law.

" 'What has he ever done?' the lady inquired.

"Replying, Dr. Sykes rejoined,—'Well, up in the Lehigh Valley once he talked a mocking bird out of a tree.'

"With an all around expression of good luck and high hope for keeping that rain away from the door we all went our various ways. We the Rainmakers stood to make $10,000 if every day was clear, or lose $4,000 if it rained every day.

"But where would I get that $2,000 in those Hooverized days of tight money? Why, sure enough, there he was—dear old Mike the Bite, a real natural. 'Fade my four for the Lord's sake,' as Dr. Orlando Edgar Miller would say on occasion.

"Making my way from the haunts of the Haute Bourgeoisie in the Turf & Field to the moiling fringe of the betting ring, I braced him.

"I found him in good spirits; his tip for the third race, Baba Kenny, had won, although paying only even money. That had meant fifty-three-times-two-dollars profit to him, however, as well as satisfaction, and he had bet it back on a filly named Chalice in the fifth, which was just coming up. Our conversation and the jollification in the clubhouse had consumed considerable time. 'I got it right from Ollie Thomas, the clocker,' he said to me, 'and she is 25 to 1 in the ring.' That was one occasion on which my adherence to non-speculation proved costly, for the filly came down in front, a gray by Stefan the Great, she took the lead from the first jump and increased it with every stride, a *pisseuse*.

"Availing of the auspicious moment, I said, 'Willie, I have an opportunity to make a good score, but I need the use of two grand until Futurity Day.' And I explained to him as much of the project as I thought necessary.

" 'When I see you two buzzing Mr. Widener and Mr. Schaumberg yesterday out there on the lawn I wondered what you could be up to now,' he said.

"I averred abiding faith in Dr. Sykes's powers, but Willie was a man of occult intuition himself. 'It looks like the Racing Association made a dutch book,' he said. 'You got a good bet there.'

" 'I will pay you $2,200 next Saturday,' I promised him. 'If you wish, I will give you a note.'

" 'No need of that,' the Bite said. And he got his checkbook out of the drawer of the oldfashioned cash register and wrote out a check, telling me I could have it certified at his bank next morning, but it wasn't necessary,—Mr. Widener knew him. I heard tell afterward that when Mike the Bite died, in 1946, he was worth $600,000 in securities and property.

"And that was our last major obstacle overcome. We were turning into the stretch, with a clear field in front of us and in a contending position. Such loans could be negotiated only on the Race Track, where there was to be found a breed of men and a business method, together with an instinct, found nowhere else. But the noisome breath of the mechanical maw of the mutuels has changed all that, and the Old Breed is dying out.

"I carried the check back to the Racing Secretary's office. Mr. Schaumberg smiled when he saw the signature. 'You couldn't have a better man on your side,' he said.

"Now we were set to go, but we had only about 36 hours left to install all our apparatus, for the Good Doctor declaimed he needed a start of a few hours to dispel rain clouds that might converge upon the track Saturday noon. 'It is not an instantaneous process,' he said. 'There are some types of clouds I can dispel with one punch, but others require a couple of hours of softening up before I shoot it to them.'

"My role changed. Instead of a silver-tongued advocate I now became a construction superintendent."

At this point in my reading I became a trifle boorish. "Colonel," I said to my old friend, "do you mean to say this really happened?"

A pained expression contracted the Colonel's nostrils, but he recovered quickly.

"I expected you'd ask that sooner or later, Joe," he said. "Anybody would. And so I brought along a few old clippings from New York newspapers of that period that I happen to have preserved at the Dixie. There are more in the newspaper collection of the New York Public Library."

I had not attended any race meetings in the summer of 1930 myself,—I had been working out of town,—and I had assumed as I read along that the Colonel was writing about a scheme that had abutted in fiasco. I was waiting for the point in the manuscript at which the plan of the Rainmakers would go sour.

"Allow me to introduce my exhibits at the proper place in the narration," the Colonel said. "The points at which they are appropriate are marked in the manuscript."

So I read on.

"It was agreed we, the Rain Preventers, were to have at disposal every possible facility available at trackside, including the fine old disused clubhouse at the head of the stretch, abandoned when the finish line was moved in 1926 and a constricted area of about one-half acre at the head of the Widener Course, the straightaway down which the celebrated Futurity is run off annually. Sweeping down past the long grandstand, on the afternoon of Friday, Sept. 5, 1930, the observer arriving by the old clubhouse would have seen piles of our paraphernalia and materials with workmen and installators standing about awaiting our instructions.

"Inside the old Clubhouse on the top floor, busy as the proverbial bees, Dr. Sykes and his Mrs. were directing workmen in the setting up of the two heavy Vibrator Units and the Chemicalized Repository; I am not adept in machinery so I cannot describe their aspect more technically than to say they looked ominous. The lady, noisy as a steam tea kettle, had just issued orders that no person might enter 'the laboratory' from this moment on except by presentation of a Permit Card.

"The weird-looking Detonatory Compound at the head of the Widener Course had been completed during the morning and its equipment completely installed. Under the experienced eye of the Doctor and my urgings, vehement rather than initiate, all matters had progressed as per schedule and we would open on the morrow.

"There was little architectural ingenuity employed in the design of the Compound thus established out in deep right field; it was a one-room structure made of plain lumber, a pentagon 16 feet high in height and 12 feet on a side, with an earth floor and no doors and no windows, an important point counter-espionage-wise. A veritable packing box. Entrance was made through a tunnel of 9½ feet from an entrance immediately to the north of the layout,—you had to bend down to get in.

"Sprouting from the Roof were two Vibratory Rods of shiny steel and within an evil looking contraption best described as suggesting an abandoned oldtime Refrigerator with an electric charged battery, quite concealed, and a washtub full of the most noxious-smelling chemicals outside a slaughter house."

The Colonel had next pasted up a clipping from Audax Minor's department in *The New Yorker* of that September 13, 1930.

"The rain control machine is very hush-hush. Both the negative and positive actions, which are interchangeable, are under guard. The five-sided shack in the hollow near the training track interested us most. There is something cabalistic about it, with planks and two-by-fours laid out in curious designs around it, and the five scantlings nailed to the sides of the shed that shelters the remote radio control with a spider web of wires. Then, too, there's the big five-pointed star strung with radio aerial wire and festooned with ornaments from discarded brass beds and springs from box mattresses. The star always faces the way the wind blows. I'm quite sure Dr. Sykes has read *Rootabaga Stories* and how, 'on a high stool, in a high tower, on a high hill, sits the Head Spotter of the Weather

Makers,' for he has a platform like a starter's box, several feet higher than the shed, from which he may direct the magnetic impulses—or he may be practicing to be a starter."

The Colonel's manuscript continued:

"Audax was never in a position to describe the interior. Mr. Widener himself was admitted only once to the Holy of Holies, and in negotiating the low tunnel suffered the sacrification of a $250 imported English suit draped by Carabis of 3 Creechurch Lane, London, and the wreckage of a solid gold wrist watch presented to him by Lord Derby, another racetrack promoter. Once in he looked around in amazement but received a convincer when the Good Doctor coyly edged him into contact with the rusty steel shell of the Detonatory Giant; old man John Franzel, the Lord High Executioner in the Death House at Sing Sing, never was more facile in the feathering of a switch than Dr. Sykes, for the tall Mr. Widener received an electric shock that left no further doubt in his mind but that the occult forces of nature and the Detonatory Pulsations of Higher Physics were at work in the Grand Cosmic Order.

"As a survivor, he afterwards expressed to the panting Newspapermen, a week later, that he felt lucky to escape the lair and snare of Dr. Faustus with his life. Yes sir, it's true; it's facts and history.

"The only Scribe to make the tunneled passage and live to tell the tale was Mr. Ned Brown, then the Sporting Editor, New York *World*, and he became teetotally bald within five days and has remained denuded ever since, complete and totally, yea verily.[1]

"Between the Compound and the Laboratory, a distance of a good Yorkshire Mile, ran the Ethereal Conduit upon which traveled with the speed of Light augmented 30,000-fold the initiatory Pulsations to the Vibrator, and thence, via the antennae, to the natural Air Waves and channeled Coaxial Appendixtum.

"Without the permission of Consolidated Edison, the devious Sykes pair diverted from the blue ambient some 32,400 kilowatts of electric energy daily to the Ethereal Conduit, thereby greatly annoying, and in some remote instances, totally frustrating, the good House Wives of Hempstead Plains busy with their can openers and electric stoves in the preparation of the evening meal for the lowly husbandman plodding his

[1] This is a house joke. Ned Brown, an old friend of the Colonel's, who is at present editor of the sterling publication *Official Wrestling*, was bald before he ever heard of Dr. Sykes, and denies that he ever penetrated into the Paracelsian Dungeon. He was in 1930 not sporting editor, but boxing columnist of the *World* (his column was called "Pardon My Glove") and spent most of his summer afternoons at the race track, since, as he explains, he did not have to go to work until evening and he always had a badge. As a spectator he remembers full well the Colonel's surface activities at the racecourse in behalf of the Weather Control Bureau, he says, but he did not enter into the subterranean.

"When I was a cub reporter," says Mr. Brown, recalling an era virtually Triassic, "Jimmy Macdonald was already a top turf writer. So when I ran across him at Belmont, we used to chew over the rainmaking business, in which he was then engaged."

weary way homeward at day's end. From that day to this, Edison has not even filed a bill let alone received compensation for service rendered.[2]

"But, ah, back to the good old Clubhouse. The scene suggested the gauze and tinsel of the Bazaar of Baghdad, for here in long rows stood bright-colored glass jars, containing the various elemental chemicals used in explosive composition which in turn discharged upon the Air Currents the silver-crested Eidems which dispelled aqueous concentrations on contact, thus lessening the incidence of rain precipitation. From the top of the Vibrator, similar in grotesque appearance to the one set up at the Compound, ran an insulative tubing to the Ethereal Conduit jutting out from the building's rooftop to the skies above."

"What was really in those jars?" I asked the Colonel.

"I think it was colored water," he said, "but the good Doctor never told me." I returned to my reading:

"Hours after the running of the last race the General Staff of the Rain Preventers and a numerous detail of workmen remained at the Laboratory and the Compound. Every last item had been perfected in readiness for the great scientific enterprise of the morrow.

"Lights twinkled in the clubhouse and away across midfield under the rising Harvest Moon the eerie structure of the Compound loomed in ghostly outline; across on the backstretch the Recreation Centre, where foregather nightly the Trainers, Grooms, Swipes and Gallop Boys, stood out in full glow, and a bonfire at the entrance to the main track which nightly incinerates the trashy odds and ends engendered during the busy daytime hours shone its red fire while its illuminant rays disclosed a circle of men and boys busily engaged in what appeared to the trained eye of the old Frontiersman, peering through the lenses of Mrs. Sykes's imported French Lemaire binoculars, a roaring oldtime Crap Game in full locomotion.

"The yawning Grand Stand stood out against the night skies like a hulking Naval Aircraft Carrier, stranded, silent and menacing, against the background of sentient silence, a fearsome suggestion of what might happen should it rain ten hours hence; here and there over the vast expanse the searching lights of the night patrol of Pinkertons in protectory guard of the giant plant twinkled their assurance of an undeviating maintenance of their faithful Watch. Gallant Fox and Questionnaire, entered to contend in the Lawrence Realization Stakes, worth $50,000 to the winner, next day at one mile and five furlongs, were wound up no tighter than we."

[2] I hope this passage does not bring down upon the Colonel a posse of collectors from the Edison Company. He is still non-holding.

10/ "La Grande Semaine"

"THIS IS THE DAY of days. At eight o'clock in the morning a cold gray mist came in off Jamaica Bay and overcast the whole backstretch area but only for a brief moment, for as the last batch of horses working out with their Trainers and Swipes had departed the quarter-stretch, the mists disappeared with them and a golden sweep of sunshine overspread the scene, bringing much joy and hope to the inwardly sweating coterie of Rain Preventers.

"All that happened was it cleared up, but naturally we took full credit for it. We had engaged a publicity man, at $200 for the week, and he invited all interested newspapermen to drop in at the Sykes' town house, any time after hours, and sample Mrs. Sykes' Pisco Punch, a drink whereof she professed to have the ancient Peruvian formula, delivered to her by a medium who had wheedled it from the ghost of the Inca High Priest during a séance in Riverview, California. Naturally the press was not unfavorably disposed toward us, and we were away running.

"The funny thing about it is that a lot of the other people around the track began to believe there was something in it as soon as they read it in the newspapers. Racetrack habitués are in any case given to superstition, as the Bite daily demonstrated, and I sometimes encounter old-time turfites even today who will asseverate with conviction that Professor Sykes must have had something.

"The day was a success *extraordinaire*. Twenty-five thousand persons paid admission, an excellent attendance for those depressed days, and William Woodward's mighty three-year-old colt, Gallant Fox, prevailed by a mere nose over James Butler's Questionnaire, his keenest rival. Gallant Fox had been beaten only once in his career,—in the Travers at Saratoga, on a muddy track. We of the Weather Control Bureau could flatter ourselves that we had preserved him from a second such disaster. We received, however, no token of recognition from Mr. Woodward, which saddened us, for his horse had won $29,160, no meagre increment. I shall always remember a sentence written by George Daley, of the *World*, recounting Gallant Fox's victory:

"'One hundred yards from the wire the Fox appeared to hang and looked beaten, but just when a sob went up from the throats of many, he again settled to his bitter, grinding task and he prevailed.' In the secondary feature, the Champagne Stakes for two-year-olds, Mate, a horse destined to win the Preakness Stakes the following spring, defeated the immortal Equipoise by a head.

"But the most pleasing feature of the day for us, the Rain Preventers, occurred at 6 P.M. when, without demurrer and amid general acclaim, we collected our first check for $2,500. 'Weather Clear; track fast,' the chart said.

"After cooling out we decided to pay Willie Beeson, the Bite, his $2,000 forthwith, and the $200 interest on the following Saturday as promised. So, after the proper endorsement by Dr. Sykes as President and myself as Treasurer of the Weather Control Bureau I scampered over to the stand where the Bite was making all secure for the night.

"The Bite seemed as tickled as I was at our success. He said, 'You boys just forget that $200. Getting the big chunk back is good enough for me.'

"The next five racing days were like a dream. Weather clear; track fast. We collected $1,000 every night. The newspaper men and women were our chief trouble. We wanted to avoid too detailed disclosure, because the Good Doctor and I felt that if we went through this one undefeated, we might get more racing contracts. In the middle of the week the feature editor of the *Telegram*; it hadn't become the *World-Telegram* yet,—had a brainstorm. Home radios, as the mind of man runneth not to the contrary, had not achieved perfection in 1930. People were wont to exchange remedies for static, as for horse lumbago in days of bucolic old. Dr. Sykes, unfortunately, had let it be bruited about that we had one of the most powerful radio installations in the Western Hemisphere, and the editor sent a reporter out to ask the Good Doctor if that might not be responsible for the radio interference now so prevalent in Queens and Nassau counties on both sides of Belmont Park, where the *Telegram* was trying to build circulation. The Doctor, although denying him ingress to the sanctum sanctorium, oracled that it might. The *Telegram* published the story, with one of those playful leads about how 'householders who have been wondering why their pet radio programs sound like jabberwocky can blame it all on Dr. G.A.I.M. Sykes.'

"In a couple of days two inspectors from the Federal Communications Commission appeared at Belmont and insisted on examining our installation. After looking it over they exonerated us, naurally. But some revengeful Hildy Johnson who had overindulged in our Pisco punch, a skull-popper, got wind of their visit and interviewed them. The result was a first-page story in the *World* saying that the inspectors had minimized the efficacy of our equipment, maintaining its radiaction was imperceptible.

"We chose to ignore it as a canard, standing upon results for the authentification of our claims. The beautiful Indian summer weather brought on a track lightning-fast with a dusty cushion flying at all times. Belief in the efficacy of our manipulations even caused us some embarrassment when an associate of Dutch Schultz propositioned the Good Doctor to bring on a heavy rain overnight because the boys had a good spot for a mudder in the fifth race on the morrow. 'Mud brings this mule up thirty pounds,' the emissary enlightened us. 'We been running him on the fastest tracks we could find and he hasn't finished better than next to last since Christmas. He'll go away at 40 to 1.' They offered us ten thousand down and a bet of another ten going for us. The Good Doctor wanted to take him up. It was then I began to look askance at the old boy, wondering if perchance he had begun to believe he was genuine. I talked him out of it, saying that if we failed to produce good weather for the Association we would forfeit only two thousand dollars, but if we failed to produce a deluge for the mob we would die the death horrible. 'And there is always a chance of a slipup, Doc,' I told him. So we told the hood we would do our best, but could promise nothing. When the next day dawned clear, as usual, they scratched the horse, and I breathed as with a sense of calamity averted.

"The situation was complicated by the intervention presently of another mugg, who represented himself as a friend of Al Capone, requesting assurance of a fast track for the sixth on the same day his competitor had asked mud for the fifth. They had a speed horse going and would bet a couple of thousand for us. 'We will do our best,' I said, 'but promise nothing.' The horse come in at four to one but the hoods would give us only four thousand dollars, pretexting they had been unable to get down all the money they had intended to bet. We professed indignation but pocketed the four thousand. 'You will pay us the balance the next time you come here to get any weather,' I told the plenipotentiary, 'or no dice. The Honest Rainmaker hath spoken.'

"Coming up to Saturday, Futurity Day, the last inning, it begins to look like Dr. Sykes, with good support from the Rainmakers' infield, is on the way to a No Hitter victory over the elements, and the Rainmakers could afford to sit back and enjoy the hubbub their advent had engendered on the Race Track, in Society, and within the Mystic Circles of the Town. We had banked six checks in succession, one for $2,500 and five for a grand each and were $7,500 in hand and in front at the Night & Day Bank at Broadway and Fortieth, Manhattan, beside the four-thousand-dollar bonus legitimately acquired from the Speedhorse Boys. I will note here that of the first five days of the meeting, without the intervention of the Ethereal Conduit and the Giant Detonator, on only one had there been rain. Sceptics continued to suggest we were riding with the season.

"Certainly the old Ford Model T engine in the Vibrator at the Laboratory had been servicing us just dandy, while the Galaxy of Varicolored Bottles and their chemical content had played a role in noble inspiration. There were 16 of these Bottles of all manner of shade and tint suggesting the oldtime Drug Store with its window display of tiger fat, snake serum, and good luck potion in huge glass demijohns. The ancient Cigar Store highbred wooden Indian, could he come to life, might have had a good snicker at the spectacle.

"We could win $2,500 on the last day, if the weather remained fair, enabling us to pocket our fee intact, or take only $500 if it rained and we had to cough up our $2,000 forfeit. In any case the campaign averred itself a glorious victory, and Mrs. Sykes decided to throw herself around socially and hospitably by giving a soiree at the Red Room of the Hotel Imperial, Herald Square, Manhattan, the night after the Futurity, and 330 invitations were sent out, saying bring your friends.

"On the last day there was a precipitation no more substantial than that from an atomizer, but we accepted our responsibilities, however we might have felt, inwardly, about the Bourgeoisie exacting its Pound of Flesh on such a technicality. The races drew 25,000 paid admissions, as they had the previous Saturday, and the great Jamestown, owned by George D. Widener, the President's brother, won the Futurity by a nose from the great Equipoise, with Mate third. The total stakes were $121,760, of which the victor's share was $99,600. The Grande Semaine thus ended pleasantly for all concerned: the Westchester Racing Association, which had maintained its attendance; the Widener family, and even the general public, which had heavily backed Jamestown, a favorite at odds of 11 to 5.

"But most especially was it a victory for the United States Weather Control Bureau, which showed a net profit of $8,000 in eight days including a non-profitable Sunday, not bad on an investment of zero capital, and in addition to the unofficial supplementary income of four grand from the Mob.

"Mr. Widener, in handing over the final $500 check, thanked us for our satisfactory services, and said he hoped to see us back again the following season. I understand that to the end of his days he deprecated derision of Dr. Sykes and his theories. He maintained that the United States Weather Bureau, whose meteorologist ridiculed the Good Doctor, had little cause to carp, when its own predictions for the New York area were notoriously inaccurate."

I looked up from the last page of the story of the Honest Rainmaker.

"Did you ever work the dodge again?" I asked.

The Colonel shook his head. "The newspapers killed it," he said. "But poor old Dr. Sykes assisted them. He walked right into a haymaker. I should have kept him incommunicado with his arcane impedimenta. It seems that right at the top of his success some Park Row wag had accused him of ineffectuality and taking a free ride. The old boy, incensed, had said that he would show he *could* control weather, by producing rain as soon as his contract was finished. Monday, September 15, the next racing day after the Futurity, was set for the test. The old boy, who was really pretty weatherwise, the result of long speculative observation, may have believed that with the approach of the September equinox the weather was in fact due to change. The clouds on Futurity Day bore out in a general way this prognostication. But he overweened himself.

"He promised these reporters that he would produce torrents of rain on the track between two-thirty and four-thirty on Monday afternoon. The next day's papers chronicled the event. I was not even out at the track myself, for the Doctor had purposely neglected to inform me of his foolhardy undertaking. If he had pulled it off it would have been a great publicity stunt. But when you are sitting pretty you should refrain from endangering your position; it is like breaking up a full house to draw for four of a kind.

"The day dawned bright and sunshiny, the papers reported. The mockers assembled just before post time for the first race, when the good Doctor strode out to his cavern and interred himself. Almost immediately clouds began to gather. At three he emerged from the depths and informed observers that there would be a whale of a storm at four. He explained that he needed the intervening time to assemble more clouds. It was cloudy and threatening all afternoon, but the deadline came and passed without an obedient drop, and the old Doc looked mighty chapfallen.

"Colonel Matt Winn, who had made us a tentative offer to prevent rain at the Churchill Downs meeting in Kentucky, dropped the proposition like an option on a horse that proves unsound, and the deluge of derision breaking upon our heads deterred Mr. Widener himself from extending another contract. So, as once before in California, the rainmaker's art died the death, not to be revived for a score of years. You have to have an airplane now to practice it, and I am too old to qualify for a pilot's license."

"And what happened to old Doc Sykes?" I asked.

"I don't know," the Colonel said. "I haven't heard from or of him in many a year, and if he's still alive he must be near ninety." (Dr. Sykes still is alive, or was as late as September 1952, I learned subsequently. And he is, or was, only about as old as the Colonel. But they had apparently lost contact during the biographical interstice.)

He appeared to find insufficient solace in his beer. Then a recollection cheered him.

"Joe," he said, "you should have had a snort of Mrs. Sykes's pisco punch. It was a grand party. Sherry did the catering and the Philharmonic Chamber Music Quartet entertained the guests playing everything from *Wozzeck* to 'Turkey in the Straw.' The Banjo-Eyed Kid, Coon-Can Artie, and Commodore Dutch lent their arms to the season's debutantes preferred for the grand march. But the pisco punch constituted the standout.

"It was said New York had not before ever seen or heard of the insidious concoction which in its time had caused the unseating of South American governments and women to set world's records in various and interesting fields of activity. In early San Francisco, where the punch first made its North American appearance in 1856, the police allowed but one drink per person in twenty-four hours, it's that propulsive. But Mrs. Sykes served them up like *pain, à discrétion,* as the signs used to say in front of the little restaurants in Paris, meaning you could have all the bread you wanted. As a consequence, discretion vanished.

"Two hours after the salon had gotten underway even the oldest gals were still hunting the bartenders. Many of the old-time veteran Cellini, who hadn't scaled a garden wall in forty years, made a double score for themselves that evening, a memorable amoristic occasion. It was a famous victory, said little Peterkin. What I tell you about it now will be little noted and soon forgotten, but what those women did will be long remembered."

Daylight died in Forty-fifth Street outside the Palace Bar and Grill, and the Honest Rainmaker, who seldom feels in form before electric-light-time, continued to perk up.

"Joe," Colonel Stingo said, "last summer a tout introduced me to an Argentine trainer who knows a lot of people who own cattle ranches down there. Anyplace there are ranches they must need rain. If I had the courage of my convictions I'd go out and buy myself a Spanish grammar."

11 / *The Life Spiritual*

WHEN I first worked upon Colonel Stingo to set down his memoirs, he said, "You don't know what you're getting into, Joe. I am not the fine man you take me to be."

My effort to set him right on that score resulted in an estrangement, but we became friends again.

At another time he appeared to believe I was giving him too much of the worst of it, for he said:

"It is only a boob that conducts an enterprise in such a manner that it leads to embroilment with the law. I myself have never collided with it head on. But I have had many associates less wise or fortunate. One was Dr. Orlando Edgar Miller, a Doctor of Philosophy of the University of the Everglades, Rushton, Florida. Dr. Miller, when I first met him, was of appearance pre-eminent. Sixty years old, straight as an arrow, with snow-white hair and black eyelashes. He affected a Panama hat, Palm Beach suit and white buckskin shoes even in the dead of a New York winter. He presented an undeviating outward semblance of sanctity, but he was a deviator, a dear old fellow. Having drawn the multitude toward him, first thing you know he had his hands in all their pockets.

"During the course of the revivals he conducted, frequently lasting for weeks if the supply of boobs held out, he professed a diet of one orange a day, but he was a practiced voluptuary. He did not like oranges, but he ingested plenty other comestibles. 'We eat too much and no mentality can be alert when the body is overfed,' he used to proclaim in Carnegie Hall, where he lectured to throngs, and then he would take a taxi to a speakeasy called the Pennwick and eat a steak with a coverture of mushrooms like the blanket of roses they put on the winner of the Kentucky Derby.

"After that he would plunge his fine features in eight or nine seidels of needled beer, about forty proof, a beverage worthy of revival, for it combined the pleasant Gambrinian taste with an alcoholic inducement to continue beyond the point of assuagement. Or he would decimate a black bottle of Sandy Macdonald scotch landed at Rockaway Point and conveyed fresh to the table by courtesy of Big Bill Dwyer. Scotch, like the lobster, tastes best when fresh from the ocean, a truth which we have forgotten since repeal.

"But let him, in the lobby of Carnegie Hall after one of his meetings, be introduced to a man with upwards of fifty thousand dollars and he would ostentatiously gnaw an orange peel. It was my duty to keep him informed of the financial status of the potentially regenerate, a task for which I was well qualified by my experience as credit man for Tex Rickard's old Northern gambling house at Goldfield, Nevada, and in a similar capacity for Canary Cottage at Del Monte, California, and the late Colonel Edward Riley Bradley at his Casino, Palm Beach, Florida. Many a man rife with money makes no outward flaunt. His habiliments, even, may be poor. But, Joe, when it comes to rich men, I am equipped with a kind of radar. The houses I worked for collected on ninety-five per cent of markers, an unchallenged record.

" 'Not the mythical bacilli but improper breathing causes tuberculosis,' this old Dr. Miller would hold forth in public. 'Among the ancient races who understood proper breathing there was no such disease.' The cure he espoused was by the laying on of hands, calisthenics and giving the right heart, and the women flocked to be laid hands on, even the most buxom averring a fear of dormant maladies. In his pulpit appearances he stressed spiritual values,—Biblical exegesis, personality and love. He advised women to pull their husbands' hair to prevent baldness. He was a regular cure-all.

"He was accompanied on his forays by the Countess Bonizello, a lady born in Davenport, Iowa, but who had married, she recounted, an impoverished member of the Italian nobility, since deceased. She had at any rate been long enough on the Continent to acquire that little froufrou, and spoke a certain *patois*,—French and English. She gave evidence of having been in early life a beauty, and she was full of guile and could handle men and was a real good fellow. When they hit a town she would take a suite at the best hotel and he would assume a simple lodging in accord with his ascetic pose. She would play the role of a wealthy devotee who had followed him from Europe, platonically, of course, and she would organize the social side of the revival.

"She had in fact met him in England, so they said. There, in 1914 just before the First World War, he had conducted revivals in the Albert Hall. He induced the Duke of Manchester to put the O.K. on a line of credit for him, and was going to build a sanatorium for the cure of tuberculosis by his methods when unfortunately a woman died under his ministrations, and the British Medical Association, 'captious without a point of criticism,' the old Doctor used to say, had him haled before a Court. 'As if other practitioners never lost patients,' he said. 'Why, an Austrian prince named Hohenlohe paid me a thousand quid, when the pound was worth $4.86 and several mils, because he was so pleased with the way I treated him. That was what inflamed Harley Street against me.' The Court let him off with a reprimand, but the publicity queered his act in England, and he came home. Here he emphasized the spiritual shots in his bag, preaching that right living is the road to health, but the American Medical Association suspected he was laying hands in private, and he had to put up with persecution which seldom affected his monetary success."

A look of reminiscent admiration suffused the old Colonel's countenance.

"Of my adventures with Dr. Miller I could speak endlessly," he said, "but my purpose is only to illustrate the fine line between *fas* and *nefas*. There was no need for him to transgress that line. He was a man of great animal magnetism, reminding me of the appellation by Max Lerner of General Dwight D. Eisenhower,—'the charismatic leader,' which Mr. Lerner says means one you follow because he seems to have a kind of halo around him. Dr. Miller once said he was good for $250,000 a year on a purely spiritual plane. He drew Tease from the repentant like soda through a straw.

"But eventually the day came when the old Doctor overweened himself. Some Hollywood sharks sold him the idea of becoming a movie star. The old ham could fancy himself and the Countess bedazzling unseen multitudes. There seemed to him nothing ludicrous in the proposition. Essentially he was a boob too. The idea was to form an independent producing company and sell stock to people who came to his revivals. The way of separating the sheep from the goats, to wit the holding from the non-holding, at these meetings was to distribute envelopes among the multitude, specifying that only contributions of a dollar or more were to be enclosed, and the donors were to write their addresses on the envelope if they wished free literature.

"The Doctor was not interested in the addresses of people with less than a buck. Such were requested to drop their coins in the velvet-lined collection box, where they wouldn't jingle. The jingle has a bad effect on suggestible people who might otherwise give folding money.

"We had a follow-up system on the names. Paid workers followed up each prospect. If, as occasionally occurred, they encountered a scoffer who had invested a buck just to see what would happen, the name was scratched from the mailing list. Incidentally they were pretty good estimators of a chump's net wealth. I went to one of a series of meetings an exegizer held at Carnegie Hall this winter, and the old operating procedure is still standard. We left no room for improvement.

"When we swapped towns with another big preacher, like Dr. Hall the hundred-dollar-Bible man, we sometimes swapped mailing lists. But we would always keep out a few selected prospects, and so, I suspect, would the other prophet. The ready-made list helped in the beginning, but the one you could trust was the one you made yourself. The purpose of this labyrinthian digression is to indicate that after ten years of listmaking, old Dr. Miller had a mighty lever to place in the hands of a stock salesman.

"I was assigned to write the scenario and it was unique, indisputably. It was the only one I had ever written. It was called the *Bowery Bishop* and was based on what I remembered reading about Jerry McCauley's Bowery Mission. Dr. Miller, of course, was to play the saintly missionary, and there were two young lovers. It had been intended that the Countess should play half the love interest, though her bloom was no longer of the first blush pristine, but at the last minute she backed out. She said there were reasons why she did not want her photograph too widely distributed. This was of good augury for the enterprise, the promoters said, as the film would be surer to click if the Doctor had the support of some well-known movie names.

"We engaged two great stars of the silent films to play the young lovers. With a scenario, stars and a sucker list, the promoters were all set to go. The stock salesmen were getting twenty-five per cent commission. The nature of the promotion literature was such, however, that I felt sure trouble impended. Purchasers were not only assured of a large profit, but guaranteed against loss. I declined office in the company. I went out to Honolulu to arrange a great Miller revival there, which was to begin simultaneously with the release of the picture, and when I returned to California, the inevitable had ensued.

"Stock had been sold to the amount of $320,000, of which $240,000 had been turned in to the treasury. With part of the $240,000 a picture had been made. But only a handful of theatres were available to show the film, which was, as one might expect, a turkey. The old Doctor, seized by foreboding, had hit the booze and played away the rest of the money on horses and the stock market, deluding himself that he might thus recoup solvency. I advised him to lam before the inauguration of the uproar, and he sought sanctuary in Australia, where I commended him to the good offices of some friends I had in the fight game there. The Countess Bonizello left by the same boat. I had one or two letters from him after he got out to Sydney saying he was making plenty Tease. The revival business in the Antipodes had been in a crude stage before he arrived, he wrote. The surpliced choir with which he embellished his performances and the social éclat imparted by the Countess had remedied all that.

"But such peripheral triumphs did not content him. In 1926 or so I had a letter from him dated Calgary, Alberta, and so I knew he had ventured back to the outskirts of the battlefield, and he was contemplating a new campaign. The next tidings were bad. He was under arrest, and California authorities were trying to extradite him. They did, and he got six.

"We disappeared from the surfaces of each other's conscious lives, like two submarines, interrupted in a mission of destruction, which submerge without the formalities of parting.

"Now," Colonel Stingo said, "we do a fade-out and pick up the thread of our narrative again in the winter of 1936. The place is New York and my condition is distinctly non-holding. I am inhabiting a rendezvous of the discomfited known ironically as the Little Ritz, on West Forty-seventh Street, in New York, and in the period subsequent to Dr. Miller's misfortune I have known many ups and downs, but now I am for the nonce down. I have the price of a meal, though not in a restaurant such as the Voisin, the Colony or Shine's, and I am heading for the Automat. But before eating I decide to take a walk to increase my appetite, for I may not be able to raise the price of another repast that day. Chicken today, feathers tomorrow, and dear old Dr. Miller is far from my mind.

"It is snowing, and I cannot help regretting the climate of California, and perhaps conceding the foolhardiness of my renewed challenge to the metropolis. But as I pass the Union Church on West Forty-eighth Street I see a message of hope: the Rev. Orlando Edgar Miller is conducting a service there. I enter and there he is in the pulpit, as straight as ever. The ten years, including six with time off for good conduct, have touched him but lightly. I tried to make my advent unobtrusive, secreting myself in a side pew, but the dear old rascal made me immediately.

" 'I see among us a dear good friend, Mr. James Macdonald of California,' " he said. 'I am sure he has a Message for us. Will you come forward, Jim?' So I walked down the center aisle.

"Were you abashed?" I asked the Colonel. "Or were you prepared to speak after such a long spiritual layoff?"

"I have an invaluable precept for public speech," the Colonel said. "It is to think of five topics, one for each finger of the hand. On this occasion, I remember, I thought of the Christmas season, which it was, the miracle of the loaves and fishes, the Poor Little Match Girl, Oliver Twist, and Tiny Tim. I began by saying that as I gazed upon the countenance of my reverend friend, Dr. Miller, the Ark of the Covenant of the Lord had fallen upon me, and that I was moved beyond expression to find here, at this Christmas season, when so many were in want, a living reminder of the miracle of the loaves and fishes, whereby the Lord had provided for many although the supply of comestibles looked limited. My prospects for spiritual nourishment had looked bleak as I wandered down the cold street, I said, and then I saw the name of Orlando Edgar Miller and knew my hunger would be satisfied. These were the times when multitudes, like the Poor Little Match Girl, were expiring of hunger, spiritual hunger, and cold, not knowing that just around the corner was a man who might warm them and stoke them to Divine Grace. He was not angry when, like Oliver Twist in the story, they turned to him again and asked for More, evermore,—and like Tiny Tim——

" 'We shall have to let Tiny Tim go until some other time,' that dear old rascal Doctor said, 'for we have so many other beautiful features of our services to complete before six o'clock, when we must vacate the premises according to the terms of our lease. This church is not ours alone, though I would willingly remain far into the night to hear the conclusion of Brother Macdonald's beautiful train of thought.'

"I could tell from his dear old face that he had a hard time restraining hilarity, knowing full well the purport of my parablism. He motioned me to a seat on the front bench until the end of the service. The collection, I was glad to see, was of comfortable proportions, including many envelopes. When he came down from the platform I went up and shook hands with him and he gave me the address in the West Seventies where he was living and told me to go on ahead up there and he would come along as soon as he had finished his routine of benevolent adieux. 'I must clinch my sales for God,' he said.

"I went on along up to the address, which was an old brownstone house that he had taken over *in toto*. The Countess was not in evidence but three hatchet-faced old secretaries, well past the mid-century, were. It was a ménage most circumspect, and I could sense that the field of the old scalawag's deviations had narrowed with the infirmities of age. The Florabels regarded me with some suspicion, as of an outwardly unsanctified appearance, but when the old boy arrived, he led me directly into his study.[1] There, having locked the door, he went to an old-fashioned wall safe and drew out of it a black bottle of unclerical demeanor and we went to it and had a fine time.

"We rode upon the flying carpet of reminiscence: for example how we had prevailed upon one of the leading oyster growers of the Pacific coast, a Scandinavian gentleman, to endow a two-week revival featuring hymns with special lyrics composed in his honor, as: 'Thank you, Mr. Snorensen,' to the tune of 'Onward Christian Soldiers.' The lyrics were thrown upon a screen, as those of popular songs were in movie theatres of that era. I had first used this device to publicize a fight between Burns and an Australian heavyweight named Bill Squires, at Colma, California, in 1906. After the revival proper Mr. Snorensen treated all the executives of his company and their wives to an esatoric course with graduation ceremonies in white robes and white mortarboard hats and presented them all with fountain pens. We beat that squarehead for forty grand, and he had starved hundreds of oyster shuckers to death.

" 'Those were wonderful days, wonderful,' the dear old Doctor said. 'And by the way, Jim, we parted so hastily that I never did pay you the

[1] A Florabel, in the Colonel's idiom, is the antithesis of a Lissome, his highest term of aesthetic praise for a female. It had its origin in his reaction to the newspaper photograph of a woman so named.

last week's salary you had earned.' This was a bow to convention, simply the old man's way of offering aid without embarrassment to me, for he knew full well that I had held out an ample share of the Hawaiian contributions to the revival he had never held there. So he slipped me a hundred, which in those depression days was riches.

"When we had fortified ourselves enough to face those Gorgonic old spinsters we sallied forth and took them all out to a vegetarian restaurant where they stuffed themselves with nuttose and date pudding, and then the old Doctor put them in a taxi and said he and I would walk home together, since he had not completed his daily pedestrian exercise of fifteen miles. We went to Al Muller's bar north of Madison Square Garden and got stiff as boards, and finally the Ark of the Covenant of the Lord fell upon the old Doctor, and he spake.

" 'Jim, there is just one thing I have never been able to understand,' he said.

" 'Why did they leave you outside when they put me in?' "

12 / A Day with the Analysts

IN THE FALL of 1951, as the public prints have recorded, Congress passed a bill requiring bookmakers to buy a fifty-dollar tax stamp and then pay a mulct of ten per cent on their gross business, in addition to their ordinary income tax. Shortly thereafter, I received a mimeographed letter of valediction from a bookmaker who had me on his mailing list:

> It is my firm conviction that the bill recently passed is both discriminatory and unconstitutional. . . . What balloon-head figured this bill out?
>
> Sometime, sooner or later, an injunction will be granted. Until that time, I PREFER TO REMAIN INACTIVE!! I'll go on record as saying that no one, bookmaker or not, can be assessed 10% of his gross business and still pay an honest income tax!
>
> Most of you should be very happy that all this has come to pass. For the first time in years there will be money in your pockets around Christmas time. Think kindly of the old fellow in the Santa Claus suit as you pass by him on the corner. Reflect a minute, and if you have no change, toss him a bill or two.
>
> Because, judging from the look of things, that guy in the red suit will probably be me!

A lot of other bookmakers have followed the writer of the above letter into a retirement they hope will be only temporary. Among the people in whose pockets their defection didn't leave money is a friend of the Colonel's I met not long ago named Irwin Kaye, who uses as his registered trade-mark the title "World's Master Analyst." Mr. Kaye is not one of the Johnny-come-lately type of analysts who trace no farther back than Sigmund Freud. He is a turf analyst, or forecaster of equine probabilities, a member of a brotherhood that probably derived profit from the horse races in the Greek games of the seventh century B.C. and that was certainly well established in England when Charles J. Apperley, better known as Nimrod, produced his one-and-sixpence volume *The Turf* published in 1851. "What is it that guides the leading men in their betting?" Nimrod wrote, and answered himself, "Private information, purchased at a high price—*at a price which ordinary virtue cannot withstand.*" Mr. Kaye, while withholding the price he pays for what he represents as private information, tries to sell it at one within the reach of a large public. For forty years, the margin between what Mr. Kaye paid for his information and what he sold it for kept him in comfortable circumstances. Now that bookmakers have become scarce, however, his clients, unable to bet, have no use for his information. So they don't buy it. This leaves Mr. Kaye as badly off as he would have been all these years if there had been a law against telling a man the name of a horse that is likely to win a race. He therefore suspended publication of his medium, known as "the sheet," last winter. His only remaining service, for the time being, was providing very special information by telephone. "Winners I got plenty, but nobody to give them to," Mr. Kaye told me on the occasion of our first meeting. "I got a guy at Miami and one at New Orleans, and they ain't hardly making what to eat. They call up with good things, but nobody to play them. I pass them on to a fellow what used to make a good bet. What happens? He couldn't get the bet down. At least, he gives you that story."

The would-have-been bettor's failure to find a taker starts a cycle of destitution, because if he had made the bet and won it, he would have, in accordance with a common arrangement between client and analyst, paid Mr. Kaye the full profit from an accompanying wager—ten dollars, say, or twenty, depending on previous stipulation—made on behalf of Mr. Kaye. Mr. Kaye, in turn, would have remitted a percentage of his take from the appreciative customer to the guy at Miami or the one at New Orleans. The guy would then have bought white-on-white shirts, hand-painted neckties, and neutral grain spirits adulterated with whiskey, and the whole national economy would have profited, whereas it is a well-known fact that if you let a sucker keep his money, he sits on it.

All this is an illustration of the principle formulated by Colonel Stingo: "Disasters never run singly but always as an entry." The chain of disasters started by the law aimed at the bookmakers had, in fact, reached the

Colonel himself. The Colonel continued to write his column "Yea, Verily" in the New York *Enquirer*, a newspaper that appears every Sunday afternoon dated the following Monday. The *Enquirer* also carried a column by Louis Bromfield, who was beaten off by lengths every time he and the Colonel came out of the starting gate together. But the Colonel depended for life's amenities principally upon commissions paid him on the advertisements he attracted to the paper. (Bromfield presumably has other assets.) The advertisers were for the most part turf analysts like Mr. Kaye and, until recently, Mr. Kaye's brother, Long Shot Murphy, now retired from the analytical field. Murphy was a nom de course, like Kentucky Colonel or the Masked Jockey or Si and Smudgie, to name a few Kaye competitors. The Kentucky Colonel is a partner in a candy store and newspaper route in Brooklyn, where he grew up amid the blue grass of Prospect Park. Mr. Kaye himself thinks the use of his genuine patronymic sounds more responsible.

When the analysts can't sell their information because the bettors can't bet, the analysts can't afford to advertise. This left Colonel Stingo nonholding, but he continued to compose his weekly column while awaiting a dawn that he believed could not be farther off than the opening of the New York racing season in April. Then the analysts would have potential customers among the crowds going out to the track, where betting is legal. Quite probably they would advertise again, to reach these customers. In the meantime, Colonel Stingo sometimes visited his accounts on a strictly social basis, to maintain contacts. One time he suggested I go with him on a tour of the devastated areas, and that is how I happened to meet Mr. Kaye.

I waited upon Colonel Stingo in his chambers in the Hotel Dixie at noon on the day set for our tour and found him just dressed and fixing in his lapel a slightly ivoried white carnation, which, he explained, he had bought on starting his prowl the night before and which still seemed too good to throw away. "It is a hang-over," he said. "The carnation, I mean." The only phase of inflation I ever heard the Colonel deplore is the rise in the price of these flowers. "A good carnation now will stand you forty cents," he said. The Colonel is seventy-nine years old, by his own declaration, but he still has a light foot and, when he has not been riding the magic carpet too hard, a clear eye. He is not an early riser, and attributes the short lives of most people with good habits to the inner tensions these set up.

As an example of the fatal consequences of restraint he likes to cite George Smith, the famous race-track plunger once nationally famous as Pittsburgh Phil, who was a great judge of horses and riders and sometimes bet a hundred thousand dollars on a race, usually on one of his own horses. Smith never smoked, drank, took tea or coffee. He never permitted his face to express any emotion during the running of a race or when the hole cards were turned up,—he was a heavy gambler on cards and dice too. "So naturally," the Colonel says, "he dropped dead,—the natural consequence of repression of the self-indulgent faculties."

Like most people of pronounced seniority he reads the obituary pages with attention, and had a morning of quiet triumph last winter when two insurance shamans, a past president of the Actuarial Society of America and the vice-president of a major company, died on the same day, aged sixty-two and fifty-four respectively. "I bet they avoided excitement, late hours, high blood pressure, tasty food and intoxicating liquors and had themselves periodically examined with stethoscopes, fluoroscopes, spectroscopes and high-powered lenses," the Colonel said. "The result was inevitable and to be expected, the result of a morbid preoccupation. The anxious fielder drops the ball."

I twitted him with the vigorous old age attained by Mrs. Ella Boole, past president of the Woman's Christian Temperance Union, who recently passed on in her ninety-fourth year, but the Colonel had a ready explanation of her survival.

"She must have been a secret tippler," he said.

On this particular noon, Colonel Stingo was in good form, attributable, he informed me, to his not having met with a villain on his excursion of the previous night. A villain is anybody who induces him to switch from beer to hard liquor when he is out late. Beer seems to preserve my friend like a beetle in amber. It affects his figure no more than it does Miss Rheingold's. Colonel Stingo's nose runs straight down from his forehead without indentation at the bridge—a contour characteristic, he says, not without pride, that has marked many great men of action, like Napoleon, Terry McGovern (the irresistible featherweight), and Al Jennings (the famous train robber), the two last having been friends of his. The Colonel himself, however, does not believe in what he calls "the life strenuous."

The Colonel proposed that we begin our day with a call on Mr. Kaye, whose office is in the Newsweek Building, at the corner of Broadway and Forty-second Street, hardly a block from the Dixie. The address brought back the vanished past to the Colonel. "This building used to be the Hotel Knickerbocker," he said as we entered it. "The bar was so elegant they had a printed menu for the free lunch." The door of the Kaye office, on the fourteenth floor, bore the legend: "Irwin Kaye, Publisher and Analyst." I paused with my hand on the knob to ask the Colonel what Mr. Kaye published. "A daily racing sheet," he said. "Graded selections. He had it on sale at about four big newsstands in the center of town and sent it out by mail to subscribers. But he isn't getting it out now, on account of this unfortunate situation."

The walls of the large office were decorated with framed photographs of race horses from Colin to Stymie, looking down upon the multigraphing machines and filing cabinets indispensable to any small direct-mail business. We found Mr. Kaye alone, seated at his desk and working over the past performances in the *Morning Telegraph*. He is a thin man, with a thin face that slants forward from the top of his head to the point of his long chin, the nose forming most of the incline. When we entered, he jumped up to greet the Colonel. The analyst proved to be shorter even than Stingo, by a couple of inches. "Colonel!" he shouted, pumping the Colonel's right hand. "You look six to five to live to be a hundred!"

The *Enquirer*'s star columnist appeared flattered. "We just stopped by, Irwin, to ask your views of the situation," he said, after introducing me.

"It's dead," Mr. Kaye said. "I've got plenty of good things but nobody to play them. Sometimes old customers call up and ask *me* do I know a bookmaker. So what am I—a solicitor for bookmakers? Is it my business to look for bookmakers? Cops look for bookmakers. They don't find any, they pinch a ninnocent guy, what then? A salesman probily. They got to show a record, make a narrest."

Mr. Kaye's voice rose, indignant. "It's communism, that's what it is, communism!" he howled. "They think any guy in his right mind can give them ten per cent the gross? They going to drive the solid element out, the only fellow to take a bet will be a noutnout criminal, which if you win he won't pay you. Let that happen a couple times, the player is cured."

The voice dropped to the sweetly reasonable as Mr. Kaye continued: "Let them take two per cent and give a license to operate without ice fa the cops. Why not the guvvament get it, fa crying out loud, not some feller in a cellar on Twelf Aveny? If it was depriving a baby's milk, it's different. But every person is a sucker—you got to take it that way. So why should the sucker pay all the taxes, in *addition* to what he loses? The only way to save the sucker taxes is let the bookmaker pay taxes. But *let* him."

Mr. Kaye, emotionally exhausted, sat down, waving us with a limp left hand to chairs in front of his desk.

"There is much to what you say, Irwin, from the point of view of pure logic," the Colonel said. "But there is little hope, I fear, of legalized bookmaking forthwith. I see you performing a figuration on the *Telegraph*. Are you thinking of reviving your sheet?"

"What good?" Mr. Kaye asked. "I had two girls and my daughter getting out the sheets and mailing, but I let them all go. The sales didn't pay the girls' salary, and I told my daughter she might as well go home instead wasting her time around here. I'm figurating to kill time till what way the cat jumps."

"And what do you think of Senator Kefauver's announcement of his presidential candidacy?" the Colonel asked, like a little boy poking at an unexploded firecracker to make it go off.

"I'll lay forty to one against him if he runs!" Mr. Kaye shouted, coming up out of his chair. "He's got friends? Not here! He can't even speak English. Did you ever heard such a naccent? His wife is a nice woman." Mr. Kaye's voice grew heavily ironic. "She wants to be in the White House. You and I should have their worries, Colonel!" The Master

Analysts of the Democratic Party later concurred in Mr. Kaye's figuration of the senator, deciding not to start him.

The Colonel, perhaps sorry he had teased the Master Analyst, turned the talk down happier, reminiscent channels. "Irwin is one of the most talented figurators in the profession," he said to me. "I've known him since he was a boy."

Figuration, more commonly called handicapping, is the art of picking winners off the figures, or past performances, which may be interpreted in as divers ways as the entrails of the sacrificial sheep. A guy in New Orleans is not on the telephone with a good thing in every race, but the figures are always available. A consecrated figure man, in fact, scorns tips, even from a reliable source, as mere distractions beclouding his deductions with extraneous haze.

An analyst, Mr. Kaye kindly explained to me, does not disdain information, but he weighs it. He has to be a good figure man to start with. If the information concurs with his figures, or if his figures sustain the plausibility of the information, all, or almost all, is well. "I worked with the original Clocker Lawton, whose real name was George Garside, for five years—1910 to 1915—and the old man saw I had the makings of a second Steve L'Hommedieu," Mr. Kaye said. (Lawton was so famous a figurator that his name became a hereditary title. The present Clocker Lawton is his son.) "Who was Steve L'Hommedieu?" I asked, and the Colonel answered reprovingly, "The Prince of Handicappers." I could see that my ignorance had dropped my claiming price about fifteen hundred dollars in his estimation.

"I made hundreds long-price winners," Mr. Kaye said. "So I went into business for myself. I can go back as far as Baby Wolf, which he opened at two hundred to one, but when I made him he was played down to four to one. That's the kind reputation I had."

"What was the longest-priced winner you ever made?" I asked, adopting Mr. Kaye's idiom.

"A horse named Rock Candy, at Bowie," Mr. Kaye replied. "He paid $440.80 and I hardly took a buck. I gave him to my customers, but nobody played him. They thought I was crazy. A good thing is supposed to be two to one, three to one—not two hundred and twenty to one." He did not explain why the customers who had played Baby Wolf on his say-so had shied away from Rock Candy; perhaps in the interim he had had a string of losers.

Recalling past glories cheered Mr. Kaye up; I could see from his face that the thought of Senator Kefauver had receded. "Look at my scrapbook," he said to me, holding out a black-leather folder he had had within easy reach. "I am the only analyst that ever got sued for giving too many winners. The guy was a furniture salesman and spent all his money on broads, the wife sued *me* because she said if I hadn't given him the winners he wouldn't have had any money the broads would have let him alone he would of been home with her! So she sued me for alenation of her husband's affections, as if I would have been doing her favors to give him stiffs, she would of been the first one in to complain I was rooning her husband!"

This story, not easy to comprehend when delivered orally, was both clarified and substantiated by clippings in the scrapbook. On October 18, 1933, it seems, a woman in Brooklyn had sued Mr. Kaye for a hundred thousand dollars for alienating the affections of her husband, Louis, because Lou had won so much money that he spent it, and his time, with chorus girls.

"I told him go back to his wife," Mr. Kaye went on. "I said, 'Why give it to girls, they're only a passing fancy, why give it to strangers?' I told him. So he went back to his wife and she dropped the suit."

The scrapbook showed that at one time Mr. Kaye had exploited the incident in his advertising campaign. One of his ads read:

IRWIN KAYE
FAMOUS ANALYST
THE TALK OF THE COUNTRY.
Ask a Fellow Player
I AM BEING SUED BECAUSE YOU WIN!
Read it Yourself

Another ad I liked ran:

PROF. KAYE
World Famous Analyst
SAYS:
NOW LISTEN, PLAYERS—BE WISE!
If owners and trainers make mistakes,
and they make plenty
What chance have you got?

Do you still think you can dope out horses? No! Follow the crowd, I will work for you also. You also will save many a foolish wager, also thousands of dollars. Subscribe now and you will be surprised.

All the ads included the names and prices of recent Kaye winners.

It appeared from the clippings that only after passing through the grades of Famous Analyst and World Famous Analyst had Mr. Kaye awarded himself the degree of World's Master Analyst, which he registered as his trade-mark in 1947.

I inquired of Mr. Kaye how an analyst differed from a figurator or a tipster. His answer reminded me of a passage in old Nimrod, who wrote that successful plunging must be based on "great knowledge of horseflesh and astute observation of public, running, deep calculation, or secret fraud."

"A tipster is a fellow what might know something or he might be guessing," Mr. Kaye said. "A figurator is a figure man. But some owners never try—and *that's* what I gotta analyze."

I asked him for his definition of the word "tout," but this proved injudicious. I gathered from his reaction that a turf analyst takes the same view of a tout that J.P. Morgan & Co. takes of a bucket shop. "In the first place, there ain't no such thing!" he said. "What do you mean, a tout?"

"The difference, I should suggest," Colonel Stingo said, "is that the legitimate turf consultant, adviser, counselor, analyst, or even tipster, acts in good faith. The tout is cynical."

After a few more commiserations, the Colonel and I took our leave. As we started for the door, Mr. Kaye settled down again to his calculations with the *Morning Telegraph*. "The funny part is I *like* to figurate," he said by way of farewell. "Maybe if business stays bad I'll become a horse player myself. Then I'll have to go look for a bookmaker."

Out on the street, the Colonel proposed that we walk downtown to call on a profound figurator named James Trombetta, who has an office on Seventh Avenue near the Pennsylvania Station. We might break our journey by taking lunch on the way, he said.

"The quality they all have in common is that they are impressed with their own science," Colonel Stingo declared as we set forth. "They overween themselves. They are Dr. Fausti." The Colonel, as I knew from previous conversations, hasn't bet on a horse since the administration of Benjamin Harrison, and thinks anybody who does is crazy. He prefers a flutter at faro or *chemin de fer*, games in which there are no jockeys.

"The occupational disease of figurators is betting on their own selections," the Colonel went on. "They all swear they don't, like the bartenders who say they never take a drink. But sooner or later, like the bartenders, they fall off the wagon, and the consequence is disaster. The slip may follow a string of good selections. They have given their customers two or three successive good-priced winners, and they begin to think brokerage is too slow a way of making money. ["Brokerage" is the trade term for the profit on the bet that the customer makes for his adviser.] Having been paid off by their grateful clients, they have a wad on hand. The percentage of pay-offs, I may add, is high, due less to the bettor's sense of honor, of which he boasts, than to the controlling passion—avarice. Simply stated, when a fellow has been let in on a winner at nine dollars or better, he wants to be let in on the next one. When he has been let in on two in succession, an anaconda wound around the mailbox would not prevent him slipping his check into it, correctly addressed to the tipster. Now the figurator thinks he really must have something on the ball. I have seen men of the cloth similarly affected when their prayers were answered, or so they imagined. So the figurator ventures his wad on what he considers an even more ingenious figuration than the last one—and the horse finishes down the course. His customers, who lose their money too, desert him, and next thing you know he is scratching around for his office rent, or trying to sell his list of boobs who will make a good bet if properly approached. The same recklessness may overtake a figurator when he has nothing to do but sit and brood." The Colonel sighed, and I suspected that he was worried about Mr. Kaye. "In ordinary times," he said, "a turf analyst, consultant, or adviser has no more readily convertible asset than his list. Now, however, no one would wish to buy a list of bettors who couldn't find bookmakers if you called them up."

As we approached Smith's chophouse, on West Thirty-sixth Street, where we had decided to eat, the Colonel discoursed further on the economics of the information business. "In times like these, the more names you have, the more money you waste on telephone calls, and if you make them collect, the clients refuse to accept them. I predict that the telephone company will find an unparalleled number of slugs in its coin boxes as a consequence of the situation. I once journeyed downtown to the company's executive offices to intercede as an intermediary for a handicapper who had been caught in a telephone booth by a company inspector. He had slugged the booth for $750, calling boobs as far away as Hawaii. To cap his misfortune, the horse lost, leaving him without any Tease he might make good with. Some friends, including myself, raised a total of $67.50, and I persuaded an executive of the company to accept it. It was a lucky thing, for I learned afterward that the fellow was under indictment for a mistake he had made in California. I wrote a paragraph about it in my column, and the result was a run on slugs in the one novelty store on Broadway that had the concession. It was impossible to buy a quarter-size slug for nearly a week—a striking demonstration of the power of the press."

The Colonel said that substantial analysts like Mr. Kaye and Mr. Trombetta, who have maintained offices, as well as accounts with the telephone company, for years, are not in the telephone-booth category. "But there is a disingenuous element in the business that does not advertise," he continued. "There have been occasions in the distant past when, in the fell clutch of circumstance, I have figurated a horse myself and sent him out as a special tip, gleaned from the slip of a drunken trainer's tongue. A horse like that in New Orleans once bought a gold mine for me. It came in at twenty-five to one and enough boobs paid off to net me fifteen hundred dollars. The gold mine was in Rawhide, Nevada, and a friend of mine who happened to be at the same meeting let me have it for an even thousand. But I never had an opportunity to develop it."

We strode on for a while in silence, and then the Colonel said, "My old friend George Graham Rice, the wizard of finance, used to say to me, 'All a man needs is one good gold mine west of the Missouri.' I'm still looking for it."

By the time we were at table and a waiter had brought us drinks, Colonel Stingo had apparently banished the memory of his mine. "In my youth, the great tipster—to employ a term not in favor with Irwin—was a man called Jack Sheehan. In time he sold his name and practice to a disciple whose square name was Boasberg," he said. "The original Jack Sheehan worked the Chicago tracks in summer and New Orleans in winter, and he always wore a plug hat and a wing collar and a cutaway coat, as though he owned a large stable. He stopped at the best hotels and he advertised freely—any paper would take tipster ads in those days. But he was ruled off making book against his own tips. Every once in a while, he would advise his clients to send him the money so he could get it down at the best price. They had bookmakers in those days, of course. Then he would pocket the money, having picked a horse that he figured to finish last. One of them ran in on him one day at sixty to one.

"Mark Boasberg, the second Jack Sheehan, as I have heard, migrated to New Orleans, where he became a mighty gambling man. But throughout his career he retained the Sheehan *nom de guerre*. When I last heard of him he was running easy, just off the pace, raising garden peas and broiling chickens in idyllic retirement by the banks of the Mississippi. Between you and me, I don't know how he stands it, having barely entered his ninth decade. He may be meditating a comeback.

"On the New York tracks around 1900, when I began to frequent them, the most prominent tipster was an old gentleman named Mr. Merry, who sported a long white beard in addition to formal attire. 'Get happy! Get happy!' he would cry. 'I have a winner today!' When they opened Belmont Park, they ruled that dear old man off, because they considered him undignified. I went to the Jockey Club myself and succeeded in having him reinstated. By that time, I was secretary of the New York Turf Writers' Association.

"Then, there was John W. Diestel, a very sterling figurator whose slogan was, 'I never advertise a winner I did not give.' And so many dear fellows who dabbled in the information business—the Singing Kid, the Swing-Door Kid, the Coon-Can Kid and the Banjo-Eyed Kid . . ." Moisture gleamed to windward and leeward of the Colonel's nose, and he had recourse to his bourbon-and-seltzer to steady his voice. He is very sentimental about old times. But after he had ingested a grandiose serving of lamb stew he became elucidative again.

"There is only one kind of horse player more incorrigible than a dyed-in-the-wool figurator and that is a system-player," he said. "The figurator is bewitched by his own intelligence, an empiricist. Each race is a problem that he is sure he can solve. But the system-player believes there must be some one underlying principle that will solve all races. He seeks the philosopher's stone. No salvation outside the church. There is a firm in Boston that stocks about a thousand systems, and you can buy them at from one to three dollars apiece, with fifty per cent off if you take ten or more. You can have your choice of the Getting Rich with the One-Bet-a-Day System, the Twelve Goldmine Longshot Angles, the French Marvel System, the Super Duper System, the Old Reliable System, the Logical Winning Horse Method, the Never-Die-Broke System, the Old Professor Longshot System, the Famous Movie Director's Million Dollar Racing Idea, the Mysterious Angle System, the Triple Dutch Winner, the Golden Win Producer, or the Supreme Advantage Method, to name but a few. The real system-player will go from one to another, like a fellow that used to be a communist and has to join something else to feel comfortable."

"Who invents systems?" I asked.

"System-players," the Colonel answered promptly. "The last stage of being a system-player is the invention of a system. I never knew a system-player who started out to discover a system and didn't come up with one. 'Eureka!' he cries. 'Play any horse that finished fourth in one of its last three races if he ran at a claiming price of at least a thousand dollars more than he is entered for today.' And catastrophe engulfs him."

"It is the old human need for certainty," I said. "You shouldn't be too hard on it."

"It isn't sportsmanlike," the Colonel said. "A system-player has the same mentality as the sucker who expects to be let in on a fixed race."

When we had had our coffee, we headed for Mr. Trombetta's. We found him hard at work behind his desk, in a fifth-floor office less ornate than Mr. Kaye's. "Jim Trombetta is an optimist," the Colonel had said on the way over. "He continues to advertise, although on a reduced scale." I knew this, having read in the *Enquirer* on the previous Sunday:

3 HOT HORSES A DAY
Genuine Last Minute Information
NOT FAVORITES—
FREE WITH TROMBETTA RATINGS
You'll Do Better With Trombetta
DAY'S PREFERENCE, DAY'S LONGSHOT
AT EACH OFFICE
Daily $1
Regular Mail
One Week $5
Five Weeks $20

This was followed by the customary list of recent winners picked by the figurator. Restraint was the keynote of Mr. Trombetta's copy. His advertised winners were all horses paying between $8 and $15.80—a nice, conservative return of from 300 to 690 per cent on your money.

The practitioner's appearance was consonant with his advertising—rich but conservative. A round-faced man in a dark double-breasted suit, he controlled with the right-hand corner of his mouth a long cigar. A black chesterfield on a hanger behind him and a derby on the hook over it indicated the dignity of his appearance when dressed for the street. He had evidently acquired his sense of style in the time of the late Jimmy Walker, which middle-aged New Yorkers recall with the same nostalgia Colonel Stingo reserves for the Edwardian era.

Admiration for Walker is his only point of agreement with Mr. Kaye, his bitter rival in figuration. "Walker was a crook," Mr. Kaye says, "but his motto was: 'Letchez all live!' Now we got crooks who want it all for themselves."

Mr. Trombetta was still getting out his ratings because, he informed us, he wanted to hold his organization together. It is a one-man organization. But business had fallen off drastically, he said. In a normal, pre-Kefauver winter, he used to send out about a hundred and fifty copies of his ratings every day, and things always got better in summer. Now he had only about thirty subscribers, producing a daily income that barely met the nut. "But I've been in this game for thirty years, and I'll stay until we see what happens," he said. "It ought to pick up during the New York season, anyway."

Spread out before Mr. Trombetta were the entries for the next day's races, together with each horse's biography, in the shape of a collection of race charts cut from *Daily Racing Form*, a tabloid that suspended publication in January, and from the *Morning Telegraph*. I asked Mr. Trombetta whether he missed the *Daily Racing Form*, and he said that its passing had increased his woes by one, because the *Telegraph* is a standard-sized paper, and the charts it publishes take up more room than the *Racing Form*'s did. The owner of the *Racing Form* was Triangle Publications, which also owns the *Telegraph*. One Broadway theory has it that the decline in betting and the consequently decreased demand for papers to pick horses from was what made Triangle decide to drop the *Form*. Another school of thought, more subtle, holds that Triangle was only waiting for an excuse, since the papers covered the same field and the survivor was sure to inherit the other's readers. The price of the *Telegraph*, these cynics point out, has risen from a quarter to thirty-five cents.

"The fomenters of this unfortunate legislation have made trouble for everybody, even legitimate newspapermen," the Colonel said. "I must say, however, that Frank Munsey did not await the appearance of a Senator Kefauver to scuttle the *Globe*, the *Mail*, the *Herald*, and the rest, nor the Pulitzers the *World*, nor the Dewarts the *Sun*. The march is ever toward monopoly."

Mr. Trombetta said things might wind up with everybody's having to move to California, where there is racing all year round. "Either that or build an indoor track in New York—a straightaway under glass, about five miles long," he said. "You could use the Third Avenue Elevated, which is broke. You could have mutuel-ticket sellers in the ticket booths on all the stations and sell clubhouse badges to get into them. They wouldn't be any more crowded than Jamaica on a Saturday."

"Are you getting many winners, Jim?" Colonel Stingo asked, and Mr. Trombetta said he was doing pretty well. "But I have long slumps, when if you played every one of my selections you would drop far behind," he conceded. "The trouble with daily ratings is that you have to name a horse in every race. If you wanted to hit a big percentage, you would play only six-furlong claiming races for horses over three years old. The claiming price brings them together. Two-year-old races and handicaps are too hard, and there are so few horses that can really go a distance that all long races are a gamble. And since the daily double started, racing secretaries try to make the first two races tough to pick, so there will be more double combinations. They card eight races, and the two that fill best are the ones they stick up top.

"Jack Campbell [the Jockey Club handicapper, who, incidentally, isn't a figurator but a racing official charged with imposing weights on handicap horses] once told me an important secret for beating the races," Mr. Trombetta continued. " 'Always take the last train from Penn Station,' he said. 'Then you'll miss the first race. And when you get to the track, don't hurry. Go into Harry Stevens' restaurant and have a bowl of clam chowder. Then, if you're lucky, you'll miss the second race.' But you can't tell the average player that. He wants to go out there and play eighteen dollars on the daily double, three horses and three horses, and then, if he is a small bettor, he has to play long shots to break even on the day. There aren't enough good long shots in the world."

A guilty grin turned up the corner of Mr. Trombetta's mouth that was not held down by the cigar. "Still," he said, "if you take the horses that figure fourth, fifth, and sixth in the first race and tie them up with the ones that figure the same way in the second, you can get a pretty good double sometimes."

Mr. Trombetta told me that as a figure man he followed the principles of the late John W. Diestel (here the Colonel glanced at me knowingly) —he "graphed" the horses. According to the Diestel method, the position in which a horse finishes is less important (for future reference, that is) than the rate of speed at which it runs the last portion of the race compared with the speed at which it runs the first part. "It is a tough concept to handle unless you've had a lot of experience," Mr. Trombetta said. "The idea is that a horse may have won all by himself and still have run a bad race if the others quit even faster. Horses like that become false favorites."

I was hoping to learn more, but we were interrupted by the advent of a female of most respectable appearance, whose accelerated breathing indicated a state of high tension. She wore a Persian lamb coat, which, hanging open, revealed a tailored suit, and her face, featuring a long, square-ended chin and tortoise-shell glasses, expressed the antithesis of frivolity. I thought Mr. Trombetta looked a trifle apprehensive, for the lady presented the outward aspect of a bettor's wife, and while all analysts advise their clients to play within their means, you never can tell what a boob will do.

"Mr. Pearlstein sent me," the caller said, allaying the figurator's anxiety. "Do you know Mr. Pearlstein?" Mr. Trombetta said he knew several, but he and the lady could not get together on which Mr. Pearlstein they both knew. "It doesn't matter," she said, after they had gone into the matter at some length. "This Mr. Pearlstein thought you might help me. I've been losing money."

This was one client, apparently, who still knew a bookmaker.

Mr. Trombetta, with the manner of an eminent consultant, leaned back in his chair and took the cigar out of his mouth.

"Why don't you cut down on your betting?" he suggested.

"Who can do that?" the woman asked.

"Play only one race a day, or if you go to the track, play only two or three."

"You call that action?" the woman said. "I'm too restless."

"In that case, you have a problem," said Mr. Trombetta. "I can't promise any miracles."

The woman looked disappointed and at the same time baffled. I fancied that she had come prepared to resist a sales talk.

"A flat play on all my selections over a stretch of years would show a profit," said Mr. Trombetta. "But you might run into a stretch of months when I had a lot of losers."

The woman looked resentful now, as if beginning to suspect that Mr. Trombetta didn't want to let her in on his secret. "How much is your service?" she asked. I was quite sure she knew.

"Five dollars a week, by regular mail," said Mr. Trombetta. "Where do you live?"

She gave the street number of a mammoth, mausolean apartment house in the West Seventies that I happened to be familiar with. (She probably placed her bets through the elevator boys.) "But I'm going to Hialeah next week," she added, sounding glad to have thought of a reason not to buy. "I wouldn't get your figures in time."

"We can send them by wire," Mr. Trombetta said, "but it's more expensive."

"I'll consider it," the visitor said, and departed.

"They're all a headache," Mr. Trombetta said when she had gone. "If you gave them six winners a day, they would kick because they heard from a woman friend she had a man who gave her seven."

"Nevertheless," said Colonel Stingo, "is it not a shame that a woman like that—a widow, no doubt, ill-equipped to draw the attention of the opposite sex, her children perhaps grown and married and having no time for her—should be harassed in the pursuit of her one remaining distraction? Should some detective knock off her present bookmaker, she would be in the same position as a diabetic deprived of insulin."

"She reminds me of a woman I knew, a friend of mine's mother," Mr. Trombetta said. "A wealthy widow eighty years old who spent her last years playing the horses. Fine days always found her in her box at Jamaica. When the weather was bad, she played by phone, through her bookmaker. Last fall, when her bookmaker went out of business, she had to go to the track every day. One raw afternoon, she caught a tough cold. It began a parlay of infections, and in six months she was dead."

"Kefauver killed her," the Colonel said sternly. "He should be indicted."

Just then the woman from uptown returned, still shorter of breath. She held a crumpled dollar bill, which she placed on Mr. Trombetta's desk. "Give me your sheet for today," she said. "I'll see how good you are."

The transaction was executed, and again the woman departed. "You can't cure them," Mr. Trombetta said.

The Colonel and I prepared to leave. "Well, Jim," the Colonel said. "In the words of the English poet Hutchinson: 'If winter comes, spring must be moving up to a position of contention.' And I project that when that bugle at Jamaica doth windily blow, the rush toward the mutuel windows will be like the Charge of the Light Brigade."

13 / Balmy Clime

AS WE WALKED up Seventh Avenue after leaving Mr. Trombetta, the wind howled in our faces at a rate which, if it was blowing straight up the Widener chute, would stop a field of two-year-olds dead in their tracks.

When we stopped in the bar of Shine's restaurant to take shelter, the Colonel said, "Truly it is remarkable. Saul and the Witch of Endor. The faith of man in soothsayers is unquenchable. And his capacity for self-deception is infinite.

"Joe," he said, "I assure you that the Chatelaine, if she studied the matter for two or three weeks, could take a race card and a hatpin and pick winners as well as any tipster in the business. It is a snare and a delusion."

"The Chatelaine" is his name for my wife, who is tall and lissome, although not loaded down with Tease. The Colonel constantly avers a deep though paternal affection for her. She was born in Kentucky, a fact she is not averse from acknowledging, and when we find ourselves in disagreement in the Colonel's presence, he becomes a courtly mediator. "The Chatelaine is not really angry," he will say. "It is just that old Daniel Boone spirit."

The Colonel is not loquacious about his own domestic past, perhaps because he considers it unworthy of a Long Rider. He was married in 1903, to a Brooklyn girl, and he took her with him to California in his flight from the Hughes antibetting law. For nearly twenty years they had a house near Golden Gate Park in San Francisco, and the Colonel says there were two children who attained exemplary maturity, a son and a daughter. Like Pierce Egan, that embattled Regency journalist of London sporting life, the Colonel kept his family and professional lives on separate shelves. He recounts no domestic episodia.

When we had medicated ourselves against the hyperborean blasts—for the rule of the Great Transition allows exceptions for therapeutic purposes—he said, "Joe, if I were holding, I would be at this moment in Florida, the land of lime pie and short-priced favorites. But the spirit of adventure deteriorates, and I will not venture forth unheeled, as I did in prewar days."

"Pre what war?" I inquired undiplomatically.

"Pre World War II," he said. "Release from responsibility brings to the Long Rider a second blooming, and I may say that I never felt younger in my life than in what must have been about 1935, when I checked in at a small but pleasant hotel at Miami with just seven dollars in my right breech. I discovered from perusal of the local press that a political contest of sorts was in progress, and by attaching myself to the headquarters of one of the aspirants I quickly assured my sustainance while I enjoyed myself. I ghost-wrote radio campaign talks for this Huey Long in little, and he attained a summit of eloquence which much puzzled those intimately acquainted with his illiteracy. The climate was delightful.

"I adapted myself so well to my environment that I became at one point manager of the hotel," he said, "as well as senior resident. My tenure was transitionary but notable. Managements succeeded one another in that hotel with the rapidity of Roman emperors immediately after Nero. It was in a perpetual furor of reorganization, like the French government.

"From the beginning I learned to love the life there. Upon awaking in the morning I would lie abed in my room on the second floor, and through the wide-open window would come the song of the mocking bird and the voices of Flo and Jack, a couple on the fourth floor, by inclination disputatious. The colloquy, to say the least, was startling.

"This Flo was a Miss America emerita, but of not too old a vintage, tall and still lissome and a natural blonde. Her boy friend made book on the dog races at night, and that, naturally, left them the afternoons free to play the horses, a frequent cause of their recriminations.

"Her voice would assume a plaintive, irritating timbre, and his would become denunciatory, even menacing. But just as I would begin to apprehend the sounds of open violence, a member of the hotel personnel would shove the *Daily Racing Form* under their chamber door, and the exchange of strictures would lose audibility while they read it in bed.

They got only one copy, and naturally that would bring them together, and they would become reconciliated.

"By the time they reached the lobby, ready to drive out to the track, her demeanor would be imperturbable and her attire modish, and no one could imagine her vocabularial arsenal, or the asperity of which she was capable. Similarly her consort was the personification of affability, punctiliously allowing her to precede him and never permitting her to light her own cigarette.

"She had quite a wardrobe, including the tastefully renovated vestiges of the raiment bestowed upon her when she was a beauty-contest winner, and presented what Mayfair would term a smashing exterior. Sometimes of a morning I would hear Jack complain that she had so many suitcases and hatboxes in their room that he had no place except the bed for sedentation.

"We all became well acquainted, like travelers Chaucerian at some wayside inn, and in the evenings, while Jack was at the dogs, Flo and I would sometimes sit together playing gin or cribbage. Dogs had slight attraction for her; she said the greyhounds had faces that reminded her of a snoopy little old schoolteacher she disliked in her native Alabama. Her distrust was justified. Jack became afflicted by a couple of bettors who always seemed to know which dog would win. They took him good, and from the matutinal dialogues I learned that my friends' circumstances were stringent. This naturally placed a further strain upon their relations. Adversity sometimes brings people closer together, but not when they are of different sexes."

The Colonel and I had somehow found our way to a small table midway between the telephone and the head of the stairs that led to the men's room, and the medication was having a restorative effect, so we repeated the dosage, the Colonel this time enjoining the waiter to tell the bartender to leave off all the fruit except lemon and to omit sugar.

"While their star was declining," the Colonel said, "mine was in the ascendant. The hotel had fallen into the hands of a couple of young fellows from New York who had managed to extract a profit from it, but they became enamored of change. One got married and bought himself a couple of two-year-olds. They were not good enough to win at Hialeah so he acquired a horse-trailer which he hitched to his white De Soto convertible and headed for Oaklawn Park, Hot Springs, Arkansas, with his bride. His partner had a girl too, but he omitted to marry her, possibly because the union would have been of a bigamous nature. They too began a journey, but to New York. In departing, the two hoteliers appointed me locum tenens, or manager in their absentia.

"I had had time to study the problems of the Florida hotel business, which I had found largely psychological. Tenants who missed out on one week's room rent would become diffident about approaching the cashier with a payment next week lest they be demanded to shell out the bustle beyond their capacity to pay. With each successive rent day their recalcitrance would increase, and the hotel manager merged with the jungle tracker, ever pursuing and never catching up.

"On the day I assumed office I placed an imposing carnation in my buttonhole. I put on an expression of stern grandeur and assumed an early station behind the desk, from which I could see the various delinquents descend the stairs. I called them all over one by one and accosted the moratorium. 'Beginning today we tear everything off and start afresh,' I said, 'but from now on you will have to get it up.' The new policy was universally acclaimed; I felt I had been destined for the hotel business and had mistaken my vocation.

"In midafternoon I walked across the street to the House of Usher, a bar proprieted by a couple of ushers from Madison Square Garden who in the course of long service had hustled the price of a saloon. We started celebrating my accession to power, and all would have been well save for an accident unforeseeable. Mine host who had started north with his girl had incurred a certain amount of enmity in Miami. Some troublemaker had put the finger on him and he had been halted just after crossing the border between Florida and Georgia and arrested for intent to violate the Mann Act. After a night in a disagreeable jail he and his girl, bail furnished, had returned to Miami in a state of disgruntlement, and he had entered his own hotel demanding to be assigned to a room. The bellboy had signified to him my whereabouts, and members of the lobby gab circle had apprised him that I had torn up the tabs.

"With none of these preliminaries was I, of course, acquainted, when, hearing my name thunderously invoked, I looked up from a table in the House of Usher to see this man glaring from the doorway. On his face he wore a demoniacal expression. I had barely time to brush a buxom stranger from my knee when he was upon me. 'You are fired!' he detonated, like Professor Hatfield's Gatling gun. So I reverted to my status as a guest.

"Meanwhile," the Colonel said, "Jack has gotten what seems to be a break. The big booking syndicate which has the monopoly in the leading Miami Beach hotels is continually in search of new business. A representative, unaware that Jack is in dire straits, asks him why he doesn't give the syndicate book a bet. Jack is unable to believe his ears. He bets five hundred on a horse at eleven to five. It comes in, and he and Flo are in love and business again. He has his check next day and bets five hundred on another horse. This too wins, at eight to five, and all is well. Then he has three losers, and pays each time. He bets again, loses, and omits to pay off, hoping he can recoup at the dogs.

"A couple nights later I am sitting in the lobby with Flo, playing klabiash, when there irrupt two credit men for the syndicate. I can feel the vibration. They ask Jack's whereabouts, and Flo says he will not return until late. 'All right,' say the credit men, 'we will be around to see him in the morning. It is nothing of consequence, just a small tab he has neglected to discharge.' When Jack walked in half an hour later Flo told him what had happened and he kept right on walking, up to the room to pocket his shaving kit and then out into the night until he cools off.

"It leaves Flo in a position of difficulty, but she is resourceful, and I am there, an experienced Galahad. I get her a job with this political organization, running the women's committee for Yulch, my candidate for Governor, and this takes care of her feed bill amply. Her one insoluble problem is the arrearage in room rent. Jack has enjoyed the confidence of the management. An old guest of several seasons' standing he has frequently run long tabs and squared them. But now he has vanished into the empyrean, the boys demand payment instantly,—or it will be the plug in the door, and confiscation of Flo's extensive wardrobe. They have repudiated my moratorium, accusing me of conspiracy with my fellow beneficiaries.

"I will revert to the transitional, lest I lose the thread of my narration," Colonel Stingo said, calling for a bottle of Black Wolf Ale. The waiter asked if he meant Black Horse, and the Colonel, with grave mien, said, "Black Wolf is much superior. It is brewed in the Yellowknife country, two hundred miles within the Arctic Circle, the home of the world's richest unexploited gold deposits. I have frequently seen a bottle sold for one ounce of gold dust. But Black Horse will be all right.

"I got up one week's room rent in advance for Flo," he said, "gaining for her a brief respite from the hoteliers' fury. I urged on them consideration of the possibility Jack would raise some scratch in the interim and communicate with her, in which case she could discharge all. But the rent itself, fifty dollars a week, as I remember, was excessive for her current increment, particularly as the season was now virtually at a close, and you could get a room and bath for a dollar a day at many nearly empty hotels in other parts of town. I engaged one for Flo at a distance of several miles.

"We devised a pardonable stratagem," the Colonel said. "My room and hers fronted on a lot where hotel guests parked their cars. Rosebushes and other floral ornamenta were trained against the side of the hotel. Flo would pack a suitcase or hatbox with her finery, choosing consignments in order of cherishedness, and bring them down from her room to mine, without the necessity of passing laden through the lobby, which would have entailed interception. Then she would continue on down and walk around back of the hotel to the parking lot. I would drop the luggage into the bushes and she would retrieve it and convey it to her car, a battered but rakish vehicle.

"She would drive to her new lodgment and leave the stuff, then return. We got out all her feminine frippery in this manner, but there remained two problems,—her wardrobe trunk and her parrot. The ponderous trunk, of mighty dimensions, was insoluble. She could not carry it down the stairs in the first place, and in the second, if I had dropped it from the window the impact would have caused a detonation like that of a clap of thunder, the harbinger of a new hurricane. She therefore reconciled herself to its loss.

"But the parrot, Pat, was her companion of longest tenure, antedating Jack and a number of other human predecessors. His hawking and rawking in the mornings, similar to those of a middle-aged man with catarrh, had roiled and moiled me on occasion, conflicting as they did with the songs of the mocking birds. But when I had remonstrated with Flo she had said they were a perfect reproduction of Mr. Westmacott, a banker with whom she had been associated subsequent to her elevation to beauty queen. 'Pat is in a sense my diary,' she said, 'and besides, Cunnel, honey, those are not little old mocking birds you hear in the morning. Mocking birds sing at night. What you hear is just little old Pat imitating mocking birds.'

"I had been well aware of the nocturnal habits of the generality of mocking birds," the Colonel said, "but I had assumed this was a special strain imported from Las Vegas, Nevada, which is a twenty-four-hour town.

"At any rate she could not induce herself to relinquish Pat to his fate, possible reappearance on two blue plates as halves of a broiled spring chicken. So it was decided she would tie a pillowcase around the cage, with Pat inside, and I would drop it as gently as possible into the roses, where she would be as usual standing by."

The waiter had by this time delivered the Black Horse, and the Colonel sent him back for a garniture of bourbon. "It is a moment that I cannot recount without extraordinary stimulus," he said. "I find myself overcome by retroactive emotion."

When reinforcements had arrived and he had incorporated them he said:

"As I received the parcel from her hands I could hear poor Pat muttering imprecations, but I disregarded them, reminiscent as they were of many of the departed Jack's matutinal remarks. When Flo had had time to reach her appointed post I looked out to see if the coast was clear. Sure enough all was propitious. She was alone in the lot, and I leaned as far out the window as I could, dangled the muffled cage at arm's length and let go. It plummeted down, landed in the rosebush, a perfect hit, right on the target. But the pillowcase was torn off, and I must assume that a number of brambles had penetrated between the bars, also the cage came to rest upside down.

"Flo rushed, motherlike, to the retrieval, scratching her sun-lacquered arms as she dived into the shrubbery to rescue darling Pat. When she had placed the cage right side up, the bird of retentive memory spoke, in a voice of thunder:

" 'You sonofabitch, you do this to me?' "

We paid our check, and passed out into the night.

14/"In Deathless Resolve"

IT WAS in the summer of 1943, while in New York between a trip to North Africa and one to England, that I became aware of Colonel Stingo as a major literary enigma. The Colonel had been writing his weekly column "Yea Verily" in the weekly New York *Enquirer* for nearly ten years prior to that, but I suppose I had never before read him with attention on a day when he had all his stuff.

Curiosity about a writer, for me, depends upon some peculiar combination of personality and subject matter—Stendhal on Love, for example, or Philadelphia Jack O'Brien on "Instructions for Men Handling Big Boy on Night of September 23, 1926." The piece which first impressed me with the Colonel's quality, as I recall, was one in which he played Plutarch to a man who had built a race track in Camden, New Jersey. "Loined in nonchalant Palm Beach kalsomine white duck and tabbing his program with stubby lead pencil, he is watching handy field of sprinters trot postward in Fleetwing Handicap, 3 Y.O. & U. 6 furlongs, here this afternoon," the portrait began. "He is 53% owner of newest and best-paying Gold Mine in this America of our'n. And, his name is Eugene Tomaso Mori. Throw-off kid from Mori family that run quaint old Café Mori, Bleecker & West Broadway, New York, for years.

"This fabulous Gold Mine of aforesaid Mr. Mori is the Garden State Racing Association plant, Camden, N. J. May not be yielding quite the gross bullion of Porcupine's far-famed Hollinger, nor, the Empire shaft, Grass Valley, California, but Garden State has the rich veins and soft yellow stringers indicative of tremendous Bonanza output in years to come. Yes, Mr. Mori struck it rich when he made his strike on New Jersey's unbelievably treasure trove Mother Lode ledges only three years ago. . . . And this, despite most exasperating heartbreaks and setbacks in Construction Operation & Transportation in all Race Track history. . . .

"First, that powerful and bitterly narrow Reform Element which had defamed Jersey State since Dr. Lyman Samuel Beecher's bigoted day, brought Heaven and Earth to bear to squelch Mori's enterprises. Tax schedules were enacted and thrown like a Rick in middle of road. Then the wartime necessity killed off Motor Transportation. . . . Yet, today, this Camden racetrack is pretty snug and nice-away as any you wish to see. And all this time Mori just keeps on smiling while weeding out heavy Tease and plentee.

"I'm out here to Camden's miracle Raceway last week. And what spectacle? Round about 85% attendance comes from Philadelphia. After youse leave Philadelphia's subway terminal to Camden, then youse heel and toe 2¼ miles to trackside. Or, perhaps, for a Buck hard, you can claw onto one of the weird Horse drawn vehicles that transport the hungriest Army of Straggling Fortune Hunters over on the March since 'Lucky' Baldwin's Party went over Chilkoot Pass into Klondike in 1898. Like the cavalcade in 'Jim' Cruise's pic,—*Covered Wagon*, leaving Platte River in 1849, the Quaker City saffari of dyed in wool Horseplayers sinuously winds down road far as eye could see. All ee samee Oklahoma's 'land rush' on Cimmaron in Indian Territory days.

"Moiling and Sweating in Jersey's terrible midsummer's parching sun, here they come, day after day. Women in run over heels, men in bare feet, carrying their boots, sometimes. I've seen 75-year-old wooden wheeled Bonecrackers in locomotion. Also, regular oldtime Hay Wagons, daily Victorias, creaking Democrats, swaying Buckboards, and a collection of busses which must have seen service for Wells Fargo Express in 'Kit' Carson's heyday. But on they come in deathless resolve of a score today. Perfectly oblivious to biblical admonitory suggestion,—'All Horseplayers must die broke.' Truly, this present day Pari Mutuel deleria begets a human dementia comparable only to the grand old Bank player who just had to go against Gaff for it was only game in town. And now, as I join out this coolly fastidious Old Boy Mori, in liason with Col. 'Mat' Winn, 'Herb' Swope, 'Packey' Lennon, and George Vanderbilt, to belly Clubhouse Bar for further libation of that heather creamy John Begg liquorial ecstacy, I'm told off a chunk of delectable news.

"Come devoutedly wished Peace, this Pennsylvania Railroad, its line between Philly and Atlantic City now running only 500 yards off Garden State's front gates, will haul to Trackside that Philadelphia multitude. Then, attendance will average close to 35,000 and the Handle will break up to, perhaps, $1,500,000 every day. Today, Philadelphia is one of America's red hottest gambo towns in country. May be lot of proverbial Living Dead in old Quaker City but it's surprising how quick come to life when that Paddock Bugle gol darn doth blow."

I recognized this as notable prose. Shattering all frames of reference, as the boys in the quarterlies would say, it ran off into multitudinous milieus seldom simultaneously exploited by any one writer—gold mining, horse racing, the history of American bigotry, and the *haut monde,* coolly fastidious in white duck. The genres were similarly intertwined; parts of the piece reminded me of Bernard de Voto, others of Horatio Alger, while some passages were beyond the power of anybody since the anonymous creators of the *Chansons de Geste*. The author knew the American past, the parlance of the I & Y Cigar Store at Forty-ninth Street and Seventh Avenue, and the Bible.[1] He had led a life variegated.

[1] I long thought "All horse players must die broke," was in one of the Lost Books, whose contents have survived as oral tradition. But the Colonel says it is in "Apocalypse, the Horsemen's Book."

The "Rick in middle of road" bespoke a bucolic, somewhat old-fashioned boyhood. To this the heavy Tease offered a piquant note of the incongruous, since Tease, for money, is the antithesis of a rusticism. "Soft yellow stringers indicative of tremendous Bonanza output in years to come," echoed an auriferous middle life, supported by the reference to far-famed Hollinger and the Chilkoot Pass. (It also echoed, as I later learned, the best mining-stock prospectuses of the Colonel's promotional years.) It was when the Colonel got out to that miracle raceway, though, I thought, that he drew a bead on the finish line and began to fly.

What he evoked was an irruption, like that Fourth Crusade that resulted in the sack of Constantinople. The profusion of image with which he illustrated this surge of human plankton carried forward by a tidal wave of avarice embellished but did not obscure his exposition of its motive. "But on they come in deathless resolve of a score today." And nevertheless he liked them, perfectly oblivious to admonitory suggestion as they were. They were like the old-time bank (faro) player who had to go against the gaff (the gimmick that put him at the dealer's mercy) because there was no other game. Sisyphus was out of the same mold. In instant contrast, he offered the superman, coolly fastidious, above the excitement of the crowd he mulcts, another major figure in the Stingo cosmology, I was in time to learn. Mr. Mori, smiling in the face of difficulty and weeding out that Tease, was a prototype of what the Colonel most admires and has never succeeded in being.

Above all, I could see, he was a stylist. "May be lot of proverbial Living Dead in old Quaker City but it's surprising how quick come to life when that Paddock Bugle gol darn doth blow," is a magic sentence. The "Dead" in the first clause is balanced against the "quick" in the third (the quick and the dead) and the "Living Dead" against the "quick come to life." "Quickly" would have spoiled everything. These first clauses are like the annual statement of the Guaranty Trust Company—in perfect balance. But the last clause changes the character of the whole structure. It is a Louis XV pleasure house added onto a double-spired Gothic cathedral. The sentence ends joyously like a dog wagging its tail. In fashioning this tail the author had shown his *maestria* once again. "The gol darn Paddock bugle" would have been less good. By displacing his adjective and using it as an adverb he had achieved an effect of sweet disorder, as in the phrase, "a hothouse bloody flower."[2]

I did not know, or course, whether Colonel Stingo achieved his effects deliberately or as the osprey builds its nest, but the result was there.

[2] It was Dai Dollings, a Welsh fight trainer, whom I first heard employ this phrase, in describing a brittle boxer entrusted to his care. The flower wilted in the fourth round. Horticultural similes are rare among fight handlers, but I knew another who always used to refer to Abe Attell as a honeydew melon. "He was a honeydew melon," this fellow used to say, meaning Attell was extraordinarily proficient. "Cauliflower ear" is a simile without verisimilitude. I have never seen a fighter's ear that looked like a cauliflower, save perhaps for a suggestion of *gratin* that could have been removed with a washrag.

His byline offered no more clue to the real identity of the author than the likeness which accompanied it in the *Enquirer*. This latter was a line cut of a conventional Old South gaffer with long sidehair, moustache and goatee, in working position behind a large square typewriter. In the background hovered a horse and jockey, evidently just emerged from a starting gate in the upper left-hand corner. The horse was a nose off the centered title of the column "Yea Verily," and to the right were three elbow benders gathered around a triangle of mahogany with a bartender inside it. One of the three was a soubrette. The easy symbolism, equine and convivial, failed to record the true range of the Colonel's interests, which, I could perceive, were as universal as the hand of the Clan Sullivan.[3]

I determined to seek Colonel Stingo out beneath this banal typographical mask, but in those days I had a habit of putting off all plans until after the war.

The *Enquirer*, as I have said earlier, is the only newspaper published in New York on Sunday afternoon. For the irreclaimable newspaper addict, therefore, it is "the only game in town," but although it costs ten cents there are not enough such hopheads to support a paper by themselves. To augment its chances of survival it bears a Monday dateline, so that it may carry legal notices, a class of business New York State law denies to Sunday papers that are dated Sunday. Since the Sabbatical appetite for reading matter is pretty well satisfied by the *News, Mirror, Times, Journal-American, Herald Tribune, Morning Telegraph* and *Daily Worker*, with a combined circulation of around nine million, there is not much left for the *Enquirer* except when some news story breaks too late for the last editions of the morning papers. John D. Rockefeller died for the *Enquirer*; Mussolini's executioners were similarly considerate in their timing of the Duce's departure. The Ward Liner Morro Castle burned on a Saturday back in 1934, and details were still pouring in on Sunday afternoon. Colonel Stingo, the only man in the office as the stuff came over the United Press ticker, added to the appeal of the story by filling the sea around the sinking ship with man-eating sharks, which as he said later, he penciled in because they seemed to be well suited by the conditions.

The paper hit its peak circulation, one hundred and twenty thousand copies, the Sunday of the attack on Pearl Harbor, and since it has become a fashion to start wars on week ends, it probably will have a scoop on World War III, if there is one. On less fortunate afternoons, the *Enquirer* has to use artificial respiration.

In its early days its founder, a former Hearst advertising man named William Griffin, used to assemble packs of ruffians and send them into the streets howling "Murder! Horrible Crime! Throwed a Baby Offa Bus!"

[3] *"Nulla manus tam liberalis atque generalis atque universalis quam Sullivanis."*

The horrible crimes, when you read the paper, turned out to be in three-line United Press despatches from places like Hankow or Ljubljana, but the headlines were as big as if they had happened in Columbus Circle. The vendors traveled in packs and kept the full price of the papers they sold. Griffin believed in the Hearst maxim: "There is no substitute for circulation." The wolf-pack scheme worked well through the depressed thirties, but hit a snag when the approach of war brought full employment. The supply of wolves failed.

Once the United States was comfortably in the war, however, circulation took care of itself. Something genuinely exciting was likely to happen on any Sunday afternoon. Besides, there was a boom in horse-race betting which brought the *Enquirer* a handsome volume of touts' advertising, and the tipsters' ads in turn drew circulation, as the home front was well supplied with venture capital.

The war bore seeds of disaster for the *Enquirer*, but their gravity was not then apparent.

"The wartime shortage of cigarettes and chewing gum gave rise to our gravest postwar problem," William Scott Griffin, who succeeded his father as publisher, told me a couple of years ago.

"The small neighborhood candy-and-newspaper stores, which were a vital outlet for us, took to closing on Sundays because they could sell all their smokes and sweets during the week. It wasn't worth their while to stay open just to sell *Enquirers*. The proprietors learned they could make a living by working only six eighteen-hour days a week, and now most of them still take Sunday off."

Young Mr. Griffin added that he was working on a scheme to put the *Enquirer* on sale in delicatessen stores, which do stay open on Sundays.

Thus the *Enquirer* depended more heavily than ever on headlines designed to make the paper "jump off the stands," as they say in the trade, in such outlets as it had.

THREE GIRLS RAPE
QUEENS BACHELOR

an eight-column front-page streamer in type three inches high was one such headline that minimized the number of returns from dealers, Mr. Griffin said. The follow-up the next week:

NEW YORK SEX LAWS FAIL TO PROTECT MEN

UNSUSPECTING
MALES WIDE
OPEN TO ATTACK

was almost as successful.

Last spring, the *Enquirer* was purchased by Generoso Pope, Jr., son of the late publisher of *Il Progresso Italo-Americano*. It thus embodied two family journalistic traditions. The new management of the *Enquirer*, incidentally, has eliminated from its pages the Colonel Stingo line cut with the starting gate and the soubrette, possibly in an effort to make the paper look more like the New York *Times*. In partial compensation, it has awarded the Colonel an extra "Verily." The standing head on the column now reads "Yea Verily Verily."

The old *Enquirer* combined its headline style with a reverently sentimental approach to organized religion and the Democratic Party machine in the five boroughs. In national affairs, however, its heroes were General MacArthur and Pat McCarran, and its editorial outlook would not have displeased Colonel Robert Rutherford McCormick. This has been somewhat modified under young Mr. Pope, who endorsed Governor Stevenson's candidacy in the last election.

Colonel Stingo, incidentally, never shared the Griffin political orientation. His policy was simply, "Let Paris be gay!"

Back in 1943, as I continued to read his columns, the range of the Colonel's acquaintance, like that of his specialized knowledge, amazed me every Sunday, as when he began:

"Watching finish, $25,000 Empire City Handicap, 3-year-old special, 1 3/16 miles, here this matins is Old Man 'Jim' Kirk. Saddled great colt, Dobbins, for Richard Croker just 50 years ago to dot. Though turning 82, 'Jim' still can rig nice fat boob with anybody. . . . Well-liked 'Jack' Levine, celebrated 'Jewish Cowboy,' makes sturdy Hit with Numbers this past Friday. Little over $2,800 drawdown. . . . 'Johnny' Gillieu dealing for O'Brien Bros. oldtime Bank Game outside Troy, N.Y. . . . Popular 'Big Jim' McMahoney now The Eye at Hotel McAlpin. . . . That tobacco-spitting gnat, Spindle Jack, making Midnight Handbook, Night Trots, Buffalo, N.Y., on Batavia, N.Y., nocturnal harness heats. And scoring good. . . . Duke of Windsor back on Park Ave. on hustle, incog, past Tuesday. Gurnee Munn his standbye with limitations."

This cast of characters included only two, the Duke and Mr. Munn, of whom I had ever heard before, unless you want to consider Dobbins and Croker among the dramatis personae. But they seemed more interesting than the celebrities who turned up in columns like Leonard Lyons's and Louella Parsons's. And the Nestor who could still rig a boob at eighty-two was a comfortable subject of reflection for a reader getting on to forty. As for Spindle Jack, a character who recurred in the Colonel's notes, usually reporting on aleatory conditions in the hinterland, I wondered about him until, as a friend of the Colonel, I was in a position to inquire.

"He is a gambler who acquired that sobriquet during years of peregrination with carnivals," the Colonel said. "He conducted a wheel of fortune, one of those large vertical wheels with numbers divided by brass pins," the Colonel particularized. "The wheel is set in motion by the operator and slowed down by the pins hitting against a leather spindle attached to a stationary frame. When it comes to a stop the number at the top of the wheel wins the prize. The more nearly rigid the spindle, the more deliberate the last few turns of the wheel. The operator thus has a better chance to stop the wheel just where he wants it, inducing it just barely to kiss off a number on which some yokel has wagered, and stop on a number which has not been played at all or is being played by a house shill. He effects the stoppage itself by a slight pressure on a device known as the gaffpit, imperceptible except to the initiate. Jack's fingering on the gaffpit was lighter than the pianissimo of a De Pachmann—you wouldn't think he had touched the wheel. And his spindles could make the thing stop as fast as a quarter horse trying three furlongs. In the days of hippomobile carnivalry he was known as the Canfield of the Crossroads. He graduated into dealing games like chuck-a-luck and shemmy, but the name Spindle Jack adhered."

This of course puts me out in advance of my story. I soon knew from "Yea Verily" that Colonel Stingo was a reading man. "Description by correspondents of drab London life makes you think of Charles Dickens' narrated impressions of New York in 1855," he wrote one 1943 Sunday. Market conditions of all sorts engaged his attention:

"Two mighty shipments of topgrade Scotch whiskey, July 21 and August 1 into New York and Philly reported," he wrote on another Sabbath. "Cargoes evaluated at $16,000,000. And not a case of it reaches thirst frenzied public market. Being cached under reserve for Christmas trade when John Begg, instance may retail on hustle at $11.20 a fifth."[4]

I also learned to recognize his portentous manner, one of his best, as in these paragraphs:

"Through many of these clearing houses [for bookmakers] is washed an ocean of money wagered in hundreds of Cities and Towns over the land on Base Ball, Football, and Hockey. Scores of stockbrokers in Wall Street district, today, gross more 'commission' on 'the games' than they do 'clearing' dull and slow moving Stocks and Securities in the Market, believe me. Today the players in the handbooks, off trackside, or the Punter pasting away at Pari Mutuel slots, on trackside, want daily lines from Professional Turf Information purveyors. . . .

"Truly, under legalized Pari Mutuel betting today, Coast to Coast, our Turf speculation becomes a mighty financial and social factor in the Nation itself. Ordinary laymen scarcely visualize its immensity. Futility and fallacy of attempting to 'prohibit' betting on Racing and Sporting Events is, more and more, becoming apparent to students of public order and wel-

[4] The Colonel's loyalty to John Begg, described in the Garden State column as "liquorial ecstacy," was not unconnected with an advertisement that ran regularly on the sports page of the *Enquirer*, extolling that brand of scotch. He collected a commission on the ad, which had been placed through him. Thus, in a column reviving the glories of P.T. Barnum's Jumbo, he included several gallons of John Begg in the historic behemoth's daily ration.

fare. It can be regulated, licensed and taxed but never stifled. If legal within a racetrack enclosure, why not outside that Race Track? Experience of the 'noble experiment' rises in memory like a spectral gnome at this time.

"Tonight, there is all sort of talk in Hotel Mayflower bar about this and that concerning impending tustle. One thing certain, revived Turf Committee of America is to have campaign Bank Roll which will tremendously overshadow Half Million swagged around at Albany, N.Y., in 1908 to offset Governor Charles Evans Hughes' onslaught on Racing and its Book makers, for, never in over 100 years of sport have Race Track Stockholders ever stood so deep in Dividends, thanks to crimson sister of one Arm Slot Machine, viz., sacred Pari Mutuel Slotways. They say, tonight, an Ohio henchman, big Lawyer and Senator, will Boss this fight on Racing's behalf. Liason man up in New York, and, here in Washington, would be Herbert Bayard Swope, most able Talleyrand. Our ancient Turf owes much to his talent and devotion.

"During 180 racing days, 1943 New York season, just $266,435,000 was betted through Pari Mutuel Slotways. . . . Approximately, sour faced Taxman in Albany, N.Y., will take off $17,715,500 as his share. . . . Game almost doubled in all departments in one year.

"Jockey Fred M. Smith, now retired these many years [here a couple of paragraphs on Jockey Smith's sterling career] looks little different from sturdy appearance of two decades ago. For many recent years 'Freddie' has been engaged in purveying inside Information to widespread betting clientele. Always, he is a familiar figure on Gallop Grounds of a nippy morning. His large plant and offices are at 131 W. 42nd St., Manhattan, where, periodically, many a lovely long priced winning overlay adds joy and emolument to the scores and scores of his speculative followers and admirers."

The abrupt switch in subject matter in this column was, I suspected, explained by a large advertisement which appeared in the lower left-hand corner of the page:

Jockey Fred M. Smith,
Bootin 'em In Over Quarter Century.
I Have Worked For America's Foremost Owners
—N-O-W I Am Ready To Work for Y-O-U!!
—Dealing Exclusively in "Exceptional" Moves.
I release on days when conditions are right.

Plans are made in advance,
and every "Move" bears my personal Okay. . . .
Three ($3.00) Dollars brings you all three
"Exceptional Moves."
This is merely an introductory offer.
The idea is to get acquainted and get the best.
Make all remittances payable to Jockey Fred M. Smith.

15/"*Moby Dickiebird*"

I FINALLY had to forsake the Colonel for my trip and when I returned to the United States in the last week of 1944, I found his mood funereal. Unduly alarmed by a slight temporary success of the Germans in the Ardennes, Mobilization Director James F. Byrnes, subsequently Governor of South Carolina, had shut down the race tracks. This was perhaps because they caused absenteeism from the war plants that had been prematurely reconverted to the manufacture of peacetime goods.

When I renewed acquaintance with "Yea Verily" I found that Colonel Stingo was down in Washington, judging from his dateline, trying to discover what there was left to us worth fighting for. I did not then understand his elastic use of the dateline; he holds that a writer is entitled to use in perpetuity the dateline of any place he has ever been once. Thus in the summertime he will sometimes begin a despatch: "Clubhouse, Belmont Park," when he has in fact spent the afternoon on the Hudson River, on the deck of the Bear Mountain steamer. "I have been to Belmont," he says. "I know what it is like."

The Colonel's datelines are subjective, like those of a correspondent I knew in North Africa whose colleagues called him Magic Carpet Mac. The Carpet would lunch aboard a submarine tied to a pier in Algiers and date his despatch: "Aboard an American submarine in the Mediterranean." On the next day he might take the *aperitif* with an officer of the Camel Corps at a bar in the center of the city and dateline that piece: "With the French Sahara Camel Corps."

In similar fashion the Colonel, before we began to share professional secrets, used to amaze me by sometimes dating one week's *Enquirer* piece from Yellowknife, Ontario, the scene of what he terms the last great gold rush, which is within the Arctic Circle, and the next from the Oriental Park racecourse at Havana. Considering the modest appearance of the *Enquirer*, it seemed to furnish him a lot of traveling Tease.

"One notes the sharp repercussion here today, resultant from the Kiss of Death administered the American Turf by Mobilization Director Jimmy

Byrnes when he 'requested' the closedown of racing throughout the nation," the Colonel wrote. ". . . After a week's sobering reflection, the question remains in the minds of Turf Leaders, viz., 'Why was Racing, of all professional and commercialized sports, singled out for the Crusher?' " The Colonel seemed to feel that it was because the racing people, like Dr. Sykes and the Rev. Dr. Orlando Edgar Miller, had overweened themselves. "No question the Pari Mutuel lobby is one of the most powerful 'educational' camaratti here in Washington today, and, for many years, going back to the nefarious Standard Oil, Southern Pacific, and Anti Saloon League protectory movements of 60 years ago. . . . It is said the Pari Mutuel Lobby has suffered at times from over aggressive and flambuoyant Bellwethermen, especially Col. Herbert Bayard Swope, a sincere and able devotee and Defender of the Faith of the Turf, lo these many years." ("Flambuoyant," so spelled, seemed to me so fine a description of Mr. Swope that I almost forgot my country's troubles in my aesthetic wonderment.) "Many wisenheimers around here tonight opine it would have been the simple act of elementary common Horsesense (which, after all, they of all people should have had) for the Turf leaders to have accepted the new 1945 Tax proposed for the Pari Mutuels without a Squawk, and, with ready alacrity. But no, even the smartest Lobbyist gets bullheaded."

I learned, further along in "Yea Verily," that the Turfites were preparing for a Dunkerque, rather than a Pétain armistice. They were going to sail off to Havana and continue the war there, at Oriental Park.

A "Yea Verily" in mid-January considered the sad case of the horse players who had not been able to make Havana.

"What are they going to do for 'action'?" it began. "Meaning the Gambler who had been always with us, and the Speculator who is irradicably a part and parcel of our organic economic life. Through intensive study and experted practice they hold an edge upon the haphazard Player, and, thereby, earn a luxurious living upon the Racetrack, the Stock Market, and across the Gaming Board throughout the land. Where there is one professionalized Gambler there are a multitude of Schukels [Boobs] serving as ready material for the exercise of craftsmanship. Director 'Jimmy' Byrnes picked Christmas to launch his Squelcher closing down the Racetracks, and great had been the panic of readjustment of Life for hundreds of thousands of persons, directly and indirectly effected, since then."

A month or so later the Colonel reported in "Yea Verily" that the boys had found something. This one was dated from Lakewood, New Jersey, where, I learned subsequently, the Colonel was during this period engaged in dealing a faro bank.

"Lakewood, N.J., Mar. 3rd (Special):—We've engaged in, or observed, the Tango Marathon, the Bunion Derby, the Stork Derby, the Flagpole Sitter Contest, Commodore Dutch's Annual Ball, the Pie Eater Handicap, the Frog Jumping Championship, the Irish Royal Hospital Sweep, and the Roller Skating Gold Cup, but, the White Robin Authenticity setup takes the confectionery.

"About middle of last month, 'Bonehead' Barry, the Original, surprised the weary eyed company at the All Night Drug Store, over in New York, after the shutters had clattered down at Armando's, Duffy Tavern, Golden Pheasant, Stork Club, Paddy The Pig's, El Morocco, and Hogan's Irish House, with the astounding assertion that the White Robin had come back to Lakewood. He had been seen by that distinguished Ornithologist, affable 'Abe' Potal, Commander 'Sam' Moorehouse, and 'Mike' Todd. Sure sign of early spring and a favorable Training Season for the New York Giants[1] explained 'Bonehead' Barry. Fitting in nicely with the pattern of things planned by the devious 'Bonehead,' grave doubt and challenging apprehension of Mr. Barry's assertion immediately arose. What, a White Robin? Never heard of such a thing. There's no mention of it in Frank C. Menke's Encyclopedia of Sports. Impossible, 'Bonehead,' you're sure daffy.

"Then old 'Sad Sam' Jackson, the Booking Agent and All Night Sitter Up of substantial repute, offered to lay 3–1 that no one could prove there is such a thing as a White Robin. Quick as lightning for the Overlays, 'Jack' Bart, the Pharmacist, demanded 16–5, and, on acceptance, loaded 'Sad Sam' with a hundred. That started it. The nice fat Schnuckles[2] cut in hefty, too. Night after night, the Mob had been betting off its collective head on the White Robin proposition. Over the All Night Drug Store's steaming Java many a wager, one way or another, had passed on the gentleman's word.

WHITE ROBIN CINCH

"Appears, this 'Buddy' Prior, across at the Golden Pheasant steam beer Peelau, side-kicker of Wingie of Philly, consistently laid against the White Robin proposition, still posting 12–5 right up to 5:00 O'Clock, yesterday (Friday) morning. Other good Players booked against the White Robin too. Strange how iron faced Sophisticates will take Gamble Action on anything these days,—and nights,—with the Horses on motatorium? With plenty a money around the Mob will go for anything. And, so, the White Robin was made to order.

"And now 'Bonehead' Barry was going to prove his case,—that there is a White Robin, and, that he is back in Lakewood again

[1] During World War II, when there was a limitation on unessential travel, the major-league teams forewent their training camps in Florida and other southern states. The Giants trained at Lakewood.

[2] "Schnuckles," or "Schnuckels," is correct. The Colonel's unorthodox spelling, "Shukels," in an earlier column, had drawn a blizzard of protesting letters, I subsequently learned. "Shukel" must have sounded to him like a word more closely akin to "shekel," an old word for a kind of Tease.

this Spring as pouty and chesty as ever. This past Wednesday Night the 'Bonehead' declared he had a friend, Lawyer Frank A. Murchison, whose country home on Forest Drive, beyant the Rockefeller Estate, is surrounded by the Red Berried bushes[3] of the Paunsa Tree.

PAYOFF

"This sends 'em. Schnuckles go for White Robin hook, line & sinker. Soft touch.

"The hardy Long Island Thrush, the early Spring visitor, the long tailed Bluebird, and the Robins thrive lustily on these Red Berries as well as the wild Pidgeons, fast becoming extinct, the Jersey Ravens, and the shiny owl like Toebills. 'For the past ten days,' says 'Bonehead,' 'the Birds have been appearing in the bushes, opposite the large bay window of the Murchison home, which commands a full view of the red berried feeding grounds.

" 'Several red breasted Robins have been noted, and, for the first time in many Springs the very rare specia, the White Robin. He, or she, is the same in size and contour of brother Red Breast. Has the same song, hop, and trot of Mr. Redbreast, and, is quite as chesty too. Feeding time is around 7:15 O'clock every morning, soon as the light of Dawn is tolerably clear.' Continuing, 'Bonehead' said, 'It is my Idea to have you Betting Men appoint two Representatives and let Pricemaker Prior nominate the third one. You'll all ride out to the Murchison country manor house in my car leaving Paddy the Pig's ice free Barge Landing at 3:30 A.M.' Agreed. 'I'm taking along Photographer "Ben" Cohen, post graduate pupil of I. Kaplan, and we'll see what we can do as to proving that there is such a thing as a White Robin.' Readily agreed.

PAYOFF ON PICTURE

"Quickly the Anti-White Robin Mob selected as representatives Oldboy 'Bitzy' Ascher, ancient Bookkeeper for roly poly 'Sam' Boston and 'Jack' Durnell, the Parker & May, Bar Harbor, Me., credit man. The trip was made, the Birds fed as per schedule, and Picturetaker Cohen caught a corking flash of rare White Robin through the Murchison large bay window. The illustration, poised herewith, tells eloquently that there is a White Robin, and, the Payoff of quite some money was made last night on the Committee's Report and this visual confirmation of the fact.

"And now the denouement, the finale, the Grand Sendoff, if you don't mind. This ostensibly Silly Johnnie, the red headed 'Bonehead'

[3] I am not familiar with this deciduous conifer.

Barry, may be knave or fool? I'm just after learning from Tillie the Toiler, in effect, Mr. Barry is a Brother of 'Ringer' Barry[4] who did a little Remembrandting on the good racehorse Ahmaudon,[5] $5,000 Claimer, at Havre de Gras, Maryland, ten years ago.

"Made this Ahmaudon look like a certain $1500 Claimer entered in a race that same afternoon. The conspirators got the Price and they reaped the harvest. Without customary Easel or Pastel, somebody could have done a neat job on White Robin. I'm only Saying, that's all. Ever, and always, the Honest Rainmaker, as related in Job, the 2d Verse, is among those with the Prattle of a Babe and the soul of Jimmy Hope, the Bank Robber. Some of the Lads haven't cooled out as yet. Anyway, I lay 'em down, and you guess 'em. Yea, Verily."

This was the piece that sealed my determination to meet the Colonel.

Besides the narrative merits of the story, I was impressed by a historical oddity few other readers may have noticed. Ben Cohen, the photographer privileged to photograph the white robin, is described by Colonel Stingo as a pupil of I. Kaplan, who was the first observer to report on the naked duck, another creature previously little known to ornithologists.

Mr. Kaplan, who must now to my sorrow be referred to as the late, was a photographer employed by the *Daily Mirror* in its sport department, and was not a man of the type to build a blind near the nest of a tawny pipit and then patiently wait. But, as any correspondent of the *Field* knows, opportunities a convinced bird watcher would give his best field glass for frequently fall by luck to a Philistine.

Mr. Kaplan, who told me the story in an automobile chartered by the Twentieth Century Sporting Club, on the way back from Max Schmeling's training camp for the first Joe Louis fight, related that he had accompanied the New York Yankees baseball team to their training camp in Macon, Georgia, in the early spring of 1916 or 1917, he forgot which, and that the roster had included the usual large complement of left-handed pitchers.

One evening Mr. Kaplan had wandered out to sample the native corn whiskey,—there was already a state prohibition law in Georgia,—and two of the left-handed pitchers had attended a carnival being held for the

[4]Skillful horse-ringers do not usually resort to the paintbrush. "That paint look streaky when the horse sweat," a learned clocker of my acquaintance explained to me. "What they do is get two horses that look the same to anybody but maybe me, only one of them is something and the other one ain't nothing. Then they enter the nothing in a race and they run the something." That is what Barry the Ringer did when he ran a four-year-old named Akhnaton instead of a three-year-old named Shem at a Maryland track in the late thirties. But the traditional notion that ringers do use paint is essential to this fable of the kalsomined robin, which is equally evocative of La Fontaine and Damon Runyon.

[5] "Ahmaudon" is Third Avenue Irish for a graceless fellow, a schlemiel, and is a friendlier name for a horse than Akhnaton anyway.

benefit of the Knights of Pythias. There was an artful dodger concession, with a colored man who stuck his head through a hole in a backdrop for the customers to throw at. "Five baseballs for twenty-five cents; hit the dodger in the head and win a fat white duck!" The baseballs were large and soft, which cut down on their velocity, making them easier to dodge, and also obviated any lethal result in case of a hit. The pitchers, both canebrake southerners, had brought on their persons a supply of league baseballs, which they switched with the concession's own. In consequence they scored six hits out of ten, winning half a dozen ducks and disabling half a dozen colored men, all for fifty cents.

Then they returned to their hotel, where all the sports writers were staying as well as the club, and knowing Mr. Kaplan to be out on the town, they entered his room with a passkey, filled the bathtub with water, threw the ducks into it, and left, closing the bathroom door as well as that of the bedroom.

When Mr. Kaplan came home, barely conscious, he sat down on his bed, undressed a hundred per cent, and then went to the bathroom to brush his teeth before retiring. He opened the bathroom door and was almost knocked over by a flight of naked ducks, as pink and wrinkled as newborn babies. He swore they flew, although I don't see how they could without wing feathers. They must have looked like the pterodactyls in the illustrations to Conan Doyle's *Lost World*.

The pitchers, in their haste to leave the Kaplan premises before he returned, had not noticed they were running hot water in the tub, and as often happens in hotels, the hot had been near the boiling point. It had taken all the feathers off the ducks, and when Izzy unwittingly released them, they fluttered and tumbled all over the bedroom, squawking like burning witches with head colds.

Mr. Kaplan, thinking he was going mad, flung wide the door that opened from the bedroom to the hall and ran out as nude as a scalded duck, falling in a faint at the feet of a group of baseball players who had assembled outside his door to enjoy the joke.

"Ven dey saw da naked dogs," Mr. Kaplan said (he pronounced "duck" in this unique canine fashion), "dey damn near fainted too, I betcha."

He thought it was one of the funniest things that ever happened to him.

Remembering Mr. Kaplan's story, I was reminded of the experience of a Frenchman I know who on his first visit to New York was staying at a super-palace-hotel with his wife. The wife had retired, and he, in a state of undress like Mr. Kaplan's, opened a door which he thought led to the bathroom, on a hook within which he had left his pajamas. The door he mistakenly opened was that which led to the hall, and as he gazed dismayed about him, he heard a loud bang which told him that the door had swung shut in his rear and that he was locked out. He turned, rang the bell, pounded the door, but discreetly, since he did not wish to arouse the sleepers in other rooms, who might come to their doors to see what was happening. The discreet pounding was not enough to awaken his wife, who had fallen instantly into a deep sleep. The Frenchman sold wine, and they had been out until night-club closing hours, drinking his firm's brand of champagne with proprietors. He himself had been in a moderately thick fog, which accounted for his mistake about the doors, but his situation, he told me, sobered him instantly. The best thing he could do, he thought, would be to make his way to the row of elevators, ring the bell and then flatten himself face to the wall until a lift man arrived, when he could explain his predicament and send him for a passkey. Since it was between four and five in the morning, he would probably not be seen waiting. He rang and pressed himself against the wall for what seemed an interminable time. At last he heard the hum of the approaching elevator. He was on the forty-second floor. It came nearer and nearer. His appeal had been heard. It stopped at his floor. The elevator door slid open, and my friend sidled toward it, but he heard voices within. The lift had passengers. He froze, and after a pause the door shut again and the elevator continued. As soon as it departed he worked his way to the bell and rang again. The elevator stopped again, on the way down,—and out walked four men and four women, all in evening dress. They were guests at the hotel, who had been attending a party in some other guest's suite. My friend was at the right of the row of elevators, frozen to the wall, trying to make himself *mince, mince.*

"It was as during the Resistance one time, when I knew the Gestapo was looking for me," he said. "I could hear their footsteps, their voices. . . ."

The men and women, absorbed in one another's conversation, turned left and went off in the other direction, without having seen the Frenchman. The elevator paused again, for 42 flashed on the operator's board. The lift man looked out. But the Frenchman did not dare attract his attention because the men and women, although moving toward the other end of the hall, were still in sight. The puzzled flunkey waited a few seconds and then continued downward.

"I had fear that if I rang again he would think somebody was playing him a joke and would not respond," my friend said. It seemed to him that he had been out there for hours when the ultimate horror arrived. The door of one of the suites swung open and a woman in a *robe-de-chambre* appeared in the doorway. She stood peering about, as if for the source of some noise that had disturbed her. My friend was on the point of losing consciousness, he thinks, when he heard her say, "Oh, there you are." It was his wife.

The whole incident, he said, had lasted five minutes.

This has turned into what may seem another labyrinthian digression, but I mean it to show that Colonel Stingo's writing, like that of all major authors, has the quality that Stendhal attributed to great music. It starts you thinking along parallel and then tangential lines, and reflecting on the inwardness of the meaning of experience, your friends' and your own. The Colonel's nature story is just like *Moby Dick* in that respect, except that it is about a robin instead of a whale.

16 / *The Navasota Murder*

My first encounter with Colonel Stingo, like Boswell's with Dr. Johnson, was not the result of accident but sought out. I began my active quest for the Colonel at Madison Square Garden, on the night of January 6, 1946. A long, lanky colored heavyweight named Al Hoosman was fighting an untalented but experienced fellow named Lee Savold, and the attendance was so sparse, even including a couple of thousand paratroopers who had been admitted free, that opportunity for seeing friends and visiting with them was unlimited.

I asked Harry Markson, then the Garden press agent, if he knew who Stingo was, and he said he didn't but would find out from the *Enquirer*'s boxing writer, a fellow named Billy Stevens. Markson went off and came back to my seat in a couple of minutes with a slip of paper that said on it, "Jimmy Macdonald, Hotel Dixie."

I called the Dixie on the morrow and on several succeeding days, but the operator said his room never answered. I left my name and telephone number on each occasion, and on the fifth or sixth day I got a telephone call, at my desk in *The New Yorker* office, from the author of "The White Robin."

His voice was mild, fresh and courteous, untinged with regional accent. A certain measured orotundity of phrasing reminded me of his prose style, but his tone bespoke amusement with his own rhetoric. I told him I wished to meet him because of his writing. His voice reflected a modest incredulity, but he made a rendezvous in a joint on Fourteenth Street near Irving Place. "I would suggest," he said, "that you ask for me at the bar." I acted upon his suggestion, and the bartender pointed out to me the protagonist of this chronicle.

I have already furnished, in places scattered from the beginning of this work to here, bits of description of the Colonel. It is difficult to remember, when you have known a man a considerable time, what there was about him that particularly impressed you at first sight. In the case of the Colonel, I think it was his boyishness. He seemed rather a very old youth than a youthful old man. He was as astonished at the maturity of my appearance as I at the juvenile quality of his.

"From your voice," he said, "I judged you to be a young neophyte. But

I see before me a man with the outward aspect of a Russian heavyweight wrestler."

Nothing flatters a fat man more than the suggestion that he is in fact a mass of muscle.

The Colonel, had he presented stock-subscription blanks and a fountain pen, could have signed me up right there for ten units in the American Hog Syndicate or one hundred shares of the Stray Dog Manhattan Mining Company, both promotions of which I was in time to learn from his own lips. But he contented himself with accepting a peg of John Begg.

Contemplating Colonel Stingo as he sipped his drink, I noticed he wore a bow tie, a white carnation in his lapel and a dashing suit of the period of the Great Gatsby. His neatness and dash made me wonder whether he had ever been a military man, and I was impelled to ask.

"I deny the impeachment, but I come of a military family," he replied. "One of my ancestors, a giant of a man, led the last despairing charge of the Clan Macdonald at Culloden. It is possible the genes have marked my physique." The Colonel had, I now noticed, a wide mouth, which, when he smiled, presented a full crescent of square teeth, several of them braced with wires, and his nose, wide at the base, was uptilted at the end. His confiding eyes were of the color of a washed-out blue shirt. The full face was disarming, the profile less so. The bridge of the nose was high, and so were the cheekbones. The lids hung heavy over the eyes when he wasn't looking straight at me. From the side, the head reminded me of a not particularly benign tortoise.

I asked him what papers he had worked on before the *Enquirer*, since his column offered internal evidence that he had been active long before the foundation of that organ in 1926. This is a good way to get an old newspaperman started talking, sometimes, and it worked with the Colonel. (It is never hard to get him started, I have learned since, but, like Scheherazade, he takes his own way home.)

"I began in my native city of New Orleans," he began, not at the time entering into any details on his debut, "and by the time I was twenty I had achieved the position of handicapper on the *Item*. My selections appeared on the first page of the early edition during the winter racing season. At that time New Orleans offered the most important winter racing in America. There was a track at Jacksonville, but it didn't amount to much, and neither did Florida.

"Stopping in at the *Item* office one day on my way to the Fair Grounds track I found a note asking me to call on a Mr. Charles Phillips Cooper at the St. Charles Hotel. The name meant nothing to me, but I went. Mr. Cooper introduced himself as the managing editor of the New York *Evening Sun*. He said he was in town with his wife and daughter for a holiday, and the women had played my selections in the *Item* and won thirty-four hundred dollars.

" 'That proves to me, my boy,' he said, 'that you are the best racing writer in the business, and I offer you the post of turf editor of the *Evening Sun*, at a stipend of fifty dollars a week.' I accepted his offer, but delayed my departure after he had left. When he wrote that he wouldn't hold the job any longer unless I took the next train, I finally made up my mind and quit the City of Mardi Gras, where I had been raised under the tender care of my grandmother's household slaves."

"But surely you don't go back before the Civil War," I said, astonished.

"I was born in 1874," the Colonel said. "People in New Orleans held slaves long after the end of Mr. Lincoln's war. It was like bootlegging.

"When I was a little tad my grandmother and her mother, my great-grandmother, would send two of their male slaves and a white-haired black-faced mammy over to Newtown, beyond Canal Street, to the 'big house' where I was born, to get me and return me in regal splendor in a Creole-type open barouche behind a big jack mule who could roar like a lion. He liked me, that I remember, for I always maintained an adequate supply of sweet yams for his delectability.

"On one of those cavalcades I saw General Beauregard. The mammy called him to my attention.

"It had been twenty years since Beauregard had smelled powder at Chickamauga but nevertheless he was still the Napoleon of the Promenade at Old Spanish Fort on Sunday afternoons for all the fashionable Deep South world to pop an eye and heave a sigh at the wondrous sight of the little man in large wavy black hat, encrusted with a gold ribbon and bonbon tassel, and sporting a goat whisker trimmed down to a pin point. He was the President of the Louisiana Lottery then. His shiny black Prince Albert coat caught my eye, and I wondered did he wear that black coat, almost to his knee cap, into battle.

"My great-grandmother, whose maiden name was Angelica O'Reilly, lived to be ninety-four, and my grandmother, whose maiden name was Elizabeth O'Regan, to be ninety," the Colonel said. "Since Great-grandmother had been only sixteen when she gave birth to Grandmother, the two at the age when I recall them seemed to me like sisters. They would call each other by their first names.

"My great-grandmother spoke but little English, but she was fluent in Spanish and very handy with the Gaelic tongue. She looked like the monument you see of the pioneer mother. She was rough but kindly, I recall. All the slaves adored her.

"My wonderful grandmother sang and played most acceptably on the first Steinway piano ever brought into residential Vieux Carré. She had once acted upon the stage of the French opera and could handle a Springfield rifle like a soldier at Shiloh. Well I recall seeing my grandmother, many times, smoking a big black plantation cigar while knocking off with fine appreciation Brahms or Liszt in G Minor at the Steinway. Her expectoration had remarkable capacity as to distance and accuracy, her objective being right through the open window to the green lawn in the garden across the pedestrian walk. If ever the flapping window curtains interfered with her trajectory, vent would be accorded her annoyance by an indulgence in choice profanity."

The Colonel ordered us another brace of drinks.

"It is not yet the hour of the Great Transition," he said, introducing me to that now familiar term. "I drink hard liquor only before breakfast. But I got up at five o'clock this afternoon and have not had my breakfast yet. After breakfast, on principle, I drink only the Gambrinian amber."

When the barman set down the drinks, the Colonel went on, flicking a tear off his right eyelash:

"It is the wonderful dining hall at Sarsfield House, our ancestral demesne, that sticks uppermost in my childish memory with its two immense and positively beautiful old antebellum crystal chandeliers, the soft and generous old-time Irish linen at table overspread with silver 'right from Tiffany's up there in that hateful place New York,' as my grandmother would explain. Out of forty-odd slaves who manned Sarsfield House not one accepted freedom at the close of the war, though invited to do so. Grandmother directed them with regal authority, but she was also kindly and considerate. The old-time darkies just loved her. She would get up in the middle of the night and go out into the pelting storm to help one of them in an hour of anguish or emergent necessity.

"My father was Macdonald, a descendant of the Highlanders who came to Louisiana while it was still Spanish," the Colonel said. "He was a highly successful attorney. But by and by hard times came knocking at the door, and the result was my precipitation, at an early age, into the branch of letters which first suggests itself to the non-holding, namely, journalism."

"Well, what happened after you got the job on the *Sun*?" I asked, ashamed of my intrusion upon these deeper recesses of Mr. Macdonald's early private life. I could see that every time he thought of those antebellum crystal chandeliers he felt terrible.

"I was highly successful," the Colonel said, "and by adhering to bad habits I scored one of the greatest beats in the history of the newspaper business. It happened in the summer of 1902. My work had already attracted the attention of Arthur Brisbane, who had been appointed managing editor of the *Evening Journal*, and he had sent for me. 'What are you getting over at the *Sun*?' he asked. I had the presence of mind to answer seventy-five dollars. I was getting sixty by that time. 'We'll give you a hundred to come over here,' he said. I said I would have to have time to think it over.

"I meant it, because I felt safe over at the *Sun*, and I didn't know what would happen once I entered that Hearst volcano.

"I was a perspicacious observer around the racecourses, although I never bet my own money, and one day I got a hot one and passed it on to a fellow who bet heavy Tease. It was a two-year-old filly named Navasota that hadn't been out since the Fair Grounds meeting, and she came down at ten to one. The fellow made a big score, and he slipped me five hundred.

"She ran on a Saturday, at Morris Park. It was the same day Compute won the Withers Stakes. There was no evening paper next day, so Saturday was my night of revel Babylonian. Another fellow and I took a couple of girls from a Weber and Fields show to the Woodmansten Inn, a roadhouse over by the backstretch.

"It was nothing but bubbling Irroy *brut* and *toujours l'amour* until far into the night, and we stayed right there, but the room with private bath was not so ubiquitous as it has since become. Shortly before dawn I had to go to the second floor and I was aghast to find the hall outside my room filled with the muffled bustle of clandestine activity. There were two employees of the inn carrying a blanketed form on a stretcher, and escorted by the night clerk and the owner. As I came out of my room the latter placed his finger to his lips, giving me the office to keep quiet.

"Realizing the boss would not offer physical hindrance, since he wished to avoid a row, I stepped over to the stretcher and lifted the blanket from the recumbent's face.

"It was one of the richest and most powerful men in America, a pillar of the turf, a big politician and a great thief, and he was barely breathing. I couldn't be mistaken about who it was because he was a man I talked to almost every racing day. I had seen him out at the track that afternoon. I pulled down the blanket to see what had happened to him. The nightgown over his bulging belly, an onion-shaped kiosk, was slotted with dark blood, around which fluid more freshly pumped from the interior formed a burgundy border, ever spreading. He had evidently been shacked up with a woman and opened to the wrong knock, perhaps an outraged husband or a cadet to whom she had refused an agent's commission. I gave no sign of recognition and went about my errand. When I returned to my room the hall was empty.

"The Sunday-morning papers, which I read over my coffee at the old Imperial Hotel, Thirty-second Street and Broadway, carried no account of the sensational event, so I knew I had a scoop. It was by that time midafternoon, and I proceeded to Park Row by the Elevated Railroad and went up to the city room of the *Evening Sun* which was then on Frankfort Street, just off the Row. I typed out my story, left it on the managing editor's desk and departed, feeling I had performed above and beyond the call of duty. The party of the second part in the shooting was one of the most famous men in the country. I got a first edition of the *Evening Sun* with my breakfast next morning. Evening papers then went to press at 7 A.M. with their first editions. The story was spread right across the front page. I dressed and breakfasted, feeling good, and made my way downtown again to stop by the office and receive congratulations before starting out for the track. On the way I bought another copy of the

Sun, a later edition. There was no trace of my story in it. I was perturbed.

"On entering the city room I was met by the managing editor, who asked me if I knew that the assassinee's brother-in-law owned the money behind the paper. The family had had the story jerked, and had managed to keep it out of every other paper in the city. I told him that I could not possibly be mistaken,—I knew Mr. —— well. He said he was sure I was right, but I could not remain on the *Sun*. But he invited me to continue as racing writer until the paper could find a successor. I thanked him warmly and went right over to Mr. Brisbane's office at the *Journal*, which was then published in the old *Tribune* Building. Luckily the *Sun* gave no by-lines on local stories in those days, a circumstance which I had deplored when I thought it would deprive me of public credit for my scoop, but of which I was now glad.

"'Mr. Brisbane,' I told that old fraud, when I had penetrated to his presence. 'I have been thinking over your offer and have decided to accept.' He was delighted. I worked out my two weeks at the *Sun* and then went over to the Hearst empire."

We had another round, and the Colonel said:

"The experience shook my faith in the integrity of the press."

17 / *Honesty Is Not*

THE COLONEL had told his story complete with names, and I was disappointed, when I looked the victim up in newspaper files, to learn that he had died in a hospital a couple of years after Compute's Withers, of what were described as natural causes.

Colonel Stingo, however, insists to this day that he saw the man after the shooting, and that the family hushed it up. "He may have been patched up and lived a while afterward," he says, "but he was never healthy again and that is what he died of."

This is the kind of difficulty that comes up frequently in editing the Colonel's reminiscences, but his reply, when consulted, is to say that reminiscences are not meant to be edited, but enjoyed. "Memory grows furtive, Joe," he will sometimes say when faced with a fact right out of the Columbia One-Volume Encyclopedia, the New York telephone book or Philadelphia Jack O'Brien's legacy to me, a copy of Tom Andrews' Boxing Record Book for 1913.

But with equal frequency he will maintain that his version of the past is right, and that conventional history is wrong. He believes assassination a far more common cause of decease than commonly supposed, and it is no worse than even money that any prominent figure of the past you happen to discuss with him will turn out to have been a victim of a very thin blade or of slow poison. In the Colonel's opinion, a man who avoids getting murdered is likely to live to a ripe old age.

In speaking of the heroes and demigods he has known in the past, he denotes their success by the appellations, "a rich man, a powerful man." He signifies his own approbation by adding, "a great thief," "a great old thief," or "a *pisseur.*" He reserves the three-point accolade for a group including Elbert Hubbard, William Randolph Hearst, George Graham Rice and Boss Croker. He will never refer to a man he dislikes as a thief. Brisbane, for example, he considers a petty figure. "His show of erudition was a phony," he says. "He always played it close to the chest." "For instance," he said once, "while demanding of me during my tenure as racing editor a succession of sensational stories on the turf, which he deemed salutary for circulation, he would enforce the publication on the sports page periodically of the admonitory slogan: 'Race-track betting is the downfall of millions. . . . Don't be one of them.' And while we ran more boxing news than any other paper, including much citation of the fluctuations of odds, we published often at his behest, the injunction: 'Don't bet on fights.' He was a facing-both-ways, like Double Deck Tobin, the two-headed baseball pitcher, who was able to visualize simultaneously both first and third bases while working in the pitcher's box. It is a fact that Tobin existed," the Colonel said, retracting his heavy eyelids and looking me full in the chin. "He pitched for Hanlon's Brooklyn Superbas, but only briefly, because there arose Dr. Henry Ward Beecher to protest against parading him in public, an ungodly offense, according to the great lover and pious old humbug. He could have gone with Barnum but he disdained to earn his living as a freak. So a fellow named Jim Ryan gave him a job in a loan brokerage shop, or hypothecary, as chief overseer, where he did all right, all right.

"This old Buzfuz Brisbane had me write a Sunday story in the summer of 1907,—it was a full page magnificently illustrated by Hype Igoe, then a young cartoonist,—entitled: '"You Can't Beat the Races—and Why," by J.S.A. Macdonald, Racing Expert of the *Evening Journal.*' In it I related the sad case of a one-legged man who hovered storklike about the betting ring in the grandstand at Sheepshead Bay because he had hocked his artificial limb to play a three to five losing favorite. 'Everyone is surprised at the meteoric rise of the sport,' I concluded, as if disturbed by the shadow of a bird of ill omen, 'and no one dares to think where it will end.' We were furnishing the sinister Hughes with ammunition for our own destruction."

But Mr. Hearst ranks only just behind Al Jennings the train robber, Rice and maybe Bet-a-Million Gates and Aneurin Bevan in the Colonel's all-time list of standouts. "Although," he once said affectionately, discussing his old boss, "I must admit the man was mad as Nero, and eschewed self-criticism."

Aneurin Bevan,—the Colonel pronounces it BeVAN,—is his choice in the future book among the world's statesmen. "The Red Napoleon," the Colonel calls him. This, I have learned from him, was the title of a peering-into-the-future book by the late Floyd Gibbons, in which Gibbons predicted a Communist world dictator would be English. The Colonel clips newspaper stories on BeVAN and saves them. He is probably the champion long-distance reader of the New York *Times*, which is perhaps the nearest thing the Colonel has at this moment to a wife. When he has been riding the magic carpet too hard, hovering like a helicopter over the Gambrinian waves, he shuts himself into his Hotel Dixie retreat and reads back numbers for days at a time.

"It is both soothing and educational," he says. The only drawback to this habit, from my point of view, is that he sometimes tells me Arthur Krock's column without assigning credits.

Of all the Colonel's idols, a man named George Graham Rice (born Jacob Simon Herzig) is the one he most frequently invokes.

On the first evening of my acquaintance with Colonel Stingo we walked, as we best could, from the bar in which I encountered him to the restaurant Barney Gallant ran on University Place near Eleventh Street. As we emerged from the bar, Colonel Stingo looked up at the vast Consolidated Gas Building across Irving Place. There were lights in hundreds of windows scattered along its sides.

"When George Graham Rice would see windows lit up like that," said the Colonel, "he used to say, 'Jimmy, behind every one of those lights there is a man staying up thinking how to get the better of the fellow across the way.' "

The Colonel first met Rice, he told me, when both were reporters in their twenties in New Orleans. Rice had come down there from New York, where, previous to embarking on a career of letters, he had had what he called "a very youthful past" consisting of nineteen months in the Elmira Reformatory for grand larceny and another couple of years in Sing Sing for forging his own father's name to a check. Rice, who developed into something of an author, later lumped the two episodes as, "One incident in his youth that left a blot on his escutcheon and placed in the hands of unfair opponents an envenomed weapon ready for use." He often wrote of himself in the third person.

He not unnaturally refrained from placing the envenomed weapon in the hands of his newspaper colleagues.

"George Graham Rice entered upon many and diversified fields of endeavor," the Colonel said to me as we walked toward Barney's, "but in a general sense his flaunting banner will be best remembered always on the turf and in the stock market, both reservoirs of romance, money and adventure. No baccalaureate wreathed his brow, but he soon acquired in the practical world of men and affairs a grasp of matters no formal education might afford. Down in New Orleans he was known to the rest of us as Ricecakes, a thin, wiry, young fellow with an extraordinary bump, or protuberance, on the pointed end of his cranium. He wore his top hair very long so he could comb it back over this bump. He was always fashionably attired.

"Even then Rice had foreseen the golden horizon of newspaper advertising looming in the early morning of his career, a perception that did not fade from his vision the rest of his days; it may be said truly of him that he became a master of the science. But for yet a space his genius was confined within the limits of the non-profitable, or editorial, department.

"His chance came suddenly, at a period shortly after I had left New Orleans for the *Evening Sun.* He was assigned to the hotel beat, and one night, late, he was over at the St. Charles, a block away from the publisher's office in Camp Street. He knew the rudiments of telegraphy, and he heard a call for help come in over the Western Union wire running into the Hyams & Co. brokerage office in the lobby, from Galveston, Texas; a giant tidal wave had engulfed the entire city, thousands dead, an outbreak of fire, and all communications fast going out. 'Greatest disaster of the century,' clicked the operator, which, if you held that 1900 was the first year of the twentieth century, it certainly was.

"Over to Camp Street in a hop, skip and jump went Ricecakes and got from the drowsy business office cashier a requisition for five hundred dollars and transportation over the Texas, Pacific & Western to Houston. From Houston he got into Galveston just before communications went out altogether and got out by rowboat and mule a few days later with the material for a nationwide scoop.

"Ricecakes, when he arrived at a telegraph office, didn't see why he should turn over such a bonanza to a hick newspaper that was paying him, tops, thirty dollars a week, so he queried the editor of James Gordon Bennett's *Herald* in New York, sold them an exclusive story, with a follow-up series, and cleaned up. He was a genius. He said afterward that he sent a duplicate story to the *Times-Democrat*, but that didn't make them happy. They took the narrow view that just because he was their reporter and had gone to Galveston on their money, national rights belonged to them.

"So Ricecakes, when he finished his series, came on up to New York, bypassing New Orleans en route. He had got five grand from the *Herald* for his series, and it looked like a fortune.

"Our paths crossed again, possibly at the bar of the Knickerbocker Hotel, or the old Waldorf-Astoria. He was thirty and I twenty-six. We were fortunate to be at our prime in the much discussed golden era, which embraced the halcyon period in Wall Street, upon the race tracks and in the fashionable seasons at Saratoga, and in Europe upon the Riviera,—from 1896 to 1906. To have lived it is an experience unforgettable and priceless. It exemplified the method of fine gracious living without the raucous perplexities of frenzied taxation, sordid politics, and displacement of solid social status resultant from the parlous conditions of war, past and to be.

"Ricecakes had been infected by the contagion of turf fever while in New Orleans. In New York he bought a declining racing weekly called the *Spirit of the Times*, but a printers' strike caused him to miss several issues. By the time he came out again, the circulation had evaporated and so had his five grand. His reportorial services were in weak demand on Park Row, even though he had demonstrated his prowess, because the Galveston sequel had made his reliability appear dubious. It was then, with his fortunes at a low ebb, that he made his first ten-strike.

"Ricecakes recounts its genesis in his book, *My Adventures with Your Money*. Published in 1913. It is one of my head-of-the-bed favorites. I read a chapter every other night, alternating it with episodes from *Get-Rich-Quick Wallingford*, by George Randolph Chester. But Ricecakes is not completely accurate, tending always to over-dramatism. He says that he was down to a cash capital of $7.30 when he met Dave Campbell, an acquaintance of the turf world who was flat broke. It was in March, 1901. Campbell had a letter from Frank Mead, another friend, who was at the races in New Orleans. In the letter Mead tipped a horse named Silver Coin to win next time out. He said it would be as good as ten to one. Silver Coin was entered to run next day.

"Campbell wanted Rice to bet the horse, but Rice suddenly got a better idea. He would publish an ad giving the tip free, and including an office address. If it won, he would have more suckers than he could handle coming to his door with bundles of lettuce to spend for further information. In one cogent paragraph he disposed of the dry adage frequently proffered by the platitudinist: 'If the tipster thinks the horse will win, why doesn't he back it himself?'

" 'If the seven dollars was used to bet on the horse,' he propounded, 'the most we could win would be $70. By investing seven dollars in the advertisement, it was possible for me to win much more money from the public by obtaining their patronage for the projected tipping bureau. I was taking the same losing risk as the bettor—seven dollars—with a much greater chance for gain.'

"He took all the space in the *Morning Telegraph* that seven dollars would buy,—four inches of a single column, according to his account,—and the ad ran, 'Bet Your Last Dollar on Silver Coin Today at New Orleans. He Will Win at 10 to 1. Maxim & Gay, 1410 Broadway.' In agate type at the bottom of the ad it stated usual terms for information would be five dollars a day and twenty-five a week, and that this would be the first and last free horse. They then rented an office and stalled the agent for the rent, promising to pay after the first week.

"Well, in came Silver Coin, paying ten to one at New Orleans, but the betting on the horse was so heavy in the New York poolrooms that at post time six to one was the best you could get in New York, according to the book version.

"Next day when Rice and Campbell went down to the office they found a line of men stretching all the way around the block and clear up the stairs to their door, each with five dollars to pay for the next sure thing. Mead had telegraphed another horse that morning, and they gave it to 551 customers at five dollars, taking in $2755. The horse was forty, twenty, and ten, and finished second. They had given it to win, but at a price like that, a lot of the bettors had played it across and they cleaned up. They established the firm.

"It's a good story that way, but I think Maxim & Gay had a less impetuous inception. Ricecakes during his short flyer with the *Spirit of the Times* had gained insight into how much money could be made by the exploitation of avarice. He saw how crude the tipster's ads were in the racing papers of the day, and knew that with big display and his genius of persuasion, he could draw the boobs in swarms. But he planned the enterprise with deliberation, not, as he recounts, on the spur of the moment.

"Then inscrutable Fate steps in upon the scene. Always an inveterate horse player, Ricecakes had formed the acquaintance of a hefty bettor at Sheepshead Bay through a mutual friend, Belle Corwin, afterwards to gain renown as the inamorata of John Jacob Astor. The name was Amby Small, a great theatre magnate of the age, with headquarters in Toronto. This Dave Campbell mentioned by Rice was Small's executive assistant, and knew the equine realm in all its manifestations. At Campbell's solicitation Small advanced three thousand dollars as a pump primer to start the tipping business, and the boys made careful preparations. They wanted a real good thing to advertise as their initial free tip, a premeditated stratagem.

"Both, and I, had a sterling friend at New Orleans, Frank Mead, named but not described by the master in *My Adventures with Your Money*. Mead was a sheet writer for a bookmaking firm supreme known as The Big Store. The sheet writer records the bets and does the arithmetic. This firm was so ramificated it employed two money takers and two sheet writers. No one man could grab the cash fast enough, neither any other one man keep track of it. At night Mead was a croupier in an emporium of chance, and he also wrote racing news and did a daily handicap for the New Orleans *States* under the pen name of Foxy Grandpa. He was a jim-dandy and always well occupied, conversant with the flow of money, the gossip of the in-the-knows, and the welter of commentation that always surrounds the world of turf.

"The new firm wired Mead to send them 'an advance horse that might win at ten to one.' In due course, he complied. Silver Coin, a three-year-old maiden, was the horse, entered in a modest selling stake. The good jockey, Winnie O'Connor, after the Hughes stab in the back a favorite of the European turf, but then still in dawn flush, was to ride.

"Far from being broke, they still had $825 left of the $3,000, which, considering their proclivities, was a remarkably large fractional residue, for they liked to play the wheel available then in innumerable and dignified establishments. This was ample for a full-page ad in the *Morning Telegraph.* The advertising text was in the dignified verbiage, with an artcraft spread, that only a master like Ricecakes could devise and articulate; as you read along, the vibration of a piece of copy from the house of Morgan, announcing the flotation of a new issue of United States Steel, seemed to be confronting the reader.

"It invited the turf-speculative populace of New York to visit the office, the unpretentious demeanor of which was not stressed, and receive, without charge, the name of a horse, its rider, and the stake in which it was engaged to run in two days. It would, without peradventure, win at ten to one or better.

"For two days long lines of seekers of the golden info led from the Maxim & Gay Company's office door down the street and around the corner. Each received an envelope with a slip inside containing the name of Silver Coin. Names and addresses, with telephone numbers, then not so common, were duly taken and registered in the mailing list department, keystone of Ricecakes' subsequent success in promotorial capacities. So far as history records, it was the first sucker list he ever compiled, and I would venture that on the successive peaks of his crenelated career, over a span of forty years, he continued to hold the confidence of some of the investors upon whom he created this first favorable impression.

"The day of the race comes to hand bright and early, with all the forebodings that such a situation might well hold. Repair by Messrs. Rice, Campbell and Peter Grant was made to Gallagher & Collins poolroom in Sands Street, Brooklyn, to learn what Fate might have in store—triumph or disaster?"

The Colonel paused, for dramatic effect.

During his narrative we had walked clear down to Barney's, been seated by Dominick, the headwaiter, and been served with two bourbon old-fashioneds without sugar or any fruit except lemon, which I had ordered in a whisper without interrupting the Colonel's outflow. Gallant's is gone now; I am sad when I think of the generations of good restaurants the Colonel and I have survived.

It was the first chance I had had to ask a question since the Colonel broke on top.

"Why didn't Rice and Campbell use their own names?" I asked.

"Because they wanted to be able to try again if the first horse missed," the Colonel said. I could see from the change in his expression that he was putting a couple of bugs next to my name in his roster of acquaintances. (Two bugs, or asterisks, next to a jockey's name in a program indicate that he is an apprentice, one of small experience, a neophyte.)

"It was while dining at Browne's Chop House, on Broadway next to the Empire Theatre, one evening, that the ingenious Ricecakes picked up

Colonel Mann's scandal sheet, *Town Topics*, noting a story about 'gay times at Maxim's, Paris.' Hence Maxim & Gay."

This is not the way Rice accounted for the name in his published version, but it seems more plausible. Rice says he looked at the entries for the next day's race, and took the name of a sire, St. Maxim, adding Gay "for euphony." I was to find in all my experiences with Colonel Stingo that where he diverges from recorded history, he improves on it.

"But the horse won, as he said?" I asked, wondering for a moment if Rice had known anything at all about his own venture.

"Everything came in off the call wire just as advertised," the Colonel said, "the horse, the jockey, and the price on the opening line. Why prolong the agony? The dandy Silver Coin thing got off in front and just winged all the way. Every quarter call was so much music to the sinners' sore-distressed souls, conveying visions of limitless lamb chops in the future.

"That launched the firm. On the next day they handed out Annie Lauretta, the forty-to-one shot, and then they played it safe, giving out a couple of odds-on favorites, which did not let them down, but provoked some sensation of anti-climax among the boobs,—why pay five dollars for a tip on a one-to-five shot?

"It was then Mead furnished them with the name of a mare named Brief, owned by a man named Mose Goldblatt, handy with a needle and syringe. Racing at winter tracks then was not so sanctimoniously supervised as under the aegis of the august Jockey Club in New York. Visiting a race track in Puerto Rico only a couple of years ago, I was informed by one of the stewards: 'We do not discourage the use of helpful medicines.' That, in 1901, was the practice on the mainland.

"The favorite was Echodale, strictly a hophorse, trained and owned by the notorious Bill Phizer. Echodale closed that afternoon at sixteen to five and Brief went only mildly supported at six to one, with eight to one available in spots. Both went to post frothing and preening like unto De Quincey's opium addict you read about. It was a competition in stimulative medication. Brief, a stretch runner best ridden by Jockey Redfern, just did get up to beat Echodale on the post by a head. At the precise moment of passing under the imaginary winning wire, Brief toppled over dead.

"The success of Brief, under circumstances that denoted Maxim and Gay knew the very stride a horse would drop dead on, appeared symbolic. The high-riding Maxim & Gay people were now in the lap of the gods running before the wind with all sails bellowing. The heavy play on Brief put out of action two Herald Square books, while all the newspapers carried stories on 'Broadway Cleanup of the Bookies.' Next day the boys took in ten thousand dollars, their highest gross yet.

"Mr. Ricecakes boarded a streetcar, rode down to the Stewart Building at Broadway and Chambers Street, No. 280, and rented a suite of offices of a sober magnificence commensurate with Anaconda Copper. He wired Mead, empowering him to get the very best information that money could buy, setting up a staff of clockers, figurators, and toxicologists. Mead would wire one horse a day, which the full-page ads would advertise daily as 'The One Best Bet.' It was the first time the term had been used.

"The country was race-mad and bet-mad. There were some weeks when the business netted over twenty Gs. In one Saratoga meeting of three weeks they took fifty grand. He averred to have paid a thousand dollars a week for information, and in advertising he spent an unparalleled amount, which I remember as usually twenty-two thousand dollars a month. The great Chicago firm of Lord & Thomas handled the account, and ads appeared in Chicago, Toronto, Dallas, Detroit, New Orleans, San Francisco and Los Angeles newspapers, as well as the *Morning Telegraph* and a similar sheet in New York called the *Daily America*, not to be confused with Hearst's *American*, as yet unborn but soon to be.

"His methods of advertising were unique. He used full pages wherever possible, and proclaimed to his subordinates that small type was never intended for commercial uses. He claimed to have coined the word 'clocker,' as well as 'one best bet.' If so he permanently enriched the language.

"He enlarged the variety of his services,—from sending out one horse a day, he progressed to putting out complete ratings, a Three-Horse Wire, an Occasional Wire Special at fifty dollars and a Maxim & Gay Special Release, in return for which the recipient promised to bet a hundred dollars for Maxim & Gay's account."

The prosemaster paused for purposes of imbibition, and I had an opportunity to order two shell steaks, of a variety known to Barney that sliced down the side like bricks of chilled pâté de fois gras and cost at *sotto voce* 1946 prices less than you now pay for a slab of pink gristle in a store.

Getting his empty glass on the table quickly,—he is considerate of waiters and does not like them to make extra trips for his drink orders,—Colonel Stingo continued: "I was in New Orleans myself when Silver Coin and Brief scored, covering the meeting for the *Sun*. After that I went on to Bennings, the track near Washington which filled the gap between the close of winter racing and the New York opening, which in those days occurred at Aqueduct. By the time I returned, Ricecakes was in full stride, lashed on by the divine inflatus. I remember it as a time of literary production like that of Shakespeare. Some of Ricecakes' ads were so good I still remember them." And closing his eyes reverently, the Colonel intoned:

" 'The Whole Question is one of Money, Plus Brains. We know we have one; we think we have both.

" 'We invite you to join us. You never struck a better investment proposition in any field of speculation than our Three-Horse Wire since you joined the Human Race.' "

"It's beautiful," I said.

The Colonel opened his eyes and looked me full in the nose.

"Thank you," he said. "I wrote that one myself.

"Besides this species of ad, which I may call the exhortatory," the Colonel continued, "he employed another of his own devising, the confidential, or cards-on-the-table. He had a remarkable run of luck through that summer, and he would frankly review on Sunday in the *Morning Telegraph* the results of all his selections for each week, with commentation, such as:

"Our selection for the Metropolitan, second, was beaten by a fair horse, but not the kind any sane man would pick to win such a race in a hundred years.

" 'Our selection in the Juvenile was practically left at the post and then beaten by an added starter of unquestionable class.

" "A flat bet of a hundred dollars a horse on our Three-Horse Wire for five days is only a five-hundred-and-forty-dollar winner,—a distinct disappointment. The element of racing luck will creep in occasionally, but when it does it is the exception that proves our rule of many winners. The Three Best Bets given by us daily, famous to the racing world as Maxim & Gay's Three-Horse Wire, and backed by almost every plunger of note in the country for thousands daily, is worth your serious consideration, whether a big or a small bettor.'

"The 'disappointment' about winning only $540 was the convincer. Readers could see Maxim & Gay were on the level. The money flowed in like the waters of the Columbia River over the awesome Grand Coulee Dam, spreading beneficence in all directions. The fallacy undermining Ricecakes, like so many great men standing unwittingly upon the brink of disaster,—Hitler and John L. Sullivan are examples—was that he overweened himself. He began to think he really had something.

"Like the sheik in the story, he bet on those horses. And so when his intelligence department turned up a succession of stiffs, his reserves diminished rapidly.

"On March 15, 1902, he was enabled truthfully to advise the public: 'We sold our information to sixty-four thousand individuals during the twelve months just ended. What was in it for them must be in it for you.' A few days later Maxim & Gay promulgated:

" 'This is getaway week at New Orleans. Our experts burned the wires yesterday with startling inside information, which, added to knowledge already in our possession, points to the fact that this will be the banner week in the history of the Maxim & Gay Company. We are conservative in our promises. Each word is weighed well, and when we say there will be sensational doing during the next six days the statement is a positive one. Opportunity is knocking at your door. It is the time for action! Any two days of this week should show better results than the backing of our wire during the entire fortnight just ended. We know what we are talking about!' "

It was like hearing Carl Sandburg recite his own verse.

"The results of that week compelled Maxim & Gay to assume an apologetic tone," the Colonel said sadly.

" 'New Orleans is the hardest track in America to beat on any system of selecting probable winners that is based on workouts,' the faithful readers were instructed at the end of the meeting. 'The reason for this is that the horses which race here have little or no class and cannot be depended upon to repeat their morning workouts in their afternoon races. Again, the jockeys—most of them—are a lot of pinheads who are as unreliable as the horses. In the East it is different. The horses are classy, reliable, and their morning workouts are a safe indication of their evening performances. Entire eastern season, four hundred dollars in advance.'

"The reputation of Maxim & Gay was so firmly established in a year that even after the bad week at New Orleans, a number of boobs sent in the four hundred dollars," the Colonel said. "But the Bennings meeting was barely a standoff for Ricecakes' tips.

" 'Our performance at Bennings was fair,' the next series of ads began. 'At Aqueduct it will prove to be brilliant. This week, beginning with the first race Monday, we will give the pencilers the worst dose they have had in 1902 to date. Get aboard!'

"Aqueduct was grim for Ricecakes," the Colonel said. "His policy of frankness proved a boomerang when the hypothetical flat-bet-of-a-hundred-dollar customer, mainspring of his advertising, showed a loss for several successive weeks. When he dropped this type of advertising the boobs demanded the reason for the abandonment. By midsummer his enterprise was on the verge of collapse.

"It impressed upon me indelibly the lesson that in advertising honesty is not the best policy."

18 / *Farewell to Ricecakes*

WHEN THE Colonel referred to Mr. Rice it was with the tone of Joyce's Mr. Casey talking about Charles Stewart Parnell: "My dead king."

I could see that the two experiences the Colonel had just narrated, both coming in the fateful summer of 1902, might well have engendered the cynicism he professed.

I also had a memory of Rice, more recent than the Colonel's. I had interviewed the great old thief in January, 1934, when I was a reporter on an evening newspaper and he had just come out of the Federal Penitentiary in Atlanta, where he had done the fourth, and last, prison stretch of a long and accidented life. (He had successfully defended himself against at least as many indictments, including one for evading $1,700,000 in income taxes from 1925 to 1929.)

He was a pot-bellied, round-faced man of sixty-four, with spectacles and fine white hair,—I did not remember noticing the bump,—and his asseverations of continuously misunderstood good faith had seemed to me almost comic. I remembered he had told me he had "a phosphorescent mind," and that he was "the only honest financial writer in America," for which reason the big interests had always persecuted him.

It would be unkind to tell this to Colonel Stingo, I knew, since he remembered Mr. Rice at the top of his form. That is how fans who saw the second Tendler fight remember Benny Leonard. They do not like to be reminded of how Leonard looked in his attempted comeback nine years later. Long Riders, like prize fighters, should be remembered off their best.

So I merely asked Colonel Stingo if the 1902 run of losers had meant the end of Maxim & Gay.

"No," he said, "the mind Napoleonic will never concede defeat. In Ricecakes' book he records that it was the wont of the firm's track salesmen, dressed in khaki paramilitary uniforms, to appear at the office at noon every day and receive a bundle of envelopes containing the tips. They would then go on to the track and sell them at the gates for five dollars each. The stupendous gall of the procedure becomes apparent if you reflect what five dollars was worth in 1902.

"One day, while Ricecakes was out sick," says he, "a man in his office put slips of blank paper in the envelopes. The salesmen were forced to refund money to the handful of faithful boobs who still patronized Maxim & Gay. A horse named May J. came in at two hundred to one. The next day's papers carried full-page ads of Maxim & Gay claiming they had tipped May J. Nobody could prove they hadn't.

"And such is the power of suggestion that in the afternoon a boob, not a plant, came into the office and laid down five dollars on the counter, averring that he had played May J. on Maxim & Gay's tip, and wanted more like her. They got him to make an affidavit to that effect and published it in another series of full-page ads. Business picked up immediately.

"When the clerk who performed this stunt was asked for more information as to how he came to secure such an affidavit," the Colonel said, "and I quote Ricecakes: 'He gave absolute assurance that he did not offer the customer the slightest bribe to make it, and that nothing but an innate desire to call himself "on top" had influenced the man to perjure himself.' The duplicitous employe was promptly discharged, Ricecakes says, although he does not go so far as to state that Maxim & Gay ever repudiated the May J. ads. He fails at any point in his narrative to identify the clerical scalawag, and I think his disclaimer of origination is due to modesty.

"To me the May J. coup is reminiscent of Jack Dempsey's triumph over Luis Angel Firpo, when, knocked out of the ring and groggy, he climbed back and felled that huge black-browed man, the incarnation of misfortune. Maxim & Gay gave a string of winners, and within a month net earnings again reached twenty thousand dollars a week. Shortly after May J., the president of Maxim & Gay found a bankroll man, or source of new capital if needed. He was Sol Lichtenstein, one of the mightiest bookmakers of the day.

"There grew up at about this time in the tremendous business of Maxim & Gay, engineered by this truly astounding old Ricecakes, a problem. Their nationwide advertising and resounding success had created a vast public of small-town investors who knew no bookmakers but wanted to get in on the rich profits envisioned in such copy as:

" 'This will be a bonanza week! Our Three Best Bets Wire every day this week beginning Monday should prove a bonanza! We know what we are talking about! It will sizzle with good things this week, beginning with the first race Monday. You are invited to get aboard.' "

From the Colonel's expression I could divine who had written that one.

"Rice moved his entire office staff to New Orleans at the beginning of that winter racing season. He took twenty thousand dollars' worth of display advertising to run in thirty newspapers in the United States on the same day, announcing that Maxim & Gay would function as a commission house, accepting money orders for any amount and *betting the money for clients* on Maxim & Gay information. Maxim & Gay charged ten dollars a week for the information and retained five per cent of the winnings. It was a sure method of preventing holdouts, since they knew exactly what was coming to them. They made seven thousand dollars a day for the one hundred days of the meeting.

"As offices they rented in New Orleans the entire floor above Parson Davies' Crescent Billiard Academy on Canal Street, the lurking place, Bourse and Lloyd's Clearing House of the sporting gentry. The volume of mail addressed to Maxim & Gay was so great that Ricecakes had to hire a couple of trucks to haul it from the post office.

"Nothing like it was ever seen. But Ricecakes kept betting his profits back on the losers. He became crazed with the megalomania of octopus-like expansion. Not content with selling information, wagering his clients' money, clipping them five per cent of their winnings, shaving the odds and occasionally slipping them a wrongo, he decided to become a newspaper publisher, run his own ads and make a profit off himself.

"He may have had visions of becoming a second William Randolph Hearst. In pursuit of his ambition he bought a New York racing paper called the *Daily America* and announced he was pulling the Maxim & Gay business from the *Telegraph* and giving it all to his own sheet. He might have put the *Morning Telegraph* out of business, but William Collins Whitney, one of the richest, most powerful men in America at that time, bought a controlling interest in the *Telegraph.*

"It was made known to the upstart that unless he sold the *Daily America* to Mr. Whitney there would be a Federal investigation of the affairs of Maxim & Gay. It was also conveyed to him that the Jockey Club considered the methods of Maxim & Gay injurious to racing, since there was implicit in them a suggestion that racing was primarily a form of gambling. This is a heresy denounced to this day by the owners of the patents on the pari-mutuel machines. Therefore, even if he sold the *Daily America* on Whitney's terms—a squalid pittance—the *Morning Telegraph* would refuse his ads.

"The words in which Ricecakes has recorded his defeat are ever present in my memory. They are of a sombre chastity divergent from his florescent vein:

" 'Having lost the *Daily America* and having "blown" the Maxim & Gay Company, I was again broke.'

"It is said that Stendhal, the French gambler, used to read the Code Napoleon to learn stylistic restraint," the Colonel said, just as the waiter began to cut up our steak. "It is also said there was another distinguished Frenchman, whose name I do not at the moment recall, who used every year to reread Stendhal's masterpiece about roulette, *The Red and the Black,*[1] for the same reason. Personally I read George Graham Rice."

We fell to upon the steak, which offered small test of the Colonel's mandibular powers but a brilliant field for the demonstration of his appetite. "I am a good doer," he said, and proved it.

As frequently happens when food is voraciously ingested after several rounds of drink, we became torpid and conversation lagged.

In this first meeting I had heard more about George Graham Rice than about the Colonel himself, but I felt we had established a rapport.

19 / *The Honest Hog Caller*

SHORTLY AFTER our first rencontre, I paid my first visit to Colonel Stingo at his eremite retreat in the Dixie. Having forgotten his room number, I confused the desk clerk by asking for Mr. Macdonald. He looked through

[1] Much later, when we had become habitual associates, I remarked to the Colonel that *The Red and the Black* was not about roulette. "Memory grows furtive, Joe," he said. "I meant *The Gambler*, by Volodyovski." Volodyovski, a horse leased for the occasion, won the Epsom Derby for William Collins Whitney in 1901.

the list of guests, found what room Mr. Macdonald had, and then said, "Oh, you mean Colonel Stingo."

The Dixie is a seven-hundred-room hotel with entrances on both Forty-second and Forty-third streets, between Seventh and Eighth avenues. From the Colonel's single-with-bath, on a corner of the seventh floor on the Forty-second Street side, he can look out over a block of shooting galleries, cafeterias and third-run movie houses—a block that he knew in more glorious days, when the New Amsterdam Theatre housed the *Ziegfeld Follies* instead of Tarzan pictures, and Murray's Roman Gardens Restaurant occupied the building presently tenanted by the flea circus. The ramps of a bus terminal plunge beneath part of the Forty-third Street side of the hotel, and the buses bring many of the Dixie's guests—earnest young honeymooners from the South, and servicemen with their wives. The crowd in the small plywood-and-aquamarine lobby at the core of the building is younger than the crowds in most hotels, and this, the Colonel says, is good for his mental tone. "It makes the sap rise just to look at them," I have heard him declare.

The Colonel's room is simple and functional. It contains a single bed, covered with a rough gruelly cloth, a writing desk, a typewriter table, a dresser and two chairs. It is about the size of the chief steward's cabin on a small ship, and the Colonel's gear is stowed as neatly as a seaman's. His greatest periodic dread, next to rent day, is the approach of the time when it will be necessary to change the ribbon in his portable typewriter. Usually he delays this operation until he himself is unable to read what he has just thumped out. "Have a new ribbon for Mr. Underwood," he wrote to me once. "Put it on myself, single-handed and unassisted. As great an engineering feat as a triple play in the clutch." There are a few framed photographs on the walls, the most noteworthy of which is a picture clipped from the New York *Press*, a sporting sheet. A headline over the print reads: "Grand Old Hickory Jims of the Turf Writers," and the caption underneath identifies it as a reproduction of a picture of "the organization meeting of the American Turf Writers Association, January, 1902, in the popular Old Hickory Restaurant, Jackson Square, New Orleans." There are fifteen men, nine standing and six at a table, and there are fifteen stiff collars and five handle-bar moustaches in the group. Fourth from the left among those erect is J.S.A. Macdonald, New York *Evening Journal*. The Colonel, considerably more solemn of aspect at twenty-eight than he is at seventy-eight, is wearing a white scarf and watch chain with a dark suit. His hair, quite long, sweeps low on the right side of his forehead, his cheeks are leaner than today, but otherwise he is much the same. He has his right hand on the shoulder of the racing correspondent of the Buffalo *Express*, who looks like Herbert Hoover, and stands directly behind an old deep-south gentleman denominated Captain Williams of the New Orleans *Times-Democrat*. In Captain Williams I recognized the true original of the Colonel Stingo cut, complete with white moustache, goatee, long hair, and frock coat. They were an imposing lot, the turf writers of 1902, like some weighty committee of the American Federal Bar. Colonel Stingo and a man named Harry Brievogel of the Chicago *American* seemed to be the youngsters of the band.

The Colonel first bivouacked at the Dixie in 1940, at a time when Broadway hotels welcomed residential guests at a weekly rent lower than the transient rate. When World War II brought a great rise in demand for rooms at any price, the Colonel and many another Broadway solitary sat tight, protected by the emergency rent laws, and he still pays a rent he describes as "inexorbitant."

When I first visited him I congratulated him on his *bonne mine*. He was then, by his own count, seventy-two. "I have three rules for keeping in condition," he said. "I will not let guileful women move in on me, I decline all responsibility, and above all, I avoid all heckling work. Also, I shun exactious luxuries, lest I become their slave."

He was at that time prosperous, if not precisely holding,—his relation to liquid assets, at best, is that of a conduit, not a cistern. He was making and therefore spending a couple of hundred dollars a week,[1] all in commissions on ads in the *Enquirer*, and when I called on him insisted on taking me to dinner at Dinty Moore's, a place where an order of celery costs as much as the blue-plate luncheon at the Dixie. Within Moore's mirrored walls I tried to get him to resume the train of his autobiography where he had abandoned it in favor of the great George Graham Rice's.

"Was it on the *Journal* that you began to use the Colonel Stingo byline?" I asked him.

"No," he said. "It was not until I came back to San Francisco after my betrayal by Tommy Burns, who wouldn't fight Ketchel for me, that I adopted the sobriquet. Colonel Stingo was a character in Bret Harte's *Luck of Roaring Camp*. He was a wise old fellow, held in universal reverence, who would settle all disputes among the desperadoes. And he would conclude all sessions with the solemn words, 'Yea, Verily.'[2] I was conducting a legitimate advertising agency under my own name, and I used Colonel John R. Stingo as a nom de plume in a little weekly newspaper I owned called the *Referee*."

"And what does the middle initial *R* stand for?"

The Colonel reflected.

"Randolph," he decided. "A great southern surname.

"San Francisco, in the years immediately subsequent to the Fire," he said, "was a magnificent city. Everybody had money and nobody went

[1] The Colonel told me at our first meeting that he had purchased an annuity to mature when he was ninety. When, during the plug-in-the-door flap of 1951, I asked the Colonel what had happened to the annuity, he said, "It has been hypothecated to the ultimate degree,—extinction."

[2] I have never been able to find this Colonel Stingo in Bret Harte. But when my Colonel Stingo told me about him I hadn't tried. There is an old guy in *Luck* called Colonel *Starbottle*. But I don't think the Colonel meant him, either. It seems to be a case of the Colonel's creating a character that Harte had forgotten to [create].

to bed. The insurance companies had paid off so many claims in cash that the town was a maelstrom of liquid capital. It was wonderful and remained so until the reform element got in its deadly work.

"It was a life gracious and delightful," he said, "and not at all sordid. I remember the weekly embarkation of Tessie Wall and her bejeweled girls for the races at Emeryville, across the Bay. It was like a painting by Watteau, or a story by De Mossopont. Tessie had been for years the reigning madame of the city, the arbitrix elegantrium or, as the troubadours would say, the queen of love. She wore so many diamonds she was attractive, in spite of her grenadierian mustachio and not inconsiderable seniority. But the girls were pips.

"Emeryville was across the Bay, and to get there you took the ferry to a jetty called the Mole. There you boarded streetcars to ride out to the track. Drinks were served on the ferry, going and coming, and if you didn't have a place at the long table with Tessie and her girls it meant you were an outsider, a rustic. Nobody ever ventured to order anything but champagne, which in the parlance of those days was just called 'wine.' For other sorts you said claret, hock, or any other specification.

"After the return from the track the girls and their favored escorts embarked in Stanley Steamers, Wintons and the like and proceeded to Tessie's, a noble mansion with an anteroom like the rotunda of the American Museum of Natural History at Seventy-seventh Street and Central Park West. In this anteroom the gallants would remain while the girls changed to their work clothes."

This is something that often happens with the Colonel. He contemns precise chronological sequence. You try to hold him to New York in 1904 and he ducks under your arm and turns up in San Francisco in 1910 or '11 or '13. In his handling of years he holds to an axiom of his managerial days: "It is ever the part of sagacity, in making a match, to give or take two pounds."

"I bought the *Referee* for thirteen hundred dollars," he said, "and put it over big, selling it at all the fight clubs, with enclosed in each copy a printed slip listing the boxers and their weights. San Francisco was the pugilistic capital of the nation then, the sport being obstructed by hampering laws in New York. The sporting pages of New York papers were filled with stories of California pugilistic activity, and the state contributed a disproportionate share of the fistic talent. Corbett, Jeffries, Tom Sharkey, Choynski had come out of there, and among the lighter men there were stars like Abe Attell and Willie Ritchie. Not only the boxers but the best fight writers came from the Bay region,—Bob Edgren, Tad, and Hype Igoe, all great names already in New York. The patronage of the fights largely corresponded with that of the select resorts which advertised in the *Referee*. But when the reformers, urged on by Fremont Older, an editor skillfully avid of circulation, succeeded in jailing the mayor, a man named Schmidt, who led the orchestra at the Tivoli Opera House, and also Abe Ruef, the political boss of the town, I had a premonition of woe. I sold the *Referee* for fifteen hundred dollars, glad to find a sucker in the person of a journalist recently arrived from the East.

"But I had been prematurely discouraged. Abe and the mayor continued to run the city from San Quentin. Life went on as merrily as before, the henchmen being but put to the trouble of going out to the can daily to receive their instructions, a trajectory they accomplished in an Overland automobile driven by a young friend of mine who is now a mighty advertising executive here in New York.

"So I bought for twenty-six hundred dollars another paper, denominated the *Wasp*. It followed much the same pattern. I have always found there is nothing like having a medium of personal articulation. The *Wasp* had a yellow front page, in allusion to the yellow jacket, and when we mentioned anyone we would send him or her a penny post card with the message: 'You are stung on page 8, column 3,'—or whatever it was,—'the *Wasp*.' I took care to mention about a thousand people an issue, and for a small paper it developed a mighty circulation,—fifteen thousand."

" 'Colonel John R. Stingo' was a great by-line for the *Wasp*," I ventured, but the Colonel stuck to the Bret Harte etymology.

"Disasters never run singly, but always as an entry," he said, an aphorism I was to hear many times from his lips. "The monarch of the California turf was a man named Tom Williams. He controlled the racing at Ingleside, Tanforan and Emeryville. There was no good racing in Southern California then. Tom put up fifty thousand dollars bail for Mayor Schmidt, merely as evidence of his sympathy for a musician. The incensed reformers took out after Tom too, and the result was the Walker-Otis Law, repeating in California the Hughes crime in New York. It spelled the death of the sport of kings in California, not to be revived for twenty years. It flourishes there now, but, as always happens, the vulgar pari-mutuels, while contributing mightily to dollar prosperity, have at the same time wrought a depletion of the sporting festival's charm of artistry and selective quality.

"Next they assailed the boxing ring, limiting bouts to four rounds and rendering it the most innocuous fight town in America. San Francisco hasn't sent out a good fighter since. And as the international Panama-Pacific exposition approached, the black-visaged band of ascetics assailed the robust pleasures of the Barbary Coast, the dance halls like the Thalia, the Hippodrome, the London Music Hall and the Midway, all good advertising accounts of mine. The Hearst paper, the *Examiner*, imitative of Older, supported the inroad. Coblentz, the editor, hired Pinkertons to take the names of respectable citizens entering the purlieus. Then he published them. Sex became a hole-in-corner affair, politics without savor. I sold the *Wasp* for a paltry sum and devoted full time to the boresome pursuit of legitimate profit."

The Colonel polished off an order of large oysters, drank a bottle of ale and continued.

"I dislike humdrum occupation; it lacks solidity," he said.

"Avoid merchandise, it's ethereal, whether it be coffee, sugar or butter. The only solid value is a concept. There was a woman named Cassie Chadwick, for example, who convinced a couple of hick bankers from Ohio that she was an illegitimate daughter of Andrew Carnegie and had a bank vault full of securities. She took them up to Carnegie's house in Pittsburgh in an open barouche and got out and went in right in the door. She spent half an hour inside on some premeditated pretext, and when she came out the butler carried a package to the carriage for her. Maybe she had slipped him a sawbuck. They loaned her two million dollars on the securities she said she had. If she had had a tangible house and asked them for a mortgage they would have demanded eight per cent and her right eye.

"In the early fall of a year that I recall as 1914, because it coincided with the beginning of the war in Europe, I was in the wonderful bar of the Palace Hotel in quiet contemplation while gazing rapturously upon Maxfield Parrish's vibrating canvas,—'The Pied Piper of Hamelin.' It was a spot to which I repaired when in need of spiritual replenishment. I was still in quest of a concept.

"Suddenly, the shadow of a quietly approaching man in a long black coat, homburg hat and carrying a heavy stick, falls upon me, reflection in the back-bar mirrors affording me a moment in which to effect recognition and identity of the sidling figure before he could make introduction himself. Yes, sure enough, it would be none other than Harry Brolaski, true soldier of fortune, whom I had not seen for many the year.

"This Harry Brolaski," he said cheerfully, "was a freebooting Barbary corsair of horrendous background, but a good fellow withal, although not to be lightly trusted unless you were armed to the teeth. He was bereft of the full use of his left leg, and I shall cite the manner in which he suffered this mishap as an illuminating commentary on this Long Rider. In his very early days he worked week ends for his father, owner and personal operator of a piratical craft on the Mississippi River, plying between Natchez and New Orleans. The ship never was known to have freighted more than two bales of cotton on any one voyage. The craft's chief item of revenue arose from that grand old institution of postbellum days, faro bank and stud poker.

"The Brolaskis were insatiable,—they began ascending the river as far as St. Louis. There was engendered a matter of disputation there, for a St. Louis mob suspected the character of the seemingly innocent craft. They learned of the gaff roulette game below decks, to which landlubbers were admitted while the vessel lay at dockside. It was a muscle-in job. No moving the Brolaskis, father and son, to a sense of reason. 'This is our racket, and we're a-going to keep it that way. No one is going to cut in here except over our recumbent cadavers.'

"So, one moonlit night, as the *Sea King* drew hawser and moved into the stream from the Temple Street docks, St. Louis, with the games going big guns, wheels turning and cards falling, a hefty pineapple exploded aft in the captain's cabin when the stud-poker game roared along.

"It is interesting and pertinent to note that on the casuality list, his leg fractured in three places, was young Brolaski. Tenaciously, he refused surgical suggestion of immediate amputation, but he limped for the rest of his mortal span.

"In a later period of his life he bank-rolled the Palmetto Club, a bookmaking plant in the Fair Grounds race track, New Orleans, and at Montgomery Park, Memphis, Tennessee. He was singularly prosperous at both spots, but one day he was discovered to be laying heavy odds against horses with whose jockeys he had prearranged their stoppage, while betting considerably on others for whose jockeys he had made friendly wagers. This led to his requested departure, but he little wreaked. We find him a year later as the builder, owner and operator of the sumptuous Arkansas Jockey Club, Little Rock, Arkansas, where he was both judge and jury at all times.

"He was a rare good fellow, and as expatriates from the southland we were mighty glad to see each other. His plethoric pocketbook did not increase the size of his head, and he was always full of schemes.

"After the customary salutation and the setup of new drinks by the impeccably white-appareled man behind the stick, the fat is in the fire with Mr. Brolaski dilating, with great and convincing fervor, upon the opportunity which now presented itself, whereby we two could now make a whole ton of money, without hurting anybody, says he, particularly ourselves. So we talked and talked, with many a relation of an experience shared interlarded in the intercourse to leaven the sales approach my old friend is waging unremittingly at thirty-four strokes to the minute.

"After the third Ramos gin fizz, a drink chosen as appropriate to a southland reunion, Mr. Brolaski divulged to me that he was the inceptor of a potential mint called the Great American Hog Syndicate. The beginning of the war, he pointed out, had jumped pork prices sky-high, Europe had to buy here to feed its armies, and if we went in, which he thought, with perspicuity, likely, we would have to feed an army of millions as well as civilian war workers, with plenty Tease to exchange for nourishment. 'Pork is the big chance, the main chance right now,' he said, and adduced in evidence the evening newspaper which showed that prime bacon was bringing seventy-six cents a pound as compared with twenty-four the year before. Please remember that I quote these prices from memory, so do not vouch for their exactitude, but that was the general idea.

"I said that might be all right for people without any imagination, like the Swifts and Armours, but how did it concern us? Harry looked at me reproachfully, and I am lucky that he did not konk me with the cane, which concealed within its ebon sheath a keen Toledo blade.

"His idea was fraught with that divine simplicity that denotes genius," the Colonel said, after an interim marked by the partial demolition of a portion of chicken in the pot with broth and noodles.

"At the fourth round we deem it better to sit down at a table in order better to comprehend the inviting opportunity offered by the incubating enterprise to make money in large gobs without too much exertion and no risk whatsoever.

"But before beginning operations, Mr. Brolaski divulges, he needs a farm of at least six hundred acres within an hour's motor ride of San Francisco. He must have two offices in a prestigious building and we must have ten grand for newspaper advertising. If I can supply these requisites, he says, I'm in for fifty-fifty. Generosity was never the quality for which this old Brolaski was most noted."

The Colonel tore elegantly at a drumstick and then said:

"Peculiarly enough I was in a position to comply with these demands."

"How?" I asked naturally enough.

"A Long Rider's most precious resource is a well-catalogued mental file of acquaintances," the Colonel replied. "A good friend should not be lightly used, but put away in a drawer like a good pair of pajamas, for use on a special occasion. But I shall not denoue the identity at this moment. De Mossopont once wrote that more than half the value of a story was dependent upon the maintenance of suspense, and I concur.

"It is enough at this point to say that within two days we had a suite of three offices on the ninth floor of the Crocker Building,—conveniently across the street from the Palace with its mighty bar,—and on the cuff. In a week more we're installed, with 'Great American Hog Syndicate' lettered with chaste flamboyancy across all the doors and front windows, and a staff of six handy people hired on. Behind us we have a one-year lease on a farm of twelve hundred acres at Millbrae, California, just twice the size stipulated by the wily gambling man. I also have a bank roll not of ten grand but of twenty-five hundred dollars, promoted from the same beneficent source and origin.

"We decide to invest twelve hundred of it in newspaper advertising the following Sunday."

By now the Colonel had me, and I crudely asked, "What was the scheme?"

"The first effort in preparing a sale," the Colonel said, "should be to stimulate curiosity. But I shall be clement." He ordered two coffees and, by excepiton to his rule of the Great Transition, a couple of brandies, and then said:

"I threw together the advertising display copy and it had a pull like a horny-handed backwoods dentist. I knew just how to talk to my public, having been successfully advertising 'sun-drenched apartments' for years in San Francisco, city of mists, where the sun never shines. It is what people haven't got enough of that they want to read about in advertisements. The sunshine is an example. One thing they never have in sufficient quantity anywhere is easy money. The Monday after the Sunday on which our copy ran in both *Examiner* and *Chronicle*, the corridor in front of our office was packed-jammed with boobs holding money in their hands. They couldn't wait lest they be short-circuited, excluded from this heaven-sent opportunity.

"It was a unique proposition, entirely fair and on the face of it sure to pan out good."

"All right," I said. "Put me down for one hundred shares and tell me what the scheme was."

The Colonel held up a reproving palm.

"No shares," he said. "Units. There was an important legal difference. The screaming advertisements, in effective position next to vitalized reading matter, bore the modest suggestion that Pork is King, and His Majesty has it in mind to make the reader rich and happy through a moderate investment in what might turn out to be a modern Golconda;—turning the poor into the rich, the depressed into the elated and all is to be as merry as a wedding bell.

"In my early copy-writing esquisays," Colonel Stingo said, after knocking back his brandy, "I modeled my style upon that of a man named Dr. James W. Kidd, a savant of Fort Wayne, Indiana, but a national advertiser.

" 'After years of patient study and delving into the dusty records of the past, as well as following modern experiments in the realm of medical science, Dr. James W. Kidd, Fort Wayne, Indiana, makes the startling announcement that he has surely discovered the elixir of life. State what you want to be cured of, and the sure remedy for it will be sent you free by return mail.' "

"Listen," I said, but was put off by the reproving palm again.

"Be no longer impatient," said the Colonel. "Here it is. The proposition, so adroitly, and with utmost native caution, worked out by the illustrious Mr. Brolaski, invited the reader to undertake an investment of two hundred dollars in the purchase of a unit partnership in the Great American Hog Syndicate. This, it elaborated, was a movement in furtherance of the laudable purpose of supporting the food creation campaign so necessary to our national survival in a time of crisis. Once a unit partner, the subscriber became a half owner of a high-blooded sow which the incorporated Syndicate agrees to maintain in reginal splendor at its farm in the Santa Clara Valley.

"It is important to note that the subscriber would not acquire a share in the Syndicate itself,—just in the hog.

"In addition to this commitment the subscribing unit partner would be entitled to the ownership of one half the litter of the aforesaid sow during her fecund lifetime,—generally two years. On its part the Syndicate pledged itself to acquire and maintain in stud ten of the best boars from the sales and catalogue of the National Hog Breeders Association, Kansas City, Missouri. They were to be of the finest bloodlines extant, viz.,—Berkshire, Cochin China, and Hertfordshire, with a dash of St. Simon and an outcross to the line of Commando.

"Our pulsating Syndicate did business with Long Brothers & Pidgeon, Kansas City, Missouri, in buying these ten porcine monarchs.

"On the first day of business we took in just thirty-two subscriptions to unit partnership, sixty-four hundred dollars, encouraging. But on the next day we took but one, and that by dint of concerted persuasion reinforced by a gratuitous libation at the Palace bar when the boob seemed on the point of withdrawal. It was obvious that the Hog Syndicate was the sort of promotion that must have continuously plenty of newspaper space. In such circumstances it was the wont of the great Ricecakes to use the incoming money with which to buy more display pages, a dangerous practice if carried to extremes, like continual reliance upon strong stimulants. Because of my longer and more congenial association with the newspaper racket, I improved upon this device.

"Within a week of our establishment, the Oakland, California, *Daily Post-Enquirer* thought the enterprise so unique and praiseworthy that it deserved news treatment, resulting in a two-column spread with a double-decker head and drop sublines enlivened by a startling picture of Red Alexis II, the Gold Cup winner at the New York State Fair in Syracuse in the Berkshire class. He was the Best Hog in Show, too, and had earned during the year in prize money thirty-two hundred dollars including a small purse in a trotting race and fifty dollars for fighting a pit bull terrier.

"WILL THE GREAT RED ALEXIS II COME TO CALIFORNIA?"

the headline demanded. The story, written by an enthusiastic dairy farmer named John R. Stingo, went on to say that our Great American Hog Syndicate had made an offer of six thousand dollars for Red Alexis II but without avail.

"It was the highest price ever quoted on a blue-blooded prize-winning boar in this country, and, of course, other newspapers followed with stories and layouts on the matter, all most beneficial in stimulating the sales campaign of the Great American Hog Syndicate. The newspaper stories were embellished by accounts of the reporters' visits to our on-the-level indubitably tangible farm, where Mr. Brolaski had installed a never-failing supply of bourbon whiskey under the governance of an agriculturist known on eastern race tracks as the Millionaire Kid. The Kid was glib with the figures on hog prolification. He had dutched many a book in his time, taking thirteen to five in thousands and laying it back at eleven to five, thus insuring against loss while retaining the chance of a handsome profit. He was therefore well qualified to bedazzle even the mathematically expert, especially after plying them with nectar, and the stories reflected the roseate impression the Millionaire Kid managed to slip the pressmen.

"We reinforced this free publicity, which is the best kind, with a regular salvo of paid space on Sundays, and we mowed them down. Mr. Brolaski, betraying an unbecoming lack of confidence in me, moved to bring the Millionaire Kid into the office as money taker. He himself was not qualified to occupy the spotlight, since he had a record as long as Bob Fitzsimmons' arm, and public confidence might waver if he were identified on the premises of our public-spirited venture.

"After six weeks of drum-thumping we finally offered Long Brothers & Pidgeon the spot-cash sum of eight thousand dollars,—our final bid,—for prodigious Alexis. He weighed 464 pounds, or perhaps 1,464,—memory grows furtive, and I don't think I've seen a live pig since my one porcicultural experience. He was quite young, coming up to his two-year-old season with engagements in all stakes, as I remember. In his first time at bat he had fathered seven litters of eighty-four little pigs, which is perfect, like a score of three hundred at bowling, for the mother pig is equipped with but twelve outlets for nutritional contact with the young, and a thirteenth piglet would starve to death. The residuum of information from my avatars is variegated. All this statistical data caused Mr. Brolaski to smack his thin cruel lips in contemplation of what the leviathanic Alexis would do when given a chance at the beauty chorus of piquant young sows we were assembling.

"To our surprise and delight an acceptance came through from Kansas City by wire."

20 / *Enter, the Duchess*

MY CURIOSITY now at fever heat, I demanded of the Colonel, "But who was your backer? Abe Ruef?"

He smiled cryptically, and then, with quasi-parental indulgence, said, "Since the purpose of my narration is not to beguile but instruct, I shall sacrifice at this point the veiling concealment which is the pointer-upper of the storyteller's art. With a bow to De Mossopont, whose precept I am violating, I will allow you in."

He ordered a replenishment of the aquavital supply, and said:

"It was a beautiful woman. She was a Nouvelle-Orléanaise, a true Creole, of an admixture of Spanish, Irish and Italian blood, known to me in my cub days on the *Item* as a glorious ornament of my native city.

"In her late twenties then, she was tall, dark and winsome. Willowy as a reed in the Babylonian Gardens, she was sophisticated and daring. Her true name, Frances Miro Valin, her father had amassed a fine competency in cotton and passed on as chairman of the board of a mighty steamship company. Miss Valin, our the Duchess, among her members of family and circle of friends was addressed with appreciation and affection as Frankie but in no time became known upon two continents as the Duchess. She had lost no time in precipitating a career, for she had married into the proud and brave blood of the celebrated Torlonia family of Rome and Naples, one of the foremost industrial components in the economic fibre of Italy. In the fourth year of her married life, coming to New Orleans with her noble Italian husband and her young son for a brief visit, she lost her husband, who succumbed to yellow fever. She had then migrated to California. There she had been again married, again widowed, and when our paths crossed once more there she was in her mid-forties but still enchanting,—a solitary, haunting figure."

The Colonel took a pensive slug, sighed, and continued.

"Her second husband had been one of the California Midasei, a man of coruscant wealth," he said. "Name of William Sutro Tevis, heir to a monumental concentration of Tease. At their residence of true ducal aspect, Hillsborough House, Santa Clara Valley, the Duchess held lonely court.

"We had many old touches to cut up together and we got to be great pals. The world of the Long Riders enchanted her, although she had no incentive to participate, being incurably holding. She just wanted the fun and distraction that a rich lonely woman sometimes craves. A wealthy woman, she was a power in her own right, and one of the most remarkable characters who ever lived." Colonel Stingo sighed again, and ground the end of his lighted cigarette into the ash tray, as if extinguishing the embers of an ambition he had never dared acknowledge at the moment of possibly fruitful temerity. Later I learned that during his San Francisco days he led a commendably uxorious married life.

"One characteristic thing about her, I recall," he said, "she appeared always to be lonely, searching for somebody she never seemed to find.

"When Mr. Brolaski popped his proposition, I thought of the Duchess instantly. So down to Santa Clara station I scamper next morning after duly informing the Duchess of my coming. She laughed and laughed and willingly proffered the necessary help, on condition she be allowed participation in the inner councils of the enterprise, for she liked to be on the inside of everything. All financial assistance, however, was to be in the shape of loans. Her position did not allow direct involvement in the enterprise. It was she who arranged for the farm, the offices and the initial wad. Her native caution, as intense in its way as Mr. Brolaski's, had caused her to limit the amount to twenty-five hundred dollars, lest Harry lam with the scratch.

"The journalistic furor about Red Alexis, however, and the resulting gusher of boobish Tease, hinting at the vast reservoirs still untapped, indicated to her that we had good cards to draw to, and she willingly shoved over another stack of chips. She advanced another ten thousand for purchase of Red Alexis II, but insisted we give a note to the small local bank for that amount, bearing six per cent interest. When Brolaski heard that he bellowed like a harpooned behemoth. He said he had thought of the Duchess as a sister, and now she was demanding his signature on a legal document.

"But these preliminary bellowings were nothing compared to those the great man emitted when it dawned upon him in due course that he had failed to pin upon Long Brothers & Pidgeon the onus of safe delivery and competent attendance for Red Alexis during his long trip from the Mississippi Valley. Finally, a Dr. Shepherd, a California veterinarian of repute, was engaged at a five-hundred-dollar fee and expenses to escort Big Alex to his new home at Millbrae.

"Meanwhile I had indulged in a staccato of cogitation, and come up with an idea worthy of a P. T. Barnum, of Cecil de Mille. A civic and state reception for the monster swine came to mind as a natural. The concept impressed both the Duchess and Mr. Brolaski. We agreed that there should be a representative committee of reception, and the Duchess's feminine flair for the aesthetic really developed an angle in conjunction therewith; it was that the members of the committee should all wear long red-and-gold badges and bright shiny opera hats.

"At this juncture, although protected in every case by the statute of limitations, I shall not explain the why and wherefore, but the Great American Hog Syndicate, Inc., did enjoy, even in moments that might otherwise have proved distressing,—a kind, friendly and generous press. This is a most essential circumstance in all undertakings in which the Long Riders engage.

"After five days' travel in a palace horse car, all to himself, Dr. Shepherd and an attendant, the royal Red Alexis II came home to California in all the regal glory of an ancient Caesar returning from the Carthaginian wars a mighty conqueror to receive his people's homage in spontaneous outburst of love, admiration and affection.

"This Big Alex had to be bathed twice a day, a fresh bed of imported Argentine grass laid down nightly and to satisfy his temperament not be left alone.

"The day of days had come to hand. At the snug little station of the Southern Pacific Railroad at Santa Clara, near San Jose, there had gathered the reception committee, headed by the sixty-piece band of the University of Leland Stanford, Jr., and Senator James D. Phelan, Lieutenant Governor Frank J. Moffat, representing our dear friend, Governor 'Jim' Rolph, solid citizens, crums, bums and sharpshooters in large number, buttressed by all the cameramen that Mr. Hearst's ponderous San Francisco *Examiner* could level on the momentous event, plus an army of reporters and special writers. In fact, Annie Laurie, the famous sob sister, long identified with the Hearstian press, was there as the guest of the Duchess, together with other of her friends, including Mrs. William H. Crocker, Mrs. Charles Stuart Howard, Ethel Barrymore, Helen Wills, little Poker Face, and Kathleen Winsor, youthfully innocent then, with no indication at hand of the guileful sophistication of *Forever Amber* to come some years later.

"A passer-by enquired audibly,—'What's the occasion? Who is coming home today?'

"Someone answered,—'Mr. Herbert Hoover.'

"Apparently satisfied, the interrogator went on his unlearned and elfin way, gratified at the gladsome scene.

"Mr. Washington Dodge, Jr., the cashier at the bank where we negotiated the ten thousand dollars through the gracious help of the Duchess, acted as chairman of the reception committee and made a nice speech but spoke more about Mr. Rolph's bright chances for re-election as Governor than an espousal and character study of Red Alexis II.

"Of course Mr. Brolaski, approaching the speaker's stand, where he would be in full view of friend or enemy, came forward mincingly, for who knew, there might lurk there an ancient foe from Arkansas who perchance might accord him leaden recognition, which would not be viewed as a buoyant circumstance in the upward climb of the Great American Hog Syndicate, Inc.

"Luckily there ensued no fusillade, indicating he had not been recognized, nor were any visiting prison wardens or sheriffs among the invited guests to call attention to his heroic past, so the occasion was unmarred.

" 'I am just a simple hog farmer,' Harry told the assembled multitude, 'unaccustomed to address such distinguished gatherings. But I am here to tell you that the Great American Hog Syndicate is going to bring home the bacon.' It is impossible to be too corny on such occasions, and the rustic Santa Clarans applauded as if for David Warfield. Senator Phelan said to me, sitting beside him on the platform, 'Who is that man? He would have a great future in politics.' "

At this point I made a tactical mistake which I have since learned not to duplicate when I wish the Colonel to maintain the tenor of a narration.

"I saw Helen Wills play at Forest Hills in 1922 when she was still in pigtails," I said. "She was supposed to be fourteen years old and looked it. That would make her six at the time of the reception. And Kathleen Winsor must be even younger."

"I can see," the Colonel answered, "that you are essentially interested in the unessential, a spoilsport. You will remind me next that Caesar did not partake in the Carthaginian wars. If you know better than I do who was at the reception, why don't you tell me about it? I have made my submission. I await your rebuttal."

The Colonel, as I was to learn from reading his column as well as listening to him, shares with the painters of the *quattrocento* and *cinque-*

cento the practice of placing favorite contemporaries in his historical canvases. It amuses him.

It does not detract from the verity of a martyrdom by Mantegna or his great contemporary, Calamaretti di Posilipo, that the face of the officiating centurion is that of the artist's greengrocer, whom he liked, while the holy man getting the works displays the distorted but recognizable countenance of the landlord who had him dispossessed for throwing empty wine jugs out of the window at the watch.

Nor, to cite an example from "Yea Verily," does it take away from the Colonel's word picture of the great race between Man o' War and John P. Grier that in his enumeration of those watching the finish that day in 1920 he placed me between Samuel D. Riddle, Man o' War's owner, and Kentucky Babe, a light lady from Louisville who had been associated with the Australian prize fighter, Young Griffo, in 1895. I didn't even see the race. What made the piece great reporting, though, was the Colonel's description of the sleek millionaire, a ringer for Samuel Seabury in white-haired, rubicund dignity, seeing John P. Grier gain for a few strides on his immortal champion. "The hair on the back of Mr. Riddle's neck stood straight up," the Colonel wrote, "like the bristles on the back of an enraged Deer Creek porcupine."

This is a labyrinthian digression.

On this particular evening at Moore's, though, I was sobered, or nearly sobered, by the impasse into which my brashness had got me. In calling attention to what I had misinterpreted as unwitting anachronism, I had jeopardized my chance of ever finding out what happened to the Great American Hog Syndicate.

"Please by-pass the interjection," I said. "I have a compulsive habit of blabbing out the irrelevant."

The Colonel was mollified but still hurt, like a boxer whose opponent offers to shake hands at the end of the round after sticking a thumb in his eye. He said, "Let's get out of this dump. It's getting on my nerves."

When we emerged and headed for an institution known as the Formerly Club, the Colonel looked about him appreciatively at the double alignment of marquees, stage doors, saloons and restaurants that forms Moore's block on Forty-sixth Street. "What a mighty and wonderful city," he said. "I'd die on the vine anyplace else."

As we took our way down Eighth Avenue to the Formerly, he continued in the same strain. "Some Friday nights I sit up in my room at the Dixie," he said. "Working away on my column. I finish, and it is perhaps one o'clock. If I were sagacious, I would put on my hat and go to bed. I always keep an old felt hat by my bedside," he said, "because I like to sleep with my windows wide open, and bedclothes make no provision for the protection of the thinly veiled cranium. The brain, like Rhenish wine, should be chilled, not iced, to be at its best. Women, however, are best at room temperature.

"Up there in my retreat I feel the city calling to me," he said. "It winks at me with its myriad eyes, and I go out and get stiff as a board. I seek out companionship, and if I do not find friends I make them. A wonderful grand old Babylon."

The story of the Great American Hog Syndicate apparently was finished for that night, but scarcely had we arrived at the bar and ordered drinks,—the Colonel reverting to his Gambrinian conservatism,—when there occurred a manifestation corroborating one area of my friend's reminiscences.

For as long as I could remember,—and I had been almost a founding member of the Formerly,—one of the peripheral personages there had been an old ex-bookmaker named Benny. Suffering from some wasting malady that closed in on him slowly from year to year, he became with each lustre more spectral, his nose longer in proportion to the rest of his face, the veins on his wrists more prominent. The doctors had got all his money. It is the only way they can beat the books, being notoriously incompetent horse players. Benny would earn an occasional skin by placing a bet for one of the patrons of the Formerly. If the bettor won he might slip Benny a buck, and if he lost Benny might get a commission from the bookmaker. It wasn't much of a living, since the Formerly is chiefly patronized by newspapermen, who are two-dollar bettors. But Benny might have had a couple of other places of call.

The Colonel and I had just bellied up to the bar, like Mr. Mori and his friends in "Yea Verily," when Benny entered, returning from some mysterious mission of small import. Waves of recognition passed between the two old men and they grabbed each other by the shoulders, as if they had been dressed in funny clothes and attending their fortieth reunion at Old Nassau.

"I haven't seen you since 1906, when we were both running for that train out of New Orleans," Benny said.

"I made it," said the Colonel.

"You were always an all-around athlete," Benny said admiringly. "I missed it, but I got out on a banana boat."

"This fellow used to win bets on how fast he could run around the block," he told me. "He'd race you around the block for a round of drinks."

The Colonel smiled at this evocation of his agility.

"The circumstances suggested the advisability of a hurried departure," he said. "We had touted Dynamite Jack Thornby onto a horse that had failed to justify our confidence. It had been well meant, but dear old Dynamite was irascible, and we thought it best to let him cool out."

Benny had been rapidly taking stock of the Colonel's appearance, which was debonair, and the Colonel had been casing Benny, too. It was obvious their fortunes were at this point disparate, but the Colonel fortunately remembered something to his old friend's advantage.

"I had completely forgotten that sawbuck you let me have on getaway day at Bennings the previous spring," he said. "Here it is and God bless you," and he shoved a crumpled bill into Benny's hand.

"I never thought twice about it," Benny said.

I am pretty sure he had never thought once.

This was the incident that first made me suspect the sincerity of the Colonel's representations.

It reminded me of the time I took a distinguished Armenian-American author of my acquaintance to call on an astute Armenian-British friend in London. The author opened, in English, with several of those naïve, sunny sentences that light his prose with a happy, childlike glow. My friend parried with banal observations indicative of a dull, heavy mind. Suddenly they broke into Armenian and for about twenty minutes fired volley for volley in the tongue of Tigranes the Great. Disengaging, they returned to discoursing English amenities open to the rest of the company, and when the author left the room for a moment, I asked my friend what he thought of him.

"He is what we call a false fool," the host answered. "He is really very intelligent."

Walking back across the green park in the blackout, I asked the author what he thought of my friend.

"He's a nice guy," the author said, "but who does he think he's kidding? He's not dumb."

I had an intimation that the Colonel might be a false Long Rider.

The intimation was confirmed years later when I met a man who had known the Colonel in his San Francisco days. "Jimmy Macdonald has been playing cops and robbers all his life," the man said. "He likes to think of himself as a Robin Hood, but he is really a Santa Claus.

"I hit San Francisco in 1911, as a young man of twenty-one, and went into the outdoor advertising business with a chum my own age. We had to buck what amounted to a national monopoly, the two big firms that controlled billboard space all over the United States. Any national advertiser who rented our boards would find himself denied billboard space in all the territories where we didn't operate. So we got only local accounts, and we were paid in whatever the advertiser peddled,—whiskey, automobile tires, hotel rooms or ready-made clothing. Then we in turn had to sell our takings. Jimmy was a man about town then, noted for his patent-leather shoes and his New York air, and he used to go out of his way to introduce us to saloonkeepers who would buy our whiskey. He even gave us a job selling advertising on the *Wasp*, so that we could pick up a bit of cash on the side.

"I'll never forget one day when the three of us, none well heeled, despite Jimmy's imposing exterior, were walking over from our office in the Crocker Building to the Palace Hotel bar for a drink, and the most awful human wreck I've ever seen came along, without even enough energy to panhandle. Mac walked up to him politely, handed him a ten-dollar bill and said, 'Pardon me, I think you dropped this.' Then we went into the bar and rolled dice with the bartender for the drinks. Luckily we won."

When I repeated this to the Colonel, he sulked and hinted he had once helped Al Jennings rob a train.

21 / Da Sissantina

I MET WITH the Colonel several times more before I could get him to resume the story of the Great American Hog Syndicate, about which I had by now developed a curiosity of my own. I could not see what there was about the scheme which would redound to the disadvantage of the customers, and I would have suspected the Colonel of conducting a legitimate enterprise, if I had not known that in that case he would never have mentioned it.

On occasions I expressed my misgivings to him, but he maintained a mien inscrutable, having returned, he said, to the axiom of De Mossopont that the element of surprise must be reserved for the last round in order to make a showing and catch the eyes of the referee and judges just before they render a decision. "The referee and judges in the case of a narration, either spoken or written, being the auditors or readers, as the case may be," the Colonel said, "and especially those readers who come under the classification of potential investors.

"I will concede," he said, "that the enterprise had a reassuring aspect of benevolence, since it was based on a well-known phenomenon,—the tendency of animals to proliferate, which was traditionally exploited by the patriarchs of Biblical days,—sheepherders all of them. This has imbued animal husbandry with such a respectable air that people who would shy off from gilt-edged copper stock will sink their all in a chicken farm, a vastly more speculative form of investment. The American Hog Syndicate had this quirk running for it.

"I myself, in an anterior period of my life, had devoted time, if not money, to the promotion of an enterprise known as the Mid-Continental Chinchilla Rabbitry, under the aegis of a figurator named Kelly Mason, who had become entranced by the multipular possibilities of those rodents. In Kelly's mind it presented the aspect of a progressive bet, or endless winning parlay. He had read in some newspaper, doubtless discarded by somebody else on the seat adjoining Kelly's in a race train, for he himself never purchased anything but the racing form, that the air and track conditions in Kansas were so favorable to rabbits that the state was spending thousands of dollars in the form of bounties for their extirpation. 'That,' he said to himself, 'is of a surety the place to breed rabbits.' He had seen two of these animals in a pet-shop window, marked at fifty cents apiece. Further inquiry instructed him that rabbit pelts were used in the manufacture of hatter's felts and a fur called royal seal,—there was a market for them as illimitable as for four to one against Roseben.

"He leased a farm of twenty-two acres near Wichita, Kansas, after asking the yokel who leased it to him specifically whether it was good rabbit ground. He installed hatches, a kind of coop covered with earth to make the rabbits feel at home. They are so denominated, I suppose, because the rabbits hatch their young therein. The rabbits needed little encouragement; they spawned monstrously. Kelly made contracts with furriers in Kansas City, Missouri, and with hatmakers in Danbury, Connecticut, to take all his output, but as the production increased, like a mighty gusher of oil it proves impossible to cap, he had to sell farther afield, his operations reaching the Brunswick-Balke-Collender Company, manufacturers of billiard tables, which are of course felt-covered, and also Luchow's Restaurant, the Blue Ribbon, Hans Jaeger's and the Hofbrau, New York; the Golden Ox, Chicago; and the Techau Tavern, San Francisco, all manufacturers of *hasenpfeffer*.

"Things began to look so good that Kelly sent for me to undertake a campaign of national promotion, but on the very day of my arrival we were visited by a representative of a newspaper who demanded Kelly buy a full-page ad, reading simply, 'Compliments of a Friend.' I remonstrated that this did not seem to me the type of pulling copy we needed. It said nothing about our wares. 'It better not,' the small-town newspaperman said, 'since there is a state law that makes it a misdemeanor to raise rabbits in the state of Kansas, imposing a fine of five dollars, or three days in jail for each rabbit so produced. You probably owe about sixty thousand dollars now, if anyone wanted to get tough about it.' We took the ad, and business went on as usual for a couple of weeks when another dumb rural newsman appeared from the sheet published in the seat of the adjoining county. He said they were getting out their annual centennial edition. Every year is the centennial of something, he said. He wanted two pages of complimentary advertising. So we gave him that.

"After awhile the sheriff came over for a contribution to his campaign fund, and then the fellow who was running against him, and a committee of ladies from a Congregational Church, who said it was so nice having us in the area, they knew we would be glad to donate five hundred dollars to build new pews. Then eventuated delegations from the Campbellites, and the River Brethren and the Methodists and the Greek Orthodox. They were all on the shake. Even the WCTU got us for a grand." The Colonel looked glum. "Even a stick-up man will let you keep coffee-money," he said, "but not a woman engaged in God's work.

"The reason for the ban, we learned, was that rabbits are prone to escape,—they become stir-crazy, although not, like the poor souls at Alcatraz, sexually deprivated. It is a wonder to me," the Colonel said, "that they had any energy left. Having escaped, they would proliferate extramurally, thus nullifying the efforts of the state to exterminate them. They were a menace to the great universal granary, the Kansas wheat fields. They cost more than Professor Hatfield with his Gatling gun.

"Our rabbits kept right on breeding," he said, "unaware that their activities were without legal sanction, and Kelly continued to market the pelts, because he had a bite to meet every time a strange Ford honked at the gate. He figurated by now if anybody sang he was in for a million and a half dollars in fines, nine hundred thousand days in durance laborious. 'I haven't the heart to think of it in years,' he said, 'but it's a long rap.'

"Eventually the rube who was renting him the place came around and told him he had broken the lease by conducting illegal activities, but it would be all right if Kelly and I cut him in for fifty per cent.

"That was the day before the night Kelly got drunk with the husband of the president of the WCTU and they turned all the rabbits loose.

" 'I don't want any incriminating evidence left on the place when the law comes,' Kelly told this good old countryman, so after they had run a tractor through the wire fence that surrounded the Mid-Continental Chinchilla Rabbitry they loosed a pack of beagles on the property. Next morning there wasn't a chinchilla on the farm.

" 'Here is something for your wife,' Kelly said to the benevolent rustic as we climbed into our Winton racer to depart, and he handed him a sawed-off shotgun loaded with deer slugs. The old fellow looked as pleased as a ballplayer accepting a free automobile. He promised to give it an early trial. Within the next year the state of Kansas had to pay out $723,000 additional bounty in that county alone."

The Colonel paused.

"The moral of Mr. Mason's adventure," he said, "if any, may be expressed: 'Never enter a race without reading the condition book carefully.' "

"I should have thought that experience would have made you leery of participation in the Great American Hog Syndicate," I said.

"The circumstances were radically different," the Colonel said. "We had the deal, an inestimable advantage."

The Colonel is a great coffee drinker, being particularly devoted to that black Italian brew, with lemon peel on the side, that is erroneously supposed to be conducive to insomnia. He sleeps like a lungfish.

On the evening when the Mid-Continental Chinchilla Rabbitry came to his mind, we were sitting in the Red Devil on West Forty-eighth Street, a deservedly crowded place at dinner hours, but tranquil as you could wish once the theatre crowd has gone.

The Colonel ordered a third cup of coffee and looked so soulful that I divined he was thinking of the Duchess. I thought this was a favorable moment to animadvert to the Great American Hog Syndicate, and it proved so.

"You were just beginning to tell me about the reception for Red Alexis II at Millbrae," I said, "the last time we talked about your venture with Mr. Harry Brolaski."

"Ah, yes," the Colonel said, softly. "An occasion unforgettable. To be observed all through the activities at the Southern Pacific Railroad station and the rest of the eventual day of days is a naughty twinkle in the eye of the Duchess. This is her day, and resolved she is to enjoy it to the full. The furor at the station is but hors d'oeuvre. Scarce returned to the New House in the foothills of the Coast Range, filigreed in a forested park of redwoods, fifteen hundred acres in extent, our Duchess, the perfect chatelaine, is beaming in exaltation at the thought that here now is to come the crescendo of the home-coming-of-Red Alexis festivities.

"The great manor house, a sixty-two-room job, with a ballroom as large as the Crystal Room, Hotel Ritz Carlton, New York, had undergone a special furbishment for the occasion. The splash, I afterward learned, cost her sixty-two hundred dollars, which constitutes but a trivial item when set, back to back, against an annual income from vast inherited holdings.

"So here we are at the great table, a huge oaken plank affair, 18 feet by 5, purchased by the late Frederick Charles Crocker, builder of New House, for thirty-five thousand dollars translated into pounds, from Christie's, London, many years gone by. It was originally in Tower Hall, the residence of Henry VIII at Bath, even today a favorite watering place in succoring the gout-afflicted, for centuries the national malady in well-stuffed Blighty."

The Colonel maintained a most serious demeanor. I had already informed him I am subject to attacks of gout, a circumstance which he finds inexhaustibly amusing.

"For luncheon this fine and historically redolent item, the table, is battened with cottoned mats and then overspread with Irish linen tablecloths, inherited by the Duchess from the Torlonia family years prior, and now to be activated in service to his lordship, the prolific American pig. Members of that proudly defiant Savoyan family would flop over in sepulchred rest did they but know the situation of the moment.

"So, in files for luncheon the thirty-three guests led by Mr. Dodge, the banker, and the six other members of the reception committee of the Red Alexis II welcome celebration; all in high silk hats with long red-and-gold badges displayed upon their Prince Albert-coated breasts, an impressive spectacle to be sure; there they be, the State of California sent the lieutenant governor, Mr. Will Crocker, Mr. Dudley Field Malone, Mr. Seabiscuite Howard, and Herb Fleishhacker, mighty men of politics, finance, the law and insurance. As a representative gathering it would serve to background a more consequential event, but the gentlemen were all friends of the Duchess, and it is pertinent to bear in mind their banks, brokerage offices and professional services had been requisitioned by the Duchess to their monetary advantage through the years. Such is life west or east of the Sierra Nevada, a puppetry with the strings pulled by the acquisitive instinct.

"Of course at table head appeared the urbane Mr. Brolaski, wise as a serpent, with all the top cards reposing in his capacious mitt. Dazzling in her happiness, and impatient for the business to begin, sat in queenly poise our the Duchess."

The wall lights at the Red Devil are screened by parchment tambourines, on each of which is recorded some Neapolitan saying the proprietor, Don Ciccio, considers amusing. The Colonel's glance rose to one of these as he sought Ernesto, the waiter, in order to command another cup of coffee. It read: "*Da Vinta a trenta giovane valente.*"

"Are you conversant with the Mediterranean idiom, Joe?" he asked, "and if so, pray what does that mean?"

"From twenty to thirty, a potent young man," I ventured.

"And the next?" asked the Colonel.

"*Da trenta a quaranta valente ma nu tanto,*—from thirty to forty good, but not that good," I approximated.

"Next?" said the Colonel.

"*Da quaranta a cinguanta, nu o crerere si s'avanta,*—from forty to fifty don't believe him if he boasts," I said miserably. This is the line I take most to heart.

"And then?"

"*Da cinguanta a sissanta uno ogni tanto,*—from fifty to sixty just one in a while."

"And the finale?" he demanded, pointing to the last of the row of tambourines on that wall.

"*Da sissantina a sittantina lass' e femmene e piglio o vino,*—from the sixtieth to the seventieth year, abandon women and stick to wine."

The Colonel ruminated a while and then said:

"Who wrote that, Dante? It is one of the saddest passages in all literature."

He ordered the coffee and then said, "Besides, it is prematurely pessimistic. A man of seventy is a mere boy."

22 / The Apotheosis of Alexis

WHEN THE waiter had brought the coffee the Colonel resumed his narration.

"Directly across the table from the Duchess is Mr. Dodge and the other members of the committee ranged and intermingled with the guests round about and on both sides of the huge board, which in its day had heard the flagoon and trencher platter of good King Hal impinge upon its solid fibre," he said.

"The huntsman's trusty sharp-beaked Falcon had fetched the meaty bird and vinters their tumbler of red Kent wine full to brim for ho my lads they lived high in those thumping days of old.[1]

"The ancient oaken planks of the treasured table must have felt *en rapport* as the chattering merriment of present company voculated into their creaky recesses, bringing suggestion that perhaps there yet lived the spirit and the guile of Robin Hood and of Moll of Flanders.[2] After the dishes had been cleared, and the period of pleasantries before guest dispersal had drawn to close, Mr. Brolaski and the Duchess decided much important business affecting the Syndicate would be discharged forthwith.

"And now we're in the smoking room with its high-paneled Tudor oak wainscot and marginal eaves around its expansive walls in the late afternoon of a California summer with its dry but chilly fogs which drift in from Half Moon Bay with the trade winds from the far-stretching Pacific Ocean. Suddenly, as we're seated round about, the butler announces a call at telephone for Mr. Brolaski, now in the midst of the delightful incineration of a genuine Principe de la Porta, from out the recesses of the Duchess' cherished humidor continental. 'No stinker, a real two-dollar torch,' he had boasted to me *sotto voce*.

"Returning to the company's midst this marvelous knight of opportunity brought gleesome news, in effect: 'The Millionaire Kid is on the way down with plenty dirt to spill.'

"So we awaited in expectancy but in no wise allowed this significant development to interrupt the forward trend of business at hand.

"I could see the Duchess was just bursting with some tremendous suggestion which, to her feminine mind, spelled drama and money. After Mr. Brolaski had explained to Mr. Dodge, the genial old codger who initials the credit slips for the teller at the San Mateo National Bank, that a Principe de la Porta has a more aromatic pungency on a 'relight than before,' we cuddled closer and finally came to grips. Looking back over the years it's so consoling to see Mr. Brolaski work in mind's eye. What a man!

"So it came to be the Duchess exploded all of a sudden. Breathlessly, her idea was that a swine evaluated at eight thousand dollars should have a spot in Burke's Peerage with a chronological background befitting a monarch of Berkshirian blood and ancestral distingué.

"He had already proved his capacity as a family man, a very good point in the favor of Red Alexis II.

[1] The Colonel, I fear, is not much of a medievalist. Falcons do not fetch their quarry to the table but stay with it until the falconer arrives with transportation. And Henry VIII drank French wine.

[2] George Borrow's apple woman on London Bridge called her Blessed Mary Flanders.

"He had been received in his new California kingdom with a pomp and circumstance befitting a regal liege.

" 'He ought to hit .336 in this California climate,' chimed in Mr. Dodge. 'And he is going to have nothing but chic young sows,' emphasized the Duchess, now about to retire at any moment to reappear outfitted in blue jeans and shoulder braces befitting any up-to-date manager of an American-type breeding-farm swinery.

"We had received so far bounteous publicity and the fullest co-operation from the newspapers, and Mr. Brolaski remained perfectly aware of the necessity of a continuance of that generous attitude on the part of the gazettes. On three long draws off the Principe de la Porta the cogitating president came to surface with this one; he said, with glee in his eye and competency in his voice, 'I'll tell what it is. We name this Big Red after William Randolph Hearst.'

"So it came to be that Red Alexis II, as he appears registered in the American National Swine Breeders' Association Stud Book, fell heir to a new and glorious nomenclature,—William Randolph Hearst. The Hearsts and the Stingos are only collaterally related, I may say, the two middle-name Randolphs having been mere acquaintances on their respective mothers' sides.

"Now then the butler announces Danny Haggerty, the Millionaire Kid. His affluence having come to a terminancy with the collapse of racing in New York, the Kid had come to California in that great diaspora of talent which followed the cruel Hughes holocaust, like the dispersion of the Huguenots following the revocation of the Edict of Nantes. New York, like the France of Louis XIV, lost many of its keenest minds after this triumph of intolerance."

The Colonel looked glum for a moment.

"The city has never entirely recovered," he said. "Only last week I was having a light collation of lentil-and-pasta soup and beef *braciola* at the Antica Trattoria Roman, near the Criminal Courts building, and encountered Francesco Salerno, an old friend of mine engaged in the bail-bond business.

" 'You must be in a flourishing condition, Frank,' I vouchsafed to him. 'The papers record a multitude of arrests, and high bail is set in almost every case.' 'It don't do me any good,' he replied. 'I would not write a bond for the cheap-class crooks they got nowadays. They skip.'

"It all started with Charles Evans Hughes," the Colonel said. "In American history he will rank with the chestnut blight.

"Well, to return to the main thread of dissertation, the Millionaire Kid is just chuck full of news respecting the day's operations in the offices of the Great American Hog Syndicate up in San Francisco. The headline publicity about the preparations for the arrival of big Alex has served as a hypodermic for sales, we hope.

"Mr. Brolaski, so eager to hear about it he rests the Principe de la Porta in its dying and fragant stages upon one of the Duchess's heavy Venetian gold-encrusted ash trays, arises with both hands in his money pockets. 'Is the news good, Kid, and how much, tell me quick, Kid,' Mr. Brolaski kept volleying as he approached the lone traveler.

"As the Millionaire Kid drew from his black pocket case a roll of bills a cheetah couldn't jump over, I thought Mr. Brolaski would revert to cannibalism and devour the Kid alive—boots, hat and all.

"He kept pushing and jabbing his forefinger into the Kid's mid-section, forcing him half around the table while we all looked on in amazement. Finally, the Kid sidles into a chair belching the latest advice from the battlefield's front lines in bated and hurried respiration. Mr. Brolaski, meanwhile, in menacing attitude, looking down upon his victim much after the manner of a Siamese cat surveying a captured mouse.

"Proclaimed the Kid in triumphant tone: 'We did sixteen subscriptions, and the take was thirty-two hundred today, with two hours to go. I have eleven hundred dollars in cash here and the checks I leave up in the office safe. Thought you might be wanting some of the ready, and here it is. I've got to have a cut of it myself before leaving you all.'

"Drawing himself up to a commanding poise the pleased master promoter,—how he relished that designation,—replied, 'Well, Kid, I see you took all necessary steps to assure yourself that the money would be available. You leave me without an alibi. Now I'm slipping you five hundred.'

"The Millionaire Kid thanked Mr. Brolaski, briefly but pointedly: 'That's so good of you, Mr. Brolaski,' he said. 'Three hundred would have been O.K.'

"I'll never forget the reaction on the master promoter's well-weathered face, the storms of the centuries behind it, as the realization of the Kid's remark arose within his comprehension. Fleecy clouds lacing the blue summer skies suddenly displaced by a black intruder from nowhere with the depressive forewarning of rain and bluster. But nothing happened.

"With the Millionaire Kid gone and on his way, we all reverted to the matters of moment concerning the destiny of the Great American Hog Syndicate.

"We long ago had figured that an average of ten subscriptions a day, a take of two thousand dollars, would be tops. Now it looked as if we might exceed this. To supply the necessary number of little piggies to offset this phenomenally rapid growth of the business would require more than one William Randolph Hearst at royal court.

"This wonderful Mr. Brolaski, with all the brains and nerve in the world, had overlooked nothing. At the very moment of our social amenities at New House as the guests of the Duchess, the master has working under lights until far into the night at the offices of the Great American Hog Syndicate two young actuaries from the Equitable Life Assurance Society, poring over an overwhelming number of figures cryptic to the layman, but to them reassuring right down to the last decimal point on blue- and red-lined paper marked out in quadrilaterals to keep them from going blind. They were being checked by Kid Bloggs, the same figure man I had employed in behalf of the rainmakers.

"We the board of directors and strategy of the Great American Hog Syndicate would soon know how many little piggies we must produce, how many boars in the stud, the cost and source of feed, overhead and other esatorica. Already the experts had informed us that when we would reach a thousand unit partnerships we must have twenty-five high-class, well-bred, boars of top prolificigacy, the best that money would buy, to keep the production line moving, and four thousand acres with expert trainers, grooms and exercise boys, or their taxonomic equivalents in the idiom of the hog business.

"It appears the actuaries had it down so fine they told us that after 255 days' operation we could count on at least a net profit of 37.01 per cent with pork on the hoof ruling in the market at Chicago, Kansas City and San Francisco at sixteen cents the pound or better. It was now twenty-eight cents a pound with continual uprise; to what heights nobody could predict beneath heaven's vault. A year later it did reach fifty-seven cents, and two years after that drovers were willing to pay as much as ninety-six cents a pound at the sty with a bonus of a free baseball bat and glove to the seller if a member of the 4-H Club, a nationwide organization of juvenile agriculturists."

Here, as in the episode of the rainmakers, I must trust the Colonel's figures, having no way of checking up on them. The newsprint on which papers of the period were printed is so friable that it crumbles at the touch, or I would look through the commodity price tables for the period of the First World War. I have been unable to get in touch with Kid Bloggs, now said to be an inmate of a blind men's home, where he is running a pea-and-thimble game. What I got out of the Colonel's recitation was, in a general way, that the Great American Hog Syndicate was sucking up a lot of Tease.

"As an office manager," Colonel Stingo said, "the Millionaire Kid was even better than at conning reporters. It was no time until we find him daily lunching with boobs of moment. He was a guest of honor at the weekly luncheon and gabfeist of the Rotary Club, for example, addressing the august assemblage upon the subject of 'Pork is King.' Ostensibly espousing the cause of increased food production in support of war preparedness, he did not fail to emphasize the chance to turn a clever buck in the units of the Great American Hog Syndicate selling at a sacrificial two hundred dollars a throw. All the Mr. Babbitts from Main Street perked an eye and bent an ear at the alluring prospect delineated by the Millionaire Kid.

"They showed an eagerness to try one shot anyway equaled only in enthusiasm by the rainbow trout in springtime as he contemplates the juicy angleworm covering up for the shiny hook in the sunny waters of Valley Junction Creek. The trout has the excuse of hunger resulting from the difficult foraging conditions of the winter," he commented, "but the more replete the boob is with currency the more rapaciously he reaches for another helping.

"Then there was the day when the school children of South San Francisco and their teachers, at the invitation of the Millionaire Kid, visited the farm to see the much vaunted and sensationally advertised and publicized World's Heavyweight Champion Boar, William Randolph Hearst. The cameras snapped and the Duchess, in blue jeans and heavy long boots, surrounded by her society friends from Burlingame and Hillsborough, performed beautifully as the lady of the manor. She even wanted to sing, finally moderating her enthusiasm by directing her secretary, Miss Mary Muffins, to present the leader of the school's twenty-piece brass band with a five-hundred-dollar check.

"Then came that day when Mr. Hearst, moated at San Simeon, 180 miles down the Coast Highway, must be apprised of the honor bestowed upon him by the acceptance of his nationally acclaimed monicker as the name of a very tremendous porker of expensive progenitory capacity.

"Someone had to carry the Message to Garcia and the honor devolved upon the Millionaire Kid, since, we reason, Mr. Hearst, who read his own newspapers and had an elephantine memory, might well recall Mr. Brolaski's oft-implicated name or physiognomy, frequently in the past photographed over such captions as: 'Missing from his usual haunts.' As for that distinguished agriculturist, John R. Stingo, Mr. Hearst would have known him immediately as a horse fellow, and so have doubted the solid gravity of the whole operation. So the Kid tooled down the wonderful new Pacific Coast Highway, around mountain peaks, into green valleys, and then close to the ceaseless hiss of the combing surf, in the special Jaguar job from the garage at New House, as directed by the Duchess. By prearrangement he was waved on by the postilioned castle watch in the medieval arched block house at the foot of the precipitous hill upon which crested the turreted ménage of the mighty dragon of American journalism. The Duchess's writ ran everywhere.

"Once in the presence of the august Caesar Imperator and Heliogabalus combined, the Kid duked him with aplomb. Brevitating his pitch, for the American emperor, always a busy man, had allotted him but one three-minute round, the Kid asked Mr. Hearst whether he objected to the use of his name for the furtherance of the food-production racket,—effort, rather,—he said, retrieving his verbal burble. Mr. Hearst, amused, queried, 'Why hit upon me for the honor? Why not Mr. William Jennings Bryan?'

"The Kid, returning from his mission, reported that he sensed beneath the good humor a modicum of annoyance, and the Kid was highly sensitized to such emotional nuances. His flair had enabled him on a couple of occasions to drop under a table or otherwise escape a second before opponents opened fire.

"I therefore suggested we change the big hog's name to Governor Rolph, as I could not afford to turn the Hearst papers hostile.

"A politician, I knew, would welcome publicity in any form."

23/*The Iron Was Hot*

"As I VIEW retrospectively the progress of the Great American Hog Syndicate," Colonel Stingo said, "it seems to me that the reception for Red Alexis II marked it indubitably with the stigmata of success. From that point on it proceeded on carefully stimulated impetus. We had broken on top, but like a skillful jockey equipped with a stinger we took nothing for granted, applying the whip of high-voltage advertising whenever our enterprise showed signs of going limber.

"A stage soon arrived when, left to my own devices, I would have refused further subscriptions. I trembled in thought of how we were finally going to get out with sails bulging and craft unscuttled. But Mr. Brolaski was insatiable, and the enterprise, moreover, had developed a sordid commercial aspect of tangibility. Within a year of our establishment, we were selling pork on the hoof, tons of it, and sending out dividend checks to the owners of the units that had produced the progeny sold down the river. Had not Mr. Brolaski advised me in advance of a denouement delectable to anticipate, I would have suspected him of embarking me in a simple exercise of entrepreneurage.

"With the rise in the pork market the prices of eligible debutante sows and bachelor boars of old stock naturally increased, but Mr. Brolaski refused to raise the price of unit subscriptions. 'We will breed our own stock,' he said, 'and sell it to ourselves at Kansas City on-the-hoof prices, thus saving the cost of transportation thither and consequent loss of weight, also insurance and commissions.' He was mad with greed, like an ordinary businessman.

"For the enhancement of prestige, however, and in order to harvest more publicity, we sent the vet, Dr. Shepherd, east to recruit nine more glamour hogs like Alexis. His mission was followed by the California press with the same interest that attended the signing of players for the San Francisco Seals or the recruitment of gigantic high school all-state football beehemotheye for the University of California Golden Bears. He soon apprised us, to our dismay, that prices for boars of even the allowance class had risen to an average of four thousand dollars. Sows of scrub type, not recognized by the Jockey Club, were available at their comestible or stockyards price, and Mr. Brolaski decided, while authorizing the purchase of the new lot of porcine aristocrats, to encourage *mésalliance* between them and the girls from the wrong side of the track.

" 'Half the aristocracy of Virginia,' he said, 'is descended from marriages between Cavaliers and indentured women.'

"A less recondite argument that might have influenced his decision was embodied in the contract of unit partnership. In the writ and scroll it was provided that the Syndicate owned one half of each sow and one half of each crop of sibling swinelets. At all times the Syndicate retained full ownership of the blue-blooded boars of ancestral distinction,—we were whole-hog on them.

"We therefore wired Dr. Shepherd, our scout, to close the deal,—we must have more names to exploit, like Hollywood, or we would lose our grip on the public, and the Frankenstein monster we had reared would engulf us all.

"I urged caution upon Mr. Brolaski," the Colonel said. "But he replied, 'Always step inside a punch, not away from it. It's safer.' He therefore despatched the thirty-six thousand dollars, still hot from the Millionaire Kid's hands, through which they had passed with such speed that none had had a chance to adhere on their journey from new subscribers' pockets.

"The personalization of Red Alexis II had yielded such generous dividends of free space and public interest that we immediately decided the new rookies of the year should be baptismically monickered after the best-known good fellows in California. They were accordingly denominated Doug Fairbanks, Charlie Chaplin, Ty Cobb, Jim Jeffries, Gunboat Smith, Sunny Jim Coffroth, Clark Gable, Daddy Browning and Legs Diamond."

I noted that the Colonel had here repeated the cinquecento device of historical displacement, as in the case of Helen Wills and Miss Winsor. Neither Mr. Gable, Mr. Browning, nor Mr. Diamond, I was sure, had been public characters as early as the First World War. But I had learned my lesson and said nothing, lest I never hear the end of the adventure of the Great American Hog Syndicate.

"Remember," the Colonel said modestly, "I was in charge of the general advertising and publicity activities of the Great American Hog Syndicate. And it was the style and pull of the appeal in the copy of the Great American Hog Syndicate's advertising campaign which sensationalized the whole career of the fabulously successful enterprise.

"To describe it: we used 280 agate lines by 2 columns wide, which made an area of 2 columns by 20 inches. An artcraft border, heavy and challenging, with ornamentation in the way of a drover herding a wriggling mass of little piggies out of the lush meadows into the stock pens, was used with a minimum of lettered type face.

"The appeal to self-interest was promulgated chiefly through tables in box form setting forth the rising market for pork, on the hoof, in dressed form, canned, or bottled, at the emporia of trade throughout the land. Chitterlings, I remember, had risen in value five and three quarters times in a space which had produced an increase of only 113 per cent in a selected group of twenty-four industrial and twelve public-utility common stocks. Coupled with this evidence was a mild intimation that price per unit might soon rise.

" 'Pork is King,' read the punch line, relieved with a picture of our Jim Rolph, formerly Red Alexis II and William Randolph Hearst, with a royal crown mounting his swinish brow.

"But the feature which made of each ad a conversation piece, sought after with the same eagerness as the daily standing of teams in the Pacific Coast League or the race charts, was a heavy-bordered box showing the standing of the ten prize boars in number of pigs credited to their prowess during the week terminating with the Sunday on which the advertisement appeared. We also showed monthly and lifetime product. Heavy betting developed on this feature, and also numbers games paid off on the three last digits of weekly accouchements. We published a regular price line, twelve to five against Clark Gable, seven to two Hiram Johnson, or whatever it might be. It varied according to the fluctuations in their recently recorded potency. It was surprising how some hogs would do better in warm, others in rainy weather. They seemed to fall like horses into a classification of fast-track or mud runners, also sprinters and routers. Lagging behind the others in weekly output, Governor Rolph would occasionally put on a bonanza burst, coming through when the price was right with a production like Bethlehem Steel.

"But over the route Clark Gable reigned supreme. In three years of competition, he and thirty sons produced over sixty thousand dollars' worth of pork in varied finished form and nailed Doug Fairbanks by a nose on the post. Each weekly summary was accompanied by a footnote in chartmaker's style, penned by the old master, Jimmy Macdonald, as: 'Charlie Chaplin, a prominent contender from the start with three litters totaling thirty-five attributed to him on Monday, continued in good style through Friday, but hung in the stretch. Gunboat Smith came with a rush and got all the money with a week-end four-bagger!'

"My purpose in initiating this feature was orthodox. As any county-fair promoter knows you've got to give the public a show to get them into the place. After they have been attracted they buy. I would pull them in with my race chart. Then I would sell them with my pork-production tables. But as interest in the weekly chart increased astonishingly, it became apparent that in it we had the key to another Montezuman treasure chamber of Tease. We installed in our offices a couple of bookmakers, discreetly dissembled as order takers, and the handle soon attained as much as ten thousand dollars a day. We contented ourselves with a modest 110 per cent book, not having before us as yet the national example of unsyndicated hoggishness, the pari mutuel with its bite of sixteen per cent. The ten per cent profit insured us a steady thousand dollars a day, sufficient to meet the office nut and keep Brolaski in two-dollar cigars and old Farmer Stingo in good spirits.

"It almost lost us the services of the Millionaire Kid, who said he would forego all the commissions accruing on his sales of units if we would just let him have the bookmaking privileges in the town's four leading saloons. Then the Duchess called up from the breeding farm, now extending over four thousand acres by the leasing of juxtaposed acreage and its addition to our original twelve hundred.

"She said she had caught her most trusted stable foreman out in the boar barn with a syringe, just on the point of slipping Daddy Browning a hypo which would diminish his ardor. 'He said he expected a big play on Daddy Browning this week, and he was going to lay him two points over the house price,' she said in cultured trepidation. 'Jimmy Macdonald, I think you have demoralized our employes.' "

The Colonel looked about him dolefully, and said:

"Gambling spreadeth pollution in its wake, Joe. It is like one of those ships that go up the Hudson and pump out their old bilges at night, imparting to the shad a gasolinic taste, so that after despatching a portion priced $3.50 you are afraid to light a cigarette.

"Scarcely had I put down the receiver, when I saw Mr. Brolaski, with a lowering air of conspiracy upon his trust-repelling features, standing in the door of his private office and beckoning me to enter. There, secreted from the public, he watched through a number of armored judases the operations of his subordinates, particularly the three cashiers, or money takers, constantly employed.

"When I joined him and he had snap locked the door, he said, 'Jim, I've got a great idea. We lay five to one against Gable and slip him a line of bashful sows.' 'There are none,' I said at a venture, wishing to discourage this train of thought. 'And moreover, what are we running here? A handbook or a mighty corporation? Next thing you know the cops will be in for ice. Do not let us imperil this stupendous operation for the sake of any extracurricular larceny.'

"I could see on his lowering façade an expression of agonized indecision; my suggestion that he pass up any form of booty outraged his natal instincts. But he said, 'Jim, I agree with you. We will can that lousy foreman and let it be understood around the farm that every one of them hogs is well meant.' It was a decision that demanded a great deal of moral courage."

The Colonel, having reflected on the advisability of ordering more coffee, decided against it, and suggested a bottle of Canadian ale. "It is not in the tradition of the Mediterranean cuisine, I know," he said, "but my tastes are eclectic."

Encouraged by the ale, the Colonel continued:

"In full bloom, the operation, under precise and punctilious direction, as already explained, proceeded untrammeled into pleasing fruition both for sponsor and investor. The situation arose where our earliest boobs had by now accumulated in semiannual dividends a total of $907.10 for each unit of $200, a result little typical of the average opportunity marketed by Mr. Brolaski. Others had reaped lesser profits; still more were in the clear, or nearly. Pork on the hoof ruled at a high of eighty-three cents a pound; here and there stray lots brought up to a dollar.

"Three years had passed. With the United States in full-fledged belligerency the price of hogs hit a new zenith at close of each day's market.

"It was the hour when the Syndicate's full board found the iron at furnace heat,—the fateful moment for the great move in the carefully contrived stratagem. One learns from history that whatever soars must some day recede to a rational basis. The market might at any moment break adversely. That great patriot, Mr. Brolaski, had a statesmanlike intuition of the collapse of the Hohenzollern empire, although it was apparently in ruggedly ebullient bellicosity.

" 'Suppose them bums quit?' he said. 'We are buried in lard.'

"We therefore decided to wind up the business with assured profits of gladsome proportions in the offing. The multitude of subscribers, or partners in units, as legally and speculatively set up, were duly informed to claim and remove from the four farms, which the rapid growth of the business had made necessary, the half sows and half litters pertaining to them within a week, as our lease was up. They retained the option of buying our half of the sow at current Kansas City rates, but, we informed them with regret, we would not buy their half of the sow because we had no premises suitable for porcine harborage. The countryside literally swarmed with little piggies, for the Big Ten had done a noble job in the department of genetics, and the young home-bred boars had followed their noble example.

"Consternation reigned wherever the United States mails were delivered, for our subscribers were all over the United States, and most of them were urban, unequipped to receive hogs into their domestic premises. Checks on the Syndicate treasury for all the various earned and accumulated accretions went out, together with notices to hurry, hurry, hurry, pick up those pigs. One little lady, a schoolteacher, on confrontation with the necessity of taking possession of a half sow and five pigs, wrote from New York on stationery of the Martha Washington Hotel, 'I never heard of anything so awful.'

"After a week another batch of letters went out, imploring recalcitrant subscribers to come and get their pigs, since we were being dispossessed and the animals would become a public charge and cause of destruction, rendering their proprietors of record liable for any damage they inflicted on the watermelon crop.

"If this proved impracticable, we said, we would consent to take them off our partners' hands at a nominal price, although we did not know what we could do with them. Meanwhile Mr. Brolaski was considering competitive tonnage bids from representatives of Swift & Company, Armour, Wilson, Morris, Cudahy, Timothy Shine of Shine's Restaurant, Barney Greengrass, and the Maryland Market, Amsterdam Avenue, New York.

"In the end 95.42 of the subscribers ceded their porkifers to us at a price 79.2 below prevailing market price. Yet they did not lose money in all cases; some of them broke even, a happy result which is not subject to income tax.

"Mr. Brolaski received a certified check for $512,011.30 from the successful bidder, Cudahy or Wilson, I forget which. The Duchess was happy for our sakes and offered to sell Mr. Brolaski an ancestral chateau of the Torlonia family in a romantically malarial part of Italy. 'It offers the best pheasant-shooting in the Old World,' she informed him."

The Colonel finished his bottle of ale and called over to the waiter, "Ask the man at the cigar counter if he has a Principe de la Porta two-dollar straight."

"And what was your share of the proceeds?" I asked him.

"Fifty per cent of the net," he answered without elation.

The waiter returned to say the cigar man had never heard of a Principe de la Porta, and the Colonel took a pack of Kools instead.

"There was only one drawback," he said. "Mr. Brolaski left town with the check. His object was honorable, he explained several years afterward when we met in a shop at Saratoga, where he put the bite on me for five cents to buy a glass of vichy. 'I just wanted to make another spot of Tease for both of us,' he said, 'so we would have something to show for our trouble when we cut it up.'

"So he bet the money on a horse that was going at Havre de Grace at a price of three to five," the Colonel said, "and it ran eighth in a field of nine. The last horse broke a leg."

24/ *An Exercise in History*

COLONEL STINGO does not conceive of history as a photogenic cake, with successive layers placed precisely on one another and all held firmly together by a mortar of Toynbee or chocolate goo to give it cohesion, like a picture magazine's history of Western man. He sees it rather as a slow stream, often doubling back, and while he will concede that nothing is as dead as yesterday's newspaper, he believes the day before yesterday's is already slightly less so.

"That old fraud Brisbane once told me that any first-class news story, if revived and recounted years after it happened, is fifty per cent as potent as it was in the first place," he said to me in one of our first disquisitory interchanges, "and for once he was right." It is a principle the Colonel had exploited in the redaction of "Yea Verily," in which he periodically reconstructs such mighty episodia as the burning of the steamboat General Slocum in 1904, the great Rubel Coal and Ice Company holdup of 1934 and the Battle of Gettysburg. Other events he from time to time commemorates are the unexplained disappearance of Amby Small, a Toronto theatre owner, in 1913, the defeat of Terry McGovern by Young Corbett at Hartford, Connecticut, in 1901, and the charge of the Irish Brigade at Fontenoy.

The Irish Brigade got him out of a tight spot last Christmas, as it had the Maréchal de Saxe in 1745. Lacking Tease wherewith to buy Christmas presents for his friends, he told me at the year's turn, he had sat in his room at the Hotel Dixie too dispirited to hunt up a fresh story for his next "Yea Verily." As he had not done the Fontenoyset- piece for a couple of years, he painted in a couple of new rhetorical touches and sent it in. The day after it ran he was sitting in his room again, equally dispirited, when the telephone rang and the desk informed him that there was a man below with a package to deliver.

"I instructed them to forward him," the Colonel said, "and presently there appeared a large Irishman, red of neck and countenance, carrying a cardboard carton of the size that contains a dozen fifths. 'Merry Christmas from Mr. Ignatius McGonigle,' he said, naming a member of a large firm of booze wholesalers. 'Mr. McGonigle says he always enjoys the part of that piece where they mow the redcoats down in swathes, and will you please mow down an extra swathe for him the next time you write it.' He departed, leaving behind him the remembrance, which consisted of tastefully bottled grain neutral spirits flavored with whiskey. It solved my gift problem instantaneously. I bought some seasonal wrapping paper and appropriately packaged the twelve individual bottles for distribution."

As tangible evidence of the truth of his story, the Colonel offered two bottles of the blend, which I am sure he would never have bought of his own volition.

"The incident illustrates the pulling power of an old story," he said, and then added, a trifle ungratefully, I thought, "Next season I'll *exterminate* the English. Then maybe he'll send me some whiskey worth not giving away."

Gettysburg, to which he returns in fancy at least once a year, is a flexible anniversary,—he can run it either on the date of the battle itself, in July, or of the Gettysburg Address that followed it in November. Each time he writes it he develops a news lead. Once it was an interview with Eddie Plank, the old Athletics pitcher, who lives near the battlefield, and again the fact that a boy from Gettysburg town was playing fullback on the University of Pennsylvania varsity. Last year it was the news that General Dwight D. Eisenhower had bought a farm near by. In all the years he has been writing the piece, however, he had never succeeded in getting it into the *Enquirer* intact, a failure which causes him artistic distress.

"The current Newsprint shortage raising hob," he wrote back in 1946, soon after our acquaintance began. "After our Mr. Make-up, the Great Deleter, had done with his emasculation of last week's Stingo, there remained absent several pickets from the wooden fence."

Not only Gettysburg has suffered from this species of mutilation, to which the Colonel is peculiarly susceptible. "In last week's compendium of the famous renewal of the Dwyer Stakes in 1920, wherein the heroic John P. Grier ran Man o' War, the winner, to a neck finish," he was once compelled to write, "the Kite lost its Tail through constriction due to a tight paper."

I have no copy of his 1946 Gettysburg story, but one excerpt haunts my memory: "As the sweet River Shannon began to flow softly and copiously, although I like Trommer's White Label a deal better than the local Conestoga brew. But this Mennonite cheese is surpassing."

"Gettysburg is the kind of subject I like, Joe," he once said to me. "I can really wind up and throw. The description of lesser events is like a half-mile race track, on which a horse with a long stride is at a disadvantage. The fear of hyperbole restrains. But with a theme like Gettysburg or J. P. Morgan it can be disregarded."

One November—he had chosen the anniversary of the address this time—he sent me an advance manuscript of his Gettysburg so I could catch it uncut. The unabated paper shortage precludes my reproducing it that way, but I can quote some.

"I had been here before, many times for many reasons," the Colonel says, setting the mood, "but one finds the quiet old Dutch countryside changed but little, while the sleepy old town remains just the same as ever." Then, after working through the Eisenhowers' purchase of a farm "composed of rolling land of hill and valley while the historic Cherry Creek comes in off the Battlefield nearby to scintillate the vistas," the Colonel gets into his battle. "From the long verandah of the Manor House of the General's lovely new home to be, you gain a sweeping concept of the expansive Battlefield and figurate for yourself how the awful conflict was won and lost.

"The catastrophic Third Day of the titanic struggle remains the crescendo of the momentous almost man-to-man grapple in utter death on the outskirts of the Little Dutch Town. Recently a summarization was given you of the first and second days' operations. Now let us hop to the line in respect to this vital and crucial Third Day, one of the great military episodes of all history."

Instead of hopping immediately, however, the Colonel wheels for another run, like a horse-show rider bringing his mount up to a high obstacle.

"But a final word of Devil's Den itself, centre of the Second Day's fighting. Within this gigantic Rockery are the celebrated Five Rocks. They are not of volcanic upheaval but came into the cosmic in the Paleozoic Prima Period,—some 200,000 years ago according to Darwinian Theory. . . .

"It is said that 3,700 odd youngsters, both sides, lost their lives within Devil's Den at Gettysburg, within a space no larger than the Baseball Diamond today at Yankee Stadium, New York, as explained recently.

"Night falls again. The tumult dies. There is a full moon over Gettysburg. The living and the dead are in tumbled heaps. Men breathe their last amid the overwhelming fragrance of the Sweet Clover, in Hayfields and Wheatfields ripe for Harvest. Lights burn late in the opposing Headquarters while the tired thousands of the unwounded of both armies drop where they stand and sleep. . . .

"Then comes the Third Day at Gettysburg . . . Sparked and emblazoned by the Charge of Pickett's Brigade, its result is to affect all men and history in its trend for a thousand years. . . .

"It is sublime and pitiable. . . ."

The Colonel would have made one of the great war correspondents of all time, if he had had the luck to find himself in a war.

Personally I prefer the kind of historical writing he does about his own era. For example:

"Clubhouse, Aqueduct, L.I., June 10 [1944]—Squeezed in like Monterey sardines in a tin packet case a great, and motley, throng of rabid Pari Mutuel fanatics strained at girth here this afternoon for the annual renewal of oldtime Carter Handicap, 3 y.o. & u., 7 furlongs, $10,000 added, in this tight little racetrack known as Aqueduct.

" 'How long can it last?'—It's the cry on every side. Deep students of the economic problem involved in Pari Mutuel operation now foresee the restrictive value of Bookmaking as opposed to rampant mechanized Pari Mutuel legalized gambling.

"Mayfair was well represented on Balcony and out in Box Row. . . .

"It's no secret to New York *Enquirer* that David Windsor appreciatively evaluated the parties given for him and his American Duchess by 'Her Grace' last summer which brought out the most interesting of the Belgravia. . . ."

But the kind of history in which the Colonel is at zenith, I think, is in the mid-ground between Gettysburg and the present. It is represented by his narration, last summer, of a great betting coup and its sequelae.

"Saratoga, N.Y., Aug. 11—This here United States Hotel Stakes is not so rich in endowment, but it is redolent in warm tradition as one of the most important juvenile fixtures in the entire Saratoga Book of Events. . . . In 1902, if recollection serves rightly, it was Blonde Plunger Charlie Ellison from Norwood, Ohio, who sensationalized the Ring and Club House by scoring a smart coup with his colt, Skillful, son of John E. Madden's top ace stallion, Mirthful.

"Late Kansas Price and Mose Fontilieu placed the Ellison Commission in the betting ring, Cad Daggett in the Club House and elephantine Hughie Quinn in the populous Field where quite some 80 summerily attired bookmakers operated. Joe Ullman and Kid Weller, operating the celebrated Big Store for John W. Gates and John A. Drake, the notorious prodigals in the Main Ring, stubbornly decided to lay Skillful with an opening price of 10–1. Coyly, the chalk showed 12–1 over at the mart of Sol Lichtenstein and Lucien Appleby. At crowded club house imperturbable Johnny Walters offered 12–1 as a feeler while English Bill Jackman and Humming Bird Tyler in the Field were reported to be overboard with as good as 15–1."

The Colonel's historical characters, like those of the reign of Robert the Pious,[1] have sobriquets that stimulate the curiosity. I have learned that it is unwise to interrupt the flow of spoken narrative to ask him how they were acquired, for the explanation, while beguiling, is so long that it prevents the completion of the anecdote in which they figure. But in the case of stories already committed to paper by him, I have no such inhibition. So the first time I met him after the appearance of the specimen of his art now under consideration, I asked him about Humming Bird Tyler.

"Humming Bird was a fellow who would have a horse marked up at four to one on his slate," the Colonel said, "and then some fellow who looked as if he were betting for somebody else would walk up and bet him a substantial sum, perhaps a thousand. Old George would start humming, 'On the Banks of the Wabash,' or something like that, as if he hadn't heard him, and he'd turn around in an absent-minded manner and mark that horse down to five to two before he casually turned to the stranger again. Humming Bird was a cautious type, like Circular Joe Vendig, so denominated because he would act as his own outside man and circulate among the other books, to see what they were doing."

But I must return to Saratoga in 1902:

"Afterwards, it was learned Skillful had been highly tried and the great jockey Otto Wonderly, then at the very zenith of his riding flair, was in the saddle. Blonde Charlie, then a rich man and heavy bettor himself, really represented a syndicate and Mid-Western high-money operators as well. . . .

"Well, sir, suddenly, a farmer-looking fellow, dug up by Kansas Price, modestly approached the Big Store where Kid Weller, on the block, was invited to take on $500 at 12–1. Accepted. Then a tender of another $500. 'You're on,' replied Weller. Then a proffer of a $1000. Accepted. Two minutes later the yokel came back beseeching $5,000 more at the prevailing 12–1. Hadn't Mr. Drake instructed Weller & Ullman to 'take anything offered and don't rub until you hear from me'? But now the cat's out of the bag and where is Mr. Drake? By the time that rough toss Outside

[1] For instance, Hugues Eveille-Chien, or Wake-Dog, the Count of Maine, and Olaf Krakaben, or Break-a-Bone (or possibly Break-a-Leg), the King of Norway, known after his conversion as Saint Olaf.

Man Red Sam Friedlander had knocked down [here a long catalogue of people who might have been standing around] and caught up with Drake and 'Ort' Welles cooling themselves beneath a wide spreading elm tree in the Paddock, fully some $162,000 had been eased upon the bookmakers and Club House commissioners.

"Then came the break in George Wheelock's market, followed by hurried chalk rubbing.

"To make a long ancient story abbreviate, it will suffice to say that the Syndicate got down to the last penny. Skillful closed at three, even and out.

"Next day, in New York *Herald*, the erudite Judge Joe Burke approximated the Ellison syndicate had won upwards of $470,000. It is a bye-thought today, in the speculative world of American racing, that Blonde Charlie Ellison, who afterwards won a Kentucky Derby in 1903 with Judge Himes, took down on Skillful's win a figure which surpasses all the known single top takes by either Pittsburgh Phil or Riley Grannan in their halcyon heights. Of course William Collins Whitney once won close to $2,000,000, though his Commissioners collected but $1,400,000, on George W. Jenkins, a steeplechase horse. Them were the days when men were men and women used no talcum powder."

A member of the Hearst politburo once informed me that the three only elements of news were blood, money, and sex in four letters. This particular commissar has since edited an anthology of great American reporting. By his criteria, the Colonel's story has everything. Right up to the talcum powder, it dealt only with money, but the other essentials were coming right up.

"But there is a climax to this reminiscence. The day after Skillful's win all hands are at Hotel Fort William Henry, Lake George, where Blonde Charlie had gone to escape the Bee and ubiquitous reporters, and the wrath of the Jockey Club's emissaries, who decried 'loud and vulgar betting' even as today. It was a gaudy dinner that night with Edna McCauley and Lil Russell honored guests and Diamond Jim Brady and Joe Seagram, foremost Canadian distiller and breeder and racing man, vying, one with the other, in sustaining a running river of choicest vintage, all the way, Mumm's Sec to fragrant light Paul Masson and White Seal, the champagne of the dilettante and gourmet. . . .

> "Pleasing and natural event was the presentation to Jockey Otto Wonderly by Blonde Charlie of a cheque for $25,000, apart from his regular riding fee and winning stake bonus. Joe Seagram (who had won $144,000) chipped in with one for $15,000, and Abe Frank, representing another winner, George C. Bennet, ill at Hot Springs, Ark., with another for $10,000.
>
> "There were other honoraria for Johnny Mayberry, Ham Keene and Jack the Ripper, who had a lot to do with bringing up Skillful

to point in secret undercover. Nice job. But, as I say, the Climax.

"Two days later, down at Spa, little rosy cheeked Wonderly, fat and rich now as a lamprey, did not show up to ride a pretty undercover year-old-trick for Handsome Harry Robinson, owner of New Orleans' famous mudder, Death, a descendant of Leamington. The colt was scratched and another coup nipped in the bud."

(A lamprey, having once fastened on a succulent whitefish, must swell up as quickly as a jockey who breaks training. The fluid medium of inflation in the fish's case is blood, in the jockey's champagne. The brief introduction of the apparently extraneous Robinson story is for me a high point of narrative art. It marks the continuity of that world of intellectual combat from which the jockey has absented himself, like Achilles from the siege of Troy. Where, the reader asks himself, has Otto Wonderly gone?)

"Two other afternoons came and went with no Wonderly. He had eloped with petite, youngish and most personable Wendy Ellison. Month later, they were located at Amalfi, on the Italian Riviera. Hector Mackenzie, the Prince of Wine Agents, made the trip across the Atlantic carrying the Palms of Forgiveness but the rascals declined all overtures, and remained in Villa looking out upon the assuaging Monterey Blue of the Mediterranean for years."[2]

So much for the third element of a good news story. Now the Colonel darkens his canvas.

"They finally returned to America, but like all things mundane, the stalwarts, men and women, of a former day had passed from the scene and there had come the dolorous Ides of Charles Evans Hughes and the nullity in Racing—the charm had gone. Hildebrand, a great race rider, handled by Plunger Joe Yeager, succeeded Wonderly, who finally met his end in a shooting affray at Little Rock, Ark. It all happened in front of Chambers & Walker's palatial poolroom while the Don Juanish race rider stood talking to Dynamite Jack Thornby & Harry Brolaski. Long legged Red Booger strode up and Smith & Wessoned him to death with a soft nosed slug through the heart.[3] Dark visaged Dynamite, like his friend Bat Masterson, quick on the trig, wheeled and killed Mr. Booger. Next night the poolroom was dynamited as flat as Mattie Baldwin's proboscis.[4] McCarthy[5] Boy are you on the Listening Dept.? Yea Verily Verily."

That takes care of the blood.

[2] Not the Mediterranean Blue of Monterey, as Henry James might have expressed it. The Colonel is no servile deferent to extraterritorial scenery.

[3] Only the adjective Don Juanish applied to Wonderly hints at the cause of the tragedy.

[4] Nothing even hints at the cause of this. Who blew up the poolroom? Friends of Booger or friends of Wonderly? Or did the vigilantes simply blow it up as a menace to public health? In front of it was obviously a dangerous place to stand.

Matty Baldwin, as I have often heard, was a good Boston lightweight of the first

25/*A Little Journey to Pittsburgh Phil's*

MY PREFERENCE for the Colonel's stories of his own life, or at least of the life in which he played a role, has frequently evoked the astonishment of my friend, who believes, like the authors of Greek tragedy, that only the lives of the illustrious are qualified to edify a large public.

To support his theory he cites the example of an old idol of his, Elbert Hubbard, known to Americans of the gas-log and hobble-skirt period as the Fra. Hubbard published an indeterminate number of volumes of Little Journeys to the Homes of Famous People, Good Men and Great, Famous Women (as distinguished from People), American Authors, American Statesmen, Eminent Painters, Great Musicians, and Great about everything else you can think of.

"He barely broke even on those," the Colonel says, "but he began to sandwich in Little Journeys to the Homes of Great Businessmen and Great Industries. For example he would write A Little Journey to the Home of the Hartford Lunch, or A Little Journey to Wanamaker's Department Store, or to Joseph Quincy Magruder, the shelled-pecan king. The Fra would publish the Little Journey in one of his magazines, the *Philistine* or the *Roycrofter*. The *Philistine* bore the whimsic device, 'Published Every Once In A While.' It was the equivalent of the marine expression, 'As cargo offers.'

"He would suggest that the businessman on behalf of his company purchase a hundred thousand reprints at ten cents, to distribute as the most flattering format of publicity. Soon a spirit of rivalry and emulation began. Unless you had been visited by the Fra you had little stature in the industrial world. The deals were arranged in advance; the boob signed up for so many thousand reprints before the Fra deigned to visit him.

"I served as a herald and intermediary, posing as one who knew the Fra intimately and thought I could arrange to get the boob visited if he consented to Mr. Hubbard's usual terms. It was all legal, nobody got hurt, and it was wonderful. I think you have the makings of another Elbert Hubbard, but you are in need of promotion. There is a millionaire I know

decade of the century, and his pictures show the exactitude of the Colonel's simile. The obscurity of the reference I hold as no subtraction from the pleasure of reading Stingo. The allusions in Milton and Spenser were similarly opaque to the uninitiate.

[5] Clem McCarthy, the radio announcer of turf events, an old friend of the Colonel's. They met in Seattle in about 1909, when the Colonel was conducting a medium of personal articulation known as the Seattle *Daily Sporting Times*. There was a boom in Seattle then, and a race track just outside of town.

of who manufactures poultry-laying feed down in Pennsylvania and feels he is a fitting subject for a biography in a national magazine. We could take him like the Dalton gang took Coffeyville, Kansas."

The Colonel is always trying to make something of me, but I let him down.

"I don't think I have the qualifications to be a Fra," I told him once when he was particularly urgent.

"You have, Joe," he said generously. "All you lack is self-confidence and a good advance man. Of course he had an advantage in appearance. He had hair that came down over his shoulders, and he wore a hat like Walt Whitman, with a Prince Albert coat and long-legged burnished boots.

"I remember the first time I met him out in San Francisco. He was on a lecture tour and I had been engaged to do some advance promotion. I had a committee of representative citizens and a brass band out to meet him at the Oakland Ferry. The crowd coming off the ferry cheered thinking it was Buffalo Bill, and as we drove off through the huzzaring plebes, the Fra put his hand on my knee and said, 'Little Mac, I've got them.' His creed was Sunshine, Fresh Air, Friendship, Calm Sleep, and Beautiful Thoughts,—the Sea, the Sun, the Smile, America, and the Love of the Farm. He was the sweetest, dearest human being that ever lived, and you would have loved him."

Colonel Stingo and I were in Joe Braun's Palace Bar and Grill on the evening of this particular discussion. It is a place which always disposes the Colonel to sentimentality. "There have been three Palace bars in my life," he says, "the grandiose dispensatorium dominated by the Pied Piper in San Francisco, the Palace Bar on the Bund in Shanghai, where I was entertained by Dr. Sun Yat-sen, who was then incubating the revolution, and this present Palace on Forty-fifth Street. It lacks the pretension of the first two, but it is more appropriate to my present portfolio of securities.

"This dear old Fra," he said, "perpetrated a tour de force called the *Message to Garcia*, which sold a couple of million copies. The fellow he said carried the message didn't even find the right Garcia. Cuba is full of Garcias. 'How the fellow by the name of Rowan took the letter, sealed it up in an oilskin pouch, strapped it over his heart, in four days landed by night off the coast of Cuba from an open boat, disappeared into the jungle, and in three weeks came out on the other side of the island, having traversed a hostile country on foot and delivered the message to Garcia,' the old Fra wrote, 'are things I have no special desire now to tell in detail.' That is just as well, because it didn't happen.

"The old Fra, though, used the suppositious exploit as an illustration of the kind of service employers didn't get in return for the wages they paid, in those days frequently aggregating a dollar and a half a day. He adjured the toiling masses to spit on their hands and prove themselves worthy of their bosses' benevolence.

"Sales were light among the objects of his exhortation, but this did not disappoint his anticipations. 'Slipshod assistance, foolish inattention, dowdy indifference and half-hearted work seem the rule," he fulminated, and the Pennsylvania Railroad bought the first million copies for distribution to passengers and employes.

" 'No man who has endeavored to carry out an enterprise where many hands were needed but has been well-nigh appalled by the imbecility of the average man,' that dear old humanitarian indited. 'A first mate with knotted club seems necessary; and the dread of getting the bounce Saturday night holds many a worker to his place.' But he was not incapable of sympathy.

" 'Nothing is said,' he suggested considerately, 'about the employer who grows old before his time in a vain attempt to get frowsy ne'er-do-wells to do intelligent work; and his long, patient striving with help that does nothing but loaf when his back is turned.'

"Dear old Fra," the Colonel said, swelling the tide of his Gambrinian with a tear. "He was the people's friend."

"He seems to have been a precursor of Westbrook Pegler," I said.

"He was more on the order of Al Jennings, the train robber," the Colonel said, "only he didn't need an equalizer."

Seeing him in a mood so softly reminiscent, I thought it might be a good time to bring up again the subject of his own career in conventional journalism after his discharge from the *Evening Sun* for scoring a sensational scoop.

"Did you achieve any scoops of note after your translation to the *Evening Journal*, Colonel?" I asked him.

"*Any* scoops?" the Colonel repeated ironically. "It was my function to provide at least four exclusive first-page stories a week while the horses were running at metropolitan tracks, and I may say I succeeded. Shortly after my advent to the Halls Hearstian, a Mr. Foster Coates was made managing editor of the *Evening Journal*, always under the superior aegis of that old fraud Brisbane, who retained guidance remote. Mr. Coates was said to be capable of swearing for half an hour without repeating himself. He was of a type prefiguring the hard-boiled city editor of *The Front Page* and many moving pictures.

"This Mr. Coates infected Brisbane and through him Mr. Hearst with the idea of a late edition of the *Evening Journal*, to be known as the Peach. It went to press at the unprecedentedly late hour of 7 P.M. By tacit agreement theretofore all New York evenings had put their finals to bed at five-forty. The Peach had a pink front page.

"In order to sell an otherwise redundant paper at an hour when the workaday crowds had already homeward wended, it was essential to have some startling daily item of headline import. It would in most cases concern sports, since it was difficult to assure a supply of murders or stickups between five-forty and seven. The race track would seem to be the most dependable source, since, as Mr. Coates observed, baseball did not interest women. He envisaged the Tenderloin and Broadway as the mart for the Peach, and a woman objects to the purchase of a newspaper by her escort unless she wants to read it too."

The Colonel reiterated his Gambrinian intake, and said: "The two fields that newspapers cover most inadequately are, indubitably, Wall Street and the race track. The reason is the same in both cases, hypocrisy. The motivation of both institutions is frankly acquisitive. There is however in Wall Street a sanctimonious fiction that the market exists as a medium of liquidating old ladies' estates. It is parallel to the Tartuffian claim that the pari-mutuels run to improve the breed of horses descended from the Darley Arabian.

"The professional journalists covering these beats have a jargon of veneerment which bedims rather than accentuates.

"MARKET WAVERS, for example, has not the same interest as $500,000,000 LOST. You look at Wall Street headlines and the only thing they seldom mention is money.

"Readers are not interested in trends, so denominated, but in tales of quick enrichment or spectacular impoverization—the saga of that vast gist of gelt.

"For racing news the same thing is true. People go out there to bet, and the betting is what they want to read about. The plungers of halcyon were not secretive. The income tax, with its incentive to discretion, had not yet been constitutionalized. So Pittsburgh Phil, Bet-a-Million Gates, and their ilk were public figures, outranking in interest the Russo-Japanese War and like contemporary events. By concentrating upon the ebb and flow of the oceanic tide of Tease, I was able to provide a bumper crop of headlines.

"Each day at five forty-five, when the other papers were away, I would send my Peach story from the track. Western Union facilities at the race track were limited, and, by agreement among the newspapers, no one message filed could run more than fifty-five words. There was therefore scant opportunity for fine shading and qualification. The copyreaders and make-up men, impatient to be off to their respective chatelaines, were indisposed to lavish time in the pursuit of the exact equivalent of my thought, in Gallicism, *le mot au jus*. The resulting headlines were in one or two cases the cause of embarrassment. But I survived."

The Colonel paused to help a fellow devotee of Gambrinus over a rough spot in a Sunday *Times* crossword puzzle. The puzzler, a graying fellow, had come to our table and asked: "What is an opera by Wagner in six letters, beginning with *R* and ending with *i*?"

"*Rienzi,*" the Colonel said without hesitation. "It has an overture."

After the grateful puzzler had withdrawn, the Colonel said, "A pitiful case. He spent nine months in the Death House at Sing Sing, a victim of mistaken identity. There he became addicted to crossword puzzles. Now he wanders disconsolate, in search of a saloon without a juke box or television so he can concentrate. He misses the amenities of prison life.

"One morning at Brighton," he said, reverting to the good Edwardian time, "I was standing over near the racing secretary's office when I saw George Smith, known on the turf as Pittsburgh Phil, with his trainer ascend the steps to the pagoda, or stewards' stand. I used to get out to the course early in those days, since the time for digging was before or after the races. During their running my usual news sources were too engrossed to talk.

"I was therefore the only turf writer present. Mr. Smith's presence at the track at that hour was more unusual than mine. I sensed that something must be up, though when he descended from the stand his imperturbable countenance reflected no disgruntlement. He was a man of inconspicuous demeanor, like one of those fellows who sit at their desks in the front offices of banks, waiting for their prey.

"I therefore waylaid Mr. Harry Knapp, one of the Jockey Club stewards, a dear old fellow, when he in turn descended from the pagoda, and asked him what was up.

" 'We have refused the entries of Mr. Smith's horses until the miserable showing of one he ran yesterday is explained,' he said. 'There's an investigation in progress.'

"I naturally kept my information to myself throughout the afternoon. I knew Pittsburgh Phil would tell no one, and I was sure the Jockey Club would make no announcement until the result of the investigation was determined.

"After my colleagues had gone home, I sent my Peach story: 'Entries of horses owned by George A. Smith, better known as Pittsburgh Phil, were refused today pending result of investigation of Grand Opera's showing in the fifth race yesterday on which it is known western gamblers took the books for a cool quarter million. Such investigations have often led to stables' being barred from the turf.' It was all I could do in fifty-five words.

"I started for my office well pleased, traveling by electric train to the Sands Street station in Brooklyn, where I had to transfer to a streetcar for the trip across the bridge. At Sands Street, which I reached at seven-thirty, the Peach was already on sale, but with a headline which indicated I was in Blackstonian jeopardy: PITTSBURGH PHIL RULED OFF. The copyreader, anticipating the decision of the Jockey Club, had strained the legal limits of my innuendo.

"The next day's papers announced that the stewards had cleared Mr. Smith of complicity in the capricious conduct of his three-year-old Grand Opera, and that Pittsburgh Phil was now suing the *Evening Journal*, Mr. Hearst, and J.S.A. Macdonald, the *Journal* racing expert, for a hundred thousand dollars apiece, in my case, sheer flattery. Luckily the *Journal* had published the text of my despatch in full, so I was in the clear with my superiors, but it was the occasion of much mental anguish.

"I was interviewed by a junior member of the paper's firm of libel lawyers, a neophyte trusting only to written rote. He asked me what time I had seen Mr. Smith go up into the stand? I said eleven o'clock. He said, 'How do you know?' I said, 'Because I was just outside the racing secretary's office and all the hustlers and the touts and trainers were standing around waiting to see the entries for the next day's races.' He was unacquainted with the world outside Harvard Square. However, Mr. Smith was reported implacable. The paper was clearly at fault, even if I wasn't. I squared that one myself. I waited upon him in his suite at the Hotel Imperial, Broadway and Thirty-second Street, and explained that the fellow who wrote the headline was a Sunday-school superintendent and a force in the Anti-Saloon League and was, besides, the sole support of his mother, wife, and eleven children.

"The man was in real life established in sin with a member of the Ladies' Orchestra of the Atlantic Gardens *bierstube*, and his sole support for every day of the week except payday was the magnificent free-lunch counter at Furthmann's Saloon under the El on Park Row.

"Because of the paragon's blameless past, I told Pittsburgh Phil, he was unacquainted with the terminology of the turf, a country boy who thought a poolroom was a synonym for a natatorium, and if he lost this job he would be blacklisted and the children would become public charges, while all the drunkards on Park Row would jeer at this black eye for clean living.

"Pittsburgh Phil was a man who would bet fifty thousand dollars on the turn of a card and never indicate by the slightest contraction of the facial muscles pleasure or displeasure at the outcome. But, Joe, I had him crying like a baby.

" 'Thank you for coming to see me, young man,' he said when I had finished. 'You have prevented me from committing a grave injustice. I will instruct my solicitors tomorrow to withdraw my suit. And here is five hundred for you,' he said, the dear old fellow. 'And the next time one of my horses is a stiff I will let you in on it.' "

26/ A Little Journey to Sysonby's

"THE HORSES, like the men, were of superior stature in those days," the Colonel said regretfully. "These are degenerate times, in which the race horse, sensing himself a mere instrument of greed, has lost all sense of *noblesse obligée*. A horse like the great Sysonby, by Imp. Melton, winner of the Epsom Derby, out of Optime, would never let you down. Imported *in utero*, but foaled in this country, as I recollect, this equine knight of the

Table Round lost but once as a two-year-old, and then to the great mare Artful in the Futurity. As a three-year-old he won all save for one dead heat with Race King. That made fourteen firsts in fifteen starts, and the American public waited, agape, for his *rentrée* as a four-year-old in the season of 1906. He was the predilectory possession of James R. Keene, a mighty old man of money, a czar of Wall Street and preeminent on the American turf, having survived William Collins Whitney, his chief competitor. Keene and Whitney were two of the most rivalous men that ever lived.

"Mr. Keene was by then a valetudinarian, swathed in thick-carpeted luxury and surfeited with attendance in the old Waldorf-Astoria, on the site of the present Empire State Building. The triumphs of his horses were to him the most potent of tonics, accountable, according to his physicians, for his continued survival. But the doctors adjured the members of his suite to cushion him against shock as much as possible.

"The seasonal debut of this Sysonby," the Colonel said, "was repeatedly postponed. Jim Rowe, his trainer, said he was doing well, but he was scratched in turn from the Metropolitan, Brooklyn, and Suburban Handicaps, the Wagnerian Ring Cycle for three-year-olds and up of that era, and it was bruited about in hushed whisper that he was suffering from a mysterious rash that the veterinarians could not diagnose. A minor ailment, the vets said, but he could not endure a saddle blanket on his back.

"I was standing down by the finish line at Sheepshead Bay after the last race one day in mid-June, trying to think of something to send that the boys could hang a headline on for the Peach, when Dynamite Jack Thornby breezed up to to me and said, 'Jim, you'd better get over to Jim Rowe's barn. Sysonby is in a lather and shaking like a leaf, and they're walking him in circles. He looks one to ten and out to die in an hour.'

"I ran right over there and the facts were as Dynamite Jack had reported. The track veterinary, whom I knew, said, 'He's a goner of a certainty,' and the horse's groom was crying. I hustled back to the telegraph operator, who waited for me every day before putting up his bug, and sent the *Evening Journal* all I knew: 'The great race horse Sysonby was fatally stricken by illness at Sheepshead Bay after the last race this evening.' It was a scoop. When I reached Sands Street I bought a *Journal* with the headline across the page: SYSONBY DEAD.

"The boys had pushed up the tempo on me again, but this time I thought it was safe enough. Sunday morning's papers, however, brought trepidation. The morning papers, taken aghast by my scoop, had tried to confirm it but had been unable to establish contact with trainer Rowe. They had then sent reporters to the Waldorf to check up with Mr. Keene, but had not been allowed to see the old hidalgo. Instead, a gentlemanly understrapper, a kind of social secretary, had come out from the sanctum and informed them that Mr. Keene could not be disturbed, but that they might rest assured there was nothing the matter with Sysonby. 'If the horse had died we would surely have been informed,' he said, and dismissed them.

"Every Sunday sports page carried a headline: SYSONBY LIVES—CANARD DENIED, or TURF SCOOP PROVES HOAX—SYSONBY HAS HORSE LAUGH. I had a gloomy morning. But the afternoon was even more lugubrious. I was captain of the *Evening Journal* team in the Newspaper Baseball League, which played its games on Sunday afternoons at old Washington Park, the home grounds of the Brooklyn Superbas. There was no Sunday professional baseball, and they let us use the park. I pitched," the Colonel said, and added, modestly, "I was of big-league calibre. On this particular Sunday we were playing the *Evening World*, a deadly rival.

"All the *World* boys took the opportunity of riding me. Their witticisms were uncouth but effective,—they would for instance whinny when I came to bat, and yell, 'Run it out, Sysonby,' when I hit a bounder. While I pitched, their coaches on the base lines would ask me where I expected to work after the iron ball hit, suggesting I might find employment with my old associate George Graham Rice, then promoting mining stock in Nevada. I was so preoccupied that I allowed three hits and had to drive in the winning run myself with a double in the ninth inning.

"I was by now a married man and father, and my thoughts were dark indeed as I turned in that night, after an evening of spurious good humor designed to conceal from my spouse the foreboding which was, under the circumstances, appropriate. Fortunately she was not a sports-page reader and did not know what I was thinking about. On the morrow I dragged myself to the office, then on William Street, figuring I might better go there and receive the fatal news than straight to the track and receive the blow by telegraph.

"On entering the city room at noon, I saw by my desk the ominous figure of Coates, the Peach's only begetter. I made my way bravely toward him, prepared to submit my justification but not sue for mercy. Suddenly, on perceiving me, Mr. Coates, a man of generous dimensions, rushed in my direction. I threw myself into a posture of defense, but his intentions proved amicable.

" 'That was a clean beat, Jimmy," he proclaimed, and waved in my direction a paper with headlines stating: SYSONBY DIED SATURDAY NIGHT, TRAINER ADMITS. It seems that the great son of Melton had expired a few hours after my view of him, but the trainer, fearing the effect of such dolorous news on the cardiac structure of the octogenarian millionaire, had not imparted the information until late the next day. The social secretary, in denying the receipt of the bad news, had been veracious, but the news desks, eager to throw down Peach's story, had not pushed their enquiries far enough.

"We crowed over our beat for a week. Mr. Coates expressed his pleasure, and an office boy delivered at my desk a note from Mr. Brisbane congratulating me on my performance and alleging that I would be rewarded with a five-dollar raise as soon as Mr. Hearst's finances permitted.

"In my memories of equine immortals, Sysonby holds a special place. I sometimes dream of him, a great bay horse, charging down upon me as I lie flat on my back on an unidentified racing strip. As he comes thundering down upon me I hear him singing: 'Alive, Alive-o,' to the tune of 'Cockles and Mussels,' an air I never hear in my waking moments without a shudder of grim association."

It was now my turn to surprise the Colonel. I ordered up another round of the amber, and when we had filled our glasses I said, "I challenge. I propose a Little Journey to the Home of Sysonby."

I must explain here that as a small boy resident on the West Side I had been a habitué of the American Museum of Natural History, earning a familiarity with every stuffed seal and dummy Eskimo in the joint. I had ranged from mammals to meteorites, hummingbirds to horses, and the name Sysonby struck a familiar note. Sysonby's skeleton, I remembered, had stood in the Museum, plainly labeled, and that omniretentive repository must still hold it fast.

The Colonel, for once, looked at me with astonishment, but when I recounted my recollection he readily acceded to my proposal.

"I never thought to look on Sysonby again," he said. "He was a hell of a horse."

We got a taxi and made our way to the Museum. It was still midafternoon. When we arrived we had to fight our way in through a vast circular agglutination of school children in the rotunda, forming a human aspic around a miniature whale *sous cloche*. This was labeled "Oscar, the Baby Whale," and a card under the glass explained that Oscar's mother when killed had been sixty-eight feet long and that Oscar, if he had survived the ordinary period of gestation, would have been born twenty feet overall. Oscar and the children packed the rotunda. The Colonel made a way through the juvenile plankton, making effective though surreptitious use of his pointy shoes, for a few small shrieks of pain mingled with the gabble in his wake. I fancied that, following him, I stepped on one or two small prostrate bodies. However, these may have been knocked down by their playmates and trampled to death hours before our arrival.

A girl at the information desk said that all the horse exhibits were grouped. By consulting a map she was able to inform us that they were on the fourth floor, and we extricated our legs and buttocks from the pediatric jelly mold and headed for the elevators, the Colonel hitting one little darling a pip of a backhander as we broke away.

We found Sysonby, a spirited *squelette*, in full stride in the midst of his Museum playmates: the Przewalsky horse; the wild ass, or Kiang; Grévy's zebra; and a draught horse pulling a heavy load, all skeletons grouped for ready comparison. Sysonby, the sign within his glass case indicated, is shown at the instant when the right forefoot has left the ground, and left hind foot, right hind foot and left forefoot are to follow in that order, carrying him forward one full stride of twenty-six feet. "He's hanging in the stretch," the Colonel said. "Can't seem to get anywhere. It isn't like him."

The delicacy of the horse's bone structure impressed him. "He looks so small when he is divested of his outward integument," he said. "I remember him as a big horse. It is easy to see why two-year-olds go so frequently askew," he added, regarding the complex lattice of the rib cage. "They are of surprisingly fragile construction." Another card within the case gave the date of Sysonby's demise—June 17, 1906—and noted that the skeleton had been mounted at the expense of James R. Keene and presented by him to the Museum. There was a photograph of the great son of Melton-Optime,—the Colonel's recollection of his breeding had been precise,—passing a winning post in full flesh, with jockey up and Keene's polka-dot silks flattened to the boy's small torso by the breeze.

"He was a hot tip the first time he ever came out," the Colonel said, "and I passed him up. He was three to five, and that turned out to be the best price ever laid against him."

We began the return journey to Joe Braun's. Our path led through the Hall of Mammoths, a larger and more impressive catacomb between Sysonby's glass loose box and the elevators. The Colonel, ever curious, paused before several of the reconstructed mammoths and mastodons, and was particularly attracted by a South Dakota entry called the Megabelodon, which stood about twenty-seven hands at the shoulder and was slightly longer than a crosstown bus. "If a puny creature like Sysonby could stride twenty-six feet," he said, "imagine what that thing could encompass with a bound." He stood, contemplative, before Megabelodon for a moment, and then continued on his way.

"If we could get Sysonby out of here, some night," I suggested playfully, after we had got into the elevator, "we could enter him in the last race at Belmont and he could probably still take that class of horses."

"Sysonby hell," my courtly old friend said unsentimentally. "Do you suppose I could get racing papers on a Megabelodon?"

It was shortly after our Little Journey to the Last Home of Sysonby that I suggested a Little Journey to the Home of the New York *Journal-American*, the Hearst newspaper that encompasses in its identity the old *Evening Journal*, on which the Colonel scored his scoops, along with the *Journal*, its senior, and the *American*, its junior.

The Colonel had learned from a newspaper paragraph that there was at least one man at the *Journal-American* who had been an office boy in the sports department in his day. The paragraph had recorded a testimonial dinner celebrating the man's fiftieth year of service, at which fellow employes had presented him with a watch. The Colonel had passed on the information without comment, but it was my idea to promote the reunion, in the belief that some further details of the Colonel's career in the days of halcyon might accrue. He telephoned to the man, whose name was

Harry, and the mutual recognition, to judge from the Colonel's end of the conversation, was immediate. Harry, after all these years, the Colonel informed me, was now sports make-up man, a job replete with responsibility and tension, for it means putting the several sports pages together for each of several editions, rearranging them each time to feature the latest news. Four in the afternoon, Harry said, was a good time to come and see him.

At luncheon on the day set for this Little Journey my old friend was, not unnaturally, in reminiscent mood.

"The Hearst empire of my day was, like that of the Byzantine emperors, labyrinthian," he said, "and not without occasional instances of corruption stemming from its uncontrollable ramification. Each of the Old Man's objetti d'art, it was rumored, had been paid for at least three times by officials of duplicative functions, two of the three prices being split between the art merchants and the disbursing officers. A similar tropical profusion reigned in all other departments where gelt was to be laid hands upon, and this sometimes redounded to the profit of even the reporter.

"I well remember one winter when I was covering racing at New Orleans I received, in place of my regular weekly money order for $125, including expenses, a whopping one for $750. I had sent for no extra Tease, but there it was, all properly made out to me. After a period of trepidation, waiting for the home office to announce discovery of its error, temptation prevailed and I spent the money. There followed a period of more intensive apprehension, but this in turn receded into the subconscious recesses of my mind, and I forgot all about it. Full fifteen years later, protected by the statute of limitations, I was standing in the Palace Hotel bar at San Francisco in full sartorial splendor. I was riding high on the Great American Hog. The Syndicate was proliferating profit as well as pork chops. Down the bar from me I noted a man who seemed familiar. He was a seedy character however, in so advanced a state of disintegration that I wondered he had the temerity to brave the flunkey at the door. Upon further inspection I was horrified to recognize a man with an Irish name I now forget, who had once been auditor of the *Journal*, but who had been caught siding with the losing party in some court intrigue for the Old Man's favor. So he had had to suffer legal penalty for the peccadilloes of which his persecutors were perhaps equally guilty. He had embezzled around eighty grand, the price of a bogus stained-glass window, and so he got five.

"Upon his emergence from the stocks, he had found no ready victim and had made his way west, arriving in the debilitated format which had excited my commiseration. Putting my arm around his shoulder, I said to him, 'Mr. O'Calagan'—or whatever the name was—'I am *so* glad to see you again, and by the way, here is a small sum I have owed you for years,' and I slipped him a sawbuck.

" 'It is damned little interest on that 750,' he said.

"I then realized," Colonel Stingo said, "that the man had embezzled to gratify all his tastes. One of them had been philanthropy. Heaven knows how many employes' lives he had brightened with his unexpected gratuities. He may have prevented suicides, facilitated marriages, made possible appendectomies. And the Old Man would have blown the Tease on a bogus tapestry if O'Calagan hadn't diverted it."

We rode the East Side subway down from Grand Central to Brooklyn Bridge. When we came up out of the hole we were just outside City Hall Park and diagonally across the street from the Pulitzer Building, that monument to a great publisher's posthumous defeat. The building stared down, unkempt as a deserted eagle's nest, and the Colonel looked distressed. He remembered the park as the centre of the newspaper world, with editorial offices elbow to elbow all along Park Row. Even I could remember when five daily papers of general circulation clustered around the square,—the *Sun* at the northwest corner, the *World* and *Evening World* in the Pulitzer Building, and the *Journal* and *American* in the old rookery on William Street. Now there were none.

"The deterioration is pronounced," the Colonel said. "It is even worse than Times Square."

We started to walk to the East River to find the *Journal-American,* which stands on a wind-swept barren north of the Fulton Fish Market, a site so inaccessible the company runs buses from the subway railhead to the bleak door.

As we threaded the labyrinthian East Side streets the Colonel grew progressively more depressed. "It is the road to Siberia," he said. "I haven't seen a good-looking saloon for three blocks." When we came in sight of the Hearst newspaper building at Catherine Slip and the river, he stopped and surveyed the bare, nondescript rectangle of whitewashed concrete. "It's like a factory," he said, and wriggled his shoulders as if to shake off a revulsion. But he gamely got under way again. We entered the portal, under the eye of a house cop, and went up to the sports department, which is spread out, together with the city side, on one vast loft floor, like a garment plant before the unions got strong. The fluorescent lights overhead cast a wan glow on the sweat-pearled forehead of a man on the city side whom I recognized as one of the *Journal-American's* experts on Communists. The chap, a long-legged snollygoster with a profile like Andy Gump, looked intently at the Colonel, as if preparing to identify him as leader of a cell at Tanforan race track in 1937. The Colonel was unconscious of his peril, but I was beginning to be uneasy by the time we found the old colleague, Harry.

Since Harry had been a copy boy when the Colonel was already an established racing expert, I took it that Harry was about ten years younger than the stylist of the New York *Enquirer*, but they looked to be much of an age. They began almost immediately to enumerate the men they had worked with who were dead, their words expressing regret and their voices a guilty pleasure in their survival. Harry remarked that the Colonel had put on weight. The Colonel said he wasn't pitching any more. The Colonel said Harry had lost weight. Harry said the doctor had made him cut down on his eating. He had a family and lived in some place like Jackson Heights or Gibson, Long Island, and he came to work five days a week at some atrocious morning hour like eight or nine or ten and spent his day under the fluorescents, wondering whether there would be enough championship golf scores in to put a head on for the four o'clock edition.

As they talked, Harry and the Colonel measured each other with an affectionately actuarial eye. They were glad to see each other, but it was evident that their paths had diverged since 1907, and they didn't seem to have anything more recent to talk about.

"I remember how we used to sit around waiting for your exclusive from the track: PITTSBURGH PHIL SENDS BOOKS TO COVER, or something like that," said Harry, and the Colonel smiled graciously. But he seemed uneasy, and to my surprise, did not make his visit a long one. When he started for the elevator he was walking faster than usual, and by the time we got down to the functionally bare lobby, he almost sprinted for the door. He reached the sidewalk like a booster pursued by a store detective, and tore on for a block in silence, until he spotted a saloon. It was of dismal aspect, but he headed in like a Central Park riding horse going back to a warm barn.

"I would suggest a double bonded bourbon, straight," he said to the grimy-handed bartender wearing a shirt unlaundered for a month. He was suspending the Rule of the Great Transition.

While the bartender was fumbling among the bottles to find one that did not contain neutral grain spirits, the Colonel said to me:

"Joe, it was just like a prison. Newspaper life nowadays must be like working in a factory."

He got his drink, and after he had knocked it back with one swift, untypical motion, he began to feel better. His mouth lost its unwonted tightness, and the corners turned up in his habitual happy smile.

"Joe," he said, "affluence has not crowned my endeavors—as yet. But all I need is one good gold mine west of the Missouri. And I've certainly done a lot better than Harry."

The Colonel clasped his shot glass as possessively as if it contained fifty years of episodia.

THE EARL OF LOUISIANA

Contents

1 / "Joe Sims, Where the Hell?"

SOUTHERN political personalities, like sweet corn, travel badly. They lose flavor with every hundred yards away from the patch. By the time they reach New York, they are like Golden Bantam that has been trucked up from Texas—stale and unprofitable. The consumer forgets that the corn tastes different where it grows. That, I suppose, is why for twenty-five years I underrated Huey Pierce Long. During the early thirties, as a feature writer for a New York evening paper, I interviewed him twice—once at the brand-new Waldorf and once at the brand-new Hotel New Yorker. The city desk showed what it thought of him by sending me instead of a regular political reporter; the idea was that he might say something funny but certainly nothing important. He said neither. Both times he received me in his pajamas, lying on top of his bed and scratching himself. It was a routine he had made nationally famous in 1930, when, as Governor of Louisiana, he so received the official call of the commander of a German cruiser visiting New Orleans, causing the Weimar Republic to make diplomatic representations. New York reporters couldn't figure out how he expected to get space with the same gag every time he came to town, but now I think I understand. He was from a country that had not yet entered the era of mass communications. In Louisiana, a stump speaker still tells the same joke at every stop on a five-speech afternoon. He has a different audience each time, like an old vaudeville comic, and Huey just hadn't realized that when a gag gets national circulation it's spoiled.

It was the same with his few remarks intended to be serious. He would boast of free schoolbooks, which we had had in New York since before he was born, and good roads, which ditto. Then, talking in the shadow of the new Empire State Building, he would brag about the thirty-four-story Capitol he had built in Baton Rouge. As for the eight bodyguards he brought with him, they seemed in New York an absurd affectation: didn't he know we had cops? And who would bother to shoot him anyway? It is hard to put yourself across as a buffoon and a potential martyr at the same time, and Huey did not convince us in either role. A chubby man, he had ginger hair and tight skin that was the color of a sunburn coming on. It was an uneasy color combination, like an orange tie on a pink shirt. His face faintly suggested mumps, and he once tipped the theater-ticket girl in the lobby of the Hotel New Yorker three cents for getting him four tickets to a show that was sold out for a month in advance.

Late in July 1959 I was in Baton Rouge, and I took a taxi out to the Capitol, where he is buried. Standing by Huey's grave, I had him in a different perspective. A heroic, photographically literal statue of him stands on a high pedestal above his grave in the Capitol grounds. The face, impudent, porcine and juvenile, is turned toward the building he put up—all thirty-four stories of it—in slightly more than a year, mostly with Federal money. The bronze double-breasted jacket, tight over the plump belly, has already attained the dignity of a period costume, like Lincoln's frock coat. In bronze, Huey looks like all the waggish fellows from Asheville and Nashville, South Bend and Topeka, who used to fill our costlier speakeasies in the late twenties and early thirties. He looks like a golf-score-and-dirty-joke man, anxious for the good opinion of everybody he encounters. Seeing him there made me feel sad and old. A marble Pegasus carved in bas-relief below his feet bears a scroll that says, "Share Our Wealth." That was one of Huey's slogans; another was "Every Man a King."

I walked along well-tended paths between melancholy Southern trees to the entrance of the Capitol, which is reached by forty-eight granite steps, each bearing the name of a state, in order of admission to the Union; to include Alaska and Hawaii, Louisiana will have to raise the Capitol. My taxi driver, a tall prognathous type who was a small boy when Huey was killed, had parked his cab somewhere and now sociably rejoined me. "The newspapers gave old Huey hell when he built that for five mil-li-on," he said, waving toward the skyscraper. "You couldn't build it now for a hundred mil-li-on." He talked of Huey as a contemporary, the way some people in Springfield, Illinois, talk of Lincoln.

Inside the Capitol, which is air-cooled, I paused, breathless with gratitude. Outside, the heat was pushing a hundred. The interior of the building is faced with agate, porphyry, basalt, alabaster and such—more than thirty kinds of stone, the *Louisiana Guide* says. It is the richest thing in its line since they moved the barbershop in the Grand Central Station upstairs. The rotunda, as slick as mortuary slabs on end, reminded me pleasurably of Grant's and Napoleon's tombs, the shrines that early fixed my architectural tastes forever. Marble, high ceilings and a reverential hush are the things I like inside a public building—they spell class. In addition to all this, and air-conditioning, the Capitol has its legend, and perhaps its ghost, hurrying along the corridor at the rear of the first floor. Looking around, I thought of what the Chief Justice of the Supreme Court of Louisiana had told me a day earlier about how Huey was shot in this monument he had erected to himself.

At sixty-four the Chief Justice, the Honorable John Baptiste Fournet, is still a formidable figure of a man—tall and powerful and presenting what might be considered in another state the outward appearance of a highly successful bookmaker. The suit he had on when I saw him, of rich, snuff-colored silk, was cut with the virtuosity that only subtropical tailors expend on hot-weather clothing. Summer clothes in the North are make-shifts, like seasonal slipcovers on furniture, and look it. The Chief Justice wore a diamond the size of a Colossal ripe olive on the ring finger of his left hand and a triangle of flat diamonds as big as a trowel in his tie. His manner was imbued with a gracious warmth not commonly associated with the judiciary, and his voice reflected at a distance of three centuries the France from which his ancestors had migrated, although he pronounces his name "Fournett." (The pronunciation of French proper names in Louisiana would make a good monograph. There was, for example, a state senator named DeBlieux who was called simply "W.") I had gone to the Chief Justice to talk politics, but somehow he had got around to telling me instead about the night of September 8, 1935, which has the same significance among Longites that St. Bartholomew's Day has for French Protestants.

Huey had come down from Washington, where he was serving as United States Senator, to run a special session of the Louisiana Legislature, Justice Fournet said. He controlled the state from Washington through a caretaker Governor named O. K. Allen, but whenever there was a bit of political hocus-pocus to be brought off that he thought was beyond Allen's limited competence, he would come home to put the legislators through their hoops himself. When Huey was in Baton Rouge, everybody called him Governor. Since he feared assassination, he had a flat furnished for him on the thirty-fourth floor of the Capitol, and theoretically he would retire to it at the end of each legislative day, but, Fournet said, "He was the kind of man who was always running around so they couldn't keep him in that apartment. He was a hard man to guard." Fournet himself had served as Speaker of the House—it was he who adjourned the Legislature when Huey's enemies were about to impeach him—and, after that, as Lieutenant Governor under Allen. Huey had later looked after his old friend by pushing his election as an Associate Justice of the State Supreme Court. The Court was in the front line of conflict, because, as the Chief Justice explained to me, "There was hardly a piece of legislation that Huey introduced that the other side didn't carry to litigation. Huey had what he called a 'deduct' system—ten per cent of the salary of every state employee for his political fund. It sounds raw, but he had to take the money where he could; the other side had all the money of Standard Oil to pay its attorneys. I was elected for a term of fourteen years, and on the day I took the oath of office I had to start thinking about my campaign for re-election." On September 8, 1935, the Chief Justice said, he had to see Huey personally about some friends who needed political help, so he drove up to Baton Rouge from New Orleans, where the Supreme Court sits, and arrived at the Capitol just before nine at night, when the Legislature was to recess. Here he offered a slight digression. "People from out of state sometimes ask me why the Supreme Court sits in New Orleans when the capital is Baton Rouge, only eighty miles away," he said. "I tell them the truth—that there wasn't a road you could count on until Huey got in office, so the busy lawyers of New Orleans would have spent half their lives traveling back and forth. Now you can make it in an hour and a half, thanks to Huey, but the Court has stayed in New Orleans, mostly from habit."

When Fournet reached the Capitol, Huey was in the House chamber, on the second floor, co-ordinating the efforts of his legislators, and Fournet walked in and took a seat. He had the Senator under his eye, but when the session broke, there were a number of people between them, and Huey started out the door so fast that Fournet couldn't get to him. "That man never walked," he told me. Huey headed toward the corridor in the rear of the building that led to Governor Allen's office, and Fournet followed, content to catch Huey when he came out after leaving a few instructions with the titular Governor of Louisiana. There were bodyguards in platoon strength in front of the Senator and behind him as he trotted. Entering the corridor, Fournet saw a couple of rich dilettante politicians who were always good for a campaign contribution. He stopped to talk to them and then went on. Huey had disappeared into Allen's office. Fournet, as he followed him, passed two or three men standing in a recess in the wall, talking. He paid them no heed, assuming that they had just emerged from the House chamber, as he had. Then Huey came out of Allen's door, turning, with the knob still in his hand, to shout an inquiry back into the room. Fournet heard the answer: "All of them have been notified, Governor." He started toward Huey, and as he did a young man came up on his right side and passed him, walking fast. What attracted the Justice's attention was that he had a stubby black pistol in his right hand. "It was a hot night—before air-conditioning—and I perspire exceptionally," Justice Fournet said. "So I was holding my Panama hat in my right hand while I wiped my head with a handkerchief in my left. Without thinking, I hit at the man with my hat, backhand. But he reached Huey and fired, and Murphy Roden, a bodyguard, grabbed his gun hand and got a finger inside the trigger guard, else he would have killed Murphy. Huey spun around, made one whoop, and ran down the hall like a hit deer. Murphy and the young man went to the floor, both holding that gun and Murphy trying to reach his own gun with his other hand. I was leaning over them, thinking to grab hold, and Elias Coleman, another guard, leaned, too, and fired two bullets that passed, by the mercy of God, between Murphy and me and killed the fellow. He let go his gun and lay there. He had black hair, combed down a little slick, as I remember it, and black-rimmed eyeglasses. Huey ran clear to the end of the hall and down a flight of stairs. Then the other guards pulled the body over to the wall and emptied their guns into it. It sounded like machine guns."

When Huey got to the lower hall, a couple of fellows he knew stopped him. One said "Are you hit?" and he said "Yes." The other said "Are you hurt bad?" and Huey said "I don't know." They put him in their car and took him to the Our Lady of the Lake Hospital. There, the examining surgeon found that the bullet had perforated Huey's colon and part of one kidney. "I couldn't ride with Huey, because it was a two-seated car," the Chief Justice said, "so I went to get mine, parked not far away, and by the time I saw him again he was on the examining table at the hospital. He felt strong and didn't think he was going to die. 'I want you to be more charitable toward Wade Martin and Ellender,' he said." (Martin was the chairman of the Public Service Commission, and Allen Ellender is now the senior United States Senator from Louisiana.) "He knew that all three of us wanted to be Governor, but he wanted us to get along together." It reminded me of how an old friend of mine, Whitey Bimstein, described the death of Frankie Jerome, a boxer he was seconding in the Madison Square Garden ring. "He died in my arms, slipping punches," Whitey said. Huey, mortally shot, talked politics.

Alone, except for the taxi driver, in the rotunda of the Capitol, I thought I heard Huey make his one whoop, but the sound may have been a mere hallucination. In any case, I felt different about Huey when I walked out into the heat. By that time I had been in Louisiana about ten days, and I had also changed my mind about Earl Long, then Governor of the state. Earl was Huey's brother, his junior by two years and his survivor by a quarter of a century, and although Fournet had said that Earl "wouldn't make a patch on Huey's pants," it seemed to me that he was filling a pretty fair pair of country britches.

For one thing, the expression of conventional indignation is not so customary in Louisiana as farther north. The Louisianians, like Levantines, think it naïve. A pillar of the Baton Rouge economy, whom I shall here call Cousin Horace, had given me an illustration, from his own youth, of why this is so.

"When I was a young man, fresh out of Tulane," he said, "I was full of civic consciousness. I joined with a number of like-minded reformers to raise a fund to bribe the Legislature to impeach Huey. To insure that the movement had a broad popular base, subscriptions were limited to one thousand dollars. When I went to my father, who was rich as cream, to collect his ante, I couldn't get but five hundred from him—he said he felt kind of skeptical. So I put up a thousand for me and the other five hundred for him. I wouldn't pass up a chance to give the maximum for such a good cause.

"A vote of two-thirds of each house was needed to impeach, and there were then thirty-nine state senators. But before our chairman could see enough of them, Huey induced fifteen—a third plus two—to sign a round robin stating they would not impeach no matter *what* the evidence was. Earl says now that he thought of that scheme. We were licked, so I went around to the eminent reform attorney who was treasurer of our enterprise and asked for my money back.

" 'Son,' he said, 'I am keeping *all* the subscriptions as my fee.'

"I was mad as hell, and told Dad, and he said, 'Son, it shows I did right to hold out my other five hundred—I gave it to Huey as part of the contribution he levied on me to pay the fellows on *his* side.' "

Cousin Horace, who looks like Warren Gamaliel Harding, the handsomest of Presidents, imbibed deeply of a Ramos gin fizz.

"Right then," he said, after the interval, "I made up my mind that it didn't make any difference which side was in in Louisiana, and I have stuck to business ever since."

It was Cousin Horace who told me that the disparity between the two Longs was not one of shrewdness but of scope. "Earl is just as smart a politician inside the state as Huey was," he said, "but Huey saw things big.

"I'll give you an example. One evening during Prohibition, Huey came around to my dad's house and said, 'Telemon, I need a drink.' My father went down to his cellar—he prided himself on it—and brought up a bottle of pre-World War One Jack Daniel. When he started to open it Huey said, 'Don't open that bottle for me, Telemon; it's too good. I'll take it.'

"So he put it in his pocket and left. Earl would have given Dad a drink out of the bottle."

I had left New York thinking of Earl as a Peckerwood Caligula. Dispatches in the New York papers had left small doubt that he had gone off his rocker during the May session of the Legislature, and I wanted to see what happens to a state when its chief executive is in that sort of fix. The papers reported that he had cursed and hollered at the legislators, saying things that so embarrassed his wife, Miz Blanche, and his relatives that they had packed him off to Texas in a National Guard plane to get his brains repaired in an asylum.

By late July, when I arrived in Louisiana, he had heaved himself back into power by arguing his way out of the Texas sanitarium, touching base at a New Orleans private hospital and legalizing his way out of the Southeast Louisiana State Hospital, at Mandeville. Then he had departed on a long tour of recuperation at out-of-state Western race tracks that most of the lay public had never heard of before he hit them. Just after I disembarked from my plane in New Orleans I read in the local *Times-Picayune* that the "ailing Governor" had got as far back toward home as Hot Springs, Arkansas, a resort famous for reconditioning old prize fighters and race horses. He had promised to be back in the state on August 1, in time to begin stumping for renomination as Governor in the Democratic primary elections, four months away.

"You know, I think ol' Earl will just about do it again," the taxi driver said as we descended the Capitol's forty-eight states. The place had started him thinking about the Longs. "It don't set good how they done him like they done, y'unnerstand. Those doctors. And his wife. Saying he was crazy. It'll be like the last time he run, in '56. Two days before the primary, you couldn't find nobody to say he was going to vote for him. Then they all voted for him. And two days later you couldn't find nobody would admit to have voted that way."

With the Governor unavailable, I sat down in New Orleans to await his return and meanwhile try to build up a frame of reference, as the boys in the quarterly magazines would say. Politics is to the conversation of Louisiana what horse racing is to England's. In London, anybody from the Queen to a dustman will talk horses; in Louisiana, anyone from a society woman to a bellhop will talk politics. Louisiana politics is of an intensity and complexity that are matched, in my experience, only in the republic of Lebanon. The balance between the Catholics in southern Louisiana and the Protestants in northern Louisiana is as delicate as that between the Moslems and the Christians in Lebanon and is respected by the same convention of balanced tickets. In Louisiana there is a substantial Negro vote—about a hundred and fifty thousand—that no candidate can afford to discourage privately or to solicit publicly. In the sister Arab republic, Moslem and Christian candidates alike need the Druse vote, although whoever gets it is suspected of revolutionary designs.

The grand gimmick of Louisiana politics, however, providing it with a central mechanism as fascinating as a roulette wheel, is the double-primary system for gubernatorial nominations. The first primary is open to anyone who can get up the registration fee of two hundred and ten dollars. This brings out as many entries as the Preakness or the Kentucky Derby. If any candidate has more than fifty per cent of the total votes, he wins the nomination, which means that he will automatically be elected, since Democratic nomination is a ticket to the Governor's Mansion. If no one has a clear majority, the two top men have a runoff in a second primary, held about a month later.

It is unusual for a candidate to win first time around, and if one does he arouses a certain amount of resentment as a spoilsport. After the first primary, each beaten candidate and his backers trade off their support to one of the two men who are still alive, in exchange for what he will bind himself to do for them in the way of legislation, patronage or simple commercial advantage. Naturally, the runoff candidate who looks more likely to win can buy support at lower political prices than the other fellow, but by trying to drive too hard a bargain he may send the business to the underdog. Many a man has beaten himself that way. A Louisiana politician can't afford to let his animosities carry him away, and still less his principles, although there is seldom difficulty in that department.

In the campaigning days before the first primary, topics of conversation are delightfully unlimited; the talkers guess at not only how many votes a candidate will get in the first primary but what he will trade them off for, and to whom, if he fails to make the second. It is like planning carom shots or four-horse parlays.

In 1959, the date for the first Louisiana primary was December 5, and in July conversation was already intense. The talk centered on Long and whether he would be able to get to the post. I found few people, even among Long's worst friends, who believed that he was "crazy," although there were some who said he had been at the time of his deportation. (This second position, however, was hard to defend in public discussion. "Crazy" and "not crazy," like "guilty" and "not guilty," are terms that, in popular usage, admit of no shading in between; being crazy or being not crazy is considered a permanent condition, like having one leg.) In New York, the stories of his conduct on his Western tour of convalescence may have seemed clear evidence that the old boy was mad—the phrenetic betting on horse races, the oddly assorted roadside purchases (forty-four cases of cantaloupes, seven hundred dollars' worth of cowboy boots, and such), the endless nocturnal telephone calls, the quarrels with his friends and guards—but seen from New Orleans they indicated a return to normal. Earl had always been like that, fellows who knew him said. A summary of his physical condition had been released to the press by the physicians who examined him after his discharge from the State Hospital at Mandeville on June 26. The doctors' workup on the Governor looked dreadful to a layman—bum ticker, series of cerebral accidents, hardening of the arteries, and a not otherwise described condition called bronchiectasis. But there were lay experts who said that it was all a fake—that no doctor had been able to lay a hand on Earl to examine him.

A Louisiana political tipster never expresses a reservation, and when politics extends over into the field of pathology the positiveness extends with it. "I know a fella that Earl carries with him all the time, hear? and he says Earl just playing mousy, y'unnerstand?" summed up one extreme position. The opposing view could be summarized as "I know a fella told me they gave him adrenalin right in his heart, hear? and that means the old alligator is in extremis, y'unnerstand?" On my first evening in New Orleans, I received forty-two other prognoses in between.

Nor was there any agreement on the efficacy of the device whereby Earl, in entering the primaries, was challenging the Louisiana constitution, which provides that a governor may not succeed himself directly. Earl, bowing to this law, had dropped out after his 1948–52 term, and then had returned in 1956. Now, however, he was raising the point that if he resigned before election—the formal, post-primary, election, that is—his Lieutenant Governor would become Governor, and so he, coming in to begin a new term, would be succeeding not himself but the fellow who had succeeded him. Even Huey had not thought of that one.

What I heard from Long men was that it was the way the law read that counted, hear? and not what the framers had wanted it to signify. From the other side I heard that there wasn't a court in the country but would hold against a little fine-print loophole, and yeah, you resigned, but, yeah, you can't get away with that. Another point of dispute was how near the Governor stood to Federal prison.

The Income Tax people were reportedly on his trail, and apparently they were not being as hermetically secretive as they are supposed to be, or else the Natty Bumppos stalking Earl had stepped on a couple of dry twigs. The range of the opinion on this point lay between "They got it on him this time, hear?" and "Uncle Earl is just too smart to get caught so easy. Whatever he got, he'll say it was campaign contributions, same as Nixon in '52. That's why he's got to keep on campaigning, y'unnerstand?" (There is no statutory limit on campaign contributions in the state of Louisiana, and Earl Long often said, like Brother Huey before him, that he was campaigning all the time.)

Arranged in capsule form, all the areas of disagreement about the Governor, peacefully soaking his hide in the Arkansas vats, came to this: The perfect sour-on-Long man held that he was likely to die before the primaries, sure to get licked if he survived, certain to be thrown out by the State Supreme Court if nominated, and bound to be in jail before he could be inaugurated. The perfect Long man expressed faith that the Governor was as full of fight as a man twenty years younger, that he would probably win the first primary with seventy per cent of the vote, that he had the Louisiana Supreme Court in his pocket, and that if campaign contributions weren't income for a Republican like Nixon, they weren't income for a Democrat like Uncle Earl.

On my first night in town, before I had finished my third Sazerac at the little bar in Arnaud's Restaurant while waiting for a table, I was not only indoctrinated but willing to bet. An outsider, I had no feedbox information and less idea of the form, but I had an analogy, and nothing can seem more impressive to a man drinking on an empty stomach.

"When Pat McCarran was seventy-one," I said to the pair of home experts with me, "he had a heart attack so bad that they were laying eight to one against him in the Nevada Turf Club, but he recovered and lived seven years to ruin every politician who hopped off him when he was sick. He was mean. How old is Uncle Earl?"

"Sixty-three," said one expert.

"Is he mean?"

"Mean as hell," said the other.

"You see?" I said. "It's a lock." It was an insight that wouldn't have come to me if Arnaud's had not been doing such a good business, but we got a table just in time to prevent my laying money.

When we had ordered moderately—crabmeat Arnaud, filet mignon *marchand de vin*, and a bottle of Smith-Haut-Lafitte '47—we got back to politics. One of my convives, a lawyer, said that the Governor had deep pockets lined with fishhooks: "When you're with him and he picks up a newspaper, you lay down the nickel." The other man, a newspaperman and former Nieman Fellow at Harvard named Tom Sancton, whom I had known for some time, maintained that old Earl wasn't so bad. "He gives money to every kid he meets," he said. "'A quarter to whites and a nickel to niggers' is the way you hear it around here."

The "nickel to niggers" is a key to the Long family's position on the Southern issue. "They do not favor the Negro," a Negro educator once told me, "but they are less inflexibly antagonistic than the others."

"Earl is like Huey on Negroes," Tom said. "When the new Charity Hospital was built here, some Negro politicians came to Huey and said it was a shame there were no Negro nurses, when more than half the patients were colored. Huey said he'd fix it for them, but they wouldn't like his method. He went around to visit the hospital and pretended to be surprised when he found white nurses waiting on colored men. He blew high as a buzzard can fly, saying it wasn't fit for white women to be so humiliated. It was the most racist talk you ever heard, but the result was he got the white nurses out and the colored nurses in, and they've had the jobs ever since."

A Negro minister in Baton Rouge said to me, later: "Earl is a politician —and a human being." The combination, he evidently felt, was rare.

Since the Governor was not available in the flesh, my friends took me after dinner to see and hear him on film. In the projection room of television station WDSU, which is off a handsome Creole courtyard in the French Quarter, they had arranged for a showing of a documentary composed of various television-newsreel shots, and from this encounter I date my acquaintance with Uncle Earl. The cameramen had covered all the great moments of that fulminating May session of the Legislature, which began with the Governor riding high and ended, for him, when he was led from the floor, tired and incoherent, by Margaret Dixon, the managing editor of the Baton Rouge *Advocate*.

A day later he was under heavy sedation and on his way to Texas, where he arrived, he subsequently said, with "not enough clothes on me to cover a red bug, and a week later I was enjoying the same wardrobe." But within a fortnight he had talked a Texas judge into letting him return to Louisiana on his promise to matriculate at a private hospital in New Orleans. After signing himself in and out of the New Orleans hospital, the Governor had started for Baton Rouge to assume power, only to be stopped by sheriff's deputies at the behest of his wife, Miz Blanche, who had then committed him to the State Hospital at Mandeville. Thence he had been rescued by a faithful retainer, the lawyer Joe Arthur Sims, who sought a writ of habeas corpus. Once the Governor had regained temporary liberty, he completed the job by firing the director of the Department of Hospitals and the superintendent of the hospital, who, in the normal course of events, might have appeared against him to contend that he was insane.

In the opening newsreel shots Long appeared a full-faced, portly, peppery, white-haired man, as full of *hubris* as a dog of ticks in spring, sallying out on the floor of the Legislature to wrest the microphone from the hands of opposition speakers. "Let him talk, Governor, let him talk," a man in the foreground of the picture—perhaps the Speaker—kept saying during these episodes, but the Governor never would. He would shake his finger in his subjects' faces, or grab the lectern with both hands and wag his bottom from side to side. He interrupted one astonished fellow to ask, "What's your name?"

"John Waggoner, from Plain Dealing." (This is the name of a town.)

"Well, well, you look like a fine man. Don't let nothing run over you."

Some of the newsreel clips were of the Governor's press conferences, and in one, when a reporter asked him whether he thought he could manage his legislators, he said, "You know, the Bible says that before the end of time billy goats, tigers, rabbits and house cats are all going to sleep together. My gang looks like the Biblical proposition is here." This was the first good sample of his prose I had had a chance to evaluate, and I immediately put him on a level with my idol Colonel John R. Stingo, the Honest Rainmaker, who, at the age of eighty-five, is selling lots at Massena, New York, a community he predicts will be the Pittsburgh of the future.

In another remark to a reporter I thought I detected a clue to what was to set him off. The Governor said he had reduced 29 pounds, from 203 to 174, in a few months at his doctor's behest. To do this he must have been hopped up with thyroid and Dexedrine, and his already notorious temper, continually sharpened by ungratified appetite, had snapped like a rubber band pulled too hard.

Khrushchev, too, looks like the kind of man his physicians must continually try to diet, and historians will some day correlate these sporadic deprivations, to which he submits "for his own good," with his public tantrums. If there is to be a world cataclysm, it will probably be set off by skim milk, Melba toast, and mineral oil on the salad.

The newsreel also included a sequence in which the Governor sounded off on Mayor deLesseps S. Morrison of New Orleans, who for years had been his rival in Democratic primaries. "I hate to say this—I hate to boost old Dellasoups—but he'll be second again." (Long beat Morrison badly in the 1956 race for Governor. He always referred to him as "Dellasoups" and represented him as a city slicker.) "I'd rather beat Morrison than eat any blackberry, huckleberry pie my mama ever made. Oh, how I'm praying for that stump-wormer to get in there. I want him to roll up them cuffs, and get out that little old tuppy, and pull down them shades, and make himself up. He's the easiest man to make a nut out of I've ever seen in my life." The "tuppy," for "toupee," was a slur on Morrison's hair, which is thinning, though only Long has ever accused him of wearing a wig. As for the make-up, Morrison occasionally used it for television. Earl's Morrison bit was a standard feature of his repertoire, and I could see from the mobile old face how he enjoyed it. Morrison took the "dude" attacks so to heart that in his last campaign he performed dressed like Marlon Brando in deshabille.

And, as if to illustrate the old Long vote-getting method, which had worked in Louisiana ever since Huey took the stump in 1924, the newsreel anthologist had included part of a speech of the Governor's, evidently favoring a higher license fee for heavy (rich men's) vehicles. "Don't you think the people that use the roads ought to pay for building them? Take a man out in the country, on an old-age pension. He don't own an automobile, can't even drive one—do you think he should pay for highways for overloaded trucks that tear up the highways faster than you can build them? We got a coffee-ground formation in south Louisiana—it cost three times more to build a road in south Louisiana than it does in west Texas—but still the *Picayune* says they don't know, they can't understand. Well, there's a hell of a lot that they don't understand—that they *do* understand but they don't want *you* to understand. And you can say this, as long as I've got the breath and the life and the health, I've got the fortitude and the backbone to tell 'em, and dammit they know I'll tell 'em, and that's why they're against me. You can only judge the future by the past."

Almost all the elements of the Long appeal are there, starting with the pensions, which Huey conceived and sponsored, and on which a high proportion of the elderly people in Louisiana live—seventy-two dollars a month now, a fine sum in a low-income state. "But still the *Picayune* says they don't know, they can't understand" refers to the good roads whose high price the *Times-Picayune* constantly carps at, because, the Longs always imply, the *Picayune*, organ of the czarists, secretly wants *bad* roads. "They know I'll tell them, and that's why they're against me" means that the press—a monopoly press in New Orleans now—has always been against the Longs, the champions of the poor; when all the press consistently opposes one skillful man, he can turn its opposition into a backhanded testimony to his unique virtue.

"You can only judge the future by the past" is a reminder that the past in Louisiana, before Huey, was painful for the small farmers in the northern hills and along the southern bayous. It is not hard to select such an all-inclusive passage from a Long speech; they recur constantly, the mixture as before.

Then followed clips showing the crucial scrimmages on the floor of the Legislature. In the beginning, I could see, the Governor was as confident as Oedipus Tyrannus before he got the bad news. He felt a giant among pygmies, a pike among crappies, as he stood there among the legislators, most of whom owed him for favors—special bills passed for their law clients, state jobs for constituents, "contributions" for their personal campaign funds, and so on. But that day the Governor was rushing in where the dinner-party liberals who represent one or two Southern states in Washington have steadily refused to tread. Old Earl was out to liberalize the registration law, passed in Reconstruction times, that gives parish (i.e., county) registrars the power to disqualify voters arbitrarily on "educational" grounds. Except in a few rural parishes, the effect of this law has been on the decline for decades, but now a white-supremacy group in the Legislature had moved for its strict enforcement—against colored voters, of course. It took me a minute or two to realize that the old "demagogue" was actually making a civil-rights speech.

"Now, this registration you're talking about," he said. "That was put through in carpetbag days, when colored people and scalawags were running rampant in our country. You got to interpret the Constitution. There ain't ten people looking at me, including myself, who, if properly approached or attacked, could properly qualify to vote. They say this a nigger bill—ain't no such." (The old law, if enforced impartially, would also have disqualified a number—large but hard to estimate—of older white men and women who had been on the rolls since they were twenty-one but were not Ph.Ds. Needless to say, the bill's proponents did not expect enforcement to be impartial.)

At this point, the camera focused on a young man with slick black hair and a long upper lip who was wearing a broad necktie emblazoned with a Confederate flag and who addressed a microphone with gestures appropriate to mass meetings. "It's Willie Rainach, the Citizens' Council boy," one of my mentors told me. Rainach, who is a state senator from Summerfield, in Claiborne Parish, pleaded with his colleagues not to let Long "sell Louisiana down the river." (I felt another concept crumbling; I had always thought it was Negroes who got sold down rivers.)

Long, grabbing for a microphone—probably he had no legal right to be in the argument at all—remonstrated, "I think there's such a thing as being overeducated. Scientists tell me there's enough wrinkles up there—" tapping his head—"to take care of all kinds of stuff. Maybe I'm getting old—I'm losing some of mine. I hope that don't happen to Rainach. After all this is over, he'll probably go up there to Summerfield, get up on his front porch, take off his shoes, wash his feet, look at the moon and get close to God." This was gross comedy, a piece of miming that recalled Jimmy Savo impersonating the Mississippi River. Then the old man, changing pace, shouted in Rainach's direction, "And when you *do*, you got to *re*cognize that *niggers* is human beings!"

It was at this point that the legislators must have decided he'd gone off his crumpet. Old Earl, a Southern politician, was taking the Fourteenth Amendment's position that "no State shall make or enforce any law which shall abridge the privileges or immunities of citizens of the United States . . . nor deny to any person within its jurisdiction the equal protection of the laws." So sporadic was my interest in Southern matters then that I did not know the Federal Department of Justice had already taken action against Washington Parish, over near the Mississippi line, because the exponents of the law that Earl didn't like had scratched the names of 1,377 Negro voters, out of a total of 1,510, from the rolls. (When, in January 1960, six months later, United States District Judge J. Skelly Wright, a Louisianian, ordered the Negroes' names put back on the rolls, no dispatch clapped old Earl on the back for having championed them. Nor, in February, when Louisiana appealed Judge Wright's decision and the Supreme Court sustained it, did anybody give the old battler credit for having battled. The main feature of the civil-rights bill passed by Congress was, in fact, an affirmation of the Earl Long argument that led to his sojourn in Texas, but nobody recalled the trouble that his fight for civil rights had cost him.)

"There's no longer *slavery!*" Long shouted at Rainach. "There wasn't but two people in Winn Parish that was able to own slaves—one was my grandpa, the other was my uncle—and when they were freed, they stayed on" (here his voice went tenor and sentimental, then dropped again) "and two of those fine old colored women more or less died in my Christian mother's arms—Black Alice and Aunt Rose." He sounded like a blend of David Warfield and Morton Downey. "To keep fine, honorable gray-headed men and women off the registration rolls, some of whom have been voting as much as sixty or sixty-five years—I plead with you in all candor. I'm a candidate for Governor. If it hurts me, it will just have to hurt."

He didn't believe it would hurt, but it did. In any case, he was taking a chance, which put him in a class by himself among Southern public men.

This was the high point of the Governor's performance, an Elizabethan juxtaposition of comedy and pathos; weeks after witnessing it, I could still visualize Senator Rainach up on his porch in Summerfield, looking at the moon, foot in hand, and feeling integrated with his Creator. As the session continued, the old man, blundering into opposition he hadn't expected, became bitter and hardly coherent.

The theme of one long passage was that many legislators had Negro or at least part-Negro relatives in the bar sinister category, to whom they now wanted to deny the vote. He told a story about his own uncle who, climbing into bed with a Negro woman, had given umbrage to her husband, then present.

Here the Governor's voice was sad, like the voice of a man recounting the death of Agamemnon: "He shot my poor uncle—" a one-beat pause—"and he died." If white men had let Negro women alone, he said, there wouldn't be any trouble.

The squabble continued, Uncle Earl growing progressively less effective, but with flashes of humor: of some fellow on his own side, he said once, "Why does the *Picayune* hate him—is why I like him. When he makes the *Picayune* scratch and wiggle, he is putting anointed oil on my head."

The others snarled him down, and Mrs. Dixon led him from the floor.

The light in the projection room went on, as if at the end of a first act, and there was a pause while the operator loaded a new reel. When the show went on again, I saw a shocking change. The Governor, between his exit from the screen and his reappearance, had made the tortuous journey to Texas and back. Extended on a pallet in a dusty little hotel at Covington, where he lay after winning his way to freedom by firing the hospital officials, he recalled old newsreel shots of Mahatma Gandhi. His pale, emaciated arms and chest showed over the top of a sheet that covered the rest of his body, and he addressed the reporters in a hoarse whisper that was hard to understand because he had mislaid his dentures. It was the beginning of the second chapter of the legend of Long-family martyrdom: following the assassination of Huey, the crucifixion of Earl.

"I'm very happy to be relieved from hijacking, kidnaping, punctures, needles, and everything they could use," he said, "and one of the first things I'm going to do is see that no person, colored or white or what, has to go through the same humiliation, the same intimidation, the same hurts and bruises that I did. I think it was politics—I think some of my enemies thought that this was a way to get rid of old Uncle Earl.

"In my opinion, instead of hurting me politically, I think this is going to make me," the old boy moaned happily, transmuting his hurts into votes even as he ached, "I b'lieve our state and nation needs a few senior statesmen to hold the younger ones down—when you get to be sixty you realize what it's all about."

Here he closed his eyes, as if in mystic prayer, and one of the Faithful around him, a woman with a big chin, hauled off and recited W. E. Henley's "Invictus," the Long family anthem since Huey's day—it was the only poem Huey ever liked.

His appearance and weakness at this interview had set many reporters to predicting that his death was imminent. But his performances within the next month had stimulated a counter-rumor that the whole episode was from beginning to end a fake, put on to build up a defense against income-tax prosecution. The second report credited its hero with a yogi's gift of physical retraction—he had lost another thirty pounds between the Baton Rouge and Covington scenes.

Now, in a motel near Covington, a day later, he was on the subject of his wife, talking with a touch more vigor as he picked up strength: "There hasn't been a woman employed by me that she didn't worry about—any decent, nice-looking woman. How can an old man like me take care of three or four of them when I'd do well to take care of one and know I'm doing a bum job at that—that's why she tried to get rid of me—I don't blame her."

The next sequence was pastoral—on the veranda of Earl's old-fashioned farm at Winnfield, in his home parish, where it is politically inadvisable to paint the house too often. The horrors of Texas and Mandeville were beginning to recede. "Now I'm at my little ol' peapatch farm in Winnfield, where I raise some billy goats, shoats, cows, got two or three old plug horses, but they suit me," he said. "I knew I was a little run down in the Legislature. Only two weeks to go, and I knew there was lots of important things that would fall if I wasn't there. When they kidnaped me, I lost the loan-shark bill." This was a bill to regulate rates of interest charged by small-loan companies, and the Governor's tone made me tremble for the small debtors of Louisiana, left naked to the exactions of the Shylocks.

The respite at Winnfield was brief, however—just a couple of days, while he prepared for a few nonpolitical, pre-campaign stump speeches. The screen showed one of these stump appearances, too. The Governor was weak and had to be helped up some wooden steps set against the side of the flat-bodied truck from which he spoke. The sun, to judge from the sweaty faces of the crowd, must have been killing. He didn't say much; the main purpose of his appearances was to show the voters that Lazarus was in business at the old stand. Joe Arthur Sims, his disciple-at-law, made the principal speech. Mr. Sims is a big young man, about six feet four, with a big face windowed in tortoise shell, a big chin, and a big voice.

His delivery is based on increasing volume, like the noise of an approaching subway train; when he reaches his climaxes, you feel almost irresistibly impelled to throw yourself flat between the rails and let the cars pass over you. "When our beloved friend, the *fine* Governor of the Gret Stet of Loosiana, sent for me in his need at Mandeville," Mr. Sims said, "his condition had been *so* MISREPRESENTED—" here he took the train around a loop and up to Seventy-second Street before he started down again—"that people I knew said to me, 'Don't you go up there, Joe Sims. That man is a *hyena*. He'll BITE YOU IN THE LAIG.' But I went. I went to Mandeville, and before I could reach my friend, *the armed guard had to open ten locked doors,* and lock each one of 'em again after us. And theah, *theah*, I found the FINE Governor, of the GRET Stet of Loosiana—" and here his shocked voice backed up way beyond Columbus Circle—"without SHOES, without a stitch of CLOTHES to put awn him, without a friend to counsel with. And he was just as rational as he has ever been in his life, or as you see him here today. He said, 'JOE SIMS, WHERE THE HELL YOU BEEN?' "

2 / He's an Imam

WHEN Tom and the lawyer and I left the projection room, I felt that I had been introduced into a new world, and it gave me something to think about as we moved from cool WDSU through the wet heat toward Pete Herman's bar. The transitions between conditioned and unconditioned air are the new pattern of life in the summer South. This was a pilgrimage. Herman (his name in the prize ring), who has been blind for thirty-seven years, was the best infighter I have ever seen in my life, and I had to tell him so. As I age, I grow more punctilious about my aesthetic debts; in Paris a few years ago I met Arthur Waley and thanked him for translating the *Tale of Genji.* I had watched Herman fight fifteen rounds against Midget Smith at the old Madison Square Garden during my college holidays in December of 1921. They were bantamweights—a hundred and eighteen pounds. Herman was already nearly blind, although he was not saying so. He fought by a system of feint and touch. Until he could make contact, he would move his head to draw Smith's punches to where he did not mean to be, and then, as soon as he felt a glove or an arm or a passing current of air, he knew where he was. If he had his glove on a man's right biceps, he knew where the man's left hand and belly and chin must be as a touch typist knows where the letters are on the keyboard. He could anticipate moves, and lead and counter and put his combinations of blows together at a range of inches; I have heard it said that he could feint, and fool you, with both hands out of sight. At the Garden, I could see the beauty of what he was doing, but I couldn't understand why, when he hurt Smith, he didn't follow him up. And until he had established touch again, Herman was lost; Smith, a tough little slugger, caught him with some savage blows that Herman—inexplicably, then—failed to see, although they were a long way coming. Smith got the decision, but I thought it unjust, and until Herman's manager announced Pete's retirement because of blindness, I lacked the key to what I had witnessed. In the thirty-nine years since, I have never seen such a performance. "What Pete Herman done," an initiate once told me, with awe, "nobody could have learned him." My New Orleans companions, both of whom were children when Herman was fighting, could not fathom my compulsion to see him; they probably thought he was like what you see on television. To them he was only a hard little Italian named Gulotta, whose late brother, Gaspar, had been the official collector of the contributions to police and politicians that kept the sucker traps in the Quarter operating.

Pete's joint was a bar that had a back room with a floor show. The show was on when we arrived. There were only a couple of people in the bar, but the back room was packed. A Negro, who the master of ceremonies said was named Pork Chops, was dancing desultorily, and he and the M.C. were carrying on a dialogue:

M.C.: If you're so good, why aren't you on television?

P.C.: I'm waiting for *colored* television.

With this, everybody except us got up and left, in a disciplined, joyless group. I hadn't thought the joke was that bad, and I was almost glad the proprietor was blind, because otherwise the exodus might have hurt his feelings. But then I learned that such mass entrances and departures are routine, like the alternations of being too hot or too cold. The migrating audiences are tourists from Iowa, who sign up for rounds of the night clubs at their hotels and are carried from one joint to the next in buses. The deal apparently includes one soft drink at each stop.

When the sightseers had gone, we sent for the proprietor, who came over to us, walking briskly and only once or twice checking his course by touching a table. He had a big head and a welterweight's shoulders and thorax on short legs—a jockey's build. I told him I had seen him fight Midget Smith. "And I still think you should have had the decision," I said.

"I thought I won, too," he agreed. "I could see Smith was cut up bad." I assumed that his manager had told him Smith was cut up bad. Then he said happily, "Barney Ross was in here a couple of weeks ago with a fighter he's handling. Barney's thirteen years younger than me, and he looks older. He's gone all gray on top." Then I understood that he visualizes what people tell him and that a minute later it's all a part of his past, as if he'd seen it himself. Pretty soon he excused himself and went about his business, as a good saloonkeeper should. When he was gone, we had a round of beer and began talking about the Governor again.

"Don't let him con you," the lawyer said. "You hoid him talk about, yeah, Black Alice, and, yeah, Aunt Rose, but all he cares about is Uncle Oil." There is a New Orleans city accent (which I shall try to reproduce only fitfully) associated with downtown New Orleans, particularly with the German and Irish Third Ward, that is hard to distinguish from the accent of Hoboken, Jersey City, and Astoria, Long Island, where the Al Smith inflection, extinct in Manhattan, has taken refuge. The reason, as you might expect, is that the same stocks that brought the accent to Manhattan imposed it on New Orleans, between the eighteen-forties and the Civil War. Irish immigrants, not Negro slaves, built the levees; the Negroes, bought at high prices to work cotton, were too valuable to use on low-pay labor. "Earl doesn't care about the jigs," the lawyer went on. "He wants their votes. And he knows he'll get them if he can just make those other fellows keep their hands off the lists. They're just fakers anyway. They don't want to disfranchise all niggers—only his niggers. When they've got a nigger they can be sure of, they'll vote him every time. Uncle Earl makes sweet talk about keeping those old white people on the lists, too. He knows that any man or woman old enough to draw a pension will vote for a Long every time. And that loan-shark bill he talks about—hell, he just doesn't want to let that small-loan business out from under his thumb. It's too rich. The small-loan companies are licensed to lend sums up to a thousand now. The bill would have limited the interest on loans of under a thousand to three and a half per cent a month—that's forty-two per cent a year. But it would have given them the right to make loans of more than a thousand dollars at true loan-shark rates. The loan business of over a thousand is reserved for the banks now. So Earl's loan-shark bill would have helped the sharks more than it hurt them. I'll bet the sharks were *for* it, and the *banks* put up the money to fight it."

I said I couldn't understand the importance of the small-loan firms to a politician. We have them in New York, but they are not considered important sources of graft.

"It's because to get a license for a small-loan company you have to get a special bill passed through the Legislature and signed by the Governor," the lawyer explained impatiently. "One Shylock, one bill. It's the surest way in the world to get rich. So a man wants a small-loan license, he goes to a politician from his home parish and gives him ten thousand dollars to take up to Baton Rouge. The fellow steers it through—he gives so much here and so much there, and maybe a good campaign contribution to whoever's Governor for signing. And what's left sticks to him for his trouble. There've been seventy-two special small-loan bills passed and signed in the last couple of sessions. So now comes a bill to change the statute itself—you can *imagine* the number of jackpots there are to be split up. What makes Uncle Earl sore is that they run him off to Texas before he could get into the act. He wants his leaders to be like those trained dogs you used to see in vaudeville—the ones that hold a pose until the trainer tells them to come and get their piece of meat."

"Earl likes to cut them down to size before they get too big and fresh," Tom Sancton said. "You heard what he did to the fellow from Alexandria who got a big retainer from the theater owners to try to remove a two per cent tax on movie admissions? The fellow went to see Earl before the last campaign and came back and told his clients that it was in the bag. Then he went out and worked like a dog for Earl—speaking on television and radio, and stumping and conspiring and kissing babies and hustling votes—until Earl was elected Governor. One of the first things Earl did in the new Legislature was to *oppose* removal of the tax. The fellow from Alexandria went to see him—he was afraid he would have to refund his fee, or the theater owners would shoot him—and he said, 'I told my clients that you said you wanted their support and that you wouldn't block removal of the tax. What do I tell them now?' You know what old Earl said? He said, 'I'll tell you what to tell them. Tell them I lied.' "

"Why did he do that?" I asked. "Did somebody induce him to *keep* the tax on the movies?"

"Hell, no," said Tom. "He just didn't want the other fellow's clients to think the other fellow was that strong. He likes them to come straight to Uncle Earl." Tom, who is impressed by medical opinion, added: "I'm afraid he won't make it this time, though. My doctor told me that what the man needs is about six months of solid rest in a sanitarium if he wants to live."

"Rest is just what might kill him," I said. I have always believed in the therapeutic value of attending horse races. It fills the lungs and empties the mind. You sit a horseplayer down to occupational therapy and he will founder.

"Oh, there's lots of ways of making money here," the lawyer said, returning to what interested him. He left pathology to them that liked it. "For instance, a law says that all state property must be insured at a rate set by a committee known as the Louisiana Insurance Rating and Fire Agency. That does away with competitive bidding, so placing insurance is just a matter of dealer's choice. The Federal Housing Authority has found that on public housing, built partly with Federal and partly with state funds, the insurance rate here is the highest in the nation. And then there's the tax payable to the state on sulphur taken from the ground. It's set ridiculously low—one dollar and three cents a ton—by a provision of the state constitution. There isn't a session of the Legislature that somebody doesn't introduce a sulphur bill to amend the constitution. It's always beaten—but just. How much does it cost the sulphur companies to keep that limit on the books?"

"But old Earl is tight with his money," Sancton said. "The one thing he's never been tight about is horse betting. He can't stop. When he gets the papers in the morning, he tears them open and goes straight to the hog quotations and the racing charts. After that, he gets a batch of *Daily Racing Forms* and *Morning Telegraphs* and lays out the entries and past performances at every track going—side by side, on a long table. It's too much trouble to use one paper and turn the pages. Then he goes to work with a red pencil and a blue one, and in an hour or so he begins calling up touts on long distance—Picklenosed Willie and The Owl and Stableboy and fellows like that. Next, he starts calling bookies to place his bets—a few dollars on each of three horses in practically every race in the country, unless one of the touts has given him something hot, and then he lays it in. If he's betting a book in Louisiana and he loses, he puts it on the tab, but if he wins, he has a state trooper over at the bookie's joint within a half hour to collect."

This was the life I had always wanted to live, and I had a great fellow feeling for Uncle Earl as the lawyer took up the refrain.

"After he makes his bets, the day's business can begin," the lawyer said. "First item is to turn to the supermarket ads. If he sees something in the ads that the price is right, he buys it regardless if he needs it at the moment or not. Like the morning he saw that Schwegmann's was selling potatoes for forty-nine cents a ten-pound sack. Schwegmann's is a string of three big supermarkets here that sell everything—furniture, automobile parts, grits, steak. Earl was a couple of days out of the State Hospital and was staying here at the Roosevelt Hotel with ten state policemen, and there were a dozen politicians paying their respects. Earl says, 'Come on, boys, I can't afford to pass that up,' and he goes downstairs and gets into his eleven-thousand-dollar air-conditioned official Cadillac that he says he got for eighty-five hundred because he is always protecting the interest of the fine people of the Great State of Louisiana, and the state troopers get out in front on motorcycles to clear the way, and he sits in front, next to the chauffeur, the way he always does, and packs those politicians in the back, and they take off. They pull up in front of Schwegmann's—all the sirens blowing, frightening hell out of the other shoppers—and Earl gets out and heads straight for the vegetable department, and, yeah, there are the potato sacks, but they're marked fifty cents instead of forty-nine. Earl calls for the store manager and accuses him of misleading advertising and shows him the ad, and the manager calls over all the clerks he can spare, and they change the price on the bags from fifty cents to forty-nine. That satisfies Earl, so he buys a hundred pounds of the potatoes and tells a state senator to pick them up and carry them to the car, and then he sees some alarm clocks on sale and buys three hundred dollars' worth, and tells some representatives from upcountry to carry them. And eighty-seven dozen goldfish in individual plastic bags of water, and two cases of that sweet Mogen David wine, and he tells the new superintendent of state police to load up. By the time they come out it looks like a safari, with all them politicians as native bearers. He must have had five thousand dollars' worth of junk."

"What did he think he was going to do with the stuff?" I asked.

"Damfino," the lawyer said. "It's just one of his ideas of pleasure. Well, when they got out there on the sidewalk, under about a hundred degrees of heat, the stuff won't all go in the trunk of the Cadillac. At least, the trunk won't close. So Uncle Earl sends a couple of senators and a judge into the store again to buy some rope, and they can't find any but the gold kind that women use to tie back drapes with, so they buy about a furlong of that, and then when they get outside, the Cadillac is so low-slung they can't pass the rope under the car. By that time Uncle Earl is sitting in his air-cooled seat eating watermelon with salt, and he orders the chauffeur to get out and tell the judge to lie down under the car and get the rope around the best he can. The judge gets down on his knees, and as he does he says, 'I wonder what the governors of the forty-nine other states are doing right this minute!' "

Louisianians often tell this story, and they never fail to laugh at it. It could be the subject of a Daumier lithograph, and they have a Daumier sense of humor.

"And who are the candidates who are going to run against Uncle Earl?" I asked, almost as an afterthought. All the conversation I had heard that evening sounded as if Uncle Earl were running against hardened arteries, cerebral accidents, his wife, exhaustion, and the investigative branch of the Internal Revenue Service.

"Well," Sancton said, "there's Chep Morrison, the Mayor of New Orleans—he's the one Uncle Earl calls Dellasoups. He's a brisk, nice-looking fellow, and his boosters say he gets things done, but he has two strikes against him out of town—he's a Catholic and he's a New Orleans man. As Mayor of New Orleans he's made himself an international figure, touring South America and Europe to get business for the port, and he's improved the city physically, but the kind of mayor who looks right taking Zsa Zsa Gabor to tea looks all wrong to those rednecks up in the hill parishes. Being a Catholic doesn't hurt him downstate—our Cajuns are Catholics, too, of course—but being from New Orleans does hurt. And even in the city he beat Uncle Earl by only twenty-two hundred votes in 1956. Of course, if Earl was out, Chep would carry the city big, and he'd get all the Negro vote; Earl gets about two thirds of it now and Chep the rest. And he'd get the organized-labor vote, too—but only if Earl was out. He would have been Mayor for life, but in 1952 the city passed a law that no mayor of New Orleans could succeed himself more than once. Chep backed the new law, and maybe he wishes now he hadn't, like the Republicans who pushed the no-third-term amendment for President.

"Then there's Bill Dodd, the state comptroller. Big Bad Bill Dodd, Uncle Earl calls him. Dodd is an old Long man. He was Lieutenant Governor with Earl from 1948 to 1952, and ran for comptroller on the same ticket with him in 1956, but they're enemies now. With Earl out, he'd get most of the steady Long vote. And there's Willie Rainach, the racist, but he won't get anybody but his own kind. The race issue isn't as hot in Louisiana as it is in Arkansas or Alabama or Mississippi. Nobody will say he's *for* integration in the schools, but as for letting Negroes vote or not vote, most people are for leaving things as they are—a kind of local option. Morrison and old Uncle Earl might lose some votes by being what people call a little 'soft on the niggers,' but those people wouldn't necessarily all go to Rainach—many would go to somebody in between."

"That's why a lot of people think Jimmie Davis is the best bet," the lawyer broke in. "Jimmie is a psalm-singing fellow from up in Shreveport, in the northwest corner of the state. He used to be a hillbilly singer and composer—he wrote 'You Are My Sunshine, My Only Sunshine'—and he was Governor from 1944 to 1948. He isn't a clown; he's smart. Lately he's been making a lot of religious records. That helps him with the church people, and when he was Governor he didn't have any trouble with the gamblers either. His motto is 'I Never Done Nobody No Harm.' Davis is a country boy from a big city, but Shreveport doesn't frighten the rubes the way New Orleans does. If he could get into the second primary with either Earl or Chep, he might inherit the votes of all the candidates who lost out."

The one political element that neither of my mentors mentioned even once—nor did they need to—was the Republican party. It is the smallest of all the political sects in Louisiana. In the statewide primaries of 1956, there were seven hundred and forty thousand Democratic voters and eighteen hundred and eighty-three Republican voters. There are no Republican watchers at most polling places on primary day, because there aren't enough Republicans to go around. Of the eighteen hundred and eighty-three Republican voters, it is my impression that eighteen hundred and eighty-two are lawyers, and during a Republican administration in Washington, at least three quarters of them have Federal jobs. Aspirants to the order have to be of sober demeanor and sterling character, to live down the ripe odor left by the "Customhouse" Republican regime of Reconstruction days, so called because President Grant's brother-in-law, James F. Casey, was Collector of Customs for New Orleans.

Known as the party of plunder when they were turned out in 1876, the Republicans have become the party of purity in state affairs. Louisiana Republicans must also have better than average education, because of the high incidence of office they must cope with when the wind off the Potomac is favorable. Barring protracted accidents like Roosevelt-Truman, a Louisiana Republican has three hundred and ninety-eight times the chances of a Louisiana Democrat to become a Federal judge. Patience and self-denial are other necessary qualifications, since the novice renounces all hope of elective office when he takes the veil. His salvation can only come from outside the state, as Zeus came to Danae in a shower of gold. But it comes quite often. Since 1876, when Washington abandoned the Reconstruction, Republicans have held the White House and its appointive powers for forty-eight out of eighty-four years.

I never learned the process of induction into the Louisiana Republican cult, but the ranks are always full, and the queue does not disperse when there are long waits between buses. Even during these spells of unemployment, the Republicans suffer no outrage. No Democrat in his right mind wants to incur the wrath of a man who will be a United States District Judge or a District Director of Internal Revenue the next time the Republicans win. Like the Parsees in India and the Mozabites in Algeria, they have won respect as clean, sober and industrious people, and their attorneys get a full share of civil practice.

"And who is your man?" I asked my two mentors.

The lawyer, who had been knocking the Governor ever since I met him, said, as if there had never been any doubt of where he stood, "I'll stay with Uncle Earl unless he looks too sick to go the distance. They may say, yeah, he's crazy, and, yeah, he's got deep pockets, and, yeah, he'd cut his best friend's throat to keep him from getting elected, but how far do you think a man like me would have got in the Louisiana bar before Huey came along? Up from the bottom, ate my way free through college by playing football, studied law at night. Without the Longs I'd be limited to police-court cases. Any time I walked into court against one of those old-family boys from the big law firms that represented the banks and oil companies, I'd be dead."

The lawyer is a member of the Regular Democratic Organization, the New Orleans machine that is the spiritual equivalent of old-fashioned Tammany Hall. The Old Regulars, as they are known, fought Huey Long until he broke their power in the thirties and then joined him. "Before Huey," the lawyer went on, "the state was as tight as a drum and crooked as a corkscrew; now it's still crooked, but it's open to everybody. Maybe some judges do cut up jackpots, but they aren't working for a monopoly. In business it's the same—there's plenty of ex-wildcatters, oil-and-gas millionaires, who under the old house rules would have been crushed out before they got started. Huey was like the kid who comes along in a game of Chicago pool when all the balls are massed. He breaks them and runs a few, then misses and leaves the table full of shots for the other players. As long as the Longs are in, you have a chance."

"You got to remember that Earl carries the blood of Huey the Martyr," Sancton said. "He's an Imam. People up North see Huey's career from the wrong end. Here, a lot of voters remember him as a poor, friendless boy who stood up to the bully—the rich machine that had run Louisiana forever. He licked it. That put him in a favorable light. By the time the North's attention was attracted to Huey, he was sitting on the bully's chest. That made *him* look like the bully. The papers called for law and order, and when that fellow shot Huey in the Capitol, they said law and order had been vindicated."

3 / *Bruttally Frank*

MANEUVERS like Earl's scheme to succeed himself unimmediately enrage the Longs' opponents because they never think of them first. The opposition is personified by the rich and conservative *Times-Picayune* and its afternoon satellite, the *States-Item* (these hyphenated newspaper titles, memorials to cannibalism, are becoming a rule rather than the exception in a shrinking press). The double-barreled duo is continually getting mad at the Longs, like a fat policeman in an old-time silent film shaking his fist at Charlie Chaplin. Chaplin in the films always ran around the block and kicked the policeman in the pants, and, like the little man in the bowler, the Longs always enlist popular sympathy. This would be harder to understand in a state other than Louisiana, where the populace has always viewed its self-acknowledged betters with skeptical animosity.

The anti-Longites' fair-haired boy for thirteen years, up to and including the summer of 1959, was Mayor Morrison. I thought that I ought to talk to him to see what the Martyr was up against. I had heard that Morrison bragged of a private poll that showed him a winner with 52.78 per cent of all votes cast in the first primary for Governor, whether Long ran or not. This would insure his election as Governor without need of a runoff primary. The consensus in New Orleans' political cafés, however—a term signifying any place in town where you can buy a cup of coffee—was that he was desperate and talking through his tuppy.

"He has to go up or out," one expert said. "The fat cats who paid for his campaign for Governor in 1956 are discouraged. His charm doesn't work upstate."

The Mayor, known to the general public as Chep, is a city type. I had heard admirers, chiefly public-relations men for the city, describe him as a mélange of Jimmy Walker for looks and manner, Fiorello La Guardia for energy and probity, and Big Bad Bob Moses, the Builder, for getting things done.

People who didn't like him conceded only the energy and a certain hard neatness of appearance. They said he was terrifyingly ambitious, a complete egoist and willing to trade for votes anywhere. The gamblers and brothel keepers accused him of a double cross; before his first election, in 1946, they said, he had caused them to understand that his reformism was a sham and that if he was elected they could continue to operate wide open, *without* paying graft to the Old Regular machine.

After election he had shut them down, to consolidate his position with the church- and womenfolk. That had continued until he copyrighted the label of respectability in New Orleans, so that to run against him was like running for office against a coalition of the Holy Ghost *and* the *Times-Picayune*. Meanwhile he used municipal patronage to build up a machine that could compete with the Old Regulars.

A good number of the saloonkeepers, figuring they wouldn't lick him, joined him in return for a kind of modified autonomy—about what De Gaulle has been offering to the Algerians. New Orleans, while no Gomorrah, is certainly not a sedate town now. Cab drivers wait at the exits of the strip-tease joints to proposition the visiting firemen, rendered randy by the bumps and grinds. The cabbies pimp for the brothels across the river in Jefferson Parish. The cops operate like the New York Police during Prohibition—they move aggrieved drunks along rather than listen to their beefs.

At a dinner of Morrison people to which I was invited, a charming downstate lady, counted upon as a sure source of Morrison campaign money, alarmed her hosts by saying that she was about through wasting cash on Blue Boy, a nickname for Morrison that in itself showed a deterioration of his sentimental appeal. When, at thirty-four, he first won the mayoralty, an inspired female admirer called him Little Boy Blue, blowing his own horn to rally the forces of decency. Now, at forty-seven, he was just Blue Boy, a name evoking blue babies and blue chins.

The lady and her husband are both as physically abundant as they are agreeable—two rich people who look like rich people, with not a concavity in their contours and not a regret in their heads about being so rich.

"I don't mind the money," she said, "but I just hate having a loser. My husband can go on backing Blue Boy if he wants, but I'm going with Jimmie Davis." Her husband smiled deprecatingly, but he did not look like a man fond of backing losers indefinitely, either. The lady's announcement spread dismay among the Morrison professionals. (Later, she came back to Morrison, but the ripples stirred by her threat could not be recalled.)

I was to see the Mayor next morning at City Hall, and I arrived early for my appointment. The City Hall itself is a monument to the Morrison administration, as the Capitol at Baton Rouge is a monument to Huey Long's. An assistant to the Mayor, a Mr. Dixon, showed me over the place before His Honor showed up. We ended our tour in the Council Chamber, a modest vault of marble and blond tropical woods—woods from all the countries with which New Orleans traded, Mr. Dixon said. The difference between the porphyry and agate of the State House and the blond mahogany of City Hall is the difference between the Long-family and Morrison manner. Morrison has better taste—but not by Louisiana standards.

"Each session of the Council is opened with prayer by a minister of one of the three great faiths, Catholic, Protestant and Hebrew," Mr. Dixon said reverentially. "They take it in rotation." With an arrangement like that, the great city of New Orleans, like a prudent oil man, had money on each of the three leading candidates. I tapped my breast, to make sure my wallet was still with me.

When we emerged from this air-cooled crypt, refreshed and feeling slightly sanctified, we returned to the mayoral suite, where representatives of the entire local press awaited us—a man from the *Times-Picayune* and a girl from the *States-Item*, like a racing entry marked 1 and 1A. With three or four secretaries, a photographer and Tom, we filed into the Mayor's audience room.

It was paneled with double- or treble-autographed photographs of the Mayor with the last Pope, Perón, Trujillo, Cardinal Spellman, Bishop Fulton J. Sheen, a number of prominent race horses and various Gabor sisters. There were also United States Senators, baseball players, television personalities, and a number of Miss New Orleanses, Miss Louisianas and Miss Confederate Daughters of America. There was a picture of Mayor Morrison in a colonel's uniform at the Eiffel Tower after he liberated it in 1944, and snaps of him laying cornerstones and greeting a delegation of Uruguayan school children. In all of them he was smiling and fighting politely for the center of the picture, even at the risk of being trampled by a horse. I found the entire display an engaging disclaimer of false modesty.

When I had browsed awhile, we all sat down, and a colored man brought us coffee. The ceremonial coffee is a link between Louisiana and the rest of the Arab world. It is never omitted, even though your host is going to throw you out when you have drunk it.

We had no sooner put our cups down than the Mayor entered briskly, smiling, wearing a dazzling suit of tropical cloth and a necktie like a Persian dawn. He is a man in appearance midway between Richard M. Nixon and John F. Kennedy, and as tenacious of youth.

At an age when prize fighters are described as venerable freaks, politicians are still referred to as "young." In an effort to live up to the adjective, most politicos in their forties act downright kittenish. This puts an increasing burden on them with the years, for no performer wants his public to notice that he is aging. It is an advantage to a man who aims high not to project a public image until he is bald or gray, has a few wrinkles on his face, and is too slow to show that he is slowing up. So the great Bob Fitzsimmons, bald from youth, did not buy a toupee to make him look younger, but raised a long mustache to make him look older. Ten years later he shaved it off, and contemporaries said he looked as young as when he first came over from Australia. Grand Old Juvenile is a hard role to sustain, even with the aid of geriatrics. If I were coaching a candidate in the Nixon-Morrison-Kennedy age range, I would bid him raise mutton-chop whiskers and cultivate a limp, so that when the inevitable happened the deterioration would be less striking.

This, however, is a digression. In New Orleans, Mr. Dixon hauled at my sleeve and, when I rose, moved me into a corner of the office where I had my back to a big American flag and my left side toward the Mayor, who with practiced adroitness placed one side of a document the size of a large bill of fare in my right hand. I tried to read it, but the printed side was toward the camera.

The Mayor smiled. The photographer blazed away. The whole operation could not have taken more than thirty-two seconds, and I was now, as I ascertained when I had a chance to read the bill of fare, an "Honorary Citizen of New Orleans, the International City founded in 1718 A.D. by the French Explorer Bienville . . . a city of Old World Tradition and New World Enterprise famed for its charm, beauty and hospitality . . . one of America's most progressive communities . . . a great World Port and the center of a vast and growing industrial empire. . . ." I also got a gold-plated "key to the city."

What impressed me about the operation was its practiced efficiency. They had my name spelled right, as if they had been waiting for me to come along. All around the text were lithographed vignettes of New Orleans glories, most of them reflecting credit on Morrison; the new City Hall and civic center, built under Morrison; the Moisant International Airport Terminal, erected *au temps de Morrison*; the new Mississippi Bridge, built during a Morrison term of office; the International Home and Trade Mart, completed while Morrison was Mayor; and the new Union Passenger Terminal, uniting the Illinois Central and Louisville and Nashville stations under one roof in the center of the city, a monument to the Morrison regime. Other vignettes were devoted to the port, which the Mayor has done much to develop, and the skyline, in which he takes a proprietary interest.

"World famous Cuisine and Birthplace of Jazz," and "Vieux Carré and Mardi Gras," and the football stadium were the only depicted attractions that were not directly attributable to the Mayor—three out of ten.

While I was still looking at my new diploma, Mr. Dixon, like a Billy Graham usher with a sinner in tow, led me back to my seat, at a respectful distance from the desk behind which Mayor Morrison now took station. The *Times-Picayune* man and the *States-Item* girl poised their notebooks on their respective right knees. I now realized that I had been invited not to an interview but to an audience such as Father Divine used to grant visiting sightseers in his Harlem Heaven.

The Mayor began by expressing sorrow over the plight of Governor Long. "It is to my selfish interest to have him as an opponent," he said, "because surveys show I would be a cinch to defeat him."

But, Morrison said, Old Earl was a sick man, and Louisiana couldn't afford a Governor who "wasn't even housebroke." Therefore he hoped Earl wouldn't run. The state must rebuild its prestige in the outside world if it was to attract sorely needed new industries. And he told me quite a bit about the new industries he constantly brought to New Orleans and the civic improvements he incessantly perpetrated. It was all as spontaneous as the neat diploma and the key to the city.

I stress my unfavorable first impression of Morrison because I was to wind up the campaign rooting for him with all my heart.

Tom suggested that, for balance, we call next on Jim Comiskey, the leader of the Third Ward and chief of the city-wide Old Regular Democratic organization. Morrison kept the municipal patronage out of the Old Regulars' hands, Tom said, but they did well on the state patronage Earl fed them.

"The Old Regulars can't go with Morrison. They got to go with somebody from upstate. Before Earl blew his top in the Legislature, they were sitting pretty. All they had to do was sit tight with Earl and go in again. Now they don't know whether they got a candidate."

The Comiskey brothers, Jim and Larry, were wholesale liquor dealers on a mighty scale, Tom said. If we ran down to the warehouse now, we probably would catch them in. We had best get cracking, because it was already noon, and Jim Comiskey, if he went out to lunch, might stay out for a siesta or take a swing around the saloons where he communed with the pulse of the electorate. We climbed into Tom's battered station wagon and raced out to where the Comiskey Brothers' sheds and loading platforms lay under a sun like the Sahara's. The heat bounced visibly off the concrete like a rubber ball. It was on a wide avenue of desolation—railway culverts, streetcar rails, and the kind of businesses that deal by the ton, the carboy or the freight-car load.

Jim Comiskey was not there—he was in Baton Rouge for the day, the girl at the switchboard said—but Brother Larry was out on the loading platform, squatting on a kitchen chair, like a great, wise, sun-freckled toad, an old straw hat down over his eyes, his fat red arms akimbo as he watched the outgoing loads of lovely liquor, as hot as Tabasco sauce to the taste, that would set longshoremen swinging their fists and old women gabbling and Vidalias leching after *entraineuses* who would roll them in the dark recesses of intimate bars. "Vidalia" is the New Orleans word for a sucker from out of town. In the beginning it meant a rich planter from Vidalia, up the river, in town for a good time. And on every bottle of Comiskey's Special Private Stock Whiskey was the photographed face of Brother Jim, like Father John on the medicine bottle.

Brother Larry was not astonished that we had come to consult the Oracle of the Bottle. "He's win all his life," he said. "He knows da answers." But he disclaimed authority to speak for the house. "Wait fa Jim," he said. And, picking a whiskey bottle from a case, he showed me his brother's portrait. "Dat's him," he said. It was one of the few times in my life I have heard a pure New York accent as reported by Stephen Crane in *Maggie*. It startled me, as if I had seen a horse-drawn fire engine. The Third Ward lawyer's had been diluted by education, but Larry had stayed home.

Tom had picked up another bottle and was looking at that. Then he compared the two pictures. "Hey, they're different," he said. "He's smiling on one and looking sore on the other."

"Maybe he's winning easy on dis one," said Brother Larry, "and on dat one he's in a close race. It's a wonderful free campaign poster, dat label. A fellow is drinking and he sees dat face on da back bar, it sinks in his conscious.

"You boys catch him at da clubhouse in da ward tomorrow night," he said. "Every Wednesday night he's dere to hear confessions."

"Is that what we call taking the contracts?" I asked, and Brother Larry winked.

"Here we call it hearing confession," he said. "Everybody in da ward dat has troubles, dey come to tell dem to Jim."

"Troubles like what?" Tom asked, in quest of the picturesque detail.

"Dey all got da same one," said Brother Larry. "No money. Dey need money. Dey're broke. Dat's da disease of da ward. He never toins one away widout a hearing. Sometimes I've known him to come home at five o'clock in da morning, staying up to listen to dem."

"And what does he do for them?" I asked, although I was sure I knew the answer. For this is an American Universal.

"He gets dem a little job," said Brother Larry. "Maybe watchman, or laborer on a state contract, or doorman at a hospital. It don't pay much, but a man don't need much if you don't woik him too hard. It's like a mule, he can get along on grass if you only woik him once in a while. But if you woik him steady, you got to give him grain."

He didn't elaborate, because he saw we were men of intelligence and could fill in for ourselves. A real job, besides calling for minimal qualifications that the broke man may not have, demands presentable clothes, a car that will get him to work, money on which to eat in restaurants at noon.

"It's better to get a hundred little jobs for a hundred little fellows dan one big job for one big fella, because den you got a hundred you can count on to work for ya, instead of one dat might likely cut your troat in da bargain," Brother Larry said.

I realized that New Orleans might be exotic in some respects but that in others it was exactly like everyplace else.

"How is it Jim always wins?" I asked, just to make conversation. "Because he works so hard?"

It was here, I think, that Brother Larry got the idea he had overrated me.

"If you watch da way elections goes," he said, "you will notice it's very seldom da Assessor gets beat."

Tom had neglected to tell me that Jim Comiskey's sole public office was Assessor of Taxes for the Eighth District of New Orleans, which includes most of the big buildings. He tells the property owners what they have to pay.

"I'll tell him you're coming to confession," Brother Larry yelled after us as we departed.

Early that Wednesday evening we drove down to the Third Ward to sit in with Brother Jim, going through ghostly streets of one- and two-story white clapboard houses out-at-elbow to out-at-elbow, the obscurity broken only by the bright sign of an occasional fried-chicken shack or one-story saloon. There was no scent of magnolias, there were no lacy wrought-iron balconies here. It was like a cross between Paterson, N.J., and Port-au-Prince, and at night, with the crepe myrtles and the scraggly palms invisible, there was nothing specifically southern. The insubstantiality of the buildings could be duplicated in any run-down summer resort in the North. Here people lived in them all year round, in the winter when they would not be warm enough, and in the summer when any house at all was too hot.

Jim Comiskey's headquarters was a one-story clapboard building with a store front. Inside, there was a web of junk around the walls: ladders, lathes, Coke bottles, paint cans, ruptured Venetian blinds, tangles of electric wires, a water cooler, a clothesline with clothespins and wire coat hangers, all these objects except the clothesline looking as if they had been simply kicked against the walls to clear a space in the middle of the room. The clothesline was a *vestiaire* in winter, when Comiskey's petitioners might have coats, but provisionally a torn cotton wrapper hung on it to dry.

Down the middle of the room there were two sections of undertakers' chairs, one block occupied by a score or so of dejected white men and the other by a lone Negro. At the head of the room was an iron stove complete with pipe and an ancient golden-oak writing desk. Back of it was a foul toilet with a sheet hanging in front of it instead of a door, and behind the desk sat Mr. Comiskey, a tall man, pink-faced, blue-eyed, white-haired, benevolent of expression and dressed in sober but costly black shantung. He had the face of a popular cardinal, and looking at him, I was sure that if he had felt the vocation when young, he would be one by this time.

After he had disposed of the petitioner who was at his desk when we entered, a limpy man carrying an old straw hat, Tom and I approached the seat of power. My friend, who knew Comiskey of old, introduced me. He said I was a New Yorker interested in Louisiana politics, and that as such I couldn't afford to pass up the leader of the Old Regulars. Mr. Comiskey clasped my hand and looked into my eyes with two of honest blue. He called for chairs for us, and we sat down, like visitors to a class in session.

"They'll all have their turn," said the Assessor, with a wave of his hand toward the clients. "Everybody in the ward that have any trouble is here, and if they don't be here, they should be here. And anybody in Noo Wawlins is welcome. They all have somebody that they want to get into a hospital, or a job working for the Levee Board, or things of that nature and so forth. When I hear what they want, if it can be done, I process it to its final completion."

I could have closed my eyes and believed myself in Alderman Paddy Bauler's saloon in Chicago. There is neither Blue nor Gray when you get down to the American essentials.

I said gently that I had come to talk politics, and asked him what he had heard about Governor Long's condition, which was the *sine qua non* of the battle in the offing.

"I hear he's on da steady improve all da time," the Assessor said. "Fellas wit him at Hot Springs tell me he's champin' at da bit to go." He laughed happily. "He's like a hoss dat woik is what he needs! He'll get better as he goes along. He's a stoiling campaigner and as Governor he's doin' a wonderful outstanding job."

"But don't you think this trouble with his wife will hurt him?" I asked.

"I can't see wherein it will," he said. "Da women know da Governor. He stops to talk to even kids, and he's coyteous wit everybody. He sent Mrs. Comiskey a basket of cantaloupes from Texas."

"Did he pay the express charges?"

"To be bruttally frank," the Assessor said, "he forgot. I had to pay two dollars and seventy-six cents, and Mrs. Comiskey says she could get da same cantaloupes for two dollars a dozen at da market. But it shows how kind he is—always remembering his friends.

"You can't never count a Long out," he reminded me. "Look at da form: Morrison and Dodd are past losers. Dey have been at da post before and found lacking. You can't never tell what will happen, but if he run back to form, Earl got to win it all."

This was a degree of conviction I had not yet encountered anywhere, and I felt a bit guilty in even asking Mr. Comiskey whether he had heard talk about the Governor's income-tax trouble. But relying on his realism, I asked just the same.

"To be bruttally frank," he said, "if he has income-tax troubles possibly it might do him a lot of good wit de electorate. So many people are in da same boat dat dey might say, 'I hope him good luck!' If dey all vote for him, he's home free."

Becoming slightly more serious, he said, "You got to realize dat when somebody slips Earl money it isn't for just his personal campaign. He uses it for candidates all over da state. He needs friends. Da Governor is an enforceful man. Like last fall, we had a young fella named McGovern over in St. Bernards we thought could make state senator if he had another fifty-five hundred dollars for his campaign. I call Earl one night and he calls back next morning: 'Come up and get da green stuff.' No ifs and buts about Earl—no *mãnana*."

Comiskey's words laid open for me a plan of defense in depth that might worry any Federal man.

With friends like him, I thought, old Earl would win it all.

4/ *Race and Oil*

PAUSING FOR another cup of coffee in Thompson's Cafeteria on St. Charles on our way back from Comiskey's confessional, we heard a bit of news about the Third Force. Our acquaintance, the success from the Irish Channel, was having elevenses of apple pie à la mode and Coca-Cola. In New Orleans elevenses are P.M. and serve to fortify for the long night ahead. He was, as he had told us, a neo-Longite, but was always ready to jump to a winner. He viewed the political scene with the dispassionate glee of a horseplayer looking at the past-performance charts in the *Morning Telegraph*—entranced by the whole business, but not letting himself be swayed by affection for any particular horse.

"Perez is making his real play with Davis," he said when we had brought our coffee to his table. "He's throwing Willie Rainach to the alligators. Officially he'll be with Willie to start, but the deal's all set."

Already, although I had been in the Gret Stet only a few days, I could comprehend this jargon.

Leander Perez, the Pasha of Plaquemines Parish, was the Gret Stet's most powerful voice for the political sterilization of the Negro. ("Don't register your Negroes," a Governor named McEnery said in the nineties, "but don't forget to vote them.") He was also, even I knew, a racist of the obsessive kind often bred in regions of old admixture. Plaquemines is a coastal parish, once chiefly inhabited by muskrats, which now has more mineral wealth than any other in the state.

"A race of mixed blood, the product of various Latin progenitors, live on the islands and along the coast of the Gulf, who are termed Dagos," a political reporter named A. M. Gibson wrote of Louisiana at the end of the Civil War. "They are fruiters and fishermen. For a few dollars many of them can be hired to wield the assassin's knife." Whether all these violent men of "mixed blood" meekly accepted Negro status after 1876 is one of the small puzzles of Louisiana history, like the fate of that considerable society of cultured, ivory-tinted "colored" men and women, set free and enriched by their white fathers and grandfathers long before the Civil War, who excited J. W. De Forest's admiration when he came to New Orleans as a Union officer. (De Forest's outsider's impressions of New Orleans are one of the glories of a great war book, *A Volunteer's Adventures*. A third riddle of Louisianian history is what happened to the descendants of the soldiers in the Louisiana regiments of the *Union* Army. De Forest mentions several and tells especially of a brave charge of the First Louisiana infantry in the assault on Port Hudson. Its soldiers must have been sterile, like mules, for they left no visible descendants in their home state—either that or their offspring went underground and posed as Sons and Daughters of the Confederacy.)

It was therefore natural that Perez should support the campaign for Governor of pale, gloomy Willie Rainach, the state senator with a Confederate flag on his tie. Rainach, as chairman of a joint committee of the State Legislature on segregation, had made a spectacle of himself, and an enemy of Long, by prancing through the state purging "irregularly registered" colored voters from the rolls. In Iberville Parish, for example, the committee struck out the names of Negroes who, in the space marked "Color," had written "Negro" instead of "Black."

But though racism is a Perez obsession, sulphur, oil and gas are the revenues on which he feeds, and "local autonomy" is what he needs to preserve his domination.

"OIL and gas and sulphur! a magic combination of wealth for a parish and its people!" said an institutional ad I read in the *Times-Picayune* special supplement celebrating the centennial of the discovery of petroleum in America. "Plaquemines Parish produces more than twice as much oil yearly as any other Louisiana parish. It produces a great part of the world's urgently needed sulphur. And its gas reserves promise a bright future as the many miles of gas lines now under construction are connected with 'through pipe lines' serving the state and the nation. . . .

"SAID Judge Perez: 'We seek here to continue the traditional American way of life: freedom of enterprise, local control of our local destinies, high American standards of living.' "

With all that OIL, not to mention the gas and sulphur, he could afford the whim of staking a losing candidate in the preliminary heat, for the sake of his race hobby, but he must have a winner in the runoff to protect Plaquemines against investigation or legislation threatening "local control of local industries." The exploiting companies, no matter how mighty in Wall Street or Washington, are his captives in Plaquemines, as they used to be old Gomez's in Venezuela.

This time, our lawyer friend was telling us, Perez had decided to place his main bet on Jimmie Davis. The favorite, if he got to the post and did not break down, was Old Earl, but his condition was doubtful, and he was a declared personal enemy.

The second favorite on form was Chep Morrison. Long and Morrison were antitheses in all respects but one: they agreed on a sensible, calm approach to the color problem. This kept Louisiana agreeably free of the storms in neighboring states but made it hard for Perez to stomach either of them. Each of the two proclaimed himself a "thousand per cent," or occasionally a "million per cent," segregationist, but enemies accused both of being "soft on the niggers." School integration was not an immediate issue in the state, and neither was stirring it up. Both favored keeping Negroes on the registration rolls and giving them a fair share of social benefits. Naturally, both ran strong in colored election precincts.

The third man, Davis, was like a poker hand, open at both ends, ready to catch anything. He wanted the Negro vote *and* Perez's money.

Unfortunately, though, when you accept a man's support you sometimes have to accept his quarrels, and our lawyer friend said: "Davis people saying as little as possible until after the first primary, because if Davis known as old Leander's man, it will hurt him with the nigger vote. The Morrison and Long people going to spread the news with the jigs as fast as they can."

The lawyer, a big man, went up to the counter for a second piece of pie à la mode. When he returned, he said with relish, "Upstate the Rainach people say they got a photograph of Davis dancing with Lena Horne at a theatrical party up north, and they going to spread it all over the state. So the niggers will cut him because he's Perez's man, and the red-bones will down him for a nigger-lover."

It was the kind of paradox a politician could enjoy.

"Still, a lot of money's going there," he said. "Don't sell Davis short."

The lawyer demolished half his apple pie in a stroke and a gulp and then said, "Leander has things exactly his own way over in Plaquemines, and he wants it that way in the whole state. They're saying Davis has promised to change the name of the state flower for him if he's elected."

"What the hell's the use of that?" I asked innocently.

"From the Magnolia to the O-Leander," the lawyer explained, and he guffawed.

"He's the permanent District Attorney here," he said, "and appoints all the commissions. If you're an oil company and he don't like you, the safety commissioner will find a fire hazard so your rigs can't operate, and the highway commissioner will find your rigs are too heavy for the public roads so you can't move them. A couple of years ago when a union struck a friendly shipyard there, he arrested all the pickets on a charge of littering the public highway—they were smoking and throwing away the butts. It's an oil sheikdom, plus sulphur, and he's the sheik.

"You go over there to look up a title on land for a client that's an outsider and has a suit against an insider, and you find old books of deeds handwritten on parchment dating back to the seventeenth century. But when you come to the page about the land in dispute, it's typewritten on brand-new paper. You ask the parish clerk what happened, and he says, 'Cockroaches ate the old page so bad we had to copy it out and replace it.' " His admiration was as pronounced as his taste for pie à la mode.

"Plaquemines has so many islands and trappers and fishermen lost up bayous, that's the excuse, that it's always the last parish in the state to come in with its vote, and that gives Leander a tactical advantage, y'unnerstand—a few hundred votes can make a big difference in a close race for Congress or the State Supreme Court. We elect Supreme Court justices down here one from each of seven districts.

"He hasn't enough votes to change Governor much—he has only about 15,000 people living there, and he can't report that many votes, because you gotta allow for a couple of children here and there. But it's the oil that counts—it gives him leverage."

This, I knew, was true. In its passion for politics, the Gret Stet of Loosiana, as southern Louisianians refer to it, resembles most closely the Arab republic of Lebanon, but in its economy it is closer akin to the Arab sheikdoms of the Persian Gulf. The Gret Stet floats on oil, like a drunkard's teeth on whiskey.

"Oil is to Louisiana what money is to a roulette game," Tom said. "It's what makes the wheel go round. It's the reason there are so many big bank rolls available to stake any politician who has a Formosa Chinaman's chance to get into office." Louisianians who make money in oil buy politicians, or pieces of politicians, as Kentuckians in the same happy situation buy race horses. Oil gets into politics, and politicians, making money in office, get into oil. The state slithers around in it.

"Louisiana is now the second biggest oil-and-gas-producing state in the country, after Texas," Tom went on. "The state gets an average of twenty-five cents in severance tax on every barrel of oil released from the earth, and last year the output ran to over eight hundred thousand barrels a day, which amounted to a take of around seventy million dollars. The state also puts an ad-valorem tax on all the real property of the industry. That's ten million more, and then there's all the millions for leases on state-owned oil land, inshore and offshore. We're in a class with Bahrein and Kuwait. This is a rich state full of poor people, just like those Arab sheikdoms. Ten years ago, Louisiana ranked thirty-ninth among the states in per-capita income, and it's probably not much higher now. But where the state differs from the Persian Gulf is that here the natives vote. The hardest fight Huey Long had was to put the severance tax on oil, but now no politician would dare talk of taking it off. It's the same with the pensions that the oil tax pays. Eighty per cent of the people over sixty-five in the state are on that blessed pension. Seventy-two dollars a month. And they aren't the only ones who benefit. They've all got children and grandchildren, who'd have to support them otherwise."

"Some of the money sifts through to the parishes, too, hear?" the lawyer said. "The parish in which the oil is located gets a share of the state's share to use on roads and schools. When it's a parish with a lot of oil and a small population, that give the local boss a mighty fine jackpot to cut."

Politics in Vermont might wheel more freely, too, if the home folks knew the state was floating on an oil field.

It is impossible for a candidate to run without oil money. As in Lebanon, campaigning in Louisiana presents a high per-capita voter cost. But, since the oil men are competitive, they place their principal stakes on competing candidates, with "savers" on others and a certain amount of around-the-table baksheesh even to their sworn enemies, to turn away wrath in case the worst happens.

The oil has worked deep into the pores of the state; only five parishes out of sixty-four have no producing wells. Of these, one, Orleans, consists of the city of New Orleans, and there may be oil under that too. Politics has been a passion of Louisianians since the eighteenth century, however. Oil is an addendum. Now they are inextricably mixed.

The aleatory nature of the oil business facilitates the mixing. A safe way to pay a man a bribe is to buy a bit of worthless swamp from him for a high price, as "potential oil land." To buy it simply as real estate would appear too raw. Another method is to let him in at a low price on a well that is about to prove up.

The mysterious oil business is also a perfect instrument for decontaminating hot money; a gambler or a rackets man with a large accumulation of unreported profit buys a modest well, which immediately becomes, on his tax returns, fabulously productive. He pays tax on part of his hoard—at the lenient rates prescribed for oil men—and thereby legitimizes the rest.

If all oil men were content to remain such, except for harmless hobbies like raising prize cattle and keeping women, their effect on politics in the Gret Stet might be no worse than that of silver dollars on slot machines. Unfortunately, some of them have political ideas, an insight I acquired while lunching magnificently with two hospitable New Orleans brothers, a Republican and a Democrat. The Republican was a big man. The Democrat was the size of a grand champion Clydesdale horse, nineteen hands at the shoulder. Like all Louisiana Republicans in good times, the Republican brother was an important Federal official; the Democratic mammoth, I soon gathered, had of late years been lucky in his oil gambles. The Republican took a detached but appreciative view of the situation. The Democrat said that he liked Willie Rainach.

"He's just a country boy," the Republican brother said.

"He's a country gentleman," Big Man answered.

"My brother has more money than political sense," said the Republican.

It was evident that they had argued Rainach often, but they dropped the argument there and bore me off to Manale's, a restaurant with the aspect of a saloon, far from the French Quarter, where they provided a glorious lunch of pompanos studded with busters—fat soft-shell crabs shorn of their limbs, which are to the buster-fancier as trifling as a mustache on the *plat du jour* must seem to a cannibal. Driving me to my hotel, Big Man, the genial and solicitous host, called my attention to a pert redheaded girl walking along the street and flirting her tail in the attractive Southern manner.

"See her?" he said. "Passing for white. She's a nigger." And his good-humored double truck of a face was red with fury.

Under a state administration with Leander Perez's approval, I knew such anomalies would be rectified on a subjective basis. The registrar of births of a Louisiana parish has the right to change the status of parents retroactively by marking their child's birth certificate "colored." In such cases "common report" and the registrar's opinion of the physical appearance of child and parents govern. The registrar, usually a woman, is legally presumed to know "who is who."

The parents of a child thus ruled "colored" automatically, under law, become colored people too, or if the registrar impugns only one of them they are guilty of miscegenation, a serious crime. Challenges are usually based on gossip, malice, "intuition" or a combination of any two or all.

The parents may sue to force the registrar to change her decision, but the burden of proof is then upon them to demonstrate that all the ancestors of both for five generations back were white, a task that would tax any white person anywhere. (Name your thirty-two great-great-grandparents. Find a natal document for each, or, failing that, what was "common report.") Only the brave and relatively rich can undertake such litigation, and only a Pudd'nhead Wilson of a lawyer can win a color case. Under nonfictional conditions, Pudd'nhead Wilsons come high.

Tom, a believer in the visual approach to teaching, said that I needed a glimpse, no matter how brief, of the oil and gas business. (There was little to be gained by further palaver in New Orleans; we had reached the stage where we were beginning to pick up rumors that we ourselves had started.)

"Let's go down and look at a drilling barge tomorrow," he said.

We drove across the bridge over the Mississippi and south along the west bank to a point about twenty miles below the city, in the parish of Plaquemines. There was warm rain all the way. We drove down a side road toward the river and left my guide's station wagon in front of a cluster of Negro shanties huddling under the levee. Then we walked a slithery path along the edge of the levee to a point where we saw a catwalk out to a plank boat landing. The drilling barge lay, or stood, about one hundred yards out in the stream, a creature at once reminiscent of a giant sucking insect, a birthday cake with nine candles, and the skyline of a factory city. It was a great platform, resting on the water's surface, with the superstructure of an oil well rising from its center and eight tall shafts, like factory chimneys, towering toward the sky around its perimeter.

These shafts, called jacks, are the barge's feet. When she arrives in working position she thrusts down the lower extremities of the great rods until they dig into the sea bottom and hold her fast. She then rises on them, like an automobile on jacks, until there is a good clearance between her bottom and sea level. From a seagoing vessel she has changed to a house on stilts.

Next she extrudes from her belly the business end of the drill that she will thrust ten or fifteen thousand feet beneath the bed of gulf or ocean until she reaches oil or gas—or the charterer gives up. Then she lowers herself to the surface of the water, retracts her under parts into her hull and is ready to be towed to her next job. There is so much machinery within her hull that there is no room for an organ of locomotion.

She is a specialized succubus, a great pipette, moved about to wherever her manipulators think there may be blood worth sucking. Such a barge may work for her owner, if he has leased new undersea acreage, or, which is more common, she may be chartered to companies that have acreage and no barge. This one, Sancton said, was new and had cost four and a half million dollars to build.

She weighed four thousand dead-weight tons, as much as a fair-sized tramp steamer, and contained, in addition to the mechanisms of her gymnastic and oil-searching systems, a plant for distilling sea water for hydraulic drilling. Tom said the barge in the river in front of us was called the *Mr. Louie*, after her owner, promoter and chief conceiver, a man named Louis Roussel.

We walked out onto the catwalk and shouted and waved our arms at the barge's tender, an old LCT, or landing-craft tank, with long forward deck and a high pilot house at her stern. The LCT lay under the monster's quarter, swinging lazy at her cable. A workman on the *Mr. Louie* cast the line off and the old warrior turned toward shore and came in through the muddy water. Her one-man crew, a big mulatto bare to the waist, brought her alongside the plank and held her there by her own power as we stepped aboard, then backed her out and wheeled her under the barge. A crane man in the high superstructure lowered a rope basket cage at the end of a cable to the LCT's deck. We stepped inside and grabbed hold, and he swung us up in the air like a couple of crabs in a long-handled net, then brought us inboard and set us gently down.

From the steaming 100-degree heat of the deck, we walked through a door into an air-conditioned mess hall as cold as an iced drink. Two men in coveralls were seated at a long plastic-topped steel table drinking Cokes. One was the owner, Roussel. He explained that with one of the other men, his naval architect, he had been running final trials of his creation's jacking system.

"She can work in a hundred and twenty feet of water," he said. "When she's set she's as solid as an island. She'll carry a working crew of eleven, living in air-conditioned quarters, with unlimited fresh water, twenty feet above the surface of the sea, if it's rough."

I asked him, not unnaturally, how the owner or lessee of such an elaborate tool chose a place to use it.

"You go out in a boat," he said, pronouncing boat "bawat," with two syllables, in the Cajun way, "and you try a seismic shot." (The shot is a charge of dynamite detonated under water.) "The best way I can explain it is that the vibrations are like a rubber ball. If the ball bounces hard enough, you know it has hit something solid. You measure the bounce of the shot by its vibrations. If they show you are over what we call a dome, or salt dome, formation, there's a chance that there's oil under it. Naturally, if you're near a field that's already producing, you have a better chance. But everybody has the same idea—the area will have a higher selling price. If you're away from the rest, using your own judgment, you're wildcatting, but you get better odds if you're right."

I realized that he was describing a process necessarily complex, but he made it sound simple.

"And then, if you decide you want to drill?" I asked.

"You make a map showing what you want," he said. "That's called a lot, and it can't be more than five thousand eight hundred acres. You send a deposit of one hundred dollars to the State Minerals Board with a letter saying you want to bid on that lot. The Board calls for bids on the lot by a certain date. Then, if you bid high enough, you get the lease."

"How many acres are there altogether?"

"Quite a few, I imagine," he said. "The whole coast from Texas to Mississippi, out to a distance of ten and a half miles from the land. You know about the dispute between the Federal Government and the state, probably. The State Minerals Board runs the show meanwhile, and the money paid for leases is held in escrow." (The United States Supreme

Court has since ruled against Louisiana, but Congress may bail the Gret Stet out.)

Square-chinned and leathery, Roussel has the kind of head Norman peasants carve on wooden stoppers for Calvados bottles.

From their respective inceptions, Texas and Oklahoma have had a frontier character. Oil men there, or so it seems to me, are primarily oil men. But Louisiana is a very old community, for America, and the independents in oil are varied and indigenous types: Roussel, for example, said he had been a bus driver in New Orleans in 1930. He had made a bit of money and bought a share in a wildcat drilling venture. The well had come in, and he had gone on venturing, like a man with the dice in his hand. He had not had to move far to get from his bus route to his holes; he was as native as a muskrat, as French as his taste for litigation. He had backed five successive winners, which is as hard as five successive passes. Then he had drilled "a big one I won't brag about, because it was dry."

If he had had the bad luck first, he might still be driving a bus. But by that time he was out ahead, like a crap shooter with a big bankroll.

5/*Nothing But a Little Pissant*

THE ENTRY OF a hero on the public scene goes unnoticed, but his *rentrée* always has an eager press. Napoleon coming back from Elba, Robert Bruce from rustication among the spiders, and Jim Jeffries from retirement in 1910, all drew a heavy coverage; so, no doubt, did Odysseus after he announced his arrival at Ithaca. The betting public, sentimental only to a point, wants to know whether the hero's legs are sound, his spirits good, whether he has shed the lard of sloth, and if so, whether he has weakened himself taking off weight.

Such was the mood of Louisiana when, on the afternoon of August 2, Tom and I started from New Orleans in his battered station wagon to go to the midstate city of Alexandria, where Earl was to make the first major stump speech of his campaign for renomination on the Democratic ticket.

Opinion, all biased, was split on how the Governor would shape up. The *Times-Picayune*, like the Royalist journals in 1815, held that the man from Elba was a burned-out shadow of a hollow shell. But Jim Comiskey, boss of the Old Regulars, had assured me "Oil is on da steady improve and champin' on da bit to go." Mister Comiskey was, for the moment, a red-hot Long man.

Tom was about as neutral as a Louisianian can be during a primary fight, which is to say about as calm as a cat can stay with catnip under its nose. He erred, however, in overweighting medical testimony. This is a mistake journalists have made increasingly since 1953, when, after President Eisenhower's heart attack, the statements of physicians in attendance became more newsworthy than good triangle murders. Abruptly, any utterance of an M.D. rated as much space as the award of an honorary degree to the publisher of the paper, and editors, not content with the daily bulletins from Denver, Washington and Harvard, sent reporters out to ask local cardiologists everywhere for inside comments on the Chief Executive's viscera. These covered everything from the effect of fried mush to how many times a day a middle-aged man ought to lose his temper. Reporters, always confused between what is news and what makes sense, began to take the doctors seriously. After that the cholesterol was in the fire.

Tom was impressed because half the doctors in the South and Southwest had tabbed Uncle Earl as infected with all known diseases, from paranoid schizophrenia to warts and bronchiectasis, which means difficulty in clearing the throat. Even his own experts, who denied he was demented, said in explanation of his antislavery views that he was beset by arteriosclerosis, several small strokes, oscillatory blood pressure and an irreverent gleam in his left eye. The collective diagnosis recalled the doctor described in the great book *The Flush Times in Alabama and Mississippi,* who would "fire at random a box of his pills into your bowels, with a vague chance of hitting some disease unknown to him." It was Tom who, years before, had first called my attention to the *Flush Times,* by Joseph G. Baldwin, a happy 1853 antidote to the mystic-memories-of-magnolia school of Southern writing.

"There is an expert at Tulane they call 'Dr. Schizophrenia,'" Tom said to me. "He says Earl hasn't got it. But what he says he has is progressive deterioration of the memory caused by an occluded ventricle. Once they got that, they're gone."

I myself inclined to the theory that if a man knows enough to go to the races, he needs no doctor. A good tout is the best physician for a confirmed horseplayer, and any prescription he writes that pays 5 to 1 or better tonifies the blood, synchronizes the pulse, regularizes the functions and lets bygones be bygones.

The distance from New Orleans to Alexandria is about 190 miles. The first 90 miles, from New Orleans to Baton Rouge, are on a throughway, a straight, fast road on the east side of the Mississippi, far enough back from the bank to avoid meanders, and high enough over the marshes to obviate bridges. There is nothing worth a long look. The bayous parallel the road on either side like stagnant, weed-strangled ditches, but their life is discreetly subsurface—snapping turtles, garfish, water moccasins and alligators. The mammals are water rats and muskrats and nutria, a third kind of rat. The nutria, particularly ferocious, is expropriating the other rats. Bird life, on the day we drove through, was a patrol of turkey buzzards looking down for rat cadavers. There pressed down on the landscape a smell like water that householders have inadvertently left flowers in while they went off for a summer holiday. It was an ideal setting for talk about politics.

The old station wagon slammed along like an old selling plater that knows a course by heart.

"It's the most complex state in the South," my companion said. "In just about every one of the others you have the same battle between the poor-to-middling farmers on the poor lands—generally in the hills—that didn't justify an investment in slaves before the war, and the descendants of the rich planters on the rich lands, who held slaves by the dozen to the gross. Slaves were a mighty expensive form of agricultural machinery, with a high rate of depreciation. You could only use them to advantage on land that produced a cash crop. We had that same basic conflict, and it lasted longer than anywhere else, for reasons I'm going to give, but in addition, we have a lot that are all our own. In the other states it was just between poor Anglo-Saxon Protestant whites and rich Anglo-Saxon Protestant whites. But here we got poor French Catholic whites and poor Anglo-Saxon Protestant whites and rich French Catholic whites and rich Anglo-Saxon Protestant whites. Sometimes the Catholic French get together against the Anglo-Saxon Protestants and sometimes the rich of both faiths get together against the poor, or the poor against the rich.

"And there's always been another problem in Louisiana that no other Southern state has. There are other large collections of people living close together in the South, but they are not big cities, just overgrown country towns like Atlanta. They may have corruption, but not sophistication. They lack the urban psychology, like ancient Athens, that is different, hostile, and superior, and that the countryman resents and distrusts. So you get a split along another line—you got not only poor rural French Catholic, rich rural white Protestant, rich rural French Catholic, and poor rural white Protestant, but poor urban Catholic, not exclusively French, rich urban Catholic, poor urban Protestant (mainly Negro) and rich urban Protestant. Making out a ticket is tricky.

"Alick, in Rapides Parish, is the political navel of the state, right in the middle." (Alick is Alexandria.) "Southern, bilingual, French Catholic Louisiana, the land of the bougalees, shades into Northern monolingual, Anglo-Saxon Protestant Louisiana, the land of the rednecks. But in Rapides itself and the parishes across the center of the state you get both kinds. So there's always a lot of politicking and name-calling in Alick, and when Earl picked it to stump in he showed he was ready to fight."

He sounded as complacent as a man I remembered on the road to Baalbek, telling me of the Ten Varieties soup of politico-religious divisions within the Lebanon.

The old car banged along. Its speedometer was not working, but it had a clock in its head, like an old horse that an old trainer, set in his ways, has worked a mile in 1.47 every Wednesday morning since it was three years old.

"Orleans Parish—that's the city of New Orleans—and Jefferson, across the river, which is its dormitory country—have about a quarter of a million voters between them," my instructor said. "That's between twenty-five and thirty per cent of the state vote. All the parishes north of a line through Rapides have maybe twenty per cent and all the parishes south of it and west of the Mississippi maybe twenty to twenty-five. The central chunk, on an axis from Alick to Baton Rouge and on east, has the balance of strength. To get a majority of votes on the first primary, a candidate got to win big in one of the four regions and make it close in the others, or win big in three and lose big in one. They're so different and so opposed historically that it's hard to imagine a candidate running evenly in all four. Old Earl was so strong in 1956 that he ran *almost* even in the metropolis. For an upstate candidate that's great. He won easy everyplace else.

"If Earl is too sick to run, a Catholic from New Orleans like Morrison might win big in New Orleans and south Louisiana, but he would be snowed under in the north, and he would have to run like hell in Alick and Baton Rouge to make it. So probably there would be no winner the first time around, and then, in the runoff between the two high men, anything could happen. Generally all the losers gang up against the top guy. Hard to name a favorite in the betting until the day before the second runoff, and then often you're wrong anyway."

"Then how did Huey Long put all the bits and pieces together?" I asked.

"Huey got all the poor people over on one side," my friend said. "And there were a lot more of them. He made the poor redneck and the poor Frenchman and the poor Negro see that what they had in common was more important for voting purposes than the differences. The differences couldn't be changed by ballots. The Depression helped, of course.

"When people are living good again they can afford to fight over unessentials. The regime that ran Louisiana right on from the Purchase discouraged the idea that a man had the right to live decently. It was new stuff down here when Huey put it out: 'Share Our Wealth'; 'Every Man a King'; and remember, he got to be Governor four years before Franklin D. Roosevelt was elected President. Huey got after the out-state oil companies and the in-state oil companies, and the old-family bench and bar that held with the out-state money, and anybody that gave him an argument for any reason he blackened with being a hireling of Standard Oil. I don't know how much money he made out of it, but certainly less than a lot of politicians make taking the easy-money side.

"And whether he did it all because he loved the sense of power is moot—you could say the same thing against any leader you didn't like. I think up North you got the idea that the man who killed him became a popular hero, like William Tell or Charlotte Corday. Incidentally, Charlotte Corday wouldn't have won any Gallup polls in Paris in her day. There were editorials that said, 'Louisiana heaved a sigh of relief and raised her tear-stained head from the dust.'

"But, in fact, Dick Leche and Earl Long, who ran for Governor and Lieutenant Governor on the Long ticket in 1936, got sixty-seven and a tenth per cent of the popular vote, even though there was a fight among the Long people themselves and Leche was next to unknown then. That was a better percentage than even Roosevelt got against Landon that year. The vote came straight from the tear-stained head."

We got hungry and stopped at a glass-and-Monel-metal hangar that advertised "Shrimp, BarBQue, PoBoy" (this last the Louisiana term for what we call Italian hero sandwiches). The BarBQue was out, the shrimps stiff with inedible batter, the coffee desperate. Southern cooking, outside New Orleans, is just about where Frederic Law Olmsted left it when he wrote *The Cotton Kingdom.* A PoBoy at Mumphrie's in New Orleans is a portable banquet. In the South proper, it is a crippling blow to the intestine.

"We're hitting a new culture belt," I said. "This is the kind of cooking that goes right on up the center of the United States with the Mississippi until it hits the Great Lakes. It's nearer akin to what we'd get in a roadside diner in La Grange, Illinois, than to the poorest oyster bar in New Orleans, sixty miles behind us."

Tom, New Orleans born, of parents born there, said, "You're right on that. We're Mediterranean. I've never been to Greece or Italy, but I'm sure I'd be at home there as soon as I landed."

He would, too, I thought. New Orleans resembles Genoa or Marseilles, or Beirut or the Egyptian Alexandria more than it does New York, although all seaports resemble one another more than they can resemble any place in the interior. Like Havana and Port-au-Prince, New Orleans is within the orbit of a Hellenistic world that never touched the North Atlantic. The Mediterranean, Caribbean and Gulf of Mexico form a homogeneous, though interrupted, sea. New York and Cherbourg and Bergen are in a separate thalassic system.

Hellenism followed the Mediterranean littoral; it spread to the shores of the Caribbean and Gulf. The Hellenistic world stopped short of the Atlantic edge of Europe, but its Roman conquerors got there with a version in *Reader's Digest* form, like Irish missionaries of a Jewish religion. Culture on both shores of the North Atlantic is therefore a paraphrase, as if Choctaws had learned English from Cherokees.

The Mediterraneans who settled the shores of the interrupted sea scurried across the gap between the Azores and Puerto Rico like a woman crossing a drafty hall in a sheer nightgown to get to a warm bed with a man in it. Old, they carried with them a culture that had ripened properly, on the tree. Being sensible people, they never went far inland. All, or almost all, the interior of North America was therefore filled in from the North Atlantic Coast, by the weakest element in that incompletely civilized population—those who would move away from salt water.

The middle of Louisiana is where the culture of one great thalassic littoral impinges on the other, and a fellow running for Governor has got to straddle the line between them.

When Tom and I were sufficiently disgusted with the coffee of the inland-dwellers, we resumed our ride, bypassing the center of Baton Rouge to cross the Mississippi by the Baton Rouge bridge, and after that leaving the monotony of the throughway for the state roads with their complete lack of variety. By now I had begun to sneak compulsive glances at my watch. We had left New Orleans at four, and Earl was slated to speak at eight. The owner of the old station wagon had said he could make it to Alick in four hours easy. It began to look not all that easy.

I tried to estimate the station wagon's speed by clocking it between signposts. From "Bunkie, 27 Mi." to "Bunkie, 20 Mi.," I caught it in a consoling seven minutes, but the next post, a good bit farther on, said "Bunkie, 23." Bunkie is the leading bourgade between Baton Rouge and Alick—it has a population of 4,666—but there were other one-street-of-storefronts towns that the road ran through. By now it was dusk and the stores were lighted, so that, coming out of the dark, we galloped episodically between plywood maple-finished bedroom suites in the windows on one side of the street and mannequins with $7.98 dresses on the other, scaring from our course gaunt hounds that looked like Kabyle dogs.

The entrance to Alick was little more impressive than these others, except for two electric signs. One was a straw-hatted spook flapping great wings over the Hocus-Pocus Liquor Store and the other a symbolic giraffe and dachshund over a used-car lot. They disappeared at every other flash in favor of a legend: "High Quality, Low Prices."

Hurrying through otherwise undistinguished streets, we passed between cars parked thick along the approaches to the courthouse square and heard the loud-speaker blaring long before we got there. Somebody was on the platform in front of the courthouse steps, standing too close to the microphone and blasting. The crowd, massed immediately around the speaker's stand, thinned out toward the sidewalks.

My companion let me out and drove on to find a parking space, and I ran onto the lawn for my first look at the Imam in the flesh. As I crossed over to the forum, a boy handed me a pink throwaway, which I examined when I got within range of the light diffused from the floodlamps over the platform:

GOVERNOR LONG SPEAKS

Governor Long Opens Campaign for Re-Election

Come Out and Bring All your friends to hear the truth.
Come out and see Governor Long in person. Nothing will
be said to offend or hurt anyone.

The Governor, on the platform, was saying to somebody I could not see over in the other wing of the audience:

"If you don't shut up your claptrap, I'm going to have you forcibly removed. You just nothing but a common hoodlum and a heckler."

"Amen," an old man in front of me yelled. "Give it to him, Earl."

Whoever it was that Earl was talking to in the crowd had no microphone, so we couldn't hear him, but he must have answered in tones audible to the Governor, because the latter shouted into the mike:

"I knew your daddy, Camille Gravel, and he was a fine man. But you trying to make yourself a big man, and you nothing but a little pissant."

"Amen, Earl," the old man yelled. "Give it to him."

The fellow in the crowd, now identified for me as a lawyer from Alick who was the Democratic National Committeeman from Louisiana, must have spoken again, for the Governor thundered:

"Mr. Gravel, I got nothing against you personally. Now you keep quiet and I won't mention your name. If you don't I'll have you removed as a common damn nuisance." He paused for the answer we couldn't hear and then bellowed:

"If *you* so popular, why don't *you* run for Governor?"

It sounded like a dialogue between a man with the horrors and his hallucinations. But the National Committeeman, Earl's interlocutor, was there in the flesh. He had brought his ten children, and they were all mad at the Governor.

The night was like a heavy blanket pressed down on the lawn. Men stood in their sleeveless, collarless shirts, and sweat caked the talcum powder on the backs of the women's necks. Anti-Long newspapers the next day conceded the crowd was between three and four thousand, so there may well have been more. Plenty of Negroes, always in little groups, were scattered among the whites, an example, I suppose, of Harry Golden's "vertical integration," because in public gatherings where there are seats, the two colors are always separated into blocs.

"That's the way I like to see it," the Governor said, from the stand. "Not all our colored friends in one spot and white friends in another. I'm the best friend the poor white man, and the middle-class white man, and the rich white man—so long as he behave himself—and the poor colored man, ever had in the State of Loosiana. And if the NAACP and that little pea-headed nut Willie Rainach will just leave us alone, then *sen*sible people, not cranks, can get along in a *rea*sonable way. That Rainach wants to fight the Civil War all over again."

There were two colored couples, middle-aged, in front of me, next to the old white man who didn't like Gravel, and now one of the colored men shouted "Amen!" The old white man gave him a reproving look, but he couldn't bawl him out for agreeing with a Long. Nobody can object to *rea*sonable and *sen*sible, but Long hadn't said what he thought *reas*onable and *sen*sible were, and it occurred to me that he probably never would.

I had been looking at him with an amateur clinical eye since I got there, and his physical condition seemed to me to have improved several hundred per cent since his stump appearance with Joe Sims on the Fourth of July. Late hours and a diet of salted watermelon, buttermilk, and Vienna sausages cut up in chicken broth had put a dozen pounds back on his bones. Walking between grandstands and paddocks had legged him up, and he pranced under the floodlights that must have raised the temperature to a hundred and ten or so. I remembered when I had seen first the referee, Ruby Goldstein, and then the great Sugar Ray Robinson himself collapse under the heat of similar lights in a ring on a less oppressive night in New York.

Uncle Earl wore a jacket, shirt and tie, a pattern of statesmanlike conventionality on a night when everybody off the platform was coatless and tieless. The tie itself was a quiet pattern of inkblots against an olive-and-pearl background, perhaps a souvenir Rorschach test from Galveston. The suit, a black job that dated from the days when he was fat and sassy, hung loosely about him as once it had upon a peg in the supermarket where the Governor liked to buy his clothes.

He left the dude role to Morrison. And in fact, before the evening was over, he said:

"I see Dellasoups has been elected one of the ten best-dressed men in America. He has fifty-dollar neckties and four-hundred-dollar suits. A four-hundred-dollar suit on old Uncle Earl would look like socks on a rooster."

It is difficult to report a speech by Uncle Earl chronologically, listing the thoughts in order of appearance. They chased one another on and off the stage like characters in a Shakespearean battle scene, full of alarums and sorties. But Morrison, good roads and old-age pensions popped in quite often.

Of Dodd, the State Auditor, a quondam ally and now a declared rival for the Governorship, he said, "I hear Big Bad Bill Dodd has been talking about inefficiency and waste in this administration. Ohyeah. Ohyeah. Well let me tell you, Big Bad Bill has at least six streamlined deadheads on his payroll that couldn't even find Bill's office if they had to. But they can find that *Post Office* every month to get their salary check—Ohyeah."

It was after the "*reas*onable and *sen*sible" bit that he went into his general declaration of tolerance. "I'm not against anybody for reasons of race, creed, or any ism he might believe in except nuttism, skingameism or communism," he said.

"I'm glad to see so many of my fine Catholic friends here—they been so kind to me I sometimes say I consider myself forty per cent Catholic and sixty per cent Baptist" (this is a fairly accurate reflection of the composition of the electorate). "But I'm in favor of *every* religion with the possible exception of snake-chunking. Anybody that so presumes on how he stands with Providence that he will let a snake bite him, I say he deserves what he's got coming to him." The snake-chunkers, a small, fanatic cult, do not believe in voting.

"Amen, Earl," the old man said.

The expressions on the Governor's face changed with the poetry of his thought, now benign, now mischievous, now indignant. Only the moist hazel eyes remained the same, fixed on a spot above and to the rear of the audience as if expecting momentarily the arrival of a posse.

"I don't *need* this job," he said. "I don't *need* money." He stopped and winked. "I don't miss it except when I run out."

There were shouts of laughter, the effect he courted.

"Amen, Earl. You tell 'em, Earl."

His face turned serious, as if he had not expected to be so cruelly misunderstood.

"I'm serious about that," he said. "You know I'm no goody-goody. But if I have ever misappropriated one cent, by abuse of my office, and anyone can prove it, I'll resign.

"I know lots of ways to make a living. I know how to be a lawyer, and a danged good one. I know how to be traveling salesman. I know how to pick cotton, and have many times, although I've seen the days when to get my hundred pounds I had to put a watermelon in the bag."

There were gales of tolerant laughter now, even from farmers who would shoot any of their own help they found cheating on weight.

"All I ask," he said, with the honesty throbbing in his voice like a musical saw, "is a chance once again to help the fine people of the Great State of Loosiana, and to continue to serve them as their Governor."

Even a group of great louts in T shirts, perhaps high-school football players, were silent and by now impressed; earlier in the address they had made a few feeble attempts at heckling, like yelling, "Hey, Earl, what's in the glass?" when the Governor paused for a drink of water. These boys might be from well-to-do anti-Long families, but they had the endemic Southern (and Arabic) taste for oratory, and they knew a master when they heard him.

Mr. Gravel, down near the platform, must have again attracted the Governor's attention, but now Uncle Earl, the creature of his own voice, was in a benign mood from offering his own body to the Great State of Loosiana.

"Mr. Gravel," he said, "you got ten beautiful children there, I wish you would lend five of them to me to bring up." It was one of Earl's well-publicized sorrows that he, like the Shah of Iran then, had no legitimate heir, and he handed peppermint candies or small change to all children he saw, even in years when there was no election. "He bought those candies by grosses of dozens," an ex-associate told me.

Mr. Gravel, still inaudible except to Earl, must have declined this overture, because the Governor shouted to the crowd: "He used to be a nice fellow, but now he just a goddamn hoodlum!"

"Leave him alone, Earl, we come to hear *you* talk!" the old man near me shouted back.

"I was in Minneannapolis once, talking to the Governor of Minnesota, a great expert on insanity," Uncle Earl said, "and he told me an astonishing fact—there are ten times as many crazy people in Minnesota as Loosiana. I suppose that is on account of the cold climate. They cannot go around in their shirt sleeves all year around, go huntin' and fishin' in all seasons, as we do. We got a wonderful climate," he said, and paused to wipe the sweat from his face with a handkerchief soaked in Coca-Cola, which he poured from a bottle out of a bucket of ice handed him by one of the lesser candidates on his ticket. The bugs soaring up at the edge of the lighted area and converging on the floodlights formed a haze as thick as a beaded curtain.

"On account we got so few crazy people, we can afford to let Camille Gravel run around."

"Leave him up, Earl," the old man yelled. "You got him licked."

"Some sapsuckers talk about cutting down taxes," the Governor said, apropos of nothing he had been talking about. "Where are they going to start cutting expenses? On the *spastic* school?" (When any opponent suggests a cut in welfare expenditures, Earl accuses him of wanting to take it out on the spastics. This is the equivalent of charging the fellow would sell his mother for glue.) "They want to cut down on the *spastics?* On the little children, enjoying the school lunches? Or on those fine old people, white-haired against the sunset of life—" and he bowed his own white head for a split second—"who enjoy the most generous state pensions in the United States?

"We got the finest roads, finest schools, finest hospitals in the country—yet there are rich men who complain. They are so tight you can hear 'em squeak when they walk. They wouldn't give a nickel to see a earthquake. They sit there swallowin' hundred-dollar bills like a bullfrog swallows minners—if you chunked them as many as they want they'd bust."

"Amen, Earl," the old man said. "God have mercy on the poor people."

"Of course, I know many *fine* rich people," the Governor said, perhaps thinking of his campaign contributors. "But the most of them are like a rich old feller I knew down in Plaquemines Parish, who died one night and never done nobody no good in his life, and yet, when the Devil come to get him, he took an appeal to St. Peter.

" 'I done some good things on earth,' he said. 'Once, on a cold day in about 1913, I gave a blind man a nickel.' St. Peter looked all through the records, and at last, on page four hundred and seventy-one, he found the entry. 'That ain't enough to make up for a misspent life,' he said. 'But wait,' the rich man says. 'Now I remember, in 1922 I give five cents to a poor widow woman that had no carfare.' St. Peter's clerk checked the book again, and on page thirteen hundred and seventy-one, after pages and pages of how this old stump-wormer loan-sharked the poor, he found the record of that nickel.

"'That ain't neither enough,' St. Peter said. But the mean old thing yelled, '*Don't* sentence me yet. In about 1931 I give a nickel to the Red Cross.' The clerk found that entry, too. So he said to St. Peter, 'Your Honor, what are we going to do with him?'"

The crowd hung on Uncle Earl's lips the way the bugs hovered in the light.

"You know what St. Peter said?" the Governor, the only one in the courthouse square who knew the answer, asked. There was, naturally, no reply.

"He said: 'Give him back his fifteen cents and tell him to go to Hell.'"

He had the crowd with him now, and he dropped it.

"Folks," he said, "I know you didn't come here just to hear me talk. If this big mouth of mine ever shut up I'd be in a devil of a fix. I want to introduce to you some of the fine *sin*cere candidates that are running with me on my ticket. My ticket and the independent candidates I have endorsed are trained, skilled, and have the wisdom and experience to make you honest, loyal and *sin*cere public servants."

He turned to the triple row of men and women who sat behind him on undertaker's chairs, the men swabbing, the women dabbing, at their faces with handkerchiefs, while the Governor talked like an intrepid trainer who turns his back on his troupe of performing animals.

A reporter who had his watch on the Governor said that his talk had lasted fifty-seven minutes, and he was not even blowing.

"And first," he said, "I want to introduce to you the man I have selected to serve under me as Lieutenant Governor during my next term of office —a fine Frenchmun, a fine Catholic, the father of twenty-three children, Mr. Oscar Guidry."

The number of children was politically significant, since it indicated that Mr. Guidry was a practicing, not a *soi-disant*, Catholic. The candidate for Lieutenant Governor had to be a Frenchman and a Catholic, because Uncle Earl was neither.

Mr. Guidry, a short, stocky man who reminded me of a muscular owl, arose from his chair like a Mr. Bones called to front center by Mr. Interlocutor. He appeared embarrassed, and he whispered rapidly to Uncle Earl.

"Oscar says he has only fourteen children," the Governor announced. "But that's a good beginnin'."

Mr. Guidry whispered again, agitated, and Earl said, "But he is a member of a family of twenty-three brothers and sisters." He turned away, as if washing his hands of the whole affair, and sat down.

Mr. Guidry, throwing back his head and clasping his hands in front of him, as if about to intone the "Marseillaise," began with a rush, sounding all his aitches:

"I am *honored* to be associated with the Gret Governeur of the Gret Stet on his tiquette. Those who have conspired against him, fearing to shoot him with a pistol-ball . . ." and he was off, but Earl, seated directly behind him, was mugging and catching flies, monopolizing attention like an old vaudeville star cast in a play with a gang of Method actors.

Pulling his chair slightly out of line, he crossed his legs and turned his profile to the audience, first plucking at his sleeves, which came down about as far as his thumbnails, then, when he had disengaged his hands, picking his nose while he looked over at Alick's leading hotel, the Bentley, across the street, described by the Louisiana State Guide as "a six-story building of brick and stone, with a columned façade and a richly decorated interior." He stared at it as if it contained some absorbing riddle.

When he had finished with his nose, he began to bathe his face, his temples and the back of his neck with Coca-Cola from the cold bottle, sloshing it on like iced cologne.

"Cool yourself off, Earl," a voice piped up from the crowd, and the Governor shouted back, "I'm a red-hot poppa."

When he had wet himself down sufficiently, he drank the heel-tap and set the bottle down. Then he lit a cigarette and smoked, dramatically, with the butt held between his thumb and middle finger and the other fingers raised, in the manner of a ventriloquist. While he smoked right-handed he pulled out his handkerchief and blotted his wet face with his left.

He sat unheeding of the rumpus raised by his adherents, like a player in a jazz band who has finished his solo, or a flashy halfback who poses on the bench while the defensive team is in. The candidates ranted and bellowed, putting across a few telling although familiar points.

"In the great state of Texas, biggest and richest in the United States, there is an old-age pension of thirty-one dollars a month. Here in Loosiana we got seventy-two."

But the bored crowd stood fast, knowing that a whistle would blow and the star would throw off his blanket and come onto the field again to run rings around the forces of Mammon. Sure enough, after what seemed to me an endless session of subordinate rant, the Governor threw away the last of a chain of cigarettes and shook his head like man waking up on a park bench and remembering where he is. He got up and walked to the microphone so fast that the man using it had barely time to say "I thank you" before the Governor took it away from him.

"You shall know the truth, and the truth shall set you free," the Governor said, "but you will never get to know the truth by reading the Alexandria *Town Talk*. You all read in that paper that I am crazy. Ohyeah. Do I look any crazier than I ever did? I been accused of saying the fella that owns that paper is a kept man. Maybe he ain't, but I'd like to be kep' as good as he is. He married a rich woman. That's about the best way I know to save yourself about ninety-eight years' hard work."

"Amen, Earl, it's the truth," the old man in front of me cried, and the Negroes laughed at what was apparently a well-established local joke.

"Maybe some of you are here because you've never seen a man out of a nuthouse before," the Governor said tolerantly. "Maybe you want to see a man who has been stuck thirty-eight times with needles. Oh, the first man stuck me, stuck me right through the britches. He didn't get me in the fat part, either, and oh, how it hurt! Maybe I lost a little weight, but you would have, too. Occasionally I say hell or damn, but if it had happened to you all, you'd say worse than that. Christ on the Cross Himself never suffered worse than poor old Earl!

"Oh, not that I'm fit to walk in Christ's shoes!" he bellowed to preclude any confusion. "I'm not good enough, when a fellow slugs me on one cheek, to turn the other side of my scheming head. I'm going to slug him back."

"Amen, Earl. You tell him, Earl. Who you goin' to hit first, Earl?"

"Down there in that court in Texas in Gal*ves*ton before that Texas judge, I felt like Christ between the two thieves. He reared back his head and he said, 'Father, forgive them, for they know not what they do!' "

At this point he was interrupted by wild handclapping from a group of elderly ladies wearing print dresses, white gloves, straw hats and Spaceman eyeglasses, who had been seated quietly on the platform through the earlier proceedings. They were under the impression that it was an original line.

I next remember the Governor in his seat again, head down, exhausted, having given his all to the electorate, in a pose like Bannister after running the first four-minute mile. It occurred to me that he was like old blind Pete Herman fighting on heart alone, by a trained reflex. Pete is a friend of the Governor's.

As Earl sat there, one of the assisting speakers, a fellow with a strong voice, grabbed the microphone and declaimed the family battle ode, "Invictus."

When the man came to the part where it says:

> Under the bludgeonings of fate
> Ma haid is bloody, but *unbowed*

Earl flung up his head like a wild horse and got up like a fighter about to go into a dance to prove he hasn't been hurt. He called for a show of hands by everybody who was going to vote for him, and I waved both of mine.

I left him surrounded by children to whom he was passing out coins, "a quarter to the white kids and a nickel to the niggers."

My companion had rejoined me after parking the car, and we walked together through the breaking crowd.

"How could his wife have done him like she done?" a woman was asking another, and a man was saying, "Got to give da ol' dawg what's coming to him."

My friend saw Gravel, a handsome, tanned man in a white sports shirt and black slacks, standing where the lawn ended at the pavement, and walked over to him. Two or three reporters were already there, asking Gravel what he had said when Earl said what.

The National Committeeman said he had come to hear the speech because two or three men close to Earl had called him up and warned him that Earl was going to blacken his name.

"I wanted to be there to nail the lie," he said. He said Earl started the argument.

Six or eight of the ten Gravel children played hide-and-seek around their father's legs, and as he talked, another boy, about eleven years old, ran up and said to a slightly younger girl, his sister, "The Governor wanted to give me a quarter, but I wouldn't take it."

"Why not?" the girl asked, and I decided she had a bigger political future than her brother.

Gravel said he had to go home because there was a wedding reception there, and the rest of us walked back toward the Bentley, where all the rocking chairs on the porch were already occupied. The row of glowing cigar ends swaying in unison reminded me of the Tiller Girls in a glow-worm number.

6 / *The Bird That Kicks*

I THOUGHT Uncle Earl had been great, but a couple of press association men who had been covering him for years said that he looked over-trained. After his first speech of the day at Leesville, the seat of Vernon Parish, they said, he had had to make a detour to his home farm at Winnfield and have a half-hour nap and eat a piece of watermelon before he could continue the day's round.

Then he had gone on to Coushatta, the seat of Red River Parish, and Jena, the chief place of LaSalle Parish, picking up steam as he went along, sitting next to the driver in the front seat of the air-conditioned limousine. He keeps the rear seats free for bodyguards and the things he buys at the wayside as he travels: pitchforks, country hams, post-hole diggers, goats, and cases of Dr. Pepper, 7-Up, Louisiana and out-of-state beers, and sacramental wine. It's his way of getting into conversation with people, and he likes to bargain with them—another Arab trait.

"Do you know he came back from Galveston with fifteen pounds of okra that he bought at the nuthouse farm because the price was right?" one reporter asked me. "And we got all the gumbo in the world in Louisiana. Why, Dick Leche told me that one time when he was Governor and Earl was Lieutenant Governor, about 1938, they went to a convention out in Chicago, and the day before they left they stopped by Marshall Field's store to buy some presents.

"Dick says, 'When da salesgoil wrapped up all Oil's poichases—' you know how Dick talks, with that Orleans Parish accent—'Oil says, "How much is it?" and she says, "Twenty-two dollars." Oil says, "Dat's ridiculous, I'll give you sixteen." ' Dick tried to pretend he wasn't with him.

"The girl said salespeople weren't allowed to change prices, and Earl said he wanted to see the manager of the store. The girl went for her boss, and he sent for his, until the head man came, and Dick says Earl didn't get the package for sixteen dollars, but he got it for twenty and a half.

"When they were outside, Earl said, 'Marshall Field or a little store in Winnfield is just the same. Dey'll all take a little less if you hold out.' "

We moved into the Bentley cocktail lounge, a big, air-conditioned basement room, as cheerless as the crypt beneath the Egyptian temple in *Aïda.* The Bentley was built in 1908 by an Alexandrian lumber king who thought Alick was destined to be a metropolis; like a parent buying clothes for a growing boy, he took several sizes too large.

The reporter who had been telling Long stories continued: "Dick likes to say, 'Dey talk about da boid dat fouls its own nest, but Oil is da guy who kicks ovuh his own applecart.' "

"Dick's right," another fellow said. "When Earl is out in front, he gets too rough, and he starts acting out front as soon as he thinks maybe he will be. With all those croakers agreeing he was crazy a while back, a lot of politicians thought he really *was.* So they started cutting him out of the jackpots. Now he wants to punish all of them at once. Naturally they're going to stand together against him. What he should do is play sweet until he gets re-elected, and then go after them later.

"But instead of that he calls a special session for August 11. That's a week from Monday. And he's going after Theo Cangelosi, the chairman of the board of supervisors of L.S.U., the State University, because he says Cangelosi sided with Miz Blanche against him when she put him in the crazyhouse. Cangelosi was Earl's own lawyer, and Mrs. Long's too. Earl needs a vote of two thirds of the Legislature to can Cangelosi, and it means a row with everybody who believes in keeping the State University out of politics. Besides that there are a lot of Italian voters. He's kicking over his own applecart."

Olmsted wrote of Louisiana politicians in 1854: "A man who would purchase voters in the North would, at least, be careful not to mention it so publicly," and the difference persists, to the great advantage of conversation in Louisiana. We were joined by a lawyer who said he would like to be district attorney in his parish because that's where the money could be made. The incumbent, who had made plenty, was willing to move up to the bench, for a reasonable monetary consideration, because it was secure and dignified. The lawyer and the D.A. were sure they could swing both interim appointments, and if they did they could dig in solidly by doing favors before next election time.

But the old judge in the district, although infirm and due soon to retire for age, wouldn't quit a day sooner because he did not care to go on half pay. The fellow telling the story, the would-be district attorney, had offered to pay the judge the difference between half pay and full pay for the rest of his term, but the old fellow wanted the whole sum in advance.

"It ain't right," the attorney said, "because he don't figure to live that long, y'unnerstand?"

In a while I went up to bed, and before I turned out the light read the verso of the pink throwaway I had acquired at the meeting. It said:

A Message From
GOVERNOR LONG

This is a special invitation to my friends and all the people of this area to come out, bring your friends and neighbors, and learn the truth about what I have done, and what I have tried to do for you while serving as your Governor.

Ye Shall Know the Truth and the Truth Shall Set You Free

I also want to tell my people who have been so faithful to me just how I have been treated. I want you to personally see me and hear for yourself the harassments I have been subjected to. I want you to know the truth and not be guided by the rumors which have been spread among the people and which have been printed in the Alexandria *Town Talk*. Not all of the newspapers and reporters are bad. Many of the newspaper reporters are my personal friends. Some are ugly, and are inflicting upon their readers a great deal of sordid material that is distasteful. Some, but not all, of these newspapers and photographers, have been hounding me all day and all night like a pack of hounds after a wounded animal, scenting blood, trying to catch him and pull him down. They won't allow me—a sick man—a little privacy in which to recover from being dragged, without my permission, through three hospitals. I know you will agree with me that they have somewhat kept me from looking after our state business, which I have been daily doing even while I am trying to rest. I can tell you, as my office force well knows, that I attended to the affairs of state by giving of my time from 12 to 15 hours a day while I was out of the state. Only when you know the truth can you judge for yourself what the facts are.

Father, Forgive Them; For They Know Not What They Do

I do not propose to punish those who have had me locked behind ten doors, and had to have a key to turn on the lights, I would not hurt any one of them even though they have vilified me and almost wrecked my physical well-being. To those who have helped me in so many ways, I want to personally shake your hand and thank you for your prayers, your letters, and all the help you have given me. Were it not for your prayers, I would still be locked up by so-called friends who forbid my true friends from getting to me.

Wherefore By Their Fruits Ye Shall Know Them

As long as I have lived, I have been a friend of the less fortunate. I have always worked to improve their lot, and am still working to do so. These small-loan lobbyists who bleed the poor must be stopped! It is wrong for them to take advantage of the poor people. And it is wrong to railroad sane persons into insane asylums, where they do not belong, just because somebody wants to get rid of them for their own selfish purpose. After being dragged around, I know now personally how many of our people are mistreated in those hospitals. And I am going to wage a fight against those who thrive, prosper and live like kings on the misery of the mentally sick in this state. I want to help these poor, unfortunate people.

Your Help Is Needed

After being dragged through three different hospitals, locked up and jailed, in less than 30 days and losing 40 pounds, I am pleased to tell you that I have gained back nine pounds and hope to gain more. I continue to solicit your prayers and assistance during the months ahead. If the good people of Louisiana continue to stand by me as you have in the past, we will by the Grace of God win our battles against those who would take advantage of the poor, the mentally sick, and those of our people in less fortunate circumstances.

COME OUT AND HEAR THE TRUTH!
THE TRUTH SHALL SET YOU FREE!

The lobby was still acreep with politicians when I came down to breakfast next morning.

On the way down to the Coffee Shoppe my guide spotted our up-from-the-Third-Ward lawyer friend.

The lawyer was a Comiskey man. And Jim Comiskey had, as of Wednesday evening last, been the most enthusiastic Long booster I had encountered. This was Sunday morning.

"How do you think our boy looked?" I asked jovially, sure that with him at least I knew who "our boy" was.

"Who do you mean, our boy?" he asked. "We're going with Davis."

"When did you go off Earl?" I asked.

"He's got no chance," the Comiskey man said. "Did you hear him last night? Fighting with everybody in the state. Nobody can trust him. The sheriffs can't trust him. He'd send state troopers in anywhere if he didn't get what he wanted. The money people don't trust him either; he'd put a tax on sulphur, tax on timber, tax on gas, if he took the notion. He'll always have the newspapers on his neck. He's crazy.

"Besides, how does he know the Supreme Court will okay this scheme to resign and then come in again? What happens if it doesn't work?" There was fury in the lawyer's fair, handsome face now, the fury of a man taking a runout.

There was political logic in the move of traditionally incompatible factions to Davis. The newspapers and the money people, implacably hostile to Uncle Earl, were not sure of beating him with Morrison, whom they had backed of old. But the Mayor of New Orleans was a good campaigner, and what with the bad publicity Earl had been getting lately and the new enemies Earl delighted in making, Morrison might make it a close race in the first primary.

In the event Morrison did, only he and Earl would run off in the second primary. Then, if Earl blew his top again, or the Supreme Court turned him down, it would be too late for the Old Regulars to get behind a third candidate.

Morrison would win, and that, to the R.D.O. and the gamblers, was the worst thing that could happen. Morrison had taken away the R.D.O.'s municipal patronage. If he went to Baton Rouge he would take the state patronage too, and the R.D.O. would expire.

The forces of respectability that could not tolerate Long, and those of sin, which could not tolerate Morrison, had thus a poolable, swappable negative interest in the primary. The *Picayune* crowd had only to chuck Morrison, and Comiskey to chuck Long.

Uncle Earl had once said of Davis, "He won't say nothing, he won't promise nothing, and if he gets in, he won't do nothing." These are the qualifications of the ideal compromise candidate.

Outside, Alick lay prostrate under the summer climate of Louisiana, like a bull pup flattened by a cow. Night had hidden nothing of its charm—there was nothing to hide. I wondered what a well-kept man did with his time.

"At a place called Alexandria, our progress was arrested by falls in the river which cannot be passed by boats at low stages of the water," Olmsted wrote of Alick when he visited it in 1854. "The village is every bit a Southern one—all the houses being one story in height, and having an open veranda before them, like the English towns in the West Indies. It contains, usually, about 1,000 inhabitants, but this summer had been entirely depopulated by the yellow fever. Of 300 who remained, 120, we were told, died. Most of the runaway citizens had returned when we passed, though the last cases of fever were still in uncertain progress."

It is not much of a place now, but it must have been hell then. I have sometimes thought that the Deep South—Mississippi, Alabama, northern Louisiana and eastern Arkansas—resembles an iceberg floating upside down in the sea of history. The iceberg, dear to after-dinner speakers, shows only a fifth of its volume on the surface.

The Deep South has gone on for a hundred visible years since the Civil War bemoaning the twenty-five years of its own total history that preceded. In this submerged fifth of its past, according to the legend, great "floating palaces" went up the majestic rivers (since sullied forever by Yankees washing their feet in them) to thriving cities (like the Alick of 1854). Short-order aristocrats, rich from cotton made on new land by prime Negroes, built the great houses, and elegance busted out all over.

Joseph G. Baldwin, in 1853, wrote the pleasantest contemporary text on this period: *The Flush Times in Alabama and Mississippi.* Baldwin was an immigrant from Virginia, not a Yankee, and he lit out for the gold fields in California in 1849. *The Flush Times,* in 1853, was reminiscence. Since Baldwin wrote before the War, his work has none of the *de mortuis nihil nisi* piety of the writers during the hundred years above the waterline. He writes of a vulgar, swindling, money-grabbing time, when homicide and practical jokes about equally divided the boomers' leisure moments.

The boom was already over when he wrote. From the beginning of the rush for cotton lands, in the 1830s, to the beginning of the War, in 1861, was a span shorter than separates us from the administrations of Herbert Hoover and Jimmy Walker. This included the Caliban beginnings, the making of the money, the achievement of elegance, and the historic split-second left for the elegance to harden—like a quick cake icing. This knockabout-comedy turn in history has furnished forth the brooding squashy ancestral memories of a hundred Faulknerian heroes, *echt* and *ersatz.*

It is as if, in 2029, the whole nation should blame all intervening misfortunes on the stock-market crash of 1929, and think of the few years of money-making—for atypical people—that preceded 1929 as a thousand-year Reich of Stutz Bearcats for Everybody. I opened my mind to my friend when we got on the road again, and he, since he was from New Orleans, took no offense. In New Orleans a planter was always a figure of fun, a pigeon to pluck.

"The South doesn't believe the story," he said, "except when it seems useful to pretend to believe it. That's why I can't read Faulkner. And one of the bonds between Earl Long and his audiences is that he doesn't believe it, and they don't believe it, and it's a kind of private joke between them, like two kids in Sunday School that don't believe in God."

On the way out of town the old station wagon jogged along for a while beside the turbid, yellow Red River, celebrated in hillbilly song. The

Governor had retired for a day of rest to his farm at Winnfield, in Winn Parish, about fifty miles north of Rapides.

Tom said that the parish voted Populist in the 1890s, when the poor white-Populist leaders were taking over power in other Southern states—Pitchfork Ben Tillman in South Carolina, Tom Watson in Georgia, Jeff Davis in Arkansas. But the downstate "aristocrats," who had their counterparts in the states named, had a unique advantage in Louisiana in the alliance of the heavy-voting New Orleans city machine. The machine ran the wide-open city and the oligarchy ran the state. So the revolt within the Southern Democratic party that took place almost everywhere else was delayed in Louisiana until the emergence of Huey Long. That accounted for part of the added bitterness.

"They sat on the lid an extra thirty years," Tom said.

We ourselves were bound for Baton Rouge, where the Governor was slated to hold a press conference on Tuesday, and where, in the meanwhile, I hoped to find a couple of people I wanted to talk to. We took the route that leads directly to the Mississippi this time and followed its west bank down, instead of taking the overland diagonal between Alick and the west end of Baton Rouge bridge. This was better. There were old towns in a pastoral country like Angoulême, French names on the R.F.D. mailboxes and the general stores, cattle and even sheep under the trees in the fields by the way through Marksville and Mansura.

We stopped in a *guinguette* on the bank of False River, a long, narrow lake that once was an arm of the Mississippi, isolated by a shift in the river's course. The *guinguette* was a dicotyledon; within one plank shanty were two saloons, one for white and one for colored, divided by a partition. They had, of course, separate entrances. The white side was empty of customers when we arrived, the colored full of racket and animation. The old station wagon was the only car at the white entrance; there were two or three Oldsmobiles and an MG at the other.

To my regret we had to drink on the gloomy side. The licensee was white, a Monsieur Lejeune, who pronounced his name Ledjoon. The bottles were on the white side, but Monsieur Ledjoon spent most of his time serving the colored. We felt left out and, after a drink, pushed on, to arrive after dark in Baton Rouge, where on Sunday you can't buy a drink at all.

Baton Rouge is not only the state capital but a boom town. In 1940 it had a population of 34,000, which has risen since to an estimated 150,000. The population of New Orleans has increased only by twenty per cent in the same period. Oil refineries and chemical plants using the by-products of oil are the main factors in the industrial growth.

The factory chimneys, suggesting the laboratory of a titanic alchemist, are floodlighted at night. The old paddle-wheel steamers converted into ferryboats, crossing and recrossing the vast river, look like hansom cabs on an autobahn, or if you like to put it the other way, the factories look like paintings Niles Spencer slapped down against a Currier and Ives background. I reviewed the confusion of epochs from my bedroom in the Capitol House, a vast hotel on the bluff overlooking the river. It reminded me of the night when on the George Washington Bridge, bound for Manhattan, I encountered a raccoon determinedly padding his way back to the New Jersey shore.

I spent Monday nonpolitically, beginning the day with a drive to St. Francisville, north of Baton Rouge, to see an elegant, gracious old pre-War-Between-the-States mansion named, I think, Rosedown. (All elegant, gracious mansions dating from the Flush Times have names like pre-War-with-Spain blocks of flats on the West Side of Manhattan.) The excursion was the idea of a lady who accompanied us and insisted that not to see at least one great house would leave me with an unbalanced view of the state.

When we reached the gates of the great house, hospitably inscribed "No Visitors," we learned that Rosedown had new Texas owners (for my own sake I was glad they were not Yankees), who were home in Dallas attending the accouchement of an oil field. The caretaker would not let us in. By that time it was raining hard, as it often was in Louisiana that summer, rain that descended in nine-foot cubes with only small airholes between them, so we went back to Baton Rouge.

In the evening I was the guest of a Mr. Lewis Gottlieb, chairman of the board of the City National Bank of Baton Rouge, who gave me dinner at the City Club, the city's social hub. It was a good dinner, built around mallards shot by one of the guests, who emptied his deep freeze in the name of hospitality. There was good wine to drink. But large tears appeared in the lovely violet eyes of my beautiful blond dinner partner, when we had finished the baked Alaska.

"I shivah when I think of what you are going to write about us," she said, "having a man like Earl Long for Govunuh of the State of Loosiana. Oh, please tell the fine people up North that we ahnt all like that! There ah fine, decent people in the State of Loosiana, just as there ah in New York and Chicago."

When I told her that Uncle Earl was, for the moment, my favorite American statesman, she professed not to be able to believe me. I thought of the ghost-written *Time* speeches recited by national figures, and for the moment I believed myself. I could not imagine Robert Montgomery coaching Uncle Earl.

"Would you rather have Kefauver as Governor of Louisiana?" a man across the table asked her.

"Oh, Kefauver," she said doubtfully, "I don't know whether I would."

"Or Fulbright?" said the man, playing it straight.

"Yes, Fulbright," the lady said unexpectedly, "yes, I believe I'd rather have even Fulbright," and she looked very grave. It confirmed my opinion that Uncle Earl was the most effective liberal south of Tennessee.

"How about Warren?" the man asked.

"Warren?" the lady repeated. "What Warren do you mean?"

"The Warren who's Chief Justice of the Supreme Court," the tease specified.

"Oh, *him!*" the lady cried, in a voice that indicated a joke could go too far. "I'd much rather have little old Earl Long."

7/Henry Luce's Shoestore

NEXT DAY, with Uncle Earl expected to appear at the Mansion at four in the afternoon, I called on Theo Cangelosi, his *bête noire*, in the morning.

The attorney was a long, bony man, with the long, bony face of a Savonarola, a likeness particularly noticeable in the nose and chin. He practiced law in one half of a double white clapboard house on a wide, shady street near the Governor's mansion.

"People suffering from Earl's affliction frequently turn against their nearest and dearest," he said. "Their anger is in proportion to their affection before they took sick. Earl is under the impression that I helped Mrs. Long get a first mortgage on their new house for forty thousand dollars and that she kept the money, but I never even saw the cash. I just sent the papers to the bank. Both Earl and Blanche signed them, and if he didn't get his share it's his own fault." Mr. Cangelosi looked sad and injured. "Now Earl's putting out that Blanche shared the money with me," he said.

"Earl really turned against me when I wouldn't help him try to escape from that hospital in Texas, but I just didn't want him to get into trouble. I went down there to see him when he sent for me, and the first thing he said was, 'I'm pretty good at getting around people, and I've been talking to the guards on this floor, and I believe that if I had a thousand dollars in cash I could bribe my way out. You take this note and go back to the City National Bank at Baton Rouge and get me the money, ya hear, and I'll be all right.' "

Mr. Cangelosi took from a desk drawer a slip of ruled yellow paper and showed me the message, in the wobbly script of a man having a lot of trouble. "Treasurer, Louise Gottlieb, Earl Long Campaign Fund Account, City National Bank, Baton Rouge, Please pay over to bearer $1000 in $100 bills.—Earl K. Long"

The Governor was an old friend of Lewis Gottlieb, the bank chairman, but he had spelled Gottlieb's name Louise, indicating considerable residual confusion at that moment. (The 38 shots had not, perhaps, worn off.)

"I heard that somebody did slip him fifteen hundred dollars," I said.

"Yes," said Mr. Cangelosi, "but that was later, at the hearing, and it wasn't me. I was trying to protect him. If one of those guards had taken his money and then shot him trying to escape, I would have blamed myself forever. I have always acted in his best interests."

I thanked Mr. Cangelosi and walked out into the blood heat and down to the bank to confirm the existence of an Earl Long Campaign Fund.

Mr. Gottlieb, looking little like a Louise, said there was such an account, but it wouldn't be ethical to tell me how much there was in it. I surmised that there might suddenly get to be a lot in it if the Income Tax people ever disputed the Governor's blanket contention that the money people hand him is intended as campaign contributions. He might then formalize the status of cash in hand by making a large deposit.

"I imagine Earl is up in Winnfield making catfish bait for the special session," Mr. Gottlieb said. "He's probably putting together a program of legislation aimed to give every senator and representative something for himself: a bill to appropriate funds to widen a road in one parish, a bill to raise the salary for a kind of job some senator's cousin has in another. That's the kind of thing Earl's good at—knowing every local politician in the state and remembering where he itches. Then Earl knows where to scratch him."

Lunch in the Capitol House confirmed my theory of culture belts. The Capitol House lies within ninety miles of Galatoire's and Arnaud's in New Orleans, but its fare bears a closer resemblance to Springfield, Illinois, where a distinguished hostess once served me a green salad peppered with marshmallow balls. So Dover, within twenty-three miles of the French coast, eats as un-Frenchly as the farthest side of England.

A statewide convention of high-school football coaches was in session, and there seemed to be hundreds of them—a cross between the plantation overseer and Y.M.C.A. secretary. In the night they congregated over bottles of bourbon, building character for transfusion to their charges in the fall, and in the day they attended seminars on whipless slave-driving and how to induce adolescents to play on two broken legs.

The Governor's Mansion at Baton Rouge, like the State House, is a monument to the administration of Huey Long. The story goes that the Martyr, when he gave the architect his riding orders, said he wanted a replica of the White House so he would know where the light switches were in the bathrooms when he got to be President. Huey lived in it from 1930 to 1932, and Earl inhabited it briefly for the first time in 1939, when he filled out the term of the unfortunate Mr. Leche. After that he lived in it again as Governor from 1948 to 1952 and began a third tenancy in 1956. When I saw it, Longs had been masters of the house for ten out of the nineteen years of its existence, almost enough to give it status as an elegant old gracious family mansion. Earl and Miz Blanche had built their new house in a newer and more stylish part of Baton Rouge, before the Governor decided against moving.

Tom and I arrived half an hour before the hour appointed for the Governor's press conference. We were in company with Margaret Dixon, editor of the Baton Rouge *Morning Advocate*, one of the few people in Louisiana who could usually get along with Earl. Mrs. Dixon, handsome, stable and strong, has a firm, serene personality. She is the kind of woman motherless drunks turn to instinctively to tell their troubles with their wives.

"Earl is the funniest man in the world," she said over her shoulder as she drove. "Life in the Capitol would be dull without him. Did you hear what he said to Leander Perez, the States' Rights man, the other day? 'What are you going to do now, Leander? Da Feds have got da atom bomb.' And when Blanche went to live in the new house, he said she had 'dis-domiciled' him. He has a style of his own—he's a poet. He said he was so groggy when he got off the plane that took him to Houston that he felt 'like a muley bull coming out of a dipping vat.' I don't know why it should, but the 'muley' makes that line sound a hundred times funnier. It just means without horns."

"It particularizes the image," I suggested. "Bull is a word so general that it blurs: the dumb bulls in Spain, the tight bulls in fly-time. 'Muley' makes you see a bull of a peculiarly ineffectual kind."

"You sound more like Huey," Mrs. Dixon said. "Earl says, 'Huey tried that highbrow route and he couldn't carry his home parish. I carry Winn Parish every time.'

"He praises Huey up, but he never misses a chance to mention when he does something better—in 1956, when he won the Governorship on the first primary, without a runoff, the first thing he said was 'Huey never done that.' "

Now we were on the Mansion driveway lined with laurel and packed with press cars.

Inside, the press had taken over, as if the Mansion were the scene of a first-class murder and the cops were still upstairs. Reporters in large groups are ill at ease, and they try to make up for it by acting too easy. Each is preoccupied with his own time situation—his paper's deadlines and the accessibility of telephones. Each, before a public conference, shapes in his mind what would make a good story if the principal said it, and how he can trap him into saying it. If the principal delays his appearance, the reporter begins to wonder whether he will have time to write the story. Then, with further delay, he begins to wonder if he will have time to telephone. Next, he gets angry. He resents his subjection to the whims of his inferiors, and he vents his resentment by a show of elaborate contempt.

We turned left inside the fanlighted door and went down a couple of steps into a great reception room furnished like a suite in a four-star general's house on an Army post, where the furniture comes out of quartermaster's stores. The bleakness of such pieces, all bought on contract sale, increases in proportion to the square of their sum: two hotel sofas are four times as depressing as one; three, nine times. The Governor's drawing room, of good height and proportions, contained at least twenty-six paired pieces, all covered with pink or green brocade chosen for its wearing qualities. The mauve drapes were of the tint and gloss of the kind of spun-sugar candy that is usually filled with rancid peanut paste; the carpets were a flushed beige. There were two wall mirrors reflecting each other, a blackamoor candelabra, three chandeliers, and no pictures. There was not a piece of furniture from before 1930 nor a portrait of a former Governor or his lady. I wondered where the loot from the old Mansion was.

Huey had cleared out the lot, as a link with the hated aristocratic past. As it was, it made a perfect waiting room—a place in which boredom began in the first ten seconds.

At half-past four the Governor's press secretary, an intimidated former state senator named Fredericks, appeared at the top of the two steps. He announced that the Governor's party had telephoned from the road: they were still about fifty miles from town, and the Governor had given orders to serve cake and coffee to the reporters and tell them to wait. Negro servants in white jackets served coffee and sponge cake, both good. A couple of the bloods of the press who covered the beat regularly had found their way to some bourbon concealed from the rest of us and came smirking back.

One fellow went about canvassing colleagues to join him in a walkout. He proposed that everybody go off and leave the Governor flat—insult to the press, showing up so late. That would let him see where he stood. His colleagues, knowing where they stood, paid no heed.

An hour passed, and the Governor's party arrived. State troopers shoved us back, and the Governor's party headed straight upstairs, to "wash up and be right back." A minute later, word came down that the Governor was going to shave. The Negroes served more coffee, this time without cake. Nobody talked of leaving now.

A reporter with good connections learned the cause of the long delay from a state cop who had ridden in the convoy. "Governor stopped at a few farms along the way to buy some guinea hens, but he couldn't get the right price on them."

Forty-five minutes more, and the Governor made his entrance. He hadn't shaved but had taken a nap and put in a telephone call to a woman friend in Alick. Fortunately for the press, she had not been at home. Once on the line, he talked for hours.

Mrs. Dixon said that this was his first press conference in the Mansion since deputy sheriffs, whom he called bonecrushers, had hustled him down his own steps and into an ambulance on the night of May 30.

He was wearing a black mohair suit even less elegantly adjusted than the one at Alick, and a sober necktie of black with atom-bomb mushrooms of white and magenta. He moved to a seat in the middle of a long sofa with its back to the cold fireplace. There, crossing one leg over the other knee, which exposed his white cotton socks, he faced his familiar persecutors with the air of a country Odysseus home from a rough trip, with no Penelope to greet him.

This Odysseus didn't care if he never set eyes on Penelope again. A woman reporter asked him if he was going to make it up with Mrs. Long, and if he didn't think that would help him get the women's vote in the primary.

He said, "If dat's da price of victory, I'd rather go ahead and be defeated. After all, lots of men have lost elections before."

Somebody asked him if he was set on the special session of the Legislature and he said he was, that the call would go out before five o'clock the next day. That was the latest moment when he could call a session for Monday, August 11. The Governor must include with the call a list of the legislation he means to propose; none other can be voted at the session. He said he was readying his list.

A reporter asked him if he would include any new tax bill, and he said no, if the state won its suit against two oil companies, "we might get by with no taxes at all." But if the money did not come in that way, he would try for some new taxes at the regular session. This was a flat assumption that he would run and be re-elected.

He had already said that, rather than cut state services, he would be in favor of "any kind of a tax but a sales tax, because that falls on the poor devil."

Now he began again to lay into the rich people, who "wanted to cut out the spastic school," but the reporters, who had heard that number in his repertory, managed to get him off on Cangelosi.

"There never has been a man who *mis*used and unduly *ab*used my confidence like Cangelosi," the Governor said. "If he hadn't a done me like he done, and rubbed it in, I might forgive him, but that long-legged sapsucker made more money than any man I ever knew," he said, adding quickly, "of which I have not participated in any of the profits."

The Governor's moist hazel eyes, filled with sweetness, clouded over at the memory of what he had suffered. His voice, low and hoarse at the beginning of the conference, as it well might be after the weekend of stump-speaking, rose indignantly, like a fighter knocked down by a fluke punch.

"They misled me," he said. "The reason I was feeling so poorly at the last Legislature was I had kept on postponing an operation that I was to have at the Oshner Clinic in New Orleans. When my sweet little wife and my dear little nephew got me to go on that plane, they told me a damn lie that I was going to Oshner for my operation.

"Then when they got me to the plane the bonecrushers strapped me to the stretcher and a doctor stuck me through the britches with a needle. My wife and my nephew promised they would come right down to Oshner next day to see me. But the plane flew me to Gal*ves*ton, and my sweet little wife hasn't showed up yet, neither my little nephew. When the plane landed me at that airport, there, they told me I was going to a rest house, where I was promised a double bed and quiet. The doctors gave me pills to make me sleep. First I took them one by one, then by the papercupful. Then I got to chunkin' them in there by the wad. While I was in that condition, they got me to sign a thing that I wouldn't sue them for kidnaping. I went contrary to what my lawyers would have wanted." This, I learned long later, was precisely true. His Texas counsel believed he had his transporters cold under the Lindbergh Act.

Uncle Earl looked out at the reporters with bottomless pity in his eyes, as if he were recounting the ills, not of one storm-tossed traveler, but of all our common kind.

"They snatched me out without even enough clothes on me to cover up a red bug," he said, "and a week after I arrived in Texas I was enjoying the same wardrobe. They put me in a room with the door open and crazy people walking in and out all night; one of them thought it was the toilet."

"Pardon me," said a lady of the press, interrupting, "but what was the operation you were expecting?"

"I guess you can guess," the Governor answered, and he pointed down. "On my lower parts."

He was still intent on his sorrows. "Then, this Corner here," he said. "Wasn't he a nice judge to commit me to Mandeville when I come back? We been on opposite sides in politics as long as I remember, but if the position had been reversed, I might have given him a break. And Bankston, the superintendent, a man I appointed myself, could have left me out, but he wouldn't. But I got out, all right. I put *him* out and *got* out."

"Governor," a reporter queried, "what is your personal opinion of who's going to win this election?"

"I am," the seated orator replied without hesitation. "Uncle Earl. It's going to be a case of Katy bar the door. Little old Dellasoups Morrison will be second."

"And third?" pursued the questioner.

"Jimmie Davis, if he stays in the race," the man who picked himself said. "And little Willie Rainach and Big Bad Bill Dodd a dogfall for fourth." In country wrestling, a dogfall means that the men lose their footing simultaneously and both go down, which makes that fall a draw.

"We going to have a party here tomorrow, a homecoming party for the press," he said, "and you are all invited. Going to have something for everybody—religious music over here on one side of the room and honky-tonk on the other. But no Bedbug Blues—that's Jimmie Davis' tune."

There was a good deal of the discourse that I have not recorded. Carried away by the stream of idiom like a drunk on a subway train, I missed a lot of stations.

Somebody asked the Governor what he thought of the Luce publications' having asked for a change of venue to a Federal court in his libel suit for six million dollars. He said he didn't care what kind of court the case came up in.

"They going to find themselves lighter and wiser when it's over," he said. "The Luce people been going on too long picking on people too poor to sue them, and now they're going to get it in the neck. Mr. Luce is like a man that owns a shoestore and buys all the shoes to fit himself. Then he expects other people to buy them."

This was the best thing said about publishers, I felt, since I myself wrote thirteen years ago: "To the foundation of a school for publishers, without which no school of journalism can have meaning."

I put all my admiration in my glance and edged my chair up to the end of the Governor's sofa. When I try, I can exude sincerity as far as a llama can spit, and the Governor's gaze, swinging about the room, stopped when it lit on me. My eyes clamped it in an iron grip of approval.

I inched forwarder, trying not to startle him into putting a cop on me, and said, "Governor, I am not a newspaperman. I am with you all the way about publishers. Nor am I primarily interested in politics. I came all the way down here to find out your system for beating the horses."

An expression of modest disclaimer dropped like a curtain in front of the cocky old face.

"I got no particular system," he said. "I think I'm doing good to break even. I think horse-betting should be dissected—into them that can afford it and them that can't. I think if you can afford it it's a good thing to take your mind off your troubles and keep you out in the air."

"Do you play speed ratings?" I asked. The Governor, in his eagerness to talk simultaneously about all phases of handicapping, choked up—it was the bronchiectasis—and began to cough.

Quickly, I offered him a lemon drop and he accepted it. Once it was in his mouth, I knew, from my experience among the Arabs in the opposite end of the interrupted sea, that I had won. He had accepted my salt, now he would reciprocate. The bronchiectasis struggled with the lemon drop for a moment and then yielded.

The Governor's throat cleared, and he said: "Yo'll stay'n' eat."

"Y'all stay, too," the Governor said to Miss Dixon and Tom and a couple of the other press people. "There's aplenty." I imagined he must have a great surplus of supermarket bargains in the larder. "Just set here and wait. We got a lot to talk about."

The reporters and television men who had deadlines were already clearing out. Earl shouted after them, "Y'all come back and I'll say this—" But they, who had waited for him so long, had had enough.

8 / Blam-Blam-Blam

THERE HAD BEEN so many people in the room, and for so long, that they had taken the snap out of the air-conditioning. The men staying on for dinner—about fifteen of us—took off their coats and laid them down on chairs and sofas.

One of the women guests, a Northerner, inadvertently sat on a jacket a political gent had laid aside. It was a silvery Dacron-Acrilan-nylon-airpox miracle weave nubbled in Danish-blue asterisks. She made one whoop and rose vertically, like a helicopter. She had sat on his gun, an article of apparel that in Louisiana is considered as essential as a zipper. Eyebrows rose about as rapidly as she did, and by the time she came down she decided that comment would be considered an affectation.

A colored man brought a glass wrapped in a napkin to the Governor—"Something for my throat," the latter explained—and the members of his inner council gathered at his flanks and knees for the powwow on catfish bait. One of the bills Earl had in mind would give individual members of the Legislature scholarship funds to allot personally to young people in their districts. Another would raise the salaries of assistant attorney generals, whose friends in the Legislature might be expected to respond. There were various local baits, funds for construction. The compounders kept their voices low and mysterious, as if saying "One-half pint of fish oil, one ounce of tincture of asafetida, one ounce of oil of rhodium—that will fetch them," or "Mix equal parts of soft Limburger cheese and wall paper cleaner—never fails." Sometimes a conspirator would be unable to suppress a laugh.

A Mr. Siegelin, a political catfisherman arriving late, brought with him two children, a girl of about ten and a boy of five.

"Give them Cokes," the Governor said, and while a state cop hurried off to fill the order, he said to the little girl, "I hope you ain't going steady yet."

The little girl shook her head, and Uncle Earl said, "That's right. I went with more than a hundred before I made up *my* mind."

Made it up too soon at that, he probably thought, as he wondered about Miz Blanche and the mortgage money.

The children took their Cokes and settled down on facing identical love seats to drink them, while their father, a fair man in shirt sleeves, sat down to join in the bait suggestions, with his equivalent of "Cut smoked herring into bits. Soak in condensed milk several days." The group was still in the midst of bait-mixing when a plug-ugly, either a state trooper or a bodyguard from civilian life, came to the top of the steps leading to the drawing room and shouted, "It's ready!" By his tone I judged him ravenously hungry.

The catfishermen remained engrossed in their concoctive deliberations, and the plug-ugly shouted at Mrs. Dixon, whom he judged less engaged, "C'mawn, *Maggie!*"

Mrs. Dixon rose, and the catfishermen, Southern gentlemen after all, perforce rose too and rushed toward the dining room in her wake, the Governor dragging the two children.

The ballroom smacked of Bachelors' Hall, lacking the touch of a woman's fastidious hand, but the dining end of the Mansion, I was happy to see, was well kept up. The long table under the great chandelier was covered with a mountain range of napkins folded into dunce caps, with streams of table silver in the valleys between them, and the iced tea, Sargassified with mint and topped with cherry, was pretty near *Ladies Home Journal* color-ad perfection. Negro waiters and waitresses swarmed about, smiling to welcome Odysseus home. None of them, either, seemed to miss Penelope. The wanderer, his heart expanding in this happy atmosphere, propelled me to a seat at the head of the table.

He took his place at my left, with the Northern lady across the table from him. Around the long board crouched plug-uglies in sports shirts, alternating with the guests: Tom, Mrs. Dixon, Senator Fredericks, Siegelin, the two Siegelin children clutching Coca-Cola bottles, and half a dozen politicians I hadn't met. The colossal figure of Mr. Joe Arthur Sims, the Governor's personal counsel, dominated the other end of the table. Mr. Sims had his right arm in a plaster cast that kept his hand above his head, as if perpetually voting Aye. He had sustained an odd sort of fracture on July 4, he explained. It had followed hard on his stump speech for the Governor, a great oratorical effort, but he denied that he had thrown the arm out of joint. He said he was in an auto crash.

The Governor said, "We don't serve hard liquor here. Da church people wouldn't like it. But I'll get you some beer. Bob," he called to one of the somber seneschals, "get da man some beer." Quickly, the waiter fetched a can, two holes newly punched in the top, ready for drinking, and set it down on the table.

The beer bore an unfamiliar label, and the Governor said, "Dat looks like some of dat ten-cent beer from Schwegmann's." (He had probably bought it himself, on one of his raids for bargains.) "Dat looks like some of da stuff dat when da brewers got an overstock, dey sell it to da supermarkets. Get da man some *good* beer. And bring a glass—hear?"

He looked so healthy now that I ventured a compliment.

"You fooled those doctors, all right," I said. "You're like that Swede Johansson—you have your own way of training."

"You see dat fight?" the Governor asked, suspending his attack on the salad, which he was tossing between his dentures with the steady motion of a hay-forker. I said I had.

"I didn't see it, but I would have if I thought da fellow had a chance to lick Patterson," the Governor said. "Patterson's pretty good." (If he looked at the return fight, he was let down again.)

"I hear they've got a law here in Louisiana that a white boy can't even box on the same card with colored boys," I said.

"Yeah," said the Governor, "but dat kind of stuff is foolish. If dere's enough money in it, dey're bound to get together."

I recognized the theory of an economic resolution of the race conflict.

He sat there like a feudal lord, and his *maisnie*, the men of his household, leaned toward him like Indians around a fire. The trenchers went around, great platters of country ham and fried steak, in the hands of the black serving men, and sable damsels toted the grits and gravy. There was no court musician, possibly because he would have reminded the Earl of Jimmie Davis, but there was a court jester, and now the master called for a jape.

"Laura, Laura," he called out to one of the waitresses, "set your tray down—dere, hand it to Bob. Tell us what your husband does for a living."

"Prize fighter, sir," the girl said.

"Show us how he does when he goes in da ring," the Governor ordered.

The girl, long, thin and whippy, was instantly a-grin. This was evidently a standard turn, and she loved the spotlight. She got rid of the tray and showed how her husband climbed through the ropes, lifting her right knee high to get over the imaginary strand, and holding the hem of her short skirt against the knee as a boxer sometimes holds his robe to keep it from getting in his way. Once inside, she danced about the ring, waving her clasped hands at friends in the imaginary crowd. Then she retired to a corner and crouched on an imaginary stool until the Governor hit the rim of a glass with a gravy spoon.

The girl came out, sparring fast, dancing around the ring and mugging for friends at ringside, with an occasional wink. The opposition didn't amount to much, I could see. Laura's husband, impersonated by Laura, was jabbing him silly. Then her expression changed; the other man was beginning to hit her husband where he didn't like it. Her head waggled. She began to stagger. Even the bodyguards, who must have seen the act often, were howling.

"Show us how your husband does when he gets tagged," the Governor ordered, and Laura fell forward, her arms hanging over the invisible ropes, her head outside the ring, her eyes bulged and senseless.

The feudal faces were red with mirth. I applauded as hard as I could. Laura stood up and curtsied.

"You gonna let him keep on fightin'?" the Governor asked.

"I don't want him to," Laura said, "don't want him get hurt. But I don't know if he'll quit."

"Is he easier to live with when he loses?" a state senator asked.

"Yes, sir, he is," the jester said, and took her tray back from the colleague who had been holding it.

The meal went on.

"Dat's da way some a dese stump-wormers going to be when dis primary is over," Uncle Earl said. "Hanging on da ropes. If it's a pretty day for the primary, I'll win it all. I'll denude dem all, da *Times-Picayune* included."

Outside the air-conditioned keep the enemy might howl, but inside, the old vavasor held his court without worrying.

"Da voting machines won't hold me up," he said. "If I have da raight commissioners, I can make dem machines play 'Home Sweet Home.'" He laughed confidingly. "Da goody-goodies brought in dose machines to put a crimp in da Longs," he said. "Da first time dey was used, in 1956, I won on da first primary. Not even my brother Huey ever did dat.

"Da machines is less important dan who's allowed to vote," he said. "I appointed a man State Custodian of Voting Machines here dat run up a bill of a hundred and sixty-three thousand dollars for airplane hire in one year, just flying around da state, inspecting da machines. Good man, Southern gentleman—da *Times-Picayune* recommended him and I thought I'd satisfy dem for once. Den he got an appropriation from da Legislature to keep da machines in repair, but it said in da contract with da voting-machine company dat da company had to keep dem in repair for one year for free. So he split da money wit da company—dey sent him six thousand dollars, and den another six thousand, but I grabbed half of da second six thousand for my campaign fund. Should have took it all."

The cellarer he had sent for the name-brand beer returned with a report that none except the supermarket kind was cold.

"Dey keeping da good beer for demself," the Governor said indulgently. "You drink dis." It tasted fine.

The Northern woman, who had listened with awe to the career of the voting-machine man, asked, "What happened to him?"

"I denuded him," the Governor said. "It's an electoral office now."

"And where is he now?" the woman asked, expecting, perhaps, to hear that he was confined in a *cachot* beneath the Mansion.

"He's hypnotizing people and telling fortunes and locating oil wells," the Governor said, "and he got himself a fine blonde and built her a big house and quit home."

Outside of the *Lives of the Troubadours*, which was compiled in the thirteenth century, I had never known a better-compressed biography. I felt that I knew the denuded hypnotist well. I remembered the comparable beauty of the Governor's account of the last day of a beloved uncle in Winnfield: "He got drunk and pulled a man out of bed and got into bed with the man's wife, and the man got mad and shot my poor uncle, and he died."

I asked him what he thought of Governor Faubus of north-neighboring Arkansas, who had won a third term by closing the schools, and he said Faubus was a fine man, but nobody had told him about the Civil War.

"Fellas like Faubus and Rainach and Leander Perez and da rest of da White Citizens and Southern Gentlemen in dis state want to go back behind Lincoln," he said. "And between us, gentlemen, as we sit here among ourselves," he said, arresting a chunk of fried steak in mid-air and leaning forward to give his statement more impetus, "we got to admit dat Lincoln was a fine man and dat he was right."

Then, as he turned back to the steak, skewering it against a piece of ham before swallowing both, he caught my look of astonishment and cried, too late, "But don't quote me on dat!"

Since he has won his last primary, I disregard his instructions. It was a brave thing for a Governor of Louisiana to say and would have made a lethal headline in his enemies' hands: "Long Endorses Lincoln; Hints War Between States Ended."

We had up another can of beer, and the Governor and I shared it with a sense of double complicity.

"Laura, Laura," the Governor called to his jester, "get rid of dat tray."

"Yes, sir, Mister Governor," and the star turn passed the grits to a co-worker.

"Now, Laura," the Governor said, "can you make a speech like Mr. McLemore?" (McLemore had been the White Citizens' candidate in '56.)

This was plainly another well-used bit of repertory. The Prize Fighter and Mr. McLemore may be Laura's *Cavalleria* and *Pagliacci*, always done as a double bill. But I'd love to hear her sing Jimmie Davis.

She took a stance, feet wide apart and body stick-straight, looking as foolish as she could.

"Ladies and gentlemen," she said, "do not vote for Mr. Earl Long, because he has permitted da Supreme Court of da United States to make a decision by which, by which, Little White Johnny will have to attend da same school with Little Black Mary. If you wish to prevent dis, vote for, vote for—" and she hesitated, like a man fumbling in his mind for his own name. Then, running her hands over her body, she located, after some trouble, a white card in her breast pocket. The card, a planted prop, showed she had expected to perform. She took the card, peered at it, turned it around and finally read, "McLemore. Dat's it. Vote for McLemore."

The Earl howled, and so did all his guests and men-at-arms. I do not imagine that Penelope would have found it all that funny. She probably cramped his style.

The meal ended with a great volume of ice cream. The Governor, in high humor and perhaps still thinking of the frustrated voting machines, said to the lady across from him, "Would you mind if I told you a semi-bad story?"

She said she would not mind, and the Governor began: "There was an important man once who had a portable mechanical-brain thinking machine that he carried everywhere with him. Da machine was about as big as a small model of one of dose fruit machines dey have in a Elks clubhouse. When he wanted a answer: How many square feet in a room by so and so much? or, Has dat blonde a husband and is he home? he submitted his question and da machine answered it correctly. He would write out da question on a piece of paper and put it in a slot, da machine would read it, and pretty soon it would go blam, blam, blam—blam, blam, blam—dat was da brain working, and it would give him a printed slip with da correct answer. Well, finally da man got jealous of dis machine, it was such a Jim-cracker, and he thought he take it down a little for its own good.

"So he wrote out a message: 'Where is my dear father at this minute, and what is he doing?' He put it in da slot, and da machine says, 'Blam, blam, blam,' very calm, like he had asked it something easy, and it write out da answer, 'Your dear father is in a pool hall in Philadelphia, *Penn*sylvania, at dis moment, shooting a game of one hundred points against a man named Phil Brown. Your dear father is setting down watching, and Phil Brown has da cue stick and is about to break."

"Philadelphia, *Penn*sylvania," had the romantic sound in the Governor's mouth of Coromandel in Sinbad's.

The Governor's manner changed, and his voice became indignant. " 'Why,' da man says, 'dat's da most unmitigated libelous slander I ever heard of. My dear father is sleeping in da Baptist cemetery on da side of da hill in *Pitts*burgh, Pennsylvania, and has been for da last five years. I am sure of da dates because my dear Mother who is still living reminded me of da anniversary of his death and I telegraphed ten dollars worth of flowers to place on his grave. I demand a *re*-investigation and an *apology*.'

"And he writes it out and puts it in da slot. 'Dis time I got you,' he says. 'You ain't nothing but a machine anyway.'

"Da machine reads da message and gets all excited. It says, 'Blam, *Blam*' and 'Blam, *blam*,' like it was scratching its head, and den 'Blam, blam, blam, blam . . . blam, blam, blam, blam,' like it was running its thoughts through again, and den 'BLAM!' like it was mad, and out comes da message."

All eyes were on the Governor now, as if the ladies and men-at-arms half expected him to materialize the ticker tape.

"Da message said, 'REPEAT,'" the Governor said. "It said 'REPEAT' and den, 'RE-REPEAT. Your dear father is in a pool hall at Philadelphia, *Penn*sylvania, playing a game with a man named Phil Brown. YOUR MOTHER'S LEGALLY WEDDED HUSBAND is in the Baptist cemetery on the side of the hill in *Pitts*burgh, *Penn*sylvania, and has been there these last five years, you BASTARD. The only change in the situation is that Phil Brown has run fourteen and missed, and your old man now has the cue stick. I predict he will win by a few points.' "

It broke everybody up, and soon the Governor said to the outsiders politely, "Y'all go home. We got a lot to do tonight." But he said he might be able to see me at nine next morning.

I arose at that hour and got over there, but there were already so many cars on the driveway that if it hadn't been morning I would have guessed there was a cockfight in the basement. Inside the Mansion, the nearly bookless library on the right of the door that serves as a waiting room was full of politicians, all wearing nubbly suits and buckskin shoes, and each sporting the regulation enlargement of the left breast beneath the handkerchief pocket. (This group included no left-handed pistol shot.) The length of the queue demonstrated that the public reaction to the speeches had been favorable, and that the sheiks who had raided the herds in Earl's absence were there to restore the stolen camels.

A Negro in a white jacket came in and asked the ritual "Y'all have coffee?" Since I had no deal to offer, I just had coffee and went.

Odysseus ruled in Ithaca again.

9 / *The Battle from Afar*

WATCHING the British general election in the fall of 1959 was, for me, like being at a very dull football game where the only recourse is to watch another game on television. Luckily I received frequent batches of newspaper clippings, prefaced by wise notes, that friend Tom sent me from New Orleans, where the good game was.

The change from Louisiana was depressing; it was like trying to taste Empire hock after a dozen Sazerac cocktails.

Instead of calling each other "common damn hoodlum" or "little pissant" in the Louisiana fashion, the British candidates discussed interminably whether the country could afford an increase of $1.40 a week on the old-age Pension. The Tories, boasting the unparalleled pecuniosity of the nation, paradoxically doubted that the economy could stand the strain of the dollar forty. An option of Gaitskell or Macmillan thrilled like the choice between blancmange and Sultana roll on the menu of a British railway hotel. But there I was. I had booked my seat in advance for the wrong game.

British elections were not always so dull. William Cobett recalls for us a great moment when he stood for Coventry in 1820, at the age of 57:

"Just at this moment one of the savages exclaimed, 'Damn him, I'll rip him up!' He was running his hand into his breeches pocket, apparently to take out his knife, but I drew up my right leg, armed with a new and sharp gallashe over my boot, and dealt the ripping savage so delightful a blow, just between his two eyes, that he fell back upon his followers."

It was the kind of do that Earl Long would have appreciated. Once, years ago, in the vigor of political discussion, Earl bit a man. Later he preferred a diet of grits and fried steak. When I left, Earl looked like winning a fourth term if he had luck. I kept looking back over my shoulder until I reached the exit.

The first collection of clippings from Tom showed that Earl had run into trouble. This was normal. The fine Governor fought best when he was on the bottom. His scheme to win renomination in the Democratic primaries, resign as Governor the day before election and then be elected looked sure to succeed. The State Supreme Court, which would have to rule on the constitutionality of the maneuver, appeared firmly in his favor. His martyrdom in Texas had won him the sympathy of the rural voters.

"Wouldn't you rather have a tried and true man, half crazy and half intelligent, than some bladderskite?" he asked one cheering crowd.

One of my last political memories before I left the Great State was of the Governor devising political catfish bait. The cat is not a fish to be taken on bird feathers with whimsical names. It demands the solid attraction of chicken guts surrounded by an aura of asafetida: "Smells bad, but cats love it," the manual says.

But other hands had been setting other trotlines with baits even more persuasive to the legislators, I learned from Tom's first note. The statesmen showed up as in law bound at Baton Rouge on August 11 to answer the Governor's call, but once there and in session they voted instantly to adjourn. They left the baits on his hooks untouched; they did not seem to be hungry.

Even in the face of such wholesale defection Earl had maintained tradition, I was glad to note from the enclosed clippings. His Lieutenant Governor had said to him, "Now, Earl, don't get upset," and the fine Governor had answered, "I am upset-proof." This was in the spirit of "Invictus."

Earl was still the betting choice, Tom wrote, but he no longer had an organization he could rely upon. When some of Earl's hand-fed legislators turned on him, he felt like a British colonel in the Sepoy rebellion. But, after all, British rule in India survived the uprising by ninety years. Tom wrote that with the field for the nomination still wide open Earl was the favorite at 4 to 1, with other serious possibilities at prices ranging from 13 to 2 upward.

The relative showing of the candidates who finish third, fourth, fifth, and on down the line in the first primary, and so are eliminated, has its own significance. It serves to establish the price each expects to be paid for his support in the second run.

The rerun system gives them a chance to salvage part of their losses. In a close race between the two top men, a candidate who finishes a good third can often turn a handsome profit. Even a man who finishes down the list can sometimes make a good thing of it if his votes include a particularly deliverable bloc—say a group of parishes where his family bank owns a mortgage on every farm. It is all delightfully Middle Eastern.

I read Tom's letter and the accompanying clippings from the *Times-Picayune*, over tea in the Central Hotel in Glasgow, where I was fortifying myself for a great Tory mass meeting in a moving-picture cathedral—admission by ticket only. Mr. Macmillan, aggrieved and sniffling, would read his voters a lecture on how they had never been so well off and how chaps who wanted to spend the dollar forty had better look out where they were going to get it. I was glad, for the sake of the people around me, that there were no runoff elections in Great Britain. Two such campaigns in one year would be beyond bearing.

Nostalgic, I read a quotation from Uncle Earl: "Jimmie Davis loves money like a hog loves slop."

The next tidings I had from New Orleans were more serious for the fine Governor of the Great State. The Democratic State Committee had declined to receive his candidacy unless he resigned as Governor before September 15, the day on which entry fees were due. This was not law, but house rules, and the Committee made up its rules as it went along. Earl had farsightedly pre-ascertained the attitude of the Supreme Court, but he had failed to win the State Committee first. The ultimatum left him with a hard choice.

If he resigned at once, in order to run, he would forfeit seven months of power and patronage, from September 15, 1959, to April 18, 1960, the day before the vestigial election. During that time, the Lieutenant Governor would be Governor, free to fire all Earl's appointees and put in his own, and to make all the deals that Earl would otherwise have the opportunity to make. More, an ex-Governor is in a less advantageous position to campaign than a Governor. Worse, the Federal people, all Republicans, were known to be hot on Earl's trail with a mess of Income Tax charges.

"I'm the most investigated man in history," he said.

Earl was sure that in an age when States' Rights are again fighting words, the Feds would not seek an indictment against a Governor in office. Out of office was another matter.

These were heavy immediate advantages to risk on a chance of winning what looked like a hard campaign for renomination (and would be harder when he lost control of the state payroll). A *Times-Picayune* report of an attempt to interview him showed that Earl was preoccupied. The reporter called the Governor's hotel room and asked to speak to him.

A voice, Earl's, answered, "He's just gone up in a balloon."

Tom's next letter apprised me of the hero's decision. "Our boy apparently got what he wanted and can now pull down," the letter said.

Tom is the last independent source of news left in New Orleans. He is in the situation of the RAF hero who was 30,000 feet in the air, without an aircraft.

A couple of accompanying clippings carried denials by Internal Revenue officials and by United States Senator Allen Ellender, Senior Senator from Louisiana, that Ellender had talked to Federal officials and squared the Internal Revenue rap against Long. Denials, in Louisiana, are accepted as affirmations, and it is held a breach of the code for a public man to deny anything that isn't so. Ellender is an old protégé of Huey Long's. The Senator is therefore the last man in the world to suspect of denying anything you couldn't bet your bottom dollar on.

Tom continued, "The Old Regulars have bolted to Davis." There was a whiff of magnolia about the item. It is *de rigueur* that the first leader to declare himself for a candidate should also be the first to cut his throat.

Jimmie Davis, to whom Comiskey had bolted, was, I knew, a singer and composer of hillbilly music ("You Are My Sunshine," "Nobody's Sweetheart Now") who had been Governor of Louisiana from 1944 to 1948 but had spent a good part of his term in Hollywood making a movie about a hillbilly singer who got to be Governor.

Tom now turned to deLesseps S. Morrison, who, when I left, seemed Earl's most formidable rival for the nomination. "Chep, the progressive conservative, had chosen quietism and decency in making his play for the rational crowd here," Tom wrote. "He went back to Pointe Coupee, his home parish, to announce for Governor last weekend. Then he got on water skis and sprayed up and down False River, speaking to the crowds at the boat piers. Chep is making the Chamber of Commerce approach: no gimmicks, only a circus bandwagon and a jazz band, which he is using on his stumping tour through the towns. But Davis has a good thing going in Old Rugged Cross. Looks like he's going to whip Chep by a parasang, but you never know about Louisiana."

The "Old Rugged Cross" referred to Davis' campaign technique of visiting men's church clubs with a choir of professional hillbilly singers who harmonized on hymns. They accompanied the hymns on guitars.

When I read this letter I was in a "small hotel in a good neighborhood" in London, struggling with the vertebrae of a kipper, which refused to come loose from the flesh.

I tried to imagine the Prime Minister stumping Clydeside from the Clyde on water skis or Mr. Gaitskell playing a guitar to the electors, but I failed.

I tried to imagine the kippers were soft-shell crabs just bursting out of the old carapace, full of fat stored against the ordeal of fasting while the new shell hardens. Busters, they call such crabs in New Orleans. I failed again. I was in the wrong country, politically and gastronomically.

Clippings of a later date accompanying the letter said the fine Governor had decided not to run to not immediately succeed himself.

The next batch cheered me. Tom's covering letter was dated September 19, and as it had been mailed to New York and then forwarded, it reached me late in the month. The British campaign was well bogged by that time. Since neither party produced any news, the newspapers had taken to headlining the public-opinion polls. The polls found an ever increasing number of people who said they didn't know how they were going to vote. The headline writers christened these the "Don't Knows." Headlines on a day, as the struggle approached its climax, were: "Don't Knows Swinging to the Tories," or "Don't Knows Lean to Labor," or just "Don't Be a Don't Know."

In Louisiana, Earl had induced an old political enemy named Jimmy Noe to form a ticket with him: Noe for Governor, Long for Lieutenant Governor. In the days of Huey, Noe had been a red-hot young politician, but he had subsequently devoted himself to oil wells and radio stations and had not run for office since 1940. He was rich. But Long would supply most of the strength for the ticket. Tom said anti-Long people feared that if Noe were elected Governor he would resign immediately in favor of Long.

Tom also sent along the official entry list. There were eleven candidates for Governor, and as many for each of the state offices. Of the gubernatorial candidates five were likely to poll a sizable state-wide vote. The others were small investors, hoping to scrabble together enough votes to trade in for small state jobs if they endorsed the right man in the runoff primary. One, Tom wrote me, was a specialist in soliciting subscriptions to his campaign. He had a sucker list of country people to whom he would promise high office after his election if they would just send him a couple of bucks. This pro sometimes made as much as five thousand dollars running for Governor.

The serious candidates besides Davis, Morrison and Noe were Willie Rainach, the professional segregationist, and the schismatic Longite whom Earl called Big Bad Bill Dodd. There are false Imams as well as Imams among the Longites. All Longites agree, though, on a program of soaking the oil companies and raising up the humble. Noe and Dodd, therefore, would hurt each other.

There was no great political profit in race hatred in Louisiana, because Morrison and Long, for years the chief rivals for the crown, both favored Negro voting rights and a "reasonable" race attitude. The White Supremacy people had no place to take their votes. They had to let them be guided by other issues or else stay home on Election Day.

Earl used to contain the Rainach threat by equating him with the NAACP in "trouble-making." ("I suspect Rainach and the NAACP are just playing 'You goose me and I'll goose you,' " my hero once said.)

As to Dodd, Tom wrote, "Bill Dodd's campaign isn't getting anywhere, so he has made a deal to throw to Morrison in the runoff."

He added, "I keep thinking of that Morrison going Jesus-like on water skis to the assembled throngs on the shores of the Galilee of Pointe Coupee Parish. 'I will teach ye to be fishers of men and not fishers of fish.' Election night ought to be a good show here. It always is. Will you be back in the U.S.A.?"

The date set for the first primary was December 5, 1959. I was back in the U.S.A. a couple of days after Thanksgiving. I emplaned at LaGuardia on the afternoon of Thursday, December 3, and was at Moisant Airport, New Orleans, a few hours later.

The banishment of Aristides because his townsmen were tired of hearing him called "the Just" was one of the triumphs of the Mediterranean mind. It constituted public recognition that a crook is more easily tolerated than a man who makes his virtue a damned nuisance.

When I got to New Orleans, it appeared that the electorate had slated Chep Morrison for the Aristides treatment. In the plane on the way south I read a great bale of clippings that had been waiting for me in New York. The star item was a front-page editorial from the *Times-Picayune* of Sunday morning, November 15, under the heading

ELECTION OF DAVIS AND AYCOCK RECOMMENDED

For fourteen years the paper had been plugging Morrison, the debonair reformer. His white plume was the highest feather in its hat. He had accepted the Reform nomination for Mayor on three days' notice in 1946 and had won.

Morrison has suppressed open public gambling in New Orleans—the horse rooms are now across the river in Jefferson Parish—and at least has forced lamp shades on the red lights. Concurrently he has permitted the strip-tease joints to flourish. He has thus aided in the substitution of vicarious lechery for the real thing, keeping New Orleans in step with the nation. It is my guess that he has kept the town tighter than his political rivals will admit; this guess is based on the hostility he inspires among cab drivers and bellboys.

In addition to these negative activities, in which the *Times-Picayune* took editorial satisfaction, he has transformed the city. These building feats have given Morrison the fame, rare in the South and usually repugnant to its voters, of a man who gets things done. These facial transformations are the only extant monument to the paper's political effectiveness. In state politics, the *Times-Picayune* has been to the Longs what the Austrian armies were to Napoleon. It made their reputation by being easy to lick.

His social graces endear him to news weeklies—he neither drawls nor gets his elbows in potlicker, and he can shake a hand as briskly as Richard Nixon. Each time Morrison has been candidate for Mayor, the *Times-Picayune* has supported him and claimed credit for his victory over the Organization, which usually appeared in its cartoons as a hog with a high hat wallowing in a trough labeled "Corruption." In 1956 it had backed him for Governor against Earl Long plus the Organization, and he had been resoundingly beaten.

Now the *Picayune* was dropping its perennial candidate and joining the hog in the high hat behind Jimmie Davis. The editorial said:

"This newspaper urges Louisiana voters to support Jimmie H. Davis and C. C. Taddy Aycock in the December 5 election. . . .

"Our recommendation of Mr. Davis is no disparagement of the achievements of Mr. Morrison. We simply do not believe that Mr. Morrison would be in a position to rally various political factions and consolidate diverse legislative elements in support of a forward-looking and effective program for the whole state. . . .

"In making our choice of Mr. Davis over Mr. Morrison, we undoubtedly will be accused by some of playing politics. . . .

"Many knowledgeable experts feel that Mr. Davis will surely win and that Mr. Morrison, even if he should reach a second primary, will lose to any of the major candidates who may oppose him. This may be true and may serve as a basis for some for preferring Mr. Davis.

"But it is not our basis."

Clipped to the editorial was a report of a stump speech by Willie Rainach, the States' Rights man, at a metropolis called Napoleonville. Rainach quoted a *Times-Picayune* editorial in 1947, when Davis was in office, that said, "When the going gets hot, the Governor disappears."

The "little pinheaded nut," as Earl called Rainach, had picked up one recruit of stature, in fact of the most stature of almost anybody I know—"Little Eva" Talbot, once a legendary football lineman at Tulane, the leading New Orleans university. "Rainach called attention to the fact that New Orleans attorney and oil operator W. H. Talbot had joined his campaign as a member of the advisory committee," the clipping said.

"In a statement from New Orleans, Talbot said he was disappointed in Davis, and therefore had joined Rainach."

A vast, gusty man, Little Eva is a landmark in downtown New Orleans as he makes his way from his air-cooled office to his air-cooled automobile and back, waving a hand the size of a football at admirers. He is one local athletic hero whose shadow has never grown less. He has made a lot of money.

The *Times-Picayune* quoted Talbot as saying, "Senator Willie Rainach is the only man in the race who will help us fight the States' Rights battle.

"States' Rights includes segregation but it includes a lot of other things too, such as making the Federal Government keep its nose out of the gas and oil business in Louisiana."

It was a powerful and succinct statement of what lies behind much in the South that otherwise seems irrational.

Big Bad Bill Dodd, who had already pledged his support to Morrison in the runoff, was denouncing Morrison in a town called Rayne. Dodd said, "The nothing Davis rendered and the nothing of Chep's promises are a poor substitute for Dodd's proved record and practical progressive platform." As for Rainach, Dodd compared him with John Brown and Hitler.

Tom's brief note of interpretation said: "Davis is running a nothing campaign, but I guess maybe the early form chart making him the favorite was right. Morrison is running a better campaign. But Davis seems to have access to those mysterious submerged factors of power in La. You figure it out. The conniving between first primary and runoff ought to be fantastic."

For added entertainment on the way down I had a couple of handouts from Rainach headquarters. One, a mimeographed sheet, said:

WORKERS FOR RAINACH

No other candidate in this present contest can begin to match the record of Willie Rainach in fighting off the attempt of the Federal Government to control every phase of our existence. The record of DeLesseps S. Morrison is by far the worst, inasmuch as he has consistently refused to even protest the racial integration ordered by Federal despots in Washington. It is common knowledge that the New Orleans Police Department has planned to cooperate with any Federally ordered integration of New Orleans Schools. No man in the Police Department relishes this plan, but the Police, under Morrison, will be powerless to stop him. The United States District Court has ordered this integration in New Orleans schools to be carried out in March—NO LESS THAN SIX MONTHS FROM THIS DATE.

With Willie Rainach as Governor of Louisiana, Morrison and his NAACP and negro Longshoremen henchmen will have no chance to control the City of New Orleans. With Morrison as Governor, all of Louisiana will quickly find itself in the midst of strife such as that presently being experienced in New York City, Detroit, Chicago and other cities where politicians permitted the NAACP to have its way. THE FIRST CHILD MURDERED IN AN "INCIDENT" MAY BE YOUR OWN!

Jimmie Davis sings and says nothing. Davis is content to be known as a "sweetness and light" candidate and refuses to "be critical of my opponents." This is the proper attitude for a glass-house dweller.

DO NOT BE TAKEN IN BY THE PROPAGANDA THAT "RAINACH IS A GOOD MAN BUT HE HASN'T A CHANCE," OR BY THE COMMUNIST COINED CLICHE THAT "SEGREGATION IS NOT AN ISSUE." Ask the parents of the murder and rape victims of the Eastern cities what happened when segregation ceased to be an issue. The white people in these areas are now fighting for their very existence.

The other was a printed pink throwaway that read:

REPRINT OF LETTER TO JIMMY DAVIS FROM F. A. WALLIS
Zachary, Louisiana, Oct. 12, 1959

Dear Jimmy:

I voted for you when you ran for Governor before. I like you personally, and have been inclined to vote for you again. However, I have been doing a lot of soul-searching on this Governor's race. I have reluctantly come to the conclusion that I cannot vote for you this time. I think I owe it to you to tell you why:

The next Governor of Louisiana is going to be under tremendous pressure to integrate our public schools. The South is slowly but surely winning the battle for public opinion in the minds of the white people of the North. But if we are to win, we must stand firm and unyielding during the next administration. We don't want our children to be the guinea pigs in sociological experiments. The rapes, murders and violence that have followed integration of the schools in New York, Chicago, Philadelphia, Washington and other Northern cities must not happen to our children. And if we are to win, we must have a Governor *who will not yield*. Jimmy, you are a professional entertainer. We all know that the NAACP has the entertainment field by the throat. Why, you—as a professional entertainer—if you were Governor of Louisiana, would be at the mercy of the NAACP! The NAACP forced the entertainment world to rewrite the great songs of Stephen Foster! Will this crowd be easier on you than they were on Stephen Foster?—

If you as Governor of Louisiana dared to fight the NAACP, not a record of yours would be sung over television, radio or in a juke box over this Nation. You would be blacklisted from the night clubs and entertainment halls of this country. If you as Governor of Louisiana should dare to lead a fight on the NAACP, you would be through as a professional entertainer, and you know it—and I know it!

I shall vote for Willie Rainach, who has led the fight for segregation in this state, who has shown that he has the courage and ability to lead us to victory—a man who is not vulnerable to NAACP attack!

Sincerely your friend

/s/ F. A. Wallis
Zachary, Louisiana

Neither emission said anything about the oil department of the States' Rights question.

They served to distract my attention from the dismal airplane dinner dumped down before the passengers at five-thirty in the afternoon, as if we were patients in a military hospital. The steak was of some plastic material like Silly Putty, and only as warm as the small glass of domestic champagne that accompanied it. At current air speeds, the dinners aboard are redundant, but they are kept on, I suppose, because they are a part of the fixed rate the companies are allowed to charge for transportation. This is as if railroads were allowed to include in the price of a ticket from New York to Springfield, Massachusetts, a handsome charge for a bad meal whether you wanted it or not.

10/ *Oysters and Larceny*

THE TAXI DRIVER who took me in from the airport to my hotel did not think a Catholic could win. (Morrison is a Catholic.) So he would stay on as Mayor until 1962, when he will have to retire.

"What do you think will happen to him?" I asked.

"Oh, he's well fixed," the driver said. "Got all that money hidden down in Argentina."

A New Orleans taxi driver whose favorite candidate was accused of honesty would feel hurt. It would mean that you thought the driver capable of backing a damned fool.

My hotel, the St. Charles, had been since the previous summer officially styled the Sheraton-Charles, but is never so referred to. The first two versions of the St. Charles burned; the present was built in 1891. I was glad to see the hotel chain had changed nothing but the name, and that, as I have mentioned, ineffectually. It is a bit as if they bought Grant's Tomb and then named it the Sheraton-Grant's Tomb. The hotel was still a warren of austere rooms above a colonnaded lobby of Sistine magnificence—an architectural allegory of the Old South.

Tom was in the lobby when I got there. There was just time to catch the end of the great Davis windup rally at Jerusalem Temple of the Mystic Shrine, he said.

The meeting was just breaking when we got there. Davis is a Shreveport man, and Shreveport is a dilution of Texas, even to big hats.

His New Orleans partisans, contrastingly, were members of the Old Regular Democratic Organization, historically known as the Choctaws, and the Old Regulars, male and female, are Hellenistics to the core. They are home-bred descendants of the famine Irish who came in '47, their assimilates, the German Catholics who came in '48, and their political feudatories, the Sicilians, who came much later. They intermarry. Morrison, with his Crescent City Democratic Organization, has cut them off from municipal patronage. Their leaders consequently live by alliances with the barbarian princes from the north, like the Athenian faction that supported Philip of Macedon.

They run fatter, redder and jollier than either upstate or French Louisianians. The crowd streaming from the Temple could have been coming out of a Jim Curley meeting in Boston or a gathering of Paddy Baulerites in the Forty-third Ward of Chicago. From the Temple, we quickly learned, a good part of them were going over to a television studio, where the gubernatorial candidate and his supporting cast were to re-enact the meeting for rediffusion.

We went along and entered as part of the crowd of enthusiastic partisans. As we went in we were handed "Davis and Aycock" signs on 18-inch cardboard squares. We were to be part of the spontaneous demonstration the television audience would see. The studio was a kind of bus barn. We milled about among the undertakers' chairs provided for enthusiasts until the candidate and his music took their places on a platform facing us. Then we sat down. Then we rose and waved the signs.

I did not recognize Davis, although I had seen hundreds of newspaper and poster portraits of him. This, I discovered when he arose, is because all the pictures were taken head on, with the candidate smiling, and about twenty years ago. Newspaper photographs of Earl Long were usually taken without warning when he was scratching his pants, or when a reporter acting as the photographer's picador had provoked him into a scream of rage.

Davis, I saw, was a sandy-gray man of medium size with a profile like a box tortoise.

He sang a few verses of his campaign song:

Live and let live,
Don't break my heart—
Don't leave me here to cry.

His male chorus, all wearing big hats, helped him out on the refrain. (When he was Governor before, he had most of his band on the state payroll.) Davis then said he had run a clean campaign without trying to hurt anybody's feelings.

John Gremillion, the incumbent Attorney General, who had joined the rush to Davis, next spoke briefly, saying that he had run his own office in "a manner characterized with aggressive efficiency." (Earl Long once said, "If you want to lose anything real good, just put it in Jack Gremillion's law book.")

We all jumped up on signal and waved our signs some more, and a few spontaneous enthusiasts began shouting, "Sunshine!"

The candidate, in response to this demand, rose again and sang all the verses of his greatest hit:

You are my sunshine,
My only sunshine,
I really need you, when clouds are gray . . .

Then the television time ran out.

By that time I was hungry again, and we drove downtown to Felix's, an oyster bar that stays open all night, where you can sometimes hear betting talk.

Sam Sais, the proprietor—I don't know why it is called Felix's—said the primary was so open that he could not quote a betting line. The question nobody could answer was how and in what proportion the four upstate candidates, Davis, Rainach, Noe and Dodd, would split up the Protestant vote.

In New Orleans they eat oysters all year around, but in fairness to the oysters they shouldn't—they are much better in winter. The Louisiana oyster in winter is still a solace to the man of moderate means, sold across the counter, opened, at sixty to seventy-five cents a dozen, and therefore usually eaten a couple of dozen at a time. (I prefer three dozen to any other number of dozen before a meal.) They are wilder and freer than the oysters of Maryland and Long Island and frequently come two or three in a cluster, with rough shells like the little oysters in Trinidad. The oysters share the passionate nature of the human inhabitants of the littoral. They stimulate themselves into what in the less aphrodisiac waters of Gardiners Bay or Chincoteague Island would be considered a population explosion. This accounts for their reasonable price.

The patrons mix their own dope from a variety of condiments oysters do not have to contend with in the North—hot-pepper sauce and olive oil as well as catsup, horse-radish and straight Tabasco. Mixing oyster dope is done as solemnly as the Japanese tea rite.

Tom suggested to me that we go down to Curley Gagliano's place from Felix's because it was the campaign headquarters of a candidate for Governor I had not yet encountered, a statesman named Allen Lacombe, number seven on the ballot.

Gagliano owns the gymnasium where fighters train, on Poydras Street, and an adjoining athenaeum called The Neutral Corner (Poydras and St. Charles Avenue), where good conversation is to be had. Loungers are allowed to buy drinks if they wish, but they are never urged to. Some of the leading philosophers bring their own wine, or Sweet Lucy, and are allowed heat, seat and the privileges of the men's room simply in exchange for their thoughts.

White and colored boxers are allowed to train in the same gymnasium, although a Louisiana state law forbids them to spar with each other. They may not, however, drink in the same saloon. Curley therefore runs a second athenaeum, called Curley's Other Corner, a couple of blocks away. It is for colored.

Curley is a barrel of a man, an old lightweight who never got anywhere and is now unregenerately fat. Men like him are more sentimental about the game than ex-champions, who are often bitter about managers who stole their money. The never-was is less neurotic than the has-been.

Curley is a prosperous bookmaker in Jefferson Parish, across the Mississippi, where he has protection. The gymnasium and the two Corners are his foundations for the arts and he runs them like an endowed retreat.

Curley wears a hat indoors and out. "They call him Curley because he ain't got a stitch of hair on his head," one of the guest philosophers told me.

Curley is a gregarious man but silent, preferring audition to discourse, and is considered a famously easy touch. He maintains solvency only by spending long hours in moving-picture theaters, where he sleeps. "By that way nobody can find him," the philosopher said.

Curley was present, though, when Tom and I entered. So was his candidate, Lacombe, a young-looking man of forty, whose jet-black hair and brows and lashes pointed up a mild, sleepy face, round and pink-and-white. Lacombe, Tom had told me on the way over, was a hustler about town, at times a one-show boxing promoter and at others a handy man around the race-track publicity department. The candidate wore a wide-brimmed, high-crowned oyster-white hat, a string tie, a black worsted jacket and striped pants, the stock cartoon getup for a Southern statesman. His expression was faintly worried, his voice, when he acknowledged Tom's introduction, sweet and almost plaintive.

"Allen is known as the Black Cat," Tom said.

"Bad luck, you know," the candidate explained. "I am the only newspaper handicapper in Louisiana who ever picked seven straight winners at the Fair Grounds and came home broke. I was working for the *Item* then. I got touted off my own selections," he said. He smiled generously, like a small boy showing a festered thumb.

"But I got lucky on the draw for places on the voting machine. I got Number Seven, right between Davis and Morrison. I have to get at least three thousand votes by mistake. I figure to run a good sixth."

He handed me his election card: "Vote for Number 7, Allen G. Lacombe, for Governor," above a picture of his open, honest face and candid eyes, and below it "Vote for Earl Long, candidate for Lieutenant Governor on my ticket."

"Earl gave me the hat," he said, "but he won't come across with nothing. I'm going to get a lot of votes. You'd be surprised how many fellows I talk to that promise me their votes. I take a guy's name and the precinct he votes in, and then I say, 'If I don't get one vote in that precinct, I'll know you're a lying sonofabitch.' "

We sat down at a table with the candidate and Curley and four to six others, and Curley sent to the bar for Cokes or beer, according to tastes.

At that point, a drunk sleeping at a table in a corner of the room woke out of a nightmare and screamed. Disgruntled philosophers, waking off other tables, began to shout, "Throw him out, Goddamighty, can't a man sleep no more?" The man ridden by the nightmare continued to scream, and Curley said, "Take him to the door, Governor." Lacombe got up, and a small, curly-haired man named Blaise said, "Better get that other one over there while you're up, Governor. He wet himself half an hour ago."

Blaise is a journeyman butcher in the French Quarter, I learned later, but he is a volunteer manager.

Lacombe walked over to the screaming man and took him by the hand. He took the other drunk by the hand, too, and led them both gently to the Poydras Street door. He opened the door for them, and they went out without protest.

A moment later they came in through the St. Charles Avenue door. By that time Allen was back at the table with us. Curley laughed. "Cleared their heads," he said. "No harm in them. Toledo Slim, the one who yelled, is a great panhandler when he's sober."

The candidate said, "Like all the other candidates tell, I had a humble beginning, but unlike the other candidates I'm still humble. That's part of a speech I made in Echo, where I was born. That's one town I'm sure to carry. All the voters there are my relatives. It's up near Marksville.

"I hitch-hiked up to Echo a couple of weeks ago, and you'd have thought I was Nelson Rockefeller."

He tried to show that he was not serious, but in the weeks of mock campaigning, his role had grown on him. He was going to miss it when the primary was over. Meanwhile, he was a public figure.

I asked him how it happened that he was embarked on this masquerade, and he said, "Well, I don't have much to do, so I figured I might as well run for Governor. I told Curley I needed two hundred and fifty dollars to post for an entry fee, so he staked me. Afterward he found out I only needed two hundred and ten dollars, and he tried to get the forty back, but I told him I had to have a campaign fund.

"That's the only contribution I've had except for a speech I made to the Pari-mutuel Employees' Union, out at the Fair Grounds. They passed the hat and collected seven dollars and forty-one cents. I got the Volkswagen filled with gas and bet two dollars on the double and blew it. The Volkswagen belongs to the press department at Jefferson Downs that they let me use, but only inside Orleans and Jefferson parishes. So when I go out of town, I hitch-hike."

A customer came over from the bar and said, "I'm going to vote for you, Governor; you're better than them other sonsabitches, anyway."

"What precinct you vote in?" the candidate asked and, after the man told him, said, "Well I'm going to look at the returns Sunday, and if I don't have one vote in that precinct I'll know you're a lying sonofabitch."

The man went away laughing, and the candidate said, "I might even beat Rainach and finish fifth."

"Who do you think will win it?" Tom asked.

"Chep Morrison," the candidate said, "and old Earl will top the list for Lieutenant Governor."

Little Blaise bounced right up on his feet with rage. "Don't tell me Morrison," he said. "You can't walk down the street without somebody mug you and stick a knife in your back. Why? Because all Mr. Morrison's cops are looking for gamblers to shake down. It's easy to catch a gambler. All you got to do, suppose you a cop, is watch da newsstand. A man buy a racing form, all you got to do is follow him. He's going to a bookmaker, ain't he? That's a gambler.

"If I had my way, I'd make a law—a cop catch one gambler, he won't be allow to bring in another *until he arrest a burglar.* You follow me? The cops would catch every burglar in town so they could have a chance to shake down another gambler.

"So how is the element going to vote for Morrison?" He pronounced "element" with accent on the last syllable: "Ele*ment*."

"The ele*ment*, you know what I mean, has got all the money in the state. They running wide open in every parish except Orleans. You think they going to back Morrison? He can't beat the ele*ment*. My predicament is—Davis."

An elderly man, lean, worn and wise, joined in: "I hope you're right. The cops own this town. You can't give them an argument. They make a charge without anything to substantiate or coopberate it, and they pull you just the same. If they see a fella in the street and they don't like his looks, they incarcinate him for lerchering and d.a.s.—that's dangerous and suspicious behavior."

A heavy-shouldered old fellow who had been standing up against the bar now pulled himself away and came toward us. When he got away from the bar, he still leaned forward. Tom addressed him politely as "Ice Cream."

The old pushcart man said, "Mister Tom, I went up to the Jimmie Davis meeting, way up in th' balcony, and Jack Gremillion made one of the most powerful speeches you ever heard. Goddamaighty, it was a great oration. But I heard the old men saying, all around me: 'When Davis was Governor before, he cut the old-age pension to twelve-fifty a month.' And I thought, 'Goddamaighty have mercy on the poor people.' I'm going to vote for Jimmy Noe."

"Jimmy Noe ain't got a chance to be elected dogcatcher," the old cop hater said. Dogcatcher is apparently the hardest office to be elected to in Louisiana. As the campaign wore on, I heard it said of every candidate in the race by his opponents that he couldn't be elected dogcatcher.

"Goddamaighty have mercy on the poor people," Ice Cream repeated.

The argument could have got nowhere, but another gray-bristled ancient entered, and the volatile Blaise went off on a nonpolitical line.

"Balloons," he said, "I heard you had your foot on a twenty-dollar bill and didn't have guts enough to pick it up."

"How could I pick it up?" the old man grumbled, embarrassed. "The fellow that dropped it was looking at me."

"So they tell me you asked the fellow in back of you to pick it up, and you'd split," Blaise said. "And he pretended it was a ten and only gave you five."

"Don't you believe it," Balloons said. "It was a sawbuck, I seen it, and he give me a fin as soon as we got outside."

Blaise said, "Balloons only works once a year, at Mardi Gras. Curley stakes him and he sells balloons. He lives the rest of the year on the profits."

The old man began a chant in Hebrew, and then, breaking off, he said to Blaise, "That's a prayer for the dead, and I'm saying it over you, you should croak."

Blaise, magnanimous, said, "Never mind, Balloons, I'm going to show you what to do when a drunk drops a bill, so you'll know the next time."

He stood up again, looked down, saw the hypothetical bill, no, two bills—Blaise had an inflationary imagination. He stamped his feet down: One, two! covering both imaginary treasures.

"All right, you got them," he said. "One under each foot. Now, watch." He reached into his hip pocket, drew out an extra large handkerchief, spread it for action and then, as he raised it to his nose, dropped it. The handkerchief fluttered toward the floor and Blaise, bending, followed it down as it covered his toes. He reached under the handkerchief and brought it up again, with the putative bills inside. "That way, Balloons," he said, "you don't have to split with nobody."

It was like a program of technical aid to backward countries.

11 / Dellasoups Tops the List

It was between three and four in the morning that I returned to the Sheraton-Charles, and I fell asleep to dream of Mr. Macmillan in a big hat and string tie, lecturing the Royal College of Pari-mutuel Clerks on the evils of gambling. Curley Gagliano and Blaise were in the back benches, rising to shout, "Hear! Hear!"

Waking not long before noon, I called the Governor's Mansion at Baton Rouge and, as I rather expected, failed to get through to Uncle Earl. Tom had told me he was at feud with the press and was seeing nobody. But he would be in New Orleans in the evening for a joint live broadcast with his running mate, Jimmy Noe.

There was so much money behind Davis, and Morrison was waging so strong a campaign, with the support of his New Orleans personal organization, that they figured to run one-two. Nevertheless, Earl was expected to eclipse the nonentities running for Lieutenant Governor. I talked on the telephone with Cousin Horace, the ex-reformer who is renowned for cold, cashable political judgment. He said he had made a good bet that Earl, running for Lieutenant Governor, would get more votes than Chep Morrison would have on the gubernatorial line. And Bob Maestri, a former Mayor, whom I met later in the day, said in his batrachian voice: "Earl will be headada list."

This is the kind of romanticism that sometimes fuddles hardened veterans, like the marshals who threw in their lot with Napoleon after he returned from Elba. It is the effect produced by what Max Lerner would call a charismatic personality.

The romanticism did not affect Earl himself; he knew by then he was on a long shot. It is impossible to organize an effectual campaign around the prospect of electing a lieutenant governor, because a lieutenant governor has no means of paying off. He has no power to initiate legislation or veto bills. He has no patronage to distribute. Thus he can neither do favors for big backers nor get bread-and-butter jobs for the indispensable small workers. For a candidate to use his own money in an election would be as eccentric as a playwright risking money on his own play.

I went down to the coffee shop for a late breakfast and encountered Governor Noe in the lobby. Noe was Lieutenant Governor in 1936; he briefly succeeded Governor O. K. Allen, who demised in office. Naturally, he has been called "Governor" ever since.

Noe is a big-headed, short-legged man, protuberating prosperously in the middle; his appearance recalls the Herbert Hoover of Prosperity-is-just-around-the-corner days. Those were also the great days of "Share Our Wealth" and "Every Man a King" in Louisiana, when Huey was putting on a show as Governor that made the sit-tighters in Washington look even duller than they were.

If Hoover by some disastrous miracle had been re-elected in 1932, Huey might within two years have crystalized around himself all the discontent, rational and irrational, in the country. Roosevelt and his New Deal intervened.

By 1935, when Dr. Seymour Weiss shot him, Huey was in slashing opposition, and there is a myth in Louisiana that wealthy Republicans supplied him with a secret campaign fund of a million dollars to be used for a flanking attack on Roosevelt in 1936.

The attack would have been a national radical Share Our Wealth party, based in the South, that would take away electoral votes in Louisiana and Arkansas and cut heavily into the left of the Democratic popular vote everywhere. The money was never found, which to the politically conditioned mind of the Great State is proof that it must have existed. Old partisans of Huey's have been watching each other suspiciously ever since.

Noe owns radio stations in Monroe, his home town, and New Orleans, besides the number of oil wells normal in his social group. His New Orleans station has a broadcasting studio in the hotel. He said he didn't know when Governor Long would be coming to town. When I asked him how they were going to run, he was affable but without conviction.

"I think we'll surprise a lot of folks," he said. "They thought old Harry Truman was beat in 1948, but he surprised them."

Truman is the patron saint of short-enders; favorites never invoke him.

Over the coffee, I read the morning paper. There is only one, the *Times-Picayune*. The *States-Item*, same ownership, is alone in the evening. The *Times-Picayune* was full of candidates' advertisements. It is a bitter pill for a candidate to have to advertise in a paper that has been beating him over the head, but there is no other way, until the voters get to the polls, of telling them where, on the scrambled face of the voting machine, to find the names of the candidates forming one "ticket."

Since the election is a primary, there are no symbols or party lines on the machines, nor are the allied candidates aligned vertically. So each advertisement carries the injunction "Tear Out and Take to Polls."

The Noe-Long state-wide candidates on the machine were, for example, numbers 9, 18, 21, 22, 30, 31, 38, 44, 47, and 58, while the Morrisonites had 8, 14, 20, 25, 30 (they endorsed the same man for State Treasurer), 33, 40, 43, and 55.

Only about one voter in two is methodical enough to bring the ad along or not to mislay it. Right at the polls is where the well-organized (tantamount to well-heeled) ticket must have plenty of watchers, plainly labeled as rallying points for the well-disposed, so that they may advise voters.

To rub salt in the wounds of the candidates opposed to Davis, the *Times-Picayune* gave the best spot in the paper, the middle of page one, to a free two-column box headed "This Newspaper Endorses: Governor, Jimmie H. Davis, No. 4," and then the names and numbers of all his running mates down to Custodian of Voting Machines, James Fontenot, No. 57. At the foot of this box was the addendum "See Sec. 4, Page 8, for other endorsements by the *Times-Picayune* in Orleans, Jefferson, St. Bernard and Plaquemines parishes." These were for candidates for the Legislature and for parish offices, from sheriff down.

It is one of the consolations of a town with one paper, and a dull one, at that, that you have plenty of time to read it. But it is about the only consolation that increasing millions of Americans have, as in more and more cities monopolists buy out the competition.

The owner who sells has the superior consolation of an inflated price, based not on the earning power of his property but on the multiplied earning power of the monopoly after swallowing it. And of this price, if he has owned the property more than a year, the lenity of the capital-gains law allows him to keep seventy-five per cent. If he retains his paper and earns even a moderate profit, graduated income tax will leave him a much smaller proportion. So he has every inducement to sell. This is a fiscal policy aimed at encouraging competitive enterprise by making it more profitable not to compete.

Taking my time about it, I gazed through the advertisements. "The GO Team is the NOE Team," I read; "Elect Noe & Long and Entire Ticket"; "Keep NOE-how in Louisiana's Government a LONG time." There was a portrait of the two candidates, apple-faced and white-shirted, wearing jackets and ties for their city audience, Earl's right arm amicably around Jimmy's back.

The ad got full mileage out of the old Huey Long brags: Charity Hospital Programs, Free School Books (a landmark in Louisiana education when Huey brought them in) and Better Roads and Bridges.

Number two paragraph, "Peaceful Race Relations," was illustrated with a vignette of two clasped hands. Both were white. The text said:

> This state has had less racial trouble than any other state in the South under the Long administration. Yet, the Noe and Long ticket stands 100% for segregation and the continuance of every southern principle and custom. But it will not foster or incite racial or religious unrest.

The first boast was veracious.

The saddest line was at the end: "Paid for by James A. Noe."

Morrison was photogenic, dynamic, and particularized less:

> LOUISIANA NEEDS Chep Morrison: The only Man with Proven Leadership, Experience, Ability to serve *all* Louisiana—Chep and His Ticket will Work for You—More New Industry, Higher Salaries for Teachers, Maintain Segregation, Better Roads & Highways, Increased Old Age Pension, No Increase in Taxes, Better Care for Needy and Sick.

And, of course, the names and numbers of the running mates.

Davis had two photographs, both full face and smiling. He was genially affirmative: he favored Good Government, Long-Range Planning, Citizen Participation in Government, State Cooperation in Rodeos, Civil Service, Honest Elections, Public Access to All Records Except Those Exempt by Law, We Believe that Law Enforcement Can Best Be Achieved by the Local Authorities, Complete Segregation with Equal Facilities, No New Taxes, a Balanced Budget, Reduction of State Debt, the Independence of the Legislature, Home Rule for Local Authorities, Harmonious Labor-Management Relations, the Interests of Agriculture, Extra Pay to Firemen, Increased Pay for Teachers, Undiminished Public Services, Tourist Travel during the Summer Months (when it is mighty hot), Bids on Contracts (this would be an innovation), History and Traditions and the

Continuation of the Algiers and Gretna ferry services. The only things he acknowledged opposing were Juvenile Delinquency and Subversion.

The Rainach advertisement, unlike the others, emphasized an issue rather than a candidate. The art was freehand and showed two dainty female children, the puffed skirts of their crisp frocks midway up their plump thighs, picking flowers that looked like daffodils from dandelion plants in the deep shade of a spreading tree with the silhouette of a bunch of celery. One little girl kneeled and culled, a frilly bit of the bottom of her panties innocently peeping from beneath the skirt, and turned a precociously provocative face toward her sister, who stood and held the basket. There was a carefully planted suggestion of eligibility for rape. The copy read:

> This is a fight to curb Louisiana's disastrous financial policies. This is a fight to preserve States' Rights. This is a fight to protect the individual rights of the laboring man [*i.e.*, restore a right-to-work anti-union bill repealed by the Long legislature] and a fight to return Home Rule to our towns and parishes. But even more than that, THIS IS A FIGHT FOR OUR CHILDREN! WE CANNOT . . . WE *MUST* NOT leave them a heritage of integration to struggle against! WE MUST DO FOR THEM WHAT THEY CANNOT DO FOR THEMSELVES. Senator Rainach has led our fight for us for five years—when those whose DUTY it was to lead refused because it might have hurt them politically. He is the ONE candidate with the determination, the will and the ability to turn back Northern Radicals and the NAACP. FOR THE SAKE OF OUR CHILDREN, we *MUST* elect William Rainach Governor! Elect the entire Rainach ticket.

The names and numbers followed.

A consolation was that Rainach had no chance. Louisiana politics for nearly forty years had been a contest between Longites and antis, with the Longites in favor of a welfare state, soaking the oil companies and sharing the spoils.

The anti-Longites, at first battling to return the state to its hereditary owners—themselves—had given up on that; they now fought chiefly to lick the Longs and get a share of the gravy, as in Britain the Tories, with no hope of restoring a respectful pre-Labour Britain, declare themselves the party of the Average Man and concentrate on winning office.

This followed a pattern set by the great Huey. If in the beginning of his revolution he had followed other Southern demagogues and attacked the Negro, his opponents would have had to outbid him by attacking Negroes even more violently. He had no need of the race issue; white poverty and the backwardness of the state gave him all the ammunition he needed. He adopted a policy of speaking disrespectfully of Negroes in public to guard against being called a nigger lover, and giving them what they wanted, under the table, to make sure they would vote for him. As the poorest Louisianians of all, they benefited disproportionately from his welfare schemes; it would be a dull politician who would try to disfranchise his own safest voters.

Earl inherited and emphasized this policy, and Morrison, starting in New Orleans, where the Negro vote is important, competed for it. To be fair to both, Earl genuinely liked Negroes—and for all I know, Huey did, too—while Morrison believes in their rights. Both were inevitablists and shrewd in the law.

Morrison sees no chance of stemming the tide of Federal court decisions. He suffers under the disadvantage of living in the contemporary world, while the Perezes and Rainachs remain in the Jurassic. It was the gift of the Longs that they could straddle the intervening million years.

The Davis people were working through the Old Regulars to round up all the Negro vote they could in New Orleans. Peace and harmony was their war cry.

Davis, to sum up, had the support of the big money men who need a winner, the "ele*ment*" of gamblers and the local sheriffs who live off them; the *Times-Picayune* with its boiled shirt of respectability; the Old Regulars with their aura of venality; and a mass, hard to estimate, of upcountry people who like peace and hillbilly music.

Morrison had his own highly efficient New Orleans organization, all of French Catholic South Louisiana (except Plaquemines and St. Bernard, where Perez's authority overrides sectarian considerations), and the idealistic good-government people, earnest amateurs, with whom he had become a habit and reason for political life. These last formed a strong corps of volunteer workers. Noe and Dodd between them had the dyed-in-the-wool Longites, estimated by experts at a constant 40 per cent of the state vote. This was an overestimate. The Longites needed a Long to head their ticket, not merely to grace it.

These promised to be the three largest divisions of the electorate, and they turned out to be so, though not in the order or the proportions most observers expected. The racists were the smallest of all the factions.

That evening Tom Sancton and I listened to Jimmy Noe and Earl on WNOE, the Noe station.

"Chep Morrison is one of the ten bes'-dressed men in America," Noe said, "and Jimmie Davis hasn't got a backbone as big as a jellyfish. Ah'm pretty well fixed now, but as a young man ah pulled a cross-cut saw for fifty cents a day and wrestled an oil rig for a dollar and a half. It's an honor for me to pay my taxes. We stand for the people, the common people, the working man, the working woman, and if you don't elect us, *you will be the loser*. Who is the opposition? The old anti-Long crowd, the *Picayune* crowd. Huey Long was killed by newspaper persecution." This was the argument, familiar to all his hearers, that the newspapers had inflamed the assassin. "The same old crowd is here to fool you into throwing away the things Huey Long fought for. It's the same line they used when they fooled you into electing Sam Jones Governor in 1940. They couldn't elect Jones *dogketcher* today."

Uncle Earl, when he came in, said Governor Noe was a disinterested gentleman and had one of the best-raised families it had ever been his pleasure to meet.

"Vote for a candidate that the *Picayune* knows they can't tell what to do," he said. "They want to tell you what to do and what not to do, and they don't care which of those two sapsuckers, Morrison or Davis, gets elected."

Noe's speech sounded as if he had been away from politics too long and was still talking in 1940, and Earl sounded good-humored and perfunctory.

Next day, the date of the election, Sancton and I made a round of assorted precincts, or polling places. The approaches to them for a block in either direction were adorned with placards bearing candidates' photographs—a true Lebanese touch—and around the polls beribboned and besashed ladies on undertakers' chairs handed out sample ballots. There were, I think, two hundred and eleven names on the voting machine in most precincts, and to vote a complete Jimmie Davis–R.D.O. ticket in any ward a voter had to pull fifteen levers.

In addition to the sedentary ladies, there were roving, and in a surprising number of cases limping, males, to support challenged voters who appeared well-disposed. There were also flocks of small boys, who, however, appeared unreliable, like other irregular troops. The gutters leading up to most polls were deep in sample ballots, and so were the apertures to the mailboxes.

Morrison and Davis workers showed en masse, the Morrison watchers looking like virtuous dilettantes, the Davis people like Tammany block leaders. But in two precincts out of three there was nobody at all for Noe and Long, Rainach or Dodd. A political organization cannot be improvised: you either have to build one yourself, like Morrison, or rent a going one for the occasion, as the Davis people had chartered the R.D.O.

Down in Comiskey's ward the Davis ballots were going like Clocker Lawton cards at the races. In a couple of mainly colored precincts where Tom stopped the station wagon, the voters were providing themselves with sample ballots of both kinds, to maintain the mystery.

When the poll-hopping palled, we drove back downtown to Curley's gym and watched a visiting colored fighter spar against a couple of local hopes, who began by trying to knock him out and then held like grim death. There were bleachers on two sides of the ring, one for white, one for colored, and, naturally, only colored inside the ropes. We got to talking with white old-timers there about when the color line invaded boxing in Louisiana.

As in other forms of race relations, there has been regression. In 1892,

George Dixon, illustrious in history as Little Chocolate, fought Jack Skelly, an Irishman from Yonkers, for the featherweight championship of the world in New Orleans, and the mixed match was taken as a matter of course. None of the old-timers remembered when the color line came in. Over a long period relations improve slowly; then, very rapidly, they get a lot worse.

In 1872 there was a public meeting between fifty white and fifty Negro leaders, as equals, in New Orleans to discuss civil rights. Many of the white leaders were ex-Confederates. One was General Beauregard, whose committee report "advocated complete political equality for the Negro, an equal division of State offices between the races, and a plan whereby the Negroes would become landowners. It denounced discrimination because of color in hiring laborers or in selecting directors of corporations, and called for the abandonment of segregation in public conveyances, public places, railroads, steamboats and public schools."*

You couldn't get a leading Louisiana white to such a meeting now without a subpoena, and Beauregard, the Confederate Bonaparte, would be charged today with sabotaging the "Southern way of life."

The afternoon wore on, and toward sundown I made another tour of polling places, this time with Lacombe, the Neutral Corner's candidate for Governor; we used the Jefferson Downs Volkswagen. The lines in the working-class wards were heavy with men and women voting on their way home. Saloons were open, suppositiously for the sale of beer only. Bottles on the back bars were ostentatiously covered with newspaper. The Black Cat diminished as I watched. The dream was coming to an end. The polls closed at seven.

"I'm going to await the returns with my faithful workers at the Neutral Corner," he said. I wondered where else a man could have so much fun for $210, especially when another fellow put it up.

The result of the first primary was an upset. Morrison won handily.

The Morrison people had set up an election headquarters in a suite of two big banquet rooms off the mezzanine of the Sheraton-Charles, with wall charts on which to write the parish returns as they came in, television screens, Scotch and canapés and the rest of election-party paraphernalia. By about eleven o'clock, when Tom and I arrived, after a leisurely dinner and a bottle of Smith-Haut Lafitte 1947 at Arnaud's, the atmosphere was hopeful but scared, as I remembered it had been at radio parties in New York in the Truman-Dewey election of 1948. It was not only that Morrison was running as well as had been expected in the city, but that the other four candidates were cutting each other up in a manner that the Morrison faction had not dared hope for. People kept reminding one another that the returns from the country districts were not in yet.

The partisans at the Sheraton-Charles were predominantly scrubbed,

* T. Harry Williams, *P. G. T. Beauregard: Napoleon in Gray.* Louisiana State University Press, 1955.

well dressed and earnest, with the look of the dilettante in politics who feels he or she is doing a civic duty. Some of the women, steadying their nerves with whiskey, were already a trifle high. It was the kind of group that seldom has a winner, politics being what they are, and that is almost as astonished as pleased when it gets one.

Typically it is attracted to candidates like Willkie or Stevenson, or, on a municipal level, Bob Merriam in Chicago and Newbold Morris in New York. When it gets a consistent winner like La Guardia or Franklin D. Roosevelt it loses part of its regard for him. It is then obvious that its taste is shared by a large number of less discriminating people, and that devalues the candidate.

Morrison had been elected Mayor so often that he might have suffered from this prejudice, if he had not failed so dismally when he ran against Earl Long for Governor in 1956. That reinstated him.

As the evening wore on, no doubt survived that Morrison was in. In Orleans Parish, where in 1956 he had beaten Uncle Earl by barely 2,000 votes, he led all the four other serious candidates combined. He led Davis easily. The R.D.O., which had gathered 69,000 votes for Earl in 1956, had been able to get Davis only 40,000. Morrison took a lead of 46,000 upstate with him, and although he lost in many parishes outside, it was to different rivals in different places. On the whole he held his lead over Davis, and as the morning went on he increased it.

As the returns came in, a man named Paul McIlheny, a fervid Morrison buff, jotted down the votes for Big Bad Bill Dodd as regularly as the Mayor's and lumped the two totals. Then he would compare them with the total for the other three candidates. Dodd had already made his deal to throw in with Morrison for the runoff.

Dodd, unfortunately, was running badly, and watching McIlheny's honest distress, you would have thought he was Dodd's brother. The returns showed Willie Rainach running, I thought, surprisingly well, a not-too-distant third, but Tom said that the racists had expected even more. The great blow to me was Earl's showing. He was running far ahead of Jimmy Noe, his principal, and the Rainach and Dodd candidates for Lieutenant Governor, but he would fall far short of making the runoff. His effort to pick a soft touch had failed, and he was going to be shut out by a pair of four-round politicians.

About midnight Tom and I walked over to the Davis headquarters at the Hotel Monteleone, where there was considerable gloom. They had not yet lost the war, but they had lost a battle and would have to dicker for reinforcements. The Davis combination would now have to retain Willie Rainach, and possibly Uncle Earl, to help in the stretch. When a political side becomes all-inclusive, there isn't enough gravy to go around.

Practical politics is like pari-mutuel betting: with everybody on the same horse, the payoff is small. Worse, the *Times-Picayune* was the keystone of the odd construction, and might hedge. Should it decide on a gesture in favor of unity, it might suggest editorially that the party waive the runoff and nominate Morrison unanimously, now that Earl Long, for once, was beaten out of the picture.

"If they do that, Chep will be more powerful than Huey was," Tom said. "He'll have state and city patronage both, plus a favorable national press. He can put in a safe Mayor here when he goes to Baton Rouge and leave a safe man in Baton Rouge as Governor while he goes on to the Senate in Washington. It will be a thousand-year Reich."

Tom sees things big and dramatically.

"There's no limit to his energy or his ambition," he said, "and he might turn out to be not only the first Catholic President of the United States—if Kennedy doesn't make it this time—but the first President from a Southern state since the Civil War. He's only forty-eight, and he walks on the water. Earl was the only one that could handle him. Now that Earl is out of the way, the genie is out of the bottle. Earl was the stopper."

We decided to return to the happier mood of the Sheraton-Charles and stopped for coffee at Thompson's on the way. There we encountered Blaise, too sensitive to show at the Neutral and be needled about his predicament that Davis would win.

"Morrison preys on da nigger vote and da woman vote," he said, and pretended he had business down the street.

At a table across the room, Tom pointed out Rainach, two children, his wife, and three or four members of his *Oberkommando*. All except the children, who seemed merely sleepy, looked down at the mouth.

"This marks the beginning of a new era in Louisiana politics," Tom said. Then I went to bed.

12 / Back to Racism

WHEN I awoke, I had a feeling of sadness, and could not remember why until I recognized my surroundings. Then I knew it was because I had come back to Louisiana to see Earl play Foxy Grandpa and run rings around the righteous, and he hadn't done it. From the time I had first heard his voice on a sound track in a television studio in New Orleans and seen him on the screen, wagging his tail and shaking his fist, I had liked the old stump-wormer.

I could still hear him saying to Willie Rainach with the Confederate flag on his tie: ". . . *you got to recognize that niggers is human beings. . . .* To keep fine honorable gray-headed men and women off the registration rolls, some of whom have been voting as much as sixty or sixty-five years—I plead with you in all candor. I'm a candidate for Governor. If it hurts me, it will just have to hurt."

The law that Earl had been attacking then allows any two registered bona fide voters of a parish to challenge any name on the voting list because of irregularity in the voter's original application. A misspelled name, an omitted initial or an error in calculating age *to the day* is sufficient. The parish registrar then "segregates the name"—always that verb. The challenged voter—if he gets the notification the registrar is legally obliged to send him, if he can read the notification (literacy per se is not a requisite for voting), if he cares enough to gather three witnesses to the legality of the first registration, if he can afford to pay a lawyer, and if he has guts enough to buck intimidation for the sake of a useless protest—may ask a hearing before the registrar. At this hearing he will be asked to reestablish his fitness to vote by answering impossible questions.

Rainach, as chairman of the Joint Legislative Committee on Segregation, was encouraging members of the White Citizens' Council and the Southern gentlemen in each parish to push the right of challenge to its ultimate length against Negroes.

The Department of Justice had brought action against white citizens of Washington Parish, on the Mississippi Line, for cutting 1,377 (out of 1,500) Negro voters from the list, and the case was before a Federal District Judge born, bred and legally trained in New Orleans, who, in due time, would order Washington Parish to restore the names to the rolls.

(I don't remember reading, in any of the voluminous accounts in Northern and Southern newspapers of Uncle Earl's uncouth conduct in the Legislature, any praise for the justice of his stand. In the dictionary of newspaper prejudices, which is seldom revised, Long was still a name of fun and fear.)

But the old boy was in there slugging, in a period when the accredited Southern liberals, of the kind exhibited at Washington dinner tables, talked about something else every time civil rights was mentioned. Kefauver tried to weaken the Senate bill on voting rights, and Fulbright filibustered against it.

And I remembered his gift for prose: "You know the Bible says that before the end of time, billy goats, tigers, rabbits, and house cats all are going to sleep together," and "If you give me the right commissioners, I can make them voting machines play 'Home Sweet Home.'" You also need workers at the polls to tell the voters what chords to hit, as he probably realized by now.

I called the Hotel Roosevelt, where he stayed in New Orleans, and when the desk said he had checked out, I tried the Executive Mansion at Baton Rouge, where a state trooper said he had not arrived. The old sapsucker was licking his wounds, I imagined, and went back to sleep.

My telephone rang after a while. It was Tom Sancton, of the opinion that we should drive up to Baton Rouge in his station wagon and force our way in on our hero. "Once you get to him he'll talk," Tom said. "It's his nature. He can't resist." Tom is the old-fashioned kind of reporter who believes in giving every story the old college try. I was against it, but I had no other suggestion for what to do on Sunday.

Waiting for him, I read a Sunday newspaper that had been printed before I went to bed. It had Morrison leading by 46,000 votes at 12:25.

We left in the early afternoon and were on the porch of the Mansion in Baton Rouge in two hours. In the driveway I had left crowded in early August, there was only one car parked besides Tom's.

I was sorry for the poor old Governor, abandoned by the Old Regulars, alienated from his wife, held at the other end of a telephone wire by his favorite woman friend, and so surrounded by snooping newspaper reporters that he could not even peacefully enjoy a visit with a strip-tease girl. He was alone, but without enough privacy to cover up a red bug.

I was astonished, when I went inside, to be told by the state cop on the door that the Governor wasn't available because he was closeted with Camille Gravel, the Democratic National Committeeman from Louisiana, a leading Morrison manager. The last time I had seen Long and Gravel together, in Alexandria, Gravel's home town, they had been jawing each other at close range in public. Earl had called Gravel a common damn hoodlum and a little pissant, and Gravel had called Earl a doublecrosser and a lifelong liar.

I asked the cop to send in word that I, the Governor's great and loyal admirer from New York, was there, having driven up from New Orleans to condole with him. The cop said the Governor had instructed he wasn't seeing *anybody*, but he sent in word. After a while a colored man came out from the direction of the conference and said the Governor said to run me away from there.

I promptly sent Tom to look for Margaret Dixon. His departure gave me a stay of sentence. Even the most inhuman official will not chuck you out *on foot*. In our country the thought of pedestrian locomotion is so abhorrent that even a policeman who would gladly beat you up would be ashamed to make you walk. It is the twentieth-century equivalent of dropping a man at sea in an oarless rowboat.

In the Tunisian steppe, I knew an infantry company, brave under fire, that quailed at the notion of moving to a new position five miles away on foot. It stayed where it was for twenty-four hours after receiving the order to move, waiting for trucks to come and move it. The division commander, when he heard about it, said, "Why can't the goddamn infantry walk?" His harshness led to a Congressional inquiry.

Tom had just departed when the door from the library, where the conference was in session, opened, and a young lawyer I had met in New Orleans came out and spotted me. He was in politics, like everybody else, and, as is natural for an energetic young liberal in the Great State, was a Morrison man. (Energy and liberalism are both used in a regional, or relative, sense.) I hailed him and asked if the Governor and Gravel were still calling each other names, and he said no, they had business to attend to. I asked him to intercede with Earl and get me an audience, and he said he would try. I did not see him again that day.

The cop said to stand on the porch, as the Governor was in a hell of a temper. He shunted me out on the porch that the *State Guide* calls a colonnaded portico. I stood there thinking of all the important people who had been *glad* to receive me in other days: Pola Negri and Henry Luce and Joe Louis and the two fellows who wrote "The Music Goes Round and Round." The list is endless. Now I had fallen so low that I couldn't get in to see a defeated candidate for Lieutenant Governor of Louisiana. After a while, Tom drove up with the gracious Mrs. Dixon, but it was no good. The troopers turned all three of us away. Mrs. Dixon, fresh from the teletypes in the *Advocate* office, said Morrison's final lead looked to be about 65,000.

As Tom and I drove back down to New Orleans later, he said, "That's Earl for you, every time: In victory unbearable, insufferable in defeat."

He still thought Morrison sure. "Earl wouldn't be sweet-talking Gravel if he didn't think so too," he said. After being up all night listening to the returns, Maggie said, Chep was out stumping at noon. He held the first meeting of his campaign for the runoff election today at New Roads, on False River, the town where he was born.

At this point in my narrative, my hero, Earl Kemp Long, was in the side pocket.

By the time we sat down to dinner in New Orleans—three dozen apiece at Felix's and then shrimp and crabmeat Arnaud and red snapper *en court bouillon*—the early editions of the *Times-Picayune*, with all but complete returns and tabulations, were on the street. Morrison had about 272,000 votes; Davis 210,000; Rainach 138,000; poor Jimmy Noe 96,000; and Big Bad Bill 86,000 (the two Long factions between them 182,000). Rainach, although third, represented only the fourth biggest segment of the electorate. For Lieutenant Governor, Morrison's running mate, Bowdon, had about 223,000 votes, Davis's man, Aycock, 215,000, and Uncle Earl 156,000. He had run wretchedly in New Orleans, where he had lost the services of the Old Regular Organization.

Morrison had carried five congressional districts out of eight, including not only New Orleans and Baton Rouge, but all rural southern Louisiana. Davis had carried only two districts, in northwest Louisiana. In the remaining one, the Fourth, which included Davis's home city of Shreveport and Rainach's rustic constituency of Claiborne, Willie had topped the poll, getting more than Davis and Morrison combined.

It gave one to think, and Davis's managing directors clearly had thought.

The editorial page, on which the Morrison rooters had hoped to see a flag of truce, talked instead of a hard-fought second primary, pointing out that Morrison had 33 per cent of the vote, Davis 25 and Rainach 17. "The disposition of the Rainach voters, numbering nearly 140,000, will be of more than slight importance."

More interesting than the statistics was Davis's statement. Peace and harmony had gone out the window with his failure to cut into Morrison's Negro vote.

"There has been one sinister and disturbing element injected into this election," said the Sunshine man, "which is clearly apparent after an analysis of the precincts in the state dominated by the minority elements." Any Southerner knows that "minority" is the plural of "nigger."

"My personal conviction coupled with the overwhelming vote of confidence placed in Mr. Jack P. F. Gremillion, who has been re-elected Attorney General, confirms my faith that the voters of this state are concerned with the preservation of State Rights as guaranteed by the Tenth Amendment to the Constitution of the United States." This paragraph was set in blackface.

"The Vote that has been cast in this first primary has proven several points. One is that the majority of the voters in Louisiana want to preserve state sovereignty and the right to self-determination in internal matters.

"The second point that has been graphically established is that there are forces at work that will undermine, by tactics fair or foul, the rights of an overwhelming majority of citizens."

These forces, of course, are the Communist party and the Elders of Zion, of whose fornications the NAACP is a byblow, as any initiated grass-eater knows. Grass-eater was Earl Long's term for the race nuts. Davis was now talking their language, and the violence of 1960 was in the making.

The act of the Louisiana Legislature creating the Rainach committee begins: "Whereas, the rights and liberties of the people of the United States are threatened as never before by enemies, both foreign and domestic; and

"Whereas, these enemies have concentrated their attacks upon the States in the South and are there employing what has been described by these enemies as the Party's most powerful weapon—racial tension; . . ."

Back to Davis: "I will campaign on this mandate. This, coupled with the genuine record established during the time I served the people as Governor, and underscored by my platform for the future, will lead to an inevitable victory at the polls in the second primary election." He was, in the elegant language of politics, sucking up to the grass-eaters.

In the column adjoining the second half of the statement, the *Times-Picayune* make-up man had thoughtfully placed an item on Camille Gravel, re-elected to the Democratic State Committee. A paragraph in blackface type read:

"Gravel, 45, said the vote gave him the right to speak up as a 'segregation moderate.'

"While he hasn't made a public endorsement, Gravel is backing the gubernatorial bid of deLesseps Morrison."

I said to Tom, "It reads like Arkansas. It's going to be a White Supremacy election. But in Little Rock at least they had a newspaper with guts, the *Arkansas Gazette*, that resisted the regression. The *Times-Picayune* is pushing this one on."

We were not in a truly merry mood when after dinner we headed for the Neutral Corner (White) to congratulate Lacombe on his showing. The chart by parishes in the paper showed he had gathered 4,895 votes for Governor, finishing a hot seventh. He had got 292 votes in New Orleans and been skunked in only two parishes out of 64. His best totals were in a number of Cajun parishes that he had never visited. He had the most clearly French name on the program.

"We murdered them in Echo!" the candidate said, triumphant.

"Where are you going to throw your support in the runoff, Allen?" Tom asked him.

"I have already endorsed Chep Morrison," the recent candidate said. "There is a job at the city jail I have my eye on."

Blaise squeaked with joy. "The Black Cat never picked a winner in his life," he said. "Now the ele*ment* can ozoom Davis is elected."

By Tuesday, when I flew back to New York, the two survivors of the first primary were squared away on the last leg. The *Times-Picayune* reported:

NAACP TARGET OF DAVIS TALK

In Louisiana this is as safe as opposing incest.

"'As for the NAACP, I hope not one of them votes for me because I don't want their vote,'" the candidate was quoted. "He referred to the National Association for the Advancement of Colored People."

"'I'm not a hater but there comes a time when you must stand on your principles,' Davis added. 'We know what is good for the country and we don't want someone from New York running our state.'"

Meanwhile poor Morrison, in a town called Raceland, was disclaiming ever having a kind thought about anybody with less than 32 quarterings of Norman albino blood. He said he had taken "vigorous positive action to maintain segregation," but he spoiled it by saying that in fighting the NAACP "I have used my head instead of my mouth."

The mouth is the traditional weapon. Some great author should write a companion volume to Cash's classic *The Mind of the South.* It would be called *The Mouth of the South.*

Vainly, I felt, though accurately, Morrison denounced Davis for "the overnight change of heart that prompted him to finally make a statement on the issue."

The Negro-inhabited precincts had voted for *him*, and that was as fatal as having your social standing vouched for by Elsa Maxwell.

I felt, too, that there was an out-of-date look about Morrison's quoted plea that he had "met this problem successfully because he 'provided through vigorous action and timely performance adequate and equal opportunities and facilities for the 235,000 Negroes in New Orleans.' "

The grass-eaters consider "adequate and equal" a sign of softness. "Vigorous" is another word that Morrison uses too often. It has connotations of hard labor that displease voters in a warm climate.

"Aggressive," which has associations with violence, goes down better.

In the lobby of the Sheratonized St. Charles, I met the lawyer I had seen at the Mansion on Sunday, and he said that Earl had promised to come down to New Orleans and confer with Morrison but had not appeared.

"The Davis people must have got to him between Sunday night and Monday morning," he said mournfully. And Morrison, by going campaigning early on Sunday, had missed a chance to make an offer to Rainach.

Davis's people, rising late, had seen him first. Vigor can be a vice.

By now the *States-Item*, the *Times-Picayune* Company's afternoon coda, bragged the first primary as, on the main issue, a resounding *Times-Picayune* victory. Its lead editorial on Monday was headed "Longism Takes a Beating," and began: "Last Saturday's voting left many important nominations still to be made in a Democratic runoff primary, but on that Louisiana political phenomenon called Longism the action was decisive.

"Gov. Earl K. Long, seeking the Lieutenant Governor's post, and his handpicked candidate for governor, James A. Noe, were eliminated from further consideration.

"Unless one of the two surviving tickets in the second primary becomes prominently identified with the Long faction, the perennial choice between Longism and anti-Longism will not be the paramount issue of the runoff.

"That is a development for which the voters can rejoice. It is heartening to realize that other factors, other reasons, will bear more heavily on the runoff choice. . . ."

The "other factors, other reasons," that were to "bear more heavily on the runoff choice," were racism and the denial of civil rights—"the segregation cause."

The result reminded me of one of those automobile accidents in which a driver, swatting at a wasp, loses control of his car and runs it into a bayou full of alligators. The sequel was to prove that the *Times-Picayune*, in its eagerness to get rid of the Governor, had helped move Louisiana back into the class of Alabama.

13/*Earl Joins* Times-Pic

I HAD a chance to study the alligators in the plane on the way back to New York. Stopping by the Rainach campaign headquarters on the day before election, I had picked up a batch of literature that I had neither time nor taste for reading in New Orleans, but the boredom of the air lends itself to catching up on distasteful homework.

The windows of the Rainach store front on Union Street had been pasted over with blow-ups and reproductions of newspaper pages denouncing Davis for having led his orchestra in a drive-in dance place in California where Negroes were allowed on the same floor with Whites, and for having later himself managed an "interracial honky-tonk" of the same sinister nature in Palm Springs. But these sins of youth were to be forgiven in view of Willie Rainach's own defeat and Davis's promise to mend his ways.

The first article of indictment against Morrison that I read was a throwaway headed

MORRISON WORKS TO DESTROY SEGREGATION

Under this head was a photograph of the Mayor between two well-dressed colored men. Under that was another photo, of a number of Negro boys diving into a swimming pool surrounded by massed Negroes, some of whose faces and bodies looked white in the glare of the photographer's flashlight. No form of reporting lends itself better than the camera to equivocation.

A caption read: "The above picture was taken from the Saturday July 31, 1948 LOUISIANA WEEKLY, a New Orleans Negro Newspaper.

"In the course of his speech dedicating the Negro swimming pool shown in the above picture, the *Louisiana Weekly* quoted Mayor Chep Morrison as having said that he '*plans for full integration of the Negro community in expanding the educational and recreational program of New Orleans. . . .*'" The word "integration" did not pick up its additional special sense until after the United States Supreme Court's school decision of 1954, when it began to be used as an antonym of "segregation." Morrison's 1948 "integrate" meant, as in the dictionary, "to fit in as a harmonious part," under the old "equal and adequate" scheme:

"Facts from the record reveal that Mayor Chep Morrison urged upon leading New Orleans Hotels to register Negroes; that he attended the testimonial banquet for the Negro lawyer Tureaud who represented the

NAACP in all their suits to force racial integration in our public schools, colleges and LSA;

"That as a member of the Board of Directors of the Pelican Baseball Team, he advocated measures which would 'desegrate' the Pelican Baseball Stadium as well.

"The only streetcars and buses in the State of Louisiana which are racially integrated are those in New Orleans, under Mayor Chep Morrison."

Before I came to Louisiana, I would have thought all these statements recommendations for Mayor Morrison's good sense. Such is the force of conditioning, even in two brief visits, that I now sought to find mitigating circumstances to explain each. Morrison, not wanting the city to be boycotted as a site for national conventions, had asked the hotels to lodge Negro delegates to some of them. He had felt that the Pelicans needed new strength and the patronage of Negro fans in order to survive. (Failing on both counts, the Pelicans perished.)

It was true, I knew, that a Federal court had ordered the Orleans Parish School Board to produce a plan for the admission of Negro pupils to the same schools as whites. The plan had to be brought into court by the end of the current school year, and a whole new cycle of litigations would then begin, the judge defining what he would accept as a minimum of compliance with the law, the Board trying to whittle down the minimum. I felt sure, too, that Morrison knew that the court's order could not be completely evaded without shutting down all the schools, and, since he himself was intelligent, I assumed he preferred that schools remain open. I could not believe, though, that he had initiated a plot to force the School Board's hand. (I would have liked him better if he had.)

Before reading the White League's offering, I had been on the fence about Morrison. The White League converted me to his side. It seemed hard that a man should be punished precisely for his best point.

Davis, merely negative before the election, now was the White League's color-bearer.

I spent part of the rest of my short journey reading another piece of White League documentation: "Three Steps to Mongrelization—A Blueprint for the Destruction of Our Christian-American Civilization. The Three Steps are: 1. Mix the schools—Their immediate goal is the integration of the schools; their ultimate objective is the bastardization of the white race; 2. Teach Them 'Tolerance'—The second important step toward total mongrelization is the indoctrination of our white youth with 'tolerance' propaganda; 3. Integrate the Churches—a project dear to the heart of a great many of our social gospel clergymen. They know to begin with the mere presence of Negroes in white churches will eventually result in interracial marriages."

The tract was illustrated with smudgy photos of mixed couples: "This girl, on honeymoon with her Negro husband, will make her parents proud some day—with mulatto grandchildren," one caption said.

By the time I reached home I thought that Morrison's campaign in Louisiana might be a watershed in Southern history. If the Mayor, a Catholic and a realist, could win, intimidated liberals and moderate-liberals might take heart throughout the South, which is not monolithically insane.

The grass-eaters like to say of militant Negroes that the majority are prisoners of a few thousand who force the others to conform by threats. The *Colons* say the same of the Algerians, and the Afrikanders of the Africans. It is more true of Southern whites than of an yother group.

A Senator as ostentatiously civilized as Fulbright of Arkansas abstained from battle against Governor Orval Faubus in his own state, telling friends in Washington that it were better he knuckle under than that Arkansas be represented in the United States Senate by a troglodyte like Faubus himself. This was in 1957, and Fulbright was not due to face the electorate until 1962. The Senator was so sure that independence would be fatal that he quit five years early.

On the morning I left New Orleans the *Times-Picayune* carried the announcement that the Morrison supporters had expected: "Dodd Declares for Morrison," but it was a question of how many of the 86,000 votes Dodd had collected in the first primary he would be able to deliver. The Dodd voters, for the most part, were upstate, living among the Davis and Rainach voters, and the "new issues" were bound to appeal to them, especially if the newspapers continued to advertise Morrison's Negro vote.

A *Times-Picayune* I bought at the out-of-town newsstand in New York shortly after arriving carried a first-page story on the slightly increased registration in New Orleans for the runoff. Part of the headline read: "2262 more Negroes on Roll; 1087 Whites." A paragraph, the only one in the story that was printed in blackface type, reprised:

"The new total represents net increases of 2262 in the number of Negroes registered and of only 1087 in the number of White persons on the rolls."

This could be translated into a clear indication that the Negroes, for dark reasons of their own, were out to elect Morrison, but in order that not even the dullest should miss the point, the paper added:

"In the first primary, Mayor deLesseps S. Morrison, among the candidates for Governor, received the overwhelming majority of the Negro vote in New Orleans and state-wide."

There were about 150,000 Negro voters registered in the state, as compared with 850,000 whites. In New Orleans there were 34,000 (including the sinister accretion) and 170,000 whites. Negroes comprise about 24 per cent of the state's population, and the discrepancy between this and their 15 per cent of state-wide registration reflects in part the obstacles thrown in their way to the polls. It reflects in other part an apathy founded on skepticism.

With only two men running, Davis could turn the Negroes' adherence to Morrison into an asset, and the *Times-Picayune* and the Shreveport *Times* did all they could to exaggerate it.

A Louisiana election is fun to watch even from New York. Thus Bill Dodd, who before the first primary had said, "Chep Morrison got soft little hands like a girl's," now told a crowd:

"I'm a hillbilly from up North Louisiana, where the people are going to vote for Chep Morrison just like you folks down here are going to vote for him.

"Chep Morrison is as far ahead of Jimmie Davis as a rocket is ahead of a mule. One is a fighter and the other is a fiddler—now which do you want?

"One of them will do something, and the other will do nothing. Now which do you want? If you want nothing you got nothing running for Governor—Jimmie Davis!"

Davis stumped the state, spurning, in every speech, unproffered aid from the NAACP or the Teamsters' Union. He wanted the votes of all decent people, he said every time. "However, I have repeatedly said, and I say again, that I am not accepting support of the NAACP, Teamsters' boss Jimmy Hoffa, or that ilk." Back in 1947, when he was Governor, the *Times-Picayune* had accused him editorially of kowtowing to Hoffa during a strike. Now that counted no more than a base hit in a different inning of some other ball game.

Going down to the Cajun country to attack Morrison in his own stronghold, he carried with him a legislator named Angelle, "who spoke in French." "Davis and his hillbilly band entertained a crowd gathered at the Arcadia Parish courthouse at Crowley. He sang one number in French." It was here that Davis again declared he wanted no part of the NAACP and the Jimmy Hoffa Group.

"I have been criticized for saying that I do not want the vote and support of the NAACP and the Jimmy Hoffa crowd," Davis said, "but I will say again that I do not want their help." I wondered who had criticized him.

Morrison said he was for segregation too. But then, why had the Negroes voted for him? The answer, the newspapers implied, was obvious to any white man who could recognize a woodpile when he saw one.

"Ex.-Gov. Davis tried to give the impression during the first primary that he was such a nice old soul who just loved everybody and everything," Morrison said in a speech in a place called Baker three days after the primary. "He was not a hater, he said. . . .

"But the first words to come out of his mouth the day after election carried the old practiced ring of all professional haters—namely, the denunciation of minorities. . . .

"He didn't say one word in the three months of stumping prior to the first primary about segregation or states' rights.

"He made his livelihood for many years operating an integrated honky-tonk in California, yet now he says he is all for segregation and states' rights." (Davis later denied this story, first publicized by the Rainach people, who were soon to join him. Morrison, however, stuck to it.)

"Just who is he slurring now? Is he criticizing the Catholics of our State, or the Jews, or the Italians, or the Syrian communities scattered throughout Louisiana—or is he complaining about the good Cajuns, like myself, who, all over South Louisiana, saw through his peace and harmony pitch and voted for the Morrison-Bowdon ticket, which, to them, meant industry, progress and prosperity."

Editorials in both New Orleans papers attacked as disingenuous this attempt to twist the accepted Southern meaning of the word "minorities." Herman Deutsch, the dean of New Orleans columnists, said it was one of the things that had disillusioned him with the new Morrison, who had undergone a sinister metamorphosis since the day when the publishers changed their minds about him.

The newspaper with this speech in it brought also word that Jimmy Noe, Uncle Earl's candidate for Governor, had thrown in with the Mayor for the runoff. His long written statement lacked the Tabasco of spoken Louisianian, but it had its points.

"In truth and fact, Jimmie Davis is only a half-citizen of Louisiana, as his long residences in unsegregated California prove," Mr. Noe wrote, as if unsegregation were a contagious itch and Mr. Davis ought to be quarantined and decontaminated before Louisiana was again exposed to him.

What bothered me about the story from Baker, though, was the lead:

"Gubernatorial candidate Chep Morrison claimed last night that Jimmie Davis, his opponent in the second primary, has accepted the endorsement of Governor Earl K. Long.

" 'And don't pay any attention to any denials,' said Morrison. 'I know for a fact that Long has gone with Davis and Davis has embraced him. . . .

" 'It's plain to see that all the discredited, disreputable political machines in the state have gotten together behind Davis in a frantic attempt to keep their hands in the political trough.' " There is no animal that eats out of a trough with its hands, I thought here, irrelevantly—but no matter.

"At the Governor's office in Baton Rouge," the paper interpolated, "a staff member said the Governor had informed him, 'I have not endorsed anyone for Governor in the second primary.' "

There is a shade between "I have not endorsed" and "I have not agreed to endorse" that can save a man from telling a lie.

I was sure that Morrison would not have made the charge while any hope remained of landing Earl.

Bill White, who had run for Lieutenant Governor with Dodd, was now working for Davis. (There is an old Hellenistic proverb: "Two hands in two troughs are better than one hand in one trough.")

I was entertained but not convinced by an Associated Press story describing Earl's detachment in defeat. "Earl K. Long is taking life easy since his disastrous bid for the Democratic nomination as Lieutenant Governor," this one began. "Long is not in seclusion. But few can reach him.

"After the December 5 election, Long spent several days at his Winnfield farm—doing the things he loves most." Here I could picture him with a half acre of past-performance charts spread out before him as he played the races by telephone. "Once he was reported hunting wild hogs, perhaps his only active outdoor sport.

"When in the mood, the Governor and his workers, with horses and dogs, chase down the animals, bring them into pens and put them on a good diet to prepare them for butchering."

Combining direct and circumstantial evidence, I estimated that old Earl must have been signing up with Davis on the afternoon that the *States-Item* published its editorial "Longism Is Dead" and said voters could respect either of the runoff candidates providing he did not get mixed up with Long.

Rainach, meanwhile, kept as mum as Long. Davis continued to say there was no use side-stepping the fact that the NAACP had delivered a bloc vote to Morrison. The Mayor said that if Davis wanted to talk about bloc votes, he should talk about Plaquemines Parish, where District Attorney Leander H. Perez, racist and richest of oilmen, had "evolved a dictatorship that would make Khrushchev look like a piker."

Perez, operating in French Catholic territory, had created a solid Davis enclave in Morrison territory.

The counterattack had no effect. Perez's bloc was not a Negro bloc, although it included Perez's Negro vassals. In the *Times-Picayune*'s eyes, blocs *as* blocs were benign. The only malignant bloc was a bloc for Morrison.

"In Plaquemines, Perez has thrown the U.S. Constitution into the Mississippi River," Morrison said. "If I'm elected, we'll see some daylight and fresh air and freedom come back into Plaquemines."

That kind of talk was like giving Davis a blank check signed by Perez, I reflected regretfully. Morrison was losing his temper.

He lashed out at the gamblers, too, and this, I felt, remembering Blaise's talk of the "ele*ment*," was another mistake in the field of finance. (Forty-one sheriffs out of sixty-four declared for Davis before the runoff election date.)

The last ten days of the campaign saw a classic double envelopment of the Mayor's faction. Rainach gave Davis his official blessing on December 29. It was the extreme faction of the bug-eyed—of whom I shall exhibit a sample before this essay ends—that only Rainach in person could reassure. As the battle loomed increasingly dubious, the value of the prophet's intervention rose. He secured as part of his price the promise of a spot to be created for him in the new administration that would keep him in the public eye for four years.

As a sober Associated Press dispatch on the first page of the *Times-Picayune* had it:

RAINACH BACKS DAVIS FOR POST

> Shreveport, La.—Segregation chief William Rainach ended his long silence Friday and named former Governor Jimmie Davis as his candidate in the January 9 Democratic runoff for Governor.
>
> *The State Senator from Summerfield, head of the Joint Legislative Committee on Segregation, said Davis made a number of commitments on the segregation issue when the two conferred two days ago.*

(Common report also had it that he made a commitment to reimburse the Senator for his first-primary campaign expenses, plus a substantial *pourboire.*)

> Rainach, third man in the December 5 primary, was critical of both Davis and New Orleans Mayor deLesseps Morrison during the campaign. There were reports Rainach might remain neutral during the runoff.
>
> The Rainach statement said Davis, second to Morrison in the first primary, agreed to support creation of a state sovereignty committee to handle states' rights and segregation matters with Rainach as its head.
>
> Rainach's old job as head of the legislative segregation committee would go to Representative John Garrett of Claiborne Parish under the agreement with Davis, the statement said.

Rainach had had to give up his Claiborne senate seat to run for Governor in the first primary. Garrett, as Claiborne member of the house, was presumably a trusty friend.

> All other members of the committee would be reappointed, and Garrett would have the right to fill vacancies. . . .
>
> *The sovereignty commission would work across state lines, Rainach's statement said, to form a Southern coalition to fight the South's cause and conduct a national advertising and public relations program to carry the South's story to the North.*
>
> Camille Gravel of Alexandria, national Democratic committeeman from Louisiana, is Morrison's chief political adviser, Rainach's statement continued. Gravel is "close to Paul Butler, national Demo-

cratic Chairman, *and other Northern* radicals." [*Those* italics are mine.]

Gravel is also "closely tied to the NAACP bloc vote that went unanimously to Morrison," the statement said.

Rainach has been in a Homer hospital since the first primary, in which he polled 143,500 votes.

The segregation prophet's stay in the hospital had been due to depression and exhaustion from overwork, the same kind of thing that hospitalized Earl in the spring that now seemed ages ago. The newspapers did not suggest that he was crazy.

The Shreveport *Times*, up in Caddo Parish, at the northern edge of the state, where Rainach had whipped Davis in the first primary, published the speech of absolution in full, four columns of close-set type. Here are a few paragraphs:

"I don't think there is anyone running for Governor among the entire eleven—or anyone else in the State of Louisiana—who would take as strong a stand as I would take, but I do believe Jimmie Davis would take the next strongest stand in the State of Louisiana.

"I know there have been a lot of rumors about Jimmie Davis practicing integration in an integrated nightclub in California. [His own organization had put them about.] We had a detective agency to check Jimmie Davis for our own satisfaction to see whether or not this was true.

"We had other reports from California running down rumors about photographs [dancing with Lena Horne] and so forth out there. And in all those reports we never found that matters were as they had been reported.

"All of you saw a clipping—an ad that was run in the Shreveport *Journal* showing how Mayor Morrison got the NAACP bloc vote in New Orleans and Baton Rouge and other places in the state. It is listed by ward and precincts. It is unquestioned that he got the NAACP bloc vote in the first primary on December 5.

"On the other hand, Governor Davis has disowned the NAACP bloc vote in the State of Louisiana. He says he does not want it. He'll get elected Governor of the State of Louisiana without it.

"He also agreed to use interposition to interpose the sovereignty of the State of Louisiana, the police power of this state, to protect the people of this state from Federal oppression. He also told me that he will go to jail if necessary to protect the people of Louisiana from Federal oppression....

"I am in a better position than others to judge the background of the candidates for Governor of Louisiana. I want to urge everyone to get out and get to the polls on January 9 to politic their neighbors for the Jimmie Davis ticket...."

As to poor Morrison, Rainach said, "He has given ground to the NAACP in Federal courts in every instance of the City of New Orleans."

In White League Citizens' Council language, an official obeying a court order obeys not the court or the Government of the United States, but the power *behind* the Government. This is of course the National Association for the Advancement of Colored People, an organ of the Soviet Union.

"He has denied that they have integration in the City of New Orleans. But I have here a clipping from the Shreveport *Times*—the same appeared in the *Times-Picayune*—dated December 22, 1958, where they ended segregation in the New Orleans City Park and swimming pools and various and sundry other facilities in New Orleans City Park. . . .

"Mayor Morrison has also integrated the police force of the City of New Orleans—contemplating integrating the fireman force of the City of New Orleans."

There was nothing much Morrison could do about that, I knew. A man who let colored and white people walk in the same park was beyond political redemption in northern Louisiana, and to put Negroes on a force that Negroes paid taxes to support was the most inequitable proposition I could contemplate. (Headline: "Davis Welcomes Rainach Stand—Hails Success in Uniting Segregation Forces.")

The Governor ended *his* long silence a week later:

DAVIS GETS HIS VOTE, SAYS LONG

"Governor Earl K. Long Tuesday ended a month-long silence after his political defeat and said he will vote for former Governor Jimmie Davis in the Democratic runoff for Governor.

"The 64-year-old Long, looking rested and healthy, said he cast an advance absentee ballot for Davis Monday while in Winnfield, his home town." (Until he joined Davis, newspapers had invariably reported Earl looked gaunt, sick or fatigued.)

" 'The reason I'm voting for Mr. Davis,' " Long emphasized, " 'is that I think Mr. Davis is a kind man, a tolerant man, a Christian man, and I've always found him truthful—that means more to me than anything else.' " (Forgotten: "Davis loves money like a hog loves slop.")

" 'I don't believe Mr. Davis has any rancor or hatred toward any group —Italians, French, colored or anyone.'

"If he thought Davis would try to punish Catholics, Negroes, or anyone, Long said, 'I wouldn't vote for him.'

"In a suddenly announced press conference, Long said, 'It looks like the trend is for Davis. It looks like Davis has gained more in the last few days.' "

Then, like a practiced barroom fighter, he said the man he slugged had swung at him but missed.

"He called the news session, Long said, because Morrison, an old foe, 'has been saying I've been calling up people night and day and asking them to vote for Davis.'

" 'I've called a few friends, Mr. Morrison would be surprised how few.'

"Long avoided the terms 'endorsement' or 'support' in mentioning his vote for Davis.

"The Governor stressed that Davis didn't solicit his vote. He said he offered it immediately after the first primary. 'And I didn't ask Davis for as much as a soda cracker.' "

If Earl had indeed promised his "vote" to Davis before going up to Baton Rouge that Sunday, he had certainly fooled Gravel and his younger colleague in the afternoon. They came away thinking they had him half hooked.

I inclined to think he had not committed himself finally until the next day, after weighing both bids and giving the Davis people a chance to top the Morrison offer. Afterward I heard that he had been on the point of going on the stump for Morrison because he was so angry at Jim Comiskey and the Old Regulars for having let him down, but that he had telephoned to his estranged wife for counsel and she had talked him out of it. Morrison and his late wife, with their snooty city ways, had said things to rile Miz Blanche in previous campaigns, and she hadn't Earl's thick hide. Neither had Morrison, for that matter; he had never forgiven Earl for calling him "Dellasoups," and the old boy may have sensed it. Davis, Earl probably felt, was a fellow he could handle when the time came. Sunshine Jimmie had no personal organization like Morrison's Crescent City Democratic club.

"Oil has da best of both woilds," an old associate said enviously when he saw the statement. "If elected, he gets office, and defeated he gets money." But this was merely an informed guess.

As to why Earl came in on the same side as "that little pinheaded nut, Willie Rainach," and the other grass-eaters, he would have answered that if he stayed neutral, Davis would probably win anyway. Then Perez and Rainach would have full control of his policy. If Earl came in, he might speak for sweet reason.

After all, the *Times-Picayune* was in there with Earl Long, and the gamblers, Comiskey, and the race cranks. It was like what he had once called a "Biblical proposition." Who was he to be more saintly than the *Times-Picayune*?

14 / Who's Crazy Now?

I READ ABOUT the second rupture of silence, Earl's, the day before I returned to New Orleans to watch the final heat. The trip was becoming a habit. There was the same departure out of the overheated cattle shed at

La Guardia, with the abutting fellow passengers' hand luggage jammed into kidney and groin, the same toothpaste-ad-smile welcome aboard the brand of jet that falls apart with cheery regularity when I am not flying, and the same dreadful airplane meal. I had, as always, a bundle of *Times-Picayunes* and Shreveport *Times*es to read on the way down—my homework.

Morrison was in there battling, as if "Invictus" were *his* house song instead of the Longs'. He had women's Morrison broom brigades organized among the Junior Leaguers to sweep corruption out of office, and schemes for multiplying oysters and breeding muskrats and building roads where they were needed in whatever part of the state he found himself campaigning. He had been saying all along that Earl and Davis were in cahoots—a Davis administration would be "an Earl Long deal with a Davis front." In another art this is called riding a punch—getting in on it before it picks up snap.

"At Franklinton," a story of one Morrison meeting said, "Morrison displayed Jimmie Davis Song Books, in which he said were songs too filthy to quote in public. He said the chorus from a reported Davis song called 'Sewing Machine Blues' reads:

"'I'm going to telephone Heaven to send me an angel down,
But if they don't have any angels,
Then send me a high-stepping brown.'"

Now that Earl had broken silence, Chep said, the opposition was "caught red-handed in another lie—I have said it before and I repeat it again—all Earl Long needs is a weak-kneed, part-time Governor like Davis for him to continue running the state as he has for the past four years."

Instead of old Earl's "Biblical proposition" he called the consortium a jambalaya, a kind of Louisiana stew with everything in it but the kitchen stove: "We ask, isn't this a fine jambalaya, with Earl Long, the *Times-Picayune*, Leander Perez, the Shreveport *Times*, the Old Regulars, all together in one pot?"

But the odds appeared too great. He was like a man with a high pair on the deal who fails to draw, while the Davis combination had landed that third deuce. Davis had had 25 per cent of the vote on the first primary, and added to it was Rainach's 17 per cent—the segregation bit had done the trick. In Southern professional politics, it is known as "the black ace off the bottom of the deck." That gave him an edge over Morrison's 33 per cent of the first vote. Earl had certainly canceled out any influence Dodd and Noe may have had over the old Longites—that segment of the central and northern Louisiana rural mass that had learned under Huey to vote for its own stomach, without any flummery about the Southern way of life. Most Longites, with the encouragement of the hereditary Lama, would treat themselves this time to the luxury of a vote for prejudice. Dodd and Noe between them had drawn 21 per cent of the vote, and at least three quarters of that, I imagined, would now go to Davis.

When I arrived in New Orleans, I learned that to bet on Morrison you could get seven to five, but if you wanted Davis you had to lay eight to five. A bellboy at the quondam Hotel St. Charles said that things ought to pick up a bit, soon; with Davis in, the gaudy gambling halls in Jefferson Parish, just across the river, would be jumping again. Jefferson Parish proliferates with small places, but these, having a sordid aspect suggestive of chicanery, have little appeal for hotel guests. The big places needed a guaranteed immunity from state police interference to justify their high overhead. I have been for several years a satisfied subscriber to the Las Vegas, Nevada, *Sun*, and I knew the bellboy's view was shared out there.

Paul McIlheny, a faithful Morrison man I met in the hotel lobby, said he was going down to Iberia Parish, where he lives, to vote and shoot a deer on Saturday and would not come back to New Orleans to listen to election returns in Morrison headquarters.

Next morning I called a Louisiana elder statesman, and he said, "Chep has run rings around Davis in the campaign, but the logistics are against him. In the first primary, it was one city Catholic boy against four Protestant country boys. Now there's just one of them. It's a shame."

Morrison, I read in the paper, was still full of fight.

He said: "The most shocking fact of the campaign is that the newspapers who have almost universally stood for what is right and proper have thrown their arms around the combination of Davis and Long."

For the hell of it I telephoned John F. Tims, president of the *Times-Picayune* Company, to ask him why they had dumped Morrison, but Mr. Tims, while courteous, sounded testy. (He did not ask me to run around to his office and share a jambalaya.) He said they just liked Davis better. Morrison, he admitted, had "made a reasonably good Mayor." I could have asked a number of rhetorical questions, but they would have come under the head of twitting, so I said goodbye.

It was clear that Tims was not afraid of lining Louisiana up with the grass-eating states like Mississippi, nor ashamed of Rainach and Comiskey, so long as the *Times-Picayune* could say it had elected a governor. There was still less use asking him if it didn't feel silly to take a swing at Earl and wind up with Earl in his whiskers. He bought the shoes to fit hisself.

It was the result of the primary election that was to steel the Negro college students' hearts for the April demonstrations in New Orleans and Baton Rouge. They knew by then that gradualism was no good.

I dressed and went down to breakfast, regretting, as I walked the worn old zodiac carpet, that after the election I might not have a reasonable excuse to return to New Orleans for a long time. I could not think of anything more useful to do that afternoon than to go to the races at the Fair Grounds.

But Tom, who is a more thorough reporter than I, joined me in the coffee room and said there was something I must see before I left, in order to understand what I meant to write about: a white-on-white, like a gambler's shirt, bleached-in-the-bone, like a dead camel, segregationist of superior social standing. (It is an affront to speak of a "dyed-in-the-wool" segregationist, because "wool" suggests African origin.)

Tom is obsessed with the South, and particularly with his littoral, where he was born. He went North once, in about 1940, as a Nieman fellow at Harvard and became an editor of *The New Republic*, but New Orleans drew him back before he could get it in perspective.

It is one more city of the Graecia Maxima that rims the Mediterranean, and the professionally reputable New Orleans surgeon he took me to see was the counterpart of the anti-Semitic doctor I had visited in Oran in 1942. Both were white-haired and clean and suggested dowagers; both were amiably amused at their visitors' "ignorance" of "basic truths" about history (and ethnology, sociology, economics) although withholding blame, because a world conspiracy of educators worked against truth.

Both had an inverted understanding of all these subjects, like a Mennonite's of geography or an astrologer's of causation. They were initiates, objective and without rancor. The man in Oran said he rather liked Jews, personally, although it was a taste that, regrettably, few others shared, since ritual murder, a well-attested practice, put people off, as did Jews' lascivious character and general complicity in a world conspiracy of bankers and Bolshevists. My New Orleans surgeon said that *he* liked Negroes, or at least the good old ones he had known in Clinton, Louisiana, when he was a boy, who took in good part the Divine limitation of their intelligence.

"Allow me to read you a line or two from this book that illustrates," he said, pulling from a stack a foot high a copy of a pamphlet that he later gave me: "God Laughs at the Race-Mixers, 101 best jokes on Mixiecrats versus Dixiecrats," compiled by Rev. Carey Daniel, Pastor, First Baptist Church of West Dallas, Southern Baptist Convention.

" 'We usually quit calling White men "boys" when they have passed their twenty-first birthday. But it is not at all uncommon to hear someone say, "Hey, boy," when addressing some mature black man who may be up in his fifties or sixties. Mentally he is still an adolescent, and he doesn't feel the least bit offended by that implication—unless, of course, some white agitator has "done been talking to him." ' "

The doctor put the pamphlet down and folded his soft white hands over the gently rounded surgical smock. He leaned back in his swivel chair. "Good, isn't it?" he said. He picked up his Golden Treasury again and read another delightful spoof:

" 'A good old-fashioned coal-black Negro has summed it up in a nutshell: "It sho do look like some of them there *Negroes* is gonna get us niggers into a heap o' trouble." ' "

Having finished with the *amuse-gueules*, the doctor rubbed a hand over his profile—like a white-haired Robert Morley's—and then shoved the pamphlet over to me as a gift, to which he added others called "God the Original Segregationist," by the same Rev. Carey Daniel (who is the brother of the Governor of Texas), and "Which Way the Nation, Which Way the South?" an address by the Rev. James P. Dees, Statesville, North Carolina, to the Citizens' Council of Greater New Orleans.

I still read them from time to time, whenever news from South Africa puzzles me.

"To revert to seriousness," the doctor said. "There are well-meaning people who object to the Supreme Court's interpretation of the Fourteenth Amendment, both as to voting rights and the Black Monday integration decision. The essential fact is that the Fourteenth Amendment does not exist. It was never legally enacted. *That* is the point that has never been debated before the Supreme Court yet—and when it *is*, the whole structure of tyranny imposed upon the South is going to fall, like a house of cards. The Fourteenth Amendment was imposed on the United States by one mulatto woman—Lydia Smith, the mistress of Thaddeus Stevens. To please her, Stevens forced it upon the prostrate body of the disfranchised South. *It was never legally ratified.*

"The so-called Legislature of the Southern States that under pressure ratified the three Reconstruction amendments did not represent the white people of the South. Let me clarify." And pulling out another pamphlet from the inexhaustible pile, he read, pausing frequently to wet his lips:

" 'Lying in separate graveyards in Lancaster, Pennsylvania, are the bones of Thaddeus Stevens and his mulatto mistress of many years, Lydia Smith.'

"You see what kind of fella brought us into this situation," the doctor said jovially. "A hundred per cent integrationist." He resumed reading:

" 'Thin white bones they are now, deceptively still, as inert, apparently, as the dust to which they are returning. Yet out of those graves there seeps to this day the vapor of a hatred so intense that it has lived to curse our nation for nearly a hundred years.'

"Lydia started it all," the doctor said. "I'll be glad to give you the book, to peruse at your leisure. Now I'll just skip to the end, to give you the essence of it."

He read again:

" 'The conspirators'—that's Thad and Lydia—'realized that a Constitutional Amendment would be necessary to supersede States' Rights and override forever the objection of either individuals or State Legislatures. Stevens admitted to Lydia that because of the manner of its adoption, the Fourteenth would not be constitutional, and it is recorded that he admitted as much to several Senators as cynical as himself.'

"And they got away with it," the doctor said. "I'll just leave you with the author's conclusion and then let you have the book:

" 'On July 28th, 1869, when the sticky Washington summer was at its height, the Fourteenth Amendment, bastard child of Lydia and Stevens, became the law of the land.

" 'At that moment Stevens' mind blacked out forever. He knew he had revenged his Lydia. Life smoldered fitfully within his frame for two weeks longer, but consciousness was gone. He had died in the full knowledge that his curse upon the South could spread like a black stain until it engulfed the entire country. . . .

" 'In view of the evidence gathered from history, we submit that in no single way can the Fourteenth be regarded as constitutional. Pull down the Fourteenth, even as Samson split open the supporting pillars, and the whole structure of intolerable laws, based upon it'—He has laws in parentheses," the doctor said, with a chuckle—" 'will dissolve into the dust.' " He put the pamphlet down and looked at me with friendly superiority.

"You're supposed to be an educated man," he said, "and I'll wager you never knew that before."

I confessed I hadn't, and that it put the matter in an entirely new light for me. I had always thought of the Fourteenth as a defense of liberties rather than a violation: "No State shall make or enforce any law which shall abridge the privileges or immunities of citizens of the United States . . ." and the rest of it.

"But to be realistic," I said, "do you think there's a chance that in any near future you could get Congress and three quarters of the states to repeal it? And what can you do in the meanwhile?"

The doctor said that one thing Jimmie Davis could do, if the United States Court ordered the New Orleans School Board to open the way to race mixing by admitting a Negro to a white school, was to enjoin the School Board from complying. A peculiarity of the cult is that they all believe Negroes sexually irresistible. "He could put the Board members in jail, if they didn't comply with his injunction," the doctor said. "He has promised to do that, if the occasion arises, even if he has to go to Federal prison himself."

That night, another segregationist, a Mr. Emil Wagner, speaking from a New Orleans television station, made the same promise, in the candidate's name. Governor Davis had assured him he would go to jail for the Cause, if necessary, Wagner said.

I added the historical pamphlet—Lydia Smith and the Fourteenth Amendment—to the bundle and thanked the good physician, who said it was nothing at all, he was always glad to help a Northerner understand the South.

"You can't always believe what you read in the press," he said with a chuckle. "Did you know that after the War Between the States, when the Yankee newspapers were trying to stir up hard feelings about the Ku Klux

Klan, Yankee correspondents used to come down here and dress up in white sheets and go out and kill niggers to stir up excitement? It's all in that book. Now don't you go killing any. Ha, ha."

When we got outside and I saw the palm trees in the front yards, I said to Sancton that it was all just like Oran, but he said the resemblance was superficial.

I said we weren't going to waste the morrow in any such fashion as we had today. Come hell or high water, we would go out to the races. That evening by luck we met Glen Douthitt, one of Morrison's staff, outside Kolb's German restaurant on St. Charles Avenue, and when we said we were going racing he gave us two seats in the Mayor's box, which is one away from the Governor's over the finish line. In Kolb's they serve planked redfish steak, snapping-turtle fricassee, jambalaya and gumbo, as well as pig's knuckles and wursts, so that their diapason is wider than a German restaurant's in less favored regions. The cuisine has undergone a sea change, like that Alsatian joint's in Tunis.

Kolb's is noisy and as full of politicians as rye bread of caraway seeds. At dinner, Tom and I met another elder statesman, who said there had been only one true thing said in the whole campaign: "And that was when Chep Morrison said he would do anything to win. But he took it back."

Next morning I awoke cheerful, because I was going racing. The *Times-Picayune*'s front page reflected a lip-licking calm. Davis predicted a victory by from 75,000 to 150,000 in the state. A Mr. Wogan, Morrison's campaign manager in New Orleans, predicted Morrison would win by 115,000 in the city and then sweep on to take upstate again, but this was obviously a dream—there were only 200,000 voters registered, and positing a 90 per cent vote, which was high, the Mayor would have to beat Davis *and* the RDO by a margin of 5 to 1, to live up to Wogan.

In the event, Morrison beat Davis by 33,000 votes in New Orleans, 103,000 to 70,000. This was a fairly notable performance. In 1956, against Earl Long, who, like Davis, had the aid of the Regular Democratic Organization, Morrison had had the dithyrambic endorsement of the *Times-Picayune and* the then breathing *Item*, and even with the newspapers dancing before him like priests of Adonis had won by only 2,000 votes. With the *Times-Picayune*'s aid, or even neutrality, this time—if it be supposed that a monopoly newspaper influences even 10 per cent of its captive audience—Morrison would have beaten Davis in the city by 120,000 votes to 53,000.

As I lay abed in the old St. Charles, in the sunlight of a cold, clear day, I could not help ruminating, with the delight of the contemplative, on how many changes in the sand-whirl politics of the westernmost Arab state I had witnessed since I had arrived, in late summer, to report on Earl Long's madness. Nobody talked of that any more, least of all the doctors who had predicted his instant disintegration. I remembered with pleasure a report I had read in the *Times-Picayune* of a manifesto put out by some psychiatrists in North Carolina, protesting because old Earl had fired the doctors who said he was crazy and replaced them by doctors who said he wasn't. Doctors, like publishers, detest insubordination.

(My own amateur diagnosis had been that all he needed to calm him down was a square meal of fried steak, grits, busters, pompano, guinea hen, country ham and watermelon, and a case of 10-cent beer, and then perhaps twenty-four hours to digest it.)

When I arrived, Earl, with only Jim Comiskey and the Old Regulars to help him, had been the betting favorite for Governor. Lined up against him had been Morrison the reformer, Rainach the grass-eater, and Peace-and-Harmony Davis, with the *Times-Picayune* assumed to be for Morrison because of its pious past.

Subverting Comiskey, the rest had ganged up on Long, and then, when he was out of the way, all but Morrison had ganged up on Morrison. Lastly they had had to invite the Imam in again, and now all were dancing in a ring, old Earl holding hands in turn with Comiskey, who had held his hand before, with the *Times-Picayune*, the enemy of the Longs and Comiskey forever, with Willie Rainach, who had been his opponent in debate when the Governor blew his top defending Negro rights, and with Davis, the easiest of all for Earl to understand.

The *Times-Picayune*, which had always been with Morrison against Long, was now with Long against Morrison. It was like that other oil region where at lunch time Nasser was with Ibn Saud against Hussein, and at cocktail time Hussein was with Ibn Saud against Nasser. And, like those other Arabs, these were good at their own style of street fighting. When I came down to the street, I bought an early edition of the *States-Item* that carried a glaring front-page story:

NAB ARMED DEPUTY AT POLLS

which began:

> A Negro deputy sheriff serving as a poll watcher was arrested this morning and booked with carrying a concealed weapon.
>
> Felix McElroy, Sr., an official watcher for gubernatorial candidate Mayor Chep Morrison, was arrested shortly after 7 A.M. at the polling place of the 15th precinct of the Twelfth Ward, 2600 Peniston.
>
> Frank Manning, chief investigator for the Attorney General's office and a supporter of former Governor Jimmie Davis for Governor, made the arrest.
>
> *Gun, Blackjack*
>
> Manning charged McElroy, wearing a gun and carrying a blackjack in his hip pocket, was "walking around polls in a manner which

> was intimidating to voters." *McElroy was wearing a Morrison lapel badge.* [my italics]
>
> Manning disarmed McElroy and turned him over to Police Sgt. Jules Michel, who booked the deputy at Second District.
>
> Michel said McElroy *was not intimidating voters or threatening them* [mine again], but was carrying a sidearm and blackjack partially visible under his jacket. . . .
>
> McElroy was booked at 8 A.M. and paroled by Criminal District Judge Shirley G. Wimberley at 8.50 A.M.

The story of the armed Negro with the Morrison badge intimidating voters although the cop said he wasn't was a neat clincher to the Morrison-nigger axis stories put out throughout the campaign. The "investigator" who made the arrest was a Davis worker. The story disappeared inside the newspaper after the polls closed at 7 P.M., when it lost its news importance.

By that time Tom and I were back from the races and thinking of dinner, and when we had finished that, toward ten, word was already around town that the favorite was in.

In the first primary the Davis people had waited in vain for the count from upcountry to wipe out the Morrison lead. This time, though, the ratio of the Davis lead in the early returns from upstate to the Morrison majorities in New Orleans and the southern parishes pointed an ineluctable finger.

"Looks as if the town will open up, man," the lean old news vendor who sold me an early *Times-Picayune* at Royal and Canal said brightly. (Out in Las Vegas, the *Sun* headlines said: "Election of Davis Big Victory for Gamblers—New Governor Promises 'Normalcy' in Louisiana.") That was fine with me; I like roulette in a clean, well-lighted place.

"Within four years, Rainach be Governor," I heard a cab driver with a redneck accent say to the talker in front of a strip-tease bar.

We walked about the old town, getting the results piecemeal on radios in different bars. It wasn't a great victory, but the consortium candidate ate into Morrison's early lead steadily.

When Davis went ahead, we were in a new place Pete Herman had opened on Bourbon Street. Pete wasn't at ease in the new place because he couldn't remember his way around. Watching him in the old one, where he had been for thirty-five years, you would have trouble telling he was blind. (He has gone back since, and he's all right.) Pete had no radio going in his joint because the sound would have clashed with the strip-tease music. So he got the returns by telephone; I don't know who was at the other end, but they kept coming.

Pete would put down the phone and say, "Morrison only leading by eight thousand now," and next time, "Davis is still coming on," as if it were a fight. He could tell by the music what stripper was on the stage, and he would say, "That's a sweet kid," or "She got quite a novelty there." Sometimes there would be a busload of tourists in the joint, and sometimes the three of us would be sitting alone.

The strippers went right on, even when there was no one there. He talked about infighting, his great art, but he made it sound simple, as if Daumier had said to you, "All there is to it is drawing." "All you want," Pete said, "is get that left hand under your arm, and keep hitting. You don't want to hold, do you? What good does that do you? Keep hitting."

The bull shoulders twitched with a remembered pleasure.

The phone clicked, and he picked it up again. When he put it down he said, "Davis goes ahead three thousand."

We walked over to Morrison headquarters as we had on the first primary night a month earlier. Symptomatically, even the locus had changed. The Morrison people had lost their lucky election-night suite at the Sheraton-Charles, because it had been reserved months earlier for some convention. They were at the Jung, a less famous hotel, on Canal Street, and when we got there hope had already fled.

Some of the women workers were in tears. There were only petits-fours and empty bottles left on the buffets. Television operatives were all over the place, and there were a couple of depressed reporters. Reporters usually root against their employers, and they are distressed when their paper has a winner. With nearly all the state's precincts in, Davis had it by 70,000 votes—about 480,000 to 410,000.

The television people were waiting for the Mayor to concede, a gruesome ritual of the profession in which the loser is led before the cameras like the leading character in a lynching. And, like the prospective lynchee, he is expected to show spunk. The Mayor did, thanking all the people who had worked for him and pretending that he did not feel terrible.

One of the politicos told me that Earl Long had already been on the phone to Camille Gravel, bragging on having pulled Davis through. He claimed all the credit. He said Davis had been well licked when he pitched in and saved him. Morrison had carried Jefferson, the dormitory parish across the river, where the householders were not as happy as the parish officials about the return of big gambling. He had run well in southern, Hellenistic, littoral Louisiana, with the exception of Plaquemines, where Perez, holding his votes until he saw how many would be needed, had checked in late with a three-to-one majority for Davis. (If the contest had still looked close, the boss might have bettered that.) But the north, the region in which only Earl could have cut into the Davis vote, had gone completely, lopsidedly Protestant country boy–White League.

"What Morrison needed," the politico added, alluding to the Davis songbook, "was 35,000 less Baptists in the state and 35,000 more high-stepping browns."

As for Uncle Earl, in whose welfare I had begun to take a deep interest in the days when I first realized that he was the only effective Civil Rights man in the South, he was doing fine when I last saw him.

Out at the Fair Grounds that afternoon, I had lost three straight ten-dollar bets sitting in the box that poor Morrison was too worried about other matters to be in, when, happening to turn to my right, I saw a wide, healthy, sun-reddened hog-hunter's face grinning at me from under a wide, parsnip-colored hat.

It was the fine Governor, and would be until his term ended in May, of the Great State of Louisiana. His work was done, and he had nothing to worry about—it wasn't his election. A commissionaire had just brought him a couple of fresh handfuls of hundred-dollar bills. The system he had declined to tell me about was evidently working, and he appeared to be up to the weight he had been before he started dieting and got into all that trouble.

Later I was to read a speech he made at the State Labor Convention in which he said, "Don't you sell old Uncle Earl short—there's a lot of good reading in old books."

As he stuffed all that money in his pocket, another stout, jolly, ruddy man, also a winner, strolled over to his box and leaned over the edge, and they had a good laugh together. It was Jimmy Noe, who had endorsed Morrison, and the two companions of the Prophet looked as happy and well-attuned as Laurel and Hardy, except they looked more like two W. C. Fieldses.

I hate to bother a man about Louisiana politics when he is engaged in a serious occupation like handicapping, so I just waved to him. Earl looked to me like one of the sanest horseplayers I have seen in years. I once knew a psychiatrist who played "best bets" supplied him by three nationally advertised touts every day and hardly ever collected a dime.

15/ *The Last Race*

IF THE RACE meeting at the Fair Grounds had not ended, as it always does, in early spring, Earl Long might be with us today. Continuing in the salubrious pursuit of overlays and sleepers, he would have stoked the glow of health in his cheeks by day and relaxed his arteries in the company of squirmers in the evening. A squirmer is a strip-teaser who, having exhausted the possibilities of the vertical, exercises her art horizontally, recumbent on a chaise longue above the back bar with its array of spuriously labeled liquor bottles. Prone, she produces alternate clockwise and counterclockwise ventral vibrations, synchronized with opposed mammary rotations and what she conceives to be a facial reflection of extreme passion. With her legs, meanwhile, she performs a calisthenic of easily penetrable symbolism.

Between squirms, as presented in New Orleans, there are long intervals designed to induce the customers to leave, making place for newcomers who will pay the minimum cover charge of two and a half dollars for a drink. Nobody in his right mind ever takes a second. During the intervals the girls have time for long abstract conversations with their friends. The fine Governor, a lively lame duck, enjoyed these dialogues. They took his mind off politics. He averred that his interest in the squirmers was strictly avuncular.

Under Louisiana law he had four months in which to get his things together before leaving the State House. The theory behind the hiatus is either that a Governor of Louisiana must have accumulated during his term of office at least twice as much loot as a President of the United States, who has only two months in which to clear out after *his* successor's election, or that he must be twice as tired. This should have been a period of continued recuperation for Earl. His system had been subjected to a strain that would have mashed a Marciano to the ground.

To have been forcibly dislodged from the executive mansion, like a limpet from an oyster shell, and then to have waked in a madhouse, ticketed insane, is about as near nightmare as a man in his senses can come. The long struggle back to freedom must have taken a lot more out of him, and he had followed that with six months of uninterrupted campaigning, of the sort I had witnessed in Alexandria in the summer of 1959. Each of us has a threshold of endurance, and his was much higher than most men's. But there are limits.

The closing of the horse track interrupted the healthy regime, and he began to think of politics again. Some men carry in the backs of their minds the names of books they mean to read when they have time. Earl carried grudges to get around to. In 1958 his elder brother George, an ex-dentist, had been Congressman from the Eighth District of Louisiana, which includes Winnfield. The dentist died, and the fine Governor supported an old friend and campaign contributor, a man named Teekell, for nomination-election to fill the vacancy. He considered the nomination within the family gift. But the Eighth also includes Alexandria, and a man named Harold B. McSween out of there beat Teekell in the primary. Behind McSween was Camille Gravel, up to that moment a trusted Long man. That was when Long and Gravel split.

Now, free of office, Uncle Earl determined to get even with Representative McSween and, through him, get evener with Gravel, whom he had already hurt through Morrison. He entered the 1960 congressional primary in the Eighth District. (Congressional primaries are not held at the same time with gubernatorial primaries in Louisiana, even when they fall in the same year. Politicians in the Great State believe in staggering their pleasures so there will be no closed seasons.) In the first primary, with a mixed bag of candidates, McSween topped the list by a couple of thousand votes, with Uncle Earl a good second. The two candidates then made their customary deals with the losers and them that had voted for them. At this kind of retail dickering Earl was a master.

It was a mastery particularly helpful on the scale of a congressional election. The second primary was set for August 27. I had a letter from Margaret Dixon dated August 22 that said Earl was "running up a storm" and likely to be elected. I was in Rome for the Olympic Games, and would have thought the weather there hot if I hadn't experienced Louisiana in the previous summer. But I could imagine the old man speaking from a truck at the crossroads in the villages with funny names: "I'm the best friend the poor white man, and the middle-class white man, and the rich white man, so long he behave himself, and the poor colored man, ever had." Probably six or eight speeches a day, and six or eight bottles of Coca-Cola used as ice cologne.

He beat McSween in the runoff by about 4,000 votes. That ended a tumultuous fifteen months beginning with his own exportation to the nuthouse.

Earl went into a hospital at Alexandria on the night after his victory, complaining that he had eaten a piece of bad pork at a barbecue. In fact, he had had a heart attack the night before the primary election, but would not admit it because it might have deterred people from voting for him. It reminded me of Pete Herman not letting Midget Smith know he was blind. Instead of going to the hospital when he had the attack, Earl had spent the primary day gasping with pain on his bed in the Hotel Bentley, that monument to municipal over-optimism where we all had spent the night after his 1959 speech in the courthouse square. He didn't allow himself to be taken to the hospital until after the polls had closed and the news couldn't hurt his chances.

Earl would have been a great addition to Congress, where nobody of his stature has sat since John Quincy Adams and John Morrissey, but he shifted the field of his activities in another direction. On September 5 he died.

A man he had staying with him for company at the hospital, one of the succession of driver-handyman confidants Earl always had about him, said, "He just drank a cup of coffee and went."

Like Hannibal, who lives in history only through the accounts of his enemies, Uncle Earl had to depend on a hostile press to write his obit. But the *Times-Picayune* and its afternoon caudal appendage and the press associations did him proud. Most reporters had liked Earl, and even those who didn't had the pride in him that a groom has in being associated with a "big horse." Their feelings showed in their stories, now that they were too late to do him any good.

Robert Wagner in the *Times-Picayune* implicitly recognized Earl's status as an Imam when he recorded that followers "greeted his death almost with disbelief."

"With single-minded tenacity, Long ran for Congress, despite warnings that he couldn't win. . . .

"He out-campaigned McSween, used hillbilly singing, free groceries, hams and watermelons to lure out the voters. But the rigors of the campaign were apparently too much for the seemingly indestructible Long. . . .

"Some Longites felt he had been more resigned to 'meeting my Maker' after vindicating himself, in his own mind, by defeating McSween."

Camille Gravel, quoted by the Associated Press, said the death "closes the amazing career of the most aggressive, determined and resourceful man of politics ever known to Louisiana and perhaps in any other state. I regret his passing."

Theo Cangelosi, the L.S.U. supervisor Long had called a special session of the Legislature to get rid of, said, "Earl possessed more raw courage and determination than any man I ever knew or read about." And he said Earl had a stronger personality than Huey. He said that when Huey wanted to resign during the impeachment fight, long ago, Earl made him stay in there and fight it out.

James McLean of the A.P., who covered the fine Governor for a long time, said, "Earl just didn't organize, and the reason was, said politicians who obeyed him, he never believed in letting two fellows in the camp know the same thing at the same time.

" 'He was psychic,' insisted Ed Coco of Marksville, one-time state director of registration and staunch Long colleague. He played a harmonica for campaign crowds in Long's recent Congressional fight. . . .

"In Coco's words, 'Earl was closer to the ordinary people than Huey. Earl really knew the poor people, the little people. He'd go back in the woods to shake hands with them, white or Negro.'

"If Long had reached the Congress, Coco said, 'he'd have exposed a lot of secrets. He believed in breaking up political nests. He just loved to do it.' "

A State Senator called Rayburn told McLean: "Long was a jovial kind of fellow, for us who knew him, with a heart bigger than most people will ever know. Long could have been selfish in some of his motives, but he would go out of his way to help a person in need. And he was a man not afraid of anything."

"David Bell, a 47-year-old cousin, . . . said, 'Earl always was a head-and-head politician. Give him 20 minutes with a local leader and he could almost sell any idea. Huey appealed through oratory and organization. . . .

" 'Earl must have died happy,' Bell insisted, 'because he died after doing what he loved best—politicking.'

"Dr. Felton Clark, president of Southern University, the largest land-grant Negro University in the South, said the three-time Governor, 'within the framework of his political outlook and philosophy, showed an active sympathy for the education of Negro people.

" 'He did so in big and little things, and with blunt, sudden speed,' the university president said. . . .

"The tale is told how a disgruntled supporter said he would look for Long with a .38-calibre pistol.

"Long, hearing this, so it is told, roared, 'Mr. Smith and Wesson makes them .38's all the same size.' . . .

"The stories about Long are endless."

Editorially the two kernels in the Tims peanut were less affectionate, but they had the tone I would expect of Billy Graham if he heard a reliable report of the demise of the Devil. They had nothing left to oppose except the Supreme Court of the United States.

Hardly had Earl's head fallen back upon the pillow when the onset of the mourners began, led by Miz Blanche, his widow, who said they had made up before he died, and United States Senator Russell B. Long, his nephew. Involuntarily, I remembered the fine Governor at Baton Rouge: "But the plane flew on to Gal*ves*ton, and my sweet little wife hasn't showed up yet, neither my little nephew."

But it was a moment of general forgiveness. Representative Herbert B. McSween, whom Earl had just beaten out of his seat, was quoted saying, "His death, coming as it did, is a terrible shock to the district."

Earl's lying in state at Baton Rouge, whither he had been transported from Alexandria for the last time, with the state troopers' sirens blaring in front of him as always as the cortege clipped along at fifty miles an hour, was incessantly interrupted by the necessity of changing the blankets of flowers over his casket. Friends and ex-enemies had sent them by the gross, and whoever it was that ran the funeral felt they should all have a showing. He started under a blanket of white chrysanthemums sent by Huey's widow, who was in Colorado, and finished under white and violet orchids presented by some millionaire Longites who fell into temporary misfortune in the post-Huey scandals of 1940.

"The quantity of flowers, which had been meager early in the day, had mushroomed into a garden of flowers later in the evening," Wagner wrote.

All day long viewers passed the coffin at the rate of ten a minute—most of them, but not all, Long people like the taxi driver I had talked to in Baton Rouge and the old man in the crowd on the courthouse lawn. The *Times-Picayune* reported, "An unexpected visitor was Blaze Starr, showgirl friend of Long." (I expect Long would have expected her, though; she had been on his side when a lot of the political mourners weren't.) "She arrived with a sister, Debbie, and two friends, Jose Martinez, manager of the Bourbon St. 'Sho-Bar,' and Polly Kavanaugh, worker at the bar."

The *Times-Picayune* I saw printed a poem by a Mrs. Delma Harrell

Abadie of Donaldsonville, written "while en route here on a bus." I venture to reproduce it:

> The farmer-politician is gone, oblivious to friend and foe,
> You can't say he was a quiet man, for he talked with force,
> long and loud,
> And whether it was his words or actions, he always drew
> and held a crowd.

It is a requiem that I think Uncle Earl would have liked.

16 / La. Without Earl

LAST SUMMER, while Earl was still slugging it out at the crossroads with McSween, I had a letter from a man in Louisiana consisting mostly of a copy of the following United Press International dispatch published in the *States-Item* of August 6:

> BATON ROUGE (UP)—The newly-formed state welfare board yesterday approved a welfare spending cutback of $7,640,000 this year, made possible by a purge of illegitimate children from assistance rolls.
>
> After electing Alexandria banker James Bolton its chairman the board heard a report that 22,650 children have been struck from the state aid rosters because they live in common-law marriage homes or because their mothers bore illegitimate children after taking state aid.
>
> The purge was responsible for a cut of $6,300,000 in state aid [the Federal Government's contribution to the support of these children] federal funds. The children are dependents of 6,014 families.
>
> The report was presented by assistant administrator O. C. Sills who said about 90 percent of the children taken from the rolls were Negroes.

My correspondent added:

"The above is a result of legislation passed by the Jimmie Davis legislature disfranchising people of bad moral reputation.

"Perhaps you should come back and do a profile on Jimmie Davis."

The net saving to the state of Louisiana, I calculated from this dispatch, would be $1,340,000—a handsome return for starving 22,000 children to death. It works out, roughly, to a saving of $61 on each small victim. If the state withholds its portion of the funds it automatically blocks off the Federal contribution, too, because Congress has a fixed ratio of Federal to state aid. With each $61 of savings, the grass-eaters running the state under Davis thus got as a free bonus another $244 worth of revenge on a child for being colored.

Remembering Earl's great appeal to the Legislature, I wondered how many of the fathers were white.

In retrospect the fine Governor ("Niggers are human beings"; "Lincoln was right") seemed more than ever the most effective liberal in the South. While he was in office he had barred this kind of thing. The action seemed so atrocious, however, that I surmised something—perhaps a protest by the now remorseful, repentant *Picayune*—would occur at the last moment to stop it from happening.

Louisiana was only occasionally on my mind while I was in Rome, and the only tidings I had from there came in occasional notes. But on Sunday, September 11, while reading a copy of *The Observer*, of London, which reaches Rome by air on the date of publication, I came upon the following story, which moved the Great State minus Earl into almost the international prominence of the Union of South Africa.

Chep Morrison had long made conscientious efforts to direct international attention upon the city of New Orleans, but the results were puny compared to what the new regime had achieved:

Louisiana Shocked by British Offer

Help for Starving Negroes

From GEORGE SHERMAN

NEW ORLEANS, Louisiana, September 10. Racial prejudice and the complicated machinery of welfare administration in the United States are frustrating efforts to save 6,000 unmarried mothers and 23,000 children from starvation in Louisiana.

Ninety-five per cent of these people are Negroes. They were struck from the State welfare rolls at the end of July, when Governor Jimmie Davis—armed with a new State law—ruled that public money could no longer support "immoral" women who had illegitimate children.

A letter in a local newspaper expresses the prevalent sentiment among whites: "It is doing an injustice to the people to place this burden of taxation on our shoulders; it is encouraging a great evil and is a disgrace to this State."

But there are some small signs that the white public is beginning to realise that more is at stake here than local politics. News of national and international protest is filtering through. Critics are saying that the final result will be a boomerang against the strongly segregationist Governor.

Morning newspaper readers were shocked when they read a front-page dispatch from Newcastle-upon-Tyne saying that 15 women members of the city council had begun a campaign to send the "starving and illegitimate" Negro children to England.

Athlete's Return

Up to that point the local Press had relegated reports of misery and pleas for help to small items on inside pages. Money has come from Britain to help the children and more is on the way.

The tension between the races has all but destroyed whatever easygoing relationship existed. The bitter fight over integration of the schools and equal rights for the Negro has destroyed the middle ground of moderation for the time being at least.

The atmosphere to-day bears little resemblance to that in another Southern State, Tennessee, farther to the north, which is preparing to give a young Negress, Wilma "Skeeter" Rudolph, a welcome home from the Olympics in Rome, where she won three gold medals.

Supporters of Governor Davis's action in Louisiana admit that it is a punitive measure against Negroes. The new law itself is part of a "segregation package" passed in May in the State legislature. The parts of that package establishing a segregated school system under the Governor's direct control have subsequently been ruled unconstitutional. Schools in New Orleans will be integrated on November 14.

Prostitution Warning

Meanwhile implementation of the Welfare Act is having the effect intended. Negro leaders feel the State is showing how "tough" it can be if they persist in their efforts at integration. The door has been opened for removing "immoral" Negro women from voting rolls, as well as welfare rolls. And this spotlight on the high rate of illegitimacy among Negroes has effectively reinforced fears of the white people about "mixing" their children in integrated schools.

The practical result has been a flight of desperate mothers to the private welfare agencies. The hardest hit is the biracial Urban League of Greater New Orleans. Seven hundred women have appealed to the league in the past two weeks. "In the mood these people are in they will do anything for food. The rate of prostitution is bound to rise," said a young white social worker.

Representatives of the dozen most powerful white and Negro social and Church organizations in New Orleans have announced that they cannot cope. They estimate that 5,000 children in New Orleans alone are nearing starvation.

Funds Run Out

"The question is no longer integration versus segregation, white versus Negro, State responsibility versus Federal responsibility; it is a question of feeding hungry children," said Mr. Revius Ortique, president of the Urban League. He, like the other spokesmen, did not condone immorality, but said the law was punishing children for the sins of their parents.

Mr. Ortique said the Urban League had had to close its emergency food dispensing headquarters. Funds had run out. The Rev. A. W. Ricks, Negro representative of the New Orleans Council of Methodists, said he had turned his church into a relief centre for 36 families, but he could no longer find the necessary money to support them.

Father Ray Hebert, Director of Associated Catholic Charities, said no single private agency could handle the demand. Children in Catholic parishes throughout the city were begging for food. Some were rummaging in garbage bins.

Federal Intervention

Seventy-five per cent. of the $29 million annually spent in Louisiana on dependent children comes from the Federal Government in Washington. The State is really the administrator of national funds. To qualify, it must conform to a national code of rules laid down in the Federal Social Security System. State welfare workers here say that Federal intervention is the chief hope for saving the situation.

According to Federal rules, illegitimacy *per se* is not ground for refusing relief. The unmarried mother, like the married mother, must prove that she maintains a "suitable home." The Louisiana legislature has simply made illegitimacy one proof of an "unsuitable home."

The Federal Government has taken the first step towards cutting off Louisiana funds. The Department of Health, Education and Welfare wrote to State welfare authorities voicing concern over the dropping of the 6,000 cases in one month. All Federal money is to be stopped, unless the State can provide some evidence that illegitimacy has not been made the sole criterion for determining the suitability of the home.

I am not one of those Americans who think we should pattern our way of life—the Southern way of life, the Northern way of life, the Western way of life, or the Eastern, Northeastern, Northwestern, Southeastern or Southwestern ways of life, or for that matter the Hawaiian or Alaskan ways of life—primarily to win the approval of a lot of piffling foreigners. I therefore discounted the *Observer's* story as an example of that precious British sentimentality that led British humanitarians to invade the Soviet Embassy in London in 1957 to protest against putting dogs in rockets. Many unmarried mothers try, illegally, to get rid of their children before they are born, and letting them starve to death is a time-tested and, in Louisiana now, a state-sanctioned method of getting rid of them as soon after they are born as possible. It is better than abortion because it saves the mothers from committing a Mortal Sin, and better than letting the children live because they would then grow up in unsuitable surroundings and some might eventually become members of the NAACP. The Louisiana law is a promising demographic innovation in the Western world, and I was amazed, shortly after my return to these shores, to read an editorial in the New York *Times* that, in slavish imitation of the meddling foreigner, denounced it.

The Longs, Earl and Huey before him, blocked such ameliorations of the Southern way of life in Louisiana, and whenever I read about the fine things the State Administration is doing down there now I remember the triumphant and original political cartoon in the *States-Item* after the first gubernatorial primary, which showed a tombstone with the inscription "Here Lies Longism."

In the *Herald-Tribune* of October 8, for example, I read a story that began: "New Orleans, Oct. 7 (UPI)—Louisiana Attorney General Jack Gremillion, who last summer bellowed that a Federal court was a 'den of iniquity,' today sobbed with joy when he was spared a jail sentence for criminal contempt of court.

"Federal District Judge Edwin F. Hunter said Mr. Gremillion was 'a fighter, and the world loves a fighter, but he fought out of bounds' when he called a three-judge integration suit panel a 'kangaroo court' Aug. 26. He sentenced Mr. Gremillion to eighteen months on his own good behavior.

" 'He told me I'm free,' the overjoyed Attorney General told reporters and well-wishers after adjournment. 'I'm very satisfied with the sentence and grateful to Judge Hunter for his fairness.' . . .

"Pleading for a light sentence, State Rep. Wellborn Jack likened Mr. Gremillion to 'the manager of a ball team which hasn't won a game in six years' [a figure of speech for the segregationists in the Federal Courts]. He said such a losing streak would cause any one to lose his head 'in the heat of battle.' " It would also cause a bright manager to suspect he had a bad ball team.

This item, peculiarly enough, made me think of what Earl had once said about isms: "I'm not against anybody for . . . any ism he might believe in except nuttism, skingameism and Communism."

Longism may be dead with Earl, because the junior United States Senator is a toned-down, atypical Long, which is the equivalent of a Samson with a store haircut. He is also howling publicly about the Supreme Court's persecution of Louisiana, to head off grass-eater opposition in the Senatorial primaries by showing that his teeth are as green as any man's.

But nuttism is doing fine.

P.S.—November 18, 1960:

As I send this manuscript finally to the publisher, the grass-eaters and the nuts have taken over the streets of New Orleans, cheered on by the State Government the *Times-Picayune* helped elect.—A.J.L.

THE JOLLITY BUILDING

Contents

* *The Jollity Building* was originally published as a miscellaneous collection of A. J. Liebling's essays, most of which had been gathered in previous collections.

In *Liebling at Home*, "The Jollity Building" is found in *The Telephone Booth Indian* (page 28), where it had been collected originally.

"Yea Verily" was adapted from a section in *The Honest Rainmaker* and titled for inclusion in *The Jollity Building*. In *Liebling at Home*, it is again incorporated in *The Honest Rainmaker* (page 291).—*Editor*

Broadway Storekeeper

THE I. & Y. cigar store at Forty-ninth Street and Seventh Avenue is open twenty-four hours a day every day of the year except Yom Kippur. During daylight hours it performs the same function as any other cigar store on a fairly busy corner. People coming up from the B.M.T. station or going down into it often buy cigarettes at the I. & Y. The essential character of the place is not apparent until nightfall, when it becomes the neighborhood's nearest approach to a country store. After dark the I. & Y. expands into a forum of public opinion and an arena of practical jokes. Permanent chairman of the debates is the proprietor, Izzy Yereshevsky.

Izzy has to keep his store open all night because one of the main props of his business is selling cigarettes to nearly every night club in town. The hat-check concessionaires, whose stakes in the resorts also entitle them to sell cigarettes at twenty-five cents a pack, never seem able to estimate their needs in advance. Izzy gets emergency telephone calls at all hours for cartons of cigarettes; his nephew, Little Izzy, is on the go making deliveries from dark to dawn. In addition, Izzy supplies those long-legged dolls and beribboned Teddy bears which cigarette girls hawk between the tables in night clubs. Izzy stays open because of the night-club trade and he gets the night-club trade because he stays open.

This stuffed-animal sideline of Izzy's is likely to puzzle the casual visitor to his cigar store—a fairly deep but narrow shop, about twelve feet by thirty. In the show window on Seventh Avenue sit three Cubans making cigars by hand. Clustered around the Cubans' feet in the window are ranks of Teddy bears and dolls, some pert, some droopy, and all well cured in the aroma of tobacco leaves.

Izzy Yereshevsky is a Jewish peasant. Because he is essentially a countryman, his store has acquired a communal, bucolic atmosphere. Izzy performs all sorts of community services that pay him nothing. "On Broadway," Izzy sometimes says, "you got to be werry good, werry sweet to everybody. And even then they stick you in the back." Remaining an outlander, he feels it necessary to placate the local gods.

Most of his evening guests—their purchases are so infrequent that it would be misleading to call them customers—wear white felt hats and overcoats of a style known to them as English Drape. Short men peer up from between the wide-flung shoulders of these coats as if they had been lowered into the garments on a rope and were now trying to climb out. To Izzy his guests are the people of Broadway. They are the big talkers and, on the rare occasions when they have cash in their pockets, the big spenders. In truth the boys in the white felt hats and the English Drapes do not love money for its own sake. Each fosters a little personal legend of lost affluence; fifty grand dropped on the races in one day, twenty grand blown on a doll in a brief sojourn at Atlantic City. Never to have been in the chips marks one as a punk or a smalltimer. It precludes conversation in big figures. Continuous prosperity, to the boys, however, hints of avarice and is discreditable.

Until 1913 Izzy worked on a tobacco farm in the Ukraine, and when he first came to America he went from the boat to a place in Connecticut he calls East Windsor Ill. His brother had a job on a tobacco farm there. Izzy worked with him for a year and saved eight hundred dollars. Then he came to New York to learn the trade of cigar-making. Eighteen years ago he opened the I. & Y. two blocks down Seventh Avenue from its present situation.

"I am the 'I.' And I am the 'Y.'," he explains. "Two initial sounds more responsible."

Izzy is famous for the power of his handshake. He pulls his right hand back level with his shoulder, holds it cocked for a moment, then crashes it against the hand of the person he is greeting. It is as if you have been hit on the palm with a nightstick. "Hol-*lo doc*-tor," Mr. Yereshevsky invariably shouts as he strikes. "Doctor" is his conventional salutation. In Izzy's store, as on the East Indian Island of Buru and among certain Australian aborigines, it is considered bad form to speak a man's real name lest one unwittingly give an enemy power over his future. It is also bad form in addressing a customer who has been away to ask him where he has been. He may have been in Hollywood or he may have been in jail. If he has been in Hollywood he will say so.

Izzy is a man of slightly less than medium height, with broad shoulders and gray, crinkly hair. The color is somewhat deceptive, because Izzy was young enough to be drafted in the World War. A generous and often bluish jowl offsets the effect of Izzy's sensitive nose and mouth. He further masks his inner nature by clenching a large cigar of his own manufacture in the right corner of his jaw. The effort to sustain the cigar twists Izzy's mouth into a hard, jaunty smile hardly in keeping with his timid nature.

Izzy accepts more bad checks than anybody else on Broadway. To make his books balance in the face of such odds, he finds it necessary to work eighteen hours a day. He comes to the I. & Y. at noon and leaves at six o'clock the next morning. He likes to say he has been "thirty-six years on Broadway; eighteen years days, and eighteen years nights." After the midtown night clubs close, concessionaires and headwaiters foregather at the I. & Y. to discuss business conditions, and the cigarette girls drop in to buy their dolls and Teddy bears. Even then, Little Izzy, the delivery boy, is still darting out into the night with orders for late-closing places. On an ordinary night Izzy's nephew hustles up to Harlem or down to Greenwich Village at least half a dozen times.

Izzy does not drink, gamble, or patronize night spots. He works very hard, and most of the men who spend their evenings in his store find this irresistibly amusing. When Izzy announces that another check has bounced, his friends have been known to go out and roll with mirth on the sidewalk in back of the Rivoli Theatre. To them the calamities of virtue are exquisitely comic. They revel in unmerited catastrophe and sometimes cite Izzy as an example of the uselessness of honest toil.

Izzy shows no resentment. He feels that Broadway people who write bad checks are actuated not by greed but a need for self-expression. They want money to lose on the horse races. Izzy thinks horses are parasitic organisms that live on his human acquaintances. He blanches at the sight of a policeman's mount.

"Win money on a horse race?" he echoes, when asked his opinion of the sport. "How did you think them horses get feeded?"

Every fortnight or so he heads a subscription to bury some horseplayer who has died broke. There are always impromptu collections under way at the I. & Y. for the relief of various indigent nocturnal characters, and the boys subscribe freely. They take an equal pride in giving charity and bilking their creditors.

Izzy has another nephew, Max, who is a graduate of James Monroe High School and a deep student of human nature. A slender, pale young man with a scraggly mustache, he assists Izzy behind the counter. "Everybody who comes in here wants money so he can be a sucker," Max says. "You have to be in the money before you can be a sucker. Only out-of-towners think being a sucker's a disgrace."

One of the favorite amusements among the boys is improvising tall tales to bewilder strangers. A regular habitué of the I. & Y. will shout to another, as if they had just met for the first time, "Say, ain't you the feller that I seen with an animal act at the Hippodrome fifteen years ago, where the camel dived into the tank with you on his back?"

"Sure," the other will come back, calmly, "but it wasn't a camel; it was an elephant I was on."

A friendly stranger, just stopping in to make a purchase, may remark incredulously at this point, "I didn't think the Hippodrome tank was big enough to hold an elephant." Then everybody laughs like mad.

Some of the members of Izzy's cénacle have lovely names. A large, emphatic fellow who usually talks about big real-estate deals, rocking on his heels and shouting, is called Hairynose because of a clump of red hair sprouting from his nostrils. Everybody knows that in workaday life he is a necktie salesman, but Izzy likes to hear him talk of big land deals. Then there are Skyhigh Charlie and Three-to-Two Charlie. Skyhigh is a ticket speculator with an office on Forty-seventh Street, a large, florid man who buys Izzy's three-for-fifty cigars. The fortunes of the theatrical season may always be gauged by a quick glance at the little finger of Skyhigh's left hand. He wears a ring with a cluster of bulbous diamonds on it, buying larger stones when he makes money, pawning them and wearing smaller ones when things are dull. Three-to-Two Charlie is a betting man with a predilection for short odds which his more reckless intimates find detestable. One elderly lounger with a long goatee and a mane of hair is invariably addressed as "the Doctor." He used to have an office where he grew hair on bald men and is the court of last appeal in all I. & Y. disputes on scientific subjects. At present he is waiting for Izzy to find him a job as a washroom attendant.

The election of Thomas E. Dewey as District Attorney* did not please all of the political observers of the I. & Y. "After all, what did he do only sperl a lot of t'ings dat gave people what to eat?" a friend of Izzy's called Monkey the Bum argues. "It's tough enough to make a living now. There's plenty of guys walking the streets today without where to flop, without who to ask for a dime. And in 1926† those same guys didn't have nothing either."

Izzy deprecates such gloom. When the hat-check concessionaires ask him about business conditions he tries to cheer them.

"Me they ask how's business," he says. "So I always tell them something nice. If good, I say'll stay good. If bad, I say it's the bad weather, people are staying home. Or the weather's too good, they're going to the country. Or it's coming Christmas, they're spending money in the stores. Or it's gone Christmas, they spent all their money."

Like all storekeepers of the old tradition, Izzy carries on a number of free public services. Among them he accepts telephone messages for workers in the neighborhood. Most of the messages are from wives, and when Izzy talks to them he indulges a healthy, earthy wit. One whose calls are cleared through the I. & Y. store is a newsdealer called Chopsie who used to be a song-and-dance man in vaudeville. Mrs. Chopsie calls up often.

"Yass, Mrs. Chopsie," Izzy will shout when he answers the telephone. "Sure I seen Chopsie this evening. He was walking down the street with a blonde, weighed maybe three hundred pounds, he wouldn't say where he was going." While he talks to Mrs. Chopsie Izzy rolls his eyes, holds his right hand on his stomach as if in pain, and sometimes weeps with mirth. But he usually gets the message straight—Chopsie is to bring home half a pound of bologna or a copy of True Love Stories.

The I. & Y. is also a free employment agency for hat-check and cigarette girls who meet concessionaires there. On winter nights, too, a few bedraggled ladies without escort come in to warm their feet. Izzy lets them sit on chairs in the back of the store where, since they are always tired and usually slightly drunk, they often go to sleep. Once Izzy tied one to a chair as she slept. It was a great joke when she awoke and started to

* A sour fellow, of ephemeral repute as a Reformer, or Killjoy, now quasi-forgotten, although elected President of the United States by the Press on the day before the real election in 1948.

† I.e., before the formal public onset of the Hoover depression.

yell, but afterward Izzy felt badly because he had humiliated the girl. So he presented to her a box of Danny's Special Cigars, which she likes to smoke. Izzy names all his cigars after members of his immediate family. Danny is his five-year-old son. He has two daughters, too, Dora and Della, both in their teens. Izzy long ago combined their names to make a high-class title for a cigar—the DoraDella.

Certain essential facilities of the store are so popular that Izzy has nailed up a permanent sign, "Lavatory out of order." Only strangers are deceived. All through the evening neighborhood people buttonhole Mr. Yereshevsky, asking "Will you O.K. me, Izzy?" Izzy always nods, and the suppliants march toward the rear of the shop in successful defiance of the sign.

Fanciful signs are a feature of the I. & Y. Several steady customers feel gifts for chirography and, in gratitude for being saved from frostbites, they devote hours to lettering testimonials for the walls. A sample is:

My name is Izzy
I'm always busy
Making I. & Y. cigars.

Mrs. Mollie Yereshevsky, Izzy's wife, works in the store during the day. She is a pink-fleshed, country-looking woman, plump and cheerful. They live in the Lincoln Apartments on Fifty-first Street west of Eighth Avenue, a block populated largely by theatre and night-club people. Mollie has a hard time controlling Izzy's generous impulses. When he opened his first store he readily believed his customers' stories of immense wealth gained quickly through theatrical productions or hat-check concessions in speakeasies. Anyone who bought a box of cigars appeared to Izzy an American millionaire. If the man said the cigars were good, he became on the spot Izzy's friend. When friends asked him to cash checks he always obliged. When the checks bounced, he was sorry because the friends often stayed away as long as two weeks. Reappearing, they would explain that, just before Izzy presented the check at the bank, a wonderful opportunity to buy a night club had come their way and to grasp it they had had to draw out all their cash. But to square everything they would offer to sell Izzy the hat-check concession in the club. All he had to do was pay from one to six thousand dollars in advance.

Every time Izzy invested in a concession, he says, one of three things would happen. "Or the night club wouldn't open," is the way he puts it, "or it would open and close in a couple weeks, the fellow would keep the concession money, or the club would start to make money and they would sell the concession over my head to somebody else. Contracts you didn't have with speakeasies."

Izzy likes to pretend he is less ingenuous now. He adopts a knowing and secretive manner toward strangers, deliberating several seconds before answering even the most innocent question, such as "When did you move here from the Forty-seventh Street store?"

"Six years ago," he will finally whisper.

"Where were you during the War?"

"Fort Totten," Izzy will breathe faintly, after looking around carefully for concealed dictaphones. It sometimes takes as long as three minutes to secure his confidence. When he has given it, he will pull out a drawer in back of the counter to show you his collection of rubber checks.

"About fifty thousand dollars," he boasts, with the pride of a man showing a particularly impressive scar from an appendectomy. "Who shall I collect from, responsible people? I am de most wictim on Broadway." He is very proud of it.

Izzy sells wholesale to the night clubs, limiting his profit to two per cent. The cafés make his cigarette business larger in volume than his trade in cigars, but cigars are nearer to Izzy's heart. Because he has room for only three workers at a time, the cigar makers work in day and night shifts. Luis, the oldest Cuban, sometimes remains in the window making panatelas or perlas until three in the morning. The Cubans sit in a kind of cage, shut off from the rest of the shop by a metal grill. Izzy buys the leaf tobacco and pays the Cubans piecework rates for making the cigars. He keeps the cigars in a large humidor until he makes a sale. When he has an order for a box, Izzy takes it from the humidor, pastes on the revenue stamps, and hands it to the customer.

Izzy believes in cigars. He always recommends them for a hangover—probably because he has never suffered from one.

Tummler

TO THE BOYS of the I. & Y. Hymie Katz is a hero. He is a short, broad-shouldered, olive-complexioned man who looks about forty-two and is really somewhat older. In his time he has owned twenty-five night clubs.

"Hymie is a tummler," the boys at the I. & Y. say. "Hymie is a man what knows to get a dollar."

Hymie at present is running a horserace tipping service in an office building on Longacre Square. "What is a night club made of?" he sometimes asks contemptuously. "Spit and toilet paper. An upholstered joint. The attractions get the money and the boss gets a kick in the pants." His admirers understand that this is only a peevish interlude. Soon he will open another night club.

The tipping service requires no capital. Hymie reads out-of-town telephone books for the names of doctors and ministers fifty or a hundred miles from New York. Then he calls them, one by one, asking the operator to reverse the charges. Hymie tells the operator, let us say, that he is Mr. Miller whom Dr. Blank or the Rev. Mr. Doe met at Belmont Park last summer. If the man accepts the call, Hymie knows he has a prospect. The man probably hasn't been at Belmont, and certainly hasn't met a Mr. Miller there, but thinks he is the beneficiary of a case of mistaken identity. Hymie tells him about a horse that is sure to win. All the doctor or minister has to do, Hymie says, is to send him the winnings on a ten-dollar bet. Sometimes the horse does win, and the small-town man always remits Hymie's share of the profits. He wants to be in on the next sure thing. Doctors, Hymie believes, are the most credulous of mortals. Ministers never squawk.

Hymie picks his horses very carefully from the past-performance charts of the *Morning Telegraph.* He usually tips three or four entries in each race. Naturally, the physicians and clergymen who get bad tips send him no money, but the supply of small-town professional men is practically unlimited. Hymie says it is an ideal business for a man satisfied with a modest, steady income. Personally, he is resigned to opening another night club. "If I wasn't ashamed," he says, "I would put a couple of hundred dollars in it myself." The investment of his own money, according to Hymie's code, would be unethical.

All Hymie needs to open a night club is an idea and a loan of fifty dollars. There are fifteen or twenty basements and one-flight-up places between Forty-fifth and Fifty-fifth Streets that cannot economically be used as anything but night clubs. They have raised dance floors, ramps, numerous light outlets, kitchens, and men's and women's washrooms. Because they are dark during the day, or can be reached only by staircases, they are not adapted to ordinary restaurant use. Such a place may be worth six hundred dollars a month as a night club. Dismantled, it would bring only a hundred or so as a store. The owner of a night-club site makes out pretty well if his space is tenanted for six months of the year.

Hymie has been around Broadway since 1924. He is a good talker. In the past, some of his clubs actually have made money, although none of it has stuck to him. As a matter of ritual he always tells the owner of the spot he proposes to rent that he is going to spend forty thousand dollars to fix it up. The owner does not believe this, but the sound of the words reassures him. If Hymie said less than forty thousand dollars, the landlord would sense a certain lack of enthusiasm. If more, the landlord would feel derided. It is customary to mention forty thousand dollars when talking about redecorating a night club. If the owner appears to be hooked, Hymie goes out and spends the borrowed fifty dollars. He pays it to a lawyer to draw up a lease. The lawyer Hymie patronizes is the only man in the world Hymie has never been able to put on the cuff. But he draws a fine lease. It contains all sorts of alluring clauses, like "party of the first part and party of the second part agree to share equally in all profits above ten thousand dollars a week, after reimbursement of party of the second part for outlays made in equipping the Dopey Club (said outlays for this purpose not to exceed forty thousand dollars)." It makes provision for profits of Aluminum Trust magnitude.

Hymie takes the lease to a hat-check concessionaire. This is the really critical phase of the enterprise. He must convince the concessionaire that the place has a chance to do business ("Look at the figures in the lease, you can see what we're expecting"). He must fill the concessionaire with enthusiasm for the entertainers, who have not yet been engaged. For it is up to the concessionaire to provide the cash that will make the enterprise go—three thousand dollars in advance, in return for the hat-check and cigarette concession for six months. Hymie is a great salesman. He does impersonations of his hypothetical acts. He tells about the Broadway columnists who eat out of his hand and will give yards of free publicity. While Hymie talks, the concessionaire distills drops of probability from his gallons of conversation. In his mind he turns Hymie's thousands of anticipated revenue into fifties and hundreds. If the club runs three months, the concessionaire knows, he will get his money back. If by some fluke it runs six months, he will double his money. If nobody financed night clubs, there would be no concession business. So the concessionaire lets Hymie have the three thousand.

Hymie goes back to the landlord, signs the lease, and pays him a month's rent in advance—say six hundred dollars. That leaves twenty-four hundred dollars for the other expenses. If possible, he saves himself from headaches by renting out the kitchen. The kitchen concessionaire provides the food, cooks up a stew on which all the night-club help feed every night, and even pays half of the cost of the table linen. (Linen is rented, not bought.) The proprietor of the club gets from twelve to twenty per cent of the gross receipts for food. Since night-club food is absurdly high, the food concessionaire, like the hat-check man, is bound to make a good profit if the place lasts a few months.

The club may contain tables, chairs, and any amount of miscellaneous equipment abandoned by a former tenant in lieu of rent. If it doesn't, Hymie goes to a man named I. Arthur Ganger, who runs a Cain's warehouse of the night-club business on West Forty-fifth Street. Ganger can provide out of used stock anything from a pink-and-onyx Joseph Urban bar to a wicker smörgasbord table. Some of his silverware has been in and out of ten previous clubs. Usually Ganger will accept a twenty-five-per-cent down payment, which for one of Hymie's clubs amounts to a few hundred dollars. He takes notes payable weekly for the rest. Ganger is amenable to reason when the notes fall due. He has a favorite joke for customers like Hymie. "Your mother carried you only nine months," he says, "but I been carrying you all your life." The supply man retains title to his things until they are entirely paid for, and if the club folds he carts them back to his warehouse. Ganger decorates some clubs, but Hymie would not think of hiring him for such a job. Hymie gets a girlish young man to perform a maquillage for a hundred and fifty dollars, including paint.

Of the three thousand dollars received from the concessionaire, Hymie has now disbursed at most twelve hundred. He pays another six hundred dollars for a liquor license good for six months, and puts the rest of the money in the bank as profit in case the club flops. The remaining preparations are on the cuff. Hymie hires acts for his new club on the understanding that he will pay off a week after the place opens. He engages a band on the same terms. If there is to be a line of girls in the show, the girls rehearse free. But Hymie is not a bad fellow. He sends out for coffee and sandwiches for the girls during rehearsals. Once or twice he has been known to lend a girl five dollars for room rent before a club opened.

Liquor is harder to buy on credit these days than before repeal. Mob credit was flexible, and if you bought from a bootlegger independent of the gangs, Hymie says, you never paid him at all. Wholesalers now are allowed to extend only twenty-one days' credit, according to the regulations of the State Liquor Authority. But matters sometimes may be arranged by paying a bill on the twenty-first day and then borrowing most of the money back from the wholesaler on the twenty-second.

A few days before the opening Hymie effects a deal that always puts him in especially good humor. He sells twenty waiters their jobs. The headwaiter pays four hundred dollars, two captains pay two hundred dollars each, and ordinary waiters fifty dollars. Waiters like to work for Hymie because he lets them take what they can get. He wastes no time watching his employees. "Most of the stealing they do is from the customers, so what do I care?" says Hymie.

Despite all his forethought, exigencies sometimes arise which demand fresh capital. Perhaps an unusually stubborn landlord demands three months' security, or a police official must be heavily greased before he will let the club stay open after hours. In some places, especially black-and-tan or crudely bawdy spots, all the money comes in during the illegal early hours of the morning, after the bigger clubs have closed. In such emergencies Hymie sometimes has to take in partners. He usually bilks his partners for the principle of the thing. He is not avaricious. Dollars, Hymie thinks, are markers in a game of wits as well as a medium of exchange. He refuses to let his partners keep any markers.

Once he had to take a partner in a roadhouse he was running near Babylon. He sold the fellow fifty per cent of the place for one season. It happened to be a very good season, so Hymie built a sliding metal roof over a garden one hundred feet square, installed a swimming pool, and presented all his employees with a large bonus out of the receipts.

"I thought I would make some improvements and build up good will for next year, when Milton would be out," he says.

Some persons may wonder why even a concessionaire would trust Hymie with his money. But concessionaires know that he will not skip before the club opens, for he is under a compulsion as strong as the drive of a spawning salmon to swim upstream. His clubs satisfy his craving for distinction.

A week before an opening Hymie gets out a mailing list of exhibitionists which he has accumulated through a decade of night-club operation, and sends out his announcements. Then he makes the entertainers write letters to their friends inviting them to buy ringside tables. He insists on the attendance of every salesman who has ever sold him anything for the club, even if it all was on credit. The costumer who has dressed the show is expected to take part of his pay in trade. Since this may be the only part of it he will ever collect, the costumer usually brings a large party. It is a nice arrangement for Hymie, because he pays off on the costumer bill with Scotch at about six cents on the dollar. The costumer has made a profit of about ninety-five cents on the dollar, so this makes them both feel good. The band leader, if he has any considerable reputation in the trade, forces music publishers' pluggers to reserve tables. If the pluggers don't spend money, the leader slights their tunes.

A week after the opening, if it was profitable, Hymie gives his entertainers three days' pay. He tells them he is holding something back so they won't run out on him. Of course they never get it. If the opening has been bad, the entertainers and the concessionaire are likely to find the door locked the next night. In the event of a sour opening, Hymie takes the thousand or fifteen hundred dollars of concession money remaining to him out of the bank and lays it on a ten-to-one shot at some obscure race track. He shares the weakness for betting common to most night-club people, but he has it in an exaggerated form. He has never played a horse at less than eight-to-one in his life, because he is sure that every race is fixed. When a favorite wins he attributes it to a double-cross. Hymie almost always loses.

Occasionally the personality of one of Hymie's entertainers catches on, or the décor hits the fancy of the Broadway high-life crowd, and the club begins to make money legitimately. Under these circumstances Hymie sells it to a corporation called Hymie-club, Inc. As manager for the corporation he kicks out the hat-check concessionaire and sells the concession over again for a higher price. The entertainer who draws the crowd gets a manager and demands more money. Hymie pays blackmail in the form of weekly raises. He spends a great part of his receipts in competitors' clubs to show how prosperous he is. He stalls off all creditors on general principles.

"Sometimes you can hold them off for six months," he says. "Meanwhile everything that comes in is profit."

Finally the creditors close in, or the entertainer either loses his brief vogue or goes on to a larger club. Hymie returns to the horse-tipping business. He has written one more chapter in his saga; he has been in the money again.

Hymie admits readily that it was vanity that drew him into the night-club business in the first place, and that keeps him at it.

"Take a fellow who is born in Brooklyn," he says, "and he is a cloak-and-suiter or a shoe clerk, which he would feel honored even to talk to a trumpet player in a famous orchestra. He goes into this business and in two years celebrities like Rudy Vallee and Harry Thaw are calling him Hymie. It makes him feel wonderful. But it don't mean nothing."

Take, more specifically, Hymie Katz. He was born in Brooklyn, in the Williamsburg district. The record of his early days is shadowy, but he says that once he was a fur stretcher, and once he drove a taxi, and once he was married to a wealthy woman who died and cut him off with a dollar in her will because she didn't want him to spend anything on other dolls. Hymie got his start in the night-club world as a singing waiter in a pseudo-Bavarian joint where people drank spiked near-beer at fifty cents a glass and sang "Ja, das ist ein Schnitzelbank." He had not been there long before he had invented a new technique for reaming the customers. When one of the parties he was serving asked for a check he would delay bringing it, if possible, until he had a similar request from another party of about the same size. One check might be for sixteen dollars, say, the other for twelve. Hymie would put the twelve-dollar check in the hip pocket of his leather pants and collect the sixteen-dollar check from both parties, one after the other. The customers seldom became aware of the mistake.

After he got used to late hours, Hymie decided to open a night club for himself. That was in the winter of 1924, and many buildings between Longacre Square and Sixth Avenue had a joint on every floor. There would be a shabby night club at street level, a speakeasy-restaurant on the second floor, and two or three ratty bars on the levels above. Hymie picked a second-floor loft that had a dance floor ten by ten and forty tables with pink lampshades on them, left by a former proprietor who had not paid his beer bill. Hymie put down two hundred dollars for an option on the place—he could not then afford his present scruples against using his own cash. He dropped in at the I. & Y., where he was beginning to be known, and sold twenty per cent of the club for a thousand dollars to a fellow we will call Johnny Attorney. Johnny came from Attorney Street originally, but he was quite a big beer-man by then, and had moved uptown.

Hymie and Johnny were able to sell the hat-check concession for another thousand because Johnny was in on a couple of speakeasies where the hat-check man did business. Then they took in the no-good brother of a famous night-club hostess who was the surest draw in town. They gave the brother twenty per cent, and all they asked was that he stay away from the place as much as possible. The hostess was working for a man named Denny Boylan, who had a large, elaborate club (for those days) about five doors up the block from their place. The Boylan club was on the street level, with a uniformed doorman and a marquee, and it had to close at two or three o'clock in the morning. Drawing her ermine wrap about her and jiggling her head-dress of egrets two feet long, the hostess would then suggest to the best spenders present that they accompany her to a little intimate spot down the street, where the party could continue. Down the street they would stagger, and up the stairs to the Daylight Club, as Hymie and Johnny called their stuffy loft. After the second week the hostess demanded a share for herself, so Hymie sold her half of his sixty per cent for five thousand dollars.

"The prices we got for liquor those days were brutal," Hymie recalls happily. "Twenty-five dollars for a bottle of champagne a guy made for us down on Mott Street. But the price didn't mean nothing. It was the bottles you could stab in on a customer's check that really counted. I mean the bottles you charged him for that he had never had at all. I remember a big patent-medicine man from Baltimore that used to come into the place that once paid me twenty-eight hundred dollars for one bottle of wine. He ordered the wine and then he fell asleep with his head on the table. I had the sense to have empty bottles in ice buckets put next to every table. When he woke up, I slipped him the check. 'What's this?' he says. 'Well,' I says, 'you ordered wine for everybody in the house. A hundred and twelve bottles at twenty-five a copy. The one on your table is on me.' He couldn't remember whether he had or not, but the money didn't mean nothing to him, so he paid."

After the Daylight Club was fairly launched, Hymie devoted late afternoons to the manufacturing department. Hymie doesn't mind work when it's fun.

"I made Black-and-White so good those millionaires wouldn't drink nothing else," he says. "There was a big towel man from North Carolina who would take cases of my Black-and-White home with him every time he come to town. Once a fellow in another joint gave him some of the McCoy straight from St. Pierre, and the towel man spit it out. 'You trying to poison me?' he says. 'This don't taste nothing like the genuine Black-and-White I buy from Hymie.' He would never go back to the joint."

Hymie thinks most of his customers in those days were temporarily insane. There was, for example, a wholesale whiskey exporter from Canada who, on his business trips to New York, had the quaint conceit of carrying only fifty-dollar bills. He would toss one of them on Hymie's bar and order drinks for everybody. If there were thirteen drinkers in the house, Hymie would charge him for about twenty-nine drinks at a dollar apiece. The Canadian never counted. He would leave his change for the bartender.

"When he come in," Hymie says, "I used to go behind the bar myself."

Hymie thinks that many of his former customers still have money, but have been afraid to throw it around in public since the depression. In a select spot like the Daylight Club, he says, "they knew they was among their own kind."

The end of the Daylight Club came when a squad of twenty prohibition agents raided the place and padlocked it.

"The reason you couldn't do nothing about them big raids," he says, "is that there was never twenty Feds who would trust each other. Each one would think one of the others in the squad was trying to put him in the bag, so you couldn't talk business. But when just one fellow or two or three come in, you knew they was on the shake. If you felt good-natured, you slipped them fifty. If you didn't, you kicked them down the stairs."

Hymie likes harness cops, but not detectives. He says the latter are like Feds, always on the shake.

"The cop on the block was a kind of doorman," Hymie explains. "When you threw a drunk out, the cop picked him up and walked him down to the corner to sober up, so he wouldn't remember where he was thrown out of." Each place on the block paid the policeman on beat from two to five dollars a night, according to its volume of business. On a good block, Hymie estimates, it might have run to as much as a hundred dollars a night. He doesn't believe that the cop on beat was allowed to retain all this, but he says he never paid money to a police official higher up. His guess is that it was divided in the Department.

Hymie always enjoyed bouncing people in a nice way. When a big tough fellow heckled the hostess, Hymie would go to the cashier and get a roll of quarters. He would hold it in his right hand, with one end of the roll protruding, and he would lean over the fellow's table and slug him on the side of the jaw with it. Then a couple of waiters would carry the gentleman out and lay him on the sidewalk, where the cop would find him.

Mickey Finns, the pacifying pills slipped to obstreperous customers in many places, do not amuse Hymie. "Any fool can go into a drugstore for a dollar and buy a box of Mickeys," he says. Mickeys are purgative pills designed for horses, and act so drastically that one may kill a drunk with a weak heart. "But even with Mickeys, there is an art in the way to serve them," says Hymie. "Some fellows wait until the customer orders another drink, which may be too long, and others offer him a drink on the house, which maybe makes him suspicious. The best way is to tell the waiter, 'A little more ice in that glass, please.' The waiter has the ice on a spoon and the Mickey under the ice. He drops them in the drink together."

The Daylight Club ran fourteen months, during which, Hymie says, the partners earned about a quarter of a million dollars. The race tracks got most of Hymie's share. He remembers days when he went out to the track and lost five thousand dollars in an afternoon, then came back and delivered a case of bathtub gin to make six dollars. "Money don't mean nothing to me," he says. "Maybe I'm crazy."

After the Daylight was padlocked, Hymie and his associates opened a far more pretentious place on Fiftieth Street, which he called the Club Chez Nous. He pronounced it the Club Chestnuts. The partners continued to make money. The place went out of existence because of the hostess's sense of humor. The adolescent son of a statesman then prominent came into the club drunk one night. She persuaded him to go out on the floor and do imitations of his father, who was flirting with a Presidential nomination. The father used his influence to have the place padlocked.

Hymie's third place, the Club Monastery, was a hard-lucker. It had been open only three weeks when a party of mobsmen dropped in and began shooting at Johnny Attorney and some friends. Two men were killed and Johnny Attorney disappeared. It is popularly supposed that his body was run through a rock-crusher and that he is now part of the roadbed of the Pulaski Skyway in New Jersey. The police, however, hadn't heard about this and thought that Hymie knew where Johnny was, so they gave him a terrific beating. Hymie was not the kind who would appeal to the American Civil Liberties Union. When the police let him go, some of the gangsters took him for a ride. Fortunately they forgot to gag him, and he talked so fast that they brought him back to his hotel and loaned him twenty dollars. It is one of his proudest memories. But the Monastery was "out on the street." Whenever there was a shooting in a speakeasy, the New York police closed it. That was the reason patrons about to shoot each other were always asked to leave.

The cares that might be expected to attend such a frenzied existence have left no mark on Hymie Katz. There are scars on his face from the beating the police gave him when they questioned him about Johnny Attorney, but no worry lines. He is not as handsome as he was twenty years ago, before he began to put on weight, but he has nice white teeth and pleasant features that wear a habitual unforced smile.

Hymie is unmarried at present. Wives, with Hymie, are symptoms of prosperity, like tailored shirts. His father is still living and owns a small jewelry shop on the Bowery near Canal Street. When Hymie visits him, the old man comes out to meet his son and locks the door from the outside. Then they talk on the sidewalk. Hymie is not offended by his parent's caution; he is flattered. Whenever he meets anybody new, he tells him about his father.

Hymie is living in a hotel on West Forty-ninth Street on a due bill. He pays the due-bill broker with due bills for entertainment at his next club, which he hasn't opened yet. When the club does open, the broker will sell the accumulated due bills for half their face value to couples who arrive via the bus lines and want to see New York night life.

Shortly before noon every day Hymie goes to his office, which he shares with a man who puts on stag shows, to see if any money has come in by mail. If there is any, Hymie spends the afternoon in a poolroom betting on races. If there is no money, he puts in a hard day at the telephone as Mr. Miller of Belmont Park. Generally he has dinner at an Italian Kitchen on Eighth Avenue, where he gets spaghetti, meat balls, and coffee for twenty-five cents. He smokes six cigars a day, five nickel ones and a fifty-center, buying them all at the I. & Y. He smokes the fifty-center after his twenty-five-cent dinner, so he will feel prosperous. Evenings he usually leans against a stack of cases in the cigar store and discusses his plans—never his real plans, of course, but vast enterprises like taking over the Paramount Theatre and turning it into a night club with a ski slide and a five-dollar minimum. With ribald arguments he maintains the feasibility of projects which he improvises on the spot. The other habitués of the I. & Y. listen with respect.

"You know who was in here?" Izzy asks friends who come in after Hymie has departed. "Hymie Katz." Izzy shakes his head admiringly. "He's a real tummler, that Hymie. He knows to get a dollar."